STEERING THE POLITY

STEERING THE POLITY

Communication and Politics in Israel

ITZHAK GALNOOR

SAGE PUBLICATIONS
Beverly Hills / London / New Delhi

For information address:

SAGE Publications, Inc.
275 South Beverly Drive
Beverly Hills, California 90212

SAGE Publications India Pvt. Ltd.
C-236 Defence Colony
New Delhi 110 024, India

SAGE Publications Ltd
28 Banner Street
London EC1Y 8QE, England

Printed in the United States of America

Library of Congress Cataloging in Publication Data

Galnoor, Itzhak.
  Steering the polity.

  Bibliography: p.
  Includes index.
  1. Israel — Politics and government. 2. Communication in politics — Israel. I. Title.
JQ1825.P3G34   306'.2'095694   81-21485
ISBN 0-8039-1340-0   AACR2

FIRST PRINTING

CONTENTS

Preface   xi

1. Political Communication   1
   Communication and the Study of Politics   2
   Political Development   9
   Democratic Political Development   20
   The Israeli Case Study   31

2. Israeli Society and Politics: An Overview   35
   Challenges in the External Environment   35
   The Internal Challenges   41
   Integration and Potential Cleavages   48
   The Political System: Formal Features   64
   Modes of Operation   74

3. Common Political Contents   79
   Communality   80
   Areas of Collective Identity   81
   Nonpolitical Common Contents   88
   Political Symbols   101
   The Boundaries of Consensus   107

4. The Political Network   111
   The Political Center   112
   The Periphery   130
   The Dynamics of Network Links   146

5. Channels: The Political Parties   159
   Political Channels   160
   Parties as Channels   161
   Parties in Israel   163
   Penetration   165
   Maintenance   177
   The Parties and the Target Groups   185

6. Channels: The Bureaucracy   189
   The Bureaucracy as a Channel   190
   Israeli Bureaucracy   193
   Penetration   199
   Maintenance   209
   The Bureaucracy and the Target Groups   214
7. Channels: Mass Communication Media   218
   Mass Media as Political Channels   220
   Israeli Mass Communication   222
   Penetration   231
   Maintenance   242
   The Mass Media and the Target Groups   259
   The Channels: Summary   261
8. Steering   265
   Prerequisites and Facilities   266
   Outcomes   268
   Steering Capacity   269
   Israel: Steering Capacity and Political Development   288
   Profiles of Steering Capacity   297
9. Access   300
   Democratic Tenets in Israel   301
   Access to Channels   306
   Access to the Political Communication Network   325
10. Participation   328
    Sense of Efficacy   329
    Modes of Participation   331
    The Peripheral Groups: Access and Participation   348
    Impact on Steering   359
11. Conclusion   368
    Israel: A Developed Political System   368
    Israel: A Democratically Developed Political System?   372
    Comparative Political Communication   375
References and Bibliography   379
Index   400
About the Author   411

LIST OF TABLES

1.1 Communication Components in Political Development   8
1.2 Social Integration and Common Political Contents   11
1.3 Modes of Participation in Terms of Political
Communication   26
2.1 Selected Indicators of Economic Development   45
2.2 Structure of the Economy: Employment and
Production   46
2.3 Jews Living in Israel as Percentage of Total
World Jewry   49
2.4 Origin of Jewish Immigration to Palestine and Israel   56
2.5 Ideological Camps According to Parties and
Election Results in Selected Years   60
2.6 Differences Among the Political Camps on Major Policy
Issues in 1948 and 1951   62-63
2.7 Histadrut Members as Percentage of Total Population   71
2.8 Results of Knesset Elections (120 Knesset Members)   72
3.1 Contributions to Zionism   89
4.1 Election Results to the Histadrut Assembly   115
4.2 Changes in Socializing Agencies   146
5.1 Mapai Membership Compared to Number of Mapai
Votes in Elections   169
5.2 Ratio of Mapai Members to Mapai Voters
in Different Types of Elections   170
5.3 Comparison of Mapai Membership and Eligible
Voters to the Knesset   171
6.1 Distribution of Civil Servants by Their
Previous Place of Work, 1949   196
6.2 Elections of Delegates to Civil Servants
Union Compared with Histadrut and Knesset Elections   197
6.3 Penetration and Maintenance by Political
Parties and by the State Bureaucracy   215
7.1 Use of Hebrew   225
7.2 Circulation of Daily Newspapers in
Hebrew and Other Languages (1972)   226
7.3 Comparison of Mass Media Editors and Knesset
Members, 1948-1977   251-52
7.4 Comparison of Communication Channels Used in
Election Campaigns   254
8.1 Major Threats During the Yishuv and
the State Periods (1930-1967)   282-83

8.2 Israel's Profile of Steering Capacity
During the Yishuv (1930-1948) and the
State (1948-1960s) Periods   297
9.1 Access to the Main Channels (early state period)   325
10.1 Voter Participation in National, Local, and
Histadrut Elections   334
10.2 Israeli Arab Votes in National Elections   351

LIST OF FIGURES

1.1 Communication Infrastructure of Politics   5
1.2 Information Flow Within Political Systems   18
2.1 Schematic Distribution of Observant and Nonobservant
Jews in Israel   52
10.1 Schematic Sequence of Conditions and Activities
Resulting in Citizens' Impact on Steering   329
10.2 Combinations of Access and Sense of Efficacy   332
10.3 Gap Between Knesset and Local Voter Turnout   335
10.4 Number of Yearly Strikes in Israel (1949-1969)   344

To Doron

PREFACE

This book grew out of my previous work on the dilemma of secrecy in democracies. There I pondered government's privilege — and need — to control information versus the people's right — and need — to know as a prerequisite for participation. The more I studied information flow, channels, and barriers, the more aware I became of the communication context of politics. Indeed, the previous book ended with the conclusion that changes in the practice of government secrecy in democracies signal changes in the internal political processes of these countries.[1]

Once I embarked on this road, the difficult question was how much faith one should have in the study of politics from a communication perspective. The approach could have been either very timid — limiting itself to the study of those aspects of political life in which communication is visible and paramount (for example, the relationship between government and the mass media) — or very ambitious — suggesting that the study of politics *as* communication should replace all other forms of political analysis. I leave it to the reader to decide whether this book is too timid or too ambitious.

The purpose of the book is to propose a theory of political communication, outlined in Chapter 1.[2] One may find it abstract and tight without reference to the Israeli case study. Chapter 2 is a brief overview of Israeli society and politics available for the uninitiated reader. Following this is an application of the theoretical framework to Israel's political development (Chapters 3 through 8) and to its democratic political development (Chapters 9-10). Chapter 11 draws general conclusions about the case study and outlines its comparative value. It might be useful to return to Chapter 1 after reading the case study.

The analysis of the development of the Israeli polity ends in the mid-1960s for reasons explained at the end of Chapter 1. Data and references to subsequent developments are included whenever present-day insight is helpful.

The twin foci throughout this book have been the generation of theoretical propositions and the analysis of the democratic political development in Israel. Running in two parallel tracks imposes limitations and gets out of control occasionally, as the sharp reader will discern. In particular, not all the propositions could be fully "tested" in the case study of Israel. In addition, there were socioeconomic factors in the development of the Israeli polity which do not come to light adequately because of adherence to the political communication components of the theory. Nevertheless, it is my hope that the reader will find his or her understanding of political steering to be enriched by an analysis of Israel's political development.

Acknowledgements

The project was supported in its early stages by the Leonard Davis Institute for International Relations at the Hebrew University and its previous and present directors: Nissan Oren and Dan Horowitz. I am thankful to David Curzon, who read initial drafts of the manuscript and helped me crystallize my thinking about this book. I would like to thank my colleagues who read parts of the manuscript and made important comments: Michael Brecher, Dan Caspi, Shmuel Eisenstadt, Yaron Ezrahi, Emmanuel Gutmann, Dan Horowitz, Elihu Katz, Hanan Kristal, Moshe Lissak, and Pinchas Medding. The first chapter was presented in the seminar of the Department of Political Science at the Hebrew University, and I am grateful for the spirited criticism I heard there. I was also fortunate to obtain valuable help from several of my graduate assistants: Amir Bar Or, Allyn Fisher, Harriet Gimpel, Itzhak Haberfeld, Meir Nitzan, and Shlomo Raz.

The actual writing of this book took place in the cozy environment of the Van Leer Institute in Jerusalem. I owe a great deal to the hospitality of the institute, its director, Yehuda Elkana, and particularly to my good friends in the library there.

Finally, the hand hidden yet in full command of steering behind the completed version of this book is my Israeli editor, Gila Brand. Being also a dear friend, she knows how grateful I am for all she has done to improve the book.

I. Galnoor
Jerusalem

NOTES

1. See Galnoor (1977: 313).
2. This appeared in a concise summary, "Political Communication and the Study of Politics" (in Nimmo, 1980: 99-112).

1

POLITICAL COMMUNICATION

"Government" comes from a Greek root
that refers to the art of the steersman
(DEUTSCH, 1963: 182)

The study of politics is such a fragmented field of inquiry that the question with which we must begin our discussion is, "why offer yet another approach, especially one that adopts the foreign terminology of communication?" Deutsch was the first to provide a communication approach to politics, suggesting that a study of the nerves of the body politic — its decision-making processes — gives insight into the performance of its bones and muscles — the exercise of power (Deutsch, 1963: xxvii). "Political neurology" is perhaps the right term for this approach, but the analogy can run too far afield (for example, what are political neurons?).

In analyzing politics through the conceptual framework of communication, we are searching for the raw material of political systems, the infrastructure of human interaction. Bentley, as early as 1908, suggested that communication analysis could appropriately be applied to the study of politics because the raw material of government "is never found in one man by himself. . . . It is a 'relation' between men . . . the action of men with or upon each other" (1908: 176). Certainly the acquisition and use of power remain central to an understanding of political processes, but here we wish to probe the communication roots of that exercise of power, the conditions that lead to it. The study of human organizations in general has been enriched by the perspective brought to

1

it from the field of communication (Barnard, 1938; Blau, 1955; Simon, 1957; Leavitt, 1964; Guetzkow, 1965). Political organizations structure the behavior of the political system through processes such as political interaction, political socialization, interest representation, rule-making, and regulation. These structures and mechanisms can be analyzed in terms of interactions, networks, channels and information flows. In other words, we are not asking, "What is the decision?" or even "Who made the decision?" but rather, "What were the circumstances that brought about certain decisions?"

In this book, the political system is examined as a network of communication. It is my belief that one can distinguish between "political development" and "democratic political development" through an analysis of political variables discussed in their communication context. Israel is presented as a case study for such a demonstration, and it is proposed that this approach can be used for comparative as well as single-country studies of political systems.

Communication and the Study of Politics

COMMUNICATION

Communication implies a departure from one's private circle. Communication takes two, even if one partner says nothing or the other does not listen. Communication provides the opportunity for human interaction, which in turn creates the cement to bind and maintain social organization (Barnard, 1938: 89; Wiener, 1954: 16; Pool, 1973: 3). For our purposes, it is enough to say that communication creates human linkage by means of words, gestures, symbols, pictures, and a host of other verbal and nonverbal codes; and that the function of a communication system is to transmit information.

In this book, communication is a neutral term and not synonymous with goodwill and harmony. Communication may lead to interaction or to nothing. Interaction may result in agreement or disagreement, understanding or misunderstanding, cooperation or conflict. " Good fences" might indeed "make good neighbors" on occasion, just as the intentional barring of communication may prevent friction and even social disintegration. In other words, not all human problems stem from lack of communication.

The *contents* of a particular communication language — its symbols, signs, and messages — distinguish one system from another (Cherry,

1970: 75). Some common content is prerequisite if communication and interaction are to take place. In fact, the boundaries between social units can be delineated in terms of communication contents and intensity: These boundaries indicate that internal interaction exceeds interaction with outsiders (Deutsch, 1953: 87).

When communication develops into relatively stable patterns of human contact, a *network* can be distinguished. This happens when random communication and interaction are repeated a sufficient number of times so as to lead to the crystallization of message content, meaning, and channels. Communication may thus become "institutionalized" and conducted through more permanent modes and codes of behavior. Conversing in the street, for example, is a random form of communication; family interaction is more permanent because the channels have prescribed roles and functions; tribal ceremonies or military mobilization require a network with interrelated channels. A network, in other words, is a number of channels or points of contact with a higher degree of organization.

A network is easy to spot, especially in politics. Two people — or a million — complaining about high taxes are communicating a message. If some of them join forces, they establish a channel, and if they become a political party running for election, they add a new branch to the political network. Note that this particular example of network is closely related to some permanence, internal organization, and even control. In analyzing political networks, we are very much interested in these aspects, especially the degree of network institutionalization.

The distinction between networks and channels in physical communication systems is based on interrelationship. In a network a change in one element is followed by changes in related elements, whereas a channel is more isolated (Wiener, 1961). A *channel* is a relatively stable communication linkage independent of particular messages. A street is a channel linking physical objects, as is the "hot line" between Washington and Moscow. Organizations and groups are also communication channels, and, ultimately, so are all human beings (Miller, 1967: 47).

In analyzing communication channels we are interested in transmission capacity, technical fidelity, and measurable attributes such as "traffic" and "noise." In political channels we are more interested in distinctions such as "vertical" and "horizontal" channels. The kinds of questions we ask are: What are the links established by channels (Schramm in Pool et al, 1973: 116)? Do these channels lead to a political center? What is their degree of social penetration? Who has access, and who can receive or send messages through particular channels?

Lest one think I am interested only in the structural aspects of communication, let me reemphasize that networks and channels are only communication devices. What counts ultimately is the *flow of information:* meaning, direction, and impact. "We communicate to influence" (Berlo, 1960: 12). The analysis of information flow aims at revealing the connection, if any, established between specific sources and specific audiences. The very existence of a channel is more essential to the analysis of political communication than the fact that it may be used only to transmit and not to receive messages. Such a distinction between "existence" and "usage" will help us draw a line between different types of political development.

There remains the old question about cause and effect relationships: Do social characteristics determine communication, or vice versa? Lerner (1958: 56) tried to answer this question by pointing out two conclusions that emerged from his study. First, the direction of change is always from simple face-to-face communication to more complex and modern ones. Second, the rate of change to modern communication is highly correlated with other social changes, such as education and urbanization. Hence, communication is both an *index* for and an *agent* of social change once the process of modernization has begun.

Communication is an opportunity to interact, to do something collectively. Successful communication requires that exchanges of messages be understood more often than not. The more two people interact, the better the chances are that they will do it again and more effectively. The more a group exchanges messages, the better the chances for channels to become permanent. The more members of a whole society have opportunities to communicate, the better the chances for the communication network to develop. A developed communication network provides an infrastructure for coordinated efforts aimed at achieving collective goals. This is the realm of politics.

POLITICS AND POLITICAL SYSTEMS

Without communication, there can be no collective effort and therefore no politics. To speak of politics is to speak of relationships between members of a community (Rae and Taylor, 1970: 26). What are the unique characteristics of political, as compared to nonpolitical, interactions? Heller's answer still applies: "Political activity is the effort to develop and utilize organized social power" (1933: 301). Power is probably the most important unit of analysis in political science, but there is no need to draw artificial boundaries between power relationships and information exchanges. The two are not separate processes in which

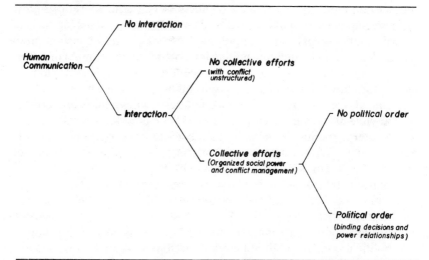

Figure 1.1   Communication Infrastructure of Politics

entirely different signals are transmitted. Communication analysis must be combined with power analysis because neither can fully replace the other. Etzioni's attempt to draw a distinction between communication and power is not very helpful for the study of politics. Both are based on previous information, and each contains transmission of messages as well as energy. Power relationships, too, are expressed through human communications and interactions, and there are no parallel networks of power and communication (Etzioni, 1968: 338). By definition, there is only one network per political system, although it can be used differently for different purposes. Political behavior in terms of power, pressures, influence, and sanctions takes place in the context of communication and interaction. One need not worry whether the coercive aspects of power are more important than the relational ones, or whether power *is* politics or only a "currency," a medium of politics, much like money in the economy (Parsons, 1969: 352-404).

In Figure 1.1, communication precedes politics; but it is also present in every part of the political process. For instance, when two groups are not isolated, their members can communicate (travel, talk, exchange messages). Such communication can result in one encounter and no real interaction; or it can lead to social interactions with more meaningful and more repetitive exchanges (transactions of goods and ideas). Once there is social interaction, it can be aggregated (again, a communication process) into collective efforts aimed at using organized social power to pursue common goals and handle conflicts. When collective efforts grow into mechanisms for making binding decisions (and establishing rules of power relationships), we have politics. Politics is thus a constant process of defining and redefining human interactions in the context of power relationships: formally — rules and procedures for applying sanctions — and informally — personal and group influences. For anyone still unconvinced, we can say that studying politics in communication terms is worthwhile at the very least because so much of politics is talk.

The term "political system" is suitable for our purposes because it is shorthand for all political interactions in society. Most definitions of political system will suffice because they refer to interrelated mechanisms that translate human wants and conflicts into "dependable coordination" (Deutsch, 1963), "bindingness" (Parsons, 1969), and "authoritative allocation of values" (Easton, 1965a). These mechanisms constitute a communication network which siphons the actual or potential political content of all human interactions into the polity. Accordingly, the political system is that part of society which is held from within by exchanges of information.

Hence to distinguish between "social interaction" and "political interaction" in human behavior is impossible. In the sociopolitical compound, these elements are intermingled and fluid. The analytical convenience of presenting political systems as separate elements for observation should not be accompanied by the assumption that politics has a meaning unto itself.

POLITICAL COMMUNICATION

At present, politics and communication are two separate fields of inquiry. Any attempt to use a monocle to view both is likely to fail, because scholars in each field have been exploring different terrains. I suggest the term "political communication" as the title of this joint inquiry, although admittedly some confusion is possible.

Current literature on political communication is often confined to the political aspects of the mass media or, more broadly, any communication considered political due to implications for the political system (Fagen, 1966: 20; Nimmo, 1978: 7). According to Mueller (1973), political communication depends on social class, language, and socialization patterns. A different framework has been suggested by Gurevitch and Blumler (in Curran et al., 1977: 270-290), in which political systems and communication systems are compared. Political communication has been a cornerstone of many studies of political development (Lerner, 1958; Pye, 1963; McCrone and Cnudde, 1967). Fagen (1966) moved one step further and defined political communication as any communication within the political system and between the system and its environment. He also suggested studying the communication network (organizations, groups, mass media, and specialized channels) together with the economic and social determinants of communication patterns. Almond and Powell maintain that instead of reconceptualizing all political science in terms of communication, political communication should be regarded as one "political function" among others (1966: 165). They add, however, that the communication function constitutes "a necessary prerequisite for performance of other functions" (p. 166). In the 1978 edition, the authors write that "on reflection [we] have decided that communication is best considered a system function" (p. 16), along with political socialization and recruitment. The following quote is very close to describing the approach suggested in this book:

> Political communication is a basic system function with many conse-
> quences for maintenance or change in political culture and political
> structure. One can assume, indeed, that all major changes in the
> political system involve changes in communication patterns, usually as
> both cause and effect. All socialization processes, for example, are
> communications processes, although communication need not result in
> attitude change. Similarly, the coordination and control of individuals
> in different organizational roles require communication of information.
> Hence, establishing new socialization patterns and building new or-
> ganizations both require changes in communication performance
> [Almond and Powell, 1978: 152].

Easton's theory (1965a, 1965b) is also a politics-as-communication approach. Easton, however, is mainly interested in the broad categories of information flow (demands, supports, decisions) and in the function of the system in processing information and coping with stress. Because of his different purpose, he is less interested in the communication network itself, its development, and the influences of flow on the content of politics. The network is taken more or less as given, except for the important discussion of communication "gatekeepers." Easton's concepts have served as a basis for further development of communication-oriented studies (see Chaffee, 1975: 85-128; Brants and Kok, 1976).

The approach of this book follows Deutsch's analysis (the subtitle of his book is "Models of Political Communication and Control") and regards political communication as the infrastructure of politics — a combination of all social interactions and information flow pertaining to collective efforts and power relationships. Deutsch maintains that politics can be explained through a cybernetic model of communication and

TABLE 1.1   Communication Components in Political Development*

I. General Prerequisite:	(1) common contents (symbols, social integration, cohesion, nation-building)
II. Political Development:	(2) political network (institution-building, state-building, control)
	(3) information flow (communication, coordination, decision-making)
	(4) channels' penetration and maintenance (political socialization, mobilization, and recruitment)
	(5) steering (governing, policy-making, leadership)
III. Democratic Political Development:	(1) through (5) above plus:
	(6) access (political mobility, modernization)
	(7) political participation (efficacy, elections)
	(8) impact on steering (democratization, polyarchy, citizens' rights, accountability)

*The closest noncommunication terms from political science and sociology are given in parentheses.

control. All governments, "as all communication systems, depend upon the processing of information" (1963: 145). Accordingly, social and political phenomena can be explained as acts of communication. Communication is regarded as not just important for social interaction: It *is* social interaction. Politics is thus a special kind of information transfer, one that has to do with governing — that is, steering. Governing a social organization, like steering a ship, relies primarily on information flow and feedback.

Deutsch's conceptual framework for a communication approach to politics is broad and original, ranging over a wide spectrum of topics, and perhaps this is the difficulty in applying his approach to the study of a concrete political system or for comparative analysis.[1] Although Deutsch's ideas have penetrated political science research (*The Nerves of Government* has been among the most quoted books in the field), his pioneering intellectual enterprise has not been broadly applied or significantly developed since its publication in 1963.

In seeking a more operational framework for the study of political communication, I propose a model in which political development is analyzed in communication terms. This is presented in outline form in Table 1.1.

In this table, common contents are regarded as a general prerequisite for political development. The four additional components that are evident in political systems are the political network (center, secondary centers, and periphery), information flow (horizontal, vertical, and diagonal), channels (penetration and maintenance), and steering. In addition, I will focus on components of *democratic* political development defined in communication terms with respect to access, participation, and impact on steering. To avoid confusion, I should mention here that the distinction between "political development" and "democratic political development" in Table 1.1 represents "stages" only if one regards the experience of Western political systems as a model. We now know, however, that there is nothing necessarily sequential about these components. The distinction is aimed only at mapping varieties of political development.

The remainder of this chapter will be devoted to an understanding of these concepts of political communication. Subsequently, they will serve as the basis for analyzing political development in Israel.

Political Development

Compared to the literature on economic development, there is a paucity of studies of political development. One prevailing assumption has been that the polity will develop after the economy when the latter reaches a certain stage, or takeoff point (for example, Rostow, 1960). However, this is one trap into which students of political communication have not fallen (Lerner, 1958; Deutsch, 1961; Cutright, 1963; Fagen, 1966; McCrone & Cnudde, 1967; Binder et al., 1971). The study of communication and development has had a different and more integrated perspective of overall social transformation.[2] (Pye, 1966: 155).

The attempt here to demonstrate a communication approach to the study of political development need not become enmeshed in the controversies surrounding the topic of development. Political systems will "start to develop" for different reasons: external — the displacement of a colonial regime, for example — or internal — evolutionary social processes or revolutionary efforts of leaders. That which bridges the gap between social and political development is the emergence of "common contents." This is the underlying condition without which social interactions cannot be translated into politics.

COMMON POLITICAL CONTENTS

A political system cannot grow without a common political language. In order to move from "cultural" communication and interactions to organized collective efforts, a cluster of people must agree on certain meanings, such as the symbols of power. Even if these collective efforts are imposed by an authoritarian leader, he still needs a common political language of coercion, compliance, or violence. This is a reference not to more communnication or more intensive interactions, but to an increased sharing of political meanings.

Sometimes more contacts breed more friction, while a minimum secures political cooperation. This raises the question of whether our emphasis on communication entails a *cooperative* model of politics rather than a *conflictory* one (Baldwin, 1978: 1229-1242). The answer is negative. Political communication requires common contents because otherwise conflicts, too, would not be structured and not handled through binding power relationships (see Figure 1.1).[3] The outcome of a political process could be more cooperation, more conflict, or both.

The common contents of political communication such as simple identification with the national anthem and the flag, or the internalization of political roles, are rooted in culture and society (Parsons, 1971: 9). The basis for the functioning of any political system is minimal social integration or the emergence of links among the various parts of society. Law, rules of membership and citizenship, economic markets, and bureaucratic organizations are examples of integration methods. Loyalty to a nation as a central collective norm is the most common basis for the functioning of political systems in modern times. The state as a concrete expression of this norm is the most prevalent manifestation of national integration. For those who view political development primarily as a process of national integration, the study of communication is a natural ally (Fagen, 1966: 124-128; Pye, 1955: 62-67).

What is the minimum amount of integration required for political development? The existence of a state is perhaps evidence of minimal integration, at least as far as concrete boundaries are concerned, but there are states in which the political system barely exists. Conversely, the Zionist movement will be presented as an example of a political system which existed long before the State of Israel was established. Cultural and social integration could stop short of politics — collective efforts capable of producing public goods. However, although social integration requires common political contents and meanings and increases the opportunities for collective efforts, the road is not inevitable. Integrated communities might find it difficult to agree on political action. In contrast, despite social cleavages that pose obstacles to integration, there are systems that function adequately because there is agreement on a limited political agenda (say, in defense or in economic regulations).[4] In the terminology of this book, these systems have acquired a

TABLE 1.2   Social Integration and Common Political Contents

	Social Integration	Common Political Contents
(1)	yes	yes
(2)	yes	no
(3)	no	no
(4)	no	yes

minimal common political vocabulary which provides some cohesion to political life.

Theoretically there are four possible correlations between social integration and political contents, as presented in Table 1.2. Cases 1 and 3 are developed (modern) and underdeveloped (traditional) systems, respectively. Case 2 can be visualized as a socially integrated society about to become independent and create its political system. As noted above, case 4 is possible when, despite low social integration, leaders and elites develop intensified collective efforts. This case also points to the possibility that politics can sometimes be the independent variable in social processes. I now present the above four cases in terms of political communication.

(1) When a society is relatively integrated, the probability of developing a modern and differentiated political system is higher. In such a system, politics has a separate language which is expressed in symbols, offices, laws, regulations, and "rules of the game." Members know that the prime minister does not judge and that the judge does not collect taxes.

(2) The social bonds are there, but they have no common political meaning as yet. Social interactions encompass all aspects of life, and political communication is merely a part of social communication. In such systems (isolated communities, or newly created states), we find political leaders who also issue divine orders or make no distinction between their private and public purses.

(3) There is no political language and there are no solid social bonds. The level of interaction is low, and chances are small that common social meanings will become a basis for developing common political contents. Individuals, groups, or communities interact, but this does not necessarily lead to collective political efforts.

(4) Social integration is low, but certain segments or subcultures of the society develop the ability to talk to each other politically. People in such a system may live separately, may speak different languages, and

seldom interact because of cultural, religious, and other cleavages. Nevertheless, they share a political language in order collectively to attain security, economic gains, technological advantages, and so forth. Here the language is indeed unique, because its contents are primarily political and often removed from the subcultures from which they sprang. We can even find national politics conducted in a foreign language. In such systems, the flow of information with high political content is paramount.

According to Pye, integration as a basis for development depends on the amplifying function of communication whereby "man-sized" acts are transformed into "society-sized" acts (1963: 60). This ability to imbue human interaction with new sociopolitical contents and meanings usually requires modern means of communication, such as channels provided by political parties or mass media.

We need not settle here the dispute about whether modern communication media created new contents or vice versa (Bauman in McQuail, 1972: 61-74). In the case of common political contents, it makes a big difference if the political messages are carried on horseback, along roads and railways, or through media such as television or satellites. It is therefore not surprising that case 4, which is low on integration and high on common political contents, has appeared concomitantly with electronic mass media. These media can diffuse and infuse common political contents even before the social ground has been properly prepared. In this respect, modern media are much quicker — although not necessarily more effective and enduring — than conventional socialization and integration structures such as schools. Modern communication enables the different interests scattered in society to coalesce and to enter into political cooperation or conflict before they understand each other. Short of war and civil disturbance, such a process also supports the political system in its role as chief arbitrator in society.

THE POLITICAL NETWORK

A minimal political vocabulary is a prerequisite for political development, and the first task toward this end is to build a political communication network. What is the difference between a "communication network" and a "political communication network"? A network is "any system characterized by a relevant degree of organization, communication and control, regardless of the particular processes by which its messages are transmitted and its functions carried out" (Deutsch, 1963: 80). The political communication network is more specialized. Because of its gravitation toward institutionalization, it is more organized, more structured, and more task-oriented than the general network in the society where it belongs. In modern societies, the political network establishes permanent contact between the "centers" and the "noncenters" of the political system. Note that we do not assume the existence of a separate political network, only the possibility of distinguishing some special attributes.

A network means some form of institutionalization, and this requires organizational instruments (Selznick, 1956; Huntington, 1968: 8-11). In a newly developing political system, these instruments are the institutions that specialize in politics. Institution-building takes place when (a) a higher level of differentiation in society makes politics a separate domain (Eisenstadt, 1970: 15-17) and (b) there is a consolidation of power which enables these institutions to gain both the authority and the ability to act.

Equating institution-building with the construction of a communication network is not new to those familiar with organizational theory. Simon, following Barnard's lead, introduced communication as the essence of any organization (1957: 154-157). Since then the scope has been greatly expanded by empirical studies of communication processes (Blau and Scott, 1962: 116-139) and systems theories of networks and information flow (Brown in Baker, 1973: 236-246; Hall, 1972: 269-293). In Barnard's words:

> In an exhaustive theory of organization, communication would occupy a central place, because the structure, extensiveness, and scope of the organization are almost entirely determined by communication techniques [1938: 91].

Similarly, the politics in a political system is carried out through the communication network. Political institutions such as the executive, courts, public bureaucracy, and parties shape the structural attributes of the network, and there are many formal and informal linkages as well. In other words, the political network establishes links among those who steer (the center), co-drivers (secondary centers), and passengers (the periphery).

In brief, constructing a political communication network means (1) a higher level of differentiation and a specialized network for the circulation of political information, (for example, the development of a national bureaucracy); (2) formal channels for the flow of support to the political center (for example, votes) and for the diffusion of political decisions, laws, and propaganda to the periphery; (3) a hierarchical quality of institutions which gives some immediate order to the complex of channels; and (4) efforts by the center toward coordination and control, which supplies the cement for the whole system.

A good place to begin a discussion of the political communication network is from the location of its switchboard: the political center.

The Political Center: The political system requires a center for coordination and control. According to Shils (1975: 3), a "center" is a central zone in the structure of society, the hub of its order of symbols, values, and beliefs. The center is the hub of action as well for the activities of its people and institutions. A political center also serves as a focus for identification — with the roles performed by political actors and organizations — and the technical locus of coordination and control. Although it is not identical with the chief executive or any other concrete institution, the political center carries authority and symbolizes the system as a whole.

Above all, the political center is a communication concept, a theoretical point within the communication network. It is what Gross calls the "central guidance cluster," serving leadership, managerial, and other critical roles (1965: 103-106). A political center can — and in a democracy it should — be accessible to all members. Once aware of the distinction between the center as a role and the central institutions as concrete entities of organization, network-building can be defined as the process of creating the means — especially the core channels — by which the center can function in handling the flow of political information. This function is here called "steering capacity," and it refers to the use of specific channels as well as to controlling the direction of information flow.

Secondary Centers: The notion of one center per system makes analysis easier, but it is not an accurate reflection of reality. A society may have more than one center in terms of values or economic activities, but such a situation cannot be tolerated for long, much like a ship with two helms. Political development by its nature moves toward the consolidation (or hegemony) of one political center. This, of course, does not imply that the political center holds a monopoly: The more modern a system, the more the center must rely on the coordinated performance of secondary centers and share with them the handling of information and power.

The nature of secondary centers differs from system to system. They may exist in the form of subcultures divided along religious or ethnic lines. There may be even secondary national institutions which play an active role in policy-making. In Israel, the labor camp and its institutions are an example of a powerful secondary center. But regardless of their power and the extent to which secondary centers reduce the centrality of the political center, they do not assume the dominant position in the network. They occupy the space between the center and the periphery, the government and the public, and they perform important communication tasks such as serving as screens, preventing information overload, and reaching into nonpolitical segments of society.

The Periphery: In Shils's terminology, the periphery is the hinterland of the political center — those parts of society that are connected to the center through the network but are not fully politicized. Without a periphery there is no political center; hence the term must refer to those who recognize the authority of the center. Yet there are groups that are more marginal than others, and the degree of incorporation within the communication network can be expressed in terms of the relative distance from the center.[5] In analyzing the Israeli political system, two kinds of peripheral groups will be identified. First, from the vantage point of the center, there are target groups that the center or the secondary centers try to penetrate; second, from the vantage point of the periphery, there are marginal groups that try to gain access and participate.

The development of the political network, in Shils's terms, is the invasion of society by the political domain. There are, however, penetration efforts from below, and they can criss-cross the formal communication network with many ad hoc channels.

THE CHANNELS

What distinguishes a modern political system from a traditional one, according to Eisenstadt, is the constant interaction between political institutions and leaders on the one hand and broad social components on the other. In modern societies, even totalitarian ones, all rulers are to some degree accountable to the ruled (Eisenstadt, 1973: 74-75). Any political system, even if it does not provide the popularly desired collective goods, needs political support. This support can be obtained only after the communication network penetrates the politically relevant parts of society.

Organizations which extend communication channels into society include the bureaucracy, the political parties, and the mass media. Literature on political development usually divides the tasks among them as follows: the bureaucratic channels are used to mobilize money (taxes) and manpower (military recruitment); the party channels, to mobilize political support; and the mass media channels, to inform, educate, and propagandize. In practice, each channel, singly or in combination with others, can carry two-way communications about all these subjects and many more.

Political penetration means crossing both geographical and social boundaries. Naturally the main efforts of the center are directed toward the more problematic peripheral groups, and they become prime penetration targets. *Political maintenance* means preserving the fruits of penetration and retaining the loyalty of the periphery with its recognition of the legitimacy of the center. The unique attributes of the society determine the kind of channels employed for penetration and maintenance.

We can identify the major channels used at one time or another, but we cannot generalize about their absolute advantages and disadvantages. Mao and Gandhi used "mass line" channels of leadership to reach millions of widely scattered Chinese and Indians (Singh and Gross, 1979). In many developing countries, bureaucratic channels were the most important (LaPalombara, 1963: 3-61). In Israel, party channels dominated for a long time both before and after the state was established (Galnoor, 1977: 191-193).

Parties and bureaucratic agencies are political organizations whose structures and hierarchies serve as communication channels. They almost always intervene in the flow of information to modify, aggregate, direct, and discard political messages. As mediators, they also have great potential for employing the channels in a two-way flow. Sending political messages from the elite to nonelites, from the authorities to the public, is a central function of the party and bureaucratic channels. Also important is their function not only in mobilizing support but in sending upward information about demands, restlessness, frustrations and disobedience.

In the case of mass media, their precise function is disputable; in any event, their channels carry more than just political information. Nevertheless, a political system cannot ignore the penetrative and maintenance potential of newspapers, radio, television, and movies. Yet if the society still comprises traditional communal entities, penetration through the mass media is not so simple.[6] The media are usually used in combination with other social instruments. They become more independent and perhaps also more powerful as the society becomes more atomized and the culture acquires "mass" characteristics (Kornhauser, 1959: 32; Etzioni, 1968: 443-446).

The role of the mass media in political development is intriguing because the media are independent technological instruments whose product is accessible to great numbers of people (Gerbner in McQuail, 1972: 40-41). Side by side with the party and bureaucratic channels, the mass media have emerged as a formidable instrument for reaching, mobilizing, and maintaining the support of most members of society.

Institutional channels are "core channels" (Fagen, 1966: 35). Information also flows in various other types of channels: periodical (voting), occasional (boycotting), voluntary (monetary donations), private (rumors), and public (billboards). Political systems also use nonpolitical channels, such as families, groups, associations, clubs, schools, and factories. But the task of extending a communication network to all parts of society — an essential component of political development — is usually carried out by organizations. This is why institution-building must precede channel penetration. Without a political center, any network, even if it possesses elaborate channels, provides only for flow and no direction.

INFORMATION FLOW

For purposes of simplicity, let us assume that the political center is monolithic and the only internal problems are the horizontal flow of information among leaders. Below the center are other political bodies such as parties, trade unions, and associations. (In the Israeli context they are referred to as "secondary centers" because they share political power with the center.) In the communication network, they operate as mediators and gatekeepers and exercise a great deal of control over the withholding and release of information as well as aggregation and recombination (Easton, 1965b: 95-97). They are not automatic relay points and informational exchanges. Their position vis-à-vis the center could be described as "diagonal" — partly between equals (horizontal) and partly between superior and subordinate (vertical). The information relationship between the secondary centers and the public is also diagonal. The vertical flow of information is between the center and the public. The public consists of an attentive part — those who are politically mobilized — and the nonattentive parts — the "target groups," those who have not yet been fully incorporated into the political system. For the center, the main communication problem with the mobilized public is one of maintenance. The target groups pose a penetration challenge.

Figure 1.2 illustrates the directions of information flow within a political system. All types of information flows could be face to face, organizational, or through mass channels. Newspapers, for instance, operate in a, b, c, and d. Similarly, leaders talk to foreign leaders (a), to each other (b), to representatives of other organizations (c), and occasionally to private citizens (d).

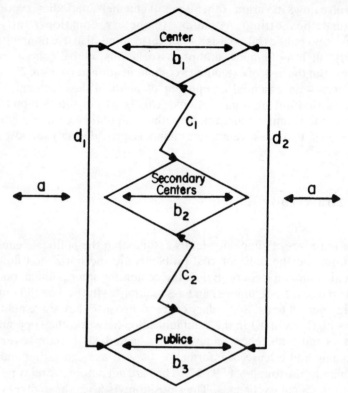

a. Information flow to and from environment
b. Horizontal information flow
    b_1 within the political center
    b_2 among secondary centers
    b_3 within the public (social or political)
c. Diagonal information flow
    c_1 between the center and secondary centers
    c_2 between secondary centers and the public
d. Vertical information flow
    d_1 between the center and the public at large
    d_2 between the center and specific peripheral groups

Figure 1.2   Information Flow Within Political Systems

NOTE: This figure does not reflect communication exchanges between countries (Brecher, 1974).

STEERING

The concept of steering (Deutsch, 1963) suggests a markedly different view of politics and political development. Governments, of course, formulate policy, make decisions, allocate resources, and go to war; but their most important role is steering the system. What is referred to here as the political center or the "central guidance cluster" is identifiable by its main function — keeping the system steady and guiding it toward some future goal.

The extent to which goals are achieved, however, is not the foremost measure of the development of a political system. A system is developing when it starts to acquire the capacity to secure its self-survival, to adjust to environmental changes, to make decisions that are binding, and to invest in its own viability. Without goal-seeking facilities, no goals can be achieved. A political system without steering capacity is a ship with a disconnected helm: It can drift, but it cannot develop purposeful movement.

Political development is thus defined as a movement in the direction of creating "steering capacity." It is proposed that this capacity can be evaluated according to the following criteria, briefly outlined here:

(1) *Autonomy* — the relative independence of the political system to conduct politics as a separate social function.

(2) *Monopoly on official symbols* — a monopoly on official information and on the creation or representation of political symbols associated with common contents, such as the nation or the state.

(3) *Exclusiveness* — one steering locus per system, centrally located in the communication network, and with monopoly on coercion.

(4) *Transmission and intake* — the ability of the center to engage in selective exchanges of information with external and internal environments.

(5) *Diffusion and legibility* — overcoming communication barriers through controlled channels which transmit information with minimal loss and distortion.

(6) *Avoidance of breakdown* — ability to survive damages to the steering mechanism and retain control of the system, or at least the politically relevant parts of it, in crisis situations.

Note that item 1, autonomy, alludes to the general status of the political system within society and to the extent that the polity is differentiated enough to perform the specialized steering role. Item 6, avoidance of breakdown, brings us close to the *results* of steering: to what extent steering is capable of keeping the system on a steady course, or guiding it toward orderly and purposeful changes. And items 2 through 5 correspond to the relationships between the development of the center's steering capacity and the evolution of common contents, the building of the communication network, the flow of political information, and the penetration and maintenance capabilities of channels.

A developed political system has high marks on all six criteria of steering capacity. There are also many intermediate combinations: A political system may be autonomous and possess exclusive control, but it may have low legibility in its information contents and lack of transmitting channels to reach all parts of society. A full understanding of these criteria is possible only in a specific context; thus steering capacity will be discussed in terms of the Israeli political system in Chapter 8.

Steering capacity is neutral in terms of the normative direction of change. None of the six indicators presented above is necessarily tied to questions of popular support or government responsiveness. Steering effectiveness is evaluated according to its ability to overcome "noise" and "disturbance" and not by its responsiveness to social demands. Indeed, better steering means a greater capacity to achieve goals, regardless of one's view of the desirability of those goals. Thus, building a communication network and channel penetration could be completely coercive.

The most important point in this discussion is that *political development, when stripped to its basic communication terms, is not inherently related to democratization.* This statement contradicts many theories in which democracy and political development are needlessly confused. The rest of this chapter will present the additional communication components that are needed in order to achieve democratic political development.

Democratic Political Development

Political development has been discussed in terms of building the communication infrastructure in such a way as to reach every member of society. Now the focus shifts to the efforts of members of society to reach the political system. The goal of democratic political development is therefore not just steering, but members' impact on steering through inclusion and participation in the communication network.

Although steering the political system requires a certain level of obedience and compliance on the part of the individual citizen, political awareness or voluntary participation is not necessary for high steering capacity and political development. But how can individual citizens and groups take part in and influence steering? What are the communication aspects of civil liberty and citizens' rights?

Information flow will be examined in order to determine whether a system is developing politically and whether the direction that has been taken can be termed "democratic." In pursuing this new set of questions, we are not repeating the discussion on common contents, the center, the network, and the channels; rather, we are asking how they operate once the public is added as an independent component in the steering process.

Even though the communication network itself does not necessarily change under different political circumstances, it will behave differently if, for example, the downward flow is supplemented by independent autonomous messages from the periphery. Political development is ostensibly neutral — it entails the refinement of steering capacity that can be used for different purposes and can result in the emergence of different political systems. If we happen to be interested in the possibility of a system becoming democratic (this being a normative concern), we should ask if there are indications that steering is influenced by individual citizens who have access to the communication network and use it. The two research items offered in response are "access" and "participation."

ACCESS

When does an individual become a factor in politics? The usual answer is when he or she influences the political affairs and collective decisions of his or her community. But "influence" is elusive. A remote village is being connected by a road to the main city — does this prove the village farmers have political influence? Would the answer be "yes" if the farmers demanded the road and "no" if they were not consulted about it? Moreover, a political leader is expected to anticipate what is good for the people and to act accordingly. These people are apparently political factors, but do they really have influence?

It is not enough to discuss entrance into and membership in the political system. I shall distinguish between members and groups which have gained *access* to political resources and those which actually *participate* in the allocation process — that is, influence political decisions. Access here means the opportunity open to individuals and groups to join the political system through *a voluntary linkup with the political communication network*. Thus, access to information is a means for reaching other political resources.

Access in this sense is closely related to social mobility, expressed in changes of residence, occupation, family setting, institutional affiliations, and personal behavior and expectations (Deutsch, 1961: 494). These changes have political consequences reflected by new affiliations to political institutions. Indicators of social mobility — such as urbanization, education, and income — are therefore good predictors of political mobility. Individual political mobility means entrance into the political system — what Easton terms "membership" (1965a: 56-57).

In the case of involuntary mobilization, individuals are sought for their contribution of tangible political resources to the military, the labor force and the tax authorities. Their general support of the regime is important but not crucial. In the case of voluntary access, on the other hand, individuals want to find out what they stand to gain through the use of political channels, and it is they who link up. Even if approached by party officials or bureaucrats and consequently linked up with the network, individuals' predispositions make the critical difference between being passively mobilized or actively using the channels. In the latter case, the network adjusts itself to this predisposition through content of messages and frequency. Individuals become a political factor to be considered, at least as far as the flow of information is concerned.

What are the predispositions of those who seek access to political channels? First, they are already fairly well integrated, if they are aware of the political messages around them. Second, modern technology, and especially the mass media, are not alien to individuals, and they slowly develop a concern for issues beyond their immediate environment. Finally, they are ready to move from face-to-face to more elaborate modes of communication. They are mobile, socially and politically, and have the skill to obtain access to information (Lipset, 1959: 190-200).

Mobility and access are closely related to the description of the modern person presented by Inkeles and Smith: an informed participant-citizen, efficacious, independent and autonomous, flexible and open to new ideas and experiences (1974: 289-290). This modern person is a potential "atom of political power," gained through the influence of modern institutions such as schools, factories, and the mass media (p. 146). He or she is an avid consumer of political information and, consequently, subject to endless efforts on the part of the authorities and other institutions to communicate ideas, attitudes, and information. This modern person is "wired." At this stage we are not interested in whether he or she also *sends* messages (participates), because even if not, he or she is already a factor in the political communication network. According to our definition, gaining access voluntarily means becoming an interested, but not yet active, part of the "attentive public" (Nimmo, 1978: 263-265).

Access is the opportunity to send political messages upward from periphery to center, from individuals to leaders. Mobilization may be guided or forced, but access is a voluntary and autonomous decision to become political. One way to evaluate the degree of autonomy in a political system is to observe access, not only of individuals but also of groups; and not only to the main channels such as the bureaucracy but also to intermediate channels such as trade unions, interest groups, and voluntary associations. When access is almost nil, the political system can establish its network and channels with practically no regard for the needs of individuals. This is when, for example, leaders use cultural contents for enforced political messages; oaths of loyalty are included in prayers and school materials; political speeches are broadcast through public speakers; and a party functionary is present at all communal gatherings.

When there is an awareness of the potential of political channels, the communication network begins to change and grow more complicated. Secondary centers and mediators such as special radio programs are then used to "translate" political messages to local and individual meanings. The two-step flow of communication becomes prominent, because both the political center and attentive individuals need noninstitutional intermediate channels to understand each other. Members start to become political factors, however weak, and government must respond. Although regional offices and youth organizations may be established and the mass media used extensively in order to hold back the tide of growing awareness, the pressure toward access increases. The network, channels, and contents of the political information can no longer ignore the new and noncenter factors.

When persons become voluntary members of political organizations, they have gained more than just access: They are ready to *use* communication channels and participate in political life.[7] At this stage, political organizations and other channels of communication start to adapt their structure and performance to the possibility of voluntary entrance (and exit) of members. We find, for instance, at least one forum that distributes information to all members, such as an annual general assembly or a leaflet. This process leads to increased informational activity and competition throughout the political system, and the center cannot afford to stay out. Access is accompanied by the appearance or increased use of state radio and television, official newspapers, and governmental information offices. Simultaneously, the number of consumers of political information increases, and the mass media technology is developed (or imported) more rapidly.

At this level of democratic political development, the political system can reach and is potentially accessible to members of society. We do not know how many are reached (obey political rules) but cannot themselves reach (gain voluntary access). We do not know which groups are excluded and on what basis (language, race, ethnicity, geography) and what is the real political importance of having gained access. A politically attentive person who listens to political news, belongs to a professional group and a local branch of a party, and votes in elections is a relevant factor, but can he or she influence politics?

Lindsay (1943) warned us that the answer to this question — how to keep government responsive — is not simple even where we have democratic voting, because the general approval or disapproval conveyed in votes is "only one among several ways of ensuring this [popular] control" (p. 285). When members gain access, they have only acquired potential political power.

PARTICIPATION

Political mobility and access to the communication network are prerequisites for political participation. Political participation means the utilization of the communication network and its channels by private citizens and groups in order to influence the actual steering of the system.[8] Whereas access is concerned with attitudinal involvement in politics, participation involves behavior (Nie and Verba, 1975: 9-12; Huntington and Nelson, 1976: 3-4). This separation between the passive and active aspects of membership in the political system is rather arbitrary (Benjamin, 1972: 23-25), but useful for understanding political communication. Participation includes efficacy — the belief in one's ability to influence politics. It is an attempt to *act*. The act itself is initially a communication effort directed toward others in the system. Even spectacular activities, such as violent riots, are ultimately messages containing political information. Thus, political participation includes one of the most important components of democracy: the autonomous initiation of information flow by independent groups and individuals.

Political participation entails some acquaintance with the network — how to initiate a message, demand something from the system, or respond to something already done. In other words, participation is an attempt to *use* the communication network and its channels autonomously, not as a result of mobilization from above. It is motivated by the desire to have an impact — to send power messages influencing the system's steering.

Political communicators have an impact on the *content* and *direction* of information flow and may add new channels and perhaps reshape the whole network and steering behavior. They must be counted twice: as both recipients and senders of political information.

Table 1.3 presents Nie and Verba's four modes of political participation (voting, campaign activities, contacting officials, and group cooperative activity) in terms of network and channel utilization and direction of information flow. There are, of course, other forms of participation, but these four titles capture the main types.

Table 1.3 illustrates that all four modes of active political participation transmit (a) low to high amounts of information, which ultimately register as a weak or a strong tremor in the steering mechanism, depending on (b) the degree of pressure. They all require (c) some form of citizen's autonomous initiative. Voting and contacting officials are rather close in terms of (d) — the vertical and mainly upward direction of information flow; (e) — the low probability of adding new channels to the communication network; and (f) — the low potential of having a significant impact on the network. These two modes of participation are in many respects a natural extension of mobility and access: gaining the ability and the political knowledge to use existing arrangements in order to express general preferences (voting); and the use of political and bureaucratic channels in order to complain or seek a particular benefit.[9]

Campaign and cooperative activities by citizens are generally highly developed modes of participation because the utilization of the communication network itself is autonomous and requires political skills and more intimate knowledge of the process.

When individual members interact politically with one another, they raise the probability of changing the structure and performance of the political communication network. Campaign activities, and especially cooperative activities of citizens, establish also a horizontal flow of political information [(d) in Table 1.3]. Moreover, if volunteers are engaged in door-to-door campaigns, or if people join to raise an issue, new channels are created. Participation of this kind implies commitment and investment of time. These resources do not guarantee political influence, but they do have a stronger impact on the communication network. The more persons participating in multidirectional transmission of political information, the more they become "political communicators" and the higher the probability of further democratic development.

TABLE 1.3 Modes of Participation in Terms of Political Communication

Modes of Participation	(a) Information Transmission	(b) Degree of Pressure	(c) Initiative Required	(d) Flow of Information	(e) Probability of new Channels	(f) Potential Impact on Network
1. Voting	low	high	little	vertical, upward	low	low
2. Campaign activity	low-high	high	some	horizontal	high	high
3. Contacting officials[a]	high	low	a lot	vertical, upward	none	low-high
4. Cooperative activity[b]	high	low-high	some or a lot	vertical & horizontal	high	high

SOURCE: Based on a similar table presented by Nie and Verba (1975: 12), with the addition of items (d), (e), and (f).

[a] Citizen-initiated contacts with "government officials."
[b] Citizens who join others and act in informal groups, or within interest groups and formal organizations.

On the basis of this analysis, a tentative sketch of two types or profiles of democratic political development can be offered. The first, given mobility and access, involves *responsive participation* — people vote, complain to public officials, and perhaps express a point of view with bumper stickers. Their conception of politics, however, is still of "subjects-participants," and their role as autonomous political communicators is relatively restricted (Almond and Verba, 1963: 24-26). In this case, the communication network resembles a fixed sound system: The listener has not composed the music and has no control of the channels and their content. He or she does have the ability to activate the system (access), to choose among a limited number of programs (voting), and to adjust the volume and noise knobs (complaints). But for the most part responsive participants are listeners. They can sometimes modify steering, but their chances of having impact are not very high, and the communication network is still likely to be dominated by central control.

In the second case, there is *committed participation* — people campaign and organize themselves because they believe their efforts can make a difference. Their commitment is related to a high level of efficacy and proved by investment of their personal resources: time, money, contacts, and reputation. Committed participants are personally involved in politics. Unlike responsive-participants, they try to control the means of communication in order to affect steering. While the purpose of the center is mainly control and monopoly, a network dominated by citizens aims at diminishing central control and making channels multidirectional — or even, if necessary, creating new channels that can reach all the way up. This may produce competition between two or more broadcasters of political information: participant citizens who influence the center, and the center, which tries to translate this participation into support.[10]

The transformation from responsive to committed participation is related to general social changes, but it depends on the development of the communication network. Such a transformation requires the emergence of communication channels capable of activating commitments: new groups, multidirectional utilization of the mass media, different ways of conducting election campaigns, and so on. In this connection, it is important to evaluate the access and participation opportunities of outside groups — those who are more peripheral than others and try to break into the political system. The place to look for democratic political development is in the circulation of political information and the way channels are utilized. The important question is, what difference do access and participation make in terms of steering the polity?

IMPACT ON STEERING

In the prior discussion of steering, the outcomes were ignored in favor of the concept of steering capacity. Impact of steering is also an aggregate concept referring to the potential of independent citizens and groups to influence their system's steering. Thus, democratic political development is a movement toward creating the opportunity for citizens to have an impact on steering. This impact is based on access and participation.

Democracy requires a strong belief in the wisdom of the "plain man" (Lindsay, 1943). One may add that modern conditions also necessitate a citizen's awareness, and this presupposes a certain measure of autonomy (Thompson, 1970: 17). An autonomous citizen should be able to lead and to respond. He or she should have the opportunity to develop both committed and responsive participation. Ideally, there should be a circular flow of information: from citizens to government (expressing preferences and reacting to government programs); and from government back to citizens (expressing leadership, preferences, and responding to demands and needs).

Political Equality: For our purposes here, political equality means that citizens have a right to transmit information about their preferences and that information transmitted by different citizens has an equal chance to exert pressure and influence steering. Citizens' political autonomy is a function of their individual rights — starting with equality before the law and ending with the right to express themselves and to discern what the government is doing.

Impact on steering requires a general condition of political equality, and political equality means that individual rights are normatively shared and legally guaranteed. One important freedom in this context is access to official information, popularly known as "the people's right to know." Without this right to information, there can be no impact on steering. This is a prerequisite for participation because it enables citizens to secure facts about the political activities of the center and the secondary centers and to gain access to critical information flowing horizontally and diagonally (Galnoor, 1977: 299-309). As for the equal opportunity to exert pressure and influence steering, one important indicator of this is the ability of peripheral groups to gain access to and participate in the political system.

Democratic political development is contingent also on two interrelated and important systemic conditions: feedback mechanisms and openness.

Feedback: Much of the information that originates from citizens and is flowing in upward vertical channels is what Easton calls "systemic feedback": "information that is fed back to the authorities about the nature and consequences of their decisions" (1965b: 363, 376-381). Deutsch's definition of feedback is broader: "a communication network that produces action in response to an input of information, and *includes the result of its own action in the new information by which it modifies its subsequent behavior*" (1963: 88, italics in original). Feedback in this sense means citizens conveying to the center information which is either corrective or aimed at changing the course of steering. Responsive participation, such as voting or contacting officials, is usually corrective feedback; while committed participation, particularly through group activities, is often change-oriented.

Any political system needs feedback for ascertaining that official information has reached its destination and for obtaining some kind of response (even if the feedback is completely enforced). Feedback is secured also through intermediary channels which are needed both by citizens (who individually can transmit very little) and by government (whose official institutions are not sufficient to secure penetration and widespread support). Regardless of the type of regime, a political system cannot exist without this feedback. It is absolutely necessary for steering: It may be used for central control or may signify committed participation and citizens' attempts to have an impact on steering.

Openness: Unlike feedback which refers to any response and thus is neutral as far as the goal of the system is concerned, openness is not a neutral concept. It refers to specific conditions not only in the political communication network but also in the society as a whole. It assumes a collective social goal: the desirability of citizens' access and participation as a means for enhancing political equality and for enabling feedback to influence steering. Complete openness exists when there is no deliberate interference in the free flow of information — there is no restriction on listening to political information in all channels and no control on channels or the right to create new ones. Openness means that there is freedom to discharge demands — complaints as well as support — and that the communication network is open for all messages at any time. (All these freedoms include the right *not* to use access and channels and *not* to initiate information flow.) There, as in other variables of democratic political development, the question "open to whom" and "closed to whom" must be carefully examined.

"Complete openness" is as evasive a concept as "full democracy." We suggest, therefore, that one regard the process of citizens gaining an

impact on steering through access and participation, as a movement
toward greater openness. The more a political system develops democratically, the more open will be its communication network and channels to members who seek response to their feedback.

Specifically, the continuum of closed-open political systems is based
on the degree of interference with the flow of information by the political
center. A completely closed system is an imaginary one in which the
center has full control of the communication network and a monopoly on
information flow; a completely open system would be a chaotic situation
in which no one controls channels or information flow. A political system
in which the principles of access and participation are accepted and
generally observed is more open than a system in which they are not.
There is no such thing as zero control of channels or no barriers on
information flow, but systems where such interference has to be justified
or can be contested are more open than those in which deliberate
interference is the rule.

Of interest are some general questions regarding the system's attitude toward the idea that citizens ought to influence steering. Citizens'
actions are in themselves a way of establishing such a climate in the
political culture,[11] but we prefer to present openness as if it were a
dependent variable — that is, contingent on general societal conditions
which enable citizens to gain access and to participate. This concept of
openness is narrower, but it is still close to Dahl's "liberalization" (1971:
4). He also refers to a systemic dimension — the opportunities for
citizens to formulate their preferences and to oppose, contest, and
compete with those of others. Political openness is therefore connected
to broader social characteristics.

> Attitudes favorable to participation within the political system play a
> major role in the civic culture, but so do such non-political attitudes as
> trust in other people and social participation in general [Almond and
> Verba, 1963: 30].

Instead of trying to define the exact parameters of openness in a
political system, I shall regard a system in which there are more opportunities for access and participation as more open. This is another way of
saying that in democracies or polyarchies, all citizens must have unim-
paired opportunities: "(a) to formulate their preferences; (b) to signify
their preferences to their fellow citizens and the government by individual and collective action; and (c) to have their preferences weighed
equally in the conduct of government." (Dahl, 1971: 2).

Let us assume there is "complete openness" — information flowing
freely in all directions and all channels. Now what? Does openness
indicate that members actually have an impact on central steering?

If we forget for a moment that there may also be distortion in openness and that the *image* of openness (Edelman, 1964) may be effective for information manipulation, the answer must be yes. The lack of restrictions on access, control of channels, and information fed into the steering process of a political system is bound to influence the center's responsiveness to participants. Moreover, participants need not be informationally active all the time -- their access and potential utilization of the network and the channels are often enough to generate anticipatory responsiveness. The potential of openness is the key to maximizing the number of sources of impact on steering.

Nondemocratic systems must also absorb different kinds of information from different sources in order to retain their steering capacity and survive. Open flow of information — actual or potential — in a system that tries to be nonresponsive must generate such enormous efforts to keep the lid on that, in fact, the system must do something about it, often ending with coercive measures. As will be seen clearly in the case of Israel, openness and nonresponsive steering do not go well together. Nonresponsive politics means programmed processes. Nonprogrammed steering requires frequent adjustments and even periodic goal modifications. Openness enables feedback information to circulate freely and increases the probability of influencing the steering process and its responsiveness to members' input. Openness could also result in political chaos — an extreme form of totally uncontrolled flow of information — in which all steering capacity breaks down.[12] Note also that openness is meaningless if the prerequisite of common political contents is not met, as is the case where the whole process of political development has just begun and the communication network is barely functioning. It does not follow, however, that openness comes necessarily after the exclusiveness over steering has been established by the center, or that participation must wait until the channels are firmly established.

The Israeli Case Study

> Judge: I have read your case, Mr. Smith, and I am no wiser now than I was when I started.
> Witness: Possibly not, My Lord, but far better informed.
> (Earl of Birkenhead, *Life of F. E. Smith,* Ch. 9)

Democratic political development is a special case of political development. It requires certain components which, in addition to steering capacity, will sustain citizens' impact on steering. This proposition will be tested in the examination of the Israeli political system as a case in

point. Political development in Israel will be presented in terms of
common contents, the political network, the main channels (with their
penetration and maintenance capabilities), and steering capacity; and
democratic political development in terms of access, participation, and
impact on steering.

The cutoff period in this book for the presentation of political development in Israel is the mid-1960s. The main reason for stopping
early is that many of the fundamental processes of political development
which had begun long before Israel's establishment in 1948 had reached
their culmination by that time. The Israeli political system by the 1960s
had become established, relatively consolidated, and stable and had
proved itself through twenty years of government, despite severe tests in
the areas of economics, social integration, and — above all — security.
The 1960s brought three critical challenges to the Israeli political system:

(a) The "Lavon Affair" — a major political crisis which started in 1960
     and continued on and off until the 1965 general elections[13];

(b) a severe economic recession (1966-1967); and

(c) the 1967 war between Israel and the neighboring Arab countries.

Although the political system successfully withstood these challenges, their cumulative impact on Israeli society and politics was so
profound that it would not be misleading to state that a new era ensued in
their wake (Galnoor, 1980: 119-148). Thus, the decision was made to end
the description of Israeli political development around 1967 with reference to subsequent events when a longer perspective seemed to be
helpful.

In the final chapter, the Israeli case study will also serve as the basis
for conclusions regarding comparative political communication.

Two points must be emphasized before the reader turns to the Israeli
case study. First, the theoretical framework presented in Chapter 1 is
broader than the specific application to the study of the Israeli political
system. This is necessary not only because any first attempt to use such
a general approach must be tentative, but also because every political
system is, after all, a unique case that may not precisely "fit" the more
encompassing theoretical framework. The additional utility of such a
theoretical approach should be tested by applying it to different political
systems on a comparative basis. Second, despite the definition here of
democratic political development as a special case of political development, some readers may gain the impression — from the order of
chapters in this book — that the reference is to "stages" of development.
Let me reiterate that nothing in the general framework or the Israeli case
study should suggest that development processes have an inevitable

sequence and that democratic development is a "natural" outcome of political development.

Communication concepts can sharpen the comparative study of political systems and their development, as well as being usefully applied to single-country analyses. While it is true that not all aspects of politics are covered by this approach — some of these limitations will become evident during the case study — nevertheless, the communication approach captures some of the richness of political life and illuminates the unique road that democratic-aspiring systems must travel.[14]

NOTES

1. There has been criticism that Deutsch's work is too "mechanistic" and that the cybernetic model fails to capture the richness of political life. Kuhn, for example, objects to Deutsch's cybernetic model of government because it deals almost exclusively with the communicational aspects of government organization and ignores the transactional (1974: 277). As illustrated in Figure 1.1, communication is not just one aspect of government; it is part and parcel of political transactions.

2. The study of political variables as independent causes of development started much later and was followed by studies of political development in developed and modernized countries. See, for instance, Sharkansky (1975).

3. This approach comes close to embracing the general implications of game theory for political analysis. The assumption is that politics, especially of international deterence relationships, takes place within a minimum set of accepted rules. See Luce and Raiffa (1957) and Schelling (1960).

4. Lijphart (1977) presents the full scope of this idea in his typology of democratic regimes, with strong emphasis on elite behavior (pp. 99-109).

5. Horowitz and Lissak (1978: 39-40) perceive the concepts of center and periphery as two extremes of a continuum along which different groups and subcenters can be located according to their distance from the center.

6. On problems of *exposure* to political communication not accompanied by persuasion, see Sears and Whitney (in Pool et al., 1973: 256-259). Our discussion of *penetration* through the mass media is from a different angle.

7. Compare with Apter's concept of "expansion of choice" (1971: 10-11).

8. We are focusing on utilization of the political communication network only, not on the actual influence and impact of participation.

9. Citizen-initiated contact may have more impact because citizens are in control of the timing and the agenda. When many citizens contact many public officials on the same issue (or express dissatisfaction about many issues), the impact on the communication network is significant. The authorities may find it necessary to respond collectively (an official statement), to establish new channels (a new bureau, an inquiry committee), or to pay the political consequences.

10. For an interesting distinction between "mobility channels" and "organizational channels" for political participation, see Huntington and Nelson (1976: 80-115).

11. The assumption is not far-fetched, since many studies suggest that the political debate in the community determines more than anything else the degree of participation in a certain society. See Huntington and Nelson (1976: 28) and Apter (1971: 3).

12. Participation may also lead to the weakening of existing political institutions, instability, and even the elimination of democracy through external or internal takeover (Huntington, 1968: 32-58).

13. See note 3 in Chapter 2, page 43.

14. On the hazards of unfounded comparative expectations, see Sartori (1970). On the desirability of developing the field of comparative political communication, see Blondel (1969: 223-243).

2

ISRAELI SOCIETY AND POLITICS:
AN OVERVIEW

"We came to this country to build
and to be rebuilt"
(FROM A PIONEERING SONG)

Israel is a new state. In this book the focus is on the development of the political system. It offers neither a historical analysis of Israeli politics nor a full account of all the social and economic developments. The selection of components has been dictated by the general theoretical framework presented in Chapter 1 and seeks new insight into Israeli political development by analyzing it through a communication vocabulary. This chapter is designed to provide a general background on Israeli politics: the external and internal environment and the interface between society and politics.

The period under review starts with the inception of the political system under the British Mandate in Palestine in the 1920s and ends in the mid-1960s. The main focus is on the years 1948-1967. Readers who are familiar with Israel may wish to skip this chapter.

Challenges in the External Environment

Although the focus in this book will be on internal political communication, what follows is a brief discussion of the system's performance in the external environment.

The story of the Israeli polity begins with a group of Jews who called themselves "Zionists" and began to view themselves as a nation without a state. The lack of a national territory was the most concrete challenge to face the infant political system of the Zionist movement. Many other national movements have had to fight foreign powers and overcome internal divisions on their road to independence. They have also had to face great challenges of nation-building after obtaining independence. The unique challenge — indeed the puzzle — of the Jewish national movement was the conceptualization and concrete definition of the nation itself. Not only were Jews scattered all over the world, but the basis upon which other movements define their national substance — physical boundaries — was missing. Many of the external challenges facing the Israeli political system stem from this fact.

THE STATE

Immigration of religious Jews to the Holy Land continued throughout the period of exile. In the 1870s several small groups of Jews living in Jerusalem and other towns decided to abandon their old way of life and to found agricultural settlements. In 1881 the first wave of politically conscious Jewish immigrants arrived in Palestine[1] from Eastern Europe to settle the land. Some seventy years later, the Jewish community in Palestine, as part of the world Zionist movement, achieved its most important goal — the establishment of a state. Not every national movement has been successful, and among the successful ones, the indigenous political system has not necessarily been the most important instrument in transforming aspirations to national independence. In the case of Israel, however, the politics of the Jewish community in Palestine and of the Zionist movement has been crucial. Through their political system, the Zionists in Palestine and abroad managed to acquire the tremendous political resources required to achieve statehood.

The odds that such an event would take place were poor, even in simple terms of time and space. On the one hand, the Zionist movement missed the emergence of nationalism in Europe. On the other hand, it appeared a bit too early to be part of the liberation movements of the peoples in Asia and Africa. Before World War II there was only guarded hope, even among the half-million Jews in Palestine, that it would be possible to achieve an independent state in an area closely watched by powerful international interests and bitterly disputed between Arabs and Jews. The struggle for independence required unusual political capabilities to conduct simultaneously the external diplomatic campaign and to mobilize the resources required for the local violent conflict. In terms of sheer political logistics — the gaining of external support, the struggle for internal unity, and the victory in the 1948-1949 war — the Jewish community possessed a powerful political system.

The political system that carried the burden of the struggle for independence and the establishment of the state in 1948 could not be regarded as fully developed or mature. Nevertheless, it already possessed two or three decades of experience in state-building. The foundations of the Israeli political system existed before the state was established and long before the present population of over three million were there.[2] This is a reverse order of political development — the political elite came before the masses (Arian, 1973: 140).

The establishment of Israel and the successful conduct of the war for independence created an aura of miraculousness around the political system and the leaders. They embarked upon the less glamorous process of running a state with a credit of proven ability. But the task of survival has remained crucial because of the continuation of the state of war between Israel and her neighbors, and therefore external challenges have continued to play a decisive role in the formation and development of the Israeli political system. Matters of security and foreign relations not only preoccupied the political leaders but also served as a criterion for their selection and a measure of their success. Mobilization of solidarity, popular support, volunteer work, and readiness to sacrifice were closely associated with the external threat. This also explains the willingness of Israelis to accept far-reaching obligations toward the state, such as long military conscription, very high tax burdens, severe emergency regulations and censorship, and many other restrictions.

In the period under review, the more conventional tasks of political systems and leaders, such as economic development or maintaining law and order, have been less important in Israel compared to the perform-ance tests in foreign affairs and security. In Israel, there was not only a widespread, firm belief in the primacy of politics, but also an almost sacramental attitude toward the state. This phenomenon is well known in other states (Geertz, 1964; Coleman in Binder et al., 1971), but the unique circumstances of Jewish revival after 2000 years of diaspora and the continuing threat to its survival gave the state and its political system a very special meaning in Israel.

WARS

War is a critical upheaval in the environment of a political system. It often subjects the system to the supreme test — proving its ability to guarantee the society's most decisive collective interest. A political system which fails this test forfeits its powers of survival and must change or disappear.

This is particularly apparent under Israeli conditions. The turbulent environment is an important constraint on the development of the Israeli political system. Deterrent capability and success in winning wars have been the decisive expression of the system's capacity to sustain the society and govern the state.

The Israeli political chronology of the last thirty years has been rent frequently by wars:

- The War of Independence (1947-1949) — during which the State of Israel was established. Ended with the signing of the Armistice Agreements between Israel and Lebanon, Syria, Jordan and Egypt.

- The Sinai Campaign (1956) — occupation of the Sinai peninsula by Israel. This was returned to Egypt in 1957.

- The Six Day War (1967) — closure of the straits of Tiran and massive concentration of forces by Egypt in Sinai led to war and subsequent Israeli occupation of territories from Syria (Golan Heights), Jordan (the West Bank), and Egypt (Sinai and the Gaza Strip). Ended with cease-fire agreements.

- War of Attrition (1969-1970) — artillery exchanges and brief encounters, mainly along the Israeli-Egyptian line on the Suez Canal. Ended with a resumption of the cease-fire in August 1970.

- The Yom Kippur War (1973) — joint attack by Syria and Egypt which ended with Egypt regaining parts of Sinai while Israel occupied territories west of the Suez Canal and in Syria. The cease-fire agreements were later supplemented with disengagement agreements between Israel, Syria, and Egypt (1974-1975). In 1979, Egypt and Israel signed a peace treaty.

In addition, during the periods between the wars, there were many clashes along the borders, terrorist activities, fierce rivalry in international bodies, economic sanctions, and political propaganda.

The wars of 1948, 1956, and 1967 — whose results were perceived by Israelis as successful — and the short periods of tranquility that followed them contributed to the survival capacity of the Israeli political system. On the other hand, the outcome of the other wars and a number of military operations were perceived as failures or not clear-cut successes. They include the abortive intelligence operation in Egypt in 1954,[3] the War of Attrition and, above all, the Yom Kippur War.

Five wars in but three decades have placed great economic, social, and emotional burdens on Israeli society. The effects of this situation are also evident in the role of military symbols in Israeli politics and in leadership credentials (Luttwak and Horowitz, 1975; Perlmutter, 1969, 1978). Wars have had a profound impact on the whole political system and especially on its capacity to preserve the existing structure and to continue its mode of operation.

Changing physical borders pose an additional and extremely sensitive problem. Since the early days of Zionist settlement in Palestine, the concrete borders of this political entity have been changing, creating an atmosphere of flux and instability. Different governments in Israel have ruled over a country with different borders. Since 1967, the issue of borders has been a divisive topic within Israeli society. To understand the functioning of the political system, this critical issue must be taken into consideration, including an intangible aspect called "acceptance."

ACCEPTANCE

The struggle between Israel and its Arab neighbors has not revolved around the size of the country and its precise boundaries, because until the 1970s no Arab leader agreed to recognize openly Israel's right to exist. Thus, one central task of the Israeli political system has to do with acceptance.

From the beginning of Zionism, the issue of acceptance has had both a pragmatic and a symbolic meaning. Zionism aimed at transforming the Jews into a "normal" nation — providing a Jewish state as well as getting other nations to recognize and accept it. This mix of tangible and intangible needs has had many repercussions on political self-images and policies. No political actor in Israel can be insensitive to the "state of acceptance" of Israel among the nations. Israeli foreign affairs have therefore had the additional burden of seeking acceptance as a nation among other nations. Part of the urgency is a result of the rejection by Arab and Moslem countries. Another important aspect is the sensitivity of Christian countries to the emergence of a Jewish state. For instance, the complicated relationships of Israel with West Germany and with the Vatican deviate from normal patterns of international relations. Furthermore, Israeli foreign policy was influenced by the need to be affiliated with and part of the modern western and democratic world, as well as a desire to be counted among the nations of the Third World (Brecher, 1974).

THE DIASPORA

Once the State of Israel was established, the Israeli political system became the legal authority for the people who were defined as Israelis.

In many substantive areas, however, there are theoretical and practical problems regarding the scope of this authority. Who, for example, should have the responsibility for state-owned lands — the Israeli government or the worldwide Jewish organizations who had spent years both acquiring and managing this land? Who should be responsible for encouraging immigration to Israel — the government or the internationally based Jewish Agency? Who should handle Jewish education abroad? Who should control the expenditure of money contributed by Jews outside Israel?

The few who carried on their shoulders the Zionist mission of returning to Zion and building a new Jewish society never regarded their group as representing only themselves. They were pioneers, and their mission was to educate, to persuade, and to set a personal example. In addition to goals similar to those of other national movements — independence and integration — there has always been another: the ingathering of the exiles. The nuclear groups of Zionists in the Diaspora and in Palestine regarded themselves as the political system for *all* Jews, regardless of their location or attitude. Most Jews did not then and do not now agree with this broad definition. The role played by the Zionists in the life of Diaspora Jews was always on a voluntary basis. Nevertheless, the political system, in addition to its authority to make rules for the Jews in Palestine and now Israel, has always had a broader circle of concern: a sense of solidarity with and moral obligation toward Jews all over the world. What are the main manifestations of this concern?

Shelter. Israel was founded on the assumption that it must provide a place for every Jew who wants to come. The Law of Return (1950) accords citizenship and state support to all immigrant Jews upon arrival.

Spokesman. Israel considers itself the spokesman for Jewish causes and the protector of Jews who are discriminated against as Jews (Brecher, 1972: chap. 11). The Nazi and Nazi Collaborators' Punishment Law (1950), for example, extends Israeli court authority to acts done abroad and before Israel was established. Israel was also an official spokesman along with Diaspora-based institutions, for all Jews in the reparation agreement with West Germany. Israel's foreign policy is explicitly aimed at securing the rights of Jews "in every land and regime to a national, cultural and religious life without discrimination and the free exercise of the right of every Jew who so desires to depart to his Homeland" (Facts About Israel, 1973: 102).

Cultural and Religious Center. Israel aspires to become the center from which the revival of Judaism and Jewishness in their secular and religious versions will emanate. Emissaries — teachers, rabbis, artists, academicians, and others — are sent by Israel to Jewish communities all over the world, and many Jews spend some time in Israel. Part of this exhange is aimed at persuading Jews to settle in Israel.

Financial Support. The Jews abroad contribute large sums of money to Israel, which establishes a bond of mutual responsibility for the future of the country, especially in areas such as absorption of immigrants, economic development, and social welfare.

Political Support. Israel requests and usually receives political support in the international arena from Jews and Jewish organizations abroad.

This list points up the lack of symmetry between Israel's definition of its "boundaries of concern" and the bond of solidarity and support as viewed by Jews abroad. The first three are self-imposed concerns by which the Israeli political system assumes the responsibility for sheltering and speaking for every Jew and for continuing the Jewish cultural heritage. The last two delineate the actual boundaries of concrete support given by Jews outside Israel who are nevertheless attached to the country. This circle is somewhat wider if we include not only those who provide tangible support but also the many Jews who have a strong sense of affinity with Israel for numerous reasons. In any case, even the widest circle is far from encompassing a majority of all Jews.

In sum, the political system of Israel has a narrowly defined field of legal authority, a very wide field of concern, and an intermediate field of support.[4] These different circles have had important implications for both the structure and performance of the Israeli political system. For instance, when Israeli leadership was reluctant to make decisions on sensitive issues such as the preparation of a constitution, the separation of religion from state, and the future boundaries of the country, the argument was often advanced that such crucial decisions should be left for future generations, when most Jews will reside in Israel. The issue of the Israel-Diaspora relationship will reappear in many other parts of this book in the context of integration, political symbols, and penetration of target groups through political communication.

The Internal Challenges

Any political system is shaped and reshaped by its encounter with the society's most pressing problems. In Israel, as in many other new countries, the political system has been compelled to do too many things at once. For instance, the 1948 war was fought during a period of mass immigration and economic crisis. A hectic pace, a sense of urgency, and helter-skelter solutions have characterized almost permanently the mode of operation. In introducing the Israeli political system, three well-known goals will be presented: nation-building, economic development, and social integration.

NATION-REBUILDING

"To build and to be rebuilt" — not only a new country for a homeless people, but also a new and different kind of society. Parallel to the wish for acceptance and normalization runs the desire to create something new, to change the way of life adopted by the Jews in exile. The 1948 Declaration of Independence expresses this mix of old and new:

> The Land of Israel was the birthplace of the Jewish people. Here their spiritual, religious and political identity was shaped. Here they first attained statehood, created cultural values of national and universal significance and gave to the world the eternal Book of Books. . . .

> In recent decades they have returned en masse — pioneers, immigrants, and defenders. They made deserts bloom, revived the Hebrew language, built villages and towns and created a thriving community. . . .

> It is the natural right of the Jewish people to be masters of their own fate, like all other nations, in their own sovereign state.

Zionism is an ideological movement: Its goals are much more ambitious than the mere establishment of a Jewish state. Not just a pragmatic solution to the "Jewish problem," Zionism was also an expression of aspirations, idealism, and social reforms strongly influenced by European ideologies of the time. Originally a pioneering movement of the young (Elon, 1971: 132), Zionism combined modern ideologies with the vision of the Biblical prophets: a revolution based on identification with the Jewish past (religious or secular). Zionism is utopian: a return of the Jews to their own history in modern times. The question of whether Zionism is a new beginning in the old land of Israel or an integral part of a long and continuous Jewish history has been hanging over the rebirth of Israel from the very early days (Scholem, 1974: 18-19). In any case, the movement of Jews to a new land and a new way of life signified a social revolution.

The image of the new society included equality, justice, hard work, and cultural excellence. The image of the new Jew in that society was one of a farmer and laborer belonging to a pioneering community and carrying the Jewish renaissance on his shoulders.

There was also, naturally, the pragmatic side. The Jewish community in the prestate period was busy implementing the revolution through day-to-day work in acquiring land, building water projects and new communal settlements, and setting up the organizational machinery for employment, education and health services, housing, industrial development, and — on an entirely different plane — the revival of the Hebrew language. The small and rather homogeneous Jewish community in Palestine regarded itself as the pioneering avant-garde for the task of nation-building: the creation of a territorial basis and the formation of a new national society.

Because of the traditional and religious elements of the Zionist movement, it can be said that the task was one of nation-*re*building. But there was also a rejection of the Jewish past in the Diaspora and especially of its narrow religious contents. This evolved later into an attempt to emphasize the *Israeli* contents of the new society as antithetical to Diaspora characteristics. The results have been mixed; the old-new nation has been both Jewish and Israeli.

The formation of this national society has been marked by a variety of new phenomena: the appearance of a Jewish-Israeli farmer, laborer, soldier, or artist. Israeli songs, dances, and other cultural artifacts were created in the rapidly evolving lingua franca of the newcomers — Hebrew. The first kibbutz (Degania) was established in the same year (1909) as the foundations of the first new Jewish city (Tel-Aviv) were laid. Every school pupil in Israel can recite a long list of firsts which paved the way for the establishment of the state in 1948. But the formation of Israel has also been deeply affected by the Holocaust and the destruction of six million Jews during World War II.

The process of nation-rebuilding continued after 1948 at an accelerated pace. The small tribal-like community of about half a million Jews more than tripled in size by 1952 and again doubled within twenty-five years. The accomplishments during the formative years and later, during the early period of the state, were quite astonishing, while a profound social, cultural, and economic transformation was taking place. Although a revolution of such proportions cannot be attributed to politics alone, the political system has played the central role in nation-building. Moreover, nation-building through the years became less a voluntary, social task and more a goal of the political system, to be achieved mainly through state organs.

DEVELOPMENT

By any set of indicators, Israeli social and economic development was rapid in the first three decades of statehood. The average standards of living, housing, health, education, and social services have been rising steadily. Until the 1960s, for example, there was an average per capita growth of five percent. There is little resemblance between an average Israeli family in the 1950s and the same family in the mid-1960s or the early 1980s. In the first period, an average urban family would have lived in a small apartment of one or two bedrooms; they would have possessed no large appliances such as refrigerator or washing machine and certainly not a private car; their daily food consumption per capita would be low; and they would spend little on private consumption. A comparison of some aggregate economic indicators of development is presented in Table 2.1.

Israel has been transformed in the short space of thirty years from an underdeveloped community living in small towns and villages to a modern, urban society. As can be seen in Table 2.1, many of the changes occurred in the first eighteen years. Table 2.2 shows that during that period the percentage of the civilian labor force engaged in agriculture, for example, dropped from 18 to 10 percent. There were also major changes in construction, transportation, and educational and health services. The period until the mid-1960s can be regarded as the development of the economy to its takeoff point. The 1965-1967 recession slowed the process, and the leap forward occurred after the 1967 war. Quite rapidly, the Israeli economy acquired the services-oriented structure that characterizes postindustrial societies (Ofer, 1967).

The Israeli political system has played a central role in this transformation. Development has been centralized: Projects were set, financed, and executed by the government and public institutions. For instance, development in the 1958-1968 decade was due mainly to government investments financed through the reparations agreements with West Germany and other sources of capital import. In the agricultural sector, modernization was greatly helped by direct government support and huge investment in the construction of the National Water Carrier and in modern technology (Galnoor, in Bilski et al., 1980).

Parallel to direct intervention in economic development, the government has pursued welfare policies. For instance, the National Insurance schemes were expanded to include many more individuals and many new categories of benefits (Avizohar, 1978). State support for education, which began with free primary school education, has been extended to high schools as well as subsidies to institutions of higher learning. Health clinics, community centers, and cultural, youth, and sports clubs have been set up by the government and local authorities or with the assistance of public funds.

It is difficult to estimate the extent of government involvement in the society and the economy. The socialist ideology that dominated Zionism

TABLE 2.1   Selected Indicators of Economic Development

	1950	1968	1978	Change Factor First 18 years 1950-1968	Change Factor Next 10 years 1968-1978
Population (10³)	1,370	2,841	3,738	2.1	1.3
GNP per capita (I.L. 1975 prices)	6,721	15,668	21,875	2.3	1.4
Gross domestic capital formation (I.L. 10⁶ 1975 prices)	4,656	11,799	20,172	2.5	1.7
Net imports of goods ($10⁶)	300	1,093	5,658	3.6	5.2
Net exports of goods ($10⁶)	35	602	3,716	17.2	6.2
Cultivated area (dunam 10³)	1,650	4,132	4,270	2.5	1.0
Industrial production (index)	100*	306	635	3.1	2.1
Industries engaging 100+ employees	163*	332	456	2.0	1.4
Electricity production (10⁶ KWH)	543	5,327	11,476	9.8	2.2
Vehicles (10³)	42*	158	435	3.8	2.8
Telephones (10³)	31	419	1,051	13.5	2.5

SOURCE: Statistical Abstract of Israel, No. 29 (1978: 3-11) and No. 30 (1979: 3-11).

*1958

TABLE 2.2 Structure of the Economy: Employment and Production (%)

	Employment Distribution				Share in Net Domestic Product		
	1949	1958	1968	1978	1958	1968	1978
Agriculture	18	18	10	6	13	8	6
Industry	22	22	24	24	22	24	25
Construction, electricity, & water	11	12	9	9	10	9	10
Services (commerce, transport, finances, public & private services)	49	48	57	61	50	59	59
Total	100	100	100	100	100	100	100
Wage earners as percentage of all persons employed	63%	66%	71%	77%			

SOURCE: Statistical Abstract of Israel, No. 30 (1979: 5, 8).

for a long period called for central planning and intervention, and there was no reluctance on the part of the central government to undertake and control socioeconomic development. Generally, three stages can be discerned in the involvement of the political system in socioeconomic growth.

(1) In the prestate period, there was a division of labor between the British authorities and the voluntary Jewish institutions. The latter carried out their social and economic functions through the parties and the affiliated organizations of the Jewish community.

(2) The establishment of the state entailed a natural transfer of functions to state organs and a relative decrease in the role of partisan organizations. Accordingly, the responsibility for education, welfare, and employment were transferred to the central government. Other functions, notably health services, immigration, and water supply, remained in the hands of nongovernment bodies.

(3) The beginning of the third stage is more difficult to determine. Elements of a welfare state ideology were part of the socialist parties' platforms as well as those of the liberal, national, and religious parties. Clear manifestations of a new welfare policy started after 1967, however, with the impetus of demonstrations by underprivileged groups, such as the (Israeli) Black Panthers and with government universalistic programs such as direct payments for children (1970) or unemployment insurance (1971) (Galnoor, 1974; Avizohar, 1978: 65-88, 105-125).

In Israel, the initial starting level of modernization was relatively high compared to other new countries, so that rapid change occurred without the traumatic effects of dislocation and reorientation. Furthermore, if political instability occurs "when men become dissatisfied . . . and when their achievements and capabilities fall below their aspirations" (Huntington and Dominguez, in Greenstein and Polsby, 1975: vol.3 p.8), then conditions were not ripe for it in Israel. Political stability was assured during that period by the steady increase in the standards of living and the relatively high level of satisfaction with the performance of the political system.

The political system has been successful in meeting the external challenges, in nation-rebuilding, and in socioeconomic development, which resulted in modernization and individual prosperity. This was felt most prominently in the daily life of the individual. In the 1950s, very few Israelis had a checking account or life insurance, not to mention a private car or the means to take a trip abroad. Within one generation, the society and the economy have been radically transformed to the point where Israel can be counted among the modernized nations of the world (Textor, 1967). Where there is such intensive political involvement in socioeconomic development, politics must be taken seriously.

Integration and Potential Cleavages

Integration is the emergence of more permanent links between parts of society. The basis for the functioning of any political system is minimal social integration. The system in turn is usually interested in fostering integration in order to translate cultural and social bonds into collective efforts. Nevertheless, both old and new political systems have to cope with the possibility that ethnic, religious, linguistic, regional, or other differences may turn into unbridgeable gaps and ultimately into disintegration.

The main integration issues, or potential cleavages in Israel, evolved around specific subdivisions between Israelis and non-Israelis, Jews and non-Jews, religious and secular Jews, Oriental and Western Jews, and the various ideological camps. A discussion of the penetration problems these subdivisions posed for the political system can be found in Chapter 4, but here an overview of each is presented.

ISRAELI VS. NON-ISRAELI JEWS

In 1897, when Theodore Herzl convened the First Zionist Congress to float the idea of a Jewish state, there were about 11 million Jews in the world, only 50,000 of whom lived in Palestine. Twenty years later, when the Balfour Declaration stated that Britain favored the establishment of a "national home for the Jewish people," less than one percent of the Jews lived there. From the very beginning, Zionism aimed at ingathering all the exiles, including assimilated ones, and the state was considered the home — or at least the center — of all Jews.

Zionism was not the only alternative open to Jews. Some preferred universal ideologies such as communism; others viewed Zionism as false messianism, which is in conflict with the Jewish religion. The vast majority continued their lives in the Diaspora. Despite the Holocaust, which shattered the universalist credo of Jews around the world, the fact is that most found alternatives to Zionism.

Israel's goal of becoming the national home of *all* Jews has not been fulfilled (Table 2.3). However, the fact that the percentage of Jews in Israel has risen steadily is some testimony to its success.

Many of those who chose not to immigrate have maintained emotional ties with Israel, and their loyalty and support are of inestimable value both politically and economically. Nevertheless, the relative failure to convince Jews in Western countries to move to Israel has caused a gradual shift in purpose. By the late 1960s, it became clear that Israel was asking Diaspora Jews primarily for support and solidarity. Concurrent

TABLE 2.3   Jews Living in Israel as Percentage of Total World Jewry

Year	Total World Jewish Population	Jews in Israel as % of Total
1940	16,700,000	2.8%
1948	11,300,000	5.7%
1958	12,035,000	14.6%
1968	13,786,000	17.7%
1978	14,396,000	21.8%

SOURCE: Statistical Abstract of Israel (1979: 33; 1980: 33).

with this development is the emphasis on Israel's role in the Diaspora as an effective means of preventing assimilation. The relationship with world Jewry has caused a great deal of soul-searching in Israel, especially in the late 1970s, when only a fraction of the Jews who were allowed to leave the Soviet Union decided to settle in Israel.

The main division between Israeli and non-Israeli Jews revolves around the issue of Judaism as a nationality and not just a religion.[5] This potential cleavage poses a serious dilemma. Are Jews who remain outside Israel part of the nation? What should be done to prevent their assimilation? Can Israel serve as their spiritual, cultural, and religious center? Should Israel be responsible for defending persecuted Jews all over the world? Should Israel demand moral, political, and financial support of Diaspora Jews? What should be the relationship between Jewish and Israeli institutions?

There is a lot of agreement between Israeli and non-Israeli Jews regarding their historical past, common fate, and religion. There is also a high degree of solidarity with Israel felt by Diaspora Jews. As for national identity, obedience to the state, and political loyalty — the Jews living outside Israel are obviously not "integrated."

JEWS VS. NON-JEWS

Whereas the previous division is a unique phenomenon, in that it extends the field of concern of the Israeli political system across its legal boundaries, the division between the Jewish and non-Jewish citizens of Israel is a crystallized national cleavage (Rae and Taylor, 1970: 1-14). One of the solutions considered to resolve the struggle between the Jews and the Arabs living in Palestine was a binational state, but this was not acceptable to the great majority of Jews and Arabs. In 1947, the United Nations voted to partition Palestine into two states,[6] but this resolution was rejected by the Arabs. The 1948 war resulted in a de facto partition,

which left about 160,000 Arabs (14 percent of the population then) within
the borders of the Jewish state. The total non-Jewish population of Israel
in 1948 was divided as follows: Moslem Arabs, 77 percent; Christian
Arabs, 15 percent; and Druzes and others, 8 percent. Thus, Israeli
Arabs became a minority within a Jewish state which is itself a minority
within the surrounding Arab and Moslem world.

The Arab-Jewish cleavage separates the two communities in terms
of nationality, religion, culture, language, and regional concentration.
There is almost no overlap in the few joint cities and virtually no social
cross-cutting. The only common denominators are the state, citizenship
(except for military service), economic relationships, and observance of
political rules and procedures. The Israeli political system has never
sought to integrate the Arabs socially or to subject them to a "melting
pot" policy. Its main concern has been to maintain loyalty through the
military government (until 1965), economic development, citizenship
rights, and cultural, religious, and local autonomy. The number of Arabs
in Israel increased naturally to 299,000 in 1965 and 596,000 in 1978 (about
16 percent of the total population).

Until 1965 the movement of Israeli Arabs within the country was
restricted for security reasons. Legally, this was another manifestation
of the existence of an almost total cleavage between Arabs and Jews
within Israel. Politically, however, the Israeli Arab population was
incorporated into the system. They were not mobilized in terms of civic
participation, but they did not remain outsiders. The social fabric of the
extended family, the village, the region, as well as the internal feuds
became part and parcel of Arab participation in national and local
elections or interaction with authorities. In 1965, the military government was abolished, signifying a trend toward liberalization of Arab
participation in the political and economic life of the country. But the
most significant transformation occurred as a result of the Israeli
takeover of the West Bank and the Gaza Strip in 1967. Since then, Israeli
Arabs have had free access to and contact with about one million Arabs
who live in these areas. The legal separation — the latter live under
military rule — does not sever the natural and strong ties between these
two Arab communities.

Even though there are a few signs of duality in Israel, such as Arabic
being the second official language, and despite the existence of formal
citizenship equality, Israel is a Jewish state.[7] Its symbols are Jewish and
its Zionist goals are alien to non-Jewish citizens. Politically, the Arabs in
Israel have not been full participants. The number of Arab members of
the Knesset has never reached their percentage in the voting population.
The political organizations of Arabs in Israel have usually been dominated by the Jewish parties (Landau, 1971). The source of the cleavage

between Israeli Arabs and Jews is rooted in the broader context of the Middle East conflict.

RELIGIOUS VS. SECULAR JEWS

The exact distinction between "religious" and "secular" Jews in Israel is fuzzy and the numbers unknown (Deshen, 1978). If the criterion is votes for religious parties in the Knesset elections, then the percentage of religious Jews has remained approximately 14 percent since the mid-1950s. But many observant Jews vote for nonreligious parties, and some do not vote at all. On the basis of respondents' reports of their religious observances (Gutmann, 1960; Antonovsky, 1963a; Arian, 1973; and Samet, 1979), the approximate continuum locating religious and secular Jews in Israel is presented in Fugure 2.1.

The main conflict is between about one-quarter of the population, who call themselves "secular" Jews and are opposed to the present lack of division between religion and state, and another quarter, who are observant or ultra-orthodox and favor a Jewish state along religious lines. (The hard core of ultra-orthodox Jews would have the Jewish state run strictly according to Halacha, religious law.) In between these two groups are the partly observant "traditionals," who are moderate on this issue. The latter do not keep most orthodox precepts but do attend synagogue at least twice a year and define their Jewishness in both national and religious terms.

The disputes between nonobservant and observant Jews are deep and bitter, and they often touch on the role of the state (for example, how to define a Jew legally, or the conscription of religious girls into the army). Yet, Jewish identity and sentiments are widely shared by both groups as long as precise definitions are not required. Any attempt at such a definition would mark a division between a religious versus a cultural interpretation of Jewish history and national identity. For the observant, the Bible is a sacred book of binding law, while the seculars regard it as a historical/cultural document. The difference is captured well by the declarations of allegiance taken by a judge and a dayan (a judge in the Rabbinical Court). The judge pledges "to bear allegiance to the State of Israel and to its laws" whereas the dayan omits the phrase, "to its laws."

Besides the traditional group, religious Jews can be divided politically into three groups.

(1) There is a tiny faction of extremist Jews called Neturei Karta, founded in 1934, who are completely outside the political system and who do not appear in Figure 2.1 (Friedman, 1979; Schnall, 1979: 125-137). They do not vote, do not use their organizations for advancing their purposes within the political system, and try not to utilize state and

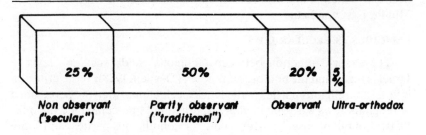

Figure 2.1 Schematic Distribution of Observant and Nonobservant Jews in Israel (%)

municipal services. Financial support is obtained directly from abroad and not from institutions within Israel. In reality, total seclusion is impossible: The city of Jerusalem — in which their quarter is located — is responsible for their health, sewage, garbage collection, and other public services. Sensitive issues such as payment of income taxes are tactfully avoided by all sides. But when it comes to issues close to their religious way of life, these groups do not hesitate to "participate": they do not allow cars into their quarter on Saturdays and holidays and do not tolerate people walking in their streets immodestly dressed. On such occasions they organize demonstrations and sometimes resort to violence against people and property.

(2) The groups labeled "ultra-orthodox" are mainly identified with two political parties — Agudat Israel and Poalei Agudat Israel — which constitute about four to five percent of the voting population. This group is within the system but very close to its periphery. Most members of these ultra-orthodox groups live in Jerusalem and some in Bnei-Brak, and they are subdivided among themselves according to their European country of origin. They are quite separated from the rest of the society not only residentially but also socially and culturally. They tend to marry within their own circles and to confine their relationships with others to the minimum economic and political essentials.

The position of these groups within the Israeli political system, albeit near the outer boundaries, has been determined by expediency and not by legitimation or support. As political organizations, the Agudah parties appeared in Palestine in the 1920s (Schiff, 1977: 66-85). Their roots were European, and they drew their support in Palestine from the indigenous religious communities.

From their inception, these orthodox groups had no intention of integrating with the secular Jewish community in Israel. It was a separatist movement, limited exclusively to Western Jews, and strictly non-Zionist. They did eventually seek a modus vivendi with the Zionist organizations — due to security needs and the inevitable direct contact with Zionist/secular groups which moderated their own position. Nevertheless, they did not hesitate to attack the Zionist movement before the League of Nations and the British Mandate authorities. Agudah orthodox Jews were against the establishment of a Jewish state in Palestine as late as 1944, when the idea was indirectly endorsed for the first time. But the movement was not a monolithic one, and in time the moderates were willing to cooperate more closely with the authorities of the *yishuv,* the Jewish community in Israel. A worker's branch of Poalei Agudat Israel even established religious kibbutzim. By 1948, they decided to recognize and cooperate with the State of Israel.

The two Agudah parties participated in the Knesset and municipal elections from the beginning and joined the cabinet coalition in the first years of the state. Their main purpose of participation in the coalition was to guarantee religious interests and receive government funds for their institutions. The regular participation of the National Religious Party in the cabinet also satisfied some important demands of the ultra-orthodox groups. By agreement, they have not sent their daughters and sons to the military and have not used the secular law courts.

(3) The biggest group by far in the Israeli religious camp is the "observant," shown in Figure 2.1. These are Jews who, by and large, accept the Zionist religious doctrine of Rabbi Abraham Kook (Avineri, 1980: 216-227): They observe religious law and at the same time emphasize the national dimension of their Judaism. What is more, they believe Zionism heralds the beginning of redemption. About half of them — 10 percent of the total population in Israel — have been politically identified with the National Religious Party (NRP), while the rest vote for nonreligious parties.

The NRP, together with the Aguda parties, reached the so-called religious status quo agreement, with the secular parties dominating the cabinet coalition. According to this agreement, religious arrangements are maintained wherever such an arrangement had already been established by the time of the early years of the state. The most obvious example is the Rabbinical Courts Law of 1953, which recognized the exclusive jurisdiction of these courts over matters of marriage and divorce. The great majority of the observant support the political system and participate in it, but for many support is conditional: as long as the system is willing to observe the status quo agreement. Even the moderates among them have used the threat of a *Kulturkampf* to prevent any drastic changes in the status quo.

The central role of the observant in Israeli politics will be discussed in detail in subsequent chapters. Here it may be said that — in contrast with the two marginal groups of extremist and ultra-orthodox Jews — this group is completely inside the political system. They chose to be politically incorporated and established political organizations for this purpose. In return, the system responded with religious and economic concessions.

Despite the political accommodation between most religious and secular Jews, the cleavage here is real, and the danger of disintegration is ever-present. Compared to the other cleavages, this one has continued to pose a constant problem across time. The gap between the observant and the nonobservant Jews is manifested in separate school systems, youth movements, sport clubs, kibbutzim, political parties, and even neighborhoods. The religious way of life imposes severe restrictions which separate the two camps. There is relatively little social interaction between young people and even reluctance regarding "intermarriages". Of course, Zionism serves as a powerful common denominator. Dividing lines are mitigated by shared loyalty to the state and by institutions such as the army, place of work, and the economic market. But the cleavage is deeply rooted in belief systems and periodically arises to preoccupy and paralyze the political system.[8]

ORIENTAL VS. WESTERN JEWS

At the beginning of the nineteenth century, there was little interaction between the various Jewish communities around the world or even within Europe, where the great majority resided. There were marked differences among these groups, manifested in the color of their skin, distinctive dress, customs, and language. Nevertheless, Jews from all over have always shared the Bible, religious beliefs, a collective sense of identity, and a spiritual bond to their ancient land and Jerusalem. This mixed background gives some indication of the roots of the ethnic cleavage, which is the most important new issue that appeared after 1948 in the Israeli political system.

The terms "Oriental" and "Western" with reference to the Jews in Israel is often misleading because of the many differences within each of these groups. Among the Orientals, there are Jews from enlightened Alexandria, the mountains of Kurdistan or the deserts of Aden; and among the Westerns, there are Jews from the parochial towns of Poland and Russia, as well as cosmopolitan Paris or Berlin. There is, however, a common denominator based on this geographical distinction that makes these terms useful. For the Jewish communities of Europe, it was the shared process of enlightenment, modernization, and the experience of the Holocaust. For the Jewish communities of Northern Africa and Asia, it was the religious and traditional way of life, where the family and the community played a central role, as well as the experience of Israel's birth and their encounter with Western Zionism.

When Oriental Jews arrived in Israel en masse, even their dark skin set them apart as a group. As in other Jewish diasporas, they had adopted local customs and spoke languages such as Arabic, Turkish, Persian, Kurdish, and Amharic. But above all, Oriental Jews *became* different because the brand of Zionism they found in Israel was European both in its origin and in its spirit.

Before 1948, most of the Oriental Jews in Palestine had been part of the urban community in the yishuv and well established in old cities such as Jerusalem, Safed, and Tiberias. They usually did not belong to the agricultural settlements founded by the immigrant Europeans. Their Zionism entailed personal fulfillment and was not originally political, so they were not among the founders of political Zionism.

The different patterns of immigration to Israel of the Oriental and the Western Jews is illuminating. The Oriental presence in Israel stretched back centuries to the migration from Spain during the fifteenth and sixteenth centuries. Throughout the twentieth century, the Oriental Jews were going to Israel, but the large wave came in the 1950s, in response to the establishment of Israel and the anti-Zionism in the Moslem countries. Since then, the Diaspora of the Oriental Jews has almost completely disappeared (with the notable exception of North African Jews in France and Canada and small communities in Iran and Morocco). The immigration from Europe, except for small groups of religious Jews, began at the end of the nineteenth and the beginning of the twentieth centuries, with a small core of pioneers who developed the ideas of what we call today modern political Zionism. Immediately preceding and after World War II, there were massive waves of immigration from Europe as a result of the Holocaust.

Part of the tension between these two communities in Israel is rooted in the attitude of some Western Jews that the Oriental Jews came to Israel due to their expulsion from other countries, while the Western Jews came for pure Zionist motives. The above thumbnail history should serve to illustrate that this claim is ill-founded. Most Jews came to Israel because they were forced to, and that includes the great majority of Western and Oriental Jews. The Zionism of all these forced immigrants was manifested in the fact that they went to Zion, rather than

TABLE 2.4   Origin of Jewish Immigration to Palestine and Israel

	1919-May 1948	1948-1968	1969-1977	1948-1977
Western	90[a]	46	80	53
Oriental	10[b]	54	20	47
Total %	100	100	100	100
N	452,000	1,291,000	320,000	1,611,000

SOURCE: Statistical Abstract of Israel (1978: 137).

[a]Most of them from Poland, Germany, Russia, and Rumania (based on Horowitz and Lissak, 1977: 344).

[b]Most of them from Yemen, Turkey, Iraq, and Iran (Horowitz and Lissak, 1977: 344).

elsewhere. The Jewishness of the Oriental Jews had long turned on the twin poles of religion and national identity, and the creation of the State of Israel meant the crystallization of both. In fact, out of the total number of Jews in each respective community, the proportion of Oriental Jews who left for Palestine before 1948 was as high or even higher than the proportion of Jews who emigrated from Western communities (H. Cohen, 1968: 10-11). The Oriental Diaspora was much smaller, however, and therefore fewer came in absolute numbers (until 1948); furthermore, their presence in the yishuv was not as politically significant.

Table 2.4 shows that the number of Oriental immigrants who came to Palestine during the heyday of the Zionist revolution (1919-1948) was relatively small compared to that of the Western immigrants. By the time the massive immigration of Oriental Jews began, the Westerners were already the dominating social and political elite of the country. Thus, from the outset, the problem of integration has had something to do with the fact that the Oriental Jews were not part of the waves of immigration that carried the founding fathers to Israel.

Also detrimental to the evolution of mutual respect between the Western and Oriental Jews has been the ongoing war between Jews and Arabs. Oriental Jews, whose cultural heritage is strongly influenced by Moslems and Arabs, began to deny their own culture, which drew heavily on the culture of their present enemies. Israeli society has been dominated by the modernized Western Jews. This has made the Oriental Jews feel inferior and, at the same time, required enormous changes on their part. Only in the 1970s did there emerge signs of change and genuine attempts of Oriental Jews to adhere openly to their Arabic or North African cultural heritage.

The socioeconomic gap is a significant one: Oriental Jews have lower levels of income, housing, education, and employment. During the

1966-1967 recession, Oriental Jews constituted the great majority of the unemployed. In the period of economic prosperity after 1967, many Oriental Jews succeeded in "jumping over the fence" economically and joined the prospering mainstream of society. Those who did not felt their discrimination more strongly than ever. This accounts for the appearance in 1970 of a significant ethnic political movement: the Black Panthers. The relative powerlessness of Oriental Jews as a group in the Israeli political system was manifested in the proportionally lower number of Oriental Jews in the Knesset, the government, public institutions, and the elite of the country in general. They have succeeded, however, in gaining power in the local authorities, in regional branches of workers' committees, and in the Histadrut.

Originally, the ethnic conflict was not expressed in political terms. There were no significant ethnic parties in the state period, and ethnic lists have usually failed to get their members elected to the Knesset. The level of conflict was mitigated also by cross-cutting memberships in terms of the religious-secular division or the ideological camps (Smooha, 1978: 230). The conflict has been primarily cultural and socioeconomic, but more recently it has also become political.

The demographic ratio in Israel between the two ethnic groups evened out by the 1960s. Jews of Oriental extraction accounted for about 46 percent of the population in 1964, compared with 42 percent for Jews of Western extraction. "Extraction" refers here to those born in the Diaspora or whose fathers were born in the Diaspora; the remaining 12 percent represent those who were themselves *and* whose fathers were born in Israel (Statistical Abstract of Israel, 1979: 57). It should also not be overlooked that the proportion of native-born Israelis has been rapidly growing: from 35 percent in 1948 to 54 percent in 1978, a fact with implications for the integration of these two ethnic groups (Statistical Abstract of Israel, 1975: 42; 1978, 57).

Both Orientals and Westerns were immigrants upon arrival in Israel, but most of those who came from Asian and African countries were at an obvious disadvantage. The distance they had to travel culturally, economically, and politically was far greater than that of their European-born counterparts. What united the different Jews who came to Israel from Iraq and Lybia, Morocco and India, was their total unfamiliarity with the political culture they found upon arrival.

Both communities in Israel have accepted the idea of national integration and the desirability of erecting a homogeneous society in the new country. Nevertheless, the question arises: *Whose* Jewish tradition, religious customs, or even Hebrew accent will dominate the new national Israeli identity? Will the new Israeli culture be a new breed made up of the various Jewish communities that have made their way to Israel? The role of the political system as a vehicle for this integration has become increasingly problematic. The problem between Orientals and Westerners is not expressed in different concepts of national identity or loyalty to the state. It is mainly expressed in a struggle for the attainment of economic, social, and lately also political equality.

THE IDEOLOGICAL CAMPS

There is no justification to include ideological divisions as an integration problem, unless there is more to it as far as the political system is concerned. If we insist on viewing human differences as obstacles to integration, then the number of obstacles is infinite. Conversely, if we define the elimination of all differences as a goal of the political system, we are talking about uniformity, not integration.

Beyond the Zionist consensus, Israel is politically very heterogeneous. In the prestate era, and to some extent also after 1948, the main division has been into three ideological camps: the labor camp (socialist Zionism), the civic camp[9] (general and revisionist Zionism), and the religious camp (the religious Zionism of observant Jews). These divisions only partly overlap the secular-religious cleavage, because there are religious people in the two nonreligious camps, although not vice versa.

The ideological differences within the Jewish community are included in this discussion of cleavages because they also represent socioeconomic values and beliefs and pose integration problems for the political system (Lijphart, 1977). As political movements, they have never been isolated entities, and they did not evolve into full-blown subcultures with womb-to-tomb membership, as in some other societies. Nevertheless, their ideologies served as a basis not only for different parties but also for the establishment of separate institutions, political alliances, economic organizations, and social services. This meant that during the yishuv period one's schooling, housing, place of work, health plan, youth movement, and sports club — to name a few — were connected with membership in one camp or another.

Almost all the parties that formed the core of these political camps emerged in Europe in the beginning of the century and were active in the Zionist movement before the emergence of the political system of the yishuv. The different parties within the labor camp rallied around a belief in manual labor, agriculture, collective settlements, and a comprehensive Jewish-socialist revolution. The labor camp, which dominated the yishuv and Israeli political systems from the 1930s, developed powerful institutions. These included the kibbutz movement (collective communities), the Histadrut (the Federation of Labor), as well as major construction and transportation companies. The political significance of these institutions is evaluated in Chapter 4.

The religious camp was also subdivided into different parties and organizations, some of which (The Agudah parties) were non-Zionist or even anti-Zionist. The more moderate wing — the two Mizrachi movements — were mainly concerned with preserving the Jewish tradition in Zionism. Politically, the religious camp drew closer to the labor camp, as evidenced by their active role in the yishuv. In later years, there was a long-standing coalition between the main labor party (Mapai) and the main religious party (NRP).

The civic camp was a loose conglomerate of parties and organizations whose common denominator was a laissez-faire economic orientation, which caused their socialist opponents to label them derogatorily "bourgeoisie" or "landlords." The members were drawn primarily from the self-employed population. This description applies mainly to those in this camp who belonged to organizations such as the Industrialists Federation, the Farmers' Association, or the Craftsmen's Guild and who eventually rallied around the General Zionists Party.

The revisionist movement was ideologically part of this camp in its opposition to socialism, but in fact it had been a separate political force since the late 1920s with a strong emphasis on nationalist ideology and an opposition to the collective bodies of the organized yishuv. Their organizations were primarily political (The Revisionist Zionists and the New Zionist Federation) and military (Etzel, Lehi) rather than social or economic. After 1948 the Herut party was formed and joined the General Zionists Party in 1965 to establish what subsequently became the Likud bloc.

In addition to the parties that belonged to these three camps, during the yishuv period there were also small ethnic and Communist parties. Table 2.5 shows the different size of each camp, based on the results of the general elections. (For a full discussion of the camps during the yishuv period see Horowitz and Lissak, 1978).

Starting in the early 1930s, the labor camp remained the dominant political power for nearly fifty years. The structure was preserved by virtue of the central holding power of Mapai (later renamed the Israel Labor Party), and the rather stable voting patterns that perpetuated the camps as shaped in yishuv times until 1977.

In terms of national identity, there was little disagreement among the camps about the ultimate Zionist goal of establishing a Jewish state, or about the importance of the historical heritage, the Hebrew language,

TABLE 2.5 Ideological Camps According to Parties and Election Results in Selected Years (%)

| | "Representatives Assembly" | | | | | Knesset | | | |
	1920	1925	1931	1944	1949	1959	1969	1977
Labor parties	37	36	42	59	53	55	50	26
Civic parties	20	42	33	21	21	24	28	36
Religious parties	20	9	7	17	12	15	15	14
Other[a]	23	13	18	3	14	6	7	24[b]
Total %	100	100	100	100	100	100	100	100

SOURCES: Prestate period — Horowitz and Lissak (1977: 142); poststate period — Statistical Abstract of Israel (1978: 604).
[a]Many different lists and groups.
[b]Includes the new Democratic Movement for Change (11.6%), the Communist Party (4.6%), and other small lists.

and certain national symbols. The religious-secular cleavage did not polarize the camps because the main religious party became a political ally of labor and nevertheless remained close to the civic camp because of Herut's moderate stand on religious issues.

During the yishuv period there were, to be sure, policy disputes regarding the positions to be taken regarding the British authorities, the Arabs, immigration, labor strikes, the role of agriculture, the preferred socioeconomic order, and power struggles within the voluntary organs. The major conflict was between the Labor camp and the revisionist movement. It brought about the decision of the revisionists to leave the Zionist Organization in 1935 and to conduct their separate war against the British in Palestine in the 1940s. The conflict came very close to an internal civil war. After the state was established, the Herut Party was excluded from all coalition cabinets until the first National Cabinet in 1967. But the notion that they were altogether outside the political system is incorrect. While the revisionists, under Zeev Jabotinsky, had left the Zionist Organization, they did continue to participate in the yishuv institutions in Palestine and returned to the organization to participate in the 1946 elections to the Zionist Congress. Further, despite their separate policy, there were periods of coordination with the official defense organization of the yishuv (Haganah) and with other organs of the Jewish community. Their military organizations were eventually disbanded in 1948, and their members joined the Israel Defence Forces. Finally, Herut members were elected to the Knesset, were represented in the Jewish Agency, and, since 1965, were also in the Histadrut.

The ideological differences between the camps in the first years of the state were still sharp (Table 2.6) but rapidly waning. By the late 1950s, the distinctions were blurred and there were many overlapping areas of agreement between the camps and their components. Instead, the actual distribution of political and economic resources became the main bone of contention.

The main achievement of the voluntary yishuv political system and later of the state has been its ability to accommodate the different ideological camps and most of the factions. They all had roles in the Zionist Organization and/or in the voluntary yishuv organizations. The survival of this political structure has been extraordinary, particularly in view of the upheavals brought about by the establishment of the state and the transfer of many functions to the central authority. The pitched ideological battles between camps did not, however, prevent a united effort in 1948 to establish the state and form a provisional government. Once Israel achieved independence, the old ideological fervor slowly subsided. The issues of loyalty to the state and the legitimation of its

TABLE 2.6 Differences Among the Political Camps on Major Policy Issues in 1948 and 1951*

	The Labor Camp	The Civic Camp	The Religious Camp
Socioeconomic Affairs	socialism; state ownership of means of production; controlled economy; support for Histadrut policies and companies	laissez-faire; development of private economy; decrease in state intervention; less power to Histadrut	no specific commitment; Labor Mizrachi supports labor positions and is close to Histadrut
Religious Affairs	status quo in religious affairs; against religious coercion (Mapam more extreme in antireligious demands)	no specific commitment (Herut supported some religious demands)	preservation of religious status quo; separate schools and other institutions (Aguda parties: religious laws should prevail)

Middle East Policy	compromise with Arabs; discreet diplomatic negotiations; peace on the basis of the 1949 Rhodes cease-fire agreements (Mapam: alliance of Israeli and Arab workers to achieve peace)	General Zionist — same as Mapai; Herut — both banks of the Jordan River belong to Israel; against the Rhodes agreements and for more militant policy	no specific commitment; in general, same as Mapai
Policy Toward Big Powers	Mapai: nonalignment and later pro-Western orientation; Mapam: nonalignment and pro-Russian orientation	In general, pro-Western orientation (Herut: anti-British and self-reliance)	no specific commitment; close to Mapai

*Based on the parties' platforms for the First (1949) and Second (1951) Knesset elections.

political system came up infrequently — as, for example, in the violent clash with Herut over Israel's relationship with Germany in 1951-1952 (Brecher, 1974: 56-110). Since 1948, all camps and their factions have been partners to democracy. They took part in advancing the legitimacy of the state institutions and the rules of political participation. The 1967 war accelerated this process because it brought about the first cabinet coalition that included all the major parties. In addition, the division into ideological camps lost its importance because of other long-range transformations that took place in Israeli society and economy.

The Political System: Formal Features[10]

In this section, only the main formal features of the political system in Israel are introduced. Many of them will reappear in following chapters in a communication context.

DEMOCRACY

In the annals of the Jewish community in which the debates about the future state are recorded, democracy was taken for granted. There was no formal resolution or ordinary statute which suggested that the State of Israel be a democracy. On November 29, 1947, the United Nations General Assembly recommended that Palestine be partitioned into two independent and *democratic* states, one Jewish and one Arab. In Israel's Declaration of Independence, "democracy" was not explicitly mentioned, but it was assumed in the references to instruments such as "elected authorities" and equal political rights for all inhabitants. We can surmise that an orthodox party such as Agudat Israel was basically indifferent regarding the type of political regime. Nevertheless, since a theocracy would take place only in the future Jewish commonwealth, it also preferred a democracy. There were sharp differences regarding the exact constitutional structure, but the decision of the great majority was to continue with the prestate political structure and modify it only to meet the new requirements (Sherf, 1959).

In the prestate period, the problem of democracy was both an ideological and institutional challenge to all political movements in the Jewish community (Horowitz and Lissak, 1977: 207). On the operational level, all movements and parties professed and practiced the democratic rules. This was imperative because of the heterogeneous nature of the community and the voluntary nature of all the Jewish institutions. There were shades also of nondemocratic and "predemocratic" positions in all parties for different reasons. The more Marxist-oriented groups, such as Hashomer Hatzair, believed in "collective ideology," while revisionists espoused the principle of a powerful leader (1977: 207-211).

An important contribution toward democracy was the "deviation of the dominant party (later Mapai) from the Russian pattern of non-cooperation with bourgeois parties" (J. Shapira, 1975: 203-204). Once this party decided also to encompass certain parts of the nonlabor sector and gained the upper hand through elections, the basis for the Israeli pluralistic and accommodating form of democracy was laid.

By conventional standards, Israeli democracy is expressed in regular national and local elections, the existence of nongovernmental centers of power, equality in political rights and so on. Mansen and Russett (1973: 17) use five indices to measure polyarchies: number of internal security men per thousand citizens, freedom of the press, partisan divisions, elections frequency, and leaders' control index. By all these criteria, Israel registers relatively high (Dahl, 1971).

The Declaration of Independence in 1948 served as the legal basis for the first Provisional Council and Provisional Cabinet. These bodies proceeded to establish the legal basis for other state organs such as the courts and decided on immediate issues such as state currency, stamps, and military ranks (Bernstein, 1957: 32-37). What were the legal and practical origins of the constitutional framework? Leaders such as Ben Gurion and Sharett openly admired the British system and regarded it as a model for the Israeli system. But by far the most important source was the legacy of the existing bodies — the yishuv institutions and the national Jewish institutions. These included the following main features: proportional system of elections and representation; unicameral house of representatives (the Knesset); coalition cabinet responsible to the Knesset; and division of functions between the political center and secondary centers, such as the Histadrut.

Unlike what happened in other former colonies, the British influence on the Israeli political system was selective and predominant in the following areas: the legal and court system; the parliamentary code of behavior and regulation; the formal structure of the civil service; and some specific areas such as the tax system, police, comptroller general, and certain ministries (for example, posts).

As of 1981, Israel does not have a written constitution, and the reasons have nothing to do with the British precedent. The Declaration of Independence called for the first elected assembly to adopt a constitution. The first elections were held in Israel in January 1949, and the elected Constituent Assembly enacted the "Transition Law," which laid

the constitutional groundwork for the political system. It also transformed itself from a Constituent Assembly to the First Knesset and
decided to defer the task of preparing a constitution for reasons that
reflect internal conflicts that still exist in Israel.

The strongest opposition came from the religious parties that maintained that a constitution already exists — Jewish law. They could agree
only to those legal arrangements that did not pose the dilemma of
choosing between their religious and political loyalties. A related argument was advanced by those who claimed that Israel's constitution
belongs to the whole Jewish people. Since most Jews still live outside
Israel, the final formulation would have to be postponed. Others realized
that the formulation of the constitution would cause a dangerous rift in
the new nation. They preferred a gradual approach as the only practical
method of solving fundamental conflicts in such a fragmented and
ideologically bent society. Ben-Gurion, too, was willing to wait, hoping
to be able to change the proportional system of election without a
constitutional constraint.

Finally, there were those who were simply not sure what *kind* of
constitution would be the most appropriate for a young and inexperi-
enced country. They were saying — perhaps naively, in retrospect — that
the political system inherited from the yishuv should continue for a while
until a new one, more suitable for the new state, emerges.

The supporters of a written constitution objected to all these arguments. They maintained that a constitution would strengthen democracy, the state, the government, citizens' freedoms and would enhance
the separation of state and religion. They were against the gradual,
piecemeal approach on the grounds that every political system — indeed, every state — must set clear rules and limits to its functioning.
Provisional arrangements become permanent, they argued, because
time is no less sanctifying an instrument than formal decisions.

The outcome of this debate was a compromise. Instead of a comprehensive constitutional document, there have been several Basic
Laws enacted over the years which eventually will be combined into a
full-fledged constitution. As of 1980, the main Basic Laws that have been
enacted are as follows: The Knesset (1958), the Israel Land Regime
(1960), the President (1964), the Government (1968), and the Defence
Forces (1976).

STATE ORGANS

The most important formal features of the state organs that have
evolved in thirty years are briefly presented below.

A ceremonial president. The president is elected by the Knesset for a five-year term. He symbolizes the state in direct contact with the people as well as in formal functions such as nominating the prime minister designate, accrediting foreign ambassadors, and signing all state laws. One central task of the president is to relieve the prime minister of ceremonial burdens. Little has changed in his functions over the years, except that each of the five presidents who served until 1980 has emphasized differently one or another aspect of his task. The personality of the prime minister dictates the degree of competition between himself and the president over the limelight of state ceremonies.

The Knesset – public arena of politics. The Knesset comprises 120 members elected for four years through a proportional system of representation. The important decisions — including issues of war and peace — are made by the cabinet, while political dealings are carried out among the parties, various organizations, and government ministries. Therefore, the Knesset serves as a public arena where the outputs of politics, usually predetermined, are displayed and occasionally argued. The political, economic, and budget debates in the Knesset reflect the partisan divisions on issues and nuances within the parties, which are further elaborated and explained by the press. The legislative work of the Knesset has been quite substantial, but, again, over ninety percent of the legislation has been introduced by the government (Weiss, 1977b; Yaacobi, 1980: 49-70). However, there are very few constitutional constraints, and the Knesset is potentially a very powerful body. In supervising the executive the Knesset is assisted by an independent comptroller general, who is also the citizens' ombudsman.

Strong executive. The cabinet is responsible to the Knesset and based on the support of a majority of its members. As of 1981, all cabinets have been a coalition of a number of parties. Government in Israel is big and powerful, and the executive is by far the dominating state organ. Israel shares this development with other democratic countries, especially parliamentary systems. Strong partisan discipline, the control of capital import, and the weakness of local governments have further strengthened the Israeli executive. Party discipline is the key reason for Israel's strong executive vis-à-vis the Knesset and all other institutions. Government ministries are divided among parties by coalition agreements.

An independent judiciary. Judges are nominated by a special nominating committee comprising three Supreme Court judges, two representatives of the Lawyers' Association, two cabinet ministers, and two Knesset members. In a highly politicized society and a highly interwoven network of political bodies, the courts have become practically and symbolically an island of independence. No doubt British impact in this sphere has been most influential. Particularly independent is the High Court of Justice, to which citizens can apply directly against alleged malfunctions of the state and the bureaucracy. Generally, the courts steered away from highly controversial political issues. Formally, the Supreme Court does not interpret the "Constitution" (that is, the Basic Laws) or the legality of new laws passed by the Knesset.[11] The courts have ruled on controversial subjects in Israeli politics, particularly religion and security.[12] But compared to the centrality of these issues in Israeli life and politics, the courts have been only marginally involved. The Supreme Court also declared its supremacy over the religious courts, but the issue has not come yet to a direct collision. In matters of security, in the past the courts have tended to accept the reasoning behind state claims of secrecy, but this, too, has changed in recent years (Galnoor, 1977: 180-83, 186). Individual judges have been involved in fact-finding and inquiry commissions investigating very sensitive issues (such as the Lavon Affair or the 1973 Agranat Commission of Inquiry), but the prestige and independence of the judicial system as a whole was spared despite the fact that the findings of such commissions became politically controversial.

A politically involved civil service. The civil service shares some features with the British bureaucratic system, but the accumulated result is distinctly Israeli. It is run by an independent Civil Service Commission, and during the years it has developed a merit system and has become less influenced by party politics and increasingly professional. The civil service, however, is in charge of numerous social tasks and cannot be completely independent or "professional" in a political system which is so densely occupied with parties and other powerful organizations. The civil service has evolved in accordance with the principal characteristics of the political system. It is delineated into separate areas according to the ministries. It is highly involved in political bargaining and confrontations and often serves as mediator for politicians, other bureaucracies, and clients.

Weak local authorities. Unlike the British system, there is no tradition of viable local government. Before 1948, the British government of Palestine discouraged the emergence of strong local governments because it did not want to vest too much power in the hands of independent Jewish or Arab cities or to force an ethnic face-off in mixed cities. The establishment of a strong political center after 1948 did not foster the development of independent local authorities. Members of local councils are elected for four years through the same proportional election systems. Since 1975 the head of the local authority is elected directly by the citizens but remains responsible to the council. Local authorities continue to be supervised and financed by the Ministry of Interior.

Lack of politicization in the military and the police. The Chief of Staff of the Israel Defence Forces (IDF) is appointed by the cabinet and responsible to it through the defense minister. The Israel Police is a national organization and responsible to the minister of interior (previously to the minister of police). Both institutions, especially the IDF, play critical roles in Israeli society, but there has been little direct involvement of the military and the police in politics. There have, however, been cases of party influences on appointments or controversies over nominations of ex-military men to political jobs. Moreover, the top military officers have been personally involved in high-level decision-making. Nevertheless, the politicization of these two institutions — at least until 1967 — has been minimal (Horowitz, 1980).

OTHER INSTITUTIONS[13]

During the prestate period, there were several other clusters of political power. There were the various world Zionist organizations which brought together Jews in Palestine and abroad around the idea of a Jewish homeland. These institutions included the *Zionist Congress,* an assembly of representatives, convened first by Theodore Herzl in 1897 and meeting periodically thereafter. The *Zionist Organization,* founded at the First Zionist Congress, was an organization of all Zionists based on a territorial representation. The Zionist Organization created the Jewish National Fund (Karen Kayemet) for purchasing land in Israel for Jewish settlement. The governing board of the Zionist Organization was the *Zionist Executive (Hanhala),* appointed by the Zionist Congress.

In 1929 the *Jewish Agency* was founded, according to the League of Nations mandate for Palestine, as the Jewish representative vis-à-vis the British administration, foreign governments, and international bodies. In due course, the terms World Zionist Organization and Jewish Agency became synonymous, and during the yishuv period the Jewish Agency was the principal political body outside and inside Palestine. The establishment of the state raised the issue of dividing the functions between the government of Israel and the Jewish Agency, and this has not yet been fully resolved. In 1952, the Knesset enacted a special Jewish Agency (Status) Law, and the government signed a covenant with the Zionist Executive defining the respective status and functions of the state and the Jewish Agency. The latter, financed by voluntary contributions of Jews outside Israel, was given authority over immigration, agricultural settlements, land reclamation, afforestation, welfare services, higher education, and youth centers.

The Jewish Agency still serves its original purpose of uniting the Jewish people around Jewish contents and Israel. Even though it ceased to be an independent factor in Israeli politics in 1948, it continues to play an important role in channeling political influence of Jews to Israel. The direction of significant influence, however, takes the reverse route — from Israel and Israeli political parties to Diaspora Jews.

A nongovernmental institution in Palestine was the General Federation of Labor — the *Histadrut* — founded in 1920. This organization aimed at creating a Jewish working class, and such an undertaking defined a much broader scope of activity than merely trade unionism. The Histadrut was the "government" of the labor movements in the yishuv and was active also in defense, training, industry, housing, health, education, social services, and agricultural settlements. "It was founded," wrote Medding, "to remove from the parties all functions except purely political ones" (1972: 9). It included, in various forms of affiliation, members of both the labor and religious camp and originally excluded members of the civic camp who were organized in other federations: industrialists, tradesmen, farmers, and professionals.

The sphere of influence of the Histadrut was considerably reduced in the state period. It lost control of education and employment in the early 1950s, which were transferred to the Ministries of Education and Labor, as well as its nearly monopolistic position in such areas as public construction, housing, and irrigation. But the Histadrut's role in many economic and social activities has not disappeared. It still predominates in health services through its General Sick Fund, and in public transportation through its two affiliated bus cooperatives.

In the prestate period, the Histadrut had been a vehicle for the labor parties to achieve domination in the political system. More than a third of the adult Jewish population was incorporated into the Histadrut (Table 2.7) — members of agricultural collectives and cooperatives as well as salaried employees: industrial workers, artisans, and professionals. In the state period, the Histadrut's ability to provide political support for the labor parties declined gradually, despite the increase in membership. This was due to the marked change in the whole occupational structure of Israel and, subsequently, in the Histadrut. The percentage of industrial and service workers increased relative to agricultural workers, and the Histadrut recruited them as members. It also made room for the self-employed and for white-collar workers, whether

TABLE 2.7   Histadrut Members as Percentage of Total Population

Year	Adult Members of Histadrut	Members of Histadrut as Percentage of Adult Population
1920	4,400	11.2
1930	28,500	26.8
1940	109,200	34.6
1950	257,600	36.7
1960	709,800	59.2
1970	988,200	62.1

SOURCES: Gil (1950: 32); The Histadrut Since the Establishment of the State (1969: 13, 15); and Histadrut Annual Yearbook (1977: 8).

wage-earning or independent. In 1960, Israeli Arabs joined the union. The result of this drive was that by the 1960s, the Histadrut incorporated the great majority of all employed persons in the country. This expansion in both membership and scope of activities came at the expense of its original aim — creating and representing the working class. The ideological aspects of trade union activity have subsided, and membership in the Histadrut became a means to gain access to certain jobs or services, notably the Sick Fund. Thus, the Histadrut could no longer count on its members for automatic political support to the labor parties.

ELECTION AND POLITICAL PARTIES

The Israeli multiparty parliamentary system is based on an electoral method of proportional representation. The Knesset is elected by universal suffrage under proportional representation. Citizens vote for fixed national lists of candidates. Most of the contenders are regular parties, but some are lists which appear just for the elections. Seats in the Knesset are allocated in proportion to the number of votes obtained by each list, provided it gains at least one percent of the total. The aggregate results of the ten elections held thus far in Israel are presented in Table 2.8.

No party has thus far achieved a majority of the votes, and thus all cabinets have been based on a coalition among several parties. Nevertheless, until 1977, Mapai was the dominating party and the pivot of coalitions formed with both labor and nonlabor parties (Diskin in Arian, 1980: 213-229). The NRP and the Independent Liberals (formerly the Progressive Party) were almost constant partners in the coalition. In

TABLE 2.8 Results of Knesset Elections (120 Knesset Members)

	1949	1951	1955	1959	1961	1965	1969	1973	1977	1981
Mapai[a]	46	45	40	47	42	45	56	51	32	47
Ahdut HaAvoda[b]	—	—	10	7	8					
Rafi[c]	—	—				10				
Mapam[d]	19	15	9	9	9	8				
Liberals[e]	7	20	13	8	17					
Herut[f]	14	8	15	17	17	26	26	39	43	48
NRP	16	10	11	12	12	11	12	10	12	6
Two Aguda Parties[g]		5	6	6	6	6	6	5	5	4
Arab Lists	2	1	4	5	4	4	4	3	1	—
Democratic Movement for Change								—	15	—
Indep. Liberals[h]	5	4	5	6		5	4	4	1	—
Communist Parties	4	5	6	3	5	4	4	5	5	4
Others	7	7	1			1	8[i]	3	6[j]	11[k]

[a] Joined with Ahdut HaAvoda in 1965 and the other labor parties in 1969.

[b] See note a.

[c] Ben-Gurion's party; joined the Labor Alignment in 1969 minus the "State List."

[d] Ahdut HaAvoda included in Mapam in 1949 and 1951.

[e] Until 1959 known as "General Zionists," joined Herut in 1965, and part of the Likud in 1977.

[f] Jointly with the Liberals since 1965 and part of the Likud in 1977.

[g] Poalei Agudat Israel and Agudat Israel.

[h] Included in Liberal Party in 1961 and independent again since 1965.

[i] Includes the "State List" (4 members), the Free Center (2 members), and Ha'olam Hazeh (2 members). The first two joined Herut and the Liberals in 1973.

[j] Includes Shlomzion (2 members), which joined the Likud after the elections, the Citizens' Rights Movement (1 member), and Flatto Sharon (1 member).

[k] Includes Ha-Tehiya (3 members), Tami (3 members), Telem (2 members), Shinui (2 members), and the Citizens' Rights Movement (1 member).

1977, the Likud — a united bloc of Herut, Liberals, and other small groups — gained 43 seats in the Knesset and formed a cabinet coalition with the religious parties and the Democratic Movement for Change. Despite many changes, the Israeli political system is still fragmented (many parties), fractional (many small parties), and polarized (great distance between the extreme ends).[14] In the 1981 elections, there appeared a greater concentration of votes, with the two big parties together, gaining about 79 percent of the votes.

Party politics have not been confined to the national level. The same main parties played roles in local elections, public organizations, and even in the internal elections in a workers' committee, the bus cooperative, and the student associations. Israel has been a prime example of a "party-dominated state." The following is a brief presentation of the principal parties currently in the Knesset.

Mapai (Israel Labor Party) appeared under this acronym in 1930 and was the dominant party in the yishuv and afterwards until 1977. It formed the first *Alignment* with Ahdut HaAvoda in 1965. These were joined by Rafi in 1968, and the union was called the Labor Party. Mapam joined them in 1968, and the combined title is again Alignment.

Ahdut HaAvoda (United Labor) split in 1944 from Mapai. Based predominantly on the kibbutz movement, it became part of Mapam in 1948 and independent again in 1954. It has been part of the labor alignment since 1965.

Rafi (Israel Labor List) is a new party, founded by Ben-Gurion in 1965. It rejoined the labor party in 1968.

Mapam (United Workers' Party) is a left-wing party with a strong constituency in the kibbutz movement. It has been part of the Alignment since 1968.

Liberal Party is a new name for the General Zionists Party, the cornerstone of the civic "bourgeois" camp. The General Zionists participated in the 1952-1955 coalition cabinets. It has been aligned with Herut since 1965 and part of the ruling Likud Party since 1977.

Herut (Freedom) was founded in 1948 by the people who belonged to Etzel and the Revisionist movement. Together with the Liberal Party, it formed *Gahal* in 1965 and, with some other small groups, the *Likud* in 1973. Herut has been led by Menahem Begin since 1948 and was excluded from all coalition cabinets during Ben-Gurion's premiership. It joined the national cabinet in 1967-1970. The Likud formed the cabinet in 1977 and 1981.

National Religious Party (NRP) originated in the prestate period as part of the Mizrachi movement and has appeared under this name since

1956. It participated in almost every coalition cabinet since Israel was established, including the cabinets headed by the Likud. It is more moderate on religious affairs than the two smaller religious parties. The NRP dropped to only six Members of Knesset in 1981.

Poalei Agudat Israel (Israeli Workers' Association), an ultra-orthodox labor party, consistently retained about one to two seats in the Knesset but did not win any in 1981.

Agudat Israel (Israel Association), an ultra-orthodox party with about four Knesset members.

Arab parties have appeared over the years, and all those which gained seats in the Knesset were affiliated with Mapai and the Alignment. Together they obtained at most five seats in the Knesset. There has not been an independent Arab party, and the Communist list received most of the Arab votes until 1977. No seats retained in 1981.

Democratic Movement for Change (DMC) was a new (1977) party and a new phenomenon in Israeli politics. Unlike other parties, which have been either splinters of old ones or obtained only a few seats in the Knesset, the DMC was instrumental in the 1977 turnover by gaining about 12 percent of the vote. Its appearance is connected to the aftermath of the 1973 war and the disappointment with the Labor government. The DMC joined the coalition cabinet headed by Prime Minister Begin, but soon afterwards it split into small factions and became extinct in 1980.

Independent Liberal Party (formerly the Progressive Party) is a small, moderate party and a constant partner of Mapai in the coalition cabinets. It did not make it to the Knesset in 1981.

Communist Parties appeared under various names during the years and suffered from splits mainly along the lines of Jewish-Arab membership. It obtained at most six seats in the Knesset.

Other small parties. The proportional election system enables the appearance of tiny parties with one to three members in the Knesset. For instance, in 1977 only 17,478 votes (one percent of the valid votes) were required to gain one seat in the Knesset. Many try, but only a few make it. An average of twenty lists and parties participated in the Knesset elections up to 1977 and only about 13 succeeded in entering the Knesset. In 1981 there were 31 lists, only eleven of which entered the Knesset.

Modes of Operation

In Israel, the composition of the Knesset is regarded as a true reflection of the attitudes, opinions, and even the social mosaic of the society. Therefore, the governing bodies of many public institutions are structured to parallel the representation in the Knesset. Appointments to the Board of Directors of the Broadcasting Authority, for example, or of department heads in the Jewish Agency, the Water Council, or dozens of other institutions, have been allocated accordingly. This practice is known as the "party key," which was developed during the yishuv period together with the politics of proportional representation, bargaining, and accommodation. The result is that most public organizations in Israel share the same mode of national representation. This limits their ability to base their operation on their specific (regional, for example) interests alone. The rewards, however, are found in better communication and coordination.

Israeli democracy is equated with the existence of the Knesset, majority rule, and elections. Other manifestations of political pluralism, such as extraparliamentary political groups or nonaffiliated interest associations, are less prevalent. They are often construed as a danger to solidarity and cohesiveness. The traditional division of ideologies and parties is still a popular benchmark for placing and evaluating any political idea or act, even though it is obvious that for a long time the parties have not kept up with social changes and are themselves split on major issues. One indirect result, to be explored later, is the lack of balance in democratic development in Israel. Important components, such as civil rights, minority rights, free press, or the people's right to know, have received less attention.

The tendency to observe democratic rules, but not to hesitate to circumvent them and to "cut corners," is also rooted in the prestate period. The Jewish minority in Palestine often faced the dilemma of how to circumvent British law in vital issues such as settlement, immigration, and military training. It sometimes resorted to illegal activities. Remnants of this legacy, including some disrespect for the law, can be found even today in Israel. The government is no longer foreign, but some tax requirements and other regulations still seem to be.

Politicization of the civil service in Israel is not precisely of a party nature; however, it has two other manifestations (Galnoor, 1980: 138-141). First, government employees display greater loyalty to their own ministries than to the civil service as a whole. Since the ministries are allocated by coalition agreements, there is still a significant link between the minister's party and the senior officials in a particular ministry. Second, the civil service is still political in the wider sense of the term: It has relationships with sectors and pressure groups, is considerably involved in channeling information to the communications media, and is an excellent springboard for political posts (see Chapter 5). Many have reached the top administrative echelons because of their ability to function in the labyrinth of interrelationships among the government, parties, affiliated organizations, and special interest groups.

Since it has been impossible to implement policy without the cooperation of all these organizations and groups, government ministries have maintained close contacts with them — confiding with their representatives while policy is being considered, and enjoying their support when it is being implemented. In this fashion, the Ministry of Agriculture's water policy was worked out with the representatives of the principal consumers (the farmers); the capital market was administered with the assistance of the banks; and the settlement policy was closely coordinated with representatives of the various movements. The most prominent examples were the relationships between the government and the Histadrut and between these two and the Industrial Association. Even consumer protection organizations belong to the Ministry of Commerce and Industry, the Histadrut, and the local authorities.

In his description of a consociational democracy, Lijphart (1977: 25-52) lists four main characteristics. Do these apply to the Israeli political system?

Proportional system of representation, appointment to public positions, and allocation of public funds. All three exist in Israel. The proportional principle, especially in the system of elections, is rigidly applied as compared with other countries.

Mutual veto rights are granted to the various camps, including the minor ones. As noted, this is applied in Israel mainly in the relationship with the religious camp. It is manifested also in the lack of a written constitution, or the special majority required for changing certain laws, such as the election system law.

A high degree of autonomy for each camp in conducting its own internal affairs. This used to be an accurate description of the yishuv and the early state periods. It has changed considerably in recent years. Still, the complicated organizational structure of the Israeli political system permits each secondary center and affiliated organization a certain degree of freedom in conducting its internal affairs, except in the sensitive area of defense, which has been excluded from the usual domestic political process and elevated to national politics.

A grand coalition of political leaders enables them to govern the country despite the cleavages. Lijphart maintains that this characteristic is only partly applicable to Israel (1977: 129). This is also one of the reasons why Israel's political system is classified as only "semi-consociational" (Gutmann in Lissak and Gutmann, 1977: 410). True, the cabinet has not usually been a grand coalition (except during the period of the National Cabinet, 1967-1970). Yet the grand coalition principle —

what is called the "party key" — was applied in the political system as a whole, especially with regard to the Zionist organizations and, to some extent, also in the Histadrut. Broad participation in the Jewish Agency and its affiliated organizations (and funds) is a clear example of this principle. The main purpose of grand coalition is to achieve compromises on the elite level and to execute the politics of accommodation, and this mode of operation was highly refined in Israel's political system.

NOTES

1. Palestine was the official name of all the territory west of the Jordan River under the British Mandate, 1919-1948.
2. The analysis of state-building in new nations often implies an organic model of political development: A political system grows out of social forces mainly through leadership roles. But there were also many cases in which the state preceded or coincided with the establishment of the political system. See Shils (1958), Almond and Powell (1966), and Binder et al. (1971).
3. In 1954, while Pinhas Lavon was Minister of Defense, a foiled Israeli intelligence operation ("The Mishap") in Egypt resulted in death sentences for two Egyptian Jews and long imprisonment for several others. The question, "Who gave the order?" — Lavon or a senior intelligence officer — remained unanswered despite numerous hearings and inquiries. In 1960, Lavon demanded that his name be cleared, and the matter quickly deteriorated into a major crisis involving all parts of the political system: The Mapai party removed Lavon as secretary-general of the Histadrut; Ben-Gurion resigned from the cabinet; and the Knesset was dissolved and early elections were held (August 1961). Ben-Gurion's final resignation as prime minister in 1963 and his decision to leave his party and form a new one in the 1965 elections are also related to the Lavon Affair.
4. It is difficult to estimate the number of Jews in the intermediate circle — those who actively support Israel in one way or another. Most observers agree it is well below 50 percent of the total number of Jewish households in the world. See Sheffer and Manor in Bilski et al. (1980: 315-317).
5. See Chapter 3 for a more complete discussion of these concepts.
6. On partition as a general solution for integration problems, see Huntington and Dominquez in Greenstein and Polsby (1975: Vol. 3, 83,89).
7. On the legal aspects, see Rubinstein (1974: 67-71, 103-104, 173-174).
8. For further details, see Birnbaum (1970), Don-Yehiya (1975), Goldman (1964), Yaron (1976), Deshen (1978), Samet (1979), and Ben-Meir and Kedem (1979).
9. The word in Hebrew is the *Ezrachim* (civic) camp. On its blurred boundaries and organizational weakness, see Lissak and Gutmann (1977: 133).
10. There have been few comprehensive attempts to analyze the whole Israeli political system. Among the first books are Bernstein (1957) and Fein (1967). Lately, there has been a revival of interest among Israeli scholars: Horowitz and Lissak (1977) and J. Shapira (1977). Among the many studies dealing with some central components of the system are Arian (1968, 1971), Landau (1971), Brecher (1972), Medding (1972),

Luttwak and Horowitz (1975), J. Shapira (1975), Aronoff (1977), Etzioni-Halevy (1977), and Smooha (1978).

11. The High Court of Justice did intervene in the well-known case of Bergman v. The Finance Ministry in 1969, and ruled that the criterion for distributing state financial support to the parties violates the principle of equal opportunity in the elections. See Rubinstein (1974: 239-244).

12. In religious affairs: problems related to the definition of a "Jew," marital and divorce laws, work and transportation on Saturday, television on Friday night, and so on. In security affairs: the Lavon Affair, the Kfar Kassem trial (1957), the Agranat Commission of Inquiry into the Yom Kippur War (1973), and settlements in the West Bank (1979).

13. On the role of the mass communication media in Israeli politics, see Chapter 7.

14. For a full discussion see Gutmann in Lissak and Gutmann (1977: 122-170); an early but still illuminating analysis of the role of the parties in Israel can be found in Akzin (1955).

3

COMMON POLITICAL CONTENTS

"The word *Arachim* (values) has always had an important place in the
internal debate. It connotes near-absolute ideological and moral
fixities. Values are always 'basic': 'Jewish values', 'socialist values',
'Zionist values', 'moral values', 'national values', 'pioneering values',
'cooperative values'. Values are both a flag and a fig leaf."

(ELON, 1972: 291)

In Chapter 1, political development was defined as "movement in the
direction of creating steering capacity." Starting with this chapter, the
general theoretical framework is applied to the Israeli political system.
The components of political communications that will be presented are
common political contents (Chapter 3); the network of communications
(Chapter 4); and the main channels — party, bureaucratic, and mass
media (Chapters 5, 6, and 7). Discussion of political development concludes with a chapter on steering (Chapter 8), followed by the presentation of democratic political development in terms of access and participation (Chapters 9 and 10).

In the following discussion, we assume that a minimum amount of
common political contents is a necessary — but not sufficient — prerequisite for the beginning of political development. The first question is,
what were the common political contents that helped the Israeli political
system emerge and develop?

Communality

The First Zionist Congress, a major collective effort of Jews from different countries to organize politically, was held in Basel in 1897. About 200 delegates from all over the world attended the congress. They dressed differently, spoke different languages, and devoted more time to "reviewing the Jewish situation" than to operational decisions. But out of this Congress a political movement was born. Fifty years later, in May 1948, the State of Israel was established.

As a political movement, Zionism — the return of Jews to Zion — is less than 100 years old. The goal of the Basel Congress was to "lay the cornerstone for a home in which the future Jewish nation can dwell" (Belkovsky, 1946: 11). By the end of the nineteenth century there were about 7,000 Jewish farmers in Palestine living in small settlements established during the preceding twenty years. At the same time, 30,000 Jews were immigrating annually from Europe to the United States (1946: 90). In the years 1881-1914, about two million Jews immigrated to the United States, mainly from Eastern Europe (Segre, 1971: 26). Nonetheless, within a relatively short period the Zionist movement became the carrier of organized Jewish efforts to establish a state. We can assume that a minimum of common political contents already existed when the first congress was convened and that this minimum was expanded in a relatively short period, enabling the movement to grow into a system and ultimately a state.

While the Zionist movement started about a century ago, the development of the political system of the yishuv commenced much later. The Balfour Declaration (1917) and the first elected Assembly in the yishuv (1920) are two important landmarks in the beginning of this political system. In the prestate period, the Jewish people were a nation without a country and the Zionist movement, a political system without a state. It was a voluntary political system which possessed neither a territorial basis nor formal enforcement power and therefore had to rest on more than just a minimum of common political contents.

These more than minimal contents can be regarded as a sense of communality and will be presented under the label "Jewishness." The achievements of the Zionist political movement indicate the enormous reservoir of political energy that was latent in the European Jewish community by the turn of the twentieth century. The Jewish national movement emerged out of different forces: external threats, the breakdown of the religious tradition of the ghetto, and disillusion from the emancipation and secular enlightenment. As a movement, it was deeply divided from the very beginning on ideological, religious, and tactical issues. Nevertheless, the central elements of identification proved strong enough to sustain not only the Zionist movement but also the formation of the political system of the yishuv.

In most revolutionary movements, politics is an agent of change: It articulates, leads, and is the cornerstone of cultural, social, and economic aspirations. This agent, what we have called the political center, can emerge and act only if it represents a central value system — an object of identification which transcends and transfigures the immediate concerns of the individual (Shils, 1975: 7). The Zionist movement proved to be this central value system for those Jews who sought a collective solution to their "Jewish problem." There were, to be sure, other collective solutions, such as the Bund — the revolutionary movement of Jewish workers in Russia and Poland (established in 1897) which was anti-Zionist, anti-clerical, and later became Communist (Vital, 1978: 239-240). At the other extreme, there were the ultra-orthodox communities which did not believe in self-initiated national restoration.

In political systems whose appearance marks a break with the past, politics as "organized social power" (Heller, 1933: 301) is, at least initially, an instrument of communication and cooperation. It provides the vehicle for translating diffuse sentiments and scattered interests into a cooperative activity (see Baldwin, 1978). With this sequence, politics is the independent, rather than the dependent, variable in the historical equation. Thus, the study of the emergence of Israel begins with the study of Zionism as a *political* movement.

Areas of Collective Identity

Integration based on loyalty to a *nation* is the most common basis for the functioning of political systems in modern times, and the *state* is the most concrete expression of this norm. In order to understand the basis for Zionism as a nation-oriented norm and "Israeliness" as a state-oriented norm, we must start with two other areas of identification: orthodox Judaism and Jewishness. The following schematic presentation of each area is aimed at outlining the common ground which enabled Zionism to move from interaction to collective efforts — that is, to politics (see Figure 1.1).

(a) Orthodox Judaism — a strictly religious interpretation of Jewish being. Orthodox Judaism is an all-encompassing religion with implica-

tions for personal and family conduct, culture, national affiliation, and
economic behavior. The main loyalty of orthodox Jews is to the Jewish
faith, to religious law, and to customs that were developed through the
long years in the Diaspora. Orthodox Jews uphold the concept of the
community implied by the "People of Israel." They reject all nonorthodox interpretations of Judaism as well as any kind of assimilation and
even contact with other religions. Both culture and nationalism are
perceived as part of Judaism, and this also entails an instrumental
attitude toward the state. For some, Zionism is premature and even false
messianism; for others, even though the modern State of Israel is not yet
a fulfillment of God's promise, Zionism is fully supported because it has
religious meaning and is located in the land of Israel.

(b) *Jewishness* — a sense of kinship and solidarity, a cultural interpretation of Jewish heritage, including religion, tradition, and "common fate." This is a modern and usually secular interpretation of what it
means to be Jewish. The main loyalty of those in this area of identification is to Jewishness as ethnicity. They reject orthodox Judaism and/or
Zionism as the only valid expressions of Jewishness. Their attitude
toward religiosity may be positive (as the faith of Jews), but they do not
regard the cumulative traditions of Judaism as authoritative. Zionist
nationalism is also accepted as one possible expression of Jewishness,
hence their solidarity with the State of Israel and their willingness to
support it without making a formal citizenship commitment. Most Jews
fall into this area of identification, and most of them live outside Israel.
They preserve their Jewish identity mainly as a cultural heritage and as a
sense of kinship. Their Jewishness is expressed primarily by not marrying non-Jews, observing the High Holidays, having a passive knowledge
of Hebrew letters, and financially or morally supporting Israel as a
shelter for oppressed Jews.

(c) *Zionism* — a national interpretation of Jewish history including
religion. The reference here is to the value system, rather than to the
instrumental role. The core of the Zionist value system is Jewish national self-determination and personal fulfillment through immigration to
Israel. Zionists reject the idea that the Diaspora is a natural and irrevoc-
able Jewish condition. Their attitude toward religion is ambivalent —
not necessarily negative — because religion could be viewed as part of
the national and cultural heritage. The state is regarded as the essence of
modern Jewish nationalism and, as such, as the potential center for all
Jews.

(d) *Israeliness* — a territorial interpretation of modern Israel confined to the boundaries of the nation-state and formally encompassing
non-Zionist and non-Jewish identification. This term connotes the grop-

ing and uncertain identities of Jews (and a minority of non-Jews) in the State of Israel. Israeliness as an area of identification is a more recent phenomenon than the others, as it is rooted in loyalty to the state and the new Israeli identity, and may include rejection of the Diaspora as part of that new identity. The attitude toward religion ranges from total rejection to a grudging acceptance (as "the faith of some Jews"). Israeli culture is perceived as something new in the process of emerging in Israel. This definition of Israeli nationalism is more narrow than Zionism. It contains strong etatist elements and is based primarily on language, territory, and state sovereignty.

These areas of identification rarely exist in their pure form. Most prevalent are the overlappings and combinations; several illustrations may be helpful.

THE EXTREME ULTRA-ORTHODOX

There are Jews in Israel and abroad whose religious interpretation of Judaism transcends any modern definition of nationality or state sovereignty. As for all orthodox Jews, Judaism is not just a religious identification in the narrow sense: It is an all-encompassing way of life. They accept Jewish law (the Halachah) as authoritative, and their connection to the Land of Israel is an integral part of their faith. They pray daily for the "return to Zion," but this has a spiritual meaning and the actual execution is delayed until the coming of the Messiah. What distinguishes the *extreme* ultra-orthodox groups is their total rejection of secular culture and modern Jewish nationality as part of it. Jews with these loyalties do not use the holy language (Hebrew) in everyday life, and they reject interpretations of Judaism which are cultural, ideological, nationalistic in the Western secular sense, or etatist. For them, the people of Israel are a holy nation which requires a total commitment. This particular form of Judaism did not appear in the Oriental Jewish communities: Ultra-orthodox Jews are trying to continue the way of life that existed in the destroyed communities of Europe before the era of emancipation and enlightenment. This group includes the Neturei Karta, as well as other extremist communities, but it does not include the other ultra-orthodox Jews affiliated with the Aguda parties (see Chapter 2). Their exact numbers are unknown, but in Israel there are probably no more than 10,000, a very small percentage of the total number of religious Jews who practice orthodox Judaism.[1]

THE WESTERN DIASPORA

Cutting across the areas of Judaism and Jewishness are modern, observant Jews who are not Zionists. European Jews of the "Mosaic confession" in the nineteenth century, or the early Reform movement in Europe and later in the United States, were clearly in opposition to Zionism. Others conceded that Zionism is a solution for oppressed Jews, but they rejected its nationalistic program. They believed in the mission of Jews as a "kingdom of priests and a holy nation" to be discharged while the Jews are scattered among the nations. Subsequently the Reform movement also recognized the importance of Palestine and the obligations of Jews to aid in its upbuilding. A splinter group, the American Council for Judaism, remained anti-Zionist after 1948.

The majority of Jews are in the Jewishness category, and most of them are in the Western Diaspora. They regard their Jewishness mainly as a cultural heritage and as a sense of kinship. For some, this heritage dictates behavior; for others, religious (nonorthodox) commitments. Many are rather assimilated in the cultures of their countries. Their assimilation is still two or three generations deep at most, and it is difficult to predict how much the phenomenon resembles assimilation in Europe in the late eighteenth and early nineteenth centuries. The nonassimilated Jews in this group are usually also secular or nonorthodox, but they regard themselves as Jewish in the ethnic sense. They may support the state of Israel, yet most reject Zionism as the sole manifestation of personal Jewish fulfillment.

THE ORIENTAL DIASPORA

In an entirely different way, much of the Oriental Diaspora combined Judaism and Jewishness in the traditional manner, but without the rejection of Zionism and the nation-state. Modern and secular interpretations of religion and kinship were not relevant for them. They could not find such interpretations in the traditional environment of their Moslem communities. The great majority of Oriental Jews immigrated to Israel after 1948 and by doing so, became Zionist and Israeli. Their undivided Jewish identity represented a possible amalgamation of the religious, cultural, national, and territorial areas of loyalty. However, they were quickly influenced, at least in the short run, by the Western orientation of the emerging common contents in Israel (Deshen, 1978: 162-166).

RELIGIOUS ZIONISTS

Most observant and traditional Jews in Israel (see Figure 2.1) and some in the Diaspora are in an overlapping area of orthodox Judaism and Zionism. They have incorporated in their religious belief a more modern interpretation of culture, nation, and state. As such, they have been an integral part of the Zionist political movement (for example, the Mizrachi movement). They envisage the State of Israel as an instrument for fulfilling God's promise to restore the Third Commonwealth and strive to ensure the state's Jewish character. The loyalties of Jews in this area are above all religious, and any other national loyalty, including Zionism, is part of that. They reject the secular, strictly cultural Israeli interpretation of Jewish nationalism.

ZIONISTS AND THE DIASPORA

The overlap between Jewishness and Zionism has been one of the most controversial areas. When an amorphic cultural interpretation becomes a deep sense of kinship and solidarity, the distance between that and national identity is very small indeed. Yet, can a Jew in the Diaspora with a strong "Jewishness" identity be regarded also as a Zionist? This has been a permanent question on the agenda of Zionism since its inception. Ben-Gurion's answer was swift and polemic: Zionists are only those who come to Zion. The answer of Jews living in the modern Diaspora has been that assimilation is not weakness of character, but an inevitable historical process. While Zionism rejects the possibility of a genuine Jewish life in the Diaspora, an assimilated Jew rejects Zionism as too parochial ("nationalistic") for a modern person living in a pluralistic Western society. For the Jew who severed his ties and went to Israel, the merger between Jewishness and Zionism is relatively easy — either secular or religious nationalism.[2] For the Israeli who continues to maintain his sense of affiliation with the Diaspora and rejects Israeliness as a new culture, the synthesis is problematic. He regards Israel as the place where the "true" Jewish culture is bound to emerge, yet he is not sure as to its exact meaning and future contents.

ALL KINDS OF ZIONISTS

The Zionist identity is made up of several complex identities: religious Zionism, secular Jewish nationalism, and secular "Israeli" nationalism with weak Jewish identity.

The Zionist national movement maintained that the anomaly of Jews without a state must be ended. Once the state was established, it maintained that the anomaly of the Diaspora must be ended. Zionism rejects the strictly religious interpretation of Judaism, as well as the strictly cultural or ethnic one. For Zionists, the return to the ancient Land of Israel, the Hebrew language, as well as self-determination composed one package containing the essence of modern Jewishness. Those who attended the First Zionist Congresses were mostly secular and partly assimilated Jews who had learned from their own experiences that a narrow definition of Jewishness (as a culture and not a nationality) is irrelevant simply because of anti-Semitism. Zionists were not necessarily anti-religious, but they fought the concept of a Diaspora as a natural condition of the Jews and demanded that every Jew personally immigrate to Zion. At the same time, "Zion" was more than just a state: The tie with Jews who had not yet arrived was to remain an essential ingredient of Zionism before the state was established and afterwards. The revitalization of a past that goes back 2000 years and the link with the Diaspora are the two elements that make Zionism different from other modern national movements.

In addition, there were also the territorialists: those who believed in a national solution for the Jewish problem, but not necessarily in Zion and not as a personal obligation. The suggestion in the Zionist Congress of 1905 of establishing the Jewish state in Uganda was supported by Herzl and testifies to the willingness of some Zionists to drop Zion as the sole territorial solution for the Jewish problem. On the other hand, the subsequent willingness of Israeli leaders to share the title of Zionists with Jews outside Israel who do not immigrate indicates that the boundaries between the areas of Jewishness and Zionism are not so clear-cut.

THE NEW HEBREWS

Israeliness is a much later phenomenon which obviously could grow only in Israel itself. There were Jews in Palestine and later in Israel who carried to the extreme the definition of Zionism as just another national movement. Once the goal of establishing the state is achieved, they argued, the Jewish and Zionist definitions of "Israeliness" should be dropped. They maintained that the Israeli national movement does not have to be only Jewish in character — that is, non-Jews can join the new state not only on a citizenship basis but culturally and nationalistically as well. They can join the new "Hebrew" nation that is being created in Israel. Accordingly, the Israeli national movement should sever its ties with the Diaspora because non-Israelis cannot be part of the new Israel.

The small and marginal "New Canaanites" movement that appeared in Palestine in the 1940s is an example of such a trend. This was a movement of young people who rejected their Jewish identity in its religious or non-Israeli forms and even the "too-narrow" Zionist interpretation of nationalism. For them, Jews are not a nation, particularly in light of the differences between Western and Oriental immigrants.

The basis for a new Hebrew nationality is forged through the link with the land of Israel and the Hebrew language:

> The new generation [in Israel] is beginning to detach itself from the Judaism of the tradition; sooner or later, it is bound to establish a new modern form for the national ethos — a form destined to expand and grow. The conditions for a Hebrew renaissance include the rediscovery of the Levant as a single country and hence, the difinition of the national Hebrew entity as a territorial, cultural society open to any man, no matter what his race or faith [from an article in *Aleph*, a Canaanite publication, June 1951, translated in Kurzweil, 1953: 3].

This total rejection of the contents of the other three areas of identity was not widespread, and the movement never became politically significant. Its importance lies in the fact that it presented in an extreme form the seeds that were sown in the overlapping area between Zionism and Israeliness. As Kurzweil points out (1953: 8), these elements were indigenous and represented deep resentment against the "decaying Judaism" and the links of Zionism with the Diaspora. The desire to redefine modern Jewish nationalism in etatist terms was not devoid of mythical concepts about the unifying role of language and schemes of grandeur to absorb non-Jews into the Great Hebrew Nation.

ISRAELIS

Perhaps the most interesting area is the overlap between Israeliness and Zionism with which most Israeli Jews are identified. There are Israelis for whom the state is the epitome of Zionism, Jewishness, and even Judaism. They have not drawn extreme conclusions from this attitude as have the Canaanites. For instance, they have not advocated the nationalization of non-Jews who live in Israel in order to make them part of the new Jewish Israel. Nevertheless, rejection of the Diaspora and the abnormality of being a nation without a state has been a rather dominant sentiment in Israel, especially in the early days of the state. From its inception, Zionism was predominantly secular, and the return to a broader Jewish definition came later (notably during and after the 1967 war, when Jews in the Diaspora and Israel shared a common feeling of isolation and threat). Perhaps the return to a stronger bond with Jews outside Israel was inevitable because of the broader goals of the Israeli political system, as explained in Chapter 2.

All the possible combinations have not been examined here; however, the above discussion is sufficient to illustrate the great complexity of the content that forms the substance of political communication in the

Israeli system. What follows is an attempt to flesh out the common
denominator.

THE COMMON GROUND

The political content which is most common to all the areas discussed above is Zionism. The extreme groups of ultra-orthodox Jews
and the new Hebrews have very little in common. The ultra-orthodox
reject any modern interpretation of their Judaism — ethnic, Zionist,
Israeli or otherwise. The "ultra-Israelis" are extremely secular and
etatist, rejecting a historical, cultural, or religious interpretation of their
Israeli identity. In between lie the great majority of Jews in Israel and a
certain portion of the Jews outside Israel. Some of the most significant
common contents that served as the common ground, or evolved in the
100 years or so of the Jewish political movement, are listed in Table 3.1

Despite all the differences and divergences between the Jewish
people and the Zionist movement, Zionism served as a firm basis for
national commitment of the individual and for a wide consensus.
Moreover, despite the fierce ideological debate within the Zionist
movement, the bonds held. They held because identification with the
Jewish state expressed the identity of the vast majority of Israelis as well
as many Jews who cared about being Jewish. The Zionist political
movement incorporated religious and secular Jews, Marxists and
capitalists, socialists and liberals, traditionalists and modernizers. It
developed a capacity to overcome disintegration tendencies caused by
the potential cleavages described in Chapter 2. One of the main reasons
why this capacity could develop was the existence of a vocabulary for
political action. Eisenstadt (1967: 389-390) points out the importance of
Jewishness, as well as other values, traditions, and orientations, as basic
elements in the Israeli identity, and concludes the following:

> The adherence to . . . collective commitments has shown great vitality
> and persistence in the face of many possibilities of erosion, enhanced
> by the numerous social conflicts for which no adequate regulative
> norms were found.

Nonpolitical Common Contents

Common contents are an integral part of communal and social bonds.
They are useless politically unless they serve the function of providing a
basis for interaction and collective action and of being instrumental in
these actions. In the preceding section, Zionism was discussed as the

TABLE 3.1 Contributions to Zionism

	Orthodox Judaism	Jewishness	Israeliness
Content	The concept of one nation; the duty to settle in the Holy Land	Kinship; solidarity; mutual support	Immigration; territory; sovereignty; state; language
Symbols	The Bible; the ancient kingdom; prayers; holidays; the Land of Israel	Common languages (Yiddish, Ladino); homeland; stereotypes of Jews	Hebrew; the state; official symbols

central locus. In this section, I propose that nonpolitical values and symbols serve as common denominators in politics. All of the five following examples have been extremely important in providing the communication infrastructure of the Israeli political system and are present in various permutations in all areas of identification.

THE LAND OF ISRAEL

The essence of the Jewish renaissance was expressed practically and symbolically in the "return to the land." The image of the wandering, rootless Jew was closely related to this lack of permanent attachment to land. The Land of Israel — as a spiritual locus of identification, as a concrete economic resource, or as the political bone of contention between Jews and Arabs — is central to my discussion (Kimmerling, 1973: 8-9). In a meeting of Jewish teachers in Palestine in 1939, the head of the Jewish National Fund, responsible for acquiring land, articulated the tangible and intangible value attached to the Land of Israel:

> There came a period when the new Jew arose and said: yes, land is important, but it must be in the homeland. This homeland is not located in the vast and rich territories of Russia and the Ukraine, but in a small and impoverished country, the Land of Israel. And here began the second phase, the movement to redeem our homeland, the movement to develop an attachment to nature in that homeland. [Ussishkin, 1943: 9-10].

The Land of Israel is, first of all, a religious symbol — the Holy Land. For religious Jews, Moslems, and Christians, the holiness of the land has important political repercussions. For Jews, this holiness is derived from the Bible and prayers and is expressed in rituals and ceremonies connected to the seasons, nature, and to specific places. Jerusalem is not just a holy city. It is also a spiritual center: It symbolizes a cultural heritage and is an object of identification for religious and nonreligious Jews alike. For Jews who are not Zionists or Israelis, the origin of the people and the spiritual inspiration are embodied in the Land of Israel.

For Zionism, Zion was the essence of national survival. Despite its secular character and some attempts to solve the Jewish problem in other areas, Zionism was born and has remained a movement of return to the historical entity called the Land of Israel (Eretz Yisrael). The emphasis on growing roots, working the land, becoming farmers — all demonstrate the salient aspect of land in the process of normalizing the Jewish people. The dominating socialist ideology of the labor camp emphasized the need to invert the pyramid of Diaspora Jewish occupations and to base it on a large number of Jews working the land in Israel.

The role of the Jewish National Fund was to acquire land and develop and retain it under collective ownership, according to the Biblical dictum: "The land shall not be sold in perpetuity" (Leviticus, 25:23). Similarly, the popularity of archeology — officially encouraged by the state — is an attempt to reestablish tangible links with the past (known also in other "revivalist" nations, such as Turkey and Iran). This "old-new land" (the name of one of Herzl's books) was to be built by pioneers who named themselves after Biblical locations, such as Jordan, Carmel, Sharon, Shiloh, and Hermon. The words Eretz Yisrael had a national and political meaning for the yishuv, and therefore the British authorities refused to allow their official usage. The term used was "Palestine (EI)" (EI being an abbreviation of Eretz Yisrael).

For some native Israelis the land itself is merely the territory upon which the state exercises sovereignty. As such it has no special religious or cultural meaning. The picture, however, is more complicated, even for the Canaanites, whose territorial basis is expandable but starts with the Land of the Hebrews. This symbol is emotionally and politically charged because the boundaries kept changing. Since the British Mandate of 1921, the east bank of the Jordan River was separated in 1922 and became the Kingdom of Transjordan. The UN resolution of 1947 called for partition and new borders. Later the borders changed in 1948-1949, 1956, 1957, 1967, 1973, 1974, 1975, and 1980.

Land is the most concrete expression of a modern nation-state and of the jurisdiction of the political system. But in Israel, the lack of definite borders and the differences between the religious, cultural, national, and legal definitions make the issues of land and borders the source of international controversy as well as internal disputes. There are real differences between those who regard the Land of Israel in spiritual and symbolic terms and those who view it as a definite territorial entity. Nevertheless, the concept of Eretz Yisrael as the "old country" provides common contents because it eventually came to be regarded by all concerned Jews as the only viable place for Jewish self-determination. The goal of gaining a territory for the Jews, located in the Land of Israel, has been the most important political common denominator of the yishuv. The preservation and defense of this territory are still unifying goals of Israelis and Jews abroad.

THE BIBLE

The Bible has always held deep religious, cultural, and ethical meaning for Jews. The opening statement of the Israeli Declaration of Independence points to its centrality, noting that the Jewish people "gave to the world the eternal Book of Books." In the context of my discussion here, the Bible is also part of the values shared by members of the political system. After all, the return to Zion was a return to the land of the Bible. Biblical images of the free people of Israel living in their own country and working on the land were an integral part of Zionism. Biblical motives were common among the pioneers of Hebrew literature: Avraham Mapu, Yehuda Leib Gordon, Moshe Leib Lilienblum, and Chayim Nachman Bialik. The names of the first settlements in Palestine were taken from the Bible (Mikve Israel, Petach Tikva, Nes Tziona, and so on). To be sure, these references to the Bible were "secular," but they provided a sense of continuity and a bridge to a common history.

The emphasis on ancient sources was selective: Socialist Zionists embraced the spiritual significance of the Bible, for example, but rejected later religious books, such as the Talmud (Don-Yehiya, 1980: 33). The attitude toward the Bible is a good illustration of the mix between religious motifs and secular political ideology in Zionism. In 1958, during the tenth anniversary of Israel, the first International Bible Quiz was held in Jerusalem. Here is how T. Kollek, the organizer of the quiz and current mayor of Jerusalem, describes the event:

> The winner was an Israeli. . . . He caused great excitement in our small nation. . . . His victory and perhaps the whole quiz led to the formation of a Bible study group in Ben Gurion's house. Suddenly Bible study groups started springing up all over the country and throughout the world [Kollek and Kollek, 1979: 141].

Alterman wrote a special poem for the occasion in which he praised the Bible Quiz, despite its gamesmanship, because of the childlike love expressed toward this spiritual source by so many Israelis:

> But even if it's a desire for play, perhaps there's
>   no harm done. . . .
> For if the Bible is the progenitor of our people, then
> In playing a Bible game, it's as if they play with their father . . .
> And if there's a touch of frivolity, there's also a closeness
>   of hearts which is mysterious. [Alterman, 1972].

Although the Bible is, above all, a sacred book for religious Jews, it has also become an object of historical, literary, and moral identification for secular Jews in Israel and elsewhere. While the land of Israel and immigration to it were more tangible symbols, the Bible could unite a variety of Jews. Bible studies were incorporated into the curricula of the first Hebrew schools set up in Palestine during the second wave of immigration (1904-1914). These were nonreligious studies; the stress was on the historical and philosophical meaning of the Bible. Ever since, the emphasis has been on the periods of the First and Second Temples, which for the Zionist movement, represented a vital link between ancient and modern periods of Jewish independence. Like the Land of Israel, the Bible has been an important object of identification for the people who supported Zionism and their divergent values and ideologies. For instance, the Biblical aspect of Zionism was attractive to the traditional orientation of Oriental Jews. The secular ideology was generally unacceptable because Oriental Jews' ties with the Holy Land had strong Biblical and Messianic elements (Shuval, 1963: 180).

The return to the Land of Israel is often portrayed as an attempt to pick up the thread of Jewish history which was severed 2000 years ago with the destruction of the Second Temple. The image of the ancient Hebrew farmer and warrior appealed more strongly to Israelis than the image of the Diaspora Jew, especially the image of those led to German gas chambers. In Biblical times, the Jews were free and had their own independent kingdom. This attachment to the ancient past explains the great popularity in Israel of archaeology and the importance assigned to every new discovery from the Israelite periods. Ben-Gurion talked about reviving the ancient glory and applying the moral teaching of the Biblical prophets; others could draw self-assurance from being recognized as descendents of the Children of Israel; still others were interested primarily in the specific laws which the Bible requires every Jew to observe.

The Bible is pervasive in all aspects of Israeli life. It is quoted (and misquoted) in cultural affairs and political speeches. Biblical verses provide words for popular songs and ideas for babies' names. Archaeological findings from Biblical times appear in the state emblem, stamps, and coins. Commercial trademarks of public and private companies use Biblical names and symbols. A booklet published by the Government Division of Information starts the description of Israel's history as follows: "The Bible is the principal source for the history of the first thousand years of the People of Israel" (Facts About Israel, 1973: 20). In its matter-of-fact official tones, it picks up history where the Bible left off, referring to the present State of Israel as the *third* period of Jewish independence — following the two periods of the ancient Temple commonwealths.

THE HEBREW LANGUAGE[3]

A land and a language! They are the ground beneath a people's feet and the air it breathes in and out. With them all things are possible, for each is an inexhaustible treasure [Halkin, 1977: 153].

Hebrew is the language of the Bible, the Mishna, and part of the Talmud. Every Jew who studied these holy books or the prayer book is familiar with Hebrew. Since the Babylonian exile (586 B.C.E.), other languages were used by Jews, but throughout the generations, the Hebrew language did not die. There were periods of decay (when Aramaic displaced Hebrew in Babylonia) and periods of revival (notably in Spain in the tenth to twelfth centuries). By and large, Jews in the Diaspora spoke the local languages as well as originating new languages — Judeo-German (Yiddish), Judeo-Spanish (Ladino), and Judeo-Arabic — but even these were replete with Hebrew words and expressions. Jews in the Diaspora learned Hebrew as a holy language to be used in prayers and religious studies, but there was usually a passive knowledge of letters and sounds, if not of meaning.

When Moses Mendelssohn translated the Bible into German (1778-1783), he started the language battle between those who regarded it as a liberating act of modernization and secularization and those who regarded it as a betrayal of Judaism. For the Jews who tried to assimilate in Western cultures, Judaism was only a religion and not a culture, and Hebrew was a menace. They considered German, the language of German Jews, as part of their culture. In Russia, on the other hand, a strong movement for the revival of Hebrew as a written and spoken language started to grow. There, Hebrew was viewed as a means of countering the threat of assimilation and the strong influence of Russian culture on Jewish intellectuals. It was in Russia that the new Hebrew literature started with writers such as Yehuda Leib Gordon (1830-1892) and Peretz Smolenskin (1842-1885); and the first Hebrew newspapers, *Hamaggid* (1856) and *Hashachar* (1867), made an appearance. This revival of Hebrew became part of not only a cultural renaissance but of national aspirations:"a return to our land and to our language."

The battle to establish Hebrew as the language of Jewish revival was not won easily. Originally, Zionist politics was conducted in many different languages. Herzl spoke no Hebrew or Yiddish and conducted the First Zionist Congress in German. According to one participant, the delegates there spoke in no fewer than 15 languages, and the protocol of the meeting was written in German (Belkovsky, 1946).

Eliezer Ben Yehuda was one of the most prominent advocates of Hebrew revival. He came to Palestine in 1881 and set out to coin new words, modernize the language, and win the support of the Jews living there at the time. The many communities of the old yishuv spoke different languages: Yiddish and European languages by the Westerners; Ladino, Arabic, and other Eastern languages by the Oriental community. Hebrew was used for prayers and occasionally as a lingua franca among the various Jewish communities. Ben Yehuda did not encounter resistance on the part of the first groups of pioneers (Chovevei Zion) who came in 1882. But Hebrew was rejected by the old yishuv population, especially the ultra-orthodox, who ridiculed Ben Yehuda and his efforts.

The revival of Hebrew in the Land of Israel began to flourish with the wave of immigration known as the Second Aliya (1904-1914) and the newcomers' insistence on spiritual and cultural revival as part of Zionism. Their contribution to the renaissance of Hebrew and its establishment as the common language of the yishuv is one of the most important cultural developments in Zionism (Eisenstadt, 1967: 35). Once the leadership of the movement moved from the Diaspora to Palestine, most Zionist politics, despite its cosmopolitan nature, was conducted in Hebrew.

The language battle in Palestine was waged primarily with Western languages. Landmarks in this vehement struggle are the decision by the Technical Institute in Haifa to use Hebrew as the language of instruction (1913) and the establishment of a Chair in Yiddish at the Hebrew University (1928). Both these decisions came after much conflict within the yishuv and opposition from abroad (A. Shapira, 1980: 146-148, 234-235).

The main thrust of the opposition to Yiddish was unwillingness to extend populist values to it or to any other language except Hebrew (Eisenstadt, 1967: 36). Eventually Hebrew gained the upper hand, mainly because it was not exclusively attached to one particular group. By the 1970s, about 80 percent of the population in Israel used it as their principal language (Statistical Abstract of Israel, 1978: 655). Until this day, however, many groups of immigrants maintain their native tongues, and Yiddish has even experienced a cultural revival in recent years. This is now tolerated only because the language war was unequivocally won by Hebrew and its predominance in Israel is no longer endangered. Significantly, despite pressure, Hebrew letters were not changed to Latin notations, as was the case, for example, of the Turkish language.

The use of Hebrew as a vital, national language was a revolution undertaken and almost completed within one generation. Hebrew had been a fossilized holy tongue at the end of the nineteenth century. For the new immigrants to Palestine, it was a necessary medium of communication in their new country. And for those born in Israel in the twentieth century, Hebrew is their mother tongue (see Blanc, 1957).

Today Hebrew is the language of all Israelis and a concrete option for Diaspora Jews who wish to identify with Israel. Hebrew is one of the few common contents that cuts across ethnic, religious, ideological, and even national cleavages in Israel. The Arabs in Israel speak Hebrew and through it gain a means of understanding Israeli Jews. But what is significant for our interest here is that social interactions in Israel — tensions, conflicts, cooperative activities, and politics — are expressed in Hebrew. It is a symbol of revival and of unification, a modernized bridge to the past, to religion, and to the ancient culture of the Hebrews.[4]

ALIYA

Aliya in Hebrew literally means "ascent" — rising physically and spiritually by immigration to Israel. The notion of aliya and the role of Israel as a shelter for Jews is one of the most important collective values. Conversely, the attitude toward the Diaspora is one of the most debated subjects among Zionists. The "return to Zion" motif is shared by different groups of Jews. For the ultra-orthodox Jew, there is a religious duty to settle in the Holy Land of Israel, although some interpret it as an obligation that can be delayed. Jews came to Palestine for religious reasons before Zionism appeared and continued to do so afterwards. For the ultra-secular who espouse "Israeliness," immigration has nothing to do with the ingathering of the exiles. For them, immigration is primarily a means of strengthening the state, and they welcome all immigrants willing to join the new nation, not necessarily Jews. On the other hand, secular Israelis who believe in the Jewishness of the state support aliya because of the demographic factor — they want to maintain the proportion of Jews in the total Israeli population.

Aliya is strongly supported by most Israelis and Jews. There are differences regarding its meaning which are related to the different conceptions of the Diaspora — as a source of identification or rejection. For the first generation of pioneers, the places they came from represented all the things they wanted to change and forget. They tried to become "new Jews": farmers, laborers, blue-collar workers — self-sufficient and proud of their Jewish national identity. In the new Hebrew textbooks used by schools, the rootless Jew of the Diaspora was replaced by the new, resilient Israeli. It should be remembered, however, that most of the Jews who came to Palestine and Israel were forced to leave their countries. They did not make a deliberate decision to change their way of life — country, occupation, and all — and to start all over again in the new country. They escaped or were expelled, and their attitude toward their native countries and toward the Jews who remained there was ambivalent. While they resented the anti-Semitism (in Europe) and the anti-Zionism (in Moslem countries) which had caused them to leave, they still regarded themselves as part of those cultures. Sometimes the emotional tie with the old country, particularly of European Jews, was stronger than the rational rejection. Unequivocal rejection was left for the next generation, those who were born in Israel. These young people, through a deliberate process of socialization, acquired negative attitudes toward everything that had to do with the Diaspora and the image of the wandering Jews, disparagingly labeled "refugees." In this stereotype, the Jew who chooses not to come to Israel is rejected both for his "Diaspora mentality" and for his tendency to cling to the foreign fleshpots.

Yet Israeli Jews had to face the fact that Jews remained in the Diaspora. Perhaps this unwittingly contributed to what Deutsch calls the link of a community with its past and the need to recall information from collective memory (1963: 129). Israel assumes responsibility for all Jews, whether they oppose or are neutral to aliya. Israel admits them and gives them citizenship without delay (The Law of Return[5]); it acts as an agent for prosecuting crimes against the Jewish people (the Eichmann Trial); and it preserves and teaches Jewish history and Jewish suffering (the Holocaust Museum in Jerusalem).

Thus, aliya serves both as a common goal and a symbol of the Zionist national revival. From the early days of Chovevei Zion (Lovers of Zion) in Russia at the end of the nineteenth century, through illegal immigration during the British Mandate, and until the immigration of Russian Jews in the 1970s, there has been a consensus in Israel regarding aliya. Aliya as a common value should not be confused with full agreement regarding the immigration policy. In 1955-1956 there was a policy of restrictive immigration regarding Moroccan Jews. The Israeli government justified this policy in terms of objective economic reasons.[6] A different opinion is presented by Smooha:

> The Orientals were not Israel's first choice, but there was no other alternative but to accept them. . . . In such circumstances it is understandable that Oriental immigration should have been accepted, but not pursued with the same degree of zeal as Ashkenazi immigration. Quotas were imposed on newcomers from Morocco supposedly because of health deficiencies — which apparently existed to no lesser degree among the Ashkenazi survivors of the concentration camps who came at the same time. [1978: 86-87].

The consensus regarding aliya reached beyond Israel, but there have been differences of opinion about its meaning as an obligation for all Jews. Many Israelis maintain that every Jew must "make aliya," whereas Jews in the Diaspora maintain that aliya is a personal decision and an opportunity — mainly for persecuted Jews. Nevertheless, broad support for aliya as a viable option is a way of expressing Jewish solidarity and support for Israel. It serves as a personal link between Israel and the Diaspora and supplies common contents to a central political goal (the ingathering of the exiles) by providing it with

depth: a link to Jewish history;

breadth: a link with the non-Israeli Jew who identifies with the State of Israel and its national, cultural, or religious meaning; and

a future: a link with the possibility that Israel will become the spiritual or national center of all or most Jews.

JEWISH HOLIDAYS AND THE SABBATH

"More than the Jews kept the Sabbath, the Sabbath kept the Jews" (Ahad Ha'am, 1856-1927). Ahad Ha'am, an influential essayist, was one of the first Zionists to emphasize the need to build a truly spiritual center in Israel based on the Jewish heritage and a careful selection from modern enlightenment.

The Jewish holidays, the Sabbath, and various customs and rituals have been observed by Jews throughout the world. For instance, remote communities in the East and West share a special attitude toward Yom Kippur (the Day of Atonement) whether or not they speak the same language, are orthodox or secular, Zionists or non-Zionists. Similarly, Jews celebrate the miracle of Hanukka when independence was regained under the leadership of the Hasmonaean family (165 B.C.E.). The holidays illustrate well the encompassing meaning of religion in Judaism. Jewish holidays are observed by those who adhere (according to our titles here) to orthodox Judaism, Jewishness, or Israeliness. In Israel, Jewish holidays are state holidays, a shared national experience. They are officially observed and deeply rooted in the way of life of Jews. Yet content and meaning are different.

Independence Day, on the other hand, poses a problem inside and outside Israel. It is not celebrated by those for whom Judaism is purely religious because it is a secular holiday, nor by those for whom "Jewishness" is purely cultural because it is clearly a national holiday. It is also problematic for non-Jewish Israeli citizens who are asked to celebrate the birth of their state but cannot identify with its Jewish character. Zionist religious Jews celebrate Independence Day and include special prayers and ceremonies. Likewise, it is celebrated by Diaspora Jews who support Israel and identify with the general meaning of the state for the Jewish people.

In Israel since the early days of the British Mandate, the Jewish holidays and the Sabbath have been recognized as official rest days for the Jewish community. The Work and Rest Hours Law of 1951 requires that Jewish employees be given rest days on Sabbath and the Jewish holidays. Permits to work on these days, in factories and restaurants, must be specially issued by the Minister of Labor. In addition, there are municipal ordinances that determine the extent of observance in the various cities. Most shops are closed throughout the country, and public transportation is generally prohibited, except in Haifa. Notwithstanding the legislation, however, there is a difference between those who observe the holidays religiously (attend synagogues and keep religious injunctions, such as refraining from traveling), those who observe it culturally (in family gatherings, traditional foods, and selective customs, such as lighting candles on Friday evening, eating no bread on Passover, and fasting on Yom Kippur), and those who regard it as just a time for leisure activities. The common contents of the holidays are not clear (Katz et al., 1976: 82-89), and the status of the Sabbath in Israel is a good example (Gurevitch and Schwartz, 1971).

Despite its secular meaning for most people, the Sabbath is evident in Israel, and foreigners cannot fail to notice that it is more than just a day of rest there. Yet the rules pertaining to the observance of the Sabbath have been among the most enduring and sensitive subjects of conflict between religious and secular Jews in Israel. In Bnei Brak and Jerusalem, there have been violent clashes with ultra-orthodox Jews who oppose any transportation on this holy day. Israeli public television began broadcasting on the Sabbath only after the intervention of the Supreme Court in 1969. Prime Minister Rabin resigned in December 1976 after an official state ceremony was held just before the beginning of the Sabbath, thereby causing those who attended to violate the Sabbath by traveling home on the holy day. Political crisis over religious issues have been common in Israel, but this was among the more extreme ones.

The uncertain meaning of the Jewish holidays and the Sabbath in modern Israel testifies most vividly to the somewhat confusing bonds of an ancient people faced with the problem of a new national identity. For some, holy days are holy indeed; for others, they are cherished customs and ceremonies; and for many, they are an ancient framework in need of new content and meaning. The kibbutzim attempted to develop new and nonreligious meaning for the traditional holidays. They rewrote the story of the Passover Hagada, emphasizing the motifs of freedom, spring, and agricultural festivals. Since most of these holidays were related to the agricultural cycle of ancient Jews in the Land of Israel, it was possible to extract from them the parts that signify attachment to the land and to nature. Yet without the prayers, synagogue attendance, and other religious rituals, the essence of these holidays and of the Sabbath, as it has developed in the Diaspora, has been significantly altered. "We do not know how to celebrate our holidays" is a frequent statement made in Israel during festive days or even Independence Day. This uncertainty is part of a broader dilemma: how to create an authentically secular Jewish culture that will be at the same time an organic continuation of the past.

The holidays are problematic for Israeli Jews whose identification with Jewishness and Zionism seems to contradict their secular sentiments. The pendulum has been swinging from an extreme rejection of Judaism as a religion to a rivival of observance and attendance of religious ceremonies.

The issue is far from being resolved. Zionists like Weizmann and Ben-Gurion were against a religious content of Zionism and yet in favor of a generous accommodation with religious Zionists. Socialists such as Ben Zvi and Shazar became identified with the tradition when they served as president. Jabotinsky was against the intrusion of religion into all corners of life, but the Herut movement which is heir to his ideology is willing to go a long way toward accommodating the demands of the religious parties. Orthodox Judaism and its legal system (the Halacha) have not been used *directly* as a main source of Zionist and Israeli identification. There has also been opposition by some secular Israelites to the usage of religious symbols in state affairs. Nevertheless, specific contents, such as the holidays and the Sabbath, and the general meaning of tradition have served as an important common denominator for the Israeli political system.

POLITICAL SIGNIFICANCE

The above illustrations of nonpolitical common contents show that the minimum prerequisite for collective and political activity was met. In the last part of this chapter its contribution to consensus will be presented. This section can be concluded by pointing out the common contents of the Zionist identity and their expression within the Israeli political system:

- The Land of Israel is regarded as the only place where Jewish national independence can take place.
- The Bible is the source of cultural heritage and of national, political symbols.
- The Hebrew language is the medium of the new culture of Israel and the official language of the state. It is emerging also as the lingua franca of all Jews.
- Aliya is regarded as the responsibility of all Jews — either to fulfill personally or to support those who do it. It is also recognized as an obligation of the State of Israel.
- Jewish holidays and the Sabbath bind the Jews culturally and are recognized officially by the State of Israel.

Political Symbols

Nonpolitical values, like those discussed above, are ultimately a matter of belief and sentiment. In this section, I shall expand on the nature of some more clearly political symbols.

Politics is enhanced by a wide range of common beliefs and identifications that are captured in tangible objects and events and are used as symbols. Politics regularly produces symbols for mass consumption — this aspect of politics is evident to anyone watching an official ceremony. "Mass publics respond to currently conspicuous political symbols," wrote Edelman (1964: 172), "not to 'facts' and not to moral codes embedded in the character or soul, but to the gestures and speeches that make up the drama of the state." Symbols are both a cultural input to and an output of the political system.[7]

The revival of Jewish nationalism and the establishment of the state gave birth to a whole cluster of symbols centered on *historical continuity,* a Jewish *national homeland,* strong *attachment to the land,* and ultimately *state sovereignty.* In addition, there was a preoccupation with political ideologies as both fundamental and operative value systems (Seliger, 1976: 175-185). These values, in the sense of belief systems and as symbolic facades, were very significant in Israeli politics.

CONTINUITY

The Israeli novelist, Agnon, in his Nobel Prize acceptance speech in 1966, said that only because of a historical catastrophe — the destruction of the Temple by the Romans — was he born in the Diaspora, yet he always considered himself a man born in Jerusalem.

Israel is the "old-new land" (Herzl) or even the "Third Jewish Commonwealth." The name "Knesset," used for the community of the yishuv and now for the Israeli Parliament, and the number of its members (120), are derived from the historical gathering of the elders during the early Second Temple period. Israeli coins and stamps carry symbols found on ancient coins or other archaeological discoveries. The emblem of the state is a candelabrum (Menorah), an ancient symbol, but the official version is copied from the arch of Titus in Rome on which "captive Judea" is inscribed. The national flag is made of the same colors as the prayer shawl (tallit). The star on the flag — representing the "shield of David" — was found in many archaeological excavations, but it gained its status as a Jewish symbol in the European Diaspora. This became the emblem of the Zionist movement, was used by anti-Semites for purposes of identifying Jews, and became the symbol of new Israel.

Perhaps the best expression of the old-new mixture is the national anthem called Hatikvah (Hope) and composed by Russian Zionist N.H. Imber in 1878:

> As long as deep in the heart
> The soul of a Jew yearns,
> And towards the East
> An eye looks to Zion,
> Our hope is not yet lost,
> The hope of two thousand years,
> To be a free people in our land
> The land of Zion and Jerusalem.

These lines contain most of the political symbols of new Israel: Jewishness and Jewish fate, 2000 years, the Land of Zion, free people, and Jerusalem.

The new national symbols were often mixed with or derived from historical, traditional, and religious motifs. For instance, the words of many new Israeli popular songs are Biblical verses. Another example is the holiday of Shavuot, in which the first fruits of the land were brought to the ancient Temple; today this is transformed into an updated and often secular ceremony in which agricultural produce is donated to the Jewish National Fund. This process of selection from traditional Judaism is illuminating in understanding political symbols. Don-Yehiya (1980: 41-44) shows that socialist Zionism actually borrowed traditional concepts and gave them new meanings: a *mitzvah* (religious commandment) became an ideological imperative; *brit* (covenant) was used to denote the links to the land and nature; and *korban* (sacrificial offering) meant the sacrifices of the pioneers. This last word has been used also to mean "war victim." Symbol displacement from religion to politics is well-known in other systems. Israeli politics was secular, however, and the terms "God" or "miracle" were carefully avoided (Don-Yehiya, 1980: 39).

This mixture of values and symbols reflects the uncertainty about where the old ends and the new begins. There is a strong need to stress continuity, and more recent surveys show that young Israelis regard themselves as a continuation of the Jewish people and not as a new people (Herman, 1973: 169); and that "most Israelis do indeed feel that they are part of the Jewish people" (Levi and Guttman, 1976: 39).

Archaeology as a national hobby — as well as a subject of massive state support — testifies to the desire to demonstrate the ancient Hebrew roots buried in the ground. Israeli political symbols stress both continuity and revival. In 1960, when the letters of Bar Kochba, the leader of the lost Jewish revolt against the Romans (132-135 C.E.), were found in the Judean desert, there was a feeling in Israel that the historical circle had been closed and a bridge thrown across 2000 years.[8]

NATIONALISM

Zionism as a movement was strongly influenced by European nationalism, but idealistic and romantic notions of national revival could not impress Zionism after the pogroms in Russia at the end of the nineteenth century and particularly after the Holocaust. The Jewish expression of nationalism was characterized by a sense of urgency and lack of choice. There were, however, many borrowings from other national movements: Edmondo De Amici's *Heart* (1886) — full of romantic, patriotic notions — was one of the most popular books for children in Israel.[9] Education and socialization of the young were based on both local and foreign material. The influence of Russian literature was predominant, and many classic Russian novels were translated into Hebrew. Other imports were heroic books, songs, dances, and art, which joined the local arts in expressing love for the land and nature and praising the new liberated person working his land. The plow was one of the most popular drawings to appear on the stamps issued by the National Jewish Fund. On Hanukka, Handel's oratory "Judah, the Maccabee" was played, along with Hebrew songs praising the bravery of the new Israeli Maccabees. The mood was heraldic, nationalistic, as well as naive and innocent, as in the popular pioneering song: "We shall build our land, our homeland; It is the command of our blood; it is the command of generations."

The generation of native-born children personified the image of the new free Israeli. Education in schools was openly geared to implant the pioneering ideology, collective values, and service to the nation and country. Art, literature, music, and journalism all reflected the collective mission. Given the dominance of the Zionist-socialist ideology, education and socialization during the yishuv and early state periods resembled those in the Soviet Union in terms of mobilization and collective orientation. Little reflects this spirit better than the popularity of pageants presented in the schools and youth movements, where identification with the new symbols of Israeli nationality were spectacularly proclaimed.

Once the state was established, the means for expressing and presenting national symbols became more available. Efforts were now focused upon *implementation* of symbols through state organs (for example, the offer made to Albert Einstein to become president) and the *distribution* of symbols (such as preparation of special education programs for new immigrants, including an "immigrants' theater"). Yet the tension among the Jewish, Zionist, and Israeli contents grew and was reflected in the political symbols and in the school curricula.[10] The symbols of nationalism, however, were stressed in all: selection of phrases from the Bible, Jewish holidays, harvest festivals, or the Hebrew names of the first Israeli ships.

ATTACHMENT AND PIONEERING

Along with this set of revived old Hebrew and Jewish political symbols, a new set emerged, emphasizing the pioneering ideology: settlement, conquering of the desert, water development, afforestation, as well as simple dress, exploration of the country, outings, and return to nature activities (Eisenstadt et al., 1970: 677). In 1953, an international exhibition and fair was presented in Jerusalem called "The Conquest of the Desert." It attracted a great part of the entire Israeli population, veterans and newcomers alike, and symbolized the attachment being forged between the people and their land.[11]

Political symbols in Israel have been predominantly influenced by the labor movement — its socialist ideology and its political leaders. Names like Borochov, Sirkin, Gordon, Katznelson, and others are associated in Israel with the slogan "return to the land" in its double meaning: national revival as well as farming and manual work. It is impossible to understand early Israeli politics without concepts such as the liberation of the land, settlement, Hebrew (=Jewish) work, and the repetition of lines such as, "Work is our entire life; it will save us from troubles" (from a pioneering song). The entire saga of return to the land cannot be captured in the narrow context of political symbols. Nevertheless, it is instructive to point out that the kibbutz — more than any other style of life in Israel — epitomized the combination of these symbols: It represents a continuity of Jewish attachment to the ancient homeland plus a new vision of simplicity, equality, and pioneering spirit.

As noted, the yishuv was a voluntary political community. Pioneering was a matter left for individual fulfillment and realization (*hagshama*) but implemented by the settlement movements and aided with public funds. Socialism and collectivism were interpreted as part of the Zionist ideology and the goal of building a new society and achieving national independence (J. Shapira, 1977: 23-34). As will be seen in subsequent chapters, the establishment of the state necessitated a reexamination of many values, including pioneering, voluntary action, and Zionist socialism. On a more fundamental plane, the state itself represented a new content and required new symbols of attachment.

SOVEREIGNTY

Jewish sovereignty, embodied in the State of Israel, is the source of the latest set of symbols, some of which have already been mentioned. Sovereignty was a novelty in 1948 and a problematic issue. Elazar (1976b: 218, 220) notes that there is no generic term for politics in classical Hebrew and that until the rise of Zionism the concept of a reified state found no place among those Jews concerned with political matters. In addition, there are some difficult general questions: Is Israel the state of Israeli Jews, or of all the Jewish people? Is Zionism to be content with the boundaries of the state which do not coincide with the Biblical concept of the Land of Israel? In what follows, the focus is on the more tangible symbols of state and sovereignty.

The prestate military organizations (Haganah, Palmach, Etzel), in addition to their practical role in the national struggle, were an outlet for expressing the new identity of a fighting Jew, in contrast with the image of the Diaspora Jew. Thus, while serving the pressing defense needs of his people, the Israeli soldier in the prestate military organization or in the Jewish units of the British Army in World War II also served as a national symbol. After 1948, the Israeli Defence Forces became a source of enormous pride and an object of national identification.

Independence Day in Israel is a complex symbol containing mourning for the fallen, prayers for the future, state ceremonies, and a military parade. For many years Israelis stood for hours in the streets to watch this miracle — Jewish soldiers and tanks — and to see their own relatives march in military uniform. The novelty would have faded were it not for the recurring wars in which this "national symbol" had to prove itself time and again on the battlefield.

The Eichmann trial in Jerusalem (1960) combined all three sets of symbols. It was "Jewish" in the sense that Israel took the responsibility of avenging crimes committed against the Jewish people. It was "pioneering" because bringing Eichmann to trial required a daring and unconventional intelligence operation. It was also "nationally Israeli" because Eichmann was brought to trial before Israeli judges and the whole affair became a symbol of historical justice and a link with Jewish fate and self-assertion (Guri, 1962).

Yad Va'shem, the memorial for those killed in the Holocaust, serves also as a symbol of Israel's present sovereignty and future responsibility toward the Jewish people. In an ill-defined but strongly felt way, Zionism and the State of Israel are regarded as a guarantee that Jews will never again be led to the slaughter.

Everything that exemplified Israeli sovereignty became a source of pride: the picture of the Israeli flag in the United Nations, foreign ambassadors presenting their credentials to the Israeli President, an Israeli sports team in the Olympic Games, or Israeli writer Agnon receiving the Nobel Prize (1966). For many years, public speeches started with, "We have now, for the first time in two thousand years . . ." and the phrase is still a standard joke in Israel.

The political symbols of Israel are closely connected to the concept or even the cult of the state. The emphasis on *mamlachtiut* (statism) was a reaction to the dangers of fragmentation and too much party politicization. It was also an attempt to make the state and the newly acquired sovereignty the main objects of symbolic identity. This term was expanded: "pioneering statism" *(mamlachtiut chalutzit),* which had the advantage of combining two major symbols. The concept itself was attacked by many and is still controversial because of the assumption that the previous voluntary pioneering can be replaced by state activities or direction. Alterman (1972: Vol. 2, 306-307) defended the idea and suggested that the government define pioneering tasks for the entire population and see to it that they are implemented. He thought that the powerful instruments of state would thereby serve their real purpose and that the fading "voluntary spirit" could only be enhanced by such central measures.

A list of positive symbolic terms that have become common currency in Israeli politics include state, peace, defense, IDF, ingathering of the exiles, integration of the exiles, pioneering spirit, conquest of the desert, settlement, and economic development. The negative terms include Diaspora, assimilation, divisionism, careerism, self-indulgence, and nonproductive work.

Some concepts and symbols are problematic, because either they were subjects of ideological differences or their meaning has changed with time. Socialism and its symbolic representation in the red flag and May Day were strongly opposed by the civic camp and certain parts of the religious camp (Birnbaum, 1970: 201-210; Don-Yehiya, 1980: 35). Purely capitalistic symbols such as the stock exchange *(Boursa)* or landlords were opposed by the socialists. Certain religious symbols that could not be interpreted in an ethical sense (such as modes of dress or head covering) were opposed by the secularists. Time has also influenced the viability of symbols. Israel's independence is not as novel and exciting as it was thirty years ago. "Zionism" is sometimes placed in quotation marks to represent the empty phraseology practiced by the older generation. Yet in an interesting symbolic development in recent years, many new movements have advocated a return to Zionism and the removal of the degrading quotation marks.

The review above has pointed to some of the most important meanings associated with political symbols in the Israeli system. There are other widely shared meanings, such as universalism and modernization (Cahana, 1968: 39-56), as well as many other common partial symbols. Societies need sets of integrative symbols in order to function politically. Common contents provide the basis for political communication, and shared symbols are a critical part of that because they imply an element of consensus.

The Boundaries of Consensus

From what has been said about common political contents as a prerequisite for political development, it may seem that social needs cause political communication, interaction, and eventually political development. It is also, however, an iterative process in which social needs and leaders "find each other" and build the political network, its channels, and its steering capacity. The less developed a political system, the more important is the role of the political actors in translating common contents into political action. Lijphart emphasized this crucial and independent role of political elites in developing the political system and especially in securing its stability (1968: 3-44; and 1969).

The success of the political actors who were involved in the development of the Israeli political system is largely due to the fact that there were common contents and symbols. At the same time, the leaders were instrumental in the development and personification of this collective identity. The revolutionary setting of Zionism called for heroes, and they did appear to perform the roles of leadership and symbolism. In a broader sense, however, leaders as "carriers" of common contents are just one aspect of our concern with the political center and its communication role. The center can function as a center because it embodies more of the values and contents than the noncenters. In Israel, as will be discussed in Chapter 4, the translation of common political contents to political activity (and results) was carried out more through an institutional network and less through the personalities of famous leaders.

A political system does not require consensus or even permanent agreement in order to emerge, develop, and survive. It does require, however, a minimum of common political contents in order to be given a fair chance. Out of many sentiments and divergent historical events, a locus of identification called Zionism emerged. Zionism was nurtured by the rich sources of Jewish religion, history, and culture and, in turn, fed the new focus of identity called the State of Israel. Politics could appear and take charge of these social forces only because there was a significant area of common identity. This area contained enough central components (for example, land, Bible, Hebrew, aliya, and holidays) to bridge the gap between the social and political spheres of human activity, individual aspirations and collective efforts, scattered efforts of self-expression, and an integrated political mechanism for binding decision-making. From this base leaders could recognize the ripeness of a social situation and the existence of historical opportunities for collective political action.

A principal characteristic of Israeli politics has been the considerable degree of consensus concerning Zionist ideology (with the exception of the ultra-orthodox Jewish circles, the New Canaanites, and the Arab citizens), and the legitimation of the Jewish state as an instrument for attaining Zionist objectives. This consensus has transcended the boundaries of the state and embraced important sections of Diaspora Jews, at least those with links to Israel. Common contents provided the basis for unity around fundamental objectives. They also contributed to a climate of political tolerance and the practice of attaining collective goals by means of a coalition structure and political compromises. On this fundamental plane, Israeli political culture was not fragmented.

The integrative basis of the Israeli political system proved to be strong enough to produce an independent state under unfavorable international conditions. It was apparently solid enough and had a sufficient capacity for further development to sustain a political system involved in a continuous military struggle and in a task of state building and socioeconomic revolution. The system and its underlying common basis have stood firm thus far against strong internal divisions and disintegrative pressures. Even the politics of protest that spread in Israel in the 1970s — on social issues (the Black Panthers), economic policy (young couples), and general structure and policies (the 1974 protest movements) — was still within the basic consensus (see Etzioni-Halevy and Shapira, 1977: 118-129). Nevertheless, the society is heterogeneous, and the political culture within which the political system has functioned was naturally affected by the cleavages and disagreements over many social, ethnic, economic, and religious issues. In the course of time, new pressures were generated for social and political reforms in many areas. There was an attempt to permit coexistence between the demands of the present and the ideological imperative or, at least, to prevent a head-on collision between them (Bilski et al., 1980: 86-90). The old consensus has been disappearing, and disagreements over fundamental values as well as concrete policies have reached all the way down into common contents.

NOTES

1. For a short summary, see Laqueur (1972: 407-416) and Schnall (1979: 125-138).

2. The relationship between Jewishness and Zionism is carefully analyzed in Liebman and Don-Yehiya (1979). The new Israeli "civil religion" is expressed primarily in the belief in Israel as a Jewish state (p. 10).

3. Sociolinguistics, the study of the relationship between language and social structure and social interaction, is extremely important for the examination of common contents in politics. See the review in Grimshaw (1973) and, on political aspects, Deutsch (1953) and Mueller (1973). Mueller discusses the semantic space within which politics is conducted (pp. 18-29) and the way language and socialization influence the ability of a political system to gain legitimation (p. 11).

4. The definition of the "Hebrews" by the modern Canaanites was based on language. Accordingly, they regarded the Hebrew language as the most important common denominator for all those who would be part of the "Semitic East." Hebrew has also been secularized in Israel, and even religious terms have a different meaning when used in a secular context (Don-Yehiya, 1980: 40-44).

5. The attitude of the State of Israel toward aliya is enunciated in the Law of Return, enacted in 1950, according to which every Jew has the right to come to Israel as an immigrant. An immigrant visa is granted to every Jew who expresses his or her desire to settle in Israel, unless the Ministry of Interior determines that the applicant (1) is engaged in an activity directed against the Jewish people or (2) is likely to endanger public health or the security of the state or (3) is a person with a criminal past, likely to endanger public welfare. The Nationality Law (1952) states that every immigrant under the Law of Return shall become an Israeli citizen.

6. The most moving and influential outcry against selective immigration came from poet and political commentator Nathan Alterman, who, in a series of polemic poems published in the daily *Davar,* called for changing the policy (1972: Vol. 2, 53-67).

7. On the more theoretical aspects of symbolism in politics, see Lasswell (1949, 1958: 31-45), Merriam (1945: 81-93), Lasswell and Kaplan (1950: 103-141), Gallie (1966), and Pool et al. (1970: 1-58).

8. On the symbolic role of archaeology in Israeli culture and politics, especially with regard to the Dead Sea Scrolls and Massada, see Elon (1971: 284-289).

9. Jewish nationalism has often been compared to the Italian *resorgimento.* Moshe Hess's book, *Rome and Jerusalem* (1862) was perhaps the first expression of Zionist aspirations inspired by the Italian national movement. Italy also had a strong influence on Jabotinsky, who once lived there and regarded it as his "spiritual homeland" (Avineri, 1980: 185-187).

10. State symbols became problematic for non-Jewish Israelis because of their strong Jewish content. "Israel," the name of the state, is synonymous with the Jewish people (usually "Children of Israel"), and in many cases "Israelis" and "Jews" are used interchangeably.

11. See Sharett (1978: Vol. 1, 40) for a description of the enthusiasm generated by this event.

4

THE POLITICAL NETWORK

Labor Zionism was creative and pioneering through two power
sources: first, the ideological element; second, a movement — an
organizational structure and a political machinery that knew what it
wanted
(BEN-AHARON, 1977: 54)

Shared common contents is a prerequisite to translating social interactions into political activity, and the instrument for doing this is the political network. In Chapter 1, a political network was presented as an organizing concept for the structure and activities of the polity. The political network is identified by a center (and often secondary centers) and a periphery linked by patterned flows of information. These topics will be examined in this chapter with respect to the Israeli political system both before and after the establishment of the state. In the subsequent three chapters, three specific channels through which information flows in the Israeli political network will be studied.

The network under discussion is mainly that of the Jewish community, but this network also transcends the geographical boundaries of the state to encompass outside Jewish groups. The Arab community in Palestine and, later, Israel poses a special problem for the network, as will be noted.

The Political Center

Shils's concepts of center and periphery focus on the relationship between the center of society and the distribution of deference. There is a generalized "central zone," defined in terms of the values, beliefs, and symbols which govern the society. In addition, "the center is also a phenomenon of the realm of action. It is a structure of activities, of roles and persons, within the network of institutions" (Shils, 1975: 3). What, then is a *political* center? First it is part of this general central zone. It is also more in the realm of action than other components of the center. It is, above all, a communication concept, a theoretical midpoint within the network. The center, according to Shils, is basically a *value system* supported by society and espoused by its ruling authorities. The elites of the economy, religion, the sciences, and other areas require some means for affirming, observing, and operating on these values. The political center provides this means. This center can activate the network and its channels. For this purpose, it is usually armed with legal, coercive, and administrative authority. Construction of the political communication network is aimed at enabling the political center to function — to handle the flow of information.

Generally, a political center could be a major one with many satellites, or it could be a cluster comprising more than one center. The image of the political center as one institution or as a definite location with specific boundaries is highly misleading. It must have at least two channels for the simple reason that even dictatorial control requires some form of feedback. There is no need to attach to the political center, or to any center, the qualities of omniscience, omnipotence, and benevolence (Sturman, 1979: 96). Following Shils, we may say that the center has the same values, beliefs, and symbols as the periphery, only more so.

What was the political center during the formative years of the Jewish community in Palestine? I shall first describe the more concrete process of institution-building and then analyze the emergence of the center.

INSTITUTIONS IN THE YISHUV PERIOD

The success of the pioneers from the second aliya as a nation-building elite can be attributed to their efficient political organization (J. Shapira, 1977: 59). This organization, however, more closely resembled many separate contraptions, rather than one efficient, humming machine.

Groups of immigrants who came to Palestine tried to maintain a separate identity and often also an autonomous communal structure. This variegated background is responsible for the mushrooming of different entities and subsequently for the organizational maze of the Israeli political system. During the yishuv period this maze was made up of many small organizations: the committees for distributing money raised abroad; the workers' associations; the settlements run by Baron Rothschild (from 1883), later the Palestine Jewish Colonization Association (established 1924); and the settlements supported by Baron Hirsch, the Jewish Colonization Association (established 1894), to name a few. The list of organizations operating in Palestine by the 1920s is long and impressive, especially considering that the total Jewish population amounted to only about 84,000 in 1922.[1] Out of this maze — whose parts did *not* disappear and which did *not* become less complex — a national political network emerged in the 1930s that had holding power and institutions capable of reaching into and representing Jewish society. By that time this community already "spoke" national politics and referred to itself as a "state in the making."

In the beginning of the Israeli political system, there were the parties. Most of the approximately 20 parties that existed in Palestine in 1920 had been established abroad, primarily for the purpose of representation in the Zionist Congresses. The differences among them were predominantly ideological and, when transferred to Palestine, could be sorted into three camps: labor, civic and religious, plus some ethnic groups (see Chapter 2, pp. 58-64).

An examination of the politics of the yishuv in the 1920s shows some features which later became a familiar pattern:

- The bulk of political activity was carried out by the parties, which established themselves as the central organizations in the network.

- The network was extended rather quickly through other organizations which had some autonomy in their respective fields but reported politically to the parties.

- As a rule, the network was composed of a hard core of clearly identified members and wider circles of people affiliated at other levels and on different bases. Thus, the Histadrut included nonsocialist workers; the national Jewish institutions in Palestine embraced labor and nonlabor groups; the Zionist organizations included Jews residing outside Palestine; and the Jewish Agency encompassed non-Zionist Jews.

The parties fulfilled a dual role. They were primarily political organizations, but they also operated intensively in social spheres by creating special "nonpolitical" organizations to take charge of these areas. These organizations operated in their respective cultural, professional, and economic fields, but their subordination was clearly to the political parties.

This tendency to establish a centralized network through a process of institution-building and to use it for the accumulation of political power and for central coordination was prevalent in the labor camp and, with important variations, in the religious camp as well. It was much less evident in the civic camp (Etzioni, 1962; Horowitz and Lissak, 1977: 97).

In the 1920s the parties in the yishuv were still relatively weak organizations, and their main contribution to the overall network was in the aggregation of political interests and the legitimation of political activity. Their main functions were to formulate ideology, supply loyal cadres of leaders, and supervise other affiliated organizations. In overall Zionist political activity, the leaders of the yishuv played a rather limited role at that time. Moreover, the Zionist organizations were controlled then by nonsocialist leaders. Although the labor parties were the largest in the yishuv, together they held less than a majority and were forced to work together with nonsocialist parties in the yishuv bodies. Ahdut Ha Avoda, for instance — the dominant labor party of that time — was relatively small, although it controlled the Histadrut, in which a majority of the workers of the country were already organized in 1926 (J. Shapira, 1975: 22).

In 1930 the two major labor parties (Ahdut Ha Avoda and Ha Poel Ha Zair) formed Mapai (later the Israel Labor Party), which became the dominant party in Zionist and Israeli politics for more than four decades. Mapai's immediate task, however, was to become the central political power not only within the Histadrut, but also in the yishuv and the Zionist organizations. In the words of Ben-Gurion, "Zionism will be fulfilled by the formation of a large Jewish working class which will build the economy, maintain the Hebrew culture and become a new nation" (from "Davar," 1930, in Gorni, 1973: 323). From the beginning, Ben-Gurion perceived Mapai and the Histadrut as the vehicles for nation- and state-building, forging the transformation "from class to nation."[2]

The development of affiliated secondary centers enabled the parties to extend their spheres of influence to other areas and to penetrate wider social circles. Each of the major parties made an effort to establish "as comprehensive a range of institutions as it could, a kind of nonterritorial state of its own, but within the framework of the overall Zionist efforts" (Elazar, 1976b: 228). The religious parties were more successful than the civic parties, but their sets of institutions were never as complex, wide-spread, and powerful as those of the labor camp. The organizations of the civic camp, such as the Farmers' Association and the Artisans'

Association, were more professional in nature and less effective as political bodies. By the mid-1930s, the parties — especially Mapai — became the main channels and the chief coordinating devices within the political network (see Chapter 6).

In the 1920s, the Histadrut started to emerge as a major institution within the yishuv political network. As Horowitz and Lissak point out, the Histadrut positioned itself at a critical junction of channels of communication and resource flow, from which it could control the communication between the national center and the important secondary centers and between parties affiliated to the Histadrut and their members (1978: 97).

As we noted in Chapter 2, the Histadrut was established because of ideological and economic reasons, but the political need to invent it was also rooted in the inability of the labor parties to extend their network through the party system. There is evidence for this, for example, in that only a few of the new immigrants to Palestine in 1919-1920 joined Ahdut HaAvoda, despite the fact that most of them were workers (J. Shapira, 1975: 39). The idea for doing "nonpolitical" work through a separate socioeconomic organization probably came from the Bolshevik practice in the Soviet Union. But the refinement that this organization was both a trade union and a "government of the workers" — during the prestate period — was original. Unlike the labor parties, the Histadrut proved capable of reaching a wide circle of new members. Even Communists who were not Zionists and therefore regarded as "traitors" could become members of the Histadrut. The Histadrut was controlled by the three main labor parties which together held a great majority of the seats in its Elected Assembly (see Table 4.1). It was dominated by Mapai because all the executive positions in the Histadrut itself and in the other affiliated organizations were filled in proportion to the votes received by the parties. Table 4.1 presents some basic figures regarding the party structure of the Histadrut.

The Histadrut attracted politicians, especially at the middle level, because of another reason: Party members were paid for their work in the Histadrut, while their activities in the party remained voluntary. Against this background, the merger that created Mapai in 1930 and the emergence of Ben-Gurion as both secretary-general of the Histadrut and leader of the party was important. Slowly, without impairing the strength of the Histadrut and without subordinating it completely, the party reestablished itself (Gorni, 1973).

The Histadrut did not lose its autonomy in matters relating to the working class. It was simply forced to recognize a different kind of division of labor. All the national political work belonged to the party

TABLE 4.1   Election Results to the Histadrut Assembly (%)

	1923	1927	1934	1942	1944	1949	1956	1960	1965	1969	1973	1977
Mapai[a]	71	80	82	69	54	57	58	55	51	62	58	55
Ahdut HaAvoda[b]	—	—	—	—	18	34	15	14				
Hashomer HaZair[c]	3	—	8	19	16		13	17	15			
All other groups[d]	26	20	10	12	12	9	14	14	19	21	19	17
Blue-White List (Herut)[e]	—	—	—	—	—	—	—	—	15	17	23	28
Total %	100	100	100	100	100	100	100	100	100	100	100	100

SOURCES: For prestate period — Horowitz and Lissak (1977: 98); for state period — *The Histadrut Since the Establishment of the State* (1969: 24), and Histadrut Election Results (1977).

[a]The united party (1930) previously comprised Ahdut HaAvoda and Hapoel HaZair.

[b]Separated from Mapai in 1944.

[c]Hashomer HaZair eventually became Mapam.

[d]Nine groups in 1923, three to four in the 1940s and after, with about ten in the 1970s. Rafi received 12% of the votes in 1965 and the DMC, 8% in 1977.

[e]Joined the Histadrut in 1965.

(and later to the party leaders in the national institutions), while the Histadrut operated as an executive arm in social and economic matters. Symbiotic relations between the labor parties and the Histadrut also included exchanges of political and financial support and close coordination.

In the 1930s, the Histadrut became the main secondary center in the yishuv and, in certain areas, was even more powerful than the national institutions (J. Shapira, 1977: 74-89). It became the parent institution for other organizations within the labor camp and, through this, for the system as a whole. The Histadrut was the first to establish a military organization to defend the Jewish community, the Hagana. (In the 1930s the supervision of the Haganah and the responsibility for security policy were transferred to the national institutions.) In the economic field, the Histadrut set up powerful companies, such as Solel Boneh (construction), Shikun Ovdim (housing), and Mekorot (water distribution). During the prestate period, these companies retained an almost monopolistic position in their respective fields. In the social services, the Histadrut's Kupat Holim (Sick Fund) was, for all practical purposes, the national health insurance for almost all the Jewish population.

It should be noted, however, that not all the people in the yishuv, especially those in the cities, were workers and Histadrut members. In addition to the kibbutzim, the nucleus of political power of the Histadrut in the urban areas was its deep penetration into almost every workplace — industrial, service, and professional. The Workers' Committees in every region were tightly organized into numerous local labor councils and some 40 national trade unions. The Histadrut represented real political power because it provided its members with direct access to the center, dominated by the same party. Workers' representatives gained opportunities for political mobility through the same channels. Mapai thus had a clear advantage over the other parties:

> The party's task was facilitated by these direct and familiar channels of communication to the mass of workers via well-known party members and activities in the plants themselves to whom workers were often indebted. This enabled it to dispense with the many officials and organizers needed to transmit the party's message. Such access was particularly valuable at election time, when Mapai members of Workers Committees actively sought support for Mapai, on a direct, informal and personal basis, either at the plant, or by visiting the workers' homes [Medding, 1972: 50].

As long as there was a rather firm consensus around the grand goals of the society and the pioneering goals of the Histadrut, the aggregation of so many different — and often opposing — interests was possible. It took a long time for long-range socioeconomic processes and the first cracks in the consensus to undermine the political strength of this elaborate institutional and economic structure.

THE NATIONAL INSTITUTIONS

During the 1920s and early 1930s, the Jewish community in Palestine can be described as politically cohesive, socially segmented, and institutionally chaotic. From the beginning there were three sets of institutions: those which represented the yishuv; those which represented the worldwide Zionist movement; and the British colonial government. The British authorities were in complete charge of security, police, the courts, transportation, radio broadcasting, and a variety of other services. The Jewish community, however, slowly struggled for and eventually won a high degree of autonomy beyond the "internal affairs" stipulated by the British regulations.

The overall organized community of the yishuv was given a collective, official name, Knesset Israel (the "Israel Assembly"). But even before it was recognized by the Mandate authorities (in 1926) as the official representative of the Jewish religious community in Palestine, the institutions of the yishuv had coordinated their activities sufficiently to have elected (in 1920) a central body of representatives, the *Representatives Assembly*. According to the Mandate Regulations, this was meant to be a religious assembly, but in reality it was more political than religious and included almost all of the factions and groups in the Jewish community of that time. In 1920, the 314 delegates were elected by 20,000 voters, and the 20 different parties ranged from 70 delegates to one (Table 2.5). The very small lists represented commercial associations or religious and ethnic communities. The Assembly had an executive arm — the National Committee (Va'ad Leumi) — of about 36 members and a small committee for day-to-day operations (Va'ad Poel). These institutions became, in fact, the voluntary government of a growing Jewish political community.

Once the yishuv institutions were formally recognized in 1926 as the representative bodies of the Jewish community, they demanded (a) to be the representative of *all* Jews in Palestine; (b) to extend their authority beyond religious, health, and welfare services; and (c) to be intensively involved in all aspects of life and especially to have a right to collect taxes (Horowitz and Lissak, 1977: 55-57). In all three areas the battle was not won easily or completely. There were, first of all, Jewish groups which did not belong to Knesset Israel, and there was a constant threat that others would drop out, an act encouraged by the British authorities. Second, any attempt of the yishuv institutions to extend their sphere of activities — for example, to form a police force or militia for self-defense — was strongly opposed by the British. Third, these institutions lacked the ability to raise money from independent sources and therefore could not become a central factor in the two primary activities of the community: immigration and settlement. At that time, the status and continued existence of the national institutions were conditional on the voluntary support of the Jewish community. They lacked formal authority and were clearly overshadowed by the more powerful Zionist organizations. Nevertheless, despite their weakness, the elected bodies of the yishuv served the purpose of expressing Jewish independence, if only symbolically at first. The Assembly, in its first session in 1920, proclaimed that it "had laid the foundations of the self-government of the Jewish people in Palestine" (Sager, 1971-1972: 40).

The beginning of the yishuv's political center can be placed in the early 1920s, because that is when centralized collective action started to take root. Yet, the real political work was being carried out by the Zionist organizations and their affiliated bodies and funded by money raised in Diaspora Jewish communities. The relationship between the Zionist organizations and the yishuv national institutions reflected a superior-subordinate hierarchy. The Zionist organizations (see Chapter 2) provided the institutional basis of the center. The political network was naturally clustered around these institutions, and the Palestine Office of the Zionist Organization was a link connecting the Palestine-based Zionist institutions and the world Zionist movement.

The Jewish Agency, established in 1929, was recognized by the League of Nations and the British Mandate as an official representative of the Jewish community. From the yishuv point of view, the Jewish Agency was both a means for obtaining external, formal recognition and an institutional device for enlarging the political network. The agency enabled the Zionist Organization to expand and include members who were not Zionists but who were nevertheless devoted to the idea of building a home for the Jews in Palestine. Officially it was empowered to advise the British Mandate authorities on ways and means of advancing the Jewish "national home" in Palestine. As such, it had the broader task of representing both the local interests of Jews living in Palestine and the overall interests of the Jews in the Zionist enterprise. In due course, it took over responsibility for immigration, agricultural settlement, and economic development. Thus, side by side with the Zionist Organization, the Jewish Agency applied itself to the proliferating organizational challenges. The leadership of the Jewish Agency included a few "non-Zionists" but was otherwise almost identical with the leadership of the Zionist Executive.

At that time, the dominant locus of Zionism was worldwide and not local. The organizational setting was mainly Europe and the United States, even though the target was the settlement of Jews in Palestine. Already in the offing, however, was the shift of the center from the worldwide Zionist network to the local yishuv. This was a gradual process. In 1929 and again in 1936-1939, there were major Arab attacks on Jews in Palestine, and thus the most pressing task of the Zionist movement became the preservation of the yishuv. This development also marked the rising importance of yishuv leadership in the Zionist Organization.

In the 1920s, yishuv representation in this body was not significant, despite the fact that from 1921, the vote of the yishuv members to the Zionist Congresses carried double weight compared with the votes of members from outside Palestine. Although the labor parties were the most powerful in the yishuv, they were weak in the Zionist Organization compared to the General Zionist Party. In fact, Ahdut HaAvoda would not join the coalition in the Zionist Executive until 1926, as it was dominated by a nonlabor majority. In 1927, all the labor parties together won only 22 percent of the votes in the Zionist Congress elections.

By 1930, however, Mapai had already become the "morally and ideologically dominant" party in the Zionist Organization (J. Shapira, 1975: 187). In 1933, Mapai, together with the other labor parties, gained 44 percent of the votes and became the dominant member of the coalition in the Zionist Executive. Ben Gurion, who in 1935 was secretary-general of the Histadrut as well as head of Mapai, also became chairman of the Zionist Executive. Thus, the necessary link was established between the dominant party (Mapai), the dominant secondary center (the Histadrut), the yishuv national leadership, and the worldwide Zionist Organization.

Other factors served to consolidate the power of this newly created political bridge. In 1932, the responsibility for educational services in the yishuv was transferred from the Zionist Organization to the National Committee (Va'ad Leumi). This paved the way for a continuous flow of financial support from Zionist funds to the local bodies. Simultaneously, the growing tension between Arabs and Jews in Palestine increased the importance of the defense measures taken by the yishuv. The Histadrut illegal defense body (Haganah) became subordinate to the Jewish Agency in 1930 and part of the central collective network rather than of only one sector. The need to cope with the British anti-immigration policy also contributed to a higher degree of integration in the yishuv.

Simultaneous with these efforts of network consolidation were the workings of powerful disintegrative forces. In 1935, the Revisionist Party left the Zionist Organization and established the New Zionist Organization. In 1937, one group left the military arm (the Haganah). A number of years later, a separate National Military Organization (Etzel) was established, and a great deal of political violence and friction developed between these two organizations. There were also many rough disputes within the organized yishuv and within the labor camp. Nevertheless, there appeared a national center in both the instrumental and the symbolic meaning. The Jewish Agency emerged as the overall "government" of the Zionist movement in Palestine and abroad and became the unrivaled central institution in the network. Together with the Va'ad Leumi, it formed the Provisional Assembly and, eventually, the Provisional Government of the State of Israel.

ESTABLISHMENT OF THE STATE

The major changes that appeared with the establishment of the State of Israel in 1948 were the disappearance of the British authorities; the formal separation of the Jewish population from Arabs in the West Bank and Gaza Strip (until 1967); and the appearance of self-government. The "leading elite" was transformed almost overnight into a "ruling elite" (Eisenstadt, 1976-1977: 1) and brought about a number of changes in the institutional base of the already established network.

The parties remained the most important institution in the political network, but slowly other contenders emerged: the government itself, its bureaucracy, the mass media of communication, and other nonaffiliated institutions. During the yishuv period, there had been no real separation of power within the political system, especially because of the existence of public officials whom J. Shapira calls "bureaucratic politicians" (1975: 205). These were noncharismatic leaders whose power stemmed primarily from their party's control over the network's channels and information flow. Mapai was the prototype of this kind of machinery since it became the major party, holding approximately 30 percent of the votes — more than any other party.

After 1948, Mapai became identified with the State of Israel (Etzioni, 1959; Arian, 1973). As will be seen in Chapter 5, it served as the main channel in the Israeli political system — a focal point for a loose federation of many institutions and organizations, some of them partly independent. It dominated the labor camp, the Histadrut, the Knesset, the cabinet, the Jewish Agency, and the Zionist organizations. Its existence gave some coherence to an othewise complex and fragmented political network.

After 1948, the yishuv pattern of strong, partly autonomous, centrally controlled multiple institutions did not disappear. The Histadrut continued to be a powerful economic, social, cultural, and political organization of workers and wage earners, as well as a major employer through its many enterprises and companies, and hence an anomaly within an otherwise centralized network. But Histadrut activities were coordinated through the labor parties (primarily Mapai), and Histadrut leaders worked closely with their counterparts in the Knesset and the cabinet. The Mapai government did prevent Histadrut involvement in security and foreign affairs, as well as restricting its activities in areas that were "nationalized," such as welfare or housing. Yet the Histadrut remained a powerful institution, providing direct links with certain groups not reached by any other organizational channel. The continuous existence of such a giant institution within the national network shows again the tolerance of Israeli politics for secondary centers whose networks cut across and even duplicate that of the national political center.

Another major change in the network during the state period concerned the Zionist institutions' position within the national center. In the 1930s, the external challenges required centralized leadership, particularly in security and foreign affairs. At that time, the expression "organized yishuv" was used to describe those who belonged to the Jewish political network of the majority, as opposed to the Revisionist Party and the separate military organizations (Etzel and, later, Lechi), whose members were referred to as "dissenters." The Jewish Agency was the core institution of this organized yishuv, and its leaders became the leaders of the state after 1948.

As a provisional government of the Jews, the Jewish Agency completed its task in 1948, and the government of Israel assumed exclusive jurisdiction. But as a link to Diaspora Jews — and as a means of obtaining support from them — it has been retained despite the obvious duplication with government ministries.

The formal division of labor between the Israeli government and the Zionist Organization was resolved in a special Knesset "Law of Status" (1952) and a Covenant (signed in 1954). According to this agreement, the Jewish Agency would continue to serve as the link between Diaspora Jews and Israel and to raise money abroad for Israel. Within Israel, the agency was to be responsible for immigration, housing, welfare, health, higher education, agricultural settlement, and youth villages. In practice, however, these internal matters have been determined by and large by the Israeli government. Periodically, the suggestion arises either to abolish the agency's functions within Israel or, conversely, to expand them. In the late 1960s, the responsibility for absorbing new immigrants was transferred to a newly created government ministry (for more recent developments, see Stock, 1972).

The continuing role of the Jewish Agency is only one example of the phenomenon during the state period of using institutions to enlarge the scope of the network, even if this entailed a certain amount of overlap and increased friction in the decision-making process. Similarly, the Zionist Organization's fund-raising body (Keren HaYesod) and the Jewish National Fund (Keren Kayemet) continued their operation after 1948, but the ownership of state land was transferred from the JNF to the Israel Land Administration.

These institutions offer a broader representation of the Israeli political spectrum than does the cabinet. Distributing power according to the "party key" (see Chapter 2), the Jewish Agency represents almost all of the parties in the Knesset. Thus, a party like Herut, which was not part of a government coalition until 1967, did have a role within the decision-making apparatus of the Jewish Agency. (When the Likud came to power in 1977, the chairmanships of the Jewish Agency's Executive as well as some key departments were turned over to members of the Likud Party.)

The overall network could afford the redundancy of institutions because coordination was achieved through party linkages. Mapai was the dominant party in both the Israeli and Jewish parts of the networks; it could afford duplication because of its penetrative capacity. Some Zionist institutions retained a measure of influence after 1948, but, in effect, they could be regarded as an extension of the Israeli network.

An example of the relative weakness of nonstate institutions is the position of municipal authorities in Israel. During the yishuv period, most Jewish municipalities were small, affiliated with political parties, and entirely dependent upon them. There was, however, some counterbalance. Mapai's control in most institutions was partly checked by the civic camp, which tried to develop alternative centers of power in local governments, especially in the cities. In Tel Aviv, the largest Jewish city in Palestine, the civic camp was dominant in all municipal elections after 1928. The same phenomenon could be observed in some other growing towns, such as Petach Tikva.

After 1948, the central government established a patronizing relationship with the local authorities. The first elections to local authorities in the State of Israel were held in 1950 on the basis of Mandate laws[3] (Weiss, 1973). These were not powerful governments with significant authority of their own, and they were subordinated to six district commissioners appointed by the Minister of Interior. Elections of local authorities are usually conducted at the same time as the national elections. Since the same parties are represented in the elected local councils, national parties also coordinate local decisions and policies. In addition, the economic basis of the local authorities even in the big cities is not sufficient to cover all expenses. Thus they are dominated both politically and economically by the political center.

The political network of the Israeli system is similar to that of other modern countries in the sense that it has government as its central institution and parties as its main political channels. It is unique in terms of the dominant role played by the parties, the existence of secondary centers that to some extent diminish the centrality of the center, and the lack of important voluntary, nonlinked organizations and interest groups. The yishuv phenomenon of an organizational maze that resembles a "big head over a small body" (Horowitz and Lissak, 1977: 145) continued after 1948. But gradual changes started to take place, and they pointed in the direction of erasing some of the unique features: weakening of the parties and their affiliated secondary centers, the emergence of new and more independent political groups, and the appearance of "nonlinkaged" organizations in the network.

CONSOLIDATION OF THE POLITICAL CENTER

The nature of the political center underwent a series of shifts throughout the yishuv and state period. Before modern Zionism, there was no single center for Jews throughout the world. The distribution of

Jewish communities could be compared to a traditional society in which each community was a separate enclave. As Jews, they were without any political center — either symbolic or institutional. There was, of course, the kinship and overall affinity to Judiasm and the symbolic meaning of the Land of Israel as a spiritual homeland, but the center of each community was in the local congregation and its leaders.

Since the beginning of Zionism, the center has changed in both its composition and as a locus of identity. These changes will be traced in this section. The different periods are also distinguishable in terms of location, leaders, and main roles, but these are not within our concern here.

The first period (1882-1918), when Palestine was part of the Ottoman Empire, is characterized by a weak and sometimes nonexistent political center. The modern Zionist immigration to Palestine started fifteen years before the First Zionist Congress, and during this period there were active political groups and the beginning of institutionalization but no real political center. The Zionist movement at that time represented the aspirations of but a few Jewish communities in the Diaspora and groups of pioneers in Palestine. From these clusters, the future leaders and secondary centers emerged later, but neither the Zionist organization nor the infant yishuv had then the ability to control the activities of the different groups. Moreover, Palestine was just one possibility as the location of the future center.

The second period (1920 to mid-1930s) begins with the British Mandate on Palestine and is characterized by the emergence of two overlapping centers. The Zionist organizations became the central political organs of the movement in terms of leadership, control, and resources. Concomitantly, the yishuv started to build an independent political center within the formal authority of the British Mandate. Concerned Jews in the Diaspora could identify with the Zionist center and, through it, with immigration and settlement of Jews in Palestine. Jews in Palestine could identify with their own emerging central zone of institutions, parties, and leaders and, through them, with the Zionist movement as a whole. At that time the secondary centers of the yishuv, clustered around the political parties, were already well crystallized. Thus, despite the existence of national institutions, the yishuv center at that time was only loosely connected to the relevant periphery and disconnected from some important groups. Moreover, while industrious efforts of institution-building took place within the labor camp and — to some extent — the religious camp as well, the joint collective efforts were tentative. The center at that time lacked not only authority but resources of its own. It was almost a center without a network.

In the third period (mid-1930s to 1948), the center shifted to the "state in the making." The yishuv in Palestine as a whole became symbolically the political center of the Zionist movement. The two previous centers became institutionally coordinated, and the Jewish Agency, dominated by yishuv leaders, became the main practical political instrument. Control of both external and internal resources became rather effective and, except for some opposition groups in the Diaspora and dissident groups in the yishuv, the authority of the center, its institutions and leaders, was widely accepted. The secondary centers within the yishuv, particularly organizations affiliated with the labor movement and the Histadrut, enjoyed a high degree of autonomy. These secondary centers were tolerated as long as the supremacy of the center in foreign affairs and security was recognized. The center was satisfied with retaining the role of coordinator of internal affairs, carried out effectively through the parties. The multiple centers were effectively synchronized into the political system through coalitions and the party key method of allocation of resources. This composition of the political center, with Mapai as a dominating channel in the network, lasted almost fifty years. The national and Zionist institutions provided the institutional base, but their functioning in the political network was made possible by the communication services of the parties.

The fourth period began with the establishment of the state in 1948 and ended somewhere in the mid-1960s. The official government of the state embodied institutionally and symbolically the political center, but otherwise the immediate changes were not great. The previous center consolidated its power, and the channels leading to and coming from abroad became almost completely subordinated. The major change occurred in the relations between the center and secondary centers. The latter lost a great deal of their autonomy and independence within the network. Whereas previously they were only coordinated by the center, after 1948 they became subsidiaries or branches of the center with a much tighter control through the parties and the governmental bureaucracy.

The fifth period started in the late 1960s with the beginnings of the disintegration of the political network carefully constructed during the 1930s. This period is outside the scope of this book, but a word about it is in order. The institutional structure has remained more or less intact until the present, but the network is functioning differently and frequently not functioning at all. The center has been forced to cope with difficult control problems: the secondary centers' independence and the parties' inability to execute their coordination functions. Furthermore, identification of the State of Israel as the Jewish center has become more problematic. There appeared, potentially at least, a possibility of the emergence of a parallel Jewish center, or centers, in the Diaspora. After more than fifty years of unchallenged position, the Israeli political center is facing legitimacy challenges from within and without (Galnoor, 1980; Bilski et al., 1980: 323-337).

THE SECONDARY CENTERS

Secondary centers, very much like the center, are not concrete or legal entities. They denote the existence of more than one center in society. For all practical purposes, the communication functions performed by a secondary center are similar to those performed by the center, except that they are usually confined to a more specific area and lack access to coercion, or a monopoly on official resources. Moreover, the same institutions or people can appear in a secondary center and in the center. Thus, the Histadrut was part of the center and, at the same time, was a secondary center of the workers' sector. However, the specific role of the secondary centers in the network is best characterized by their handling of the diagonal information flow — between the center and the various publics, including the peripheral groups (see Figure 1.2).

Israeli society reflects a mosaic of associations, but the division into subcultures is not sharp and multiple memberships are common (Galnoor, 1977: 188-194). Hence it is more accurate to refer to the Israeli political system as segmented rather than as fragmented. Israelis themselves speak of "sectors" — public versus private, workers organized in the Histadrut versus "independents," agriculture versus industry, religious versus nonreligious, Jewish versus Arab — and these are further criss-crossed by overlapping factions, organizations, and groups. These organizations fill the space between the political center and the periphery and combine to form a complex and highly divided network. Without these subunits, it is impossible to comprehend the structure of the political system and its modes of operation. The term "secondary centers" well reflects the federative structure of the Israeli political system. These secondary centers do indeed reduce the centrality of the central government. Under Israeli conditions, however, the secondary centers perform an important role in the network for the political center, or at least for its main institution — the government. For instance, the secondary center of the agricultural sector took care of most of the difficult problems regarding subsidies and land and water allocations without too much direct intervention by the government. They assisted the labor government and, in return, retained a good deal of autonomy in their internal affairs (Galnoor, 1978).

The pluralism of Israeli society finds greater expression in the multidimensionality of secondary centers than in the Knesset or party divisions. There is no yardstick for the description of their functioning or the considerable overlap in their spheres of action, tasks, and staffing. Any attempt to map out the whole system by the political camps, or by any other single measure, is doomed to failure. The cleavage between the Jewish and Arab sectors is the only one that totally separates two subcultures from one another. This is not the case for other dichotomies, such as between the workers' public sector and the private sector, or the other potential cleavages presented in Chapter 2. The division into secondary centers and their affiliated institutions is most complex, as illustrated by Horowitz and Lissak's attempts to distinguish them according to different criteria.[4].

As noted, the partial autonomy of many secondary centers decreased after the establishment of the state. Nevertheless, they continued to exercise a critical role in the political communication network during the period under review. The dynamics of network interaction, including the role of the secondary centers, will be discussed in the last section of this chapter. Here I conclude by pointing out that the secondary centers acted as intermediaries in handling the diagonal information flow. As such they performed the well-known task of "gatekeepers" (Schramm in Smith, 1966: 528; Easton, 1965b: 87-99). In addition, the structured links between the center and the secondary centers in Israel created a special situation — the secondary centers coordinated and screened the flow of information, but they also shared the political power of the center.

Thus, the institutions in the center and the secondary centers played the critical role of translating common contents into political action. But the personification of symbols as well as the actual management of information flow in the network are the tasks of leaders.

THE ACTORS

The political center is a mix of organizations, roles, and individuals. It is also the theoretical midpoint in the communication network from where the political elite operates.[5] The political elite assumes such a position by representing "more" of the political values and symbols than the periphery and by controlling a larger share of the political resources in society.

The study of elite behavior for the purpose of comparing political regimes is very instructive. Lijphart (1969) maintains that societies which are deeply divided into different subcultures can still be politically stable because of the accommodating and mediating roles played by their elites. In such cases, elite behavior is regarded as an independent variable because leaders can overcome centrifugal tendencies by anticipation of crisis and by cooperation and coalitions. More in line with what has been said here about the prerequisite of common contents, other students of elites maintain that certain minimal conditions must exist in order to enable elites to play their accommodation role and to accomplish their stabilizing task (Daalder, 1974; Barry, 1975).

The success of the elite that was instrumental in the development of the Israeli political system could not have been possible without the ideological and sentimental basis provided by the common contents.

During the Ottoman regime and the beginning of the British Mandate, the political elite of the Zionist movement comprised primarily leaders operating outside Palestine. These were the leaders who participated in the Zionist Congresses, manned the Zionist organizations, contributed money, and spread the word throughout the Jewish communities in the Diaspora. Most of them were secular; their fervor was derived from their "Jewishness" — interpreted in nationalistic or kinship terms. There were also religious leaders, men of culture, and prominent figures in their countries, as well as a small group that left the secluded orthodox community in Palestine to take part in the Zionist revolution.

In the mid-1930s, when the political center of the Zionist movement moved to Palestine, the resident yishuv leaders became the most prominent ones, with a few important exceptions. Most of them were ideologues and hard-core pioneers who personally fulfilled the Zionist duty of immigration. In the absence of a more formal political system, they became also the local political elite. Since then, the all-Jewish Zionist institutions and the yishuv institutions operated simultaneously and with a relatively high degree of coordination because of overlapping leadership. As time passed, however, the yishuv itself, or most of it, became identified as the pioneering elite of the national movement of the Jewish people — hence the proposition about the anomaly of the Israeli political system where the "elite arrived before the masses" (Arian, 1973: 140).

The yishuv had the characteristics that are usually listed in the definition of elites: It was small, clannish, intense, highly motivated, and relatively modernized. The yishuv also had a self-image as an elite of the Jewish people and possessed a strong sense of obligation toward the "yet nonpioneering" Jews in the Diaspora. They were busy trying to extend the boundaries of the system to include those Jews who were still outside. They forged and developed the common contents and built the network and its channels.

During the first period the cementing element of Zionism was weak and rather diffuse. There were disputes concerning the country suitable for Jewish national revival; there were different opinions regarding the political versus the spiritual goal of the movement; and there were deep divisions along ideological lines. The emergence of the yishuv leadership as the prime force in the Zionist movement provided a unifying element to the movement's common contents. Not that the previous differences and disputes disappeared, but they had to be accommodated within the increasingly dominant central value system of a "pioneering ideology" (Eisenstadt, et al., 1970: 673). The binding consensus of the center was based on collective goals such as settlement of the land, national revival, and the effort to build a Jewish state; as well as a personal obligation to devote oneself to these goals. Beyond that, there were many different versions of Zionism. With the establishment of the state, a more "normal" elite/nonelite relationship characterized the Jewish community, and a more conventional center/periphery distribution within the political system. The numbers in 1948 were still small, but more than half a million people cannot all be elite.

The profile of the typical Israeli political leader in the early state period was one of a veteran of the Second or Third Aliya, born in a Western country (probably in Eastern Europe), with some background in manual labor (if he belonged to the labor camp), and with a lot of experience in political work in his party, the national institutions, or one of the organizations affiliated with the secondary centers.[6] Ben-Gurion, the first Prime Minister of Israel, fulfilled this profile of the typical yishuv leader. Weizman, the first President of Israel, was also born in Eastern Europe and gained political experience in England. But he did not have a pioneering background, and was identified with the Zionist rather than with the yishuv leadership. In the state period, too, the scope of activities and the political style of the Israeli political elite were to a large extent determined by their previous yishuv background:

- The political elite was made up of people whose sole or main function was politics. They were not part, or an extension of the economic or cultural elites.

- Their career pattern was predominantly political — that is, they slowly climbed the ladder of the political hierarchy.

- There were more professional politicians in the labor and religious camps than in the civic camp. Consequently, the total number of politicians with nonpolitical professions was relatively small and the number of kibbutz members was relatively high in the political elite.

- They relied more on institutional processes than on charismatic leadership. The distance between the elite and the nonelite was too small and the weight of ideology too great to create the conditions for leaders with charismatic authority.

The first generation of leaders proved capable of manning the center without developing a personality cult. One of the reasons for this, mentioned above, is the institutional structure of the center, which had to share power with secondary centers. Thus, the skill of most political leaders was expressed in interaction, coordination, and control — that is, in political communication. In the labor movement, a few top leaders, such as Ben-Gurion and Sharett, became gradually less involved in internal politics and more concerned with external and security affairs. Others, such as Katznelson and Shazar, became more engaged in ideological and educational activities. The great majority of the leaders in all parties, however, were preoccupied with internal political communication. Leaders such as Eshkol, Meir, and Sapir had an intimate knowledge of the network and of its channels and were particularly skillful in using them. The same could be said for leaders in other parties who became members of the Knesset, ministers, or officials in the Jewish Agency, the Histadrut, the state bureaucracy, and public corporations.

The next generation of leaders, many of whom were born in Israel, presents a different picture in terms of origin, political socialization, institutional loyalties, and modes of operation. They grew up in a political system which was still predominantly institutional but became less ideological and more technocratic. As politicians, they were members of the most powerful elite in the country (Gurevitch and Winograd, 1977). As occupants of the political center, however, they witnessed a process by which the center was becoming accessible to penetration by other elites (that is, nonprofessional politicians) as well as a target for participation of the periphery.

The Periphery

"As we move from the center of society, the center in which authority is possessed, to the hinterland or the periphery, over which authority is exercised, attachment to the central value system becomes attenuated" (Shils, 1975: 10). The periphery of a political system comprises those whose share in controlling the political resources is proportionately less than those who are in the center or the secondary centers. The periphery is that part of society that has been incorporated into the political system but is only partially politicized.

The border between society and the polity — between people's general human behavior and their political behavior — is the imaginary line dividing, for instance, family life from voting behavior. The political center has an interest in invading the nonpolitical domain. One reason for this is to secure acceptance of and compliance with the existing political order. It could be said that the center, particularly in a modern democracy, aspires to the full politicization of society and the transformation of social interactions into a political order of communication. Hence, the discussion in this section will concentrate on the general issues of political penetration and maintenance, as viewed from the center.

A process becomes "political" when its collective aspect is not handled and regulated by other social entities such as the family, community, religious institutions, or economic organizations. "Politicization" therefore means that a certain matter has been included within the political system and is subject to the rules underlying this particular mode of interaction in a certain society.

There was a good deal of politicization in the yishuv and subsequently in Israeli society. The yishuv was characterized by a high degree of interest in politics and an attentive public. Political discourse was carried out at every level of society, in heated ideological battles and intensive nitpicking of political nuances. When the state was established, many spheres were entrusted to the political system which, in other societies, are handled by nonpolitical bodies or through nonpolitical processes.

Because of the extensive role of the parties in Israel's political system, there has been considerable overlap between politicization and party politicization. Consequently, a rather wide range of issues have been a bone of contention among the principal protagonists in the political system — the parties. With independence, however, the trend has been toward a decrease in party politicization and an increase in what is termed in Israel "statism" *(mamlachtiut)*. This is a natural process, stemming from the creation of a national government and the emergence of bureaucratic, military, and professional elites.

THE PENETRATION CHALLENGE

The implementation of developmental policy requires rulers to reach into the daily lives of the ruled, and this is even more crucial in a novice political system (Pye, 1966: 63). From the center's point of view, developing appropriate means for reaching the people is essential for the

mobilization of money, manpower, and general support. It is also required because in many instances, national development means changing people's ways of life. Penetration is aimed at enhancing political
integration — mobilizing social forces to achieve collective (political)
goals. And of course, the ruling elite cannot remain isolated. It must
penetrate society in order to control it and prevent others from gaining
too much power.

When the center cannot speak for the whole country, the chances of
disturbance are high and those of economic and social development
much lower. Such a system is politically underdeveloped or — in our
terminology — it has no effective steering capacity. These aspects have
been analyzed in many studies of political development (for example,
Binder et al., 1971). It is less common to analyze them in communications terms, and, again, a debt must be acknowledged to Lerner (1958),
Pye (1963, 1966) and Fagen (1966), who were among the first students of
development to differentiate systems in terms of communication. In
more general terms, Dorsey suggested that "political analysis of development should be addressed to the structures and processes whereby
communication facilitates the integration of the whole system and its
adaptation through the use of political power" (in LaPalombara, 1963:
322).

As has been shown, the political system of the Jewish community in
Palestine was different compared to other new or modernizing systems.
The yishuv, it has been noted, could be regarded as the political center of
the Zionist movement, trying to penetrate the noninterested and geographically scattered Jews all around the world. The periphery within
the small Jewish community in Palestine was indeed marginal, due to the
binding of common political contents, the wide sharing of power, and
high participation. The problem of penetration during the yishuv period
was mainly one of accommodating the divergent groups and of absorbing through the existing channels the influx of new immigrants. Other
problems, such as political socialization of young people or securing the
cooperation of separatist groups, were relatively less demanding. In this
respect, the yishuv period was characterized more by internal conflicts
over ways and means rather than by center-periphery tension. Therefore, the discussion of target groups and penetration channels will be
focused on the state period, when the problems of the Israeli center
resemble those in other political systems. These problems can be summarized in the following way:

- The center must first *penetrate* the more problematic domains within the
  social periphery. These become target groups for various reasons. In one
  system, the problem may be the geographical separation of regions; in

another, national, ethnic, or linguistic cleavages; in still others, the fact that many new members join the system in a relatively short period.

- A second task is to *preserve* the fruits of political penetration. Reaching into society is not a once and for all operation: It requires continuous efforts of *maintenance*. Loyalty of the periphery and its identification with the center must be retained and nourished.

- Penetration and maintenance are not goals in themselves. They are aimed at enabling the center to develop and activate its steering capacity. Note also that these problems are addressed here within a context in which there is already a minimum basis of common political contents and a center with a rudimentary network.

Presented below are seven target groups which the Israeli political center has had to penetrate in the period until the mid-1960s. These groups are not mutually exclusive: they are divided according to different criteria. The groups are not all equal in size or in importance, nor are the problems they pose for the center similar. The list does, however, represent the most relevant part of the periphery without which the center of the Israeli political system could not function and achieve its goals.

(1) Israeli Arabs. The Arab community in Israel is nationally, geographically, socially, and culturally separated from the Jewish community (see Chapter 2). The two are economically integrated to only a small extent. The penetration efforts of the center in this case were almost purely political, including the use of coercive means in selective cases. The purpose was to obtain their acquiescence to the state and its political system, irrespective of their identification with or alienation from an essentially Jewish state.[7] The non-Jewish population of Israel amounted to about 14 percent in 1949, 11 percent in 1965, and 16 percent in the late 1970s (including the Arabs in East Jerusalem). The predominant channels of penetration have been the bureaucracy (through the military government), the parties (mainly Mapai, Mapam, and the Communist Party), and, to a lesser extent, communications media such as Arabic newspapers (published by the parties) and radio programs.

In the case of the Israeli Arabs, the purpose was not to mobilize in terms of civic participation, yet also not to allow them to remain complete outsiders. Formally, Israeli Arabs are citizens and full members of the political system, but they posed a special penetration problem because of the hostility between Israel and neighboring Arab states. As will be seen, they have been penetrated by the political center, and rather successfully so, but the rise of Palestinian nationalism after the 1967 war posed new problems for both sides.

(2) Diaspora Jews. The world Jewish community is outside the Israeli system, but it cannot be regarded as totally external to its penetration efforts. The main purpose of the Israeli penetration activity toward this target group was to convince its members to immigrate and become part of Israeli society and polity. This goal has been augmented by others; for example obtaining financial, political, and emotional support for Israel, as well as its recognition as the "center of world Jewry." The initial purpose of increasing the percentage of Jews in Israel was partly accomplished. In 1948, only 6 percent of world Jewry resided in Israel; in 1965, 17 percent; and in the late 1970s, 21 percent. Yet it has become evident that only a minority of world Jewry will reside in Israel in the near future.

The most direct and personal form of participation for individual Jews abroad is financial contributions to Israel and involvement with the fund-raising campaign. This activity is widely supported and integrated into the social fabric of many Jewish communities to the point that it is sometimes regarded as "voluntary taxation." The exact number of Diaspora Jews involved in Israeli affairs is not available, and there are great variations from country to country, community to community, and year to year. The proportions were much higher during priods of war in Israel (Sheffer and Manor, 1980). If intangible indicators are used, such as "identification" or the existence of local Jewish education, the percentage will be still higher.

Significantly, the same penetration channels that were used for target groups within Israel have been utilized to penetrate this target group as well — namely, the parties' extensions abroad, the bureaucracies of the Zionist Organization and the Jewish Agency, as well as some more specialized channels for fund raising, education, and information distribution. The relationships are often reciprocal: Jewish leaders abroad use these channels in order to penetrate their local communities. Jewish organizations abroad that are related to Israel and Zionism are "mobilizing agencies" (Sheffer, 1980: 11): Some mobilize support for Israel, fewer are involved in fostering emigration to Israel among Jews. But by far the greatest part of their Israel-related activity abroad is aimed at consolidating local Jewish communities and meeting their social and cultural needs (Elazar, 1976a).

The two target groups described above present an unusual problem, in that the political system is compelled to reach across its national identity (to Israeli Arabs) and its sovereign borders (to Diaspora Jews). The internal penetration problems are more similar to those in other countries.

(3) Ultra-Orthodox Jews. Ultra-orthodox Jews (as defined in Chapter 2) number about four to five percent of the total Jewish population

and, like Israeli Arabs, are also isolated from Israeli society socially, culturally, geographically, (residentially) and even, to a large extent, politically and economically. Penetration by the center, in this case, has been aimed at incorporating the ultra-orthodox into the political system and especially at inducing them to recognize the state's legitimacy despite its secular laws and norms. The center would have them recognize and take part in state institutions, such as the secular law courts and the IDF.

Unlike "observant" Jews, however, who are completely within the system, the involvement of the ultra-orthodox must be explained in terms of expediency and not legitimation or support. The cooperation of this group is based on its members' evaluation of its usefulness to them. Thus, in contrast to other target groups, the ultra-orthodox could not be reached by the political center through conventional channels of penetration. Their ranks have not been infiltrated by a Zionist political party, the bureaucracy, military conscription, and certainly not by the mass media. They have developed and used channels of their own: political organizations (the two Aguda parties) and newspapers. They chose to take part in the elections and participated occasionally in the coalition cabinet, but they did not accept the legitimacy of the secular political institutions. Their participation has always been contingent upon the center's willingness to reciprocate with religious and economic concessions. In this respect, the problem this group posed for the political center has changed little since 1948.

(4) New Immigrants. Throughout its development, the Israeli political system has had to absorb masses of new immigrants — a million and a half of them since 1948. In that year, there were two immigrants for every native-born Israeli; in 1964, the ratio was one and a half to one; and only around 1975 did it become one to one (Statistical Abstract of Israel, 1975: 42; 1978: 57).

The official policy of free immigration for as many Jews as choose to come resulted in a great strain on the political system. During the years of heaviest immigration, families were settled in transit camps and later in temporary camps (Ma'abara) — formally full-fledged citizens and actually in need of public welfare and guidance. Unlike the target groups reviewed so far, the purpose here was a speedy and smooth process of political socialization — for ideological reasons, but also to sustain the political system controlled by the veterans.

Have these new immigrants become full members of the political system? Seen retrospectively, the answer is affirmative: The great majority has remained in Israel, joined the existing political institutions, and taken part in political activities such as elections (Eisenstadt, 1954; Shuval, 1963). As long as "new immigrants" are taken as one group and not broken down into ethnic components, penetration and maintenance through political socialization can be regarded as successful. There has not been a viable new immigrants' party in Israel, and the existing political network has proved capable of absorbing great numbers of newcomers without change. New immigrants were forced to adapt themselves to this network, not vice versa. The answer to the question of whether they were fully integrated into the political system is more complicated and will have to wait for the discussion in the next chapters. The channels used — a combination of Jewish Agency officials, government bureaucrats, and Histadrut functionaries, all coordinated by the political parties — worked very well as far as the downward vertical flow of information is concerned. It took many years for these immigrants, and primarily for their native-born offspring, to start using these and other newly created channels for sending their own political messages to the center.

(5) Oriental Jews. Within the group of new immigrants, those who came from Asia and Africa presented the most serious challenge for the political center. The purpose was to integrate them fully into a political culture that had been predominantly Western and based on the heritage of the Jewish communities in Eastern Europe, and to secure their support and participation in a political system controlled by veteran non-Oriental Jews.

From the center's point of view, these traditional communities posed not only a challenge of integration (see Chapter 2) but also one of political socialization. Should they be instructed on the differences between, say, politics and religion? between citizens' rights and party obligation? Such political education would have stressed the fact that not everything is "government"; that there is a distinction between the officials who tried to teach them a new vocation or a new language and those who instructed them how — and for whom — to vote.

In retrospect, it can be said that political socialization of these groups in the early years was characterized by a clear-cut quid pro quo relationship: compliance with the imposed officialdom of partisan functionaries and bureaucrats in return for work, education, health services, and favors. Naked pressure was rarely used, because — not knowing otherwise — many new immigrants from Oriental countries believed party membership was a precondition to these and other services. Furthermore, they were in no position to reject penetration efforts. The major upheaval in their lives had already occurred once they came to Israel. The other changes were just a matter of direction and content, not of occurrence (Eisenstadt, 1967: 182-185; Smooha, 1978: 86-98). In this respect, one of the most interesting aspects of Israeli political development concerns the political reeducation of these groups and their autonomous utilization — a recent development — of political channels and political opportunities. I will return to this subject in Chapters 9 and 10.

(6) *Young People.* From the center's point of view, the purpose was to develop special channels for reaching young people and for political socialization of the next generation. During the yishuv period, the youth movements were the most important mechanism for this task, particularly for implanting the pioneering ideology and for mobilizing young people for the collective goals, such as defense and settlement (Eisenstadt, 1967: 237-244). The many different youth movements were linked to the secondary centers and the parties. Taken together, their most important political impact was the successful integration of young people into the political culture of the yishuv (Shapira and Etzioni-Halevy, 1973). Conversely, the culture developed in these movements (dress, songs, and collective symbols) had a significant influence on the yishuv as well as on the initiation of young immigrants.

The penetration challenge started after 1948, when it seemed — at least for a while — that the most exciting collective goals had already been achieved. The change was manifested in the decline of the youth movements. The percentage of young people (ages 10-19) so organized was 47 percent in 1947-1948; it declined to 28 percent in 1949-1950 in the wake of the mass immigration; and reached 37 percent in 1963-1964 (Eisenstadt, 1967: 256). Concomitantly, the role of the youth movements in ideological and pioneering commitments and in political socialization also sloped downward. A tension developed between the political leaders preaching the pioneering ideology and the young, who seemed not to listen anymore. In the 1950s, there were already frequent complaints about the "espresso generation" — youth who had grown soft and lacked the pioneering spirit.[8] There was, of course, a grain of truth in these complaints, only that they were equally correct regarding all ages. Society offered young people more and more in terms of education and occupational opportunities as well as material well-being, while their numerical significance in the population was increasing and amounted to 45 percent in 1965 (Statistical Abstract of Israel, 1978: 55).

The question whether young people were successfully socialized politically in the early years of the state deserves a more elaborate answer and will be treated in the next section. They went to elementary schools run by the state, and many still belonged to youth movements and read party-affiliated children's magazines, which taught them to idealize pioneering and to implement it personally. Most, however, remained in the cities and chose an individualistic career. Nevertheless, in the period under review, they were not alienated from the adult political culture of the country and were willing, for example, to serve in the military for long periods.

The generation of young people in the state era can be characterized as being both compliant and almost apolitical. Those who grew up in the State of Israel, particularly children of Oriental Jewish families, were apathetic to and/or cynical about the ideological fervor and slogans of the political leaders. They did not become party members and were not interested in changing the political system. The emerging generational tension, particularly in Oriental Jewish families, was clearly nonideological. Until the late 1960s, there were no significant new and independent political movements in Israel — of either young or older people. As far as politics was concerned, there was a high degree of agreement between the generations in Israel. The indifference of young people to politics coupled with their general support of the system seemed to be convenient to all.

In sum, in the yishuv period the same party channels that reached other segments of society also performed the functions of socialization and mobilization of the young, predominantly through the youth movements. In the state period, Israeli youth, much like young people in other Western countries, became increasingly socialized by family and schools. In terms of penetration, the results were mixed: Until the late 1960s, general political support was forthcoming, but involvement — not to speak of participation and impact of a youth culture — was negligible. The 1967 and 1973 wars and their aftermaths changed that, too. Since then, young people in Israel started to pose difficult penetration challenges for the political system.

(7) "Nonpolitical" People. In Israel, no one can "ignore" politics. Politics is essential for collective survival; it is present in most spheres of daily life; and it is manifested in the intensity of governmental intervention in the economy. Yet the degree of involvement of Israelis in political life, and especially in party politics, has decreased considerably since the establishment of the state.

This trend is similar to the one described above regarding young people. A significant part of the Israeli population became increasingly oriented toward personal achievement and disengaged from politics. This process is not unrelated to the appearance of "mass" (social and political) characteristics in Israeli society (Shils, 1975: 91-107). More specific has been the impact of changes in occupation. In 1949, 49 percent of the population was employed in commerce, finance, transport, and public and private services. This number of "white-collar workers" increased to 57 percent in 1968 and 61 percent in 1978 (see Table 2.2, p. 46). Such an occupational structure is very much at odds with the stress of the pioneering ideology on collective goals, manual labor, and personal sacrifice.

The penetration challenge for the center with respect to the "non-political" periphery was to make sure that the political system continues to obtain its support and cooperation, however tacitly. The degree of indifference and disengagement tolerated by the Israeli political center cannot be very high because the population is requested to comply with severe collective demands such as high taxation, lengthy military service, and high state intervention in social and economic life. The chief channels of penetration and maintenance during the yishuv period were the political parties. These were supplemented after 1948 by the public bureaucracy, the mass media of communication, and other special channels. As with other spheres, great changes occurred also within the nonpolitical groups in recent years and especially after the erosion in their confidence following the 1973 war (Galnoor, 1980: 126).

The target groups described above, different as they are from each other, have remained a constant challenge throughout the period under review. For instance, the issue of political integration of Oriental Jewish immigrants, particularly the second generation, continues to pose a critical problem for the Israeli political system. The content of the information transmitted in the penetration efforts toward each group is also entirely different. Nevertheless, as will be shown in Chapters 5, 6, and 7, similar channels and communication techniques were used in all cases.

Penetration challenges are fluid, dynamic: Young people grow up; newcomers become old-timers; and Oriental Jews may cease to be a problem for the center when they move to the plush suburbs or become leaders in one of the political parties. The definition of a "penetration problem" is not only in flux, but it is also seen entirely from the point of view of the center. The ultra-orthodox Jews in Israel do not regard themselves as a problem, nor do they feel alienated from the Israeli political system. They do not recognize Israel or any other country as their state — they simply do not need one. On the other hand, there are groups which the center did leave alone for a long time, such as nomadic Bedouin tribes in the south. Finally, there are groups which the center does not have to penetrate anymore, but it must "maintain" and keep interacting with them. Once the willingness of a certain target group to cooperate politically was secured, the problem was to maintain loyalty. New immigrants and young people who were discussed above as target groups will be used in the next section to illustrate the center's maintenance efforts.

The periphery of the political system is divided into two constantly changing spheres: one poses a penetration challenge, the other requires a maintenance effort. Numerically this second sphere has always been larger in Israeli politics. More important, it was much more significant in terms of the process of resource allocation. Saying that the Israeli political system has usually been preoccupied with maintenance is just another way of explaining its relative stability. It helps also to explain why the same channels, but not the same information, could be used for both penetration and maintenance.

MAINTENANCE

In his description of how Mapai's machinery was developed, J. Shapira refers to the party branches as the "seeing eye and the listening ear." Their task was to transfer information to the center and maintain control over local affairs (1975: 151). This testimony refers to the next logical step of political development through channels of communication: Once a political system has penetrated a new social territory, it will do everything within its power to secure this achievement. "Maintenance" can be separated from "penetration" only in terms of information flow and purpose. In the penetration process, the information is primarily instrumental and unidirectional. The message to the outsider is: "Become a member and we will take care of your housing problems," or "Volunteer for party/state-organized activity and you will be considered for a public position"; or "Vote for us and your particular interests shall be duly represented." In maintenance, the channel may continue to carry this type of information, but in addition there is information whose content is more affectional and its direction circular. Of course, the system-maintenance function is based on the experience accumulated in smaller organizations according to which control of information implies the ability to assert authority (Barnard, 1938: 175-181). But the point made in Chapter 3 should be stressed again: Maintenance includes also the preservation and cultivation of the common contents — the general items of collective identity as well as the particular symbols of the polity.

The most obvious example of maintenance is the political center's efforts at political socialization. One illustration of such a "maintenance target" will be presented: newcomers to the Israeli polity.

Political socialization refers to the way a society transmits its political culture to newcomers: the new generation and new immigrants (Sears in Greenstein and Polsby, 1975: Vol. 2, 93-96). A balanced presentation of this topic would require discussion of both the content transmitted and the socializing agencies. As for content, it should be noted briefly that the common contents contributed to the success in transmitting political culture to both young people and to new immigrants (Shapira et al., 1979; Smooha, 1978: 76-77; Etzioni-Halevy and Shapira, 1977: 88-92). The above statement applies to Israeli society most vividly during the prestate period. In the yishuv, political socialization was intense and usually carried out by the political camps and their extensions. The lines of communication were simple, relatively short, and effective in terms of "noise" and other disruption. The solid basis of common contents and the easy face-to-face encounters made the usage of mediators less crucial.

The establishment of the state, the increased heterogeneity of the society, and later the rapid role of modernization have all extended the length of the previous channels. This pattern of development was observed in other countries and recorded by Lerner (1958) and Pye (1963). Mass media communication in Israel therefore became more conventional — less involved with interpersonal channels and more mediated. From the point of view of the center, such channels could now perform maintenance services better than penetration services.

For the young, the role of the family was relatively less prominent during the yishuv period, compared to that of the community and its socializing agencies. One does not need the extreme example of the kibbutz family to point out that communal influences and the socializing impact of peers were more significant during that period (Bar-Yoseph, 1959b; Talmon, 1965; Fein, 1967: 111-120). The closer one moves to the kibbutz, the pioneers, and the agricultural and collective orientation, the more intensive was this peer impact. In urban areas, on the other hand, the nuclear family was more influential, particularly among the orthodox. By and large, however, the political socialization of young people in the prestate period was carried out by agencies that belonged to or were affiliated with the political camps, especially the labor and religious ones. These agencies were the youth movements, the schools, and the paramilitary organizations.

As for newcomers to Palestine, most came with an established affiliation with a youth movement or a party in their country of origin. They had been considerably socialized before they ever arrived. In addition to the ideological motivation, it was expedient — if not downright necessary — to belong to a party. The yishuv national institutions allocated immigration certificates, settlement rights, and jobs in public organizations according to the "party key." Thus, from the moment an individual began to make concrete plans to immigrate, he or she found it necessary to be identified with a particular party. Most continued this affiliation for the rest of their lives (Horowitz and Lissak, 1977: 91).

In the 1950s, the picture described above started to change. The most impressive achievement of the existing structure was its ability to absorb and politically socialize — at least in the short run — almost one million new immigrants. This phenomenon is well-documented in the Israeli literature about immigration and can be summarized by stating that newcomers very quickly found a political nest in the form of the party-dominated agencies that were responsible for housing, employment, health, education, and cultural activities.

In the 1960s, the social forces that were released with the establishment of the state, mass immigration, and modernization started also to transform the process of political socialization. In terms of maintenance, the essence of this transformation can be traced in three areas: the increasing presence of the state; the decreasing role of the camps, the parties, and other nonstate agencies; and the more problematic role of the family.

State-Encouraged Pioneering. The establishment of Israel marked the opening of a political conflict and an ongoing ideological debate concerning the division of social tasks between state and nonstate organs. "Statism" was the answer advanced by Ben-Gurion and many of his followers to the problem of fading voluntarism, on the one hand, and too much partisan politicization, on the other. Transferring functions to the state also meant replacement of the previous party agencies as ideological and political socializers. Ben-Gurion believed "state-sponsored pioneering" could assist the parties and youth movements in promoting manual labor, agricultural settlements, absorption of immigrants, military careers, and other collective tasks. In addition, there were "new" subjects such as democracy, elections, taxation, and licensing to be implanted through the law and state organs, rather than through voluntary arrangements. Certain areas, such as education, employment, welfare, and radio broadcasting, were nationalized, while settlement, health, farming, and water allocation remained in the hands of nonstate agencies and parties. This list indicates the mixed nature of statism. In a highly politicized system, functions such as defense, foreign affairs, or the civil service had to be taken out of party politics. The same goes for the application of more universal criteria for national services such as welfare. Yet the notion that state organs can be government and also play the more intimate role of socialization (for example, encouraging pioneering) proved to be an illusion. The state could not repeat the socializing achievements of the yishuv voluntary agencies. It could only partially supplement and encourage those collective-pioneering orientations that other socializing agencies failed to achieve. On the other hand, state organizations such as the military or even the bureaucracy proved to be extremely effective in certain areas of socialization.

Military service in the IDF has been rather successful in socialization, not necessarily political. Most young Israelis regard their long and compulsory military service (two and a half years for men and two for women) as a justified necessity. There have been enough volunteers to special combat units, and — most important for this discussion — those who come out of military service are better prepared to participate in Israeli society and politics.

> Because Israel has universal military training for both men and women, the army is the most direct means of reaching all young adults. And because it has vast resources, the army has been able to extend its socializing work beyond its own ranks to concentrations of new immigrants in the civilian population . . . From teaching elementary health care and diet habits, language and civics to its own recruits, and on to sponsorship of language classes for the general population and joint service in the army and on border kibbutzim, the military has both intensively and comprehensively affected socialization [Fein, 1967: 133].

State agencies have been successful in transmitting loyalty to the state and acceptance of the democratic rules of the game. They have not, however, maintained the ideological fervor of the yishuv era. Thus, despite the official policy, state-encouraged socialization toward the collective pioneering values has not been a great success.

Nonstate Agencies. The decreasing role of the parties and other nonstate agencies was inevitable. The establishment of the state made necessary an adaptation and redefinition of their roles and scope of activities. In the early 1950s, the parties continued their socializing functions of new immigrants; in retrospect, that was both a stabilizing factor for the whole political system and a barrier to the full transformation of the parties to statehood conditions.

Socialization was not necessarily carried out by the parties directly. The space between the state authorities and the public was densely occupied by numerous bodies closely affiliated with the parties yet also partly autonomous. For example, cooperative settlements (moshavim) were more desirable by new immigrants than the collective settlements (kibbutzim). Accordingly, more than 200 moshavim were built after 1948. Their settlers, mostly Jews newly arrived from Africa and Asia, were serviced closely by the moshav movement, the Histadrut, and the Sickness Fund — all affiliated with the labor parties. Similarly, new immigrants in the new development towns and cities were organized through their workplaces and their party-affiliated immigrant associations and sports clubs. If they were self-employed, they usually became members of the Farmers', Traders', or Craftsmen's Associations affiliated with the civic parties. Although such services as housing, welfare, agriculture extension, or the building of new synagogues were rendered by the ministries' officials in the field, the services provided were identified according to the officials' party affiliations. The yishuv parties have continued to function to the present day. Over the years, however, their status has changed, and the affiliated bodies now resemble interest and professional groups in other countries. They have increased their preoccupation with maintaining their members' interests and reduced their activity on behalf of the maintenance function of the overall political system, or even their parent political camp.

The Family. The decline in the role of nonstate and voluntary bodies has exposed the family to the problems of socialization (Bar-Yosef, 1966). In traditional Jewish homes — particularly among Oriental Jews, where the family was previously predominant — the problems of being first- or second-generation immigrants were intensified by the process of modernization. The parents in such a family were typically immigrant, authoritative, conservative, and usually religious; they were not familiar with democracy, the banking system, or Hebrew. The son or daughter born in Israel was socialized in kindergartens, schools, streets, and workplaces to be secular, competitive, and familiar with a permissive society. In nontraditional families — mainly Western, veteran, secular, and modernized — a different process can be observed. The role of the close-knit and voluntary community and its socializing agencies was eroded, and this increased the pressure on the family (and the state) to act as replacements.

With increasing modernization and a rising standard of living, the family has become a more important social unit for the young, emotionally and economically. Yet, much like the situation in other modern societies, the Israeli family has been facing great difficulties in carrying out this role and in sharing it with other socialization institutions, such as schools or mass media. One frequently hears criticisms of the young and their lack of idealistic fervor, but it is difficult for the young to match their parents' previous zeal when the new challenges are really related to "maintenance" and not to pioneering. In the yishuv days, there were enough challenges to go around, especially in the military and security-related fields, but also in illegal immigration, agriculture, and educational missions in Palestine and abroad. The main burden of establishing the state fell on the shoulders of those who were in their twenties and thirties in the crucial years around 1948. This was a very hard act to follow for the next generation.

The sacrifices of the young in the military during the wars of 1956 and especially 1967 contributed to alleviating the accusation that they did not care about their country. At the same time, however, this generation of young people became increasingly apolitical and even cynical about Zionist exhortations. It was at this time that whenever the word "Zionism" was used, it was put into quotation marks — signifying bombastic rhetoric rather than the new, down-to-earth mentality of the young. Politics became associated with partisan intrigues and dirty tricks of professional politicians, collectively referred to as *askanim* ("functionaries," with a derogatory connotation). But most young people became simply indifferent. They accepted the existing political system as given. When they reached voting age, they tended to distribute their votes among the various parties according to the existing pattern. This enabled Israeli politics to remain patriarchal for a long time, with leadership confined to advanced age groups.

There is still no clear answer to the question, who are the important socialization agencies in the state era and what do they do? It seems that the family, the schools, and compulsory military service became — not necessarily in that order — the most important socializing agencies for youth in Israel. The role of the Gadna (paramilitary training for teenagers) and the youth movements in political socialization has been steadily declining (Shapira et al., 1979).

The battle over political socialization through the schools ended in 1953 when the party-affiliated schools were abolished and the Ministry of Education took over the responsibility for the school system, and the youth movements were no longer allowed to operate within the schools.[9] Of course, in most Western democratic countries, young people are not usually subject to direct political education. In the Israeli political culture, this development signified a break with the past, particularly because young people were required to make great personal sacrifices for the collective goals of the state and society.

Table 4.2 summarizes the main changes in the socializing process in the two periods. In the state period, the challenge of political maintenance became more difficult in terms of numbers and complexity. Table 4.2 refers to those who were socialized and formed the majority that was supportive of the political system. There were, of course, Israelis who were not part of this picture. This includes Israeli Arabs and ultra-orthodox Jews — both with their own socializing agencies. There were also Israelis who became alienated, and there were those who decided to leave the country altogether.

The conclusion, nevertheless, is that in addition to the accomplished penetration of the periphery, the political system succeeded in maintaining the support of the society throughout the period under review. This was sharply manifested in the submissive initiation of the newcomers — young people and immigrants. By the mid-1960s, however, the Israeli political system was facing maintenance problems resulting from both integration failures and modernization accomplishments.

The Dynamics of Network Links

The center, in its interaction with the periphery, seeks to maintain and consolidate its position. This it achieves through a variety of modes of operation. For Deutsch, "the location of control [is in] the critical connections or configurations of the channels of information and decision that keep the system behaving as it does" (1963: 130). Control is closely associated with the existence of a political network. Through the network, information flows and control is made possible. Human systems and organizations are ungovernable without communication, integration and control (Rapaport and Horvath, 1959: 91). In a political system, the communication network consists of interconnected institutions, groups, and individuals linked by patterned flows of information (Rogers and Kincaid, 1981: 140-142).

In the yishuv, the most important factor in the political development was the process of institution-building. Party channels were operative long before other components of the network — including the center itself — were of any real significance. The political network of the Jewish community in Palestine that started to emerge in the 1920s and became consolidated after less than fifteen years enjoyed a considerable amount of autonomy vis-à-vis the British authorities. It was totally separated from the Arab network and showed the attributes that enabled it to sustain an autonomous political system. Its unique structure was expressed in its being a number of distinct and yet overlapping and closely controlled centers and channels. Its unique behavior was expressed in the ability of the Zionist movement to operate in Palestine and abroad and not to let this inherent friction prevent adaptation to changing circumstances.

TABLE 4.2   Changes in Socializing Agencies

	Prestate Period	Poststate Period* (mid-1960s)
Young People	Small community Youth movements and schools Paramilitary bodies	Family Schools The IDF
Immigrants	Political parties and their affiliated bodies Place of work	Place of work State bureaucracy Professional associations and interest groups (beginnings)

*The parties were still active mainly within the labor and religious camps, but much less important compared to the yishuv period.

Thus, when the local yishuv leaders became the key figures in the movement as a whole, the network did not shrink as a result of this development. On the contrary, the growing importance of the Jewish Agency shows that the boundary expansion of the network was used to confront the difficult tasks of preparing for the establishment of the state. Within the yishuv, there was a similar pattern of an overlapping network reaching wider circles of members. The most important means of the center to keep the political network together was the control of resources. This was certainly critical for the voluntary yishuv system, but also during the state period.

CONTROL OF POLITICAL RESOURCES

The political center controls the flow of political resources to the periphery. What are these resources? Any resource is potentially "political": Money is an obvious example; identification can be channeled into political support; and the resource of manpower can be turned into bureaucrats, tax collectors, or soldiers. So far, control has been presented in cybernetics terms — that is; "means whereby courses are chosen, kept or changed" (Vickers, 1957: 4). It was also noted that the same channels that are used for communication are also used for control (Wiener, 1954: 16). In political terms, control means a regulative capability (Almond and Powell, 1978: 307-312) — the ability to receive and distribute through the network resources that are important for the steering of the polity.

The prestate political system did not have independent means of finance and could operate only with the money raised abroad by the Zionist organizations. The center could not compel the Jewish population in Palestine to pay taxes, and its main power over those who decided to remain outside the network was in the allocation of various resources. During the yishuv period the center controlled the allocation of immigration certificates, land, water, support for settlements, and employment, as well as prestigious positions in the Zionist and national institutions. The principle of allocation was the so-called party key, whereby the parties obtained an agreed share in the distribution of resources in proportion to their size. These arrangements helped the parties become the most important channels in the network. They also had a holding effect on the structure of the political system, in that they maintained a steady distribution of power among the parties and the various political actors. The mode of distribution was definitely non-zero-sum because there was a great deal of slack in the system (imported resources) and because there was a tacit agreement that no party should completely monopolize the control of resource allocation (Horowitz and Lissak, 1978: 228-229). In other words, the parties competed among themselves primarily for the *additional* resources raised abroad while their basic share in the public pie was secured. Moreover, the more a party or a group became established and joined fully the regulative and control arrangements in the political network, the more secure became its relative share of the total resources.

How have these three mechanisms — central control of resources, the party key, and the non-zero-sum mode of allocation — changed during the state period? The ability to control resources was vastly enhanced with the establishment of a legitimate government, a bureaucracy, and a taxation system. The government in Israel, from the beginning, had been intensively involved in most spheres of life. This was due partly to the socialist ideology of the ruling party and partly to the fact that the state continued to control money from abroad (Sheffer and Manor, 1980). The center increased its ability to control other resources as well, such as positions in the new local bureaucracy and abroad, economic concessions, licenses, and outright donations and financial contributions.

As for control of information, the channels used most frequently in the yishuv and Israeli political system were organizational. The most critical political information, that which is relevant for steering the system, flowed diagonally — between the center and the secondary centers, and between the secondary centers and the periphery. The arbitration role of these secondary centers enabled or forced the political center to delegate to them many of the penetration and maintenance functions.

With the establishment of the state, the vertical channels between the center and periphery, such as the bureaucratic ones that were more fully controlled by the center, took over some of the secondary centers' functions in the communication network. The vertical flow assumed additional importance because of its monopoly on the state symbols. Moreover, the ability of the center to control political communication increased through the withholding and selective release of information (Galnoor, 1977: 177-180). This enabled the center to control even more independent mediators, such as the nonpartisan evening newspapers. The bottom-to-top flow, from the public to the center, was compromised by the dominating presence of the diagonal communicator. It was not, however, totally absent or completely controlled.

Horizontal communication was problematic in the center and rare among the secondary centers. In the center, leaders had to talk to each other, and they did. Because of the fragmented nature of the center (for example, cabinet coalitions), horizontal communication actually meant hard bargaining and a great deal of friction. One main achievement of the center was its ability to carry on despite the enormous amount of energy required for horizontal communication.

Horizontal communication between secondary centers was hampered by the fact that each was a relatively "closed" ideological camp. Governing required that the leaders of the parties and the various organizations bargain and reach compromises. It did not require that lower-level officials of the Histadrut and the Industrialists' Association communicate directly with each other. Political action was rarely carried out independently by one or more secondary centers. It was done with and through the parties and their leaders in the center. The center operated on its own mainly in foreign affairs and security, because the critical information came from outside the Israeli environment. In internal affairs the diagonal channels were the busy ones in Israeli politics.

In his coalition model, Riker (1962: 32-33, 88-89) mentions the condition of "imperfect information" as one reason for an increase in the size of the cabinet coalition above the required minimum. Such an "information effect" causes uncertainty regarding resources and support and may result in a bigger coalition. In Israel, writes Nachmias, there was no such information effect because the coalition almost always included four or more parties which together controlled more than the required 51 percent (1974: 319).[10]

The horizontal information flow within the center (bargaining), the services provided by the diagonal channels (screening), and the vertical supply of political symbols and reassurances were all instrumental in developing the system's steering capacity and its control over the network. As time passed and Israeli society started to change, the importance of other channels grew, especially transmission from the periphery to the center. These changes — such as the appearance of powerful and independent interests — created new kinds of control problems for the center; these will be presented in Chapter 8.

TRANSFORMATIONS IN THE NETWORK

The communication network during the yishuv period was one of a close-knit, almost tribal, community. The national center shared power, resources, and information with secondary centers, and the periphery was not too far from all the centers. In the state period, the pattern started to change, and distances within the network began to resemble those in other countries. It was already seen that in the periphery there emerged problematic target groups which had to be penetrated and different publics which had to be maintained. Another important development was the change in the position of the secondary centers, the parties, and other organizations.

During the yishuv period, the center dominated the network through control of resources, but the parties and secondary centers were independent initiators of resource flow and rather autonomous in resource utilization. Many — the political parties, the Histadrut, hospitals, and universities, to name a few — had their own resource mobilization apparatus abroad. The central institutions also did not intervene directly in the allocation of settlements between the party movements or in the distribution of financial assistance to party enterprises through the Jewish Agency.

In the early years of the state, these regulations continued more or less unchanged. Resource allocation, however, began to be monopolized by the central government, although most of the other partners received more resources than before. The previous partnership turned slowly into domination by the central government, with the others filling the roles of subordinated agencies and extensions. The secondary centers had to compete with each other over their share in the available resources, and their position as distributors deteriorated. As long as there were enough resources to go around, this new pattern of control caused friction between the government and the former secondary centers, but it did not impair the center's ability to continue functioning. Interest groups started to negotiate directly with the central government and no longer with the partisan bodies. Furthermore, the direct relationship between the center and the periphery was enhanced by the satisfaction of most of the population with continual improvement in the standard of living. In the early years of the state, the mode of resource distribution continued to be basically non-zero-sum, even though some groups were clearly left behind. But the price a group had to pay for becoming established within the network and for gaining access to information and other resources increased all the time. There were groups, such as indigent immigrants, who could not enter into these exchange agreements.

Another change that took place is that the parties were increasingly confined to a more restricted role as channels of communication between the government and the citizens, and they started to face competition from the state bureaucracy. In a small society with an enormous public sector, where most spheres of life were politicized, control of information was a vital means of gaining and retaining political power.

Toward the mid-1960s, the secondary centers were still well entrenched in the communications network. They were guaranteed access to the national center and were able to obtain the information required for their interests. But they had lost their autonomy. The price they paid for access was both tangible (votes, money, support, information) and intangible (forfeiting public campaigns and the exercise of hostile pressure). In short, the political network developed subordination relationships, which made the secondary centers and the parties partners in the communication network and gave control of the political system to the center.

Obviously, the network could not be totally efficient. Information was leaked gratuitously in order to forward certain interests. All the same, during the period following the establishment of the state, there was centralized control of political information, with the party press constituting an integral part of the political system. The communications media displayed great restraint, partly because they agreed to the state's privilege to conceal information and partly because of the pressure exerted in the event of infringement.

As for the periphery, the position of the center did not change fundamentally when the population more than doubled. Most of the immigrants after 1948 were politically passive. Moreover, their settlement in temporary residences and their total dependence on officials made them peripheral politically but not outsiders altogether. The achievement of the political center at that time was its ability to reach every transitory camp of immigrants, every community and family, and incorporate them into the network. The unemployed had the Histadrut representative (a party official) to yell at; those who lacked housing could berate the Jewish Agency representative (also a party official); and those unhappy with their welfare allowance could throw stones at the nearby Welfare Ministry office (staffed by party officials). No wonder the ruling parties (notably Mapai) and the Histadrut were regarded as the "government" or even the "Establishment." Nevertheless, the periphery in Israeli politics was not remote and not even rural, as in many developing countries. It was penetrated and maintained by the center and, as such, was not outside the network.

In the 1960s, the center still held as a pivotal force in controlling the political network, but other links were weakening. Regardless of the exact reasons for this development (for example, modernization, weakening of the pioneering spirit, institutional fatigue, new social forces), a higher degree of differentiation started to replace the structure on which the old network was built. The roles of the center, secondary centers, and parties were changing and their grip weakening. After 1948, the center increased its hold when all residual tasks went to the new government while the secondary centers lost many important areas. The center also started to communicate directly with emerging groups such as business concerns, professional associations, and ethnic groups. Other changes included the application of more universalistic standards to housing, employment, and welfare services. Some secondary centers gained new vitality by breaking ties with their traditional camps and parties and becoming more independent — examples are the local authorities, especially in the development towns (Arian and Weiss, 1968). Most important, the old parties, operating sometimes in new combinations and under new names, were in decline.

It is beyond the scope of this book to present the full explanation for this process, as I am mainly interested in describing the communication network. One "external" explanation for this diminishing central control is that the political network, too, was undergoing a transformation induced by the socioeconomic modernization process. Where the standard of living is rising, there is also more public participation:

> In modern society, in consequence of its far greater involvement with the central institutional system, especially with the economy and the polity, the mass of the population is no longer largely without contact with the central value system [Shils, 1975: 14].

A center almost without a periphery in the yishuv period became more remote afterwards and began ultimately to be "invaded" from below. A network which was tightly coordinated in the beginning became highly controlled afterwards and, in many respects, was subsequently loosened. The invasion of the center by the periphery through new and uncontrolled channels is a known phenomenon in many "mass societies" (Kornhauser, 1959). As for Israel, it can be said that while the political network established during the yishuv period was still the basis of the political system in the 1960s, it already functioned in an entirely different manner. The center was forced to accommodate internal shifts in the patterned flows of information — that is, in the distribution of power. The transformations in the network itself started to take place later, in the 1970s.

The challenge began with new social powers seeking recognition, as well as old groups and organizations which retained enough power to break free. Professional groups, workers' committees, and local municipalities became independent in the sense that they would pressure the center directly and openly without the mediating services of the parties and other established organizations. Similarly, their degree of obedience to directives coming down from the center considerably decreased. The more established ones, such as the moshav movement or even the Histadrut, also discovered that complete loyalty and obedience were not rewarded as in the past, and this stimulated independence. No rival center emerged, even potentially, within the Israeli political system. Yet the links of the old network, and especially those of the center, started to change rapidly.

THE NETWORK: REDUNDANCY AND OVERLAP

> A commercial airliner is a very redundant system, a fact which accounts for its reliability of performance; a fact which also accounts for its adaptability [Landau, 1969: 346].

Israelis often refer to "The System" with a negative connotation sometimes implying omnipotence and sometimes excess and waste. From what has been said so far about the political network, it is evident that it was anchored in a complex organizational maze and that there was indeed a high degree of redundancy and overlap. Following Landau, we suggest that in contrast to prevailing views regarding efficiency and the need for eliminating duplication in organizations, the Israeli political network demonstrates the advantages of both redundancy and overlap.

Redundancy is a device for ensuring the reliability of communication and for the suppression of error (1969: 347). It is used in technological networks to store reserve power. As a safety device in organizations — or, for that matter, in political systems — redundancy aims at preventing small errors from turning into the failure of the entire system.

In the case of Israel, the intolerability of failure in defense and external affairs calls for redundancy as a safety device for the absorption of uncertainty. Thus the participation of non-Israeli Jews in the network secures an additional circle of support, thus making it important despite the overload on the communication network and the friction in the decision-making process. Similarly, the stubborn efforts of the center to

penetrate every target group in Israeli society is related to the significance attached to preventing any kind of dissent that could spread into
other parts of the system. Redundancy and feedback go hand in hand
and help to maintain the stability and equilibrium of a communication
network (Smith, 1966: 365).

Overlap is a device for increasing the adaptability of the communication network. It is expressed in the tendency of the network to resist
precise differentiation of functions (1966: 351). In the case of Israel, it
was necessary mainly for increasing the support of the various groups
and for securing the common contents (see Chapter 3). It was also
required for the internal political process of mutual adjustments, coalition, and compromise. With very little exaggeration, one can say that the
center was willing to extend the network and establish a special organization for every group that was willing to meet the minimum requirements and be incorporated into the system. The example of the Agudah
ultra-orthodox parties is illuminating in this respect. A very small group,
which refused to be an integral part of the political system, has nonetheless obtained many concessions in return for participation in the elections and some other political arrangements.

There are other examples of overlap, such as between politics and
administration, between the function of ministries and nongovernmental
organizations, and between two or more institutions operating in the
same area. All point to the extensive ambiguity in boundary demarca-
tions and a consistent resistance to the elimination of overlap. This is an
important reason why the Israeli network scores high on all four criteria
of political institutionalization proposed by Huntington (1968: 12-24): It
was highly adaptable to environmental changes; it was complex and
complicated in terms of subunits, hierarchy differentiation, and func-
tionality; it was to a large extent independent of other social groupings;
and it was highly unified and coherent in terms of being based on — and
nourishing at the same time — a solid consensus founded on common
political contents.

As has been demonstrated throughout this chapter, redundancy and
overlap were expressed and tolerated in the network in several different
ways:

- The division of political labor between the center and the secondary
  centers reflected duplication but created "backup systems" in case of
  failure. For instance, when the British arrested most of the national
  leaders in 1944, there were others in the secondary centers who could
  carry on for a while. Another example is the delegation of religious
  matters to the religious camp, which helped the center maintain a more
  neutral position in the non-observant public.

- The multiplication of organizations enabled the center to reach different groups through various extensions, each suited to its specific task. For instance, the Zionist organizations extended membership to the non-Zionist groups in the Diaspora. Another example is the mushrooming of immigrant associations for every country, region, and even town in Eastern Europe. These were all encouraged and supported with public funds channeled through the parties and the affiliated organizations.

- The network itself demonstrated redundancy and overlap in information flow. The importance of the diagonal flow of information was stressed: between the periphery and secondary centers and between the center and secondary centers. There was one central network, but the camps, the secondary centers, and the parties were "allowed" their own networks for penetration and maintenance, as well as for bottom-to-top information flow. The network and, through it, the political system as a whole was quite sensitive to dissenting information generated from below, as shown especially in cases of violent demonstrations (see Chapter 2).

- Finally, there was a great deal of overlap between the channels used in the Israeli political network. As will be seen in subsequent chapters, party, bureaucratic, and mass media channels were partly synchronized, partly parallel, and partly independent.

Redundancy and overlap generated friction and waste, but they permitted the Israeli political network to reach wider publics and to penetrate more deeply into many potential circles of supporters. They contributed a great deal to the system's reliability and adaptability and did not interfere with control to the extent of impeding central steering. As will be seen in the last chapters of this book, these features of the network also had a crucial impact on democratic political development.

THE NETWORK: ACCOMPLISHMENTS

In addition to redundancy and overlap, the main reasons why the political communication network worked well and fulfilled the essential requirements can be summarized as follows:

- It was anchored in organizations that provided hierarchy and division of labor.

- Despite the broad social, economic, and cultural roles of these organizations, they were essentially *political*. More precisely, they enabled specialization on political work and an intimate connection between the political and nonpolitical spheres of activity.

- The network, despite the dysfunctional qualities of noise and distortion, enabled the accumulation of political power and authority, without which there is no political steering.

From the point of view of the center, the main accomplishment of the network was its quality of endurance, as evidenced by the high survival rates of many political structures established in the yishuv period.

The smallest units in the yishuv society were not traditional families or tribes, nor just individuals, as in mass societies. As was noted, it was a small and relatively advanced community whose units — groups, places of work, collective settlements, and so on — were relatively close to the political center. Moreover, the intermediates between the individuals and the leaders were intermingled with both the center and the periphery. For all practical purposes, the political camps came close to exercising direct democracy in terms of mutual familiarity, involvement, and influence. The more organized labor and religious camps served as miniature political systems with their own secondary centers for their respective members. This situation did not lead to political disintegrations, as it could have, because there was a center — however voluntary and fragile — and there were also hierarchy and division of labor. For instance, when the political center wanted to activate the network in order to launch the massive financial campaign in 1938 (Kofer Hayishuv),[11] to mobilize volunteers for the Jewish units in the British Army in 1944, or to organize demonstrations against the British, the message was effectively transmitted through the various intermediaries, which also relayed the response. The fact that these bodies were not remote and alien created a network with "short chanels." In the labor camp, personal membership in the workers' council, the local party chapter, or the Histadrut's sports club enabled direct access to channels leading into the center. This type of network helped also a great deal in overcoming noise and distortions. It had its shortcomings in terms of waste and overloaded decision-processes, but it enabled political control without the formal paraphernalia that comes with sovereignty and statehood.

The State of Israel came into being with a relatively developed political system mainly because of the above characteristics of the network: The political center could function because it could communicate and receive political information; it could penetrate the target groups and maintain newcomers because the coverage of the old social circles was almost completed before 1948; and the network could afford redundancy and overlap even after statehood, because it gained information and support in return. The political system as a whole enjoyed stability and development because the network was strong enough to survive stress and undergo adaptation.

The combination of change plus survival is difficult for any political system, especially one under heavy external stress. In the case of Israel, the underlying common contents enabled the communication network to develop them further as a shared collective identity. The fact that no other significant ideology was developed permitted the political elite to implant the symbols of the dominating ideology in the institutional structure and to routinize it through the political network (Eisenstadt, 1976: Vol. 1, 33). In this respect, the establishment of the state did not mark a sharp discontinuity with the yishuv: The political institutions provided a crucial uninterrupted link. During the state period, the network proved capable of reaching every citizen in terms of mobilization to the army, tax collection, licensing, permissions to travel abroad, and so on. On the output side, the picture is more complicated, but all Israeli citizens benefit in one way or another from state services. The state too benefits from the existence of a political network that encompasses the entire society.

NOTES

1. For a list of the organizations affiliated with the different camps and of the nonaffiliated groups during the yishuv period, see Horowitz and Lissak (1977: 92-104).
2. This is also the title of his book, *From Class to Nation* (Ben-Gurion, 1974).
3. The elections for local authorities were identical to those for the Knesset — proportional representation. In 1978, these elections were based on a new law according to which mayors are elected by direct popular votes rather than by the councils.
4. The following are four illustrations (out of eight) proposed by Horowitz and Lissak (1978: 121-136). The examples in parentheses do not appear in their text but are mine.
  (1) Distinction by the link between the secondary centers and the parties (or the camps).
    a. Dominated by any given party or camp (kibbutz movements, Moshavim movement, Farmers' Association).
    b. Multiparty, secondary centers in which party affiliation is relevant (trade unions, Kibbutz Movement Union, Cooperatives' Center, Jewish Agency).
    c. Nonparty secondary centers (principally professional organizations, as well as the Scouts and the Hadassah organization).
    d. Quasi-political secondary centers (Craftsmen's Associations, Traders' Organization, immigrants' unions, marketing and production councils).
  (2) Distinction by the type of membership in the secondary center.
    a. Federative, membership of which is by way of other organizations (Kibbutz Movement Union, Workers' Corporation).
    b. Founded on individual membership (Craftsmen Association, youth movements, trade unions).
    c. Mixed patterns (Medical Association).
  (3) Distinction by the range of activities of the secondary centers.
    a. Countrywide (the majority).
    b. Local (labor councils, chambers of commerce, Municipal Government Center).
  (4) Distinction by the nature of the link to the national center.
    a. Direct link which makes the secondary centers into a kind of executive arm of the government (Water Council, Lawyers' Chamber, Insurance Companies' Association)

b. Mediated links by means of another secondary center or a party (sickness-insurance funds, religious councils, Agricultural Center, Aguda independent educational network).

5. On political leadership from a communication perspective, see Pool (1973: 811-814).

6. For a detailed analysis of the yishuv political elite, including its background, recruitment processes, the differences between the labor and other elites, and the personalities involved, see Gutmann and Landau (1975) and Horowitz and Lissak (1978: 147-165). Other studies of the political elite and leadership in Israel are Eisenstadt (1967: 171-188), Czudnovski (1970), Brichta (1976), and Gurevitch and Winograd (1977).

7. Lustick (1980) takes the position that the absence of conflict and instability in the relationship between Jews and Arabs in Israel is best explained in terms of *control*. This concept is very close to what I defined as penetration and maintenance, because in a control system the linkage between the center and the periphery is penetrative in character (Lustick, 1975: 330).

8. Ben-Gurion's decision to settle in the Negev in 1953 was motivated, among other things, by his deisre to set an example for the young generation. During this voluntary exile from politics, he tried to meet frequently with young groups and to rekindle the pioneering spirit (Bar-Zohar, 1977).

9. This general statement applies to the secular schools, whereas the religious schools remained attached to the religious political camp despite the overall supervision of the Education Ministry. For a general description see Fein (1967: 120-128).

10. Between 1949 and 1965 there were 12 cabinets; only the smallest one in 1955 comprised 64 Knesset Members and included three parties. The average size of the coalition in that period was 75 Knesset Members out of 120. The biggest coalition was 87 Knesset Members in 1952-1955 when the General Zionists participated in the cabinet. One of the smallest cabinets (69 Knesset Members) was in 1961-1965, after the beginning of the "Lavon Affair."

11. Kofer Hayishuv was a levy imposed by the National Committee (Va'ad Leumi) on all Jewish households in Palestine. It was a voluntary income tax as well as an indirect tax on goods and services. The only enforcing sanctions were social. The fund was managed by representatives of all elements of the Jewish community and was successful in raising great sums of money for defense.

5

CHANNELS: THE POLITICAL PARTIES

> One who believes that parties should rightly hold the center of the
> political scene can study the workings of such a system in Israel. To
> those who see in intense and powerful partisanship an undesirable
> deviation of democratic government, Israel again offers an opportunity
> to observe the details of this deviation.
> (AKZIN, 1955)

From the vantage point of the center, political development is a matter of
reaching as deeply as possible into society and maintaining a high level of
political mobilization. Once the institutional basis is sufficiently developed and there is a network capable of incorporating the relevant
segments of society into the political system, the task becomes mainly
one of regulating and controlling the flow of political information. Note
that the term "incorporation" is used here and not "participation,"
because at this stage political development is predominantly a matter of
forging central steering capacity and of ensuring members' compliance
and not necessarily responsiveness to their needs and demands. The
center determines which segments of society are relevant and should be
reached and defines the target groups for its efforts of political penetration. From the center's point of view, the channels are the instruments
through which it tries to penetrate the relevant "nonpolitical" and maintain the political segments of society. Otherwise it cannot "rule" and
"govern."

Political Channels

There is no way to determine whether a channel is political unless we examine it closely. Political channels are those whose primary purpose is collective and/or which carry information with a predominantly political content. A developing political system is characterized by efforts of the center to establish differentiated political channels that are relatively permanent. Permanence is required because, unlike face-to-face communication or a spontaneous gathering, these channels are meant to have prescribed functions and to be reused time and again.

Political penetration implies a constant interaction between the polity on the one hand and society on the other. Modern technology enables the center to reach every member of society through railroads or radio programs, but political penetration means also some form of support — tacit or stated, voluntary or enforced — for the existence of the political system.

Compared with other new nations, Israeli society was relatively secularized, urbanized, and educated. Other components, such as a market economy, advanced technology, and modern transportation, have developed quickly and, with them, the "information industry." Crossing geographical and social boundaries has been achieved in Israel through the rapid development of a variety of communication channels such as roads, telephones, mail service, and the mass media. Political penetration also needs specialized political channels that operate independently as well as in combination with the other channels.

In Chapter 1, channels were defined as communication linkages and political channels, as links between the center and the periphery. A law requiring every citizen not to drive a car without a driving license "penetrates" society to the extent that it is obeyed. It does not, however, create a channel that can send and receive messages within the political system on a relatively permanent basis. Fagen (1966: 34) distinguishes between "core channels" that serve the more permanent maintenance function of the political system and "special channels" whose functions are more circumstantial. Institutions were identified as the main vehicle for developing the political network, but it was also pointed out that there are periodic or occasional channels as well as nonpolitical channels that are used in politics.

Here and in the next two chapters, the main channels are presented and their contribution to creating the system's steering capacity is discussed. The emphasis is more on their activities aimed at meeting the penetration challenges with regard to the target groups and less on their efforts to maintain the system. The three "institutions" that proved capable of extending political communication into Israeli society and which serve as the main channels in the network have been the political parties and their affiliated organizations, the bureaucracy, and the mass media. These have been the more permanent channels that served both penetration and maintenance functions. In addition there have been some special channels, most of them nonpolitical, that served primarily for political socialization and thus contributed also to penetration. The most important ones were military organizations during the yishuv period and later the Israeli army (IDF), youth movements, some special organizations such as immigrants' associations, and nonpolitical organizations such as schools and places of work.

Parties as Channels

In developed political systems, parties are regarded as *input* agencies in the political process because they are presumed to perform the functions of interest articulation and aggregation (Almond and Powell, 1978). Furthermore, parties are distinctive institutions of a *modern* era, because only modern systems require means to organize mass participation in politics (Huntington, 1968: 88-90). In many new political systems, the parties are a source of legitimacy and authority. The state itself may owe its establishment and stability to the existence of a strong party system (1968: 91). Referring to political parties as communication channels does not ignore the richness of their functions, but it does serve to point out a role that is particularly important for the analysis of political development (see LaPalombara and Weiner, 1966). In performing this role, political parties serve as a link between social forces and the government and help to establish a political community through the integration of communal groups and the combination of social and economic interests. Societies that develop political parties early are likely to have fewer problems when political participation expands (Huntington, 1968: 397-398). How do parties perform these penetration and maintenance functions? How did the fragmented community of the yishuv period succeed in having a strong party system, and how did it help in establishing a state and keeping it stable for a relatively long period?

There is indeed an "organizational imperative" in modernization and political development, but it cannot be explained only in general terms of "power," "administrative efficiency" and "social order" (1968: 461). It is imperative because organizations serve the indispensable function of communication. Political parties are organizations capable of serving as communication channels. Furthermore, we submit that there is a relationship between the strength of political parties and their effectiveness as communication channels.

Viewing parties this way is not new. Key pointed out that political parties act as mediators between the government and the public and serve as access channels for citizens in democracies (1961: 363) Easton emphasized the role of parties as means of coping with stress emanating from social cleavages (1965b: 256-259). In trying to tie these observations together with our focus on political development, Epstein's suggestion will be followed:

> to study parties both as independent and dependent variables, that is, as intervening variables that are both influenced and influencing. . . . Parties are responses to circumstances of many kinds, *and* they are also, once existing, among the circumstances that determine political life [Epstein, 1975: 235].

Political parties are an organizational mechanism that can serve both the center (with penetration, maintenance, and control) and the periphery (with demands, pressure, and participation). The possible combinations between the two are numerous, from full central control to totally independent participation. Political parties perform so many and such varied communication functions that any attempt to summarize them would be impossible.[1] In discussing Israel, some specific examples will be used, but they are by no means exhaustive. For instance, parties are involved in electioneering, interest accommodation, socialization, indoctrination, mutual awareness, and legitimation (Marvick, 1973: 737). Penetration touches on all these activities, but it is a more narrow concept than Marvick's "effective structural extent" (1970, 1973). Penetration consists of a deliberate effort to meet a challenge, while maintenance includes more routine upkeep (see Chapter 4). Parties do both simultaneously, but there is an important difference in the type of energy that goes into each activity, especially in the consequences. In Marvick's words,

> Political parties are complex structures — attitudinal as well as corporate — for coordinating political efforts across extended domains. . . . Whatever its functions or purposes, as investigators have explored the complexities entailed by any of these tasks, they have recognized that each party was an *extensive* coordinating apparatus [Marvick, 1973: 747].

"Coordination" in this context combines penetration and maintenance. In terms of political development, it entails the ability to tap the resources of as many groups as possible in order to engage in collective efforts. For this purpose, a tool for reaching into the difficult domains is required. This is usually the first phase which, according to Lipset and Rokkan, involves penetration and standardization efforts of the national center and may also cause resistance and identity crises (1967: 9). Coordination also means a routine flow of information to the center from groups and areas already penetrated and the maintenance of their support through alliances and central control.

In reviewing what political parties do in Israel, the discussion will be confined mainly to Mapai, even though there have been many differences between the activities of this dominating party and all the others. Whether each activity was carried out by the party itself or by one if its political, social, or economic extensions also will not be elaborated. The labor camp as a whole will be treated as if it were one organization, even though this was not the case and the division of labor and friction within the camp and between the party and secondary centers was very significant. These simplifications are necessary because our subject is not Israeli political parties, but rather Israeli parties as channels of communication. Finally, the fact that parties were the main vehicle for political development in Israel does not suggest that this is inevitably so in other political systems.

Parties in Israel

Israeli parties were introduced in Chapter 2 and their place within the political network was described in Chapter 4. In this chapter, the proposition is that the central role of the established parties — those taking part in the cabinet, Histadrut, and Jewish Agency — is based primarily on their performance as channels of communication within the political system.

Israeli democracy is based on division into a large number of secondary centers and organizations, yet with considerable centralization in the allocation of political power. This centralization was attained not by coercion, but by channeling most of the public's demands and most of the government's services and rewards through the parties. The established parties acted as clearinghouses in the complex and highly divided network of Israeli politics: It was their task to regulate and coordinate the numerous and contradictory demands. They were able to do so primarily by virtue of their control over the principal resource — information and its tangible currency — power, capital (some of it raised abroad), jobs, and social status. Arrangements among the parties and the affiliated organizations to allocate each a share of the various resources were not always achieved placidly. They were adapted to changing circumstances and remained in force despite fierce competition and numerous crises.

The power of the parties, particularly those in positions of control, stemmed from the fact that functionaries — mayors of development towns, secretaries of labor councils, heads of religious councils, and representatives of interest groups — conducted their campaigns for political resources primarily through party channels. Often, they had obtained their jobs by virtue of the parties and saw no advantage in taking their tussles outside the established network and submitting them to the verdict of public opinion. The capacity of the parties to coordinate conflicting interests can be easily proved by many examples in which coordinated decisions reached in a party forum were binding on the party representatives in the Knesset, the cabinet, the Histadrut, government corporations, and so on.

The multifarious means at the disposal of the parties to perform penetration and maintenance functions enabled them to sustain a voluntary political system during the yishuv period. Most important was the organizational mechanism which in many important aspects resembled the one in Communist countries (Selznick, 1952). It also included, as will be seen, coercive means and manipulation through the party's combined political-bureaucratic leadership. There were, however, important differences already in the yishuv period. Communist parties in power cannot usually tolerate organized criticism and, above all, the existence of multiple centers of power (1952: 33-35). Mapai, however, was forced to accommodate both internal criticism that often led to splits as well as a division of labor with other powerful secondary centers. Hence, the communication role of Mapai was less oriented toward propaganda in the agitational sense and more toward penetration and maintenance through persuasion, mobilization, and recruitment.

The penetration and maintenance techniques used by parties in Israel were quickly adapted to the new circumstances in the state period and the new composition of society. The arsenal of means used to penetrate new groups through party channels was replenished to include direct propaganda, patronage, and benefits in exchange for votes. One new target was the penetration of other new organizations and associations. Perhaps the main achievement of Mapai in this respect after 1948 was the fact that most of these organizations found it more expedient to be affiliated with the center, the secondary centers, and the parties than to operate independently and outside the established network.

Penetration

The relationship between the Israeli political center and the periphery had a strong paternalistic character. An example from the early years of the state is illuminating. Prime Minister Moshe Sharett was not known for his autocratic approach to politics, yet he was deeply concerned about the growing tendency of Israelis — newcomers and veterans alike — to leave the country and settle abroad. To overcome this problem, a cabinet minister suggested controlling passport delivery to Israelis in order to prevent them from leaving the country. The suggestion was debated in the cabinet in 1953 and supported by Sharett, who wrote in his diary:

> A physician or social worker is allowed — indeed it is his duty — not to respect the foolish wishes of his patients and to subject them, on the basis of his authority derived from education, expertise and experience, to treatment or a way of life that can cure them. Similarly, the State is permitted and obliged to ignore the wandering instinct of this reckless people and not to give in to the willful forgetfulness of their past. The State should save them and their offspring — if necessary against their will — from the eternal gypsy curse with which they seek relief from absorption pains in their sole home in all the world. This is a Zionism of iron, no, of steel! [Sharett, 1978: Vol. 1, 255].

The measure was not implemented, but until 1961 Israelis were required to obtain "exit permits" from the Ministry of Interior in order to leave the country.[2] There are many other examples of economic restrictions (food rationing), legal prohibitions (on acquiring private land), or political censorship during the early years. The state, the government, and the "public sector" have been central factors in the daily lives of Israelis. As noted, this dependence was more acute in the case of weaker groups, such as new immigrants from Oriental countries. Compared to other Western democracies, Israelis have been subjected to many state limitations in the area of security, but also in their economic, social, and religious affairs. In terms of benefits and obligations, no Israeli is "outside" the political system: It reaches him whether he likes it or not. But in discussing penetration, there is a broader context than merely state-citizen relationships.

ORGANIZATIONAL EXTENSIONS

The most prominent technique of penetration was the utilization of a great variety of organizational structures and mechanisms for reaching different segments of the population. For instance, in discussing institution-building, the division of labor was noted: Mapai made efforts to incorporate the Zionist socialist workers; the Histadrut was trying to reach a broader circle — all workers; Knesset Israel tried to incorporate on a voluntary basis all Zionists in Palestine; the Zionist Organization, all Zionists abroad; and the Jewish Agency, all Jews interested in Israel. This means that a different organizational form was provided for the different areas of concern of each group with a great deal of overlap and with the parties as the chief coordinating channels.

This system of extension — penetrating different domains through different, but affiliated, organizations — was used to reach the target groups within Israel. For instance, observant Jews belonging to the National Religious Party were not Histadrut members, but through a special arrangement they could use the services of the Histadrut's Sick Fund. Immigrants' associations were ostensibly voluntary organizations, but they were supported and often indoctrinated by the parties. Teenagers were reached through the Histadrut's sports clubs and the youth movements. Every kibbutz and moshav belonged to its "federation," and, through them, the members aligned themselves with political camps. The party could use specialized, affiliated extensions as an efficient means of penetration for different groups. This technique was particularly suitable for the dominating Mapai party, which enjoyed more resources and a near-monopoly in certain services such as health and, to a lesser extent, employment. The parties developed an extensive network of branches throughout the country. The smaller and more remote the town, the greater the chances for a near-domination position of Mapai and its affiliated extensions.

Modern mass parties in Europe employed different basic units of membership: cells in the Communist parties, squads in Fascist parties, and branches or sections in socialist parties (Marvick, 1973: 729). Mapai and the other labor parties were based on an extensive system of branches interwoven with the Histadrut's local Workers' Councils and Workers' Committees. Before 1948 there were also paramilitary units affiliated with the labor parties. These were employed in the external struggle, but occasionally also in clashes with the rival military organization (Etzel). Units from the Haganah or Palmach also served as recruitment extensions of young people. All such military units were disbanded shortly after the state was established. The party-affiliated units of strong-arm men that remained were the "ushers" (*plugot sadranim),* who were employed to guard sports events, election rallies, or occasionally to disrupt the rallies of the rival party (Almogi, 1980: 22-26). Similarly, the Beitar youth movement, affiliated with Herut, had its own groups of "ushers."

The list of organizations affiliated with the nonlabor parties is shorter. The religious party was relatively more successful than the others in organizing affiliated extensions in social and economic areas such as a kibbutz movement, a housing corporation, a bank, and a youth movement. The revisionist movement has had a separate National Labor Federation (founded in 1934), a sick fund, sports clubs, and a youth movement, but its size and degree of organization could not match that of the labor parties. The fact that the Herut Party was not included in any coalition cabinet until 1967 did not help in this respect. The General Zionist Party lacked a strong organization that could unite the civic camp and serve the function of coordination. This situation was consistent with the party's liberal ideology and its opposition to strong public organizations, but it weakened its relative power within a political system dominated by party-affiliated organizations. The secondary centers that did exist, such as Ha-Ichud Ha-Ezrachi were politically weak and mainly concerned with economic affairs. The attempt to organize the self-employed could not rival the Histadrut's organization of salaried employees. The natural conveyers of these efforts — that is, the private corporations, companies, and small industries and workshops — were relatively weak in the early years of the state because of the structure of the economy, strong government intervention, and the existence of much more powerful public organizations operating in the economic field. Subsequently, the country's economic development increased the relative power of the General Zionist Party, especially its strongholds in the urban centers. One of the main changes in this area was the strength gradually acquired by private corporations in Israel and their parent organization — the Industrialists' Association.

The smaller parties tried to follow the example of the bigger ones. The Progressive Party, for example, has had a settlement extension, to which its two kibbutzim belonged. In terms of penetration capabilities, such organizations were much less effective. The pattern, however, was similar throughout the political system — all parties operated through organizational extensions. The more numerous and powerful these extensions, the more the party functioned as a coordination channel.

MEMBERSHIP

Most Israeli parties used the system of branches, but their numbers and significance were minimal in comparison with the Mapai branches. In the mid 1950s, Mapai had over 400 separate branches in cities, development towns, moshavim, and kibbutzim (Medding, 1972: 89). By 1964, in urban centers alone (that is, excluding the many kibbutz and moshav cells), Mapai branches totaled about 150,000 members (p. 89). Very much like other socialist parties in Europe, Mapai has claimed a great number of registered members. Membership was secured by paying affiliation fees. It is difficult, however, to know the exact figures of Mapai membership because up-to-date lists have not been kept, lists are not published, and the figures that were published are suspect on the overcount side. Their accuracy decreased over the years, especially because the parties ceased to insist that their registered members pay dues regularly. Once a name is on the membership list, it is not removed. Thus, in 1977, it turned out that the Labor Party membership roster substantially exceeded the number of actual voters. Subsequently the party decided to take a new census and to reimpose membership dues. Table 5.1 compares Mapai's published membership figures with the number of votes for the party in different elections.

The yishuv was a small and intimate community with a relatively high ratio of personal party membership and election turnout. Horowitz and Lissak estimated that between 1930 and 1944 the ratio between Mapai members and Representatives Assembly voters for Mapai was as high as 1:3 (1977: 114). Table 5.1 shows that this is correct also for Histadrut voters, except in 1945, when the proportion of Mapai's Histadrut voters declined. Party membership continued to be relatively high after 1948, even if reduced by 25 percent for inaccuracy.

Dues-paying membership has declined significantly, but many people were willing to add their names to their party rosters. Indeed, party membership in Israel was higher percentage-wise than in seven other countries (Nie and Verba, 1975: 24): Austria, 28 percent; India, 5 percent; Japan (political clubs), 4 percent; Netherlands, 13 percent; United States (political clubs), 8 percent; Yugoslavia, 15 percent. Party membership estimates for Israel were between 15 percent to 33 percent in the late 1950s (Gutmann, 1960: 55). Medding estimated that in 1964, about 16 percent of the eligible voters in the Israeli electorate were members of Mapai, while 37 percent of the total vote went for the Labor Alignment in the 1965 Knesset elections. If this ratio also holds for other parties, then the number of Israeli eligible voters who were party members was close to one-third and perhaps higher. If the published numbers of Mapai membership are held constant, an interesting relationship can be observed between them and the number of Mapai voters in different kinds of elections (Table 5.2).

Table 5.2 shows that around the core of party members there has been a wider circle of Mapai voters in the Histadrut. This circle roughly corresponds in size to Mapai supporters in the municipal elections. Both fluctuate less than the widest circle of Mapai voters to the Knesset.[3] The

TABLE 5.1 Mapai Membership Compared to Number of Mapai Votes in Elections (selected years and rounded figures)

Year	Mapai Membership[a]	Votes for Mapai in Histadrut Elections[b]	Votes for Mapai in Municipal Elections[c]	Votes for Mapai in the Representatives Assembly (1931-44) and Knesset (1949-65)
1932	7,000	18,000 (1933)	—	21,000 (1931)
1941	20,000	61,000 (1942)	—	—
1945	24,000	57,000 (1944)	—	74,000 (1944)
1949	62,000	79,000	90,000 (1950)	155,000
1955	152,000	237,000 (1956)	200,000	275,000
1959	172,000	266,000 (1960)	285,000	370,000
1964[d]	196,000	383,000 (1966)	344,000 (1965)	443,000 (1965)

[a]Supplied by Mapai Membership Department (Medding, 1972: 15).

[b]From supplement to *Histadrut Election Results, 1977*, Histadrut Election Unit, Organization Department (n.d.).

[c]*Statistical Abstract of Israel, 1978* Vol. 29 (1978: 604-606).

[d]From 1965, the figures are for the Labor Alignment (Mapai + Ahdut HaAvoda).

TABLE 5.2   Ratio of Mapai Members (1.0) to Mapai Voters in Different
Types of Elections

Year	Histadrut Elections	Municipal Elections	Knesset
1949-1950	1.3	1.5	2.5
1955-1956	1.6	1.3	1.8
1959-1960	1.5	1.7	2.1
1964-1966	1.7	1.8	2.3

SOURCE: Table 5.1.

table also explains why Mapai — by far the more established among
Israeli parties — could afford not to insist on formal, dues-paying membership during the period under review. Between 1949 and 1965 the total
reported Mapai membership increased three times (see Table 5.1). During the same years, the number of eligible voters in the total population
also increased three times, as shown in Table 5.3.

Most of the real penetration work was carried out by the party-
affiliated organizations, especially the Histadrut. The local party
branches, without too much fuss about formal membership, also organized effectively the relevant groups. These efforts were quite successful because "Mapai bureaucrats and officials sometimes tied the
provision of services to the possession of a party membership card. Or
else, those with instrumental demands came to believe, rightly or
wrongly, that a party card would entitle them to preference" (Medding,
1972: 68). The most important result was that the numerical increase of
Mapai voters approximately followed the voters' population growth in
those years. Note that the relative decline of Mapai in the Knesset in
1955 was also felt in the accompanying municipal elections, but not in the
Histadrut elections a year later. This relative stability and rather high
degree of loyalty underwent a marked change in subsequent years.
Mapai's success in penetrating the social and geographical domains was
due largely to its organizational strategy of extending its network
through institutionalization, redundancy, and overlap. In charge of this
variegated structure and its coordination was a hard core of party
functionaries. They were able to back the leaders on national issues
through their control of the channels linking the center, members of the
party, and loyal voters.[4]

Mapai was the only party in Israel approaching the definition of a
"mass party." The second largest party in 1949 was Mapam (15 percent of
the votes); in 1951, the General Zionists (16 percent) and subsequently
Herut with about 14 percent of the votes. In 1965, Gahal, the joint list of

TABLE 5.3   Comparison of Mapai Membership and Eligible Voters to the
Knesset

	1949 (Base)	1951	1955	1959	1964
Percentage increase in reported Mapai members	100	161	245	277	316
Percentage increase in eligible voters for the Knesset	100	182	209	240	296

Herut and the General Zionists, obtained 21 percent of the votes. This
joint list (later renamed the Likud) grew steadily in subsequent elections
and became the largest list (35 percent) in 1977. Only Herut to some
extent used its membership to increase penetration into the population.
No membership figures for Herut are available, but one could safely
assume that dues were not required for the count, especially because the
rival big party did not demand it either.

For parties like Mapam and Ahdut HaAvoda, formal membership
was not essential because their support was based on the hard core of
members in the kibbutzim. Similarly, in strongly ideological or religious
parties such as the Communist Party, the NRP, and the Agudah parties,
the majority of votes came from loyal supporters. For all practical
purposes, they could be counted as "members." Yet the Communist
Party, for instance, restricted formal enrollment to those carrying membership cards.

Compared to the yishuv period, formal affiliation with the party has
steadily declined in the state pariod. A decrease in the traditional wide-
membership party could also be observed in European socialist parties
(Epstein, 1975: 251). The numbers in Israel in the early 1960s were still
high compared to other democratic countries, but the interest of the
public in being members was waning. Nevertheless, the other instruments of penetration continued to be effective: affiliation with
politicized social and economic organizations mentioned above and
political mobilization through the parties.

MOBILIZATION

Mobilization refers primarily to the role of the party in regulating the
political behavior of society and in drawing a larger volume of resources
from it (Almond and Powell, 1966: 35). Mobilization refers also to the
role of the parties as channels for integrating individuals into the existing

political order (Kirchheimer in LaPalombara and Weiner, 1966: 188-189). The labor parties in Palestine were strongly influenced by the European Communist and Socialist Parties with their tight organizations and wide membership. In certain respects, Mapai resembled machine parties: its patronage was personalistic; the machine was rarely used to influence national policies, especially in critical security affairs; and it proved to be a very effective instrument of political socialization. The parties had a major role in the rapid process of political mobilization of new immigrants as well.

Obtaining the support and, indeed, the commitment of new groups of people was perhaps the most impressive achievement of Mapai and of the Israeli party system as a whole. If parties are primarily instruments of political mobilization within an institutional framework (Huntington, 1968: 402), then Israeli parties have incorporated most members of the population in a relatively short time and maintained their loyalty for a long period. Moreover, the consequences of the mobilization process were not confined to narrow party allegiance. They were also manifested in loyalty to and identification with the broader community, its political system, and ultimately the state. In the mobilization of great numbers of new voters, the parties and their affiliated extensions were helped by others such as the state bureaucrats. But the more difficult target groups from the center's point of view — Israeli Arabs, new immigrants, and Oriental Jews — were penetrated mainly by party channels. Very much like the American political machine, the party did not hesitate to rely on the bait of material rewards (compare Wilson, 1973: 97). Unlike these machines, however, the expected returns exceeded party loyalty. Mobilized members were expected to share the collective efforts during the yishuv period and later to identify with and make personal sacrifices for the state. For example, in 1940 the Jewish Agency and the Va'ad Leumi issued induction drafts for people to join the British Army and local defense units. Formally, there was no compulsory power behind these drafts: People could volunteer for these tasks; they could not be forced to do it. The political network, with the parties as its main channels, was put to work using a combination of national persuasion and social pressure. The response was good, and the volunteers later became the basis for an independent Jewish army (Luttwak and Horowitz, 1975).

After the establishment of the state, Israelis were still willing to be mobilized for collective purposes. particularly for security and defense-related efforts. It was also not uncommon for workers and members of youth movements to contribute working days to kibbutzim, archaeological excavations, or railroad construction in the south. Most of these efforts were organized in those years by the parties and their affiliated extensions. Mobilization was successfully extended to Diaspora Jews (financial support), Israeli Arabs (taxes), new immigrants (military service), and young people (volunteer work). These examples indicate already that such mobilization functions, performed almost solely by the parties in the yishuv and early state periods, were gradually replaced by other channels, notably those of the state. For Mapai and some other Israeli parties with penetrative capacity, such as Herut and the NRP, this entailed a drastic change in orientation. Mobilization had to be justified not on the basis of grand national vistas, but rather on a narrow party appeal: "Vote for us!"

The decline in organizational effectiveness and mobilization capacity did not reduce the holding power of the parties, at least not as far as Mapai was concerned, and not immediately. When the penetration efforts were more or less complete, maintenance took over and enabled Mapai to continue to dominate — not to grow — electorally. The less the mobilization appeal could be based on national and collective goals, the more Mapai and some other parties had to resort to the more conventional functions of maintenance, such as the "structuring of the vote" (Epstein, 1968: 77). It also affected other aspects of penetration not explicitly mentioned so far — recruitment of party leaders and officeholders and of representatives of other social and economic interests.

LEADERSHIP RECRUITMENT

The general issue of leadership recruitment by parties in Israel will not be discussed here (Seligman, 1964; King, 1969; Czudnowski, 1970), except for its implications for penetration and maintenance. In daily activities, the same organizational structure that incorporated new members, socialized them, and secured their votes was also active in recruiting candidates for offices and leadership positions. Insofar as these recruitment activities also represented an effort to incorporate new groups into the political system and enabled them to be represented in the party elite, they are relevant to this discussion of penetration.[5]

During the yishuv period, the selection of men and women for political roles was carried out exclusively by the parties. Indeed, the recruitment for other roles in society, such as pioneers and settlers, was also determined by party affiliations. This practice continued also after 1948 when

> settlers came "from ship to village" and were alloted to settlement federations and therefore to political parties by a political agreement

sanctioned by the State and institutionalized in the administration of the Jewish Agency. The element of free party choice was often entirely absent. [Medding, 1972: 39].

Recruitment was therefore based on partisan and maintenance considerations. Mapai sought to recruit new members from all spheres of society and was willing to pay the price — namely, allocating jobs and positions to representatives of target groups. These were positions in the local party branch, the local workers' council of the Histadrut, the local factory, the municipal bureaucracy, and — much more selectively — the Jewish Agency, state bureaucracy, and party's leadership.

These "representatives" of target groups were usually hand-picked by the party functionaries, and this selection method poses some questions regarding the extent to which they truly represented their respective groups (Czudnowski, 1970). Consequently, recruits such as the heads of the Arab lists affiliated with Mapai and the representatives of development towns or immigrant groups were all loyal party members, but not necessarily supported — at least initially — by their "constituencies."

The same phenomena could also be observed in other parties — for instance, the General Zionists, who attracted voters from the emerging urban middle class, or Herut, which appealed increasingly to the lower classes and to Oriental Jews. In both cases, the leadership of the party remained in the hands of the previous veteran group for a long time and did not reflect the new recruited groups. But the initial social basis of these parties was more narrow to begin with and the resources available for distribution so meager that their recruitment results were only partly successful.

The mode of party operation was to adapt to the social and economic changes taking place in the country and to coopt new groups before they joined the rival party or, perhaps worse, become an independent political threat. New immigrants, ethnic groups, young people, professionals, and even the new circle of industrialists were all actively sought by the parties, primarily by Mapai, under the assumption that they could be better controlled from within. Generosity was displayed in distribution of such resources as preferential treatment, licenses, economic concessions, and government budget allocations. This is not meant to imply that conflict over political power, leadership positions, and other scarce resources did not entail friction. But in the end, the distrubution among parties and within parties was quite effectively controlled.

Like other penetration processes, recruitment also underwent changes during the state period up to 1965.[6] An attempt to consolidate the achievements of penetration was already manifested in the way the list of Mapai candidates for the first Knesset (1949) was constructed. The founding fathers took the helm of the state, but they were careful to nominate representatives of what came to be known in Mapai's *lingua politica* as "strata" *(revadim)* and later "regions" *(mechozot)*. In addition to the veterans, the Knesset list included appointed representatives of kibbutzim and moshavim, army officers, ethnic groups, immigrant associations, professionals, artisans, women, and young people (Seligman, 1964: 70). But the process was stronger than the initial intentions, and recruitment slowly became more decentralized. As the original group of founders slowly disappeared, each "stratum" gained control of the nomination for its candidates — not for the top positions, but for promising springboards. Examples can be found in jobs such as mayors of development towns and local municipalities, the Histadrut central committee, and eventually the list of Knesset candidates, or even deputy-ministers.

Mapai was successful in turning party loyalty, organizational expansion, membership, and political mobilization into a dominant position in the political system. It was also conscious of the need to recruit new leaders who would reflect its wide reach into society. For many years Mapai was, in its own terms, "a party of the center" supported by most social strata and identified with the political center and the state. But in the long run this remarkable success of penetration and maintenance was — or perhaps was destined to be — less enduring. The wider the reach, the more strained the internal fabric woven of controlled recruitment and coalitions. The irony of this development was that the old guard, in order to block the young from taking over, finally edged them out of Mapai in 1965.

The story of the so-called young revolt in Mapai began in the late 1950s. Mapai campaign slogans in those years reveal the prevailing attitude toward the role of young people in politics. They read, "Say yes to the old man (Ben-Gurion)" or "Leave the driving in our faithful hands." The attitude was not much different in other parties, but the generational conflict emerged first in Mapai because it had more to offer and because its "young" members (they were well over 40 by then) felt they had already waited too long. These "young people" had already proved their capabilities in important public jobs before they became active in Mapai. Moshe Dayan was Chief of Staff, Abba Eban was Israeli Ambassador to the United States and the United Nations, and Shimon Peres was Director General of the Ministry of Defence. By the late 1950s, they were ready to take over. They were supported by Ben-Gurion and opposed by all the other prominent leaders of Mapai such as Golda Meir, Levi Eshkol, and Zalman Aran. The young advocated change and new vistas, but the party machinery was stronger, so they settled for cabinet and executive jobs after the 1959 elections. It was in these elections that Mapai (still separated from the other labor parties) reached the zenith of its political power in the Knesset by gaining over 38 percent of the votes.

When Ben-Gurion resigned in 1963, most of these young politicians were threatened again by the older Mapai leaders. They split from Mapai and formed a new party, Rafi. Previous tangible and intangible achievements now had to be split with a new legitimate labor party — whose head was no less than Ben-Gurion himself. In order to stay in power, Mapai had to incorporate a new leadership group right at the top. The split in Mapai and its merger with Ahdut HaAvoda in 1965 (the First Alignment) had many implications, not only for these two parties but for the whole political system, including the role of parties as channels of political penetration into society. In the 1965 elections, Rafi received less than 8 percent. Dayan and Eban were then 50 years old and Peres was 42. This was the end of the most significant "young" revolt in Israeli politics. Rafi joined the national coalition cabinet in the emergency period on the eve of the 1967 war and returned to Mapai (Labor) in 1968.

Mapai did not lose its dominating position in the political system for another decade, but it lost its unique position as "everybody's" party. Penetration by other parties into Mapai's political domain followed soon after. While mobilization and recruitment through party channels started as centrally controlled and carefully coordinated activities, they slowly turned from penetration by the established parties and primarily by Mapai to more democratic representation. The process was gradual, but Mapai's role as the leading channel of penetration started to be shared by other parties and replaced by other channels. Even internally the supremacy of the leaders was weakening. For instance, by 1973 the process of nomination to Labor's Central Committee was already entirely different. The traditional method was always rough but firmly controlled by a small and rather authoritarian nominations committee. In 1973 there were people in Mapai who longed for the old days because, "When Netzer (the boss of the machine) agreed that someone would be on the Central Committee, his word was good — and he did not fiddle with the list afterwards, as was now being done" (Aronoff in Arian, 1975: 31). Externally, groups and organizations started to act independently in the political arena — something that Mapai and indeed all the established parties formerly would not have tolerated.

All in all, throughout the 1950s and the early 1960s, the parties remained the main vehicle for leadership recruitment as well as other penetration functions. The party ladder was still by far the most important channel for anyone interested in reaching all kinds of political positions in Israel. Daalder suggests that

> perhaps the best measure to distinguish the relative hold of party elites on a political system as against that of other elites is to ask how far positions of political influence can be obtained through, as compared to outside, party channels. [in La Palombara and Weiner, 1966: 75].

By this measure, the Israeli political parties, and especially Mapai, have had a firm hold on the political system.

The slow erosion in the penetration capacity of the party channels was due, among other things, to socioeconomic development that freed many groups from the previously strong party grip. In this sense, the penetrative services performed by the parties for the Israeli political system were successful. As will be stressed in the last section of this chapter, most members of the target groups became incorporated into the system, and the parties could concentrate their efforts on maintenance. The initial purpose was to "conquer" the target groups. Subsequently, the purpose turned to continuity and stability. When the parties were strongly identified with the new political system and the state, their maintenance tasks had been much easier to perform. Once the parties — including the powerful Mapai — were more on their own (and could perhaps devote more energy to membership cultivation), the task of even maintaining their own members' loyalty became much more difficult. There were, of course, other external developments that influenced this process, as will be seen next.

Maintenance

Maintenance activities were expressed in the fact that the party channels were used to fortify the common contents of solidarity and to increase the receptiveness and general capacity of the network. I will concentrate next on party efforts to establish and control a feedback mechanism and to coordinate the information flow in the communication network.

FEEDBACK CONTROL

The survival capability of the general political network built during the yishuv period has been rather remarkable, particularly in view of the pressures exerted on it by the establishment of the state and overwhelming external and internal challenges. Upheavals within this structure, such as party splits and mergers, or the growing power of the state bureaucracy and the mass media, did not bring about changes in the political system as a whole. In the period under review, the structure was preserved by virtue of the central holding power of Mapai and its extensions and the rather stable voting patterns that perpetuated the main party divisions — at least until 1965 — which had been shaped in the yishuv. The results of the maintenance efforts of the parties, and especially of Mapai, were successful in broad terms of relative size, power, and significance.[7]

Until the appearance of Rafi in 1965, there was no significant new party in Israeli politics. In fact, with the return of Rafi to the Labor Alignment three years later, this statement remains correct until 1980. The brief emergence of the Democratic Movement for Change (DMC), which received 12 percent of the total vote in 1977 and disappeared afterwards, proves the same point. Israelis used their party affiliation not only for instrumental purposes but also as channels for expressing solidarity and agreement with the prevailing Zionist collective goals: "The Israeli voter tends to use his vote as a symbolic expression of identification with the State and the political system" (Arian, 1971: 8). The role of the parties was even broader than that. They served as channels for expressing comaraderie for groups of ideological supporters or for new immigrants who were not part of other solidarity networks of equal or greater importance (compare Wilson, 1973: 111). A great number of voters surveyed by Arian claimed that identification with the party is more important for them than identification with leaders (1973: 102). The lack of traditional or class "deference networks" in the new Israeli society, as well as the weak communal ties in a society of immigrants, paved the way for the party channels (and for the political communication network in general) to serve as a substitute.[8]

Again, the specific issue of parties as communication channels should be placed in the broader context of the political network discussed in Chapter 4. The political camps in Israel were not subcultures in the way they are in deeply divided societies. Yet they did serve as an anvil for forging the individual's sense of belonging. A new immigrant, from his or her early days in the country, belonged to a party, a labor union, a political camp, and a national state. For some, this was rather confusing and alien; for others, it meant too much belonging. In either case, channels for receiving and transmitting information were indeed available. Not everyone could use them effectively, and not every message was equally well received, yet the mechanism for feedback was there. From the center's point of view, the consoling aspect of this feedback mechanism was the fact that it was centrally controlled. In this respect, the parties performed a critical service for the center in providing it with the means of receiving as well as controlling information.

This is true primarily with regard to the role performed by Mapai and the NRP for the political center during the state period. Their masterful utilization of both vertical and diagonal flows of information made possible the coexistence of central control with relative openness of the Israeli political system. The other labor parties were also instrumental in performing this maintenance task for the center because of their contribution to the widely held values of settlement, collective farming, and security. Other parties performed such roles mainly for the maintenance of solidarity and feedback within their own circles. In doing so, they also contributed to the overall maintenance capability of the political system.

The achievements of political penetration were therefore preserved largely because these same channels also performed the broader service of maintaining solidarity. In this respect the parties in Israel served not only as means for alleviating stress caused by social cleavages (Easton, 1965b: 256-259) but also as effective channels for regulating the flow of demands as well as specific and diffuse support (pp.117-127). They proved capable of performing the function of receptiveness and — until other channels took over — also of controlling feedback.

In Chapter 1, political channels were defined as rather stable communication links that exist independently of particular messages and information. A political party is such a communication agent insofar as it is sufficiently organized so that its structure and hierarchy can serve as channels. The major Israeli parties, particularly Mapai, met these specifications. They possessed the organization and permanence to perform the important mediating role in Israeli politics. Lack of such mediating services is one significant indicator of low political development. Israeli parties, in addition to regulating the flow of messages from elites to nonelites and from authorities to the public, also proved receptive to information generated from below. The redundant organizational structure and the many secondary centers were used as sensors that could receive and send upward information about needs, demands, restlessness, frustration, and disobedience. From the early days of the yishuv, a feedback loop from society, and especially its more distant periphery to the political system, was created.

The strength of the party channels was unrivaled before 1948 because the formal British government could not reach the Jewish population, which by and large obeyed the national institutions and their arms of implementation. After 1948, the national bureaucracy was still weak, and there were more party branches than government offices in many areas. As a result, the party and bureaucratic channels were used simultaneously or alternatively during the early years of the state.

In those early years of Israel, the parties served as the most effective channels for the flow of political information, and their structures were geared to perform this function. Subsequently, the parties were matched, surpassed, and even replaced by other channels. In this respect the fate of Mapai and the other old Israeli parties in the mid-1960s resembles that of European parties:

> The party systems of the 1960's reflect, with a few but significant exceptions, the cleavage structures of the 1920's. . . . The party alternatives, and in remarkably many cases the party organizations, are older than the majorities of the national electorates. . . . The parties which were able to establish mass organizations and entrench themselves in the local government structures *before* the final drive toward maximal mobilization have proved the most viable. [Lipset and Rokkan, 1967: 50-51].

COORDINATION

It is perhaps difficult to envisage a party as a channel of communication such as a telephone. But the technical characteristics of a channel are less important than the question, What is linked, in a relatively permanent connection, by the channel? The political parties in Israel held together the network of center-secondary centers-periphery described in Chapter 4. They also provided the opportunity for vertical, diagonal, and horizontal information flows. Contrary to what is generally assumed about Israeli parties, their most important activity in the political system was not direct command or policymaking. It was their ability to *coordinate* the flow of information and to provide some order to the functioning of the political communication network.

Israeli parties operated in many spheres and succeeded in penetrating almost all segments of society. "Membership" in the political system, to use Easton's phrase, has been almost identical with state citizenship, in terms of a sense of identity, with the notable exception of Diaspora Jews. Moreover, once this initial stage of political development was achieved, the same channels proved to be effective in maintaining high political involvement and securing the stability of the system. Israel's established parties — those taking part in the cabinet, Histadrut, and Jewish Agency — served as coordinating agents, as clearinghouses in the complex and highly divided network of Israeli politics (Galnoor, 1980: 134).

Mapai, for example, was more than just a "gatekeeper" but less than an unquestioned decision center. A gatekeeper is located at critical checkpoints in the political network where it can control the flow of demands and decide what information will be passed, withheld, or rejected (Easton, 1965b: 87, 133-140; Schramm in Smith, 1966: 528; Becker in Chaffee, 1975: 40-41). Mapai was certainly an efficient gatekeeper as far as the regulation of information flow is concerned. But it could control the political agenda not only as an *arbitrator* but also as an *initiator*. Evidence of arbitration roles of Mapai can be found in books and memoirs of party leaders and government officials, such as Zeev Sherf (1959), David HaCohen (1974), Golda Meir (1975), Yitzhak Ben Aharon (1977), Moshe Sharett (1978), Yosef Almogi (1980), Shraga Netser (1980) and Gad Yaacobi (1980). The agenda of many official meetings of Mapai's Central Committee and even the Secretariat listed only one item: "information." Party officials used these forums to exchange information with other officials in order to achieve better synchronization. Around the official structure of Mapai there emerged during the years many formal and informal constellations of functions and leaders whose aim was achieving this coordination. They provided an opportunity for leaders to report confidential information in order to gain support from the party's machinery and, through them, from followers. These gatherings were also used to clear appointments to national posts as well as the Histadrut, party organs, the local authorities, workers' councils, the Zionist organizations, workers' committees, and public corporations (Netzer, 1980: 142). The party formal organs were, of course, occasionally used for decision-making, and some dramatic events in Israeli politics took place there — for example, Mapai's Central Committee decision in 1960 to dismiss Lavon as secretary-general of the Histadrut, or Eshkol's success in getting the center behind him in an open clash with Ben-Gurion in 1965. But usually, and as was pointed out in the beginning of this chapter, functionaries coordinated their activities through informal party channels. Consequently, agreements reached in party forums were binding on the party representatives in other organizations. By providing these channels for information flow, and by getting them to be used by leaders, functionaries, and ordinary members, the parties also created the capacity to coordinate conflicting interests.

Thus, the most important currency in party transactions was information. The evidence provided by Sharett's diaries (1978) shows that party channels were used regularly to share and screen sensitive information regarding national or party affairs.[9] Most of these exchanges were confidential, unless leaks occurred — and these were often deliberate (Galnoor, 1975). This complex structure of interlocking channels was

designed to keep different groups under one roof, to keep a watchful eye
on what goes on within the political system (gatekeeper role), and to
serve as the principal coordinating agent with regard to resource distribution (clearinghouse role). Moreover, Mapai's political effectiveness
was organizational — support was secured by capturing and maintaining
control of the executive bodies of other organizations in order to coordinate their policies with those of the party. It sought to "surround itself
with a network of supporting interest groups, institutions and executive
bodies that provided more permanent and assured backing" (Medding,
1973: 19).

The existence of a party system in Israel that was dominated by
Mapai for a long time did not preclude competition. The process of
political integration in Israel was not undermined by the fact that each
party established separate communication channels, because of the
influence of common contents discussed in Chapter 3 and because of the
existence of dominating channels. Furthermore, the national political
system and the national identities associated with it gradually took over
and enabled competition to be "delegated" to the sub-national level
(Lipset and Rokkan, 1967: 4).

Competition was fierce within each party and each camp because of
their federative structure. Here the coordinating impact of the party's
internal organization and hierarchy was felt most strongly. In addition,
there was competition between parties, and not just during election
times. Control of resources by the political center forced parties to
secure access to these resources. Again, competition was largely regularized as the parties substituted agreed coordination for unstructured
and open conflict. There was a tacit understanding that competition is
allowed with regard to marginal increments and not about the basic
distribution of political resources, because an open conflict could easily
turn into a disintegrating force. The party key was actually a series of
hard bargains that became accepted arrangements among Mapai, the
other parties, and the secondary centers to allocate to each an agreed
share of the various political resources. Despite numerous crises, these
arrangements worked and remained in force for a long time.

In reviewing the role of the political party system in Latin America,
Scott comes to the conclusion that it not only failed to resolve the crises
of rapid change but actually aggravated them: "Instead of providing an
infrastructure that could assist a smooth flow of political activity, such
parties block the upward and downward flow of communications and
interfere with easy interaction among regional, class, and functional
interest groups" (in LaPalombara and Weiner, 1966: 339). In stark con-

trast with this, the Israeli party system was geared toward facilitating information flow and hence toward political development. In this respect, Mapai's role as a central channel of communication resembles the devotion of the Communist Party in the Soviet Union — to organization, coordination, and mobilization of the masses (Pool, in Pool et al., 1973: 465). However, Mapai's extensions were not similar in spirit or organization to Communist Soviets, nor did they enjoy the same degree of monopoly. They had to compete with other parties and associations and operate in a relatively open democratic system.

Despite the political cohesiveness of the yishuv community, there was an opposition, and there were always a number of outspoken critics who said everything that was on their minds. For example, during the late 1920s and early 1930s, Brit Shalom was a small group of Jewish intellectuals devoted to finding a peaceful compromise between Jewish and Arab nationalism. It advocated the establishment of a binational state with political equality for Jews and Arabs, irrespective of their actual numbers in the present or the future. Such ideas were strongly rejected by the Zionist parties and leaders.

This tradition of tolerance continued, by and large, after the state was established and, perhaps more markedly so, as formal guarantees were given for the right to criticize the established system, the parties, and the leaders out of ideological, religious or personal convictions. During the state period, the Volunteers' Group (Shurat Hamitnadvim)[10] and the weekly *Haolam Hazeh* (see Chapter 7) represented two entirely different dissenting groups. The latter became established when it ran as a party for the 1965 and 1969 Knesset elections and obtained one and two seats, respectively. The Canaanites group (see Chapter 3) is another example of dissent that was tolerated even though its impact was more strongly felt in literary circles rather than political ones. After 1967, the phenomenon of independent, nonestablished groups became more common, and their opposition to the established communication network was much more significant politically (Sprinzak, 1973). Nevertheless, groups and organizations that were not linked to the network through the established channels continued to be outsiders.

The notion that parties have central social functions to perform — especially in serving as channels for penetration and maintenance — was widely shared. In the early days of the state, there was an ideological commitment to reach all members of society and to coordinate all domestic activities through the ruling parties and their affiliated extensions. Between the new state bureaucratic apparatus, the parties, and the other official organizations, there was little room for independent social agencies. But soon enough the general trend of social and political development pointed in a different direction (Sharett, 1955). Day-to-day events took over, and the roles of the parties started to change.

The overall maintenance function in the Israeli political system was performed primarily by Mapai. The other parties had to penetrate the new social groups in order to retain their share in the electorate, but they were less concerned with maintaining the overall system. They could afford to embark on direct attacks on the system and, in particular, its dominant party, with each party taking a different role.

After a brief period in 1948-1950 when the Soviet Union supported Israel, the Israeli Communist Party offered total opposition to the political system and to Mapai. Herut came next, with almost total opposition but carefully sparing the IDF and some other widely shared common contents. The General Zionist Party mainly attacked the economic system and the bureaucracy, thereby gaining a great deal of support in the 1951 elections. Mapam, the second largest party in 1949, concentrated on ideological debates, with fierce opposition to government foreign policy and to Mapai's concessions to the religious parties. Yet Mapam was part of the labor camp and the Histadrut, and it did support the system per se and labor dominance. In fact, Mapam fought for further strengthening the system and accused Mapai of relaxing its stands on socialism and a controlled economy. The split within Mapam and the appearance of a third labor party, Ahdut HaAvodah, in the 1955 elections moderated this kind of opposition as well. Both parties joined the coalition cabinet headed by Mapai in 1956 and remained partners, with short intervals, ever after. The NRP and the smaller Progressive Party were Mapai's constant partners and supporters of the existing political system.

Mapai's maintenance efforts were also expressed in its retention of certain key portfolios in the cabinet until the wall-to-wall coalition of May 1967. It monopolized the most important ministries — defense, finance, and foreign affairs — and frequently retained during this period the following portfolios: education and culture, police, and labor. The Progressive Party controlled the justice ministry: the NRP was generally responsible for the ministries of interior, religious affairs, and social welfare. As such, all these parties had a share and took an active part in performing the penetration and maintenance roles for the system as a whole. In addition, maintenance was greatly enhanced by Mapai's near-monopoly on the common contents and political symbols, as reviewed in Chapter 3.

Despite the many attacks from other parties, Mapai remained dominant and the stability of the political system was secured for a long period, indicating that the party's channels successfully performed their role in this respect.

The Parties and the Target Groups

There are a number of reasons for accrediting the parties as the most important channels of communication in the Israeli political system — certainly in the yishuv but also in the state period. First of all, the parties were involved in the penetration and maintenance activities with regard to all seven peripheries identified in Chapter 4 as the target groups. In particular, they were involved extensively and rather successfully with regard to the following four groups — Israeli Arabs, Diaspora Jews, new immigrants, and Oriental Jews (on the latter, see Lissak, 1969: 69-76). Israeli Arabs were reached through the establishment of parties, which, with the exception of the Communists, were affiliated with the Jewish parties. The main organizations linking Israeli and Diaspora Jews continued to function on the basis of a similar party key that operated in Israeli domestic politics. New immigrants were reached by the parties and responded as expected by distributing their votes more or less according to the existing political divisions. And parties were the main vehicle for political mobilization and leadership recruitment of Oriental Jews as well.

Groups that were potentially "outsiders," such as the ultra-orthodox Jews, once they decided to join the political system, did so through the best instrument available — setting up their own political parties. Observant Jews who were Zionists secured their interests by making their religious party part of the political center. The parties did penetrate the target group of young people, mainly through the youth movements, but by the late 1950s the meaning of this penetration was already problematic, as described in Chapter 4. In any case, young people did not pose a threat to the political system, and their tacit support was well maintained. The parties also enjoyed full support and legitimation from the growing numbers of "nonpolitical" people who nevertheless participated in elections and did not much change their vote distribution.

Second, the mobilization and recruitment into parties meant incorporation into the political system. Despite the great number of parties, lists, and factions and the many splinters and regrouping within the parties, the overall party system was stable. In the first six elections, between 1949 and 1965, the number of lists running for elections fluctuated between 14 (in 1961) and 24 (in 1959). But only 11-15 lists won enough votes to gain seats in the Knesset. Among the parties represented in the Knesset, only three to five had more than 10 seats and only one (Mapai) had more than 20 seats throughout this period (see Table 2.8). The parties preserved the common political contents upon which the system was established, and, with some insignificant exceptions in the early years of the state, there was no attempt to overthrow the government or to question its authority.[11]

Third, overall development of the Israeli political system was carried out or assisted by the parties. In this respect, the role of the Israeli parties resembles that of European parties in the nineteenth century. Competition between the parties did not impair the supremacy of the national system of government (Lipset and Rokkan, 1967: 4). Cultural and territorial resistance to penetration of the periphery in the Israeli case was not very strong compared to that in other places. Yet other problems, such as the need for standardization of political rules, the great variety of alliances, or the fierce competition over political resources, were equally challenging in Israel.

Fourth, the parties, as the strongest political factors in the system, did not develop into isolated centers of power. Rivalries and ideological differences notwithstanding, competition was structured. The institutional framework proved strong enough to enforce certain accepted rules of the political game. More important perhaps was the fact that the Communist Party was the only one that was left out of the political network and the arrangements for the distribution of resources. (It has remained legal, however, even during the most strained periods in the relationship between Israel and the Soviet Union.) All the other parties served as channels leading to the political center — not necessarily to the executive branch or the cabinet. Those parties not in the cabinet coalition were in the Histadrut, and those out of both — such as Herut for many years — were included in the Jewish Agency. All parties honored the election law and took part in the work of the Knesset, and there was not even one case in which a party boycotted the Israeli parliament. In this respect, the system performed better in the state period than in the yishuv, where withdrawals from and boycotts of the voluntary institutions were common.

Fifth, the parties could serve as channels of communication because they were engaged in more than just politics. In addition to serving as channels for the system as a whole, the parties were mini-networks for their different camps and secondary centers and the latters' extensions. Their penetration efforts combined social, cultural, economic, and political persuasion. There were major differences between the parties in this respect. The labor and religious parties were better organized and developed a more extensive and powerful network of affiliated extensions. The appeal of parties such as the General Zionists and Herut was more political, even though they, too, had affiliated extensions. Within such a crowded network there was little room for truly independent channels such as voluntary associations or unaffiliated interest groups.

This is one of the main reasons why, until 1965, the electoral power of the labor and religious parties was relatively more stable and that of the civic parties subject to more fluctuations (see Table 2.8 on election results). Ultimately, social and economic developments in Israel freed increasing numbers of people from the grip of the dominating parties. As the number of unaffiliated people increased, so did the significance of the floating vote. These were the people who started to vote for "pure" political reasons — that is, without belonging to a particular camp or party. In the long run, such a trend worked against the dominance of the more organized parties.

Finally, political development is enhanced by political stability. The existence of Mapai as a dominating party and a chief channel of communication helped both development and stability.[12] The success of Mapai is linked to its position in the secondary centers of the labor camp (see Chapter 4). Mapai's channels were intertwined with those of the Histadrut and, later, with those of the state bureaucracy and certain mass communications media. In addition, there were the federations of kibbutzim and moshavim, youth movements, sports clubs, extensions abroad, affiliated Arab parties, immigrants' associations, and coalition agreements with other parties. Mapai created a complex network that made its own coordinative function absolutely necessary.

The decline of the parties and especially of Mapai as indispensable prime channels started, in fact, with the establishment of the state, when more universalistic standards of democratization, professionalization, and service distribution became operative in many areas. The remarkable maintenance power of the parties is reflected in the fact that the previous mode continued to dominate well into the 1960s and is still strong in certain respects in the 1980s. However, once the possibility of utilizing nonparty channels such as the bureaucracy and the mass media became feasible, individual and group independence from party domination was only a matter of time (Epstein, 1975: 251). In due course, channels such as interest groups, corporations, mass movements, and ethnic groups made their political debut.

NOTES

1. Sartori (1970: 1048) discusses the communication functions of parties and the need to analyze party systems as mechanisms for sustaining and pressing demands all the way through to policy implementation. He also points out that there are structural alternatives to parties (see also King, 1969).

2. This was part of the Emergency Regulations issued in August 1948, and it required outgoing Israelis to obtain no fewer than six permits from various authorities before applying to the Ministry of Interior. The regulation stated that because of the emergency, "exit permits will be given only in extraordinary cases" (*Official Newspaper*, No. 17, Provisional Government, August 25, 1948). The language of the regulation was not changed until 1961, when a new regulation required only a permit from the IDF as a prerequisite for leaving the country.

3. Arian shows that among Labor voters, Histadrut membership is the best predicting variable in national elections (1973: 55).

4. For a historical survey of the development of the party machinery, see J. Shapira (1975: 150-163) and for some controversial conclusions of its impact on Israeli democracy (1977: 127-141).

5. For a survey of political elite and national leadership in Israel, see Gutmann and Landau (1975); on recruitment for local government, see Weiss (1973).

6. On the methods of selecting party candidates for the Knesset during the state period, see Brichta (1977: 103-179).

7. On the situation in the right-wing parties, see Nachmias (1976); and on the religious parties, see Schiff (1977).

8. On the role of "deference communities" and "deference networks" in nineteenth century England, see Moore (1976).

9. For example, the debates on whether Hillel Dan (a party official) could be both the head of Solel Boneh (a Histadrut company) and the government Reparation Company (Vol. 1, 259); the party Political Committee is briefed about the content of the coalition negotiations with other parties (Vol. 2, 15); the party caucus of top leaders (Haverenu) is informed of the secret intelligence fiasco in Egypt in 1955 (Vol. 3, 731); a clash between party and Histadrut officials over economic policy (Vol. 6, 163); demands of the party Secretariat to be the final deciding forum in foreign affairs and security matters rather than the party External and Security Committee (Vol. 7, 2050).

10. Shurat Hamitnadvim was a group of young academicians who devoted their time to educational activities among new immigrants on a volunteer and nonbureaucratic basis. They subsequently took upon themselves the job of raising the work ethic and the war against corruption. Between 1954 and 1957 they became involved in a number of lawsuits against a deputy-minister and a high police officer (Sharett, 1978: 54, 66, 1997-1998: Y. Gutman, 1980: 100-115).

11. In September 1948, Earl Bernadotte, U.N. Mediator for Palestine, was assassinated in Jerusalem by an unidentified Jewish underground group. Consequently, the Lehi and Etzel organizations and the right-wing Homeland Front (Hazit Hamoledet) were banned by order of the Provisional Government. In 1953 the restitution agreement with West Germany caused a deep division in the population, and violent demonstrations threatened to prevent the debate in the Knesset.

12. Israeli parties shouldered the development of the political system in all four problem areas identified by La Palombara and Wiener: national integration, legitimacy, political socialization, and conflict management (1966: 399-435). The other areas, access and participation, related to *democratic* political development, will be discussed in Chapters 9 and 10.

6

CHANNELS: THE BUREAUCRACY

> For when we speak of penetration "demands" or "requirements" we
> generally refer to the *effective presence* of a central government
> throughout a territory over which it pretends to exercise control.
> (LAPALOMBARA, 1971: 207)

The role of public bureaucracy is rule application. The literature on
public administration shows that the bureaucracy is also involved in
rule-making and even in rule adjudication (Self, 1972). We find very little,
however, on the communication function performed by the bureaucracy
for the political system. The context in which this topic arises is that of
traditional societies, modernization, and development (Riggs, 1964).
For instance, the study of "nonbureaucratic behavior" of public
bureaucracies in non-Western societies shows the existence of particularism in the treatment of different individuals (Blau and Scott, 1962;
Katz and Danet, 1973a). Such studies also suggest that public bureaucracies perform many different roles for their respective political systems, as evidenced by the special relationship between the bureaucracy
and the press in Western countries (Sigal, 1974: 131-147). In addition to
providing a link between the political leaders and the various publics in
the regions and localities, the bureaucratic hierarchy also serves as the
internal channels *within* government. It is a lifeline of communication
which "holds the entire government structure together and makes
possible coordinated implementation of policies and mobilization of
societal resources" (Almond and Powell, 1978: 146).

The Bureaucracy as a Channel

The bureaucracy is an official channel designed to link the political center and the periphery. Political development requires differentiation in political roles and institutions, extension of the activities of the center, and permeation of these activities into different spheres and regions of society. (Eisenstadt, in LaPalombara, 1963: 99). Central institutions such as the executive are not the only ones that "centralize," and parties are not the only organizations whose units or bureaus can serve as extensions. Bureaucracy is also an obvious candidate for both centralization and extension — that is, for performing maintenance and penetration functions on behalf of the political center.

Bureaucracy denotes organization, hierarchy, order, and a regularized flow of information (Downs, 1967: 241; Nadel and Rourke in Greenstein and Polsby, 1975: 374-390). In this respect the bureaucracy has several advantages over political parties. Parties are more suitable to perform the "input" (toward the center) and the bureaucracy, the "output" (toward the periphery) function in the polity. Both institutions can do either, but the bureaucracy (including the military) has the initial advantage because it is more "government" than other institutions. Parties are modern institutions, most suitable to cope with *mass* politics. Where we find parties we also find some reference, real or symbolic, to participation. Bureaucracy, on the other hand, is an old institution that proved essential for many different kinds of political systems. Bureaucracies can operate not only without parties but also without any regard to the function of aggregation of interests. As far as bureaucracies are concerned, the public interest can be defined entirely from above, and institutions such as parties, interest groups, or the press are expendable. Parties, on the other hand, can encroach upon and usurp the roles of the bureaucracy, but they cannot do without it altogether. Even in totalitarian regimes the party bureaucracy needs the officialdom of the state bureaucracy.

The bureaucracy is a natural agent of the polity and its center because it can serve all parts and branches of government. It is an execution and implementation device for the executive branch as well as for the judiciary and the legislative branches. The bureaucracy can obtain support from both the general public and the more restricted publics that depend on the bureau's services and regulation. Even in single-party systems, the task of delivering services has not been completely assumed by the party, and there is some competition between the party and the bureaucracy.

The bureaucracy's ability to play a critical role in nation-building, social integration, and socioeconomic development may lead to its supremacy, including taking over rule-making. In countries ruled by a civilian or military bureaucracy, the growth of other institutions, such as legislatures and political parties, was clearly inhibited (Riggs, 1963: 126). It affects also the steering capacity of the political system as a whole. When the bureaucracy is the most viable institution in the system, capable of exercising leadership, this has implications for *democratic* political development (to be discussed in Chapters 9 and 10). A probable "winning combination" for political development is the institutionalization of both parties and bureaucracies. Huntington explains the existence of a relatively stable, effective, and democratic government in India as a consequence of the existence of two highly developed, adaptable, complex, autonomous, and coherent institutions — the Congress Party and the Indian Civil Service (1968: 84). In Israel, this winning combination was perhaps even more evident because, among other reasons, the dominating party was somewhat less dominating and especially because the bureaucracy was less powerful.[1]

What are the characteristics of the bureaucratic institution that enable it to perform as a communication channel? LaPalombara views the public sector, particularly the bureaucracy, as an independent variable that influences social, economic, and political development (1963: 4). Without a group of officials who can handle the practical aspects of the collective efforts — for example, the acquisition of typewriters for typing government announcements — there is no politics.[2] The existence of a bureaucracy whose main task is to perform administrative functions marks the beginning of the structural differentiation required for political development. Next are the tasks that only a "public" organization can perform because they require some degree of legitimacy and "officialism." It is usually easier for the political center to use "professional" bureaucrats to collect taxes, to enforce court rulings, or even to establish a network of informers. Bureaucrats perform nonpersonalized roles. Their encounters with individuals have an air of objectivity — of being "instrumental" rather than "expressive" (Katz and Danet, 1973b: 668). They intervene, execute, speak for, and are accountable to the authorities. Even where real power is in the hands of an oligarchy, a military junta, or a party, the bureaucratic device is both expedient and effective. In short, political penetration can be carried out efficiently by the bureaucracy regardless of the type of regime and the motivation behind it. A system embarking on political development needs "officials." Agricultural experts who organize marketing cooperatives or policemen are more readily accepted if they are sent from the center and report to the official headquarters. Bureaucrats could also be "officialized" local notables nominated by the government to be village chiefs and collect taxes and graft. While penetration by political parties requires some measure of responsiveness on the part of the citizens, bureaucracies can use coersive means more directly.

The more structured and organized nature of bureaucratic institutions also enables them to perform the maintenance function. The well-known characteristics of "bureaucracy" (with the connotation of red tape) are helpful to the preservation and survival interests of any political system, particularly to its center (unless the challenge to the existing order comes from the bureaucracy itself). The bureaucracy often has an operational interest in stability:

> Public management is a stationary, not an ambulant, business. It is tied to a fixed locus. There must be offices . . . there must be workers . . . there must be space. . . . More important, each office must provide for a physical order of placement for the men of importance [Marx in LaPalombara, 1963: 87].

Bureaucratic channels may contribute to maintenance irrespective of whether there is free access and the population participates in the process. The developmental potentiality of the "bureaus" is in their solid organizational foundations (Downs, 1967: 24-28). As noted, organizations are very effective instruments for the collective enterprise of politics. Organizations with official titles and public funds radiate authority and legitimacy and can be used readily as core channels in the political network. In democratic systems parties usually perform two-way mediating services between the center and the periphery. This determines their strategic position as channels whose forte is the diagonal flow of information (see Figure 1.2 in Chapter 1). Bureaucracies, on the other hand, by definition are channels for vertical flow between the center and the periphery — primarily for implementing public policies, but also for feedback based on intimate interactions with citizens. But as with party channels, there is neither fixed direction of flow in bureaucratic channels nor prescribed content of information. The flexibility of the bureaucratic channel is directly influenced by the flexibility of the network.

Many additional variables intervene in the actual utilization of bureaucratic channels: They could be subject to a downward flow of information (policy execution), to an upward flow (policy initiative); they could also be auxiliary channels to other political or economic organizations. They could reshape the center and become a "ruling bureaucracy" (Fainsod in LaPalombara, 1963: 236-237). In all cases, the role of the public bureaucracy is much broader than administration (Gross, 1964: 241-242). It is simultaneously an instrument of unification and centralization, regulation of the political struggle, absorption and regulation of various demands, political socialization, legitimization of rulers, and political leadership and tutelage (Eisenstadt in La Palombara, 1963: 110-113). The advantage of the bureaucracy as a variegated channel of communication stems from its being capable of performance which is simultaneously "external" (between the polity and society) and "internal" (within the polity).[3] The Israeli bureaucracy is an interesting example of such a variegated channel.

Israeli Bureaucracy

THE YISHUV PERIOD

Israel's path of political development was different than that of other ex-colonial new states. In the first place, its bureaucracy was not the strongest element in the political system and did not present the familiar problem of over-bureaucratization:

> A significant problem in many ex-colonial areas is not that bureaucracy is too weak but that, as a result of the colonial experience itself, the bureaucracy in the post-independence period is the only sector of the political system that is reasonably cohesive and coherent — and able to exercise leadership and power. Where this is true, political parties tend to be ineffective [La Palombara, 1963: 23].

In the yishuv period the bureaucratic apparatus of the official government in Palestine was dominated by British senior officials (D. Arian, 1955: 345-346). Jewish and Arab employees were either professional experts or lowranking clerks. The Jewish community generally did not encourage entering the service of the Mandate government. This part of the bureaucratic history of Israel is irrelevant as far as political development of the Israeli system is concerned, except for the influence of the British legacy in Israel's government, administration, and law.

The origins of Israeli bureaucracy can be located in the autonomous bodies of the Jewish community: national institutions (the Jewish Agency, Va'ad Leumi), parties, Histadrut, and various other organizations. The pattern of Israeli bureaucratic involvement in political development emerged at that time, and the prototype was what Brzezinski and Huntington call "the political bureaucrat" (1966: 144-150; also J. Shapira, 1975: 73).

The dominant positions of party organizations in the political system of the yishuv determined the nature of the bureaucracy within all the other institutions. For instance, J. Shapira describes the fierce battle between party officials and Histadrut officials on the control of economic resources. But since all of them belonged to the party, it was essentially a conflict within the party, to be coordinated by the party machinery. "The Histadrut was an economic organization," notes Shapira, "managed by politicians according to political codes of behavior" (1975: 73). There was no distinction between elected and nominated officials or positions. The Ahdut HaAvoda party openly declared in its platform of 1923 that all party members who work in the Histadrut, the national institutions, the Zionist Federation, the Jewish Congress, and so on are to receive directions from the party center (p. 59). Shapira's conclusion is that there were in fact no professional bureaucrats — in the Weberian sense — only politicians.

A different interpretation is that bureaucratic channels were used because of their official appeal, even though they were monopolized by the parties. In this period the functioning of the dominant political party in the yishuv in many respects resembled Selznick's description of the "combat party" in Communist regimes and its use of the "cadre" for the accumulation of political power (1952: 17-20). This similarity is symbolically expressed in Ben-Gurion's proposal to establish a "Labor Army" *(tsva ha'avoda)* in 1925. He wanted to subject his party to a more disciplined and better structured organization and to turn its members into a dedicated army capable of executing the Zionist-socialist revolution. Yet the fact that he had to make such a proposal and that it was rejected by his colleagues also shows that Ahdut HaAvoda and later Mapai, as well as the other parties, were not full "cadre parties" in the Bolshevist sense. The party was surely used as an organizational weapon, and it did control the bureaucracy and part of the press but did not have total control of individual members. Not only did Mapai, despite its dominance, have to share political power with rival parties, but there were many pockets of autonomy within the party itself.

The result of these interactions during the yishuv period, especially between the bureaucrats in the Histadrut and in Mapai, was not simply that "politics became bureaucratic and not electoral politics" (J. Shapira, 1975: 206), but that bureaucratic channels were fully utilized for both power accumulation and political development. What Shapira ignores is that these political bureaucrats, or bureaucratic politicians, did create a viable political system. In a developmental context, "bureaucratic politics" has a much broader meaning. It means the utilization of organizations for the establishment of the political system and for carrying out the penetration and maintenance functions for the political center. In the voluntary yishuv community, the party — or, more precisely, a coalition of parties — performed the role of the political center. It was these party bureaucrats who were actually engaged in building the political network and using it, naturally, for the accumulation of power.

In Chapter 5 the role of the parties as channels in the yishuv period was presented. Now this role can be further clarified by pointing out that the main burden of information transmission fell on the bureaucrats who served in the national institutions and the many affiliated organizations that were active in the system. Their bureaucracies — including that of the economic, educational, or religious organizations — were coordinated by the party system to forge a consensus and to achieve a rather unique blend of national, sectoral, and party goals.

These were the most important roles of the political-bureaucratic channels during the yishuv period. In addition, certain hierarchies were almost completely transferred to the state bureaucracy. For instance, the Haganah provided the basis for the Ministry of Defence and the IDF, and the Political Department of the Jewish Agency became the skeleton of the Ministry of Foreign Affairs. Similarly, there was continuity in local government, the court system, the police, customs, and the railways. They all provided for the existence of rudimentary links within the emerging network of the infant Israeli political system.

THE STATE PERIOD

In May 1948, the provisional government of the not-yet-declared state had to perform through a nonexistent national bureaucracy. One position paper on "Government Administration in the Hebrew State" had been prepared by a professional committee for the provisional government shortly before independence, but events took over quickly (Sherf, 1959: 42-55). The structure of the top positions in the new administration reflected the existing party coalitions and divisions between the Jewish Agency and the Va'ad Leumi. Sherf, who was in charge of creating the new administration, lamented ten years later:

> It was impossible to appoint the administrators even though the lists were ready, because there were those who discovered that one party or another had been deprived. We were not surprised by party intervention — after all, we were not strangers — but we did not expect that partisan considerations would dominate the national ones, and they did [Sherf, 1959: 113].

The top positions were subsequently distributed according to the party key. Table 6.1 shows the initial distribution of all positions in March 1949.

TABLE 6.1   Distributions of Civil Servants by Their Previous Place of
             Work, 1949

	N	%
British government and army	1,724	34
National institutions	631	12
Public sector organizations	712	14
Labor sector organizations	89	2
Private organizations	1,255	25
Unknown	630	12
Total	5,041	99

SOURCE: Reuveny (1974: 24).

The senior Jewish bureaucrats in the Mandate government by and large were nonpolitical professionals. If those who came from the private sector and the "unknown" categories in Table 6.1 were also nonpolitical, then the percentage of nominations that were directly influenced by partisan considerations reached about 30 percent in 1949, among them most of the higher positions. Fifteen years later, a sample of senior civil servants showed that about 44 percent of them came from the national institutions, government and public corporations, the Histadrut, and organizations of the labor sector (Globerson, 1970: 53).

The bureaucracy grew fast in the early years of the state, and recruitments were made on the basis of what Israelis call *proteksia* (political pull). Senior positions in the various ministries were staffed with loyal party members, usually from the minister's own party. The distribution of civil service positions among the parties resembled other political distributions within the political system (Akzin and Dror, 1966: 14). For instance, in the early years of the state few civil servants belonged to Herut or Communist Parties. On the other hand, parties who took part in the cabinet coalition were fully represented or even overrepresented. Table 6.2 compares the distribution of votes to the Civil Servants' Union in 1953 to that of the preceding Histadrut and Knesset elections.

The competing lists in the elections to the Civil Servants' Union, as to other trade union organizations in the country, were affiliated with the national parties. These delegates acted as representatives of the civil servants before the party and as party representatives in the civil service. Table 6.2 shows that the domination of the labor camp (Mapai plus Mapam) was indisputable in 1953. However, representation of the General Zionists Party, the Progressive Party, and the religious parties in the Civil Service Union is related to the fact that these parties participated in the coalition cabinet in those years. In short, Israeli bureaucracy re-

TABLE 6.2   Elections of Delegates to Civil Servants Union Compared with Histadrut and Knesset Elections (%)

	Civil Servants Union (1953)	Histadrut (1949)	Knesset (1951)
Mapai	57	57	37
Mapam	18	34	13
General Zionists	9	—	16
Progressive Party	9	4	3
Poel Hamizrachi (Religious)	6	2	8
Poalei Agudat Israel (ultra-orthodox)	5	—	2
Arab list	0.5	—	1
Others	1	3	20

SOURCE: for Civil Servants Union, Reuveny (1974: 28).

flected the political reality of the country. It could not correspond precisely to the distribution of Knesset membership, but this was not necessary: the party key was based on an overall balance within the political system as a whole, not in any single organization.

Politicization of the bureaucracy stopped short of being all-encompassing. Under Mapai leadership, the bureaucratic channels, very much like the party channels, had double and triple purposes: simultaneously to strengthen the national system, the socialist movement, and the party. After 1948, the supremacy of the state and its bureaucracy was recognized in areas such as the armed forces, the judiciary, and later also in education, employment, and housing. These were more or less extracted from the party key arrangements as far as recruitment, nomination, and services were concerned (Medding, 1972: 225).[4] Being part of the political system, however, bureaucrats in these fields could not be entirely free from party influences. There is, in fact, some evidence that in the early years of the state, such official organs as the Secret Security Service were used by the ruling party and its leaders against other political rivals (Sharett, 1978: Vol. IV, 993, 1089; Bader, 1979: 75). At the highest levels of the civil service — the cabinet secretary, the chief of staff, the director of the Security Service, and director generals of government ministries — there was intense involvement in party politics (Sharett, 1978: Vol. I, 266; Vol. III, 625; Vol. IV, 987).

Before examining the bureaucratic channels as means of penetration, two facts should be reiterated. First, in terms of numbers per capita, Israeli bureaucracy is large by Western standards and not much different from those in other developing countries. It is fruitless to present comparative numbers because of the different methods of counting "civil servants" and "public officials" in various countries. The bureaucracy in Israel is large because the public sector is large. If one counts all the people employed in Israel in government, government corporations, the Histadrut, the Jewish Agency, local authorities, and the other public organizations, the percentage is high indeed (Barkai, 1964). After the first years of rapid increase, the pace of bureaucratic growth slowed considerably.[5]

Second, the politicization of Israeli society is expressed not only by the existence of a huge public sector, but also by the fact that the polity is directly (through the bureaucracy) or indirectly (through parties and many other nongovernmental public organizations) involved in most economic enterprises as well as in social, cultural, religious, and recreational activities. A traditional Jewish blessing, "May you live to 120 years" is reduced in Israel to 108, allowing for a ten percent government tax on life expectancy. Israelis complain that bureaucracy is everywhere. In 1953-1956, the income tax authority officially published the income declarations of Israeli citizens as a means of putting public pressure on those whose standard of living did not match their modest income declarations. This practice was not continued, but there are areas in which coercive bureaucratic means are used quite blatantly, such as police access to private bank accounts and the right of the bureaucracy to obtain many other types of private information. If specific groups are examined, the level of dependence on the bureaucracy is even higher. For instance, bureaucratic control of Israeli Arabs is still an official policy, coordinated by the special Office of the Prime Minister Adviser on Arab Affairs (Lustick, 1980: 169-197); or new immigrants remain dependent on bureaucratic special services for many years after their arrival in the country (Sharkansky, 1978).

Compared to other Western democratic countries, central government intervention in Israel is both more extensive and more intensive. Under these circumstances, the bureaucracy is well equipped to perform the function of a communication channel: It centralizes by conveying information flows to one center; it crosses social and geographical barriers with service delivery and socioeconomic development; it penetrates target groups through bureaucratic and nonbureaucratic means; and it performs a central role in system maintenance.

Israeli bureaucracy did not fit closely any of Fainsod's five "forms of bureaucracy" classified on the basis of their relationship to the flow of political authority: ruling, military-dominated, ruler-dominated, party-state, and representative. In certain respects, Israeli bureaucracy in the early years of the state resembled the party-bureaucracy relationship of Communist countries, or of other party-dominated political systems in which "the state bureaucracy, where it exists as a distinctive structure, is penetrated, controlled and dominated by the party bureaucracy" (Fainsod in LaPalombara, 1963: 235).

But the Israeli regime was neither totalitarian nor totally controlled by one party. Moreover, Israeli bureaucracy was also "representative" — that is, responsible to the elected leaders who dominated the government of the day and responsive to the needs of the people. This type of bureaucracy is usually also highly professional and divorced from party politics — fully bureaucraticized and impersonal. Yet, again, these traits do not fit the Israeli case well, and we may conclude that it represents a mixed form of bureaucracy.

Penetration

For any political elite, penetration refers to whether they can get what they want from people over whom they seek to exercise power. Such power clearly refers to areas of governmental policy that go considerably beyond taxation, conscription and control of deviant behavior. It would include as well the full range of social welfare activities, programs of animal husbandry, agricultural modernization, shifts in form of productive activities, demographic management, new modes of political participation, and so on. . . . The problem of gaining compliance with such policies refers not merely to geographic subdivisions of a polity, but also to social, ethnic, linguistic, racial and other sub-divisions as well [LaPalombara in Binder, et al., 1971: 209].

The history of modern political systems provides many examples of unsuccessful adaptation of existing political structures to new types of demands and organization. Israel's political development since 1948 seems to be an example of successful adaptation of the yishuv political system to the new requirements posed by the establishment of the state. It is a story of how the voluntary institutions of the yishuv transformed themselves into the state leadership and bureaucracy that managed to absorb the many changes, sustain political growth, and balance demands and policies. Note that the direct penetration of target groups, although also performed by the bureaucratic channels, was more prominent in other channels. In the bureaucracy, the penetration was expressed mainly in *centralization, service delivery*, and, to a lesser extent, in *nonbureaucratic activities* such as socialization.

CENTRALIZATION

"Centralization" refers here to a well-known attribute of the Weberian model of a rational bureaucracy and is crucial for understanding bureaucratic behavior, particularly when placed in a broader context

(Diamant, 1962). Centralization is an attempt to anticipate the impact of conflicting interests and subgoals. It is best performed through the control of information. Otherwise, the free and unstructured flow of information would evoke mutually conflicting behaviors (V. Thompson, 1973: 6). What is the contribution of Israeli bureaucracy to the consolidation of the political center as a locus of control?

Despite all the social divisions of the yishuv community — the multiparty system and the political network characterized by organizational redundancy and overlap — it was clear from the first day that the new state has one government, one army, one police force, and one public bureaucracy — that is, one official political center. The struggle over the unification of the armed forces was violent and threatening, but the outcome was decisive. By 1949, the monopoly of the center on the legitimate use of organized forces was established, and both politically connected military organizations — the Palmach (to the Mapam party) and the Etzel (to the Herut party) — had been disbanded. Since then the IDF has been depoliticized as far as direct intervention of the parties is concerned. Similarly, the national police was established as a centralized force under the civilian supervision of a cabinet minister.

The story of centralizing the civilian services is less well-known, but it is pertinent to the issue of political development. In the domestic civilian spheres, the rules of the partisanship game were established early and rather clearly: Even if a party, a secondary center, or any other organization dominates a particular sphere, activities are performed through and with the relevant government bureaucracy. Consequently, despite its growing complexity, the main organizational channels continued to be coordinated and the flow of information directed to the parties' clearinghouses and the governmental decision centers. For instance, agricultural development was dealt with both by the Ministry of Agriculture and by the Settlement Department of the Jewish Agency. In 1951-1952, Levi Eshkol served simultaneously as Minister of Agriculture and head of the Settlement Department. He established a joint Center for Agricultural and Settlement Planning and formed a personal, as well as a formal junction for bureaucratic coordination (Akzin and Dror, 1966: 51-52). Such arrangements could also be found in other areas, but in all instances, the bureaucracy played the role of official channel. As the political system continued to develop, the state bureaucracy took over some roles of the parties and other organizations. Policy-making functions, for instance, were gradually taken over by the Ministry of Agriculture, rather than the Jewish Agency Settlement Department. But this came much later and is not within the scope of this study.

Absorption of the new civilian state-bureaucracy into the existing network was not accomplished without friction. Solutions varied from area to area, but in no case was the state bureaucracy completely left out. The process was easier when previous national institutions became the basis for a new ministry, such as when the Va'ad Leumi's social services became the Welfare Ministry. The Histadrut posed a different problem because it represented only part of the population, yet in certain areas it possessed the strongest economic and social organizations. Three important areas dominated by Histadrut organizations in the yishuv period were health services, water supply, and construction (mainly public works). All three areas can serve as illustrations of the bureaucratization process because they were candidates to become state services located in the respective ministries. The Histadrut tried to retain its domination in these areas, and a fierce struggle ensued. The details of the struggle are not relevant here, but the outcomes serve as examples of three different solutions with important implications for bureaucratic centralization.

(1) *Health*. Kupat Holim, the Histadrut General Sick Fund, provided services to more than 80 percent of the Jewish population. It retained the lion's share of medical services in the country, while the new Ministry of Health became a policy and coordination umbrella organization. This was a major victory for the Histadrut, although it was forced to relinquish control over schools and the labor exchange offices. In fact, health services were not transferred to the state because Histadrut members were recruited and retained through membership in the Kupat Holim.

Mapai and the other labor parties could afford to hand over the labor exchanges to the state, but not the health services, for this would have removed the basis of Histadrut membership and their general support. Another reason was that the other contenders were weak and could not force Mapai to nationalize Kupat Holim and give up its major and ultimately its only means of direct recruitment. Namir, Secretary-General of the Histadrut, is reported to have said that Kupat Holim was the secret behind the strength of the Israeli labor movement (Medding, 1972: 235). For these reasons, Kupat Holim remained the only case where Histadrut and not state bureaucrats performed the direct penetration function with respect to all target groups except Diaspora Jews.

(2) *Water*. In this area, the situation was entirely different (Galnoor, in Bilski et al., 1980: 137-215). Water development in the yishuv period was in the hands of the Settlement Department of the Jewish Agency and the Mekorot Company — founded in 1938 and jointly owned by the agency and the Histadrut. In 1948, the new Ministry of Agriculture took over responsibility for water affairs, but Mekorot remained the most important organization in charge of construction, operation, and maintenance of the water plants and licensing of water users. Water

resources are nationalized in Israel, and on the basis of the Water Law of 1959, Mekorot was authorized by the government to be the "state water authority," responsible for supplying 80 percent of Israel's water. Members of the opposition parties demanded that Mekorot be transferred to the state in order to prevent Histadrut control of water. But the fact that the bureaucracy in both the Agriculture Ministry and Mekorot was dominated by the agricultural sector (affiliated with the labor parties) enabled a special kind of division of labor.

As far as the periphery was concerned (for example, new settlers), there was little difference between officials of the Agriculture Ministry and Mekorot when they carried out their guidance tasks. Compared to the health services, however, centralization in water affairs was complete, despite the pivotal role played by a nongovernmental company. The water institutions established a direct channel between the influential agriculture sector and the political center. Anyone who wanted to join this sector had to become a member of one of the various organizations and to comply with centralized planning and control of land, water, and crops. There was only a handful of non-organized farmers in Israel, and noncooperative "private agriculture" was relatively small. In our terminology, since the previous agricultural bureaucracy had no difficulty in penetration, it could absorb the new ministry with little effort and concentrate on reaching and maintaining the new settlers in agriculture.

(3) *Construction and public works.* This is yet another case of a state-Histadrut relationship after 1948 (Dan, 1963: esp. 208-210; Daniel, 1972). Solel Boneh was established in the 1920s as a public works company aimed at providing employment for Histadrut members. Unlike the organizations in the other two examples discussed above, it gradually became less of a public service organization and more of a profit-making company. Yet, like all other Histadrut enterprises, it was also political.

By 1948, Solel Boneh was not the exclusive company in its field, but it was by far the major one. Like other yishuv organizations, it strived to retain its dominance, and the only way to achieve this was to gain some form of official position and state legitimacy. In 1949, Solel Boneh made its bid for an official position and lost it. Instead, a Bureau of Public Works was established in the Ministry of Labor and became the official construction office of the government.

Solel Boneh failed to become the official construction authority of the new state because it operated in a field where there was powerful competition with other organizations and interests. Second, it was already involved in many economic ventures in Israel and abroad, some of them in cooperation with private capital, and this detracted from its potential as a public trustee. But third and most important, Solel Boneh did not enjoy full support from the Histadrut and from labor leaders in its attempt to obtain official status. As its former director testified, Histadrut leaders did not back the company because it was too independent and did not represent a sector or a definite "constituency" of workers (Dan, 1963: 209).

Thus, while Solel Boneh was an indispensable economic extension of the Histadrut, its direct political value — and potential for penetration — were smaller compared to other affiliated organizations. Its economic strength and independence also made it a valuable source of power, but also a difficult partner in a network closely coordinated by the party and the Histadrut.

These three examples indicate that the political system of the new state in 1948 absorbed some of the yishuv bureaucracy and not vice versa. The Israeli public administration evolved into an existing network and in most areas became an integral part of it. The new Israeli bureaucracy posed no threat to the political system. It did not become an agent of political upheaval. Despite the bureaucracy's considerable power and the inevitable friction that resulted from redundancy and overlap, interbureaucratic conflicts did not become the main form of politics in Israel. The political process was not exogenous, taking place outside the bureaucratic setting. On the contrary, it occurred with the top bureaucrats as full participants. The main contribution of the bureaucratic channels in terms of centralization can be summarized in five points:

- The bureaucracy served as an effective means for monopolizing official power and for establishing tight control over other potential contenders, such as local authorities or nonestablished political groups.

- It enabled further politicization of the society and consequently the bureaucratization of public services so as to increase the dependence of the periphery on the center and the secondary centers.

- The bureaucracy, more than any other institution, enabled the Israeli political system to turn organizational redundancy "from 'liability' to 'reliability' " (M. Landau, 1969: 346)

- In a political system with a strong ideological bent and an urgent need to sustain the political common contents, it was the bureaucracy which enabled coexistence between the ideological imperatives and the day-to-day requirements of planning and policy implementation (Bilski et al., 1980: 86).

- The bureaucratic channels were also operative in the penetration of target groups, but in most cases they were cooperating with other channels. Thus, government bureaucrats and party officials participated in the penetration efforts directed toward the new immigrants and Oriental Jews. In the case of Israeli Arabs, the local civilian bureaucrats executed the policy determined by the military government and the political parties.

The existence of a subordinated bureaucracy removed a great burden from the ruling parties. Coordination was easier because the bureaucratic channels could be trusted to handle the routine flow satisfactorily and to refer complicated matters to the proper political "switchboard." Thus, the bureaucrats in the various ministries did not require detailed instructions from the political center or the party in order to know what to do. They were directly in touch with the relevant groups and with the party-affiliated organizations operating in their fields. This is exactly the way a channel functions, and information flows vertically, diagonally, and horizontally.

The combination of party and bureaucratic channels proved to be effective initially for the steering capacity of the center and for the development of the political system as a whole. The centralization task of the Israeli bureaucracy was also facilitated by the lack of significant geographical barriers that would have posed difficult penetration challenges. In every sphere and for every target group there were actual or potential channels for penetration and maintenance. For instance, in order to solve a housing problem, the new immigrant could try (and in many cases, was obliged) to contact one or more of the following: the Housing Department in the Labor Ministry (later the separate Housing Ministry), the government corporation Shikun U-pituah in charge of housing construction, the joint government and Jewish Agency corporation Amidar in charge of immigrant housing, the Histadrut construction company Shikun Ovdim, a number of municipal housing corporations, and several other offices. In addition to red tape, bureaucratic channels also created opportunities for preferential treatment and spoils. But the important point here is that despite the apparent chaos, these channels reached every citizen and tied him or her eventually to one political center.

SERVICE DELIVERY

Centralization refers to the role of the bureaucracy in channeling information to a recognized official center and the "absorption" of this information by the political system. Other aspects of penetration through the bureaucracy are the delivery of goods and services and regulation. The mere fact that a certain group receives a new public service (for example, disease control or zoning regulation) or that a new group receives an old service (such as adult education or housing loans) is an indication that the political system has penetrated more deeply into society.

In the Israeli political system, the delivery of services served an additional purpose. The bureaucracy did not function only for the purpose of minimizing, controlling, and manipulating demands. In many cases, it *initiated* demands or responded to them with new governmental and public services. The self-image of the Israeli bureaucracy was one of a stimulator of economic and social development (Dror, 1971). For instance, the public bureaucracy played a central role in the revolution in the standard of living that occurred in Israeli society within a short time (Patinkin, 1959; Halevy and Klinov-Malul, 1968; Horowitz, 1967). The control of funds — partly raised abroad — enabled the Israeli public sector to play an "imperialistic" role in developing services, encouraging private enterprise, establishing companies and organizations, controlling the internal financial market, and numerous other undertakings. The net result of all this hyperactivity was that almost no one remained outside the political system as far as regulations and benefits were concerned. It also meant a high degree of dependence on the bureaucracy and the political center. As long as a person, a group, or an organization was willing to use the existing channels for presenting demands, their chances for partial or full satisfaction were better than of those who preferred nonestablished routes. This was equally true with regard to the establishment of a car industry or of the Israel Opera. Both these entirely different enterprises were heavily subsidized with public funds for many years.

Obviously, there were marked differences in the extent and quality of services delivered to different groups. The point here is not equality, but methods of penetration. It is impossible to generalize about the way the bureaucratic channels were used to reach the entire population and specific target groups. For the ultra-orthodox groups, for example, direct intervention of the central bureaucracy in their daily lives was out of the question. Because of their political bargaining position and effective independent organizations, these groups could mobilize a great deal of money from the public funds. They had their own housing companies, loan associations, and bank, not to mention an autonomous school system (Schiff, 1977: 138). In an entirely different way, but also due to organizational prowess, the kibbutz and moshav movements enjoyed autonomous status. In such cases, the services provided through government bureaus did not reach individual members directly. These were guaranteed services rendered collectively to well-organized groups and their recognized organizations. In principle, every group could enjoy such status — not immediately and not to the same extent, but the principal method was cooptation and penetration, not rejection. With regard to Israeli Arabs, a combination of party, military, and bureaucratic channels was used. For Oriental Jews, a mix of bureaucratic and party channels was in operation.

Israeli bureaucracy at that time did not conform either to the Weberian rational model nor to the "bureaucratic" one, in the pejorative sense — that is, a maze of impersonal offices. There was a mix of central control and service orientation; of overconformity and debureaucratization; of local initiative and independent behavior coupled with erratic responses to immediate pressures (Bar-Yosef and Schild, 1966). This flexible mode of operation served the steering needs of the political system very well. The government sanctioned the bureaucracy's use of discriminatory measures, especially in the economic field (Halevi and Klinov-Malul, 1968: 43). But despite differential terms for financing private investments, for example, or direct support given to preferred groups, the most important decisions were *political,* not bureaucratic. There was a great deal of bureaucratic leeway and discretion, but service distribution, among other things, was part of the overall penetration effort of the political center. Here again an extremely wide variety of organizational structures was used: governmental departments, public authorities, government corporations, mixed corporations, and so on. Nevertheless, the bureaucratic maze was closely integrated with the political one (see Chapter 4), and both contributed a great deal to the system's penetrative capacity.

NONBUREAUCRATIC ROLES

> Bureaucracies, it is said, depersonalize relationships; their function is, after all, to routinize behavior. How, then, are communications within bureaucracies and, more particularly, between a bureaucracy and its clients handled? Do bureaucracies retain the capacity to deal with idiosyncratic cases, or do they become entrapped by their own routine? [Katz and Danet in Pool et al., 1973b: 666]

The rather special conditions under which Israeli bureaucracy came into being made many of its activities idiosyncratic in the sense that the "special cases" outnumbered the routine ones. In a society with a pioneering ideology, even the bureaucracy is affected. More important, the burden of dealing directly with what the center regarded as the "difficult clients" (new immigrants and Oriental Jews) fell squarely on the shoulders of public officials. Unlike other new nations or immigration countries, these target groups were not traditional elements or living in remote backward regions. Most of them came or were brought to the country in accordance with the deliberate policy of "ingathering the exiles." There was a widespread commitment throughout society and the political system to help and, in fact, to integrate them. They were the "last remnants" *(she'erit hapleta)* from Nazi Europe or the "lost tribes" from Yemen. All of them were welcomed, and most needed state support. The nonbureaucratic behavior of Israeli bureaucracy stemmed from personal and spontaneous initiative combined with a deliberate policy outlined by the ruling elite which comprised both political and administrative leaders.

Consequently, the bureaucratic channels also carried a vertical flow of information whose content was only indirectly connected with the purpose of officiating, centralizing, and service delivery mentioned above. This information aimed at social tutelage, political socialization, and preferential treatment of the weak groups.

One example of nonbureaucratic and almost counterofficial behavior of Israeli low-ranking bureaucrats is Danet's study of written appeals made to the Israeli Customs Authority in 1959 and 1962 and of the nature of the bureaucratic responses (Danet in Katz and Danet, 1973a: 329-337). The unexpected finding was that there is latent particularism even in such a highly formal organization which has mandatory contacts with clients. Customs officials "gave the underdog a break" — they deviated from the rules to give unemployed Oriental Jews preferential treatment, for example.

In an earlier study, Katz and Eisenstadt (1960) showed that contacts between Israeli officials and new immigrants were nonbureaucratic in the sense that the officials took upon themselves tasks not assigned to them by their organizations. The officials developed a *personal* relationship with the clients as teachers, agents of socialization, and leaders of an incipient social movement. There are stories of a manager of a government-subsidized grocery who went into the homes of new immigrants to teach them how to use new kinds of foods; of bus companies that tried not to change drivers because the drivers knew their passengers personally; of instructors sent by the Settlement Department to teach farming to new immigrants who ended up representing them to the authorities; of officials who, in their zeal to turn new immigrants into full-fledged Israelis, interfered even in matters of religious observance; and of nurses in transitional camps who turned the clinic into a social community center and taught women their rights vis-à-vis their husbands.

Regardless of the impact of such nonbureaucratic behavior, it should be noted that in such tutelage roles, bureaucrats assumed the task of initiating newcomers to the values of the society, including its political culture. The obvious targets were new immigrants in general and Oriental Jewish immigrants in particular. Variations of the same phenomena existed also in the socialization of young people by educators in the schools, by counsellors in the youth movements, and by officers in the paramilitary organizations and the IDF (Lissak, 1971; Luttwak and Horowitz, 1975: 69-70). The more external target groups, on the other hand, such as Diaspora Jews or Israeli Arabs were not subject to these forms of socialization through nonbureaucratic behavior of bureaucrats.

There was still another aspect of this "nonbureaucratic" behavior and usage of the administrative apparatus for collective purposes. Preferential treatment was not denied even when the beneficiaries could not pay off politically, at least not immediately. For instance, the Israeli civil service was used also for the purpose of absorbing new immigrants. They were hired not on merit, but because they needed jobs and the government was one of the major employers in the country. Many of them entered the service not for permanent jobs, but in order to acquire a foothold that would enable them to adapt themselves to the new conditions and learn Hebrew (D. Arian, 1955: 347). As it happened, many stayed on. Thus, in 1953 about 35 percent of all civil servants were new immigrants who came to Israel after 1948 (Reuveny, 1974: 25). Recruitment to the civil service was influenced by partisan considerations as well as by preferential treatment of certain groups, mainly new immigrants of Western origin. It did not, however, have the same effect as the political recruitment of the parties (see Chapter 5).

There were tasks even more fundamental to the development of the Israeli polity and which were part of the penetration activities performed by the bureaucracy. The parties mobilized politically, while the bureaucracy mobilized civically — to obey the courts, to pay taxes, to become soldiers — and socially — to send their children to school or to obtain a preventive vaccination. These were also "political" activities in the broad sense because they were performed in Israel by the state (bureaucracy) and required using the services of an official bureau. The result of these extensive mobilization activities carried out by the bureaucracy was the incorporation of many relevant target groups into the political system.

The Israeli bureaucracy performed many tasks and did not become a "ruling bureaucracy." Just as the parties absorbed immigrants, the public administration absorbed professionals, representatives of various sectors, army officers, and academics without any radical change in its functioning within the system. By demonstrating nonbureaucratic traits, Israeli bureaucrats showed a strong commitment to the common social goals, including that of extending and maintaining the political system. In the short run, these efforts also served the existing regime and the dominant party, but in the long run they were a service to the development of the system as a whole.

Maintenance

The maintenance roles of the parties and especially Mapai were described in terms of fortifying solidarity, increasing receptiveness, and establishing and controlling the feedback mechanism. It was also noted that maintenance requires additional kinds of information. The purpose of the maintenance activities performed by the bureaucracy is broader: the stability and continuation of both the political and social order. During the yishuv period, the central holding power of Mapai contributed to these broader functions. The Israeli parties were well-organized and sufficiently stable to serve as the most important channels. In 1948, the infant state bureaucracy could hardly compete with the predominance of the party system. But once the state was established and the party system started to weaken, more and more of the maintenance burden fell on the bureaucracy.

In a democratic system, by definition bureaucracy is better suited to perform the overall maintenance function. In Israel, too, the bureaucracy slowly emerged as a full partner in the communication network and eventually as the senior one in certain key areas. Feedback control and coordination remained in the hands of the parties, but direct contacts with the periphery and especially with the target groups increasingly became the task of the state bureaucracy. The most important maintenance roles of the bureaucracy can be described in terms of strengthening of the state through official symbols, structural preservation, recruitment, and control of public information.

It was Barnard who first drew attention to the existence of a maintenance function in every organization and who stressed the task of the executive in developing and maintaining a system of communication (1938: 226). Downs listed among the functions performed by the bureaucracy the "maintenance of government itself" and the "creation of a framework of law and order" (1967: 34-35). In accordance with the emphasis here on *organizations* as powerful modern channels of communication, bureaucracies have the advantage over parties or mass media in that they are relatively more secure and stable. Even in non-democratic systems, parties and mass media face some competition and are exposed to some testing of public opinion. Particularly in democratic systems, politics is risky because of competitive elections; so too is journalism, because of competitive circulation. The bureaucracy and the jobs of appointed bureaucrats are also subject to uncertainties, but not of this type. Bureaucracies are more immune to and less dependent on external support and resources. If they are discreet and loyal to the political center and the political elite, they are also the most effective maintenance instrument.

There were no problems of disloyalty on the part of the Israeli bureaucracy, and it therefore became an effective maintenance channel for the four roles presented below.

OFFICIAL SYMBOLS

The bureaucracy in many new countries becomes the personification of statehood. First there are the titles, the buildings, and the signs of power. The Hebrew names to be assigned to terms such as "minister" or "civil servant" caused great excitement and long debates. More than many things, the realization of political independence was symbolized by the appearance of an "Israeli soldier" or a "Jewish policeman" with uniform, rank, and all. The regional offices and the individual bureaucrat carried the new Israeli officialdom to every corner of the country. Bureaucrats are obviously not the most suitable socializing agents for value-loaded common contents such as the Bible or ideological Zionism. Nevertheless, concrete symbols connected with nationalism (the Hebrew language), pioneering (working the land), and sovereignty (the flag) were implanted through the official channels as well.

From the outset, the administrative hierarchy was centralized: Branches reported directly to the ministry headquarters, and there was only a weak intermediate level of local authorities between the citizen and the central government. Thus government was powerful, and the national bureaucracy enjoyed a relatively high degree of respect and deference.[6] Not unlike the attitude of the French toward their powerful bureaucracy (Manor in Galnoor, 1977: 234-239), deference is mingled in Israel with a considerable amount of defiance toward any authority, and state authority in particular. With regard to the Israeli Arabs, there was no doubt that the military government and state bureaucrats represented authority and a demand for compliance. New immigrants, especially those who came from authoritarian systems, probably continued to have a mixed attitude of suspicion and respect toward the government and its representatives. Other groups were forced to be in constant contact with the bureaucracy. As long as it was new and represented statehood, it was also a respected symbol.

The implanting of state and political symbols through the bureaucratic channels contributed to the maintenance of the political system, very much like the contribution of the nonbureaucratic roles to penetration.

The two are closely interrelated because they reach deeply into people's nonpolitical orientations.

STRUCTURAL PRESERVATION

Execution or implementation is considered the main task of bureaucracy, but it is not the sole task, nor is it purely "administrative" — that is, nonpolitical (Self, 1972: 247-299). The strength of the Israeli bureaucracy as a maintenance channel stemmed not just from the direct delivery of services to groups and individuals; in this task there were also other important organizations. The bureaucracy was forced to execute a great number of government policies through other secondary centers, camps, and organizations. It was subject to central political control, zealously coordinated by the dominant party, and frequently harassed by the many other powerful organizations. The stability and survival of the complex structure that held together the Israeli system from within depended on the ability of the bureaucracy to work with and act through these organizations. For instance, it was the officials in the Ministry of Education who actually daily executed the coalition agreements between Mapai and the religious parties. Similarly, Israeli representatives abroad were career diplomats, but one of their duties was to work closely with the numerous Jewish organizations and to help the fund-raising campaigns. No doubt one central factor in all these complicated maintenance operations was the Ministry of Finance through which the actual flow and distribution of resources were controlled (Gross in Akzin and Dror, 1966: XVII-XXII; Bilski et al., 1980: 328-332). But at a certain junction, a nondescript committee with representatives from the relevant powerful organizations could be equally important and often more decisive.

Israel is a government-permeated society. It is "Big Government," to use Shonfeld's phrase (1965), and a very active one. The bureaucracy was in charge of executing development policy and at the same time of maintaining the structure. Indirect evidence that the bureaucracy carried out with loyalty the maintenance task — or at least that the political center was satisfied with its performance — is the peculiar fact that there were no significant administrative reforms and reorganization in Israeli public administration during this period. The government and parties held the power, and there were no doubt good professional reasons to examine the performance of the civil service and suggest some fundamental improvements. The attempt to change the classification and pay scales of civil servants in 1964-1965 was a failure. The reasons for this complacency were simply that the political center was generally happy with the "political performance" of the bureaucracy and estimated that changes could upset the delicate interministerial and intrasystem balance. It could, moreover, increase the trend toward professional independence of the bureaucracy. It is appropriate to note Simon's more general but very pertinent statement:

> The deliberate control of the environment of decisions permits not only the integration of choice, but its socialization as well. Social institutions may be viewed as regularizations of the behavior of individuals through subjection of their behavior to stimulus-patterns socially imposed on them [Simon, 1965: 109].

This preservation function of the bureaucracy explains the contrast between the rapid social and economic changes in Israel and the rather conservative nature of the political and administrative apparatus. What Akzin and Dror (1966: 19) call the "low inner-directed propensity to change" of the Israeli bureaucracy is due primarily to its adherence to the maintenance function.

RECRUITMENT

The parties were the most common channels of recruitment for both political and senior administrative positions (see Chapter 5). Nevertheless, in many countries — Western and non-Western, democratic and nondemocratic — the civilian and military bureaucracies have been used as channels for recruitment (Almond and Powell, 1978: 124; Quandt, 1970).

When the State of Israel was established, many politicians became senior officials overnight. The pattern of close links between the administrative hierarchy and political careers has remained a constant feature of the Israeli political system. Throughout the First to the Sixth Knesset, the number of Knesset members who listed their occupations as "party worker" and/or "civil servant" was never less than 25 percent (Zidon, 1967: 337). The figure was actually much higher. The direction, however, was reversed during the years: More and more political positions were held by former senior administrators and high-ranking military officers. The Rabin Cabinet of 1974, for example, was made up of a majority of ministers who previously held executive-military and civilian positions.

But more important for the maintenance function of Israeli bureaucracy is the fact that administrative recruitment was used for socialization and absorption of newcomers. The most obvious form was recruitment to public positions on the basis of party connections or personal favors. But, as noted, the Israeli spoils system was broader because it was used not only to reward the faithful but also to incorporate new groups through the hiring of their representatives into the bureaucracy. One prevailing method was personal cooptation: The leader of an important or noisy group got a job in the government or other public organization. Better known are the cases of collective cooptation in which whole groups and existing organizations were "recognized" by the official bureaucracy as bona fide partners for negotiations and even policy formulation in their fields.

Medding documented this method of penetration and maintenance with regard to independent artisans and craftsmen (1972: 53-59). They represented an *established* group, not a target group, which the Histadrut failed to reach previously because they were neither "laborers" nor salaried employees. Nevertheless, Mapai was interested in incorporating these people into its ranks. The first step was to establish the Artisan Bank in 1955 for channeling government loans and credits. Next came an increase in the representation of the Artisans' Associations in various public institutes and a greater share in the Ministry of Trade and Commerce's development budget. Other kinds of support followed, including some relief from the income tax burden. Finally, in 1960, an exception was made and artisans and craftsmen were permitted to join Mapai even though they were not Histadrut members (1972: 55). The result was that the group was fully incorporated through the dual usage of party and bureaucratic channels: the Department for Artisans at Mapai headquarters and the Section for Artisans and Members of Cooperatives in the Ministry of Trade and Commerce. In addition to the bank, the group got "its" Government Corporation for the Development of Artisanship. In 1959, the chairman of the Artisans' Association became a Mapai member of Knesset.

Studies of Israeli senior civil servants show that the weight of party affiliation in recruitment has been decreasing compared to personal qualifications throughout the years (Dror, 1971). But officials continued to be appointed to high posts because of their ability to function in the labyrinth of ministries, secondary centers, parties, and affiliated organizations. In combination with structural preservation, recruitment to Israeli bureaucracy provided critical assistance to the system's maintenance.

CONTROL OF INFORMATION

The power of discretion — the ability of officials to decide how the power of government should be used in specific cases — rests to a large extent on their control of vital information (Nadel and Rourke, in

Greenstein and Polsby, 1975: 385-388). Government is both a supplier and a consumer of information, which is a vital commodity in the political marketplace (Galnoor, 1975). The bureaucracy is the main channel for handling this multidirectional flow of information, and — apart from the bureaucracy's own stake in these interactions — it serves the penetration and maintenance functions for the political system as a whole (Mansen and Russet, 1973: 12-13). The well-known part of these activities is bureaucratic regulation of the flow of demands, its gatekeeping roles of selection and aggregation, and its responsibility to prevent channel failure (Easton, 1965b: 117-127). But in addition to these indispensable maintenance activities, "government offices are in the 'news' producing business up to their bureaucratic necks" (Chaffee and Petrick, 1975: 64). The actual information transactions are reciprocal because the task of governing has become too complex and officials must exchange information and maintain alliances with nongovernmental groups. Thus, both secrecy and propaganda are used by the bureaucracy to increase the added value of the information commodity.

The "culture of secrecy" is well developed in Israel, but the structure of the political system does not enable total withholding of information, just careful selectivity in utilization (Galnoor, 1977: 189-190). The "politics of accommodation" in Israel was also executed by the bureaucracy, and thus manipulation of information and partial secrecy were required in order to retain some stability. As will be seen in the next chapter, well-establlished groups were familiar with the bureaucratic channels and could obtain information that was vital to their interests. Less established groups — among them those listed as target groups — were penetrated mainly by the bureaucratic channels and not maintained by control of information. This applied to Israeli Arabs, new immigrants, Oriental Jews, and young people. Such groups had little to offer in return for confidential government information; therefore their pressure to be "accommodated" was not strong enough.

The Bureaucracy and the Target Groups

The parties were the most important channels and the dominant force behind the successful penetration of the political system into all target groups. For a iong time they also provided the organizational backing required for the maintenance activities. The role of the bureaucracy was initially secondary in both functions. It worked hand in hand with the parties, especially Mapai, in penetrating the most important and most difficult target groups — namely, new immigrants and Oriental Jews. It slowly took over the maintenance function, especially because

TABLE 6.3   Penetration and Maintenance by Political Parties and by the State Bureaucracy

	Penetration	Maintenance
Political Parties	*organizational extensions *membership *political mobilization *leadership recruitment	*Feedback control and receptiveness *Coordination
The Bureaucracy	*centralization *service delivery *nonbureaucratic roles	*official symbols *structural preservation *recruitment *control of information

of its increasing control over tangible and intangible resources, notably the flow of information. The different ways in which the parties and the bureaucracy operated are summarized in Table 6.3.

The differences between the tasks performed by these two institutions also explain their different impact on the target groups. Under the military government, Israeli Arabs were less affected by the national civilian bureaucracy. Penetration was minimal and loyalty was maintained by the existence of the military government and the creation of Arab parties affiliated with Jewish parties. These parties, and especially those participating in the cabinet coalition, received assistance in recruitment and in getting votes during elections from the military and civilian officials. In addition, the Histadrut was also an important penetration vehicle for the labor parties with regard to Israeli Arabs (J. Landau, 1973).

The Diaspora Jews were out of the direct reach of the state bureaucracy. There were, however, important contacts with Israeli officials abroad through the Jewish organizations and Israeli delegations. In addition, services and assistance were provided by the ministries to overseas investors, and there were the links between the ministries and the Jewish Agency, the Jewish National Fund, and other Jewish institutions.

Ultra-orthodox groups were outside the sphere of bureaucratic influence. The bargaining and coalition agreement were carried out on the political level, and officials in the ministries were required to conform. This usually entailed the transfer of public money to the religious parties, schools, and other organizations. The conflict between the religious and secular camps was most clearly apparent in the field of education. It came to an open clash right after the state was established in the "contest for the new immigrants" (Schiff, 1977: 174-194). The Histadrut and labor parties on the one hand and the religious parties on the other were

determined to expand — or at least to preserve — their influence through
the socialization of new immigrants in their respective school systems.
The long conflict brought about the resignation of the cabinet and new
elections for the Second Knesset in 1951.

The Labor-affiliated schools increased their percentage of the school
population in the years 1949-1953, mainly because of Labor's control
over the Ministry of Education. The compromise was that education
was nationalized in 1953 and divided into three sections: state (secular),
religious-state, and independent (ultra-orthodox). The distribution of
pupils among these three remained more or less stable over the years: 67
percent, 26 percent, and 7 percent, respectively (Schiff, 1977: 179). The
bureaucracy in the Ministry of Education was in charge of maintaining
these arrangements.

The most important impact of the bureaucracy was, as was pointed
out, on new immigrants of Oriental origin. Here the nonbureaucratic
roles were initially more important, but slowly the other activities —
especially of service delivery and representation of state symbols —
took over.

The important organizations in the lives of young people were either
nonbureaucratic or in the hands of the political parties. Schools and
youth movements were politicized, and, when education was
nationalized, the direct political influence of the Ministry of Education
was not so significant (with the exception of the religious state schools,
which were supervised by officials affiliated with the National Religious
Party). Some general influence in this direction was exerted by the
existence of paramilitary training of young people in youth units (the
Gadna) within the schools. This activity was jointly supervised by the
Ministries of Education and Defense and carried out in cooperation with
the Gadna Corps in the IDF. The most important influence on young
people has been the existence of compulsory military service. Their
service, which lasts two to three years for women and men (plus annual
reserve duty until the age of 55 for men), has had a profound effect on
their view of and membership in the political system. The "nonpolitical"
groups were affected primarily by the maintenance operations of the
bureaucracy. They have also exerted pressure to depoliticize the public
administration and have been natural allies to those bureaucrats who
fought for increasing professionalization.

Indeed, as time passed and as could be expected in a modern society
with growing ascriptive orientations, the bureaucracy grew more professional and more universalistic in outlook. Recruitment on the basis of
personal qualifications gained importance, and gradually so has the
degree of bureaucratic independence within the political system. The
early signs of this development were already present toward the end of

the 1950s. In 1959, the first law imposing restrictions on political activity of senior civil servants was passed. The Lavon Affair and the subsequent split within the dominating party in the 1960s posed a difficult loyalty dilemma for administrators and politicians alike. Once the delicate division of labor between the party and bureaucratic channels was disrupted, there followed a change in their respective roles in the political system. This change should be viewed together with the role of the mass media, the third major channel of political penetration and maintenance in Israel.

Thus, despite the high degree of bureaucratization in Israel, individuals and groups could maneuver among alternative channels because of the pluralistic nature of the society and the existence of organizational redundancy and overlap. And if "administrative ineptitude is the ultimate basis of human freedom" (V. Thompson, 1973: 15), there was enough slack in the Israeli system to leave room for this, too.

NOTES

1. On India, see Weiner, (1962) and Weiner in Pye and Verba (1965: 199-244). On comparisons between the Indian and Israeli democracies, see Benjamin (1972: 174-184) and, more generally on modernization, Inkeles and Smith (1974: 276), Heady (1979).

2. The example is taken from Sherf (1959: 132), who relates the mundane problems of preparing the first meeting of the new government of the State of Israel in 1948.

3. Lest one interpret the above discussion as a song of praise to the communication performance of bureaucratic channels, mention should be made of the distortion potentiality of these channels and of the bureaucratic hierarchy in particular (Crozier, 1964; Wilensky, 1967). The existence of informal and supplemental channels that circumvent the bureaucratic ones testify that there are many problems here too (V. Thompson, 1961, 1969).

4. For a general survey of problems facing senior civil servants in Israel see Dror (1971).

5. Based on data published in the annual reports of the Civil Service Commission.

6. The bureaucracy can perform maintenance roles also through symbolic depersonification — that is, making the leader and the government remote and majestic. This is a more traditional role of bureaucracy that was only infrequently used in Israel.

7

CHANNELS: MASS COMMUNICATION MEDIA

Modern media systems have flourished only in societies that are
modern by other tests. That is, the media spread psychic mobility most
efficiently among peoples who have achieved in some measure the
antecedent conditions of geographic and social mobility. The converse
of this proposition is also true: no modern society functions efficiently
without a developed system of mass media. . . It seems clear that
people who live together in a common polity will develop patterned
ways of distributing *information* along with other commodities.
It is less obvious that these information flows will interact
with the distribution of power, wealth, status at so many points
to form a system.

(LERNER, 1958: 55)

The mass media have a number of advantages and disadvantages as
channels capable of reaching the various publics in the periphery and
maintaining their support. The advantage of mass media such as newspapers, radio, television, and the movies over other channels lies in their
total dedication to information flow. They are established to operate as
transmitters, and they feed on information. Their attractiveness to politics stems from the assumption that the specific content of the informational product is relatively unaffected by the channel itself. Unlike the
"human" organizational channels discussed above, the "technical"
mass media channels seem to be more flexible. Theoretically, a radio
station is capable of transmitting practically any message, and this is a
useful quality for political organizations. In addition, the mass media
have an obvious advantage over other channels in that they can transmit
more information more quickly to more people.

A newspaper or a television station, however, is also an organization. The fact that it operates a powerful loudspeaker does not free it from organizational pathologies (Sigal, 1974; Argyris, 1974; Chaffee, 1975). The loudspeaker function of the media organizations enables them to serve other organizations, particularly the political system and its center. It does not follow, however, that because mass media can reach many people quickly, accurately, and with reduced "noise" that it can also incorporate them into the political system. Here the mass channels are at a disadvantage compared to organizations such as parties or bureaucracies. Information carried through the mass media can simultaneously reach most members of a target group with few transmission distortions. If the government wishes to mobilize support for a new housing scheme, for example, a radio speech by the minister will travel faster than announcements from his office or multiple personal appearances in party meetings. But will the announcement be understood? Perhaps the concerned groups do not speak Hebrew or cannot grasp the official language. Organizational channels, including bureaucratic ones, are more personal. Their advantage over the media channels is their ability to carry instantaneous feedback. There is nothing inherent in the mass technology itself to make it a few-many, center-mass channel. Nor is the identity of senders and receivers part of mass media technology. Potentially many can communicate with many, but the prevailing usage — regardless of the society's level of political development — is that the mass media operate as one-way channels carrying downward vertical and diagonal information. When they are thus employed they cannot become a real substitute for person-to-person contacts. It is possible that future generations will be acculturated to interacting over television screens and conversing through computers. Even so, for politics the adjustment will be slow and difficult because of its need to aggregate the results of human communication and translate them into collective action.

Another disadvantage of the mass media is the other side of mass appeal: the limited ability to reach smaller circles and specialized groups effectively. The local branch of a political party can distinguish between the different groups in its area, separately reaching out to each of them, and thereby form a link which is usually more permanent than one established by sporadic and impersonal messages sent through the radio and newspapers.

There are also important differences between the types of political communicators active in the different channels (Nimmo, 1978: 26-42). In bureaucratic channels, the communicators are skilled mainly in personal and group interactions. In the party channels, the forte of professional politicians is interactions, and their tools range from face-to-face persuasion to rhetorical public speeches. In the mass media organizations, there are professional communicators whose messages are not necessarily related to their opinions or beliefs. In this sense there is little difference between communicators in television, radio, public relations companies, and advertisement agencies (1978: 29).

Already mentioned was the power of combining party and bureaucratic channels for penetration and maintenance. If these organizational channels are supplemented by the mass media, the "winning combination" turns into an almost guaranteed success. Such combinations are evident in most totalitarian systems. Milder practices can be found in European democracies where political parties own newspapers or broadcasting stations (Seymour-Ure, 1968) and when the bureaucratic channels are synchronized with the mass media channels (Teherenian, 1977). These combinations eliminate the technological shortcoming of organizational channels and the interpersonal limitations of the mass media channels. Information transferred through mass media and then discussed and interpreted in small face-to-face gatherings is absorbed most effectively (Rogers in Pool et al., 1973: 290-310). In such "media forums," mass messages are reinforced by the impact of the interpersonal communication and the collective influence of reference groups. They seem to be effective in diffusing information, forming and changing attitudes, and catalyzing behavioral changes. Therefore, they are also extremely attractive to political propaganda (Liu, 1975).[1]

Mass Media as Political Channels

Mass media channels tend to be one-way channels which are high on outgoing information and low on incoming feedback. Their lack of sensitivity to the special needs of different groups makes them relatively more effective in societies that demonstrate characteristics of mass politics — that is, modern societies with atomized political actors (Kornhauser, 1959). They are relatively less effective in traditional societies where politics is still undifferentiated from other social functions. The penetration ability of mass media is impressive, but their ability to maintain and sustain the initial impact is more limited. In traditional societies, penetration must be reinforced by other channels; in modern societies it requires a constant outpouring of reinforcing messages. Mass politics without mass societies is an artificial creation of mass media. In terms of political development, this is not only superficial but also of little consequence in the long run for the effectiveness of central steering capacity. It is impossible to rule for long only through mass media channels. They need to be supplemented by organizational channels that can perform the intimate "broker" function that cannot be performed by the technological medium.

As will be seen in subsequent chapters, mass media channels alone are not sufficient for democratic political development, because they cannot secure real participation. They provide an opportunity for reaching every member of society, but by themselves they cannot mobilize. Lenin defined the role of the partisan press as the "collective organizer" of the workers; but it should not be forgotten that in the Soviet Union the newspapers' "worker correspondents" received instructions from party officials (Selznick, 1952: 48-51).

The view taken here is that neither mass communication nor mass politics is an independent variable (Bauman in Galnoor, 1971: 20-31), but that their joint appearance is mutually reinforcing. To be sure, electronic media present a challenge to politics. The most attractive feature is the opportunity to present a similar version of the world to all people (McLuhan, 1964; McQuail in Curran et al., 1977: 90), but most studies of mass media influence caution us against such a simplistic view (Blumler and Katz, 1974). The mass media are strongly planted in the political system, and without them it would be difficult to conduct politics (Seymour-Ure, 1974: 62-63). But what is the link between mass media and political development? By definition, the initial stages of political development are no longer evident in mass societies. However, one does find in less developed systems both mass political communication and attempts to develop mass politics (Katz and Wedell, 1977). The former is common even in the least developed political systems where modern electronic media may be operated by the government (Russett et al., 1964: 120-127; Teherenian et al., 1977: 22-38). Radio especially has been used as a cheap means of bringing controlled information to a great number of people, or when revolutionary regimes try to mobilize popular support quickly. The phenomenon of a coup d'etat which starts with the seizure of the radio and television stations is well known (Luttwak, 1968: 113-115).

The more limited and circumscribed task ascribed here to mass communication in political development does not contradict our previous emphasis on the central role of communication in politics. On the contrary, the critical role of communication in determining different possible patterns of political development should be stressed (see Hornik, 1980). This is done, however, through many types of channels, not only mass ones. Popular notions notwithstanding, the specific contribution of the mass media channels to these processes is limited. They can deliver to the politician an audience which, in size and composition, is unavailable to him by any other means (Gurevitch and Blumler, in

Curran et al., 1977: 274). They also enlarge the numerical base to such an extent "that previous barriers to audience involvement (e.g., low level of education and weak political interest) have been largely overcome and the audience for political communication has become virtually co-terminous with membership of society itself" (p. 274). The mass media help the political system to increase the random diffusion of political information and to overcome constraints at both the source and receiver ends (Chaffee, 1975: 87-90). However, these important political roles are not independent. Mass media serve as binding links for other channels, and their contribution to political development is strong in initial pene-tration and less so in long-range maintenance. When a highly modern mass communication technology has been superimposed on an under-developed political system, the results have not always been impressive. The Iranian experience of 1978, for instance, shattered the assumptions about the penetration and lasting influence of mass media in such a system (Mohammadi, 1980).

Once the social, cultural, legal, and political constraints affecting the mass media are understood, their contribution to political development can be more accurately assessed. In the Israeli environment, the con-tribution of the mass media to penetration and maintenance is far from negligible; together with other channels, they were indispensable for central steering. There is a difference, of course, in the influence of the various types of mass media. The press can carry a greater variety of messages and can address itself to different groups — for example, the special sections in easy Hebrew in some Israeli newspapers aimed at new immigrants. Also, the potential of the print media to serve as a two-way channel is more apparent (Rivers in Pool et al., 1973: 521-550). The press can also supplement bureaucratic and party organizations in special tasks of political tutelage and even mobilization. On the other hand, radio, television, and films are more effective in the area of instant political mass propaganda (Ellul, 1973), building leadership images, and political symbolism (Klapper, 1960).

In the following discussion of Israeli mass channels, the emphasis will be on the press because newspapers were the main mass channel during the yishuv period. In the early state period, they continued to be an important channel together with the state radio. Television was not introduced until 1968-1969.

Israeli Mass Communication

In Chapter 3, the contribution of the common contents to a highly motivated and mobilized society during the yishuv period was presented. A mobilized society *responds* to central steering. Such a response can be enforced, but in the Israeli case it was voluntary and most visibly expressed in the willingness of the Jewish community to make personal sacrifices for collective goals. Personal responsiveness facilitated the penetration success of non-governmental channels such as the parties during the yishuv period; it also explains the difficulties of adjusting to the more coercive measures undertaken later by the state in order to secure compliance. But in the early years of the state, the existence of a mobilized society had a strong influence on the role of the mass media and on their performance as channels of political communication. In addition, there were a number of other important factors which will be explored now in greater detail: the small size of the society, the general level of literacy and education, language problems, the degree of politicization, and secrecy and security.

SMALL SOCIETY

Israeli society has always been small and concentrated in a small area. Consequently, communication channels were relatively short and amenable to central control. During the yishuv period, there were fewer than 100,000 Jewish households and these could be reached easily and with simple means of communication. A general public demonstration, such as the one held in the main cities against the 1940 White Paper of the British government, drew a good percentage of the total adult population. By 1965 the total population of Israel reached 2.6 million, which still did not pose difficult transmission problems. Even before the rapid modernization of transportation and telecommunication which took place after 1948, every Jewish community could be reached from the three big cities — Tel Aviv, Jerusalem, and Haifa — within a few hours. In 1948 there were very few private cars in the country and only 30,000 telephones (compared to ten times more by 1965), but public transportation and the mail were widely used. In short, Israeli society did not face great difficulties in overcoming physical barriers of communication. All the mass media of the yishuv and almost all in the state period until 1965 were national and not local (Caspi, 1980b). Israelis throughout the country would get the same daily newspapers within hours of each other and listen to the same national radio programs.

LITERACY, EDUCATION, AND MASS MEDIA CONSUMPTION

Mass media, particularly the printed press, did not encounter distribution problems because of illiteracy. Most of the Jewish population could be reached through the written word. The percentage of literate people in the adult Jewish population was 94 percent in 1948. This dropped to 85 percent in 1954 after the influx of mass immigration and climbed back to 88 percent in 1961 (Statistical Abstract of Israel, 1958-1959: 372; 1978: 655). The average years of education in the Jewish population also increased steadily: The percentage of adults with more than eight years of schooling was 45 percent in 1961 (1978: 652). With regard to the non-Jewish population, the situation is different. In 1961 literacy among them was but 48 percent, and only 9 percent had more than eight years of schooling (pp. 652, 655). All told, however, in 1960 Israel ranked nineteenth among 125 countries in the percentage of pupils in primary and secondary schools and ninth in the percentage of university students per capita (Russett et al., 1964: 214, 218).

Corresponding to their high interest in politics, Israelis are avid newspaper readers and radio listeners (Katz et al., 1976: 179-187). Newspapers have been the main source of information and especially political information during the state period. In the late 1960s, there were 27 daily newspapers in Israel — 14 in Hebrew, 4 in Arabic, and one in each of nine languages (Bulgarian, English, French, German, Hungarian, Polish, Rumanian, Russian, and Yiddish). In addition, there was a total of 679 other weeklies, biweeklies, and periodicals.[2]

In 1969 a great majority of the adult Jewish population (80 percent) read at least one daily per week, and most of them did so four or more days every week (Statistical Abstract of Israel, 1979: 706). In daily newspaper circulation, Israel ranked twenty-third among 125 countries with 210 copies per 1,000 population in 1957 (Russett et al., 1964: 108). On weekends, the circulation increases significantly by 30-40 percent (Government Press Office, 1972-1973: 3, 5).

Radio-listening is very high in Israel compared to other Western countries. Over 90 percent of Israelis listen to news bulletins at least once a day, and the figures are even higher during periods of tension (1972-1973: 704; Katz and Gurevitch, 1976: 180-183). Thus, the educational level did not pose a problem for those who wanted to receive written or oral messages transmitted through the mass media channels.

LANGUAGES

The communication barriers in Israel were essentially those posed by the potential cleavages (see Chapter 2). The national cleavage produced a separate Hebrew and Arabic press as well as separate radio (later television) programs. Religious Jews have also had their own

TABLE 7.1   Use of Hebrew (%)

	Users of Hebrew	Hebrew as Principal Language
1920s	40	—
1948	76	69
1954	76	53
1961	83	67
1972	88	78

SOURCES: For the 1920s, Bachi (1958); other years, Statistical Abstract of Israel (1978: 655).

party-affiliated newspapers and publications, and many of them listen only to special programs and not to the regular secular ones. However, within the Jewish community, the main communication barrier has been language. Since the revival of Hebrew, the number of Hebrew speakers within the Jewish population in Palestine and Israel has been growing steadily, but there have always been sizable segments of the population for whom Hebrew was a secondary language or not understood at all.

In both the yishuv and the state periods, a great number of daily newspapers and other periodicals were published in languages other than Hebrew, particularly by the Histadrut and Mapai. Radio broadcasting was also done in many other languages. With the increase in the number of Hebrew users, there was a concomitant growth of the Hebrew press and broadcasting, but the use of non-Hebrew media remained relatively high even by 1972.

During the 1950s Israel radio broadcast over several stations and according to the following distribution of time in various languages: 48 percent in Hebrew; 25 percent in Arabic; 18 percent in the various languages of new immigrants; and 9 percent overseas broadcasts in foreign languages (Ellemers, 1961: 93). There is no detailed breakdown of those who listen to non-Hebrew radio programs. It is known, however, that very few Israeli-born Jews listen to non-Hebrew programs and that the elderly listen to these programs more than the young (Central Bureau of Statistics, 1971-1972: 3, 6).

The many languages in Israeli mass media reflect those cleavages that also contain a lingual component. Accordingly, there were two parallel efforts: first, the deliberate attempt to implant the language (hanchalat halashon) through all the media to non-Hebrew speakers; and second, the use of different languages to reach the various old and new immigrants, Israeli Arabs, Diaspora Jews, and other target groups.

TABLE 7.2   Circulation of Daily Newspapers in Hebrew and Other
            Languages (1972)[a]

	N	Combined Circulation On Weekdays[b]
Hebrew	7	430,000
Arabic	2	30,000
Other languages	9	155,000
Total	18	615,000

SOURCE: *Newspapers and Periodicals*, Government Press Office (1972-1973: 3-5).

[a]*She'arim* and *Hamodia*, the two Agudah papers, are not included because no circulation figures are available. Also excluded are finance, sports, and other specialized daily newspapers.

[b]Circulation figures may be inflated, as they were supplied by the newspapers themselves.

LINKS WITH THE POLITICAL NETWORK

Mass media in Israel are closely associated with the structure and modes of performance of the political system. There are two levels to this relationship between the mass media and the political network: the direct link between particular mass media and their sponsoring bodies, and the indirect influence of the center on the distribution of information in the nonaffiliated mass media.

The first party periodical, *Hapoel Hatzair*, appeared in 1907. Since then most of the newspapers have belonged to political parties. *Davar* (1925) started as the daily of the Histadrut; *Haboker* (1935) was connected with the Industrialists' Association and the Private Farmers' Association and affiliated with the General Zionist Party; *Hatzofe* (1937) was the daily of the Mizrachi movement (later the National Religious Party); and *Hayarden*, later *Hamashkif* (1939), spoke for the revisionist movement. Two somewhat independent dailies were *Haaretz* (1918) connected with the Progressive section of the General Zionist Party and *Yediot Aharonot* (1939), nonpartisan but with a nationalist orientation close to that of the revisionists. Under the British Mandate there were also newspapers in Arabic and English as well as many short-lived publications (Cnaan, 1969: 17-27). *Maariv* started to appear only in 1949.

Partisan controversies were the bread and butter of these affiliated newspapers during the yishuv period, but there was also a broad national common denominator that made most newspapers an integral part of the collective Zionist effort. Cnaan points out that the Jewish press was united with regard to the overall interests of the yishuv community —

free immigration of Jews to Palestine, independent economic and cultural development, settlement, self-defense, and security (1969: 17-18). The press was not only united in its opposition to certain restrictive policies of the British Mandate, it also played an important role in galvanizing yishuv resistance to such policies.

In their external orientations, the press and the underground radio stations during the yishuv period could be regarded as channels of the overall Zionist movement. Internally, however, with but few exceptions they were part and parcel of the political system. Therefore, the daily newspapers in this period were not a separate communication channel, but rather an extension of and supplement to the party channels. One of their functions was to serve as brokers of information for party members. Many messages were directed not to the general public but to insiders who possessed the ability to interpret them. One illustration of the service provided by the newspaper to the party is the complaint of *Davar's* editor against party leaders who forced him to publish their boring speeches (Sharett, 1978: Vol. 7, 2066).

This service was sometimes carried to the extreme. On August 6, 1945, the main headline of *Haboker* was a quote from I. Rokach, the newspaper's party leader. Further down the page — in fine print — was the story of the first atom bomb, dropped that day on Hiroshima. When asked about it, the editor replied that Truman would not complain, but Rokah might.

During the state period, the three independent newspapers (*Haaretz, Maariv,* and *Yediot Aharonot),* as well as the state radio station, Kol Yisrael, took on greater significance. The radio, controlled by the Prime Minister's office until 1965, became the semiofficial spokesman for the government, serving Mapai and other ruling parties only indirectly. The three independent papers, sharing more than 80 percent of the general circulation of the daily newspapers, surpassed that of all other 20 or so party dailies, which increasingly became internal channels for their respective movements, parties, and affiliated bodies. Nevertheless, the existence of state-run broadcasting services and party-affiliated newspapers gave politicians and administrators an effective weapon to fight media independence. Sanctions included preventing access to government sources and even applying economic pressure. It could be a real economic sanction in Israel to withhold the advertisements of government departments, public institutions, and parties from a particular newspaper.

The parties attached great importance to their sponsored publications despite low circulation. The economic loss was felt to be offset by the political contribution these media made. Although ten Hebrew

and three non-Hebrew dailies closed down due to financial difficulties
between 1948 and 1970 (Cnaan, 1971: 3), others which were not economically viable still survived.

During the state period, specialized newspapers started to appear —
devoted to economic affairs (Sha'ar, 1964), or sports (*Hadshot Hasport*,
1954). Specialized magazines competed with the established newspapers
in many areas and provided more independent outlets for nonpartisan
interests in the economic, professional, and political fields. Weeklies
such as *Haolam Hazeh* and *Bool* were prominent in their political gossip
columns, while monthlies such as *Molad* (Hebrew) and *New Outlook*
(English) presented articles with different political views. Nevertheless,
the political grip on the mass channels during the first two decades of
statehood remained firm.

In 1954, the Information Administration (Minhal Hasbara) was set
up as part of the office of the Prime Minister. The original purpose was
political education of new immigrants, but since then it has combined
public relations for the government with general information services. In
the hands of the central authorities and the dominating parties, it has
provided a powerful tool for the control of information distribution.
Although the Information Administration was ostensibly concerned
with increasing citizens' loyalty to the state, the service was always
headed in those years by a member of Mapai.

Another example is Gevah Newsreels, which, between 1953 and
1967, had a total monopoly of the newsreels presented every night in all
Israeli movie houses. The newsreels were produced by a private firm but
were financed by a special unit in the Ministry of Trade and Industry, and
later by revenues from advertisements. A special council incorporating
journalists, among others, was set up to supervise the contents of the
newsreel, and there is no evidence of direct government intervention.
Nevertheless, the newsreels provided a potent channel for the government to present its version of the news and current events.[3] In the
absence of television, it was also the most effective way to present
political leaders to the people and to carry the center's voice throughout
the country.

The newsreels, party newspapers, and state radio testify to the direct
linkage between the political network and the mass media channels.
These controlled channels have provided officials in government and in
secondary centers with ample opportunity to get their information and
views published.

Thus, the power of "those who know" lay not only in excluding but
also in deciding in whom to confide. Official information and leaks could
be distributed directly through the organizational channels and alterna-

tively via the mass media. Consequently, newsmen in Israel have been constantly on guard to find out what is going on in closed circles, and sometimes they solved the problem of gaining access to official information by becoming bona fide members with all the rights — and duties — involved. The legacy of the yishuv period, in which the daily newspapers were the central social, political, and cultural forums of the community, continued to have its effect. This was expressed, on the one hand, in a sense of national mission on the part of the newspapers and, on the other hand, in the relative importance attached to them and their weekend supplements on the part of the readers.

SECRECY AND SECURITY

The Israeli press has had an additional and often self-imposed constraint on its autonomy: state security. Throughout the state period, security and foreign affairs remained such sensitive matters and their importance for the country's survival so obvious that there was widespread agreement that the mass media should be restricted in these matters. Thus, most newspapers operated within the boundary of the national consensus, especially in security affairs. An interesting example was the different reactions of the newspapers to the Kfar Kassem affair in which Arab villagers were killed by Israeli soldiers on the eve of the 1956 war. As long as the government tried to impose a blackout on the affair, most newspapers cooperated, while the more independent and the radical press published censored versions (Linenberg, 1972: 60). Although the growing circulation of the independent dailies was accompanied by emphasis on commercial considerations, a sense of national purpose still lingered.

Secrecy and publicity laws in the State of Israel prescribe everything official to be secret unless disclosure is specifically permitted. The widely shared agreement about the necessity to withhold information concerning security and foreign policy contributes to general government control of information in other areas. The Military Censor is authorized to prevent the publication of any material that "in his opinion would be, or be likely to be or become prejudicial to the defense of Israel or to the public safety or to public order" (Defense Regulations, 1945, para. 87(1)). This catch-all regulation was only infrequently applied, but the power of deterrence and the potential for controlling information flow are there (Galnoor, 1977: 181-183). Such measures enable the political center to suppress legally the publication of all information. More important perhaps, they enable the release of information to carefully chosen people and at selected times. This created an effective system of cooptation according to which information is released only to those who are "reliable."

In this way the state radio was quite effectively controlled and the newspapers accepted as a natural situation their complete dependence on official sources for information about security and foreign affairs. They seldom questioned the content of an official release on these matters and usually published them as received. On security issues such as raids across the borders, Israelis knew only the official version or nothing at all. The most famous case of total censorship was the 1955 "intelligence mishap" in Egypt (see note 1 in Chapter 2). The details of the Egyptian fiasco were totally censored in Israel. When the two Egyptian Jews were subsequently hanged as spies, Israelis did not know the circumstances and were inclined to accept the official version, published in the local newspapers, that these were staged accusations. In 1960, when the Lavon Affair became a major political crisis, the story of this intelligence failure, which was the initial cause of Lavon's resignation, remained untold. Instead, coded references such as "the mishap," "the third man," and "the high officer" appeared in the Israeli press. Only after 1967 were the details — published abroad long before — made known in Israel.

Another example of the state attempting to withhold sensitive news concerned the Suez Campaign of 1956. Republications of foreign reports discussing the Israeli collaboration with France and Britain were banned in Israel and denied through the mass media. Selective publication was used in the early years of the state also with regard to news available to readers of a party newspaper. For instance, in 1952 when Mapam leader Mordechai Oren disappeared in socialist Czechoslovakia (and was later convicted in the staged Prague trials), the party newspaper *Al Hamishmar* did not inform its readers about it for nine months. Party newspapers tried to avoid the publication of information that would be damaging or embarrassing for their party. Rival political parties, however, did not hestitate to use their newspapers to mount campaigns for or against the government and to publish official information that could support their positions. Unlike the situation in countries where the press is totally controlled, damaging information in Israel did get published in one newspaper or another, and the parties learned that it is better to publish their own version rather than to ignore it completely.

The Israeli mass media were thus operating on two levels. The first level was national; here they played a central role in consensus-building. On the second level, the press continued to express the opinions and aspirations of the political movements and parties, with a great deal of missionary and educational zeal. On this level they provided an indispensable service as brokers of information for the different segments within each political camp. There were also specialized mass media appeals to the target groups, thereby reinforcing the penetration and maintenance efforts of the center and increasing its transmission capability.

The mass media in Israel thus strengthened the steering capacity of the political center. Nevertheless, the three independent newspapers enjoyed so much attention from officials and the public alike that they had a significant role in the information marketplace. They exercised a strong influence on the standards of all the mass media and were viewed, in many cases, as the only viable opposition to government. They did, however, sit uneasily on the horns of the secrecy dilemma — whether to have a cooperative or an adversary relationship with the government. Compared to their counterparts in several other democratic countries, the Isareli mass media were not fully autonomous; but compared to other subsystems and segments within Israeli society, parts of the mass media enjoyed a great deal of relative independence as well as influence.

The press became even more assertive of its independence in the 1960s, when, it has been noted, many things started to change in Israel. For instance, all newspapers participated to some extent or took sides in the controversy of the Lavon Affair (Kristal, 1974).[4] Many previous taboos in Israeli politics — particularly in security affairs — began to disintegrate. As the boundaries of the national consensus grew problematic, there was less self-restraint and a growing emphasis on the people's right to know, as well as commercial considerations. Since the 1960s, and especially after 1967, the margin of independence of all the mass media channels in Israel has grown considerably.

Penetration

How did the newspapers help the political system, especially the parties, in their penetration efforts? What were their unique roles in this respect? The focus is mainly on Mapai and later on the government dominated by Mapai.

It will be recalled that the predominant technique of penetration was the existence of overlapping organizational channels capable of reaching the target groups, recruiting new members and local leaders, and also mobilizing the public. In order to understand the role of the mass media, one should envisage them first as supplementary to the political communication which took place in direct, face-to-face meetings in the local party branch or place of work. A Mapai member could read *Davar* for both general information and specific political instructions. According to the editor of *Hatsofe,* the newspaper of the NRP,

> a daily newspaper maintains ideological and political fervor. It will fight when necessary and call upon the public to struggle. It will also sooth when necessary and call for mutual understanding. Its words echo activists' speeches, members' discussions and the party's internal public opinion [S. Daniel, 1966: 50].

The party newspaper rallied the troops or called off the battle.

THE YISHUV — IDEOLOGICAL MISSION

Jewish newspapers in the yishuv period were less concerned with the conventional task of reporting and more with their ideological and national mission (Goren, 1976: 120-122). Many contributors to those newspapers were not professional journalists but politicians and spokesmen who used the press for reaching more people and for reinforcing the efforts carried out in the other channels.

> The Hebrew press in its initial steps in Palestine was lucky to have the most prominent intellectuals as editors. They gave it its high level. These people did not regard editing a newspaper as just another vocation and certainly not as a source of income. They chose this field as their area of public activity. . . . They were leaders of the people, who knew our national aspirations and took upon themselves the central task of directing and cementing public opinion [Yosef in Cnaan, 1969: 9].

Thus the press participated in the struggle of the yishuv by relaying the official policy of the national institutions, counterbalancing the Arab press, and educating the public and new immigrants. In the party press there were also ideological and party considerations, specifically mobilization and propaganda. One could easily identify the political party to which the paper belonged just by reading the editorial. One could also predict the position of each newspaper in controversial events. Such material was useful for lower-echelon party officials who could derive from their newspapers both the official line of the party and guidelines on how to present it to followers and adversaries. Local leaders, members, and followers were "educated" to the official line through these press channels.

Radio played a marginal political role during the yishuv period. In 1936 the "Voice of Jerusalem" was heard in Hebrew for the first time. This was part of the British Government Broadcasting Services, and the hours of Hebrew programs contained literature, music, and art (Mishal, 1978). The leaders of the yishuv recognized the political importance of radio, but so did the British authorities, who controlled all news bulletins in English, Arabic, and Hebrew. The fact that there were programs in Hebrew was important in itself, and Jewish announcers used "cultural discussions" to spread the national common contents. In 1945 there were only about 42,000 radio receivers in the country, but the number of listeners was probably five times as high (1978: 12). The struggle against British policy brought about the creation in 1940 of Kol Yisrael, the Voice of Israel, the underground Hebrew station of the yishuv authorities. This ceased to broadcast after three months, but it reappeared in October 1945. Its technological capacity was weak, but it was a significant unifying element and provided the basis for the state radio. On May 14, 1948, Kol Yisrael came out openly and broadcast the ceremony of the declaration of independence. There were other underground radio stations that belonged to the different political camps, such as the Haganah stations in Tel Aviv and Jerusalem and Etzel's "Voice of Fighting Zion." All in all, however, the radio was not as influential as the press in the yishuv political system.

The Histadrut was engaged in many forms of information dissemination. At the first convention of the Histadrut (1920) the educational task of the newly formed organization was formulated: teaching Hebrew, providing formal education for workers, building libraries, and publishing a newspaper and other periodicals (Rosenstein, 1946: 500). Various departments within the Histadrut were engaged in educational and communication activities, and it even had a film department through which foreign-made movies and newsreels were distributed throughout the country. The Histadrut owned a theater — Ohel (established in 1925) — and a publishing company — Am Oved (1942). In addition to the daily *Davar* and Mapai's weekly *Hapoel Hatzair*, the Histadrut published *Davar Liladim* for children and specialized publications for farmers, Arab workers, teachers, and other interest groups. This was in addition to the 207 kindergartens and 135 elementary schools run by the Histadrut in 1945 (Rosenstein, 1946: 367). Their goal included the inculcation of the pioneering spirit and labor ideology to the children and, through them, to their parents (p. 368).

The Zionist leaders were also keenly aware of their ideological mission and sought to advance it through various means. Berl Katznelson, one of the foremost ideologues of Mapai, was named editor of

Davar. Katznelson emphasized the broad, suprapolitical concerns of socialism, noting that "the cultural and educational progress of the movement does not necessarily coincide with organizational and political achievements" (in Rosenstein, 1946: 372). He bemoaned the influence of foreign newspapers and sought to foster the growth of local means for inculcating labor movement ideology. After his death, the Histadrut established Beit Berl, a school for "active workers," where potential leaders were trained in the labor movement's ideology and taught organizational skills.

Davar as a daily newspaper was a central tool for internal communication within the labor camp. It published the schedules of the party and Histadrut meetings, public gatherings, and demonstrations; it enabled leaders to address members directly; it served also as an official spokesman for the Histadrut and Mapai. But, in the words of Katznelson, *Davar* aspired to be "a newspaper of the workers and not only for the workers."

These educational and communication efforts can be understood only within the context of the ideological commitment of the leaders and the missionary zeal of these political movements. The movement was there to build a new type of Jew in the old homeland. There was room for debate and endless discussion, but there was a firm expectation of obedience and compliance. Katznelson was fond of quoting Moses Hess, one of the precursors of political Zionism: "Freedom of debate and the unity of action" (1946: 408).

The gist of the ideological mission was presented in a speech delivered by Ben-Gurion before the Histadrut Council and published in *Davar* in 1937:

> The successful — albeit late — operation to make *Davar* cheaper and to increase its circulation shows that the usual assumptions and arguments about public decadence and alienation are not founded. . . . It is possible to expand this operation if the efforts continue not only to have more buyers but also to improve the paper and especially to better reflect the life of the worker and his problems. But there are thousands of workers from the oriental communities who cannot enjoy *Davar* because they do not know how to read a paper yet. They could be easy prey to charlatans and political adventurers who swarm about the Revisionist Party. There are thousands of workers who cannot enjoy the public and general lectures held by the Histadrut because they cannot understand what is said in these lectures. Only a weak and distorted echo reaches them of what is taking place in the Histadrut and the yishuv. Instead of lectures on subjects not understood by them, there should be special readings for them of newspapers to explain

local and world events. They should be taught how to read and write and the most elementary principles of our movement should be instilled in them [Ben-Gurion, 1974: 92-93].

Ben-Gurion's attitude was that *Davar* should cater to both its natural and potential audiences among the workers. As for the latter, the paper should try to reach them even if this required special efforts and economic loss. Moreover, *Davar* should work in close cooperation with the other channels — a classic "two-step flow" concept. Despite later developments, the concept that the newspapers are a complementary channel to the party, the bureaucracy, and the state persisted for many years in Israel.

In addition to the concentrated efforts of the party newspapers to expand and maintain the circle of their followers, they were instrumental in helping their parent organizations to penetrate the peripheral target groups. Already noted were the specific appeals of the Histadrut to groups such as religious Jews, young people, new immigrants, and ethnic groups (Chapter 2). The most difficult target group in this respect was that of Arab workers.

Arab workers were natural class allies to the Jewish socialist parties; but they were also national enemies. The Histadrut made an effort to penetrate the Arab workers by publishing a daily Arabic newspaper (1925) and a weekly (1937) and by encouraging integrated unions. The emphasis, however, was more on the symbolic importance of Arab-Jewish cooperation than on real organizational power. More leftist parties and groups such as Hashomer Hatzair (later Mapam) and the Communist Party were relatively more successful in their efforts to penetrate certain Arab groups. Again, these Jewish parties sought to appeal to the Arab workers and create an ideological alliance with them through publications in Arabic.

The general picture during the yishuv period was one of close partnership and division of labor among the political center, the parties and their affiliated organizations, and the press. The mass media channels that belonged to the "organized yishuv" were all fully mobilized to express the national aspirations and support the specific policies of the Jewish majority. Beyond that, each party used its mass channels to expand membership, penetrate the relevant target groups, and complement the work done in other channels. The channels of the dominating parties and the Histadrut had an advantage over the others, but the various parties and groups did maintain their own channels and a few independent newspapers.

During the yishuv period, the Jewish center lacked formal authority and contained strong opposition groups. Therefore the yishuv press taken together performed an important task in securing a regular flow of information from the center to the public and vice versa. For example, all important speeches or decisions would be published in the newspaper and subsequently discussed in party branches and distributed through the other channels. This provided an ongoing ideological fervor in an organizationally fragmented and voluntary-based political system. Under such circumstances, the usage of organizational channels reinforced by mass channels allowed for fragmentation and autonomy, but it also contributed a great deal to centralization (see Fagen, 1966: 152). This centralization was not the conventional unity of command, but unity of purpose based on common contents and patterned flows of information. It was symbolically expressed on May 14, 1948, when, on the first day of the state, the five major morning newspapers published an identical issue called "State Day": "The very decision to publish a joint newspaper expressed the feeling of unity in this spring-day of our people" (Sherf, 1959: 135).

THE STATE — CENTRALIZATION OF SOURCES

Establishment of the state changed the position of the mass media almost overnight. First, there was a state radio, which could announce government decisions more authoritatively than any newspaper. There emerged also state publications for publishing laws and other official materials. More important was the appearance of a powerful and legitimate centralizing channel — the state bureaucracy. It could speak for the center and carry the authority of hierarchical channels and the division of labor into specialized fields. It took some time for politicians to become accustomed to the idea of speaking through their office spokesmen. And it took quite a while for these press bureaus, information officers, and personal aides to become established. But by the mid-1950s, the government had its Information Center and every ministry had its own public relations machinery.

The party press had to accommodate to this swift change rather quickly. The established newspapers had to forego their monopoly as a direct mouthpiece for the political center and became brokers within the political system. They also had to face fierce professional and commercial competition from more independent dailies and magazines. During the state period, the party newspapers lost their position as the most important mass channels in society and politics.

Israeli politicians were also adjusting to the changes. Like their counterparts in other countries, they discovered rather quickly that mass channels could help them with their new steering problems by substituting the small yishuv intimacy with technological devices that could bridge the gap between political leaders and their audience. Nevertheless, compared to the role of broadcasting in the Third World, Israeli radio and party newspapers played a different developmental role. This is because the distance between the center and the periphery was relatively shorter in Israel due to the higher general level of socioeconomic development. In any case, the mass media are only partners in the modernization process and are most effective as supporters for other agents of change (Katz and Wedell, 1977: 181). This is true in the Third World and especially in Israel, where the mass media were less prominent as agents of change and more significant in the performance of the maintenance function.

THE STATE RADIO — MONOPOLY

The radio was a powerful penetration means because it was widely listened to and because it was controlled by the state. Despite the language barriers, the number of radio receivers increased steadily from about 150,000 in 1948 (111 sets per 1,000 population) to 400,000 in 1960 (167 sets per 1,000 population) (see Mishal, 1978: 32). In 1950, there were 16 hours of broadcasting daily and nine news bulletins — five in Hebrew, two in English, and one each in French and Yiddish. In 1960, the combined average hours of broadcasting per day in all stations doubled to 32.

Kol Yisrael was run as a government department within the Prime Minister's office and it performed the role of the official spokesman for the government using the news programs as its main device (Sharett, 1978: 44, 49, 51, 58, 60, 140, 180, 193, 430; Mishal, 1978; Kollek and Kollek, 1978).

Sharett, in his meticulous recording of events, listed numerous times when, as Foreign Affairs Minister and Prime Minister, he "instructed," "scolded," or "briefed" radio correspondents. One of the most blatant uses of the radio news to spread an official version occurred in 1953 when the government attributed an IDF military operation across the border (in Kibya) to "nonregular forces." In Israel it is impossible to assume that people would not know what really happened. Hence the government relied on its citizens' understanding that the piece of information was for external consumption.

T. Kollek who was then Director-General of the Prime Minister's office, described political intervention in broadcasting in the following manner:

> In certain respects I was responsible for broadcasting, but only rarely was there a reason to intervene and then only in foreign affairs. Some-

times, I would suggest to the director of the broadcasting station how to deal with a certain issue or Yitzhak Navon [Ben-Gurion's personal secretary and now the President of the State] would tell him what to broadcast and what not to. Ben-Gurion almost never intervened, contrary to what was usually assumed by certain people [Kollek and Kollek, 1978, 131].

During the first decade of the state, the radio was practically a channel of the political system, the prime minister, the cabinet, and the ruling party. Since there was usually agreement among them on the major national issues, the amount of friction created by the controlled channel was manageable. The radio was seen mainly as an "educational instrument" of the new state. Avoidance of controversial social issues or banning certain politicians from the air was viewed as part of this policy of not hurting the collective efforts (Mishal, 1978: 35-45). In addition, there was a military radio station, Galei Zahal, broadcasting nonpolitical programs a few hours a day. It did help, however, to bring military affairs to the attention of the general public. In emergency periods, it was also instrumental in interpreting the situation and boosting public morale.

The same general attitude toward the role of broadcasting also prevailed during the 1960s and is reflected in the language of the new 1965 law which transferred the responsibility for the radio to a public Broadcasting Authority. The task of the Authority is (Paragraph 3(1)):

To broadcast educational, entertainment and informational programs in the areas of politics, society, economics, culture, science and art, in order

(1) to reflect the life of the State, its struggle, creation and achievements;

(2) to cultivate good citizenship;

(3) to strengthen the bonds with and deepen the knowledge of Jewish traditions and values;

(4) to reflect the life and cultural assets of all Jewish groups;

(5) to increase learning and to spread knowledge;

(6) to reflect the life of Jews in the Diaspora; and

(7) to further the goals of state education.

At the same time, however, the radio became more independent of direct state control. For one thing, socioeconomic developments changed the nature of audience tastes and their listening patterns to radio programs (Katz et al., 1976: 181). The demand grew for reliable information as well as light programs. Commercial advertisements started in 1958 and also contributed to easing the solemn tone of the Israeli radio.

Concomitantly, the professional standards of journalism became more important and were reflected in the recruitment and performance of radio writers and broadcasters. In 1962, the National Union of Israeli Journalists was established and further encouraged the development of ethical and professional codes. The political events of the mid-1960s (see Chapter 2) also contributed to the breakdown of the political system's dominance in mass channels and its monopoly on broadcasting. This was manifested, for instance, in the neutrality of the radio during the Lavon Affair (Kristal, 1974: 83). The role of the radio and especially of news broadcasting did not decline altogether, even after the emergence of television in 1968. Radio broadcasting still contains a great number of hours each day of news, but there are other sources as well.

SPECIALIZED MESSAGES

The potential power of manipulation that existed with regard to the radio station could also be used with official information provided to the newspapers, news agencies, and movie house newsreels. As described in the section on secrecy, there were many examples of governmental suppression of information, as well as cases where "sponsored" items were later found to be only partially correct or even false. Sharett's diaries are full of examples of the concern of Mapai leaders with mass communication and their unhesitating use of the media for party purposes. During an attempt to prevent the publication of a sensitive piece of information, Prime Minister Sharett evaluated the situation in the following way:

> *Davar* does not require restraint; *Lamerhav* cannot be restrained; *Herut* will not listen and *Haboker* is already restrained by Rokach's promise. *Al Hamishmar* will not cause problems here and in order to influence *Zmanim* we don't need a full press conference. Under the circumstances, *Haaretz* remains the most probable candidate for a criminal act and should be approached directly [(Sharett, 1978: Vol. 3, 735].

The ability to exercise a high degree of control on political communication made possible the penetration efforts of the political center in two different ways: It extended the political domain into society, leaving few "nonpolitical" enclaves, and it enabled the ruling parties and their affiliated organizations to mount a massive effort to penetrate the target groups. An example of the first is the aforementioned government-sponsored newsreels highlighting reports on state development and achievements, the official government version of current events, and pictures of ministers inaugurating new roads and factories. But there were also more direct mass tools and more specialized messages to reach particular target groups.

(1) From 1948, the Histadrut Arab Department sponsored a daily in Arabic, *El-Yom*, with a limited circulation of about 5,000 copies. It was considered by Israeli Arabs as a spokesman for the government. The same department published special magazines for teachers, farmers, pupils, and youth and carried out many other cultural and informational activities in special clubs, lectures, trips, and social functions (Landau, 1973: 11-12). Parties such as Mapam and the Communist Party had their own Arabic publications, as well as other forms of informational activities, and were less concerned with fostering loyalty to the political system. After the 1967 war, *El-Yom* was replaced by a new daily in Arabic, *El-Anba*, sponsored by the Office of the Prime Minister's Advisor on Arab Affairs (Ahimeir, 1972: 62). Since 1968 three other Arabic dailies appeared in East Jerusalem, and the issue of Israeli Arabs became entangled with that of the Arabs in the West Bank and Gaza.

(2) Efforts to reach the relevant Diaspora target groups took a different form. Most of the political material sent to Jewish organizations abroad was published by the various organs of the Jewish Agency and the Foreign Affairs Ministry. In addition to educational and religious materials, they contained official versions of current events. Some non-Hebrew periodicals published in Israel, such as the English daily the *Jerusalem Post* (affiliated with the Histadrut), were also distributed abroad. The content of these publications varied, but they were generally aimed at strengthening the links between Jews in Israel and abroad.

(3) New immigrants and especially Oriental Jews were prime targets for the educational and informational penetration efforts. They were reached through non-Hebrew newspapers, radio programs, and the educational and movie departments of the Histadrut. In general, the political contents of these specialized messages were rarely direct propaganda. As noted, they were part of the efforts to gain support for the government and to strengthen national solidarity through a selective release of information. Most of the non-Hebrew newspapers, however, were aimed at Western groups among the new immigrants. Because of the need to distinguish between Arab Israelis and Jews from Arabic-speaking countries, all publications and radio programs in Arabic were aimed only at the former group. The sole foreign language radio programs for Oriental Jews were in Mugrabit (North African) and Ladino (Spanish) dialects. Consequently, new immigrants of Oriental origin who spoke Arabic were reached politically through the party and

bureaucratic channels, and their direct contacts with Hebrew mass media initially were limited. In 1955, only 28 percent of the Oriental immigrants were regular radio listeners, while the figures for Western immigrants reached 70 percent. However, for Oriental Jews who arrived in Israel before 1947, the rate of regular listening was 73 percent (Ellemers, 1961: 102).

(4) Most party newspapers also published weeklies, or special supplements for children and teenagers.

(5) Israeli parties even tried to curb the access of their members to rival communication media. Kibbutz members in the early state days were permitted to subscribe only to their own party newspapers, and the distribution of newspapers in the army was calculated on the basis of the proportional strength of the parties in the Knesset, plus a fixed quota for the independent newspapers.

These examples show the general pattern of the mass media's penetration efforts. Most of them were more effective with the veteran Hebrew-speaking groups in the population. They reached them in close cooperation with the other channels and were also helpful — as will be seen below — in maintaining their attention and support. There were also special efforts to reach the more problematic non-Hebrew-speaking groups through specialized channels and programs. In many cases such newspapers or programs were the only direct link of a group of new immigrants with the general society around them and its political center. Such efforts are not capable of penetrating deeply unless reinforced — as they were — by other nonmass channels.

The penetration function of all the mass channels started to decline after 1948. The number of nonpolitical groups and "nonattentive" publics grew steadily. To be sure, these people voted in elections, knew the names of their political leaders, and listened to the news regularly, but they were not very active politically. The mass channels became more successful in maintaining the existing links and loyalties than in establishing new ones.

Rapid social changes and formal adherence to standards of an open society with freedom of expression slowly yielded new independent channels and an increased independence of the old ones. In the state period, the three independent dailies — *Haaretz, Maariv,* and *Yediot Aharonot* — became more powerful (in terms of credibility and circulation) than the party-affiliated newspapers. A nonestablishment weekly magazine, *Haolam Hazeh,* has been a source of embarrassment to the political center since 1949. An odd phenomenon in "solemn" Israel of those days, it combined serious analysis with sensational reporting and sexual pictures (S. Cohen, 1973). Its actual influence was marginal, but the ideas presented therein were clearly outside the boundaries of the Zionist consensus (Brecher, 1972: 149-151). Other opposition periodicals were *Sulam* on the right and *New Outlook* on the left. These trends culminated in 1965 with the BBC-modeled Broadcasting Authority and the relaxation of many other restrictions when Eshkol became Prime Minister in 1963. *Haolam Hazeh* formed a political party in 1965, its editor was elected to the Knesset, and the magazine lost the status of an outsider as far as the political system was concerned.[5]

In sum, Israeli newspapers and the radio station did reach the majority of the audience in the political system. Their adherence to the national common contents contributed a great deal to informational sharing and ideological cohesion. The party/press parallelism helped the political center penetrate society because these newspapers were mobilized and they helped to mobilize the society and its target groups, especially the veteran ones.[6]

Since 1948, the dependence of the political system on mass media has increased, but at the same time the channels became more independent and less concerned with the political considerations of the center. Gradually Israeli mass media started to acquire the mediator characteristics of similar channels in other democratic systems. In our terminology, they became more prominent in the circular flow of information between the public and the center.

Maintenance

During the yishuv period, communication within the Jewish society and its polity was simple. The solid basis of common contents and the frequent face-to-face interactions reduced the need for "amplifiers" such as mass media. Mass events were often no more than public gatherings in the city square or kibbutz green; and mass technology was often no more than printing presses, loudspeakers, and billboards. Since 1948, the length of the previous channels was rapidly extended. Such a pattern of development was observed also in other countries (Lerner, 1958; Pye, 1963). The new mass channels of the state, such as radio and newsreels, could only partially compensate for the loss of effectiveness caused by the new social complexities. In Israel, the mass media became more concerned with their function as communication brokers.

There were three consequences of these developments. First, from the point of view of the political center, the channels could now perform maintenance activities better than penetration activities. Second, in the yishuv and early state period, the mass and organizational channels had blurred the distinction between political and social communication; during the state period, however, there was greater differentiation and more marked separation between the political and the social channels. And third, although Israel is still listed among the countries with "high parallelism" between parties and press (Seymour-Ure, 1974: 173-176), since 1948 there emerged newspapers and other political publications without parties as well as parties without newspapers. Economic, technological and professional considerations were becoming more important in the life of mass media in Israel.

In the following sections the emphasis is on the maintenance role played by the mass media in preserving the links between society and the polity.

NATIONAL SOLIDARITY

The Jewish press assumed a combatant role in the struggle of the yishuv against the British Mandate government. With very few exceptions, it expressed loyalty to national goals and placed itself at the service of the recognized leadership. It formed a united front called the "Response Committee" (Va'ad Hatguva) against British censorship and occasionally also against the "deviant" Jewish groups (Goren, 1976: 122-126). Much of this spirit remained after 1948 and the Response Committee became the Editors' Committee, comprised of the editors-in-chief of the daily newspapers in Israel. This committee has functioned as a mediating forum interposed between the government and the press. The government seeks to justify acts of censorship to this forum and presents requests for self-restraint. The editors are briefed frequently and off the record on sensitive issues by the prime minister, the chief of staff, and other high officials. This arrangement is viewed favorably because of its voluntary nature and unfavorably as it is a means of co-opting the newspapers into a secret conspiracy against the public (Galnoor, 1977: 182). In any case, it is to this forum that politicians appeal to the journalists' sense of national duty and responsibility. According to reliable accounts, these requests have almost always been granted. The first known negative response came from *Haaretz* in 1966, when it decided to publish the information that Prime Minister Eshkol had secretly visited Iran (1977: 182).

The attitude of most newspapers most of the time was one of considerable restraint. The major political crisis before the Lavon Affair, in which a security-related controversy took place publicly, was the leak in 1957 by *Lamerhav,* the newspaper of Ahdut HaAvoda, of Chief-of-Staff Dayan's planned visit to West Germany.[7]

Despite these examples of internal controversies and the existence of *Haolam Hazeh* which did not foster solidarity, the general tone was one of togetherness. Independent newspapers and those of the parties in the opposition did not miss an opportunity to attack the government and Mapai. But when it came to the common contents and to security and foreign affairs, there was a great deal of self-imposed restraint. Even *Herut* — the newspaper of an opposition party for many years and far from conformist with regard to government policies — carefully avoided stepping out of the national consensus. Kol Yisrael did not deviate from the official line and, together with the Government Information Center and the Government Press Office, it was very active in advancing national solidarity (Brecher, 1972: 189).

The notion of "national responsibility" in the Israeli mass media exceeded the mere withholding of sensitive information or the adherence to government press releases. Most Israeli newspapers continued to regard themselves as spokesmen for an intimate society with special problems and great security needs. Some messages in Israeli newspapers and radio would be incomprehensible to non-Israelis, not because of the language, but because of the assumptions that could be read between the lines by those who know. A certain type of official information, especially in security matters, was dressed up for foreign consumption, with the understanding that Israelis could see through it with very little effort. And most Israelis expected the mass media to withhold information in security and foreign affairs and to promote national goals over the individual right to know.

The flavor of mass media political reporting was unequivocally Jewish, Israeli, and Zionist. There were, of course, deep divisions concerning the Jewish and religious contents; there were accusations that the state was not exactly what the first pioneers had dreamt about; there were also demands to redefine Zionism. But the mass media expressed the new collective identity of the Jewish state day in and day out and contributed a great deal to the maintenance of national solidarity. A popular radio program in those years was called "The Treasure Hunt." A riddle had to be deciphered by a participant with the assistance of the audience. Such programs are common in other countries, but many subjects chosen by Israeli radio carried a national message: the history of the country, its struggle for independence, and its heroes.

The Israeli media are similar to those in other countries, in that they mainly reinforce preexisting attitudes and loyalties (Klapper, 1960; Katz and Feldman, 1962; Sears and Whitney in Pool et al., 1973). When such efforts are aimed at strengthening national solidarity, as in the Israeli case, mass media perform a maintenance function for the political system. In Israel, the existence of a dominant ideology and a mobilized society greatly eased the maintenance performance of the mass channels (Arian, 1971; Etzioni-Halevy and Shapira, 1977: 22). The front pages of Israeli newspapers on Independence Day, or the radio programs on holidays and Saturdays, are good examples of such a role. Other examples are the full and extensive reporting of all national events — for example, a Nobel prize received by an Israeli or soccer games played by the national teams. When a small amount of oil was discovered in the vicinity of Heletz in 1955, newspapers came out with a special edition. In periods of tension, the media not only reflect the mood of the people but also undertake the task of encouraging and boosting the national morale. During wartime, many newsmen become military correspondents and work for the state or army radio stations. But on a more profound level, Israeli mass media were instrumental in diffusing political symbols.

LEGITIMIZATION OF THE POLITICAL SYSTEM

"Legitimacy means a political order's worthiness to be 'recognized' " (Habermas, 1975: 178). To what extent was the national solidarity described in the previous section a "manipulated consensus" organized from above (Lippmann, 1961)? Lowi points out that the new information technology increases the capacity of decision centers to manipulate both the fact and value environment of the individual. He cites examples of the anti-Japanese movies in the United States during World War II and slogans such as "Yellow Peril" and argues that social control operates through consensus, but it is also a deliberate function of public policy — and consensus can be manipulated (Lowi in Galnoor, 1977: 49-50).

Obviously the Israeli consensus was advanced by a deliberate policy of the center and by communication channels such as the political parties, the bureaucracy, and the mass media. Moreover, the flow of information was not entirely free. Israelis were exposed to a "certified version" of reality in foreign and security affairs, and not only in the mass media. There were also, to be sure, attempts to use more direct means:

- In 1953, Meir Yaari, a leader of the major opposition party Mapam, discovered bugging instruments in his office. The issue was con-

sequently debated in the Knesset (Bader, 1979: 75). Many years later an
ex-security man revealed in a television program that the Secret Service
had been used by Mapai to eavesdrop on rival parties (Israeli Television,
Alei Koteret Program, Dec. 7, 1978).

- In January 1954, Sharett made a speech in the Knesset. Afterwards he
  realized that he had forgotten an important point. He went to Kol Yisrael
  and recorded anew his entire speech, inserting the missing passage. The
  edited version was broadcast. Sharett confided to his diary, "That is how
  history is forged" (1978: Vol. II, 321).

Potentially there were enough means in the hands of the political
center to follow the example of other states and maintain the political
system though coercion and massive propaganda. The Israeli version,
however, was neither fully coercive nor fully "propagandistic" (Ellul,
1973). It used both mild penetration techniques and strong identification
appeals (Liu, 1975: 3). For one thing, the "central power" (Mapai or the
political elite in general) never acquired the same omnipotence as the
ruling parties in Communist countries. Mapai had enough power to
preserve its dominating position and to control a large share of the
political resources (Horowitz and Lissak, 1978: 210), but it could not
fully control the system because there were other parties and other
rather powerful secondary centers. Second, the society had the attributes of a fully mobilized tribe which does not have or need coercive
indoctrination from above. Polity and society were not separated, and
the media did not have the problem of reflecting the former rather than
the latter (Liu, 1975: 3).

Mass immigration modified this situation in the early 1950s, but the
politically significant parts of society continued not to tolerate indis-
criminate propaganda, or blunt sanctions aimed at curbing free speech
and political opposition. Even the most severe instrument — military
censorship — was applied, since 1948, through the voluntary body of the
Editors' Committee. Therefore, the main goal of the political system
was not blind compliance but identification and — through the manipulation of symbols — the legitimization of the political system. For this
purpose noncoercive channels such as the mass media are ideally suited.
When there are enough common contents and basic solidarity to build
on, the mild means of persuasion though partly controlled channels is
sufficient. Thus, most of the symbolic manipulation was related to the
concept of statehood and was manifested in the controlled radio channel
and party-affiliated newspapers.

Political symbols have consequences for the collective pursuit of
goals and the use of power (Merriam, 1934: 104-105). Unlike other

political messages that could travel easily through the party and bureaucratic channels, symbolic messages are best conveyed through the mass media. Israeli mass channels were therefore instrumental in the diffusion of both nonpolitical symbols — aliya, the Land of Israel, the Bible, the Hebrew language — and political ones — the state, Jewish sovereignty, the IDF, the Knesset, and the flag (see Chapter 3). The name of the state radio, the "Voice of Israel," has the connotation of being a spokesman for the new state. Before television, radio news was the major source of information for the entire Jewish population. The Prime Minister's office in charge of the radio was more concerned with using this powerful instrument to reinforce statehood than partisan interests (Mishal, 1978). The known cases of distortion had to do with state rather than party affairs. It is interesting to note that many Israelis also listen to foreign stations, notably BBC (Katz et al., 1976: 182). Nevertheless, Kol Yisrael news had a clear priority in attention and no inferior position in credibility.

Radio was used as a forum for direct announcements by ministers, and it reported at length the major events of state (such as Knesset debates, military maneuvers, visits of foreign dignitaries, or the dedication of a new water pipeline). Brecher quotes a senior Kol Yisrael official who summarizes this point: "Being a state institution, we have to give the government a right to express itself; at the same time they cannot dictate to us" (1972: 189). The radio programs were loaded with Hebrew songs, reports of archaeological findings, stories of development, and events that symbolized the blending of the old and the new. The only rival was the military radio station, which was on the air only a few hours per day in those years, and, apart from the news transmitted out of the Kol Yisrael studios, it avoided programs with political contents. Nevertheless, the IDF radio station and its publicly circulated publications contributed a great deal to the general legitimation of the political system.[8] They encouraged support of and identification with the IDF — the most tangible symbol of statehood.

There are, however, other aspects regarding the role of the press and other publications in the legitimization of the political system. First, there were non-Zionist newspapers which opposed not only the government but also parts of the common contents and the state's ideology. Kol Ha'am, the daily (later weekly) newspaper of the Israeli Communist Party, was not interested in advancing state symbols or in strengthening the established system. The same could be said, for entirely different reasons, about Hamodia and She'arim, the newspapers of the two ultra-orthodox political parties. Ha'olam Hazeh for many years advocated a "Semitic" policy (a Near Eastern union of all Semitic people) and had an anti-Diaspora, anti-Zionist, and secularist outlook. There were strong disagreements with certain parts of the official line in Mapam's Arabic Weekly *Al Mirsad* and in many other intellectual and literary publications. Even the nonaffiliated newspapers could afford a wider margin for controversial issues. *Haaretz,* for instance, is well known for its opposition to a central institution in the political system — the Histadrut. It also deviated occasionally from the accepted norms even in security matters (Galnoor, 1975). *Maariv* and *Yediot Aharonot* took the government to task from time to time, and so, of course, did the newspapers of the parties in opposition. Nevertheless, the newspapers accepted the dominant role of the polity in Israeli society and most of the time worked within the constraints imposed by the political system.

Periods of external tension greatly influence the behavior of the press. Its direct influence weakens because of the rallying of the public in support of the regime. This has also been true in Israel, and, at such times, the press has tempered its critical stance (Cahana and Cnaan, 1973: 105).

The new state and its political apparatus represented a fulfillment of a common goal. As such, the emphasis in the communication media on the new army, the new Knesset, economic development, and other state achievements was the natural outcome of a shared sentiment. The media also took upon themselves activities on behalf of these shared sentiments. For example, newspapers tried to teach Hebrew to new immigrants by including special sections of "Hebrew for beginners" or "new words in Hebrew." Since 1951 the Histadrut has also published the special daily *Omer,* written in simple, vowelled Hebrew for new immigrants. Similarly, political symbols were carried to non-Hebrew speakers through the many foreign language newspapers and publications in Israel.

Legitimation was sought through diverse measures. The government tried to get support for the policy of the day, and others sought general support as well as votes. The ruling parties and the Histadrut were interested in strengthening the existing political system they dominated. This must have had some influence even on the editorial decisions of the Histadrut's publishing house, Am Oved. The government, recognizing the contributions of such bodies to its own legitimation, would include them in its official undertakings. The Histadrut, for instance, was invited to be represented in the organizing committee of the state's tenth anniversary celebrations in 1958.

One office which represents the government's ability to control information and the direct effort to win support and legitimization is that of the ministry's spokesmen. In a survey conducted in 1971, over 90 percent of the 25 spokesmen who were contacted thought the amount of information distributed by the government in Israel is similar to that of other democratic countries, and the same percentage emphasized that this amount of information is "adequate" or "very adequate," given Israel's special security conditions.[9] Most of the spokesmen who responded to a direct question about their particular ministry's information policy regarded it as "adequate" or "very adequate." They also expressed considerable satisfaction with the performance of the various mass media (television was a little less popular with them) and what is published. They did not favor a law to clarify the people's right to know or the boundaries of government secrecy. Most of these spokesmen were previously newsmen themselves, and their attitude reflected a high degree of satisfaction with the general state of affairs and the relationship between the political system and the mass media.

The public, too, was quite satisfied with the performance of government spokesmen. In a 1970 opinion poll conducted among the Israeli population, 55 percent responded that one can "always or almost always" believe what government spokesmen inform the public. Forty-one percent said "usually" and only 3 percent, "never or almost never."[10] The average satisfaction with the credibility of the information circulated by the government was even higher before 1970 and it reflects a high degree of legitimation of the political system.

Changes in the relationship between the polity and the mass media were bound to occur as the society modernized and the press became more independent. One benchmark was the treatment of the Lavon Affair in the press:

> An interesting and significant facet of the Lavon Affair was the upsurge of independent public opinion. . . The press took an active part in the debate, with two independent papers — *Haaretz* (which was on the whole pro-Ben-Gurion) and *Maariv* (which tended on the whole to be pro-Lavon) — being especially vocal. The party newspapers were generally pro-Lavon and Mapai's internal crisis was especially manifest in the Histadrut paper *Davar* which had no clear policy on the country's major issue of the day [Eisenstadt, 1967: 331].

By the mid-1960s, especially after 1967, the accusation that the mass media undermine the legitimacy of the political system started to be heard often. The relationship between the Israeli mass media and the political system was becoming more and more similar to that in other Western democracies.

POLITICAL AND MEDIA LEADERS

The mass media's contribution to political communication cannot be divorced from the cultural characteristics of the polity (Blondel, 1969: 240). But why was it so easy and natural for the Israeli press to identify with the political system and to share the generally favorable attitude toward it by the public? One explanation lies in the personal profiles of political and mass media leaders.

The comparison between those who served as editors or directors of radio and television with the members of the first eight Knessets illustrates some important points about the composition of the two groups. Both comprised primarily Westerners, although the representation of Oriental (10 percent) and Israeli-born (27 percent) members of Knesset was higher and has been increasing in recent years (Weiss, 1977b: 69-70). Both groups are also heavily represented by older people, most of whom (78 percent) immigrated to Palestine before 1946. In terms of formal education, mass media leaders have had more formal education and more academic degrees than political leaders.

Ellemers, in his 1955-1956 survey, reached identical conclusions — that almost all journalists were recruited from among immigrants from Europe and America and that it seemed to be a profession of veterans in Israel (1961: 93-95). Editors' and the journalists' backgrounds help to explain the maintenance role of the Israeli mass media channels. Mass media people in Israel were not removed from the political system.[11] Moreover, even after the establishment of Israel, there was some continuation of the politician-journalist tradition of the yishuv period. For instance, M. Bentov and M. Carmel, who later became ministers, at one time were editors of Mapam's *Al Hamishmar* and Ahdut HaAvoda's *Lamerhav*, respectively; Knesset members Y. Bader and M. Sneh had been the editors of *Herut* and *Kol Ha'am*, respectively.

Some activists of the revisionist movement found many closed doors in the new state and turned to full-time journalism in the nonaffiliated newspapers. H. Rosenblum, who signed the Declaration of Independence as a member of the Provisional Council, became the editor of *Yediot Aharonot*, while A. Disentshik and S. Rosenfeld started to work in *Maariv* and later became successive editors of that newspaper (Salpeter and Elitzur, 1973: 300-308). G. Shocken has been the editor of the third independent newspaper *Haaretz* since 1939. He was a member of the small Progressive Party and had been a Knesset member of this party in 1956. Shocken has been somewhat of an outsider to the ruling parties, and *Haaretz* took more independent positions on both domestic and foreign issues.

TABLE 7.3 Comparison of Mass Media Editors and Knesset Members, 1948-1977

	Media Editors and Directors[a]	Knesset Members[b]
Country of Birth		
Western	86	63
Oriental	1	10
Israel	13	27
Totals Percent	100	100
(N)	(80)	(428)
Year of Birth		
until 1900	14	21
1901-1910	37	23
1911-1920	26	27
1921-1930	19	17
1931-1940	5	11
from 1941	0	1
Totals Percent	101	100
(N)	(80)	(428)
Year of Immigration		
until 1915	3	8
1916-1925	21	24
1926-1935	34	30
1936-1945	25	20
1946-1950	15	13
after 1951	3	5
Totals Percent	101	100
(N)	(68)	(313)

Formal Education		
Elementary school	0	2
High school	14	24
Professional[c]	8	6
Academic[d]	79	63
Religious	0	5
Totals Percent	101	100
(N)	(66)	(363)

SOURCE: Data about the mass media editors were compiled from many different sources and are less reliable than data on Knesset Members, which are readily available in the Knesset Library. Research was conducted by Amir Bar-Or.

[a]Includes 80 editors of all Israeli daily newspapers, directors of radio and television stations, and chairmen of the Board of Directors of the Broadcasting Authority between 1948 and 1977. No information could be obtained for an additional 23.

[b]Includes all 428 members who served in the Knesset at any time between its inception in 1949 and the end of the Eighth Knesset in 1977.

[c]Partial academic studies, teachers' seminars.

[d]Universities, technological institutions, other institutes of higher learning.

However, despite the journalistic opposition of some editors and writers, by and large they were fully established members of the political communication elite (Gurevitch and Winograd, 1977). Although there was rivalry among the various newspapers and some of them often came out against the government, Mapai, or the Histadrut, their general effect — together with state radio and in combination with the party and bureaucratic channels — was to enhance the maintenance of the political system.[12]

MASS CHANNELS IN ELECTION CAMPAIGNS

The mass media generally play their maintenance role rather subtly, but during elections this becomes more direct and open. The party newspaper turns into a campaign instrument addressing itself primarily to loyal members and potential supporters. This was the case in all types of elections — national, municipal, and Histadrut or elections of workers' committees or representatives to the teachers associations or to the management of the transportation cooperatives.

In the period under review, five national elections were held (1949, 1951, 1955, 1959, and 1961). Although the style of the campaigns gradually changed with modernization, some characteristics remained stable during those years. First, a considerable amount of weight was given to the ideological component, as exemplified by the relative importance attached to the parties' platforms. Second, the voting turnout was very high — an average of 82 percent in these Knesset elections (See Table 10.1 in Chapter 10). Third, direct involvement of citizens in the campaign was low, and most of the campaign efforts were carried out by the party's regular cadres. Fourth, the press coverage — reports, analysis, and paid advertisements — remained central to the election campaign throughout this period. The radio itself remained outside the campaign, but the parties were allotted time to present their views directly. The role of the mass media changed drastically only with the introduction of television in the 1969 election campaign. Table 7.4 illustrates the changes that occurred within two decades by comparing the communication instruments used in the national election campaigns.

The trend has been very clear: from face-to-face communication either in public gatherings or in group meetings to mass appeals through television, radio, and the mail. It should be recalled that in 1949 and 1951, the society was small and so were the public meetings held in the town squares, movie houses, and open cafes. These meetings gave public leaders the opportunity to see and to be seen by their followers and this

TABLE 7.4 Comparison of Communication Channels Used in Election Campaigns

	First and Second Knessets (1949 and 1951)	Eighth and Ninth Knessets (1973 and 1977)
Public Channels		
Outdoor public meetings	++	++
Public hall meetings	++	++
Billboards	++	++
Loudspeakers in the streets	+	—
Party and Other Organizational Channels		
Meetings of ethnic and immigrant groups	++	++
Meetings in working places	++	++
Meetings of income and professional groups	—	++
Small gatherings in private homes	—	++
Mass Channels		
Articles and reports in newspapers	++	++
Paid advertisements in newpapers	++	++
Radio campaign	+	++
Television campaign	—	++
Other		
Mailings	—	++
Car stickers	—	+
Telephone canvas	—	+
Volunteer door-to-door campaign	—	—

KEY: ++ extensive use; + restricted use; — very little or no use moderated somewhat the nonpersonal character of the party list election system. Billboards were also on wide display throughout the country, and the parties utilized them to post their platforms and plans, pictures of the leaders, the symbol of the party, and caricatures of their rivals.

In the small gatherings organized usually by the local party branch, the technique was entirely different. Here the framework of existing groups was used to enable the leaders to address voters directly. For the veteran groups, the labor parties could use their natural environment — the factory, the office, and other working places. Such meetings were organized by the local workers' committees, which could control attendance quite effectively and even promise the delivery of votes. The numerous associations of immigrants — many of them based on small towns of origin in Europe — also served as effective forums for the campaigns.

With regard to newcomers, especially in the Oriental communities, the approach in the 1949 and 1951 elections was made through the head of the extended family or through the community or religious leaders. Both types of organizational channels reviewed in the preceding chapters — party and bureaucratic — were used for this purpose. Officials such as directors of employment agencies and the sick fund campaigned for their parties and used their leverage to influence the outcome of the election. In those days it was not uncommon for a head of a family, an ethnic group, or an Arab village to deliver all "his" votes in return for some concrete benefits. This was practiced by all parties, but those in control of more resources, such as jobs, had a clear advantage (see summary in Gutmann, 1960: 55-57).

Most prominent in the first elections was the press. The party-affiliated press was utilized for maintaining and strengthening support and for internal coordination of the election campaign. For the parties, the nonaffiliated newspapers were both targets and instruments in the campaign. The parties tried to win the newspapers' general support, or at least its neutrality. This was difficult, because the general political inclinations of all three independent newspapers were widely known. More important was the attempt to use these channels to reach the uncommitted public. Thus one could find long verbal advertisements of the party's principles in the non-affiliated newspapers as well as direct attacks on the opponents. Mapai attached great importance to reaching *Haaretz* readers, even though they were on the average nonsocialists and inclined to vote for the Progressive or the General Zionist Parties. These readers represented a vital economic and intellectual periphery whose general support and goodwill Mapai was eager to maintain.

The radio was much less important in these campaigns, but it was already active in the election to the First Knesset in 1949 according to an agreed formula among the parties of time distribution. Despite the prominence of the other channels, the press and radio should not be underestimated, because Israelis placed great trust in both these media (Arian, 1973: 29).

The changes that occurred within two decades in the use of channels for election campaigns are evident from Table 7.4. The first campaigns were conducted by the parties through the organizational channels, with support from the press and the radio. The pattern changed during the years, and — even before the utilization of television in the 1969 elections — the mass channels became more prominent. The previous gatherings of ethnic groups or in places of work were replaced by "home meetings" — get-togethers based on income, professional, and neighborhood criteria, which is more common in a modern and differentiated society. The general trend was in the direction of mediated campaigns. From public meetings to television, telephone, and the mail; from long doctrinal expositions to pictures and slogans; from ideological content to media-fabricated messages. The choice of channels, too, changed during the years. The organizational channels became gradually subordinate to the special technical and content requirements of the mass channels. In the 1950s, politicans made all the campaign decisions, and politicians and bureaucrats implemented them. In the late 1960s, they were helped and perhaps already overshadowed by public relations experts and advertising agencies.

It is difficult to evaluate the impact of the different styles of election campaigns, as there are no studies for the early state period. It is evident, however, that the overall political picture did not change much in the early years (see Table 2.8): The division of power among the three main ideological camps remained stable and Mapai continued to dominate. The channels primarily served the functions of reinforcement and maintenance of the ongoing political order.

But despite the ritualistic element in the elections during these years, campaigns were fierce and expensive (Gutmann, 1963), and they served some significant socialization functions. One such function was the instillment of the rules of the democratic game in a society where an increasing number of immigrant-citizens had been raised on different rules. No less important was the sense of access and participation that was conveyed. This seemed to be the effect, at least partially, of the use of face-to-face communication, reinforced by party and organizational channels. In subsequent years, the campaign became more open and the channels oriented predominantly toward a mass appeal. By this stage, the political system had become sufficiently developed to sustain less controlled election campaigns.

REGULATION AND FEEDBACK

In discussing the maintenance roles of the parties and the bureaucracy, we noted that they also performed the function of receiving and controlling information generated from below. These activities were extremely important for target groups such as new immigrants and Oriental Jews, who had few other alternatives for conveying their preferences. For the mass media, the feedback role is different in many respects. It is technically difficult, but not impossible, for the mass media to operate as two-way channels for information flow between politicians and the public. Newspaper readers and radio listeners can "talk" directly and regularly through these media to the politicians, but journalists can better perform this feedback job by reporting public moods and opinions.

The Israeli mass media during the early years of the state cannot be regarded as uncontrolled feedback mechanisms from the public to the political center. In the first place, there was the national and educational mission of the mass media, reinforced by strong ideological and partisan predispositions. Second, there was government control of information. The Israeli mass media were frequently used by the center to

- regulate the information flow, mainly through the radio news and the weekly newsreels played in the movies;
- trigger internal feedback within the political elite, mainly through coded messages in the Hebrew newspapers; and
- control feedback coming from the more distant periphery, mainly through non-Hebrew newspapers and radio programs and tailored information sent abroad.

These regulation and control activities performed by or through the mass media contributed to the system's maintenance.

There are many different methods of controlling information through the regulation of the mass media (Nimmo, 1978: 213-215) — direct legislation, the courts, and/or administrative regulations. All these methods were used in Israel. What were the methods of regulation used with and through the mass channels?

The channels used were mainly the radio stations and, to a lesser extent, *Davar,* the *Jerusalem Post,* and the affiliated non-Hebrew newspapers. The methods used were alternatively the withholding and release of information. Government secrecy in Israel is formally very strict. Legally an official can go to jail for disclosing to unauthorized persons any information (not necessarily classified) that has come to his knowledge ex officio. At the same time, classified information is divulged to selected confidants and circulates within certain channels in the network. This type of information flow generates little genuine feedback, because the source is either an authority (a government announcement) or obscure (leaks and selective disclosures). Radio news was used by leaders for making government announcements and for disseminating the official version. Before 1965 radio was only infrequently used for uncontrolled talks, discussions of independent panels, and the like. Radio had a near monopoly on the circulation of official information and was clearly a one-way channel for regulating the domestic agenda. Two famous announcements were those of Prime Minister Ben-Gurion during the October 1956 Sinai Campaign explaining the circumstances of the war and Finance Minister Eshkol declaring devaluation and a new economic policy in February 1962. Radio has also had an undermining effect on public morale, as evidenced by another famous example in 1967. During the weeks of intense tension before the war, Prime Minister Eshkol delivered a hesitant and indecisive speech over the state radio. It created a mood of despair and lack of confidence throughout the country and was instrumental in forcing Eshkol to relinquish his task as Defence Minister. Since the establishment in 1965 of the Israeli Broadcasting Authority, radio and television channels were less subject to direct government control. They also lost the previous monopoly on the flow of official information and gradually became more open to different views and dissenting opinions.

The existence of a diversified press with a tradition going back to the 1920s moderated the power of the official channels. Nevertheless, it is difficult to portray the Hebrew newspapers of those days as fully open, two-way channels between politicians and the public. Both the affiliated and nonaffiliated newspapers were largely the press of the political elite. In other countries the term "elite newspaper" is reserved for a select few such as the *Times* (Seymour-Ure, 1974), *The New York Times* (Argyris, 1974), and the *Times of India* (Arora and Lasswell, 1969). In Israel the situation was initially different. During the yishuv period newspapers served the respective political camps. The community was small, the political center was accessible, and the periphery almost nonexistent. Thus, the newspapers of the Jewish community could easily serve as effective two-way channels.

With the change of population after 1948, the Hebrew newspapers largely continued to serve the elite of the veteran, Hebrew-speaking Western community. Party newspapers remained effective feedback channels for their respective camps, but they were not capable at that time of transmitting back the needs and grievances of the new periphery. The periphery was handled much more effectively by the party and bureaucratic channels and by combined "multiple-step" flows of information. In the 1950s the two afternoon dailies assumed the widest circulation, due, among other things, to their ability to reach the new population.

It took a long time for the Israeli press to start operating as feedback channels. Consequently, the veteran Hebrew press mainly performed the other maintenance roles presented above: fostering national solidarity, legitimizing the political system, working in coordination with the political leaders, and participating in election campaigns. Most of this communication was aimed at the more established groups and at some target groups, such as religious Jews and the emerging nonpolitical professional groups. The task of reaching other target groups — and, consequently, of absorbing feedback information — was left to the organizational channels.

Thus, the cumulative impact of the maintenance efforts exercised through the mass media in Israel turned them into effective instruments of regulation and — to a lesser extent — of feedback. It should be remembered that the space between society and polity was densely occupied by parties, affiliated organizations, the bureaucracy, and centrally controlled mass channels. These all contributed to a selective process of upward information flow. Moreover, in those years there were no other significant channels capable of carrying truly independent feedback. There were no opinion polls and very few unaffiliated interest groups or voluntary associations. Thus the most important role of the mass media in Israel in the early state period was maintenance. But the vacuum for a genuine feedback mechanism was there, and in due course, as will be seen in Chapter 9, various mass channels started to perform this function.

The Mass Media and the Target Groups

The role of the Israeli mass media was generally more evident in maintenance rather than penetration, and they were thus more instrumental in binding groups to the political center.

For the immigrant periphery, non-Hebrew media were important channels for government messages. The foreign language newspapers or radio programs could exercise little discretion in selection or interpretation. They were extensions of the Hebrew channels aimed at reaching directly the non-Hebrew-speaking groups within the country. The same applied to *Omer* — the Histadrut daily, written in easy, vowelled Hebrew, and the special radio prgrams in easy Hebrew. Oriental immigrants, however, had a special problem. The Arabic programming was aimed at the Israeli Arabs and could not simultaneously serve Arabic-speaking Jews, who therefore had no radio programs or publications aimed directly at them.

Israeli Arabs could listen to a special station within the Israeli radio network, which grew in size and importance over the years and broadcast over 14 hours a day in different Arabic dialects. This station was aimed not only at the local Arabs but also at potential listeners in the neighboring Arab countries. The same applied to most Arabic periodicals published in Israel.

Among the religious Jews, the ultra-orthodox target group was little affected by the general daily press or the radio programs. They had their own newspapers and were neither penetrated nor maintained by the general mass channels. Similarly, the domestic communication channels were of little importance as far as Jews outside Israel were concerned. Foreign language newspapers such as the *Jerusalem Post* in English and, to a lesser degree, *L' Information* in French, served as a link to the respective Jewish communities abroad, but their circulation was very small. More important perhaps were the materials and publications published especially for this purpose by the Jewish Agency Information Department and the Ministry of Foreign Affairs Division of Information. The Jewish Agency disseminated a great deal of information about Israel which occasionally found its way into local publications of Jewish communities abroad. The Foreign Ministry, however, was mainly concerned with explaining Israel's foreign policy. There was relatively little reporting to Hebrew readers about the outside target groups — either Israeli Arabs or Diaspora Jews.

Thus, the messages transmitted in these mass channels had a prime objective: the simultaneous control of information and feedback. The non-Hebrew publications did not become the voice of these groups; neither did the Arabic channels speak for the Israeli Arabs. Rather, they talked *to* the various target groups in close coordination with other nonmass channels. As for the last two groups — young people and the "nonpoliticos" — they were prime targets for the mass media efforts mainly because they were relatively uncommitted.

Hence the impact of the Israeli mass media was more strongly felt in the forging of an identification with the political system. While legitimization was achieved through the manipulation of tangible political resources, the mass media channels added an important dimension through the manipulation of political symbols.

The Channels: Summary

CONTRIBUTION TO STABILITY AND CENTRAL STEERING

Reinforcement of the political camps by the bureaucratic and mass channels contributed to the stability and functioning of the political system as a whole. In a fragmented system, the fact that the mass media (in Israel, the newspapers) and the political camps were divided along similar lines was helpful for maintaining and developing the system's steering capacity. The secret of the "politics of accommodation" is that the political camps are divided, but there is a unity of purpose and performance in the political center. If the mass media channels were totally independent or divided along a different criterion — for example, ethnic or even economic — there would be intolerable dissonance between the mass channels and the party and bureaucratic ones. The more modern the fragmented society, the more chaotic and "noisy" could be the results of such crossed purposes, particularly if the political system is under great external pressure, as is the case in Israel. In other words, in fragmented societies, *consistency* in the pattern of fragmentation is a political asset, as far as central steering is concerned. In Israel, such consistency existed because of the high degree of parallelism between the main channels, and this contributed to the fact that the potential cleavages did not deteriorate into disintegration.

In the state period, there was a centralizing mass channel in the form of the state radio and there were more specialized channels of the parties, the bureaucracy, and the press, all with relatively high synchronization. In this respect, maintenance was advanced by the fact that most newspapers belonged to the parties and the nonaffiliated ones did not much deviate from the roles of fostering national solidarity and legitimizing the political system.

The party-affiliated newspapers were prominent during the yishuv and early state periods; their task was to mediate horizontally and vertically among leaders and between leaders and members of the same camp. That this task was taken seriously can be deduced from the fact that these newspapers were usually an economic burden on their parties. They continued to appear even if circulation was confined to the "convinced" party members because their mission included education, propaganda, recruitment, participation in internal and external elections, and the general strengthening of the political camp and party.

Party-affiliated newspapers did everything to help the activities of the parties and their member organizations. But what was the effect of these efforts on the political system as a whole? The usual assumption on this point is that party-tied media containing one-sided political content will also produce dissensus rather than consensus, giving rise to a higher degree of conflict among the various groups (Gurevitch and Blumler in Curran et al., 1977: 287). Although party-tied newspapers in Israel contained the one-sided political messages of their parties, the result was not a higher degree of conflict and dissensus. Partisanship was already there — the newspapers only reflected it. More important is the fact that they provided the service of connecting partial orientations to the general common contents as well as to national symbols. This service was more pronounced in the mass media affiliated with Mapai, the NRP, and other parties which generally participated in the coalition and less pronounced in the publications of the opposition, such as Herut and the Communist Party. The overall effect, especially because of the close interaction between politicians and communicators, was in the direction of allegiance plus partisanship, in that order (Chaffee, 1975: 171-177).[13] The complementary division of labor between mass media and the other channels is one of the main reasons for their respective contributions to the system's stability and its central steering capacity.

Conclusions regarding the close relationship between the mass media and politics in Israel must be qualified, lest the impression be created of total control of the mass media by the party machine. In reality, the three independent newspapers had a high percentage of the total circulation and a great deal of influence. There was also competition between the different mass channels, and as time passed there was freer flow of information.

INTERLOCKING AND REINFORCEMENT

The political parties in Israel were deeply involved in the penetration and maintenance activities with regard to the system as a whole, the periphery, and the target groups. They later lost some ground to the state bureaucracy, but throughout this period they remained a major stabilizing force for the political system. The bureaucracy gradually assumed the maintenance function and continued to work hand in hand with the existing political camps, parties, secondary centers, and their organizational units. The mass media channels served a complementary function in penetration but were more important in maintenance. They served the role of maintaining allegiance to the political system best through close cooperation with the political elite and much less through feedback services to peripheral groups.

In terms of political development, the three main channels — parties, bureaucracy, and the mass media — combined an impressive penetration capability. If to this is added the successful maintenance effort of these channels with regard to nontarget groups, it can be concluded that in terms of integration (penetration) and stability (maintenance), the Israeli political system was quite developed by the 1960s. The close links among the ruling parties, state bureaucracy, and mass media produced the steering capacity to be discussed in the next chapter. The other main achievement of these penetration and maintenance efforts was its encompassing nature. Despite the existence of potentially explosive cleavages, ideological friction, intensive partisanship, and difficult penetration targets, the distances were bridged. The whole Jewish population was politically mobilized and all parties participated in and responded to central steering. There were, of course, additional external and internal factors (see Chapter 2) and other channels which were not discussed here.[14] There were also major differences between the channels in terms of transmission capability, fidelity, traffic, and noise, not to mention channel failures or overload. Nevertheless, what was presented here was the evolution of the three main channels, the close interlocking among them, and their contribution to the development of the Israeli political system.

NOTES

1. There has been a conceptual and practical debate between the Russian and Chinese schools on political propaganda. The Russians do not believe in "mass persuasion" and the ability to increase political consciousness through agitation. They emphasize the supplementary method, in which selective mass messages are reinforced through the educational system and partisan representatives. The Chinese under Mao developed a system of mass agitation which required direct participation of millions of people in public meetings and recitations of the Red Book. This was also reinforced by family meetings, discussion groups, loudspeakers, billboards, and so on (Pool's introduction in Liu, 1975: x-xi).

2. See Central Bureau of Statistics (1978: 36).

3. In 1980 a collection of these newsreels was made into a film entitled "Oh, What a Beautiful Homeland."

4. In fact, some politicians blamed the press for the whole affair. Argov (1961: 228).

5. Compare with Seymour-Ure's (1974) analysis of *Public Eye* in Britain, and Manor's study of *Le Canard Enchaîné* in France (in Galnoor, 1977: 251-252).

6. The ideology of the party-affiliated press is presented by the former editor of *Davar* (Gothalf, 1969).

7. Ahdut HaAvoda, a member of the coalition cabinet at that time, opposed Ben-Gurion's policy of a close relationship with Germany. When the visit was approved by

the cabinet, the party ministers leaked it to their newspaper. The actual revelation of the details was left to *Haolam Hazeh* (Dec. 25, 1957), which came out with Dayan's picture on the front page and a banner headline, "The Traveller: Dayan," with a small and innocent subhead: "Ben-Gurion's Envoy to Burma and Europe." A day later *Lamerhav* could tell its leaders: "Government decision to send 'special envoy' to West Germany cancelled." There was nothing unusual about *Haolam Hazeh's* behavior, but the cooperation with Ahdut HaAvoda's ministers and newspaper in a security-related affair was exceptional. The result: a government crisis and the formation of a new cabinet.

8. The IDF publications are *BaMachaneh*, a weekly magazine with a reported circulation (1972) of 65,000; *Ma'arachot*, a bimonthly periodical with general articles on military affairs; a monthly review *(Skira Hodshit)* for officers; and periodical publications of the Gadna (youth units), Nahal (soldiers in agricultural and other special duties), the air force, Navy, armed forces, the Military Chief Rabbinate, and others. Total reported circulation of all military publications in 1972 was 162,000 (Government Press Office, 1972-1973: 16).

9. This unpublished survey was conducted by the author and his students in a 1970-1971 Hebrew University seminar on "Government Secrecy." The questionnaire was sent to the 25 spokesmen of the government ministries and agencies, of whom 21 were interviewed.

10. See the continuing Survey, No. 8, Institute of Applied Social Research, June 1970 (mimeograph), p. 14.

11. For similar findings in five other countries, see Pool et al. (1970: 321).

12. On the enforcement of social norms through mass channels, see Lazarsfeld and Merton (in Bryson, 1948: 102-105).

13. Liu presents five points regarding the interaction between the affiliated mass media and the political system in Communist China (1973: 9-11): the mass media were influenced by the social infrastructure; they played an important role in national integration; there was a close linkage between the organization of the mass media and the political structure; there was a close linkage between the content of the mass media and the ideologies; and there was a complementary division of labor between mass media and face-to-face communication. It is interesting to note that although the political system in Israel is nonmonolithic and democratic, these points are quite pertinent.

14. For instance, the kibbutz movements, the communal ties in the old small towns *(moshavot)*, the religious institutions, the IDF, and the secondary centers in general were also capable of performing crucial penetration and maintenance roles. They served sometimes as bypassing devices (Downs, 1967: 124) and sometimes as alternative channels to the main ones. On the role of the IDF, see Lissak (1971); Peri and Lissak (1976); and Luttwak and Horowitz (1975).

8

STEERING

The true pilot must pay attention to the year and seasons and sky and
stars and winds, and whatever else belongs to his art if he intends to be
really qualified for the command of a ship.
(PLATO, *THE REPUBLIC*)

Plato left the earliest statement comparing governing with the steering of
a ship and suggesting that steering entails a "union of authority with the
steerer's art" (Plato, 1945: 196). To govern implies to steer the society via
its political system toward goals that are outside the goal-seeking system
(Deutsch, 1963: 182-192). In Chapter 1 the definition of political development was reconstructed to incorporate the notion of "steering
capacity": The higher the steering capacity of a political system, the
more this system is politically developed. Steering is not a goal in and of
itself; it is an aggregate measurement of political development. Normatively, however, this measurement is far from an exhaustive one, particularly if we are more interested in citizens' impact and less in steering
efficiency.[1]

The political system is a goal-seeking system whose collective,
societal goals are outside the system. According to Deutch's analogy,
the society is a ship whose course (direction) and stability (goal) are
guided (steered) by a steering device (government). The political system
behaves much like other human organizations which require communication and central control in order to make decisions aimed at achieving
goals. However, the extent to which goals are achieved is not a direct
measurement of development. An organization or a system is develop-

ing when it starts to acquire the capacity to adjust to environmental changes, to make decisions that are binding, and to invest in its own viability.[2] Without goal-seeking steering, the polity might be drifting long enough to become a nonsystem. In this context, political development means building the communication network that feeds the steering mechanism of the political system. Note again that steering does not guarantee goal achievement. Improved steering simply means a higher capacity for achieving a goal, regardless of the desirability of that goal or the social cost involved in pursuing it.

Prerequisites and Facilities

In reviewing the links between society and politics in Chapter 2, we pointed out the influence of history (the flow of information from the past) on the functioning and learning capacity of the Israeli political system. The common Jewish memory and the historical "data bank" existed long before the political movement of Zionism started. It had also served and continues to serve other Jewish movements as well, some of them anti-Zionist.[3] Common contents are a prerequisite for the development of steering capacity. So, too, are the emergence of a political center and the concomitant development of the network and the channels. It is difficult to generalize about the precise sequence of this process, but it should be obvious from what has been presented in Chapters 3-7 that without a minimum common contents there is little political communication capable of sustaining a political center. In turn, without some patterned flows of information the political center cannot activate the network and the channels and steer the political system. Historically, the political center emerged in the early stages of the Zionist movement; this is a good illustration of the impact of elite behavior on political development.

The formation of the political center in Palestine was accompanied by fierce struggles over ideology, policy, and control among groups in Palestine and abroad. By the mid-1930s the labor movement emerged as the strongest power. The development of institutions capable of controlling resources was an important factor in this process. Once the labor movement secured domination of the center, it could extend and consolidate the political network. The emergence of strong and rather stable political institutions was a major achievement of the yishuv community. The network soon demonstrated symptoms of maturity such as multiplication, overlapping, and redundancy (see Chapter 4). Next came the extension of party channels supplemented by the affiliated press, and reinforced later by the state bureaucratic channels. They provided the political system with a penetration and maintenance capability and mechanisms for controlling political communication. The three types of channels presented in the preceding chapters were the means by which the switchboard of the political center functioned: transmitting, receiving, and screening of horizontal, diagonal, and vertical information flow. Note that such channels also can serve an intake function and that incoming information may be uncontrolled or even disruptive from the point of view of the center (see Chapter 9).

By the 1930s and certainly in the 1940s the steering components of the yishuv political system could be clearly discerned. There was a political center, operating through a network and channels with penetrative and maintenance capabilities. All this enabled the voluntary political system of the yishuv and the infant political system of the state to cope with successive critical challenges which required supreme steering performance. In a matter of five years (1945-1950), the political system had to cope with a series of almost simultaneous crises: the aftermath of the Holocaust in Europe, the struggle with the British government, the war with the Arab countries, establishment of the state, the massive influx of new immigrants, and an economic crisis. In all these tests, the political system and its steering mechanism were supported by a great majority of the Jewish community. This support met the necessary— albeit not sufficient — prerequisites that enabled the system to steer clear of immobilization or breakdowns. In retrospect, we also know that the steering facilities showed both endurance and adaptability and continued to serve the needs of the system, despite the heavy load. The system did fail on certain occasions and even came close to breakdown, but these events did not develop into a pathological process of degeneration of the system's steering capacity. We have been discussing mainly the social and organizational components of the communication network, and they are the most important ones for political development. We should note in passing, however, that the advancement of steering capacity was also based on the rapid development of the Israeli physical communication network: roads, railways, airlines, ports, mail services, and telecommunications (see Table 2.1 and Efrat, 1978).

The Israeli case shows that the development of steering capacity has a synchronized logic, as most components fall into place simultaneously (Almond and Powell, 1978: 359-362). As in other advanced democracies, however, there was a historical sequence in Israel. Common contents such as national solidarity paved the way for the emergence of the political center. Next came the construction of the network with voluntary channels and participant propensities (the parties and affiliated press). Independent interest groups played a minor role, and the bureaucracy developed much later — after the establishment of the state. Thus, the prerequisites were met and the facilities were developed for the creation of steering capacity. Considerably later, welfare expectations and access to resources were translated into citizen participation. This sequence suggests a pattern, but it should be reemphasized that the Israeli case also shows important unique features of political development. Thus the components can be used for comparative analysis, not necessarily the developmental sequence. We turn now to evaluation of the capabilities of the center to steer successfully.

Outcomes

One criterion for successful steering is the outcome — has the political system met its goals? The supreme test of the Israeli political system has been security and the survival of the state. Failing this test, or even the subjective feeling that it might happen, would have rendered all other collective goals irrelevant. Israeli governments had to worry about concrete results: deterrence, popular confidence in the government's ability to face external threats, and — if the need arises — winning wars. The turbulent external environment is the most important constraint on the steering behavior of the political system. It determines its survival and its ability to meet less crucial tests in domestic affairs. The success story of the Israeli political system in the period under review was based on the conduct of the 1948 and 1956 wars, whose results were perceived as successful (Galnoor in Arian 1980: 122-123). It culminated in the spectacular military victory of 1967, preceded by a tense waiting period in which Israel refrained from military operations against Egypt after the closure of the Eilat Straits. Conversely, military operations or wars whose results were perceived as failures would have been taken as evidence of incapacity and would have undermined the system's ability to perform in other spheres. The war of 1973 and its aftermath is a later example of such a situation.

In Israel, leaders, governments, organizations, and individual citizens are all tied together in a security predicament. Virtually everyone in Israel equates steering capacity with military performance and, to a lesser extent, foreign diplomacy. Historical evidence shows that a defeated or constantly threatened democracy — irrespective of whether the assessment is objective or subjective — decreases the political system's chances of survival and forfeits its steering capacity. In modern times a collective goal such as survival requires full mobilization of the entire social arsenal of resources and their competent handling by leaders.

Evaluation of the steering performance in Israel must begin by noting a high degree of success in meeting the survival tests. Israel remained sovereign and independent, and this is no small achievement for a political system or a new state in a hostile environment. Other important outcomes of the system's steering capacity have already been noted:

- There is a high degree of public obedience not only in meeting the survival test but also in other spheres. In addition to a universal draft system which enjoys social legitimization, by and large Israelis obey the law, pay taxes, and observe the rules of the game in politics.

- The ability of the political system to penetrate society and to maintain a relatively high level of political mobilization checked centripetal forces and disintegration trends.

- The political system by far surpassed any other social system in Israel in the control of resources such as money, manpower, organizations, and information. This provided a sound basis for its distributive, regulative, and symbolic performance.

- Because Israel is highly centralized and politicized and the government played a leading role in these developments, the achievements in economics, housing, education, culture, and science may also be counted as successful outcomes of central steering. The government contributed to economic growth and to the emergence of a viable and self-developing society.

In the remainder of this chapter, steering capacity will be evaluated as if it is not ultimately dependent on the actual outcomes. It is examined according to the six criteria presented in Chapter 1, not according to the social goals which are outside the system. Steering is a mechanism for achieving political results; it is this capacity which will be analyzed here. In real political processes, of course, these fine distinctions do not exist. Here, however, it is necessary to use the analytical distinction between "capacity" and "outcomes" in order to draw a line between the "developmental" attributes of the political system and its "normative" results. The passage from steering to political outcomes moves one across the boundary of the polity into society, wherein lies the ultimate test of the political system's steering capacity.[4]

Steering Capacity

Steering capacity can be evaluated according to several criteria, briefly presented here and then examined more fully within the Israeli context.

Self-steering refers to the degree of *autonomy* possessed by a certain society or community in combining and utilizing its own resources to achieve collective goals. It is a different concept than independence or self-determination because it refers to the modes and content of internal communication that bind the society from within (Deutsch, 1963: 128-131) and to the status of the polity in the society. In order for the political system to engage in purposeful collective actions, it must acquire a *monopoly on state resources and official symbols and the exclusive right to use coercion.*

To deserve its name, a steering device must be able to turn the whole ship, not just parts of it. Steering requires dependable links to all parts, or at least to the critical ones; hence, the great efforts invested by the political system to reach the members of society and to maintain their allegiance. In most cases, and certainly in Israel, *transmission to and intake of information* from the external environment is as crucial for the political system as interaction with the internal societal environment. The political center has to develop an ability to control the network and the main channels and to transmit information with minimal loss and distortion of original purpose. This is referred to as *diffusion and legibility.*

As concepts, steering and control are often interchangeable. Thus control is defined as the means whereby courses are chosen, kept, or changed so as to reach goals or to escape threats (Vickers, 1957: 41).[5] For Kuhn, "a controlled, or cybernetic system, is any acting system whose components and their interactions maintain at least one system variable within some specified range or return it to within that range" (1974: 25). Similarly, steering capacity means the ability to bring a system under control; conversely, control means keeping the system within a steering range.

In order to govern, a political center therefore should be able not only to transmit, receive, and screen information, but also to use information — even if it is in the form of pressure, threats, and decisions of other powers — to guide and control the system and to *prevent breakdowns.*

In reviewing the steering capacity in Israel, outcomes will be mentioned as well as criteria, especially with reference to the last — avoidance of breakdowns. Nevertheless, the questions we ask are quite mechanical: To what extent is the steering mechanism independent? Is it the only one operating? Can it keep the system on a stable course, preventing drift and overcoming threats? And what is the basis for its steering capacity — coercion or persuasion?

AUTONOMY

Autonomy refers to the status of the political system within the overall social system. The question is, to what extent is the polity functionally differentiated so that it can perform the steering role more or less independently? This focus suggests once again that political development means assigning to the polity the task of steering society. Building a political network (such as secular institutions) and channels that are primarily political (for example, parties) are steps toward steering autonomy. Likewise, the flow of information that is specifically political and the existence of specialized feedback loops for political communication (such as the bureaucracy) contribute to the autonomous behavior of the polity. In this respect even the friction that accompanies the political process provides a test of autonomous steering:

> Instead of looking simply for a "strong central power" to prevent conflicts — a power that conceivably may become precarious in certain domestic political conflicts and that in international politics does not as yet exist — we might rather ask how much central authority together with what distribution of autonomous organizations and what levels of efficiency in self-steering would be required to keep the frequency and intensity of group conflicts below the danger level for the whole system. [Deutsch, 1963: 208].

Autonomy is the relative independence of the political system to conduct its business according to the political rules. This activity interacts with and is aimed at serving other activities in other societal subsystems and in the system as a whole. But in order for steering to take place, the political helm must be attentive to, yet separate from, the other social, cultural, religious, or economic subsystems.

The Israeli political system was carved out of the Zionist movement in its early stages. During the yishuv period, despite the presence of the British foreign authority and the considerable power exercised by the secondary centers, the voluntary Jewish polity was relatively developed and rather autonomous. It may be said that the polity "invaded" society and not the other way around. Witness the high degree of politicization or the fact that there was "more center than periphery" in that society. There was no traditional authority that seriously tried to perform the role of steering, and there were relatively few "nonpolitical rules" that determined the political process.

Some challenges to the autonomy of the Jewish political system came from the old yishuv who refused to change their way of life and from ultra-orthodox Jews who did not recognize secular political rules. But those were relatively small groups which became, as was noted, targets of penetration rather than threats. There were, of course, some nonpolitical modes of behavior that influenced the political process. The intensive person-to-person communication that was transferred from small communities in Eastern Europe is one example. Another is the habit of operating in a small caucus facilitated by the solidarity of the pioneer groups and intended to conceal activities from the foreign authorities. But even such behavior was "half political."

The Israeli political culture was shaped more by political behavior than by cultural and social habits. Furthermore, there was not only "autonomy" of political steering but also domination of the polity over social spheres that were outside the realm of politics in other countries. The fact that political steering reached all the way into schools and religious services shows that the political system enjoyed a unique and powerful status. Compared to many Western democracies, Israel's political system was autonomous, powerful, and more deeply involved in social affairs. In Fein's words: "The country is small and its communication well developed; there is no hiding place from politics" (1967: 231).

The differentiation process in Israel was almost the reverse of what we find in other new nations. It was not a struggle of the polity to free itself from tradition or from other social confinements, but the gradual relaxation of political dominance over many social spheres. During the state period, the steering mechanism retained its high degree of autonomy but lost some of its dominance over other spheres. In the areas of security and foreign affairs, there was no internal rival to the government in policy-making. Similarly, the Zionist institutions abroad did not embark on a separate course, but agreed in most cases to follow the Israeli line.[6] In domestic affairs, however, the high level of friction during the yishuv period continued, and perhaps even increased, in the state years because of the struggle over resources controlled by the center. Yet despite centralization, some nonpolitical groups became more independent vis-à-vis the political center. This was an inevitable result of the process of modernization in which certain groups, especially economic ones, acquired independent bases of power. But this modification in the degree of autonomy of the Israeli political system came much later during the state period.

MONOPOLY ON OFFICIAL SYMBOLS

The internal struggle in the yishuv political system over the monopoly on official information has already been noted. During the prestate period the yishuv institutions spoke for the great majority of the community but not for all groups. There were notably the independent Jewish voices of the revisionist movement. Externally, the Zionist organizations spoke for the Jews outside Palestine; within Palestine, there was the British Mandate government and the Arab community. The issue was more or less resolved in the early years of the state. As will be seen below, the political center of the Israeli system soon developed an independent transmitting capability that enabled it to communicate with both the foreign and domestic environments. A distinction was established between the official voice of the state government and other voices. In a novice state, there are other contenders to be authoritative spokesmen, or at least spokesmen with an independent status, particularly among social and religious leaders or rival political groups. In Israel, however, the state successfully established its own official and authoritative voice and held its rivals at bay.

In 1948 there were some disputes over the legitimacy of the Provisional Government (see Chapter 2), yet the laws and decrees issued by that government were not challenged. This goes for military mobilization, state taxes, and the holding of the first elections in January 1949. Similarly, the political center faced problems with regard to its supremacy over the independent military organizations, the Palmach, and Etzel. There were also religious leaders who did not recognize the secular authority of the new state or were reluctant to do so. But by a few years after 1948, almost all these problems were solved via agreements and compromises. (The use of military power against the *Altalena* — the Etzel's arms-carrying ship — is a notable and often quoted exception in the history of the Israeli political system.) Since 1948 there has been one political center whose steering capacity has included the creation and embodiment of the state's political symbols.

The issue of monopoly over state and official symbols in Israel is more complicated. Formally no one but the state can claim to have the right to transmit government information diagonally and vertically. In all systems there is a formal delegation of authority to other bodies, such as local governments or public corporations. In Israel, however, the delegation of state monopoly is more than a formality in three specific areas.

First, there is an agreement with the Jewish Agency which was formalized in the Law of Status enacted by the Knesset in 1952. This gave to non-Israeli organizations a formal standing in central steering and detracted from the center's monopoly on internal affairs, such as absorption of immigrants or settlement. This special arrangement reflects the steering difficulties of an Israeli center which is tied to the external Jewish groups and the desire to maintain these special and complicated relationships. It also points out that the political center has a monopoly on *Israeli* symbols, but not necessarily on *Jewish* ones.

Second, judicial power in Israel is also shared and erodes the state monopoly. The religious rabbinical courts derive their rules of justice from religious law, not from the state laws enacted by the Knesset. The position of the Chief Rabbinate is also ambivalent: the two Chief Rabbis are state employees, but they are also spiritual leaders of their community and preside over the independent Rabbinical Court of Appeal. The local religious councils do not report to their municipalities, nor formally to their financial sponsor, the Ministry of Religious Affairs, but are subject to the authority of the Chief Rabbinate. Again, these arrangements reflect the potential cleavage between state and religion in Israel. They point to the center's willingness to retain the status quo ante in religious affairs in order to avoid steering problems vis-à-vis the religious groups. (Note that these arrangements do not include the ultra-orthodox groups.)

Third, Israeli Arab citizens present another steering problem expressed also in their ambivalent identification with state symbols. Israeli official symbols are predominantly Jewish. The national anthem, for instance, expresses the hope of Jews to return to their homeland and cannot serve as a symbol for Israeli Arabs. The same can be said about the IDF — an important symbol for Israeli Jews, but not for Israeli Arabs, who have been exempt from compulsory military service to avoid conflict of conscience and also for security reasons. Israeli Arabs were under military government until 1965. They were subject to state laws as well as the direct jurisdiction of the military governor. Politically, there has been a great deal of control exercised by the center but no direct state monopoly on official information because that authority was delegated to the military government.

In all these cases there was consent by the state to share its monopoly. But as far as the overall portrayal of state and national symbols is concerned, these arrangements did not diminish the steering capacity of the political center. The high status of the IDF in Israeli society is perhaps the best example of both monopoly and compliance — military service is compulsory, but this has become a positive and widely shared social norm. Similarly, despite the existence of separate religious courts, the "judicial branch" is symbolically and practically regarded with high esteem in Israel.

EXCLUSIVENESS

Autonomy refers to the boundary between the political and nonpolitical domains, whereas exclusiveness refers to the internal struggle within the political system over steering. The opposite of an autonomous political system is the nonexistence of such a system in a traditional and undifferentiated society. The opposite of exclusiveness is co-driving — a system with multiple political centers. Exclusiveness is a fundamental requirement of political development because it means one steering locus per system. A political system meets this requirement when there is only one center of control with a monopoly on coercion. In communication terms, it may be said that the network is connected through one switchboard; that the main channels run through this switchboard; and that political information — especially "systemic feedback" — flows to and from this switchboard. Exclusiveness is actually the steering aspect of the definition of the political center — the power to translate into action the fact that the center represents a greater share in the distribution of values, symbols, and political resources.

Did the Israeli political center enjoy the status of exclusiveness? During the yishuv period, the voluntary political center faced great difficulties in establishing its exclusive authority. There were other powerful institutions in the network, especially autonomous and semiautonomous secondary centers. There were uncontrolled organizations such as the dissident revisionists and the ultra orthodox parties, and even independent radio channels. It is impossible to contend that all the important political information flowed through the switchboard of the organized yishuv and its main institutions — the Jewish Agency, the Va'ad Leumi, and the Haganah. Was the center still more "central" than any other contender?

Horowitz and Lissak answer this question by listing the differences between the yishuv and other new political systems (1978: 37-40). First, the periphery of the yishuv was educated, motivated, mostly urban, and politically mobilized. The agricultural sector was not a traditional peasantry. Jewish farmers in Palestine regarded themselves as the vanguard of the new society. Second, the political center was not the primary source of innovation and social initiative. A great deal of the driving force came from the periphery and its indigenous ideals, ideologies, and pioneering spirit. Third, there was also a distinction between the distribution of institutional authority and the distribution of charisma in Shils's sense. The former was more centralized and exclusive than the latter. Fourth, even after the national center consolidated its authority in the 1930s and important peripheral groups started to regard it as such, the secondary centers continued to function as agencies of the center in certain spheres while preserving their autonomy in others. As was explained in Chapter 4, the secondary centers remained autarchic in certain respects. They also attempted to shape the new society, or at least the way of life of those they inspired.

The last point solves the riddle. The center did gain an exclusive position, but it did not and could not subject the secondary centers to the position of a dependent vassal. There evolved a division of labor in which the center gained institutional exclusiveness while the secondary centers and the periphery as a whole retained their ability to influence. In the long run, the center's institutional basis and the monopoly on defense and foreign affairs served as the basis for its exclusiveness and enhanced its overall steering capacity in the state period.

Since 1948, the possibility of establishing competitive political centers became theoretical. Rival contenders such as the Herut party accommodated themselves to the exclusive authority of the center. Other contenders which were part of or close to the labor movement and which recognized the authority of the national institutions and their military arm retained their positions as secondary centers. In retrospect it can be said, on balance, that the state's new political center imposed its authority over secondary centers such as the Histadrut and over contenders in the periphery without demanding exclusive control of political symbols, the distribution of resources, or the relationship with the Diaspora. In certain areas the secondary centers were co-drivers and sometimes chief drivers. They could force the center through the powerful party channels to share information, control, and steering.

During the state period the trend is clearly toward increased exclusiveness of the center and reduced steering performance of the secondary centers. The periphery increased in numbers and became more "peripheral," which, by definition, made the center more "central." The center became the prime mover in the social spheres, as exemplified by the slogan "state pioneering." The center acquired monopoly over the military, the police, and other coercive means and became fully established. The increased state monopoly of identity symbols was another manifestation of this trend.

The dominance of the center was expressed also in the lack of political vitality of the local authorities. Despite some beginnings of independent municipal authority in Tel Aviv and Haifa during the yishuv period and the British legacy which would have encouraged such a development, the local authorities were completely dominated by the central government and the parties during the state period. New towns were administered from the center; in many cases their head was a veteran party official who was imported to the town for this purpose. Similarly, secondary centers of the labor, civic, and religious camps did not disappear, but their "net political value" in the exchanges with the national center and with new state groups decreased relatively. They continued to serve the political system as major organizational channels and contributed a great deal to what Fagen calls "the adequacy of subsystems of communication" (1966: 98-101). Steering capacity had reached a high status of exclusiveness by the early 1950s in terms of the center's dominance over the whole political system. By the early 1960s, however, a new situation already existed, with the old center losing part of its exclusive powers and the reemergence of old contenders as well as new ones. Exclusiveness is a dynamic concept and sensitive to these shifts. As such, it is a good criterion for evaluating fluctuations in the system's steering capacity.

TRANSMISSION AND INTAKE

Since the discussion of steering is from the point of view of the center, it is not necessary to examine the independent informational performance of the secondary centers and the various publics (see Figure 1.2 in Chapter 1), but rather to concentrate on the horizontal, diagonal, and vertical informational flows in which the center is directly involved. This discussion will also be confined to the output (transmissions) and input (intake) of domestic information and not the exchange of information with the foreign environment.

Transmission and intake refer to the center's selective exhanges of information with the relevant environment. With respect to steering capacity, one may ask a series of questions: To what extent do the center's informational efforts coordinate the activities of the leaders? secure the cooperation and support of the secondary centers? penetrate the specific publics designated as target groups? maintain the cooperation and support of the public at large?

In the foregoing discussion of the main channels, it was concluded that the center succeeded in reaching the problematic target groups during the period under review, and that it maintained their support as well as the loyalty of the general public. This was accomplished through the reinforcing efforts of the different channels, the specialized messages transmitted to different groups, the fostering of national solidarity, and other means. All this indicated that the political center developed a transmission capability that enabled it to communicate with the relevant environment and to sustain its steering capacity.

Intake of information is also required for the system's steering performance. As a process, intake is not always separable from transmission, but it generates other questions. To what extent is the center capable of receiving adequate information for steering? Has it developed a memory — storage and recall facilities? Can it translate input into intelligence? Deutsch assigns critical importance to the "receptors" of

the political system and lists the following among the chief reasons for
the system's failure:

> the loss of *intake*, that is, the loss in the effectiveness of previously
> existing channels of information from the outside world, or the loss of
> entire channels, or the loss of the ability to rearrange such intake
> channels and to develop new ones [1963: 222].

The discussion of information flow, transmission, and intake is
closely connected with the concept of *feedback*, which is an absolute
requirement for self-steering systems. Feedback often determines actual performance and policy-making.

The model presented in Figure 1.2 does not suggest the existence of
separate channels for transmission and intake. The same channels that
carry information *from* the center can carry information *to* the center.
The mass media are an obvious example of a potential two-way channel.
Parties and bureaucratic offices can also receive and scrutinize political
data for the center. There are channels that are more active in or more
suitable for transmission — for example, electoral campaign through a
radio station. Conversely, voting or public opinion polls carry information to the center. Assessment of the intake capacity of the Israeli (or any
other political system) in terms of adequacy, memory, and intelligence is
very complex. Gross performance measures, such as the system's survival, are too remote from the day-to-day problems of receiving information and using it for making the right decisions. For instance, in regard to
the system's intake of security intelligence, there have been five wars
since 1948, only one of which (1973) took the Israeli government by
surprise. In other foreign affairs decisions, the results were mixed and
difficult to compare (Brecher, 1974).

But intake of information cannot be evaluated in terms of the technical facilities alone. Memory is not just a storage of relevant information:
It determines the system's learning ability (Simon, 1957: 86) and the
quality of recombination, imagination, and judgment. The same applies
for adequacy of information and intelligence. Steering without a substantial intake of information can go on for only a short time. Governments, even if autocratic or totalitarian, depend on information drawn
from the larger reservoir of the public and other subsystems. Information must first be received and absorbed before it can be used for
different purposes. The political system must develop the means for
deciding reception priorities, for weighing adequacy, and for routing
relevant information to the appropriate decision junctions. Screening
and the ability to prevent information overload are also critical for the
steering capacity of any political system.

There is no direct evidence that the strength of the Israeli political system's steering performance stemmed from the quality of its intake facilities. Its success in transmission, however, testifies to the effective intake and screening of information. After all, problematic target groups such as Israeli Arabs or even young people could not have been penetrated and accommodated politically without adequate intake facilities. It was the organizational channels located in the secondary centers, the parties, and the affiliated bodies which operated as mediators and provided effective feedback services for the political center. They helped the center in exchanges and bargaining that have been such a significant part of the Israeli political process.

Arian emphasized the importance of brokers in the Israeli political system, a system characterized by centralization and the relative stability of the electoral results. He noted that, among the various channels of communication, the most heavily used were those between decision makers (the center) and brokers (the secondary centers). Through them, "the myriad memos, reports, letters, editorials, studies, position papers, surveys, informal meetings, background interviews, and consultation flow" (Arian, 1973: 6). It should be recalled (Chapter 7) that blatant propaganda or agitation techniques were scarcely used by the Israeli political center. The boundaries of consensus were drawn around the common contents, while manipulation of information flow in the network was part of the general penetration and maintenance efforts.

As the community grew in size and complexity, the channels used for transmission and intake also became more complicated and the need for technological mediation grew correspondingly. The party remained an effective channel for leaders and secondary-level cadres, while communication with members and the public at large was increasingly carried through newspapers, radio, and public meetings. In this sense, the steering of the Israeli political system became more modernized — that is, less intimate and more mediated, as in other developed political systems.

DIFFUSION AND LEGIBILITY

Diffusion of political information refers to transmission problems stemming from penetration and maintenance obstacles. Chaffee defines diffusion as a means of relaxing constraints on communication that affect the intervening process of the political center (1975: 87). He suggests looking for structural barriers that inhibit the diffusion of political communication, mainly those that interfere with the vertical flow of information to individuals. Under optimal conditions, diffusion would be expected to follow a normal S-curve throughout the entire population, with few constraints at the source (transmission failures) or at the receiving end (receptor failures). Under imperfect conditions, diffusion could be limited as a result of source and receiver constraints. Diffusion is also affected by the structure of the network and its channels.

Israeli conditions — smallness, literacy, shared common contents and external threat — were congenial to normal diffusion. Constraints at the source were relatively manageable because of the cartel arrangements among the leaders and the effective bargaining and compromise mechanisms. Likewise, the network as a whole was rather efficient at information flow (see Chapter 4), especially in the use of organizational channels as transmitters and relay points. The most difficult constraint on diffusion was the target groups — those national, ethnic, religious, and ideological circles whose penetrability was made difficult by the objective differences as well as the groups' subjective desire to isolate themselves. Nonetheless, diagonal diffusion through the mediators and vertical diffusion through the bureaucratic channels were all instrumental in the penetration of the target groups and the high political mobilization of almost the entire Israeli population.

It was emphasized in Chapter 7 that the existence of parallelism between party and mass channels contributed to the diffusion of both specialized messages (aimed at separate groups) and the general national messages. Diffusion was also facilitated by the high attentiveness of Israelis to political information, especially on security matters. Thus, in 1968 when the Israeli submarine *Dakar* was missing with all its crew members, the rumor that it had been found reached 77 percent of the population in the telephone sample within one and a half hours.[7] Wishful expectations had caused the extraordinary rapid diffusion of a false rumor.

The center must also develop a capacity to transmit information legibly — with little loss or distortion. Legibility requires both an ability to speak in a manner that is "understood" by the recipient and the continuous control of information flow through the channels in order to prevent loss and to correct distortions.[8] Legibility is, first, a matter of language and content. The Israeli center had to speak in different political languages to the various target groups and different segments of the public. It also had to operate persuasively and to make it worthwhile for the members of such groups and publics to behave on the basis of this information. This was done rather successfully through the penetration/maintenance efforts and the utilization of various channels in which differentiated political languages and contents flowed. It was also enhanced by the development of political symbols as objects of identification (see Chapter 3).

The second aspect of legibility has to do with the quality of information transmitted by the center as a result of the feedback mechanism. Feedback flow informs the political center as to what kind of information to transmit, to whom, and at what level. The quality of such information is not an objective attribute but depends on the probability of being comprehended and acted on. There is no simple way to evaluate whether the information transmitted by the Israeli center was legible. One can only guess on the basis of the more obvious types of feedback from the public. The high rate of participation in national elections, the widespread use of citizens' appeals to public officials, and the extensive use of the courts serve as indirect indicators that the vertical flow of information has indeed reached the public and taught them the rules of the political game.

AVOIDANCE OF BREAKDOWNS

"Breakdowns" refer to damage in the steering mechanism that does not enable the political system to receive and transmit information concerning its goals and its own behavior (Deutsch, 1963: 219). A system may fall short of a certain goal (this happens all the time), but if the system loses its ability to correct its course or to pursue other goals — that is, loses its steering capacity — there is a breakdown. Every failure and every destabilizing experience may become a crisis and a potential breakdown. The steering capacity of a system cannot be evaluated according to the *number* of such events. More revealing is the system's ability to keep going. Most indicators of a political system's stability count violent conflicts, such as the number of riots (Taylor and Hudson, 1972). While such events do indicate disturbances, they are not measurements of steering capacity. A system with a low steering capacity may require a large internal security force and invest most of its political energy in securing compliance. Conversely, a system with a high steering capacity may be able to overcome a great number of disturbances with relatively little effort and no coercion.

The discussion here will be limited to a number of crises and potential breakdowns in the yishuv and in the state periods (1930-1967), arranged for purposes of convenience into two groups: threats to the system as a whole and threats to one or more major subsystem. Any of the following examples could have developed into a breakdown of the system's steering capacity (see Table 8.1). Although crises emanating from the external environment are not mentioned here, it should be remembered that the

TABLE 8.1 Major Threats During the Yishuv and the State Periods (1930-1967)

Threats to the Political System	Threats to a Major Sub-System
Establishment of Etzel (1931)	Split within the Hagana (1931)
Murder of Mapai leader Arlozorov (1933)	
Clashes over control of organized Jewish labor between the Histadrut and the revisionists (1934)	
Revisionists secede from the World Zionist Organization and establish the New Zionist Organization (1935)	
Arab revolt and economic recession (1936-1940)	Split in Etzel and the establishment of Lehi (1941)
Internal debates around the Biltmore Program, calling for an independent Jewish commonwealth in Palestine (1942)	
Yishuv authorities open conflict ("The Season") with Etzel (1944-)	Split in Mapai (1944)
Impact of the Holocaust on the yishuv (1945-)	
Altalena Affair (June 1948)	

Disbandment of the Palmach (Dec. 1948)

Mass immigration and economic austerity (1949-1952)

Reparations agreement with West Germany (1951-1952)

Ben-Gurion's resignation (1953)

Kastner trial (1954-57)

Wadi Salib riots (1959)

Lavon Affair (1960-61)

New economic policy (1962)

Economic recession (1965-1967)

Waiting period before the 1967 war

Split in the Kibbutz Me'uchad Movement (1951)

Crises in the defense system: "The Mishap" in Egypt (1954) and the Sharett-Lavon Feud (1955)

Crises in the Histadrut/government relations (1957 and 1959)

"Revolt of the young" in Mapai (1958-1959)

Lavon Affair (1960-1961)

Ben-Gurion's retirement (1963)

Split in Mapai and establishment of Rafi (1965)

successful meeting of these external tests (especially wars) reinforced the system's ability to overcome internal threats.

During the yishuv period there were two major sources of threats. The first was the rivalry between the labor and revisionist movements. This included accusations of political murder (1933), violent clashes over control of organized labor (1934), an institutional crisis in the Zionist movement (1935), the beginnings of a civil war (from 1944), and a dramatic and bloody clash on the Tel Aviv beach over a ship of arms (*Altalena*) brought in by Etzel. The center of the organized yishuv felt threatened by the separate existence and activities of the revisionist movement and the independent armed organizations mainly because they challenged the center's monopoly over the use of Jewish force. Likewise, Etzel felt hunted and betrayed by the national organizations and especially the labor-affiliated groups and the Haganah. Despite this inflammable situation, the clash did not develop into a full-scale civil war. The revisionists participated in the Zionist movement before and after their withdrawal, which lasted eleven years (1935-1946). Despite the fact that they had separate organizational and mass channels, there was cooperation, even on the military level for a brief period in 1945-1946. The breakdown was avoided due to the national common contents, the partial participation of the revisionist movement in the center and its network, and the ability of the majority to use limited force against the minority.

The second threat to the yishuv political system was less tangible and connected to the hostile external environment. The center and its leaders had to face not only problems of British policy, the violent struggle with the Arabs, and economic crises, but also internal skepticism with regard to the yishuv power to overcome these hurdles. The period starting with the Arab revolt and the prewar economic recession (1936-1940) ended with the Holocaust in Europe. The ability of the political center and the leaders to marshal the existing resources and turn the despair into collective efforts toward the establishment of the state and victory in the War of Independence are the most salient achievements of the yishuv and its political system. Any failure, or even prolonged delay, could have resulted in the system's inability to pursue its main goal.

As for potential breakdowns in political subsystems, the Israeli phenomenon of recurring splits, mergers, and remergers had its origins in the yishuv period. In retrospect, these multiple party and organizational splits may be regarded as a mechanism for solving internal feuds by allowing each factor, ideology, and interest to have an organizational variance of "self-determination." The politics of accommodation ensured that even small groups were recognized and received a portion of the collective resources. This is a different way of looking at the Israeli multiparty system, the accompanying party key arrangements, and the proportional system of representation. However, it is also true that the major political upheavals listed in Table 8.1 consumed a huge amount of energy and disrupted the political system time and again. Nevertheless, the outcome is clear: These events did not prevent the establishment of the state in 1948, nor did they cause a breakdown of the system's steering capacity (compare M. Bernstein, 1957).

During the early state period, the origin of serious internal threats was reversed: There were fewer tremors in the political system as a whole and a major one within the dominant subsystem — the labor camp. External pressures continued to pose the supreme test. The military and diplomatic victory in 1948-1949, the policy of economic and social development, the military retaliatory operations across the borders in 1953-1956, and the Sinai campaign of 1956 all contributed to the system's stability. Within a year after the state was established, the major crises were over: The soldiers of Etzel had joined the IDF, and the separate headquarters of the Palmach was disbanded and integrated into the IDF. In January 1949, before the end of the war, the first elections to the Knesset were held.

The internal rivalry among the camps did not disappear after 1948: There were clashes over religious issues, orientations toward the east or the west, and a shattering ideological split within the kibbutz movement in 1951. This was also the period of thousands of new immigrants living in transitory camps and of economic austerity accompanied by unemployment. In 1952 the Knesset approved the proposal to demand reparations from West Germany by a 60 to 51 majority. This emotional debate took place in an unprecedented atmosphere of violence, as described by Brecher:

> When Ben-Gurion rose to present his government's statement the scene outside the Knesset building was one of mounting tension with angry demonstrators in the thousands, the sirens of police cars and ambulances and sporadic explosions of grenades. Window panes were splintered by rocks, while the fumes of tear gas bombs entered from the streets. In the two hour melee 92 policemen and 36 civilians were reported injured. At 7 p.m. an army detachment arrived and by 7:30 order was restored. [Brecher, 1974: 85, abridged].

The tension with Herut continued throughout Ben-Gurion's premiership. In 1957 Herut opposed the retreat of Israeli forces from Sinai. A year later, individuals who were ideologically close to the revisionist movement were found guilty of murdering a Mapai leader named Kastner, whom they accused of collaboration with the Nazis during World War II (Gutman, 1981: 88-97). There were many other clashes and tense periods in those formative years of the state. Suffice it to say that Prime

Minister Ben-Gurion resigned eight times in fourteen years (1949-1963). Nevertheless, these events did not cause a breakdown of the system. The threat came from developments within the dominant party, and this may be illuminating with respect to Israel's steering capacity.

In 1953 Ben-Gurion resigned for personal reasons. In 1954 the intelligence "mishap" occurred in Egypt, leading to the resignation of Lavon as Minister of Defence and his replacement by Ben-Gurion in 1955. Most Israelis knew little or nothing of these events. They were handled within the party apparatus (the resignation and appointment of leaders), or within the defense establishment (the intelligence affair), and through a secret judicial investigation (the Ulshan-Dori Investigating Committee). The ability of the center to utilize its domination to screen and control the flow of information was dramatically manifested in this case. Other internal processes were taking place at the same time: tensions among the government, the Histadrut, and the party; attempts by younger Mapai members to reach positions of influence within the party; continued rivalry with other parties; and the increasing independence of both bureaucratic and mass channels.

The Lavon Affair of 1960-1961 was the most serious challenge to the political system and its steering capacity during the state's first fifteen years (Eisenstadt, 1967: 329-332; Medding, 1972: 261-180). The crisis contained almost all possible political disruptions: a cabinet resignation, leading to early elections, Ben-Gurion's final resignation, and the split within the dominating party. All the major political institutions were involved: Knesset, judiciary, Defence Ministry, IDF, Histadrut, press, and parties. This was followed by a severe economic recession in 1965-1967. For the first time since Israel's establishment, there was a feeling that not only was the political system not functioning, but that its survival was in danger. The unexpected deterioration into another international crisis and the long "waiting period" before the war in May 1967 brought the subjective feeling of breakdown to a climax. It is fruitless to speculate about the outcome of the political crisis had the 1967 war not taken place, or had its military outcome been different for Israel. The fact is, however, that the political system survived this test and reestablished itself in no small measure due to the military victory.

It can be seen in retrospect that there was some evidence of disintegration of the political system as early as the 1960s, and yet no breakdown of the steering mechanism had taken place then. So remarkable was the survival power of the previous system that the results of the 1965 elections were viewed as "a victory of the institutional setting of the existing regime" (Eisenstadt, 1967: 357). The process of change that was taking place in the political system may have been halted by the victory in the 1967 war. This was followed by a reconsolidation of the previous structure under the powerful premiership of Golda Meir (1968-1974).

But there were also internal systemic reasons for this long survival and reconstruction that may be taken as evidence for the system's high steering capacity.

Leadership: The dominating force in the political center, particularly the veteran leaders, proved capable of closing ranks by replacing the charismatic Ben-Gurion with Eshkol, a moderate leader. Eshkol's ability to reunite the group of veteran party members and to form an alignment with the other labor party warded off the challenge of the young party members.

New coalitions: The establishment of *Rafi* was a serious challenge, and the *Mapai* leadership had to respond in kind. In 1964 the Mapai Central Committee decided to form an alignment with Ahdut HaAvoda. They created a united block in the 1965 elections and obtained 45 seats in the Knesset (compared to 50 obtained by the two separate parties in 1961). Rafi gained only 10 seats in the Knesset. Under the circumstances, this was a victory for the Alignment and proved its ability to adjust to changing conditions.

Mobilization for internal struggle: In the effort to avoid breakdown, all organizational and mass channels were put to work. During the Lavon Affair, the party, bureaucratic, and mass channels were recruited for the task. Such wide-ranging political mobilization shows the other side of steering capacity in a highly politicized society like Israel. Once the internal process breaks up and the previously private feuds among political leaders come into the open, these rapidly engulf the whole political system. It is ironic that the efficiency of the system's information transmission, intake, diffusion, and legibility also fosters the spread of political crises. One is then witness to the mobilization of the entire communication network and the investment of huge resources and great energy in the internal struggle. Total mobilization is not necessarily harmful for steering, if the mechanism itself is not damaged in the process. In retrospect, it seems that the Lavon Affair and its ensuing crises contributed to opening up the Israeli political system without breaking it down.

Mobilization for external struggle: Facing an external threat, a national unity cabinet was formed in May 1967 — the first almost wall-to-wall coalition since the founding of the state. This included the Herut leaders — who, until that time, were never members of any cabinet coalition — and it reinstated the dissenting Rafi leaders, notably Dayan, in the government. (Rafi rejoined the Labor Alignment a year later.) This cabinet reshuffle was a major adjustment and perhaps sacrifice made by the ruling parties and leaders in order to regain public support and to preserve the political system. It had long-run repercussions and might have been a factor in the process culminating in the change of government in 1977. In 1967, however, it was yet another demonstration of the ability of the political system and its various components to huddle under the general umbrella of the Zionist consensus and to retain steering capacity under pressure of a security challenge (Galnoor, 1980: 125).

The reconstruction of the old political system in the mid-1960s showed not only high steering capacity, but also the other side of avoiding breakdown — political stability.

Israel:
Steering Capacity and Political Development

If a political system develops steering capacity and gets high marks on autonomy, monopoly, exclusiveness, transmission, diffusion, and avoidance of breakdowns, is it also a system with decision-making capabilities? If we assume that there is a direct causal relationship between steering capacity and political outcomes, where does decision-making come in?

DECISION-MAKING

Steering is *internal* to the political system; its results are not. Consequently, the literature on decision-making and policy-making is justly concerned with many more variables than those of communication and steering (Dror, 1968: 50-57, 69). Decision-making implies the ability to choose among alternatives as well as to implement decisions and secure certain outcomes. In analyzing political communication we are interested in the information flow and its potential for goal-oriented decision-making. From this vantage point there is no need to separate steering and decision-making — the two involve action based on communication. Deutsch discusses political systems as "decision systems" and suggests analyzing steering performance in terms of "decision points" (1963: 209-213). The term "center" has been used here and can be regarded for practical purposes as a "decision center." How should the steering performance of a decision center be evaluated? On the basis of the information presented about Israel, one can evaluate whether or not the system and its political center possess steering capacity. On this

STEERING 289

basis, however, one cannot determine whether it actually makes decisions, let alone makes good ones or is able to implement them. A communication network is no guarantee of "good steering" or of creative decision-making.[9] The communication approach to steering and decision-making is not normative in the sense of advocating, for example, network openness or the free flow of information. It does point out, however, that if certain communication requirements are met, they will enhance the system's survival and viability. Moreover, communication and understanding are not synonymous. Conflict is part and parcel of the political process, and so are collisions and catastrophes that might occur despite the communication process. Steering capacity is an *opportunity* for decisions that bind the political system as a whole and can keep it moving toward collective goals — no more and no less than that.

There are very few detailed studies of the decision-making process in the Israeli political system (Akzin and Dror, 1966, on domestic affairs; Brecher, 1972 and 1974, on foreign affairs). In a study of national planning in Israel (Bilski et al., 1980), the conclusion was reached, on the basis of case studies, that there was only partial planning in Israel's subsystems, a fact that is closely related to the other characteristics of the political and administrative system (1980: 337). In the case of water policy-making in Israel (pp.137-215), for example, it was concluded that until 1964 the success in coping with water scarcity was due to

- a continuity between ideology and policy-making, both of which were translated into planning and implementation;
- feedback from operation in the field into policy decisions and the allocation of resources:
- the implementation of water policy within a detailed legal framework (the Water Law, 1959) and with sharply bounded organizational tools; and
- the capacity to plan, develop, and manage the water system in a way that was beneficial to agricultural development and settlement — despite the many strong and often conflicting interests involved.

Decision-making in the area of water development has the advantage of concreteness, and the case study clearly shows the contribution of the organized agricultural sector to the system's steering capacity in this sphere. In other domestic areas, there was less structuring, and decision-making was more markedly based on political and administrative bargaining and improvisation. Generally, and in terms of outcomes, the Israeli political system proved capable of making decisions that affected the country's development. It possessed a communication network that enabled it to choose among alternatives and to implement decisions — at least on the subsystem level. As far as steering capacity is concerned, these were binding decisions, and they moved the entire system toward collective goals.

COMPLIANCE

In discussing Israel's steering capacity, little attention was paid to how it was actually carried out. Did steering require coercion and force? No political system, regardless of its type of regime, can exist without a certain amount of cooperation and coordination in the pursuit of collective goals. Cooperation can be achieved through voluntary or coercive means, yet the actual use of force is just a "damage-control mechanism of society" (Deutsch, 1963: 122). Coercion can also be analyzed as an attribute of steering capacity and in terms of the energy required for obtaining obedience. Thus the degree of coercion used on the various target groups in order to obtain their incorporation into the system can be evaluated. Coercion is undoubtedly the most blunt steering instrument in the arsenal of the state and its political center. It will be discussed here only in terms of its intended result — compliance.

The Israeli political system was not compelled to employ troops, secret police, massive arrests, and the like in order to secure compliance. Legal and political mechanisms never broke down to the point of massive noncompliance or threatened resistance. Despite restrictions on the flow of information and many other institutional limitations, cooperation was usually secured voluntarily and through incentives. Information flow was centrally controlled but not dictated. The network was utilized to secure compliance through persuasion, not force. The channels were used by the center to penetrate target groups and maintain loyalty, but there were abundant opportunities for political opposition as well (Dahl, 1971: 213).

Political coercion was not required to achieve integration. It was sparingly used on the Jewish population and moderately on the Arab population (Smooha, 1978: 227-228). Steering performance is sensitive to the *form* of compliance — whether enforced or voluntary — that determines the informational efforts required. The strategy used to achieve compliance is based on feedback regarding reactions. Troops might be sent to control a riot on the basis of voluntary feedback. If the disturbance persists, a special and continuous information effort is necessary and "mobilized" or compulsory feedback may be arranged. In Israel, mobilized feedback was a result of a high degree of agreement on basic goals and the development of a steering capacity to match the internal composition of society. It did not require constant or frequent employment of coercion and force.

In the yishuv period compliance was achieved through "solidarity without coercion" (Ben-Aharon, 1977: 12). After 1948 the state monopoly on coercive means was used, but compliance of the Jewish population with the steering guidance of the center, rather than its enforcement capability, was higher. There were relatively few break-downs (see Table 8.1), and therefore coercion was used sparingly and mainly for controlling damage. To say that compliance was relatively high indicates that steering was performed with a relatively low invest-ment in the coercive transmission of information. In this respect, Israel fits the "reconciliation system" suggested by Apter (1971: 31-34) — low on coercion and high on information — which is required for increasing the effectiveness of bargaining.

STABILITY

Political stability does not mean stagnation and a continuation of the status quo, but purposeful and orderly change (Pye, 1966: 41). Stability is related to a high degree of autonomy, because otherwise the polity is too easily destabilized by economic and social forces. Steering includes the concept of autonomous and stable movement, otherwise goal-seeking is impossible.

Steering performance aimed at keeping the political system on a stable course is not a normative goal in the sense of "law and order," nor is it always identical with the restoration of equilibrium (Deutsch, 1974: 157-159). Stability may mean a steady movement toward a new or chang-ing goal; thus steering aimed at stabilizing the system depends on feed-back for correcting mistakes and anticipating destabilizing forces. It is difficult, however, to evaluate political development in terms of the level of stability resulting from skillful or unskillful steering, because elegant and noiseless steering is not the most important attribute. Thus, stability does not refer to the steering mechanism itself or to the political center alone. Both are stable when there is no movement at all. Stability is significant with reference to the political system and its effect on the society as a whole. Steering capacity resulting in stability therefore cannot mean *avoiding* social conflicts, but *managing* them. When over-all stability is evaluated, one must cross the political system's boundary and examine feedback from the environment — namely, the relationship between steering capacity and the actual political outcomes.

A political system "should not" have goals of its own. As a collective instrument, all its goals should be exogenous — that is, within the social environment — but it is clear that political systems do have self-interests. The established ones pursue stability because it is more con-ducive to achieving societal goals and also because stability is a means of preserving their own power and resisting the threats inherent in change. Stability means both order — the absense of violence, force, and disruption from the political system — and continuity — the absence of change in critical components such as the legitimization and loyalty of its members (Huntington and Dominguez, in Greenstein and Polsby, 1975: Vol. 3, 7).[10]

The most extreme manifestation of instability is a revolution, and the usual circumstances for such an occurrence are the fragmentation of the political system into two or more parts and a struggle between them over exclusive control (Tilly in Greenstein and Polsby, 1975: Vol. 3, 519-521). Regardless of what follows, such a disruption engages the major components of the political system. Relatively minor disruptions — political violence, riots, or increased coercion — are not necessarily disruptive to the stability of the whole system (compare different approaches to political stability in Rosenthal, 1978). Stability is easier to conceptualize in negative terms — the absence of major disruptions in the main components of the political system:

- the sharing of common contents;
- the posture of the political center, the division of labor with the secondary centers, and the interaction with the periphery;
- the penetrative and maintenance capability of the political network and its major channels;
- the content, direction, and quantity of information flow and the amount of energy devoted to the task of stabilizing the system; and
- the soundness of the steering mechanism and its ability to avoid breakdowns, especially in feedback.

It is impossible to say whether a major disruption in just one of the above components is sufficient to induce instability. Probably not, because the ability of the political system to absorb changes in a certain component and to steer clear of isolated disruptions are themselves tests of stability. Judging stability and instability is much like assessing the aftermath of an earthquake. The fact that a certain event sends a tremor throughout the political system is merely a cue that requires further analysis. Several components are destroyed and several remain intact; others change and still others tumble down later. A stable political system may undergo radical transformations — an absence of continuity in its major components in the long run — without the incapacitation of its steering mechanism. Conversely, an absence of continuity in the short run means instability.

As for the Israeli political system, its relative stability enables us to examine the phenomenon of rapid socioeconomic changes occurring simultaneously with high levels of political order and continuity. As Medding noted, Israel is an exception among the new states established after 1945:

It has avoided political instability, coups, internal violence, military takeover and general political decay: to the contrary, it possesses a stable, effective, working, democratic political system enjoying widespread public support and legitimacy; the loyalty of citizens to the state is unquestioned; and its economic growth rate has been one of the highest in the world. [1972: 1].

Despite some major tremors and the threats of breakdown (see Table 8.1), the Israeli political system has been stable throughout the period since 1948. This is a remarkable achievement given the turbulent external environment and internal fragmentation. What are the concrete manifestations of this stability?

In terms of political order, not only have there been no coups, but the general level of internal political violence has been low. This is also true regarding the use of repressive force or intergroup violence. Continuity has been manifest in almost every facet of Israeli political life even beyond the period under review here. Between 1948 and 1981, there have been ten orderly national and local elections and only six prime ministers who presided over no fewer than twenty cabinets. The whole Jewish population of the country was mobilized to participate in five wars; five different cabinets decided on retreat from areas occupied during wars.[11] Numerous controversial laws, policies, and decisions have been made by the Knesset, the Cabinet, and the courts. Finally, the dominating party which was in power for more than fifty years was defeated in the May 1977 elections and a new party took over — peacefully.

Even more striking is the absence of significant changes in the constitutional and political structure in Israel during this entire period. Some important decisions of the Provisional Council and the Constituent Assembly (1948-1949) are still in effect. Israel does not have a written constitution, only Basic Laws. There is a unicameral legislative body, and — despite many attempts to change it — national elections are still proportional, in which the whole country is considered one region.

Israel continues to have a multiparty political system, and all its cabinets have been based on coalitions among no fewer than four parties. The formal roles of the presidency or of the law courts have not changed during this period, and the same can be said about many other political institutions and procedures. For instance, there were no major reforms in the civil service or in local government except for direct elections of heads of local authorities; and the two most important non-governmental institutions — the Histadrut and the Jewish Agency — are legally similar today to what they were thirty years ago.

This list should not mislead anyone into assuming that there have not been changes in the Israeli political system. The system adapted itself to changing external circumstances as well as to major internal transformations in the society, the economy, and the political culture. But what accounts for the ability of the system to maintain order and continuity in the face of rapid changes?

Despite all the changes and the velocity of political operations, the same Jewish, Zionist, and Israeli common contents continued to serve the system's steering capacity — at least until 1967.[12] The basic division of labor between the political center and the secondary centers and their interaction with the periphery — indeed, the whole configuration of the political network and the main channels — did not change much from 1948 to the 1960s (Gutmann in Lissak and Gutmann, 1977: 122-170). During that period the Israeli case contradicted the prevailing assumption that multiparty systems are the least stable. It demonstrated Lijphart's point (1977: 16) that heterogeneous societies with multiparty political systems can be stable. In Israel about 20 parties and lists compete in national elections, with no party getting an absolute majority of the votes. The distribution of votes among the major political camps remained rather constant and so did the need for a cabinet based on more than a minimum winning coalition. Many threats of breakdown resulted in just another cabinet reshuffle.

Throughout this period structural rigidity of institutions and organizations was a central feature of Israel's political stability. This is the main reason why, during the state period, almost all the yishuv institutions and informal arrangements such as the party key continued to be in effect.

The stability of the Israeli system was not a goal of the political center alone. Arian noted that "the conservative nature of the Israeli political system guards against radical alternatives, leaving the fundamentals of Israeli politics relatively unchanged" (1968: viii). In other words, the most important components of the system developed a vested interest in continuity. This is certainly so in the case of Mapai and the Histadrut — the "conservative elements" in the system (Eisenstadt, 1967: 314) — which were interested in maintaining and perpetuating their positions. But in the course of time, even opposition parties such as Herut and nonaffiliated economic enterprises developed an interest in perpetuating the system because they could gain more by supporting its stability than by undermining it. Even the parties and groups which did not participate directly in the coalition governments — except for the Communists and Neturei Karta — were recipients of the party key benefits. Similarly, the secondary centers acknowledged the political supremacy of the center and usually contributed to the avoidance of disruptions. Here lies an important reason for the system's stability.

The secondary centers absorbed many of the shocks and diffused much of the internal pressure, leaving the center relatively free to handle major crises, particularly external ones. The communication network and the channels served as feedback mechanisms for anticipating disruptions and for correcting performance. Through a constant intake of information, the parties and the bureaucracy supplied the political center with detailed information about the degree of support in the public at large and among the target groups in particular. Many dissenting views or actual disruptions did not need to reach the center. They were handled quite efficiently by the intermediate channels through which all important information had to pass. This structure of the network to a large extent determined the content, direction and quantity of the information flow. It enabled the political center to invest relatively little energy in the task of stabilizing the system. This role was performed effectively by loyal party functionaries and bureaucrats operating behind the scenes with the full backing of the national leaders.[13]

The most common method for stabilizing the system was cooptation. The information generated from below by the main channels was used to coopt dissenting groups, to increase a group's share in the distribution of resources, and, occasionally, to convince the leaders that a change of policy is required. For instance, the ability to learn from previous mistakes and to change policy was evident in the new settlement policy in the Lahish region, designed around an entirely new concept of immigrant absorption (Weitz and Rokach, 1968: 278-290). In previous chapters other examples were given of how the challenge posed by ethnic, religious, and other groups was met. It should be stressed that cooptation required a great deal of learning and adaptation on the part of the political center and that this learning eventually contributed to the stability of the system. The soundness of the steering mechanism of the Israeli political system and its ability to avoid breakdowns was helped by constant feedback from most relevant publics. This was a special Israeli version of citizens' participation (Huntington, 1968: 78-92), to be discussed in Chapter 10.

On the face of it, some characteristics of Israel's political system are not conducive to stability. The politics of accommodation creates a great deal of friction and waste of political energy. If the internal political process in Britain is loaded with "useless self-made friction" (Crossman, 1976: Vol. 2, 783), this is much truer of Israel. Nevertheless, the degree of stability of the system has not changed much during the four decades of 1930-1960. If anything, the steering capacity of the center in terms of retaining stability increased in the state period. The challenges remained great, but offsetting mechanisms had been developed and honed by the center, the network, and the main channels. The evidence is the way the system coped with threats and potential break-downs.

Things started to change, especially after the 1967 war. Perhaps there is a level in socioeconomic development and modernization beyond which satisfaction becomes difficult. Perhaps the rate of growth in Israel was so fast that a downfall was inevitable; and certainly there were groups that were left behind and started to demand social and political equality. In any case, in the 1970s the coexistence between the socio-economic revolution and political stability had reached a turning point, and the Israeli political system ceased to enjoy the same level of stability as before.

STEERING PATHOLOGIES

Saying that a system is politically developed in terms of steering capacity and decision-making, compliance and stability does not mean that it is free of governing problems. There are systems whose communication networks are inoperative because of the "Tower of Babel" syndrome — no common contents, especially no legibility. They have no steering capacity and are politically undeveloped. Developed political systems like Israel, however, can demonstrate many steering pathologies, such as the following:

- the "all sail and no anchor" syndrome (Huntington, 1966: 87). This is found in a system that has lost its traditional (or ideological) basis and is tossed about, responding to random pressures and other immediate currents.
- the "locked wheel" syndrome. Here there is an inability to change course because information is demanded and absorbed according to set preconceptions (Wilensky, 1967; Friedrich, 1972; Janis, 1972).
- the "high-octane" syndrome. In this case, the internal political process falls victim to excessive overlap and redundancy as most of the information flow is consumed in intensive internal bargaining. Such a situation may leave little reserve for adjusting to the external environment, for political innovations, or even for decision-making.
- the "display window" syndrome. Politics is conducted entirely up front with no backroom caucus or discreet bargaining. The network becomes leakage-prone, and the result could be an intolerable overload of information (mostly irrelevant) on the center's steering mechanism.

While the first two syndromes were not acutely present in Israeli politics in the period under review, the third one appeared as far back as the early 1960s with the beginning of the Lavon Affair. The "display window" syndrome appeared only in the 1970s (Galnoor, 1980: 141-144).

TABLE 8.2 Israel's Profile of Steering Capacity During the Yishuv (1930-1948) and State (1948-1960s) Periods

		Low	Medium	High
Autonomy	yishuv			+
	state			+
Monopoly on official symbols	yishuv	+		
	state			+
Exclusiveness	yishuv		+	
	state			+
Information trans- mission and intake	yishuv			+
	state			+
Information diffus- sion and legibility	yishuv			+
	state		+	
Avoidance of breakdowns	yishuv		+	
	state			+

In any case, pathologies such as these must also be taken into consideration when the steering profile of a political system is drawn.

Profiles of Steering Capacity

On the basis of the discussion presented so far, Israel's political system scored high on steering capacity. There is also evidence that this fact had a direct impact on the political outcomes — the system's ability to make binding decisions, to secure compliance with little use of coercion, and to avoid incapacitating breakdowns. What is the general meaning of these characteristics in terms of political development? Table 8.2 compares the steering profile of the Israeli political system during the yishuv and state periods.

The first and perhaps most interesting point in Table 8.2 is that, in general, the yishuv system was already quite developed politically in terms of steering capacity. Second, the main developments after 1948 were a greater ability to use official symbols, greater exclusiveness of the political center, and better mechanisms for coping with breakdowns. Third, in terms of information transmission, intake, diffusion, and particularly legibility, there was a turn in the other direction, because of the drastic increase in population and the change in its composition and complexity. Nevertheless, Israel's profile suggests a high steering capacity and thus can be regarded as a profile of a politically developed system.

The components presented in Table 8.2 can be used for analyzing other political systems and for comparative studies in the following ways:

- drawing the internal developments of the system in terms of increases and decreases in its steering capacity over time, and
- comparing the profile of one political system with another in a given period.

Although the components used to draw the profile of the Israeli political system may need some adjustment when used for other systems, this does not change the validity of the proposition that the development of political systems with different regimes can be analyzed and compared in terms of their steering capacity.

So far political development has been discussed from the point of view of the center. In the next two chapters I shift the focus and discuss the special case of *democratic* political development in terms of people's access and participation.

NOTES

1. This point was stressed by Deutsch (1963: 191):

While the evaluation of political systems as steering systems ought to be technically possible, it would be quite one-sided. Both Pericles and John Stuart Mill might remind us that states should not merely be evaluated in terms of their ability to function efficiently as states, but far more in terms of the types of personality and character they produce among their citizens, and the opportunities they offer to all their citizens for individual development. . . . Over-all steering performance is an important aspect of political decision systems but it is by no means an exhaustive one.

2. On organizational development, see March and Simon (1958), Gross (1964: 657-693), Starbuck (1965), Bennis (1966), and Handy (1976).

3. For instance, Jewish messianic movements, such as the Sabbatian Movement in the seventeenth century, drew their binding powers from similar facilities of recall and historical memory. More obvious examples are modern anti-Zionist Jewish political movements such as the Bund — the Socialist and Trade Union Organization of Jewish Workers in Russia and Poland, at the end of the nineteenth century — or the "territorialists" in Eastern Europe who favored Jewish colonization but not in Palestine (see Halpern, 1969: 16-19). It is interesting to note that some of them, particularly the Bund, were against using the Hebrew language and favored Yiddish instead.

4. On systems analysis presented in similar terms, see Hall and Fagen (1968).

5. Note also the following references to political control in terms similar to steering: "Regulative performance refers to the exercise of control by a political system over the behavior of individuals and groups in the society" (Almond and Powell, 1978: 307); or Simon's proposition that deliberate control of the environment is part of the decision-making process (1957: 109).

6. On the general interdependence between the Israeli center and the Diaspora and the primacy of the former, see Urbach (1979).

7. The Israel Institute of Applied Social Research, "Telephone Survey of the Rumors about the Submarine Dakar on January 1, 1968," Jerusalem, 1968 (mimeograph, Hebrew).

8. Marvick describes the careful attention to the preservation of message meanings by party outpost personnel in India, whose task is to "make spontaneous field corrections in the political communication process" (1970: 953).

9. The literature on decision-making emphasizes many other variables, such as leadership recruitment, internal dynamics, environmental constraints, effectiveness, implementation, and the decision maker's psyche. See Simon (1957), Gore and Dyson, (1964), Lindblom (1965), Dror (1968), King (in Greenstein and Polsby, 1975, Vol. 5, 173-256), and Wildavsky (1979).

10. Order is also referred to as "persistence" — attempts to overcome stress in a way that will enable the system to survive (Easton, 1965a: 78).

11. Ben-Gurion's cabinets in 1949 and 1957, Meir's cabinet in 1974, Rabin's cabinet in 1975, and Begin's cabinet in 1979.

12. Common contents became problematic after 1967 and did not serve the system's stability as before. The war of 1967 was a spectacular victory, but it did not solve the Arab-Israeli conflict and reopened many ideological questions regarding Zionism. The 1973 war, and Saadat's peace initiative of 1977 had a shattering impact on those questions (Galnoor, 1980).

13. On the way this was done in Mapai, see Aronoff, (1977), Almogi (1980), and especially the first chapter in Netzer (1980) entitled "Behind the Scenes."

9

ACCESS

Monarchy is like a splendid ship: with all sails set, it moves majestically
on, then it hits a rock and sinks forever. Democracy is like a raft. It
never sinks, but, damn it, your feet are always in the water.
(FISHER AMES, QUOTED BY BROGAN, 1945)

Building steering capacity means enhancing political development
which is not inherently related to democratization. Democratic tenets,
such as the need to obtain the consent of the governed, individual
freedoms, and people's opportunity to have an impact on government,
are not part of the definition here of political development. Nevertheless, democracy does not contradict political development: It does,
however, pose additional requirements and entails a different process of
steering. The presentation of democratic political development as a
special case of political development will be postponed to Chapter 11.
Here I will simply note that the most salient characteristic of the democratic case is that the feet of the steerers are always in the water — that
is, the public, having an independent role in the steering process, frequently tips the raft.

This "independent role" of the public was defined in Chapter 1 in
terms of (a) access, (b) participation, and (c) impact on steering. This
general conceptualization of democracy is derived from the historical
experience of western democracies inasmuch as it regards access and
participation as standards of citizenship (Thompson, 1970: 2). However,
in general the communication approach is not bounded by the usual
distinctions between Western and non-Western political systems (com-

pare Lijphart, 1977: 21-24). For instance, access to and utilization of the communication network can be exercised in many different ways derived from the distinct features of different political cultures.

The proposed distinction between gaining access and participating is based, as noted, on an examination of the communication process in which information is a means for reaching other political resources. Access is better understood in terms of *opportunities* to exchange political messages, whereas participation is a communication *activity*. Access does not lead automatically to participation. It is, however, a prerequisite, without which participation and impact on steering are impossible.

The assumption in democratic theory that people know what is good for them and only need a chance to express it must be supplemented. In modern democracies, in order for citizens to express their preferences and participate in the political process, they need information about how the political system responds to their preferences — in other words, what government is actually doing (Galnoor, 1977: 276). This notion of access thus establishes "the people's right to know" as a fundamental, democratic freedom equal to the well-established freedom of expression and freedom of the press. The emphasis on *autonomous* access is aimed at pointing out that citizens may "gain access" to false information and that participation can be distorted not only by coercion but also through public relations and propaganda. Impact on steering, therefore, is the result of autonomous access and participation.

In presenting Israel's democratic political development, I start, as has been done in other chapters, with the general environmental conditions before proceeding to individual and group political mobility and access to the main channels in the network. The main modes of participation and concluding discussion of impact on steering will be presented in the following chapters.

Democratic Tenets in Israel

In Chapter 2 the formal aspects of Israeli democracy, such as free elections and the multiparty system, were presented. By way of introducing access and participation, some additional elements are required. The internal process of democratic political development in Israel was influenced by (a) the ideological basis of political action and (b) the level of tolerance toward the social divisions.

ZIONIST IDEOLOGIES AND DEMOCRACY

There was no formal resolution in 1948 that the State of Israel be a democracy, but for almost eighty years the Zionist movement and the State of Israel did not adopt another type of political regime. To be sure, there were also nondemocratic overtones in the Zionist movement. The pioneering groups were influenced by European radical ideological movements of the early part of this century, and there were many authoritarian features in these doctrines. There was the impact of Marxist ideology on the Labor Zionist movement and especially its left wing, Hashomer Hatzair. In 1921, Ben-Gurion proposed organizing a "workers army" (Tzva HaAvoda) which would exert military-type discipline over the workers, the agricultural and urban communes, and the utilization of economic means (J. Shapira, 1975: 52-53). Inspiration for this idea apparently came from the military workers' organization set up by Trotsky in the Soviet Union in 1920. At the other end of the ideological spectrum, the revisionist movement, influenced by European radical nationalist movements and certain spinoffs, such as *Brit Habiryonim* in the early 1930s, were nondemocratic.[1] All told, the intensive internal rivalry in the yishuv did not promote tolerance, while external threats required military organization and discipline. Why wasn't the yishuv led by a revolutionary, dictatorial movement or leader, even temporarily? Indeed, given the preoccupation with security and wars, why didn't Israel turn into a garrison state?

Israeli democracy is the result both of special circumstances surrounding the Zionist movement and the values pioneering groups brought with them which were fused into a distinctive ideology. Horowitz and Lissak emphasize the first reason: "In a political system whose center lacked the sanctions available to a sovereign state, the only possibility for creating effective political institutions lay in the willingness of all parties to establish a pluralistic political structure based on compromise" (1978: 144). This is an important factor, especially because "practical Zionism" was an approach shared by all parties in the organized yishuv, particularly the dominant labor movement. It meant, among other things, that the goal could be reached only gradually and through external and internal bargaining. One major internal compromise was the recognition of other versions of Zionism and their right to be in opposition.[2]

The second factor was no less important. Zionism as an ideology embraced democracy, not only as a fundamental argumentation but also on the operative level (Seliger, 1970). Operatively, the main institutions of the yishuv, such as the Representatives Assembly and the Histadrut's, General Conference, were democratically elected. The kibbutz and workers' urban cooperatives in which direct democracy was practiced further testify to the belief in individual participation in labor Zionism. Equally important was the egalitarian vision in this ideology and its stress on the social meaning of the Zionist revolution. "How does one turn individual aspirations into a mass movement?" asked Berl Katznelson, and then answered, "by implanting social contents in our national movement" (A. Shapira, 1980: 123).

When the labor parties started to lead the national movement in the 1930s, their voluntary, noncoercive nature was largely preserved and pluralism gradually became incorporated into both practice and ideology. It was not achieved easily, and there were struggles over the independence of the kibbutz movements and many splits of dissatisfied groups. In the end, however, the line adopted — and sometimes enforced — was that despite the ideological gaps and the bitter disputes, the Zionist community of fate should be preserved and placed above all differences. Ben-Gurion presented the supremacy of Zionism in extreme language in a speech to the Mapai Conference in 1933:

> The Zionist organization which serves the Zionist ideology and activities has only one goal and one intention: the realization of Zionism. The labor movement is both Zionist and socialist — as the Revisionist movement is both Zionist and Hitlerian, the Mizrachi is both Zionist and religious and the General Zionists are both Zionists and bourgeois. . . . Even if we were not socialists and did not have an historical vision of a new human society liberated from economic, social, national and sexual oppression, even then, we would have done in this country exactly what we are doing now and we would fight for all that we are fighting now — because we are Zionists. [Ben-Gurion, 1974: 247-248; author's translation].

The Zionist movement was pluralistic and tolerated a high level of internal division. The egalitarian tenets of the socialist ideology that dominated the movement after the 1930s and the lack of traditional sources of socioeconomic inequality inhibited the emergence of a nondemocratic leadership. The existence of strong social cells within the Zionist movement, such as the kibbutz and the moshav, and of quasi-independent secondary centers, such as the Histadrut, were an additional guarantee against dictatorial overcentralization. Pluralism was not just a compromise — it represented the mosaic nature of Zionism. The fact that the labor movement had to be satisfied with "hegemony" rather than total control of the political system testifies to the pluralistic nature of its ideology as well as to its practical predisposition. Indeed, the incorporation of religious Zionism in the political center dominated by the secular labor movement was not just a tactical move. Besides the pragmatics behind the "historical alliance" between the labor and religious camps, the roots were much deeper (see Chapter 3). Their mutual tolerance was more than just a marriage of convenience because of the common contents (Avineri, 1980: 216-226). As noted, a certain degree of ambivalence on religious issues was inherent in Zionism, because of its diverse origins and its multiple belief systems. Moreover, the ideological rivals of Zionism could be found on both extremes of the spectrum: the universalists — Bundists, Communists, and the assimilated Jews — and the segregationists — ultra-orthodox Jews. Zionism incorporated elements of both: universal secular aspirations borrowed from European political thought and religious symbols emanating from Judaism. It also rejected elements of both: the assimilatory aspect of the Enlightenment and the passive outlook of the ultra-orthodox toward Jewish national revival. At the crucial moment of history in the 1940s, Zionism triumphed over its ideological rivals among Jews, due mainly to the external events in Europe but also because of the pluralistic nature of the movement.

One important influence on Zionism was that of European liberalism and the cultural tradition of openness and intellectual pluralism. The economic aspects of liberalism were incorporated into the ideologies of the General Zionists and the revisionists, while its political tenets infiltrated the Zionist movement as a whole (Horowitz and Lissak, 1977: 216). The British and American branches of the Zionist movement which advocated economic and political liberalism also exercised a significant influence on the democratic nature of the Zionist organization. That Zionism billed itself as a movement of the entire Jewish people compelled it to take into account the fact that many Jewish communities abroad would not tolerate a movement that was not based on open access and participation.

Thus, the political system of the yishuv and later the State of Israel met the formal requirements of democracy. Israel is among the countries whose "independence movements blended nationalism with the ideology of representative government and political liberalism" (Dahl, 1971: 43, 248-249). Huntington and Nelson point out that the phenomenon of political participation is largely "shaped by the priority that elites, groups and individuals give to political participation as a goal of development, its value in their eyes as a means to achieve other developmental goals and the extent to which political participation is itself a by-product or consequence of development" (1976: 159-160).

Among the common contents underlying the Israeli political system (Chapter 3), the existence of a democratic political culture was not mentioned because it is not a necessary requirement for political development. The evidence is, however, that the democratic tenet has been generally accepted by leaders, groups, and individuals as a means to other values, or as a by-product of development. The concrete manifestation of these attitudes in the Israeli political system, including the degree of participation of the more peripheral groups, are the subject of this and the next chapters.

SOCIAL DIVISIONS

One of the main barriers to a free flow of information is not necessarily intentional interference of the center, but the high walls between isolated social groups. The more divided a society is, the less open is the communication network and its political channels. The more stratified a society is, the less equal the distribution of opportunities for political influence. Citizens who are better educated, richer, or belong to "higher" social groups have better access to information and other political resources (Verba and Nie, 1972).

Modern Israeli society did not emerge out of a traditional class structure or out of separate territorial, linguistic, or kinship groups. Economic stratification in the yishuv was also relatively small due to the absence of an aristocracy and the public control of land, capital, and organizations. This was reinforced by the egalitarian and pioneering values and the uncomplicated occupational structure of the society. Social mobility was also simple because of the easy access to the most significant social role — pioneering. All it took to belong to the pioneering elite was a willingness to make personal sacrifices (Eisenstadt, 1967: 147-148). Distinct group divisions did exist, however. During the yishuv period, there were boundaries between the Jewish pioneering groups and the older yishuv community. There were also social enclaves centered on the countries of origin of the immigrants. But by far the most important divisions were the potential cleavages between religious and secular Jews and between the ideological camps, as discussed in Chapter 2.

After the establishment of the state, the stratification of Israeli Jewish society in terms of education, occupation, and standard of living gradually became significant (Lissak, 1964; Peres, 1976: 188-195). In the short period of twenty-five years, attributes such as income, occupation, education, and particularly housing became associated with voting behavior (Yatziv, 1974). The association between social attributes and political behavior (as expressed in voting) became even more prominent in subsequent years (Arian, 1980: 267-276). The cleavage dividing religious and secular Jews remained significant throughout the state period, while the social meaning of the ideological camps gradually faded. Internal divisions which became politically significant in terms of access and participation were those between Oriental and Western Jews, and between Israeli Jews and Arabs.

Social differences have remained relatively small in Israel compared to other deeply divided societies. Due to the successful penetration efforts of the political center, very few remained completely "outside" the political system. On this general level, social distinctions in Israel do not appear to prevent access to political resources or participation in the political process. The *results* of the political process, however, reveal a close relationship between social stratification based on ethnic differences and the distribution of political power. This becomes much more evident after 1967 and is documented in detailed research findings (Antonovsky and Arian, 1971; Zloczower, 1972; Peres, 1976, Etzioni-Halevy and Shapira, 1977; Smooha, 1978; Bernstein, 1980).

There are no detailed studies of the relationship between economic and political mobility in Israel, and only a few generalizations can be offered. In retrospect, it can be observed that the economic distribution of resources in Israel was initially more egalitarian than the political one. New immigrants, particularly Oriental Jews, could establish themselves economically more easily than they could "make it" politically, especially on the national level.

This last statement must be qualified, however, because — in terms of formal rights such as universal franchise and freedom of expression — there was political equality in Israel. Moreover, incorporation within the political system was almost complete, despite the social divisions: Jews and Arabs, old-timers and newcomers, Western and Oriental Jews, secular and religious had all been linked up to the political communication network. On the other hand, economic mobility of Israeli Arabs was very slow and autonomous access to political resources, almost nonexistent. Conversely, on the municipal level including local party and Histadrut branches, the political mobility of Oriental Jews had already begun in the early 1960s (Lissak, 1972). In sum, the general trend was toward social characteristics gradually becoming good predictors of actual political behavior.

Access to Channels

In Chapter 1, we posed the question: When does an individual become a factor in politics? The answer must distinguish between those who have gained access to political resources and those who participate in the allocation process. Access was defined as the opportunity for individuals and groups to join the political system through a voluntary link-up with the political communication network. Access can be perceived as the reverse of penetration: the efforts of individuals to reach the political system and particularly its center. Under certain conditions there is a link between them: the very channels which have been set up to transmit toward the periphery can provide access opportunities. But freedom — even with respect to information only — which is granted through such a process is constrained. Citizens cannot use penetration channels for transmitting deviant opinions. In fact, they are limited in their ability to choose the transmitting channel itself. Access should be viewed accordingly as the autonomous ability of citizens to reach the communication network and, through it, the center for their own purposes. Access entails choice and a scope of possible alternatives for upward transmission of information (Apter, 1971: 6). With respect to the Israeli political system, access will be evaluated here according to several criteria:

- degree of individual political mobility;
- degree of political association and organization (in terms of group activity); and
- degree of access to the main channels: the parties and their affiliations, the bureaucracy, and the mass media.

These criteria will serve as the basis for evaluating the opportunities of Israeli citizens and groups to gain access to the political communication network and its center.

POLITICAL MOBILITY

Access is often discussed in connection with the attempt to influence government decisions (Truman, 1951: 264-270). The focus here, however, is on the opportunity of individuals to gain access to information or to the various channels in the political communication network. Individual access includes the possibility of joining or forming an interest group as a means of having the desired access. Thus, access to the relevant points in the communication network is the initial interaction from which a political message or deed may spring. Access enables intake and transmission of information, which in turn may result in influence and the sharing of political power. The common shorthand "access to power" obscures the long and complicated process starting with individual political mobility.

Most studies of social mobility in Israel are concerned with the late 1960s and the 1970s, and are beyond the scope of this book. Hence, the following remarks must remain tentative and confined to the Jewish community.

During the first fifteen years of the state, the rate of social mobility was relatively high by conventional standards (Matras, 1965). Lissak also concludes his study of social mobilization among Jews in Israel by pointing out that it was pluralistic from the cultural and social points of view, but not as far as political institutions were concerned (1969: 101). Social mobility was expressed in most indices of education, occupation, income, housing, organizational affiliations, as well as personal behavior and expectations. This general process was not all-inclusive, and certain groups, particularly among the Oriental communities, were less mobile than others. Yet even deprived groups improved their condition during the 1950s. The general trend was one of a rising standard of living and open avenues for social mobility (Etzioni-Halevy and Shapira, 1977: 151-156). If the assumption that social mobility is a predictor of aggregate political mobility (Deutsch, 1961) applies to Israel, then Israeli citizens during that period became increasingly aware of the political network and opportunities for "hooking into" it. Such a development compels the network and especially the insititutions in the political center to take into consideration the increase in opportunities for access. They accordingly adjust the flow, content, and frequency of the information transmitted.

During a relatively short period, most Israelis underwent a rapid process of change and became "moderns": relatively well informed and open to new ideas and experiences (Inkeles and Smith, 1974: 289-290). They became more aware of their political environment and subject to the influence of modern technology, especially that of the mass communication media. As was pointed out in Chapter 4, even the most difficult target groups were penetrated through these concerted efforts. Most groups were thus "wired into" the communication network — they were subject to the efforts of the political institutions in the center to transmit information, attitudes, and ideas. And as a result of these efforts, the political network became accessible to most Israelis. In short, they became "political factors."

The central reason for this rapid development was the existence of powerful institutions and processes of political socialization (see Table 4.2). In many countries, political socialization is carried out through modern institutions such as schools, factories, and the mass media (Inkeles and Smith, 1974). In the yishuv period the most important institutions for young people were schools, youth movements, and paramilitary bodies; for adults, there were the parties, their affiliated organizations, and places of work. The whole community, small and clannish as it was, served as an agent of socialization.

The IDF became an important socializing and mobilizing institution for young people in the state period. To a great extent, the hero of the pioneering farmer was replaced by that of the fighting soldier (Perlmutter, 1969: 127-128). Individual mobility was enhanced by service in the IDF in the following ways (Lissak, 1971: 336-337):

- Egalitarian orientation — providing the opportunity to acquire new roles and military ranks, thus bridging social distances.

- Social mobility — through education and the raising of personal levels of expectations.

- Socioeconomic opportunities — in civilian life as a result of vocational training.

- Entrance ticket — mainly for young immigrants who, through military service, could join "the orders of the Israelis."

- Reinforcement of national identity — and of "Israeli" character traits.

This last point hints at the close relationship between military mobilization and political mobilization in the special setting of the Israeli polity.

The rise in the standard of living increased the role of the family relative to the external institutions such as schools and youth movements. Other significant changes took place in the adult population. Society became much more heterogeneous as a result of mass immigration and more stratified as a result of socioeconomic changes. The parties continued to function as socializing agents, but the state bureaucracy grew in importance. Subsequently, the presence of more specialized institutions such as professional associations and the independent mass media became strongly felt.

From the point of view of institutions in the political center, the challenge of socialization became more serious during this period. With the accelerated rate of socioeconomic mobility came the awareness of politics and of the opportunities for gaining access. This development was very slow and is far from being complete (Smooha, 1978: 40, 97), but it was already apparent in the early 1960s (Lissak, 1972). Research findings from that period show that status aspirations became more individualistic compared to the collectivistic orientation of the yishuv. The previous standards of service to the community and the pioneering way of life were replaced by new aspirations, and young people began to define mobility in terms of economic, professional, and educational opportunities as well as political power (Lissak, 1964). Within a short period, most Israeli citizens were individually skilled and prepared to take advantage of the access opportunities.

GROUP-BASED ACCESS

Access can be gained on an individual basis or as a result of group activity. In this section, I examine the opportunities to gain access to politics, specifically through group activity and the extent to which such groups acted independently of the established political institutions. Emphasis is on the changes that occurred in the status of the yishuv groups and associations once the state was established. In Chapter 10, the actual political activities of such groups will be examined.

In explaining the reasons for the political activity of some individuals and groups in Israel and the lack of activity of others, the following generalization is pertinent:

Societies differ in the extent to which parties and voluntary organizations are tied to any particular population groups and if they have such ties, in the particular groups to which they are tied. Group-based forces embodied in institutions such as parties and organizations can modify the participation pattern that one would have if only individual forces were operating. They do this by mobilizing some individuals to political activity over and above the level one would expect on the basis of their individual resources and motivation or by inhibiting the activity of others to a level below that which one would expect on the basis of their individual resources. The way in which institutional constraints on participation modify individual propensities to be politically active takes us a long way in explaining differences across nations in the representativeness of the participant population [Verba et al., 1978: 11].

One may assume, therefore, that group-based motivation and group political activity in Israel were influenced by strong community identification as well as being highly constrained by the existence of powerful political institutions.

The highly organized yishuv was characterized by the existence of many groups and associations of different kinds.[3] Most of them belonged to the ideological camps and were institutionally affiliated with the secondary centers and the parties. Despite this high degree of organization, the yishuv groups were truly voluntary, and, as such, they met the rudimentary test of being an association of people motivated to seek access through a group-based activity. This general statement applies equally to a highly organized kibbutz affiliated with a labor party as to a poorly structured chamber of commerce (Lishkot HaMishar) affiliated with the General Zionist Party.

The yishuv groups had a social base that enabled members to be concerned with public affairs beyond their immediate individual and family circles or their place of work. They were instruments for expressing solidarity and for achieving collective goals. A paramilitary organization, such as the Palmach, or a youth movement such as Betar was based completely on voluntary membership but was closely affiliated with its respective political camp and party. Moreover, "there was usually little differentiation between social, political and cultural aspects and ideals, although one or another of these would obviously receive stronger emphasis in certain groups" (Eisenstadt, 1956: 108).

The many voluntary, highly motivated, and well-organized groups and associations of the yishuv enabled their members to have access and to participate in the social and political life of the community. Yet they did not resemble ordinary voluntary groups or pressure groups in other democratic countries. In the first place, their autonomy was constrained by their parent institution, particularly the party. Second, the option of playing an open adversary role in the political system was usually closed: They had to work and exert pressure within their respective camps and institutions.[4] Third, the common Zionist content played a major role in retaining the democratic tenet of compromise and internal interaction between these groups and the center.

The result of this complicated structure of the political system was promising from the point of view of the individual. One could join existing groups or form a new one and thus gain access to the political network and to the political center. The price for access, however, was organizational affiliation and willingness to act politically within the existing structure. It should be recalled that despite the tight structure, consolidation of the national center during the yishuv period did not eliminate the autonomy of the secondary centers. They became agencies of the center in certain spheres and autarchic enclaves in others.

The secondary centers, and notably the parties, provided these groups with ready access to political resources. This was part of their belonging to the network and being established. It was difficult, however, for nonestablished groups to secure such a position or to remain autonomous afterwards. Under such circumstances, access was conditional and constrained. In short, those who knew how to get together in order to present their demands within the network had an advantage over those who did not.

The establishment of the state had a considerable impact on the political status of groups and associations. Voluntary group activity was gradually replaced by formal and bureaucratic state activity. The non-political (usually social) aspect of many groups became predominant, while some formerly affiliated groups and some newly formed ones became more ordinary pressure groups. Socioeconomic changes in the country brought about the development of new types of groups and new modes of operation. Could these developments be regarded as proliferation and institutionalization of autonomous groups in the Israeli political system?

In certain respects, passage from the yishuv to the state was a turning point in the pattern of associational activity (Eisenstadt, 1956: 111). In retrospect, we also notice many lines of continuity. Despite the multiplication of associations and the new groupings based on professional and economic affiliations, there was no increase in the *autonomous* political activity of groups in the early state period. New groups did appear and old ones disappeared, but the pattern of gaining access and of group political organization did not fundamentally change. It has also become clear that many new groups which sprang up immediately after 1948 (social and ideological groups and formal clubs) were a reaction to the events surrounding the establishment of the state, and they did not last long.

The Volunteers' Group (Shurat Hamitnadvim) that was operating in the early 1950s meets the access test in all respects, but it was a notable exception and did not last long.[5] The groups of young army veterans concentrated around the weekly *Haolam Hazeh* in 1949-1950 is another more enduring, but still exceptional, example. They were independent and had their own channel of communication (see Chapter 7). There emerged other small groups of writers, artists, and intellectuals, such as the Canaanites, which also disappeared after a while.

There were, of course, those groups whose level of organization was too low to have access and those which were deprived of access because their quiescence was secured by other means — an example is Israeli Arabs. With the economic changes in the country, some private economic and professional groups adopted independent methods to gain access. The Industrialists' Association started to flourish; similarly, the professional associations of lawyers, accountants, and physicians gradually acquired independent status. These were apolitical groups, and their authority in licensing and other professional matters was officially recognized by the state. There were occasionally attempts by affiliated groups to act independently. The workers' strike in the Ata clothes factory in 1957, without the approval of the Histadrut, is a famous example and a forerunner of a much later phenomenon (Almogi, 1980: 147-161).

By the 1960s most of the groups and associations that had lasted from the yishuv period and most of the new ones were firmly established within the existing political system. These groups discovered that cooperative rather than adversary relationships with the political institutions would secure them access to the communication network and to the political center. In Israel, in order to lobby, a group had to become established, and there were few nonestablished lobbies — that is, those that did not develop symbiotic relationships with the existing channels. There were almost no independent groups that opted for an autonomous political role in the communication network or set up their own channels in order to exercise pressure directly and publicly. The handful of public interest and promotional groups were mainly for political protest. Most independent groups had a short life span, and those that endured were affiliated with one of the political camps or even the government. Consumer protection agencies, for example, belonged to the Histadrut, to the municipalities, or to the Ministry of Commerce. Independent groups, if important enough, were quickly coopted.

But membership in an association is not alone an indicator of group-based access. The Histadrut had over 900,000 registered members (58 percent of the population) in 1965, but most had little access to the institution's decision apparatus. The percentage of Israelis who were members of different associations, organizations, and parties was probably high compared to other democratic countries, but this should not be confused with independent, group-based political access.

If the yishuv and state periods are compared in terms of the opportunities for group-based access and the degree of group independence, one finds both continuity and change. In both periods there were established groups with ready access to the political communication network and, through them, to the center. In the yishuv period, despite the high degree of structure and the absence of a significant number of nonaffiliated groups, these groups were not formed as a result of coercion from above and they enjoyed a great deal of autonomy in certain spheres. This highly structured mode of access continued in the state period because of the center's increased dominance and the smaller area left for independent group activity. Yet even in the early state period there emerged new independent groups, and there was a tendency among established groups, especially economic and professional ones, to become more autonomous and secure for themselves alternative access routes.

The fact that group access in the Israeli political system was achieved through affiliation should not be confused with "more" or "less" democracy. Such an institutional mode of conducting politics is known in democratic countries such as Austria, whereas the open lobbying style of pressure group activity is well-developed in the United

States. Israel's political culture was influenced by continental Europe, and those countries should serve as a basis for comparison. Besides, open lobbying is not a guarantee of impact on steering: Full access to the political center can be achieved through the affiliated groups, whereas access of independent groups can only be symbolic.

Perhaps the most concrete way to examine access is to find out if individuals and groups have the opportunity to transmit information, especially through the same channels that are carrying information from the center. Citizens' access to the Israeli party, bureaucratic, and mass channels is the subject of the next three sections.

ACCESS TO PARTIES

In Chapter 5, the Israeli political parties were discussed as the most important channels of communication, and their penetration and maintenance roles were analyzed. Now the role of the party from the citizen's angle must be examined: Was the party accessible and, if so, could it provide access to the communication center where decisions are made (compare Truman, 1951; Almond et al., 1973: 94)?

Access to channels is tested according to two criteria: first, whether or not there is a *choice* of channels enabling an individual to seek the one which best corresponds to his or her values, needs, and interests; and second, whether or not there is an *opportunity* to transmit information upwards through such channels to the designated places. The distinction may be illustrated in a Communist regime where the central party does not qualify as far as the range of choice is concerned, but may be providing an opportunity for citizens to transmit their feelings and opinions to leaders (Selznick, 1952: 114; Inkeles and Bauer, 1959; Liu, 1971: 37-47; Freidgut, 1979).

In Israel's *état partitaire*, there were enough competing parties to meet most individual variations of ideology and interest (Akzin, 1955; Gutmann, 1963). The prevailing attitude, a carryover from the yishuv period, was not one favoring elitist democracy; people were encouraged to become party members and many did. Moreover, as seen in Chapter 4, the multiparty system was tolerated and accommodated in various ways, including representation in the national institutions (compare LaPalombara and Weiner, 1966: 3). No party has ever achieved a 51 percent majority, and the idea of a single party as the central body in the political system is alien to Israel. Those who advocate changing the proportional electoral system are hoping to reduce the number of parties

— preferably to two — not to eliminate party competition. Thus, Israeli parties depended on increasing their membership, at least in proportion to the population growth. They also invested great efforts, as was explained in Chapter 5, in extending their branches, mobilizing their members, and recruiting leaders from politically significant groups.

During the yishuv period, when the distances between center and periphery (between elite and public) were relatively small, the parties were sensitive to the needs of the public. During the early state period, Israeli parties — with the exception of the Communist and religious parties and some other minor parties — did not develop clear constituencies. As noted, they were involved in penetration and contributed to maintenance, but the major parties tried to appeal to all groups throughout the country, and those in power became mobilization agencies for the state. The parties succeeded in incorporating almost all citizens into the political system, and a relatively great number became listed members of the various parties or their affiliated organizations. For instance, in 1965 there were 200,000 reported members in Mapai and half a million in the Histadrut Women's Organization. These figures contain overlapping membership, and they show the high degree of organizational affiliations in the labor movement. Nevertheless, if one examines membership in the other camps, parties, and their organizations, one can conclude that Israel is a very associational society. Indeed, in the early state period, the veteran population was a well-woven political and organizational tapestry into which the new immigrants were absorbed and incorporated. The question that remains to be answered is: How voluntary and autonomous was this process?

The parties in power, especially Mapai, had a clear grip over individuals and groups. Arian reports that after the 1969 elections, 30 percent of the people in his sample refused to say how they voted — a high percentage of political reticence compared to other democratic countries (1973: 39). One interpretation is that those who did not vote for the ruling parties were afraid to say so. This explanation is reinforced by the gap between reported and actual voting: After the elections, more people reported voting for the ruling party than the actual votes received (1973: 40).

If this interpretation is correct, then citizens' choice in the *secret* ballot was wider than they were willing to admit openly to the interviewers. Arian notes that the Labor Alignment was identified with the ruling power and may have been considered the "correct" answer. Some respondents may have suspected that the interviewer worked for the tax authorities, the party, the municipal government, or the police (1973: 41).

If this was true in 1969, even partially, it was certainly more likely in the early 1950s. All evidence from the early state period shows that citizens' access to the political parties and their actual affiliations were constrained by the existence of powerful institutions. Affiliations were therefore highly pragmatic. An individual joined, belonged to, voted for, or reported voting for certain parties — especially those in power — because it was the most expedient way to gain access to housing, jobs, and health services. The fewer years a citizen was in the country, the narrower his or her range of party choice and access opportunities. This applies even more clearly to the weaker groups, whose political resourcefulness was nonetheless evident in their attempts to beat the system. There are numerous stories of new immigrants carrying membership cards of different parties and producing the appropriate one according to the circumstances (Almogi, 1980).

Israeli citizens could choose their party affiliation. They also formally enjoyed free access to party channels. They could even try to get elected to the party's bodies. Yet choice was constrained by two important factors. First, despite the existence of many parties, the whole structure was rigid. Not only was it almost impossible to establish a new party, but it was also difficult to form interest groups outside the existing party-dominated structure. Second, the option of not joining any party was also limited. In order to gain access to tangible resources and services, one was often compelled to belong to a party, or the affiliated bodies. Here a distinction should be made between an individual's freedom to select a channel and the sensitivity of the party to his or her needs. In Israel, the former was constrained, yet the parties were not insensitive to the needs — as they perceived them — of the various groups and the public in general. Extensive party membership, the proliferation of branches, and the method of overlapping organizations point to penetration and maintenance, but they also show that the Israeli political system was not remote. In a paternalistic manner, the political leaders were sensitive to the public needs and could not tolerate the existence of hungry or unsheltered Jews. But they also did not tolerate independent political activity, and their efforts were geared to avoid surprises by penetrating new groups and maintaining continuous support of the old ones.

In terms of *choice,* access to parties was constrained, although a selection of channels was nevertheless possible among the available parties. In terms of *opportunity* to transmit information upward through the party channels, the picture is equivocal. The parties themselves were accessible, but they often served not as brokers and gatekeepers but as a barrier. It was usually difficult for individuals or groups to use party channels in order to gain access to the political center, particularly if their request did not conform to the party line. Thus there was little room for independent transmission outside the network controlled by the parties, and there were limited opportunities to transmit "unauthorized" information within the network. The result in both cases was that independent group activity and citizens' support of such groups was costly because the parties could easily deny the "deviants" access not only to information but also to jobs or other tangible resources. If we recall that it was difficult for Israelis to stay out of the political system completely because of its permeation of society and economy, the significance of access controlled by the parties will be appreciated.

In some cases, new groups appeared as a result of the initial efforts of a party. This enabled the party to penetrate new domains or to maintain them under control. Hence, the parties themselves acted to organize professional and immigrant associations, or even independent local party lists. But once organized, not all groups could be controlled forever. Sometimes parties found it necessary to coopt new groups by offering their leaders jobs, or by responding to the main demands — provided the negotiations were discreet and the group became affiliated. An example of this method was given in Chapter 5 — the admission of the Artisans' Association to Mapai membership. When cooptation was impossible or all efforts to negotiate failed, the ruling party sometimes resorted to political destruction of the group — thus, the end of the "seamen's revolt" in 1951. This was the attempt of a local seamen committee to press independent demands and to organize outside the Histadrut and the Haifa Labor Council. When all attempts at cooptation failed, the strike was crushed by Almogi, Secretary of the Labor Council in Haifa (Almogi, 1980: 111-178).

Parties were also the main channels for citizens and groups' access to the legislative body and the executive in Israel. There were direct contacts between Knesset Members and citizens, but access to Knesset Members did not provide Israelis with significant opportunities to enter the communication network. Because of the "arena role" of the Knesset, party dominance over Knesset Members' behavior, and the electoral system of proportional representation, the openness of the Knesset was not translated into citizens' influence on the legislative process (compare Polsby in Greenstein and Polsby, 1975: Vol. 5, 263-264). Therefore, during the early state years, direct appeals of or letters written by citizens to Knesset Members were not common, and lobbying in the Knesset, too, was conducted predominantly through party contacts (Zidon, 1967: 121-128). Moreover, the lobby in the Knesset was relatively insignificant compared to the efforts directed toward the parties and the bureaucracy.

The late 1950s marked the apex of the party structure and its domination over the Israeli political system. In 1959, Mapai and its affiliated Arab lists obtained the highest percentage of votes in the national elections — 42 percent. The labor camp controlled 55 percent of the vote in the Fourth Knesset; together with their regular partners — the NRP and the Progressive Party — they had 70 percent. They were clearly the dominant political and economic power in the country. A year later the Lavon Affair began to unfold and the structure began to crumble. As a result, Mapai and the Arab Lists obtained only 38 percent of the vote in the 1961 elections, and the wide labor coalition was discontinued.

The decline of the parties in Israeli politics was clearly a relative matter. They managed to remain strong in certain respects throughout the 1970s. The trend, however, was clear: The parties could not retain their monopoly over access. Nonparty channels such as the bureaucracy and the mass media provided the previously missing range of choice and transmission opportunities. In these particular developments, Israel resembles other industrial countries:

> The growth of corporate forms of organization in America began to reverse the flow of messages between center and periphery. Increasingly, in modern industrial and business life, these new corporate lines of communication had an administrative character, and were designed to translate central decisions into peripheral action rather than to register grass-roots sentiments in central decisional arenas, as political parties had largely been thought to do [Marvick in Pool et al., 1973: 734].

It was only a matter of time before channels such as independent corporations and interest groups would provide alternative opportunities of access to organized and unorganized individuals in Israel. In any case, easier access to the parties and to the other channels in Israel did not bring with it involvement in the party's decision-making process. As will be seen in the following chapter, rank and file participation remained indirect for a long time.

ACCESS TO BUREAUCRATIC CHANNELS

Bureaucratic channels by definition are vertical, hierarchical, and tightly controlled. By raising the question of whether citizens have autonomous access to these channels, one assumes the possibility of a "nonbureaucratic" situation in which the bureaucracy is not only executing policy (enforcing the law, rendering services, regulating) but also initiating policy by being attentive to citizens' needs or by using discretion in policy enforcement.

In a modern democracy, the bureaucracy also functions in the area of interest articulation and interest aggregation (Rourke, 1969; Marini, 1971); and citizens are interested in having access to the bureaucracy not only for services or equal treatment but also for registering demands and grievances. Their concept of participation may include taking part in the many administrative decisions that affect their daily lives as citizens. But if the bureaucracy is merely a loyal executing arm of the elected politicians, it must also be neutral as far as access and participation are concerned. In other words, the bureaucracy should be detached, rendering equal services to everyone and directing those with "policy complaints" to the proper political addresses. The fact that the bureaucracy can also be active in the policy arena implies selectivity in forwarding information and reporting it upward. Moreover, if government officials regard themselves as spokesmen for weak groups or unattended social needs, they may be inclined to let these people take part in administrative decision-making. And yet claims for citizens' participation in the administrative process are in conflict not only with the doctrine of separating politics and administration but also with the bureaucratic desire to retain its professional autonomy (Weiner in Binder et al., 1971: 179).

In discussing access to the Israeli bureaucracy in the state period, it should be noted that these official bodies were not intended to serve as channels for citizens' transmission of information. It will be recalled (Chapter 6) that the Israeli bureaucracy assumed a number of roles — official and unofficial — in the development of the Israeli polity. It contributed to centralization, was closely linked to the party channels; controlled critical information, undertook nonbureaucratic functions, performed other socialization functions, and was intensely involved in penetration and maintenance activities. These features provide the backdrop for an analysis of the central question regarding access to bureaucratic channels: Was there a *choice* for citizens in selecting alternative bureaucratic or nonbureaucratic channels to transmit demands and grievances?

The constraints on citizens' choice of bureaucratic channels were evident. Centralization prevented the separate development of independent local services. Politicization inhibited the use of nonbureucratic channels such as professional associations. Educational services, for example, were so centralized and the teachers' association so linked to the parties that there was little response to independent demands of parents or nonaffiliated teachers. Since 1953, elementary schools have been divided into general and religious categories (plus an independent ultra-orthodox one), and within each the curriculum was standardized and fully controlled by the Ministry of Education. Similarly, people interested in joining a settlement had to choose from one of the party-affiliated movements. In those years, soccer players could not switch from a labor-affiliated team (Hapoel) to a Herut-affiliated team (Betar), or vice versa.

Access was especially constrained because the bureaucratic channels were monopolistic and all-pervasive, necessary for meeting daily needs as well as the fulfillment of civic duties. When a citizen depends on a piece of information controlled by the bureaucracy — and this was often the case — access could easily be denied and the information withheld. Such manipulation of information was regularly practiced by the Israeli bureaucracy. The courts were not helpful in providing access to such information, as they conformed to the prevailing notion that everything official is secret unless disclosure is specifically permitted. This was not unrelated to the other features of the Israeli political system in which the distribution of information was skewed in the direction of established institutions.

One feature of the system was still on the side of the citizens, however, and that was the existence of alternative channels within the political system as a whole. It will be recalled that political and administrative functions were divided among governmental and nongovernmental bodies and that there was a great deal of redundancy and overlap. This situation created some circumventing routes for citizens. Some groups learned to trade "votes for benefits," for example, or sold their votes more than once. If one party official failed to deliver, another one was approached. The normal interorganizational rivalry also provided some room for maneuvering. For housing support, one could try the governmental housing department, the government corporations, the Histadrut corporation, the Jewish Agency, or several companies affiliated with the parties. Those who knew the system and learned how to use it had an obvious edge. They could gain access and exert pressure by utilizing intrabureaucratic and interorganizational competition. For the newcomer, for certain peripheral groups, or, for that matter, for the individual citizen, the overall picture was far from encouraging. In the politicized Israeli society, the bureaucracy, overburdened and under-staffed by professional administrators and experts, became notoriously Kafkaesque. Its inaccessibility, verging on the denial of having anything to do with public service, was recorded in books, films, plays, and popular music of that period.[6]

With respect to individuals, the direct involvement of citizens in the decision-making process of bureaucratic bodies was not part of the Israeli political culture. Even in party or Histadrut elections, members did not elect their leaders, only intermediate governing bodies. Notwithstanding the labor movement's ideological commitment to direct participation, rank and file involvement in the Histadrut was minimal and decisions were made by the bureaucrats and politicians. In factories owned by the Histadrut, there was no "joint management" in the Yugoslavian style. In fact, fear of workers' independence was one of the main reasons why the seamen's strike of 1951 was crushed by force with the full approval of the Histadrut and the Haifa Local Labor Council. Programs of economic and social development which were carried out by the state and executed by the public bureaucracy were conducted from above with little involvement of the recipients. This was apparent in the construction of new development towns to which new immigrants were sent directly on arrival. It also underlay the efforts to modernize the Oriental Jews as rapidly as possible. As was mentioned in Chapter 6, public officials in Israel cultivated a personal relationship with citizens, particularly members of peripheral groups; yet it was a patronizing and tutelage role and not necessarily an invitation for participation.

One way to get satisfaction in dealing with the bureaucracy was to become a bureaucrat oneself and thereby gain the savvy and contacts needed to smooth the course of interaction. Bureaucratic posts in the public sector were accessible to those who were willing to start at the bottom. Many did, and the result was an important means of personal mobility — social and eventually political (Etzioni-Halevy and Shapira, 1977: 155). Indeed, the party "spoils" system of recruitment to the bureaucracy in the early state period and the easy access to low ranks explain part of its inefficiency and the red tape. Israeli bureaucracy practiced "affirmative action" and preferential recruitment of new immigrants long before these social methods were known elsewhere under these names. Thus, although the state bureaucracy — like the other components of the Israeli political system — was run by the veteran and more established strata of the society, lower-ranking bureaucratic positions were not entirely closed, even to members of peripheral groups. And those with endurance made it all the way to the top, as exemplified by the careers of some Israeli politicians.

As has been seen, access to the bureaucratic channels, as initiated by a private citizen, was highly restricted. Involuntary mobilization by the bureaucracy, on the other hand, was also rarely attempted. Hence the picture is mixed: Citizens had some choice between bureaucratic and political channels; they did have direct recourse to officials; and there was open recruitment to low-level positions. Moreover, Israeli bureaucrats were not passive instruments in the hands of the politicians. They tried to respond to the needs of the underdog (Danet, in Katz and Danet, 1973a: 329-337) as well as to nonbureaucratic social challenges. Despite their being "delegates" of the political center, officials became transmitters to the center of their clients' needs and demands, as they perceived them. The bureaucratic channels were also highly synchronized within the political communication network, especially in their reciprocal relationships with the party channels, secondary centers, and established organizations. They operated within the boundaries of consensus and were used by the political center as reinforcement and eventually as a substitute for mobilization carried out previously by the parties. (Compare Nettl, 1967: 337). Later, as the network became more open and the bureaucracy grew more professional, access to these official channels and, through them, to the political center became much easier.

ACCESS TO THE MASS MEDIA

Access to mass media channels is usually closely related to mobility. Politically mobile citizens are the greater consumers of information supplied by the mass media. This is "politics of individuation" whereby individuals interact with the political system through the media rather than through political parties (Verba et al., 1978: 309). The mass media, particularly television, then become a source of information, as well as providing motivation to be politically active.

In Chapter 7, the supportive role of the mass media in the penetration and maintenance functions was noted, as well as the growing importance of the nonparty and nonaffiliated channels: the independent newspapers, the state radio, and, since 1969, the state television. Did Israelis have a range of choice in access to mass media channels? Writing in 1954, one observer concluded his impressions of the press of Israel in the following words:

> Israel's Hebrew press holds up a faithful mirror to the moods, the hopes, the anxieties of a small but plucky new nation whose struggle for existence amid hostile surroundings is still far from won [Stock, 1954: 490].

Is this description a faithful mirror of the role of the press and other mass media channels in Israel? There is evidence to both support and negate the above statement.

Highly politicized Israeli citizens were avid consumers of radio news and eager readers of newspapers. In security matters and foreign affairs they were fed more or less identical information from all mass channels, and there were no alternative domestic sources. In internal affairs, on the other hand, the information marketplace was more open, and the various organizations served as alternative channels of information. Information and leaks were regularly distributed through them, and citizens were therefore provided with a certain degree of choice. Yet again, this openness was constrained by the fact that the doors of these alternative channels were unmarked and only those who knew about their existence could use them. The well-established groups, and increasingly those in the private economic sector, were familiar with the communication network and had regular access to all relevant channels, using them as alternatives to the mass media. The range of access open to those citizens whose interests were diffused and less organized was limited. Moreover, the general public — or, more precisely, individuals as citizens — was outside this complicated grapevine of communication.

What about the potential ability of Israeli citizens to *transmit* information through the mass media, or to sensitize these channels to their needs? Access *to* the mass media is a relatively new subject in the literature on mass communication (Barron, 1967, 1973; Franklin in Pool et a., 1973: 887-908). Many factors, in addition to expensive technology, contributed to the concentration of mass media in few organizations. In Israel, radio was controlled by the government and most newspapers by the parties (apart from the three independent dailies and several periodicals). Under such circumstances, it was difficult for citizens to regard the mass media as "their own." Mass media editors resembled political leaders (see Table 7.4) and were well integrated into the social elite of the country. Nevertheless, these channels were not alien, and identification with society and the state was often strengthened through exposure to mass culture. This feeling was succinctly expressed by a new immigrant: "I always like to listen to the news on the radio. It is very important because only in this way can I feel that I know what happens in the state, that I am a real citizen" (quoted in Eisenstadt, 1955: 159).

Israelis tend to have confidence in the credibility of what they read, hear, and see in the mass media. In a 1969 sample, 48 percent reported that they generally trust newspapers, while 70 percent trust radio and television (Arian, 1973: 29). These are high figures compared to other democratic countries. Even if the Israeli figures are discounted due to the distrust of *some* party-affiliated newspapers and the faith in television which was introduced only one year earlier, credibility was still high and probably much higher in the 1950s. Part of the explanation lies in the fact that the mass media channels in Israel reflected the common contents and reinforced the political symbols, serving as agents for identification with the new state. The other side of this coin is the limited ability of individuals and independent groups to gain unconditional access to the mass channels during the early state period. Being so tied up in the established political network, the Israeli mass media did not contribute much to the immunity of Israeli citizens against propaganda.

As for opportunities of groups to transmit information to the center, there were frequent complaints of opposition groups that the state-controlled media discriminated against them. There is indirect evidence that an opposition party such as Herut did not enjoy equal opportunity until the early 1960s (Mishal, 1978: 55). It is impossible to confirm the assertion that there was a blacklist of political leaders in the radio in the early years of the state (p. 40), but a later survey reveals that the attitude of Knesset Members in the opposition was more suspicious toward the mass media than coalition Knesset Members (Caspi, 1976; 213). For political groups that are outside the establishment — either coalition or opposition — the independent media are a natural ally. When the mass channels become predominant in the political communication network, many groups — especially protestors — start to orient their activities to the special media needs and biases (Glasgow University Media Group, 1976). In Israel, however, such media-oriented activities appeared only in the 1970s.

Could the mass media in Israel be regarded as "society's suggestion box" through which citizens provide inputs to decision makers (Chaffee and Petrick, 1975: 11)? Although hard data are not available, it would be fair to suggest that the menu of political information in all channels during the 1950s was limited and the fare was "precooked" according to elitist recipes. Israeli radio and party-affiliated newspapers were more frequently used for transmitting information from the center to the periphery than in the other direction. Despite the differences between the high-brow morning newspaper HaAretz and the popular evening newspapers Maariv and Yediot Aharonot, all retained the educational and sometimes missionary roles from the prestate period.[7] Despite the elitist orientation, the mass channels penetrated most target groups by printing and broadcasting in their languages, thereby helping to maintain the loyalty and support of the general public to the political system.

One cannot assert that Israeli mass channels were insensitive to the needs of citizens, only that — very much like the party and bureaucratic channels — their attitude was paternalistic (Barzel, 1976). Consequently, citizens' autonomous access to the Israeli mass media and their ability to transmit information upwards was restricted; and, in the period under review, these channels did not provide uncontrolled feedback mechanisms from the public to the political center.

TABLE 9.1   Access to the Main Channels (early state period)

	Range of Choice		Opportunity for Transmission	
	Individuals	Groups	Individuals	Groups
Parties & affiliated organizations	Wide	Narrow	Wide	Narrow
Bureaucracy	Medium	Narrow	Medium	Narrow
Mass Media	Medium	Narrow	Narrow	Narrow
Access to channels in general	Medium	Narrow	Medium	Narrow

Access to the Political Communication Network

Did Israelis become a factor in politics? In Table 9.1 access to the different channels is summarized by comparing the relative range of choice and opportunity for transmission available to autonomous citizens and independent groups.

Access is a voluntary linkup with the political communication network. In the period under review, Israelis were individually mobile and modern. In election after election, they retained the multiparty system; they regularly approached public officials with personal demands and complaints, circumventing the bureaucratic channels by utilizing organizaitonal overlap; and they supported a great number of newspapers, including three independents. Nevertheless, the range of individual choice and the opportunity for transmission were restricted because the party channels were all-pervasive, and, together with the mission-oriented mass media, they did not allow for nonestablished alternatives. Moreover, the parties often *blocked* information from being transferred all the way upward. Similarly, the radio and newspapers rarely provided opportunities for citizens' autonomous transmission. The bureaucracy, too, was paternalistic, especially toward the weaker groups, and despite some legal outlets for appeals, overall it was rather rigid. The reason why individuals' access was characterized as "medium" in Table 9.1 is because all three channels displayed a high degree of sensitivity to the citizens. Their motivation was penetration and maintenance, but the method was responsiveness to needs, and thereby citizens gained access to the various political resources.

The picture with regard to voluntary access of new and nonestablished groups is less complex. The political system displayed little patience with independent groups' attempts to increase the range of choice or to transmit information outside the main channels. The center was particularly intolerant of attempts to establish independent channels such as non-affiliated pressure groups. The result was that there were few truly voluntary groups and nonaffiliated pressure groups in the early state period, and this was also the case with regard to promotional "public interest" groups or protest movements. *The institutional factor was therefore the most important variable in determining access in the Israeli political system.*

Have these levels of access of individuals and groups to the main channels allowed for overall access to the network and thence to the political center? Access to the political center means an opportunity to send political messages upwards from the periphery to the center, and it is an indicator of the degree of a citizens' autonomy in the political system. The *realization* of access to the center means political participation and a chance to influence the decision-making process and the allocation of resources. This will be discussed in the next chapter.

The general answer to the question posed above is affirmative. Access was achieved because of the democratic tenets of Zionism and because access to the main channels, however constrained, led eventually to the political center. The point here is not whether a citizen or a group actually influenced the decisions of the Cabinet or the legislation in the Knesset. Access was realized because there were opportunities to send information to leaders of the central political institutions and because the communication network was adjusted to allow for these linkups. Here the distinctions, in the Israeli case at least, between the center's efforts at mobilization and citizens' attempts to gain access became somewhat blurred. Because of mobility and access, the penetration efforts of the center could not be entirely detached from the predisposition of individuals. Because of penetration, citizens could use mobilization in order to gain voluntary access. The communication network as a whole displayed flexibility under such circumstances, and the road was paved for increased participation and for citizens' impact on steering. In Israel the communication network started to become more flexible in the 1960s, and the change was notable in the appearance of new and alternative channels and increased opportunities in the old ones. Yet even in the early state period, the political system was accessible enough to suggest that as far as this component is concerned, Israel was already moving toward democratic political development.

NOTES

1. See Aba Ahimeir, *Revolutionary Zionism*. Tel Aviv: Committee for Publishing Ahimeir's Letters, 1968 (Hebrew).

2. Amos Oz put it well when he coined the aphorism, "Zionism is not a personal name; it is a family name" (1979: 92).

3. The discussion here is based mainly on the materials and analysis presented in Eisenstadt (1956) and in Horowitz and Lissak (1978: 38-39, 167-177).

4. On adversary roles in political and administrative processes, see Gross (1964: Vol. 1, 427-429).

5. See Chapter 5, Note 10, page 188.

6. A play by Efraim Kishon, "His Name Precedes Him," tells the story of a new immigrant struggling to find his way in the labyrinth of Israeli bureaucracy in the early 1950s. Another story by the same author became a famous movie entitled *Salah Shabati*. It describes satirically the struggle of an Oriental immigrant with the veteran Israeli society and political machine.

7. Compare with the differences between the *New York Times* and *The Daily News*. See Mueller (1973: 97-101).

10

PARTICIPATION

> The more a person participates, the more politically
> knowledgeable he is.
>
> (THOMPSON, 1970: 57)

Political participation refers to the activities of citizens aimed at influencing the steering of the political system. Unlike access, which is more attitudinal, participation is expressed in acts that transmit information and utilize the political communication network. Individuals and groups transmit political information in order to signify their preferences, to influence, and to exert pressure. Participation is autonomous only if it is initiated by the individuals themselves. This emphasis on the citizen's initiative is based on the assumption that voluntary political participation creates political knowledge.[1] In modern democracies, the axiom that citizens know their own interest best must be supplemented by the corollary that they often do not know what their interests are until they participate. In Chapter 1, the main theoretical aspects of participation were presented. Figure 10.1 is an attempt to guide the reader through the more detailed sequence presented here and in the previous chapter.

The items in Figure 10.1 are not stages: The conditions and activities can take place simultaneously, and there can be "short cuts" as well as combinations. They do, however, represent a logical sequence that may clarify the role of participation in democratic political development. It is possible that individual mobility can directly influence steering, or that participation will take place even without a sense of efficacy. It is less

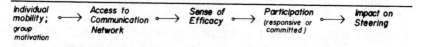

| Individual mobility; group motivation | Access to Communication Network | Sense of Efficacy | Participation (responsive or committed) | Impact on Steering |

Figure 10.1 Schematic Sequence of Conditions and Activities Resulting in Citizens' Impact on Steering

likely, however, that any one of them will occur if *all* the preceding conditions are absent.

Accordingly, the discussion of participation in the Israeli political system begins with the assumption that individuals were relatively mobile and acquired access opportunities. First, their sense of efficacy will be examined — that is, their belief that access can be translated into political action and influence. Next is a discussion of different modes of voluntary participation subdivided into "responsive" and "committed" types. This distinction is useful as long as it is clear that citizens combine within themselves both active and passive postures toward politics (Milbrath, 1965: 9). One should also keep in mind that a citizen can be "passive" by obeying the law and paying taxes or can be "active" by exiting (emigrating) from the system altogether. In the third section, the specific access and participation problems of selected peripheral groups are presented as an additional indicator of democratic political development. The chapter concludes with a discussion of the probable impact of participation on steering.

Sense of Efficacy

Bay argues that access to political knowledge is a human right and that the struggle for liberating knowledge begins with the political will of the individual (in Galnoor, 1977: 22-39). More narrowly, one may view political efficacy — belief in one's ability to influence steering — as one of the prerequisites of participation. Of course, such a belief may be totally unfounded: Efficacious and participating citizens could merely be engaged in a symbolic ritual (Edelman, 1971). Moreover, recent studies of political efficacy show that one must be wary of the reliability of the items used to measure efficacy (McPherson et al., 1977).[2] Citizens' sense of efficacy is not an absolute precondition for translating access into participation. It is more an indication of the "democratic mood" of these citizens. Although in the period under review Israelis were deeply involved with their political system — either passively as objects of central intervention or less passively as consumers of political information — did they also believe in their ability to influence the political process? Did they vote regularly because they assumed their votes do count?

Studies in other countries show that "a citizen with a high sense of efficacy is more likely to participate" (Thompson, 1970: 66; see also Campbell et al., 1960: 192-194; Almond and Verba, 1963: 261-299). There are no data on the sense of efficacy of Israelis in the early 1950s, and the data on later periods are fragmented. However, the overall findings are clear. The positive response to questions such as, "Do people like yourself have an influence on the government?" was 25 percent in Jerusalem in 1960 (Fein, 1962: 72) and between 15 and 45 percent in national samples of later years (Arian, 1971: 7; Etzioni-Halevy and Shapira 1977: 70, 77). Compared to the high interest of Israeli citizens in politics, their sense of efficacy was astonishingly low. It is even low in comparison with Almond and Verba's findings in other democratic countries of people's satisfaction with their role as participants (1963: 181). Fein's explanation for this discrepancy is the lack of a civic tradition of participation through interest groups, the weakness of public opinion, and the strength of the Israeli establishment (1967: 142-143). Arian contends that "the Israeli citizen is fundamentally a passive political animal, identifying with democratic forms, confident that the politician is concerned with his opinion, yet basically unconvinced about his own ability to influence policy (1971: 7). His data indicate that the *lower*-income groups and Oriental Jews were more likely to feel efficacious because they were less realistic about their chances of penetrating the political system. Etzioni-Halevy and Shapira point out that low efficacy contradicts the political legacy of the yishuv and is related to the fact that Israel's parties and electoral system are not sensitive to voters' wishes (1977: 78). They add that many feel that there are no adequate extraelectoral channels for participation and that the upward channels of political communication are blocked (p. 207).

This last conclusion is closely related to what was said previously about constrained access to the main channels, and to the following discussion of participation. Israeli citizens had a relatively low sense of efficacy not because they regarded politics as too complicated for them, and not because they believed voting is the only way for citizens to influence government in a democracy. Being knowledgeable about politics, Israelis realized that the direct impact of citizens on steering is always minimal, especially in their political system, which was dominated by powerful party and bureaucratic institutions. The reduced sense of efficacy in Israel stems, possibly, from a realistic evaluation of the situation and the awareness that the political communication network was designed and used mainly for downward vertical or diagonal flow of information (see Figure 1.2). Steering was performed primarily through horizontal communication within the political center and the secondary centers; and the network was virtually closed for the autonomous transmission of information by independent citizens and groups. Israelis were aware of their constrained access to the political network, and this determined, as will be seen below, their modes of participation. It also caused them to be somewhat cynical about their ability to influence steering.

One indicator of low efficacy is the widespread use of political jokes in Israel. This is a well-known practice in Eastern European countries (see, for example, Sanders, 1962a, 1962b). Waves of political jokes will sometimes spread through Israel in a short time, evidence that many people have an intimate knowledge of politics. The jokes frequently ridicule the system itself, a particular leader or institution, and they are often reshaped to fit the new person or circumstances. They appear more frequently when the situation is tense or deteriorating, and there is usually an element of popular revenge in them, as exemplified in the jokes that made the rounds through the social grapevine during the difficult economic recession in 1966-1967.[3] Political jokes are often a relatively harmless outlet for a sense of inefficacy, but they do not constitute actual participation.

Figure 10.2 summarizes the four theoretical combinations of access and a sense of efficacy. Where both access and efficacy are either high or low (cases 1 and 3), there is a congruent sequence. When access is low and efficacy is high (case 2), there is a symbolic democratic ritual — citizens believe they have influence, but in fact they cannot even gain access to the network. When access is high and efficacy low (case 4), we have a special case of democratic political development. Israel has this incongruent sequence: relatively good opportunities for individual access and a low sense of efficacy. Although individual political mobility resulted in opportunities for access, independent group-based access was highly constrained by the existence of a well-established network and institutional channels. This caused skepticism on the part of Israeli citizens as to whether they can influence government. It also affected their modes of participation, particularly those requiring a high degree of commitment. Four of these modes of participation will now be examined.

Modes of Participation

There is no need to present here all the specific types of political participation in Israel or to detail their ramifications (compare Milbrath and Goel, 1977: 10-24). Rather, the emphasis will be on *modes* of participation in order to draw some general conclusions about democratic political development in Israel. In presenting these modes we do not ignore the important forms of support given by Israeli citizens to their

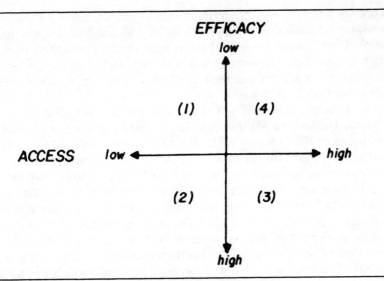

Figure 10.2   Combinations of Access and Sense of Efficacy

political system, such as their willingness to contribute to national security and to volunteer for other collective missions (Horowitz, 1980: 9-10). "Support," however, is discussed in a different context in this book (see Chapters 3 and 8) and is not regarded as an active mode of participation. Participation in Israel will be examined according to four modes of activity based on Nie and Verba (1975) and presented in Table 1.3 (Chapter 1).

VOTING

Voting exerts a high degree of pressure on leaders, but it communicates little information about specific voter preferences and requires little initiative on the part of citizens. The direction of information flow is upward vertically in the established channels. The probability of adding a new channel (such as citizens' plebiscite) or of altering the communication network through voting is low. Voting is an individual act and requires little cooperation with others.

Voting in Israel is not compulsory, and given the great number of parties, there is competition and a great variety from which to choose. The choice is confined to parties, since the electoral system does not enable the voter to choose among individual leaders nor to change their order of appearance on the party's list. Democratic requirements concerning free elections are observed in Israel: the right to vote and to be elected, secret ballot, and elections held at regular intervals. Between

1949 and 1977 Israelis voted nine times, three (1951, 1961, and 1977) before the Knesset completed its full four-year cadence. Elections for local authorities were also held regularly, usually at the same time as the national elections, except in 1949 or when the national elections were advanced. Histadrut elections are also a significant expression of participation, involving approximately 60 percent of the adult Jewish population.

Relatively high voter turnout was a tradition carried over from the voluntary yishuv institutions. It then reached 75 percent but was also as low as 50 percent (Gutmann, 1960: 58). As shown in Table 10.1, the average voting turnout has remained very high (81 percent) — among the highest in democratic countries where voting is voluntary. The figures for participation are even higher because the Voter's Register includes Israelis abroad who technically have no way of voting. High voting rates were not peculiar to specific regions, social groupings, or ethnic divisions. In fact, voting rates in both national and local elections were particularly high in small settlements, such as kibbutzim and moshavim (Avner in Arian, 1975: 205-206). Among Arabs in Israel, the voting turnout even exceeded the national average. Hence, if voting is used as an indicator, participation in Israel is high. And in light of the extraordinary sums of money spent on the campaign in Israel — even compared proportionately to such expenditures elsewhere (Gutmann, 1963: 717) — it can be said that voters' support was taken very seriously by the parties.

Local government was weak in Israel and dominated by the national parties. Local elections were held regularly — seven times in the past thirty years — and the average turnout (76 percent) was also generally high (Table 10.1). Nevertheless, there has been reduced interest in these governments which are dominated by the same national party lists. There were citizens who chose not to vote in local elections despite the fact that they were usually held at the same time and place as the national elections. Apparently the gap was not caused by differences between urban and rural populations or social divisions. Yet, on examination, a pattern can be found.

The gap was widest when local elections were held separately after the national elections in 1950 and 1978. This is understandable — people lost interest and did not bother to go just to vote in the local elections. However, disregarding these two special cases, the gap steadily decreased until the 1965 elections and has been steadily increasing since then. Moreover, the trend toward split-ticket voting became evident in the 1960s with more people voting for one party in the national election and for another in the local one. Another recent phenomoenon was the emergence of local independent lists (Weiss and Arian, 1969). For in-

TABLE 10.1   Voter Participation in National, Local, and Histadrut
             Elections (%)

Year	Knesset	Local Government	Histadrut
1949	86.9	79.6 (1950)	79.9
1951	75.1	—	—
1955	82.8	78.6	84.8 (1956)
1959	81.6	80.2	79.4 (1960)
1961	81.4	—	—
1965	83.0	82.7	77.6
1969	81.7	79.0	65.0
1973	78.6	73.2	68.1
1977	79.3	57.3 (1978)	68.5
Average	81.2	75.8	74.8

SOURCES: Central Bureau of Statistics, Special Publications, and Histadrut Institute of Social
and Economic Research.

stance, in the early 1960s independent "ethnic lists" appeared in local
elections of towns such as Beersheva and Ashdod, which had been
controlled previously by leaders appointed by the political parties
(Eisenstadt, 1967: 347-349).

In Chapter 1, the reasons for selecting the mid-1960s as the cutoff
period for the presentation of political development in Israel were given.
It now becomes clear from Figure 10.3 that in addition to other processes
which culminated in the mid-1960s, the former pattern of voting had also
started to vary. This conclusion becomes sharper when the rate of
participation in the Histadrut elections is considered (Table 10.1). Between 1949 and 1965, 75 to 87 percent of the eligible voters participated in
all three types of elections. Thereafter, the rate of participation is lower
in each type of election, and the rate of voting for the Histadrut dropped
below 70 percent after 1965. Moreover, the range of fluctuation has
increased markedly: 57-82 percent of those eligible voted in the different
elections between 1969 and 1977. It was during this period that the
dominance of the labor parties started to decline until they lost the
national election in 1977.

Participation in voting, therefore, reflects the changes that have
taken place in the Israeli political system since the mid-1960s. In the
earlier period, voting reflected the responsive nature of participation by
Israeli citizens. Voting in Israeli elections does not require a great deal of
active involvement. The voter had very little influence on the composition of the party candidate lists. There were no primaries, and in the
internal elections within the parties, only the delegates for the general
assemblies were elected. In the early years of the state, the high rate of

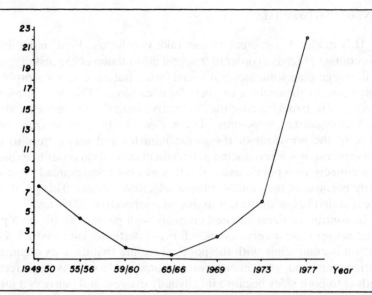

Figure 10.3   Gap Between Knesset and Local Voter Turnout
SOURCE: Table 10.1.

voting turnout can be ascribed to party pressure and persuasion, especially in new towns and urban Oriental neighborhoods, and particularly on election day. But despite the temptation, voting has not been compulsory. The findings from general election surveys in Israel confirm the general impression presented in previous chapters that participation through voting is closely related to the penetration and maintenance efforts of the political center. Thus, for example, a high voter turnout was characteristic of Israeli Arabs, who were exposed to get-out-the-vote campaigns by local party agents. Other groups with a high voter turnout were the more politically socialized, second-generation Israelis of Western origin, and the age group of 35 to 54 (Avner in Arian, 1975: 207-210).

Israeli citizens have made use of their right to participate in elections. The relative turnout exceeds that of India, Japan, the Netherlands, and the United States and is somewhat below that of Austria (Verba et al., 1978: 58). Although social and economic variables must have influenced the voting rates, there is widespread and across-the-board commitment to this mode of participation: The vast majority of the population use election day to cast their votes. And in light of the low sense of efficacy, perhaps voting turnout was so high among Israelis because they felt that this was their most effective way to have a direct impact.

CONTACTING OFFICIALS

This mode of participation can take two forms. First, individuals may contact officials in order to transmit information or express dissatisfaction regarding some general social issue, not necessarily a problem which affects themselves or their families alone. This form was not developed in Israel because the "collective issues" were in the hands of the well-organized structures. There were, to be sure, citizens who wrote to the president or the prime minister and sent letters to the newspapers, or who contacted government officials in order to express their concern on a public issue. But this was not a widespread practice, partly because of the nonconstituent, electoral system. This point will be expanded below in the discussion of cooperative activities.

In contrast, citizen-initiated contacts with public officials on a personal matter were a very common form of participation in Israel. This method is compatible with the political culture that dictates organized participation and yet encourages personal outlets. It is a preferred method to both sides because it is usually discreet and conveys a lot of information with relatively low pressure. It is attractive to the official because any politician or bureaucrat would prefer particularized contacts rather than universal standards. It is attractive to the citizen, too, who can take the initiative, choose the agenda, and use all kinds of indirect pressures to secure extra favors. This mode of participation is also congenial to Israelis who gained access as a result of individual mobility (see Chapter 9). It was seen that methods of involuntary mobilization were seldom used by the center, and citizen-bureaucrat contact was a useful and particularized link that could be applied also to the weaker groups in society.

To what extent was the bureaucracy used for complaints? Did citizens have an opportunity for external appeal about bureaucratic behavior? All indications show that Israelis complained to the various arms of the bureaucracy a great deal, and as individuals they had access to these channels. It seems as if the bureaucracy were built on the assumption that in service delivery or licensing there is a minority of normal cases and a majority of "special" ones deserving particularized attention. Of course, such personal service enables the bureaucrat to exercise a great deal of discretionary power. It is also a responsive pattern of participation because citizens usually complain about something they did not get, and this conforms to the paternalistic attitude of the Israeli political elite (Gutmann and Landau in Lissak and Gutmann, 1977: 192-221; Aronoff, 1977).

The channels in which this upward vertical information flows from citizens to public officials have been the most crowded in the Israeli communication network. In the discussion of Israeli bureaucracy in Chapter 6, the reasons for this reference-based mode of participation were underlined. Individuals will evoke old acquaintances, family ties, common ethnic origin, military service, and any other potential connections in order to avoid being "unknown" to the official. Another common method is the mediated message, the use of mediators — particularly party contacts — to exert influence or pressure on officials.

The absence of direct observations on this form of participation makes it difficult to be more precise. It is obvious, however, that the probability of adding new channels through contacts with officials is very low. In fact, this type of personal interactions is familiar in cases when the system is well established and everyone has to look out for him or herself (Sharkansky, 1978: 84).

Citizens' dependence on the bureaucracy was also manifested in the lack of simple outlets for complaints against the bureaucracy. Apart from the political channels, external control of the public bureaucracy can be exercised in Israel through the courts, the state comptroller, special means such as investigative committees, or publicity in the mass media. Appeals to the regular courts to test the legality of administrative decisions are possible but not used frequently, mainly because the regular courts have limited expertise in administrative affairs (Zamir, 1975: 17). Better supervision is exercised by the numerous administrative courts, but most of these did not exist before the mid-1960s. The High Court of Justice has been used by citizens quite effectively and has become a "means of exercising pressure on administrative authorities" (1975: 122). Yet the increased use of this device by citizens also started in the late 1960s. There were some famous exceptions during the 1950s, but in the eyes of the average citizen, the High Court of Justice was reserved for "serious cases" and for those familiar with the political network and its main channels. The nonjudiciary channels of appeal could render limited service only. The State Comptroller, an arm of the Knesset for supervising government offices, was not a tool for citizen redress until the task of the ombudsman was added in 1971. Special investigation committees were also not used in Israel for looking into citizens' complaints. The power of informal means such as public interest groups did not exist.[4] In sum, Israel resembled other countries in which the formal means for securing bureaucratic accountability were restricted (Nadel and Rourke in Greenstein and Polsby, 1975: Vol. 5, 411-429).

Opportunities for citizens' participation in the administrative process, short of joining up, were few; independent groups had even less of a chance than a lone individual. Being an integral part of the Israeli political system, the bureaucracy was clearly biased against access of independent and nonestablished groups. Israeli public administrators worked with and through the "responsible" groups only — groups affiliated with one of the existing and recognized political camps, parties, and organizations. Israeli bureaucracy did not pay much attention to what is routine activity of bureaucratic organizations in other countries — the building of a constituency and the cultivation of a supporting clientele. Public support given to bureaucratic organizations in Israel was either guaranteed or insignificant. The service ministries (Agriculture or Religious Affairs) could count on their respective clients to support them, because there were no alternative outlets. Other ministries did not need much public support, because their fate depended more on the parties and the powerful organizations affiliated with them. The development of reciprocal relationships between the bureaucracy and clientele groups came later; by that time, there were already independent groups and many other means in the hands of citizens who wanted not only to transmit information upwards but also to influence decision-making.

The judiciary is also part of the political system. Access to and contacts with the courts are an essential part of citizens' participation. It is important to find out whether the more peripheral groups in particular believe they can get equal treatment in the courts. There are no surveys of the attitudes of Israelis toward the courts and their ability to obtain justice there (compare Chaffee and Petrick, 1975: 68-75; Shapiro in Greenstein and Polsby, 1975: Vol. 5, 321-333). The importance of the courts in Israel is magnified by the fact that this is the only center of power to which access is not mediated in one way or another by the parties and other established political institutions. The court system, especially the Supreme Court, have played an important "access role" in controlling arbitrary action of the government against citizens. The most effective means for preserving citizens' liberty is the Supreme Court sitting as a High Court of Justice and empowered to "order state authorities, local authorities and officials of state authorities . . . . to do or refrain from doing any act" (Court Law, 1957, para. 7b2). Its attractiveness to the citizen stems from easy access, low cost, and quick procedure. Until 1965 this powerful means was used only infrequently by private citizens, notably members of minority groups. Nevertheless, it proved to be an effective way of restraining the government and bureaucracy (Zamir, 1975: 125).

In sum, voting and personal contacts with officials are highly developed modes of participation in Israel. Both are based on personal mobility and individual opportunities to gain access to the political network. Such citizens are aware of the political process and are familiar with the major political institutions. Their participation, however, is responsive, and their role as autonomous political communicators is restricted. Responsive participation demands less initiative on the part of citizens and is usually performed discreetly and through existing channels. It does not require much effort and does not entail personal exposure of one's political beliefs. In this sense, Israeli political culture is high on personal mobility and political involvement and low on opportunity to modify the network and to have a more direct impact on steering.

COOPERATIVE ACTIVITIES

If an individual chooses not to act alone in his or her attempt to solve a problem, and if he or she joins with others to form an ad hoc or a permanent group and this group tries to influence government, this is a more active mode of participation, because it is based on the assumption that personal commitment may work.

The most important points regarding cooperative activities in Israel were touched on with regard to group-based access to political channels in Chapter 9. When citizens act collectively to transmit information and thereby affect central steering, this may require a great deal of initiative, particularly if they form a new group and create a new channel. Cooperative participation could be of the responsive type if the participants are mobilized into an existing organization in order to transmit supportive information. The questions about cooperative activity in the survey conducted by Verba et al. (1978: 58-59) deal with membership in organizations engaged in solving community problems, group activities, and the formation of local groups to deal with a community problem. In Israel the membership form of participation is generally high. Furthermore, a high proportion of the population are members of politicized organizations or groups and are thus engaged in collective efforts aimed at solving community problems. Given the constraining features of the Israeli political system, the two relevant questions for the cooperative mode of participation are (a) Did citizens form or help form groups to influence the political system? and (b) What was the level of participation *within* the established parties and organizations?

The cooperative activity of most groups in Israeli politics was not entirely autonomous. Even economic interest groups were affiliated with the parties and their branches. There were different degrees of group affiliation, but a significant feature of many of these groups was that they were established by the parties themselves and were instrumental in the parties' attempt to enhance their power and increase their membership. The best examples are the women's and new immigrants' associations established by Mapai or the Histadrut. Moreover, some small parties, such as the Progressives, were actually interest groups (or would have been in other countries) and became parties because the Israeli political system — especially its proportional representation — encourages such a phenomenon. Thus, there are two answers to the question about citizens forming politically oriented groups. On the one hand, a survey in Israel would probably reveal that it is an "organized society" having a high degree of associational membership. This ranges from party membership to legal memberships as owners of flats in cooperative apartment buildings, in which most urban Israelis reside.[5] On the other hand, civic groups engaged in lobbying for public causes and voluntary independent associations were scarce. It will be seen in the following examples that cooperative activity was characterized by joining established groups and the utilization of existing channels.

The kibbutzim, one of the original contributions of Israeli society, are certainly a cooperative activity and a voluntary association. (Kibbutz in Hebrew means "community" or "group.") An integral part of the Zionist movement, kibbutz ideology stresses personal sacrifices, direct participation, and common social goals. Kibbutzim were instrumental in the implementation of the national, social, and economic Zionist revolution. But from the very beginning, the choice available to those who wanted to join a kibbutz was restricted by movement and party affiliation. In other words, one had to choose from among the three major kibbutz federations and a handful of smaller ones.[6] As early as the 1920s, and again in the 1930s, there were major debates on the degree of political freedom allowed to an individual kibbutz within its party-affiliated federation. In the early 1950s with the split between the labor parties, there were a number of kibbutzim which also split into two, despite the internal communal and family ties. The kibbutz is further evidence of the phenomenon of intensive group activity, operating within a prescribed network and not allowing new organizations to cut in. In those years, an individual kibbutz member could not belong to a rival party, and a single kibbutz could not be established or survive long if it were completely outside one of the party-affiliated federations.[7]

The Histadrut is another voluntary association to which individuals belong in order to advance their collective goals. It is based on the elaborate structure of trade unions, workers' councils, and workers committees in all the cities and Agricultural Councils throughout the country. There were close to a million members in the Histadrut in the mid-1960s — about 60 percent of the adult pupulation (see Table 2.7 in Chapter 2). The Histadrut provided a framework for interest articulation of workers, professional groups, independent tradesmen, and many others. The affiliated economic enterprises include Tnuva (the largest Israeli dairy products company), such urban cooperatives as the transportation companies, and Hevrat Ovdim, the holding organization of major Israeli companies such as Solel Boneh, Bank HaPoalim, Koor Industries, Am Oved Publishers, and others. Histadrut activities were conducted on both the national and local levels; this giant organization provided established channels for cooperative activity of many different organized groups. The activity was again voluntary but confined to the existing structures.

The high level of organization and dominance of the labor movement forced the nonlabor sectors to follow suit in this type of cooperative activity. During the yishuv period, the private sector was less organized. This situation started to change with the economic development in the state period, but the response of the government, dominated by Mapai, was a typical attempt of cooptation. For instance, in the 1965 elections the Labor Alignment and Rafi competed for the support of workers in the government-owned Electric Company. A representative of the group was subsequently placed on the Alignment list and elected to the Knesset (Czudnowski, 1970: 235).

There was a tightly woven web of organizations interconnecting the government, the Histadrut, the parties, and the nonlabor sector. Since the 1950s, private industry was also supported with public funds and had direct access to the relevant government ministries, singly or through its association. Ideological differences posed no serious barriers. The Histadrut construction company, Solel Boneh, was partner to many joint ventures with private companies and even individual capitalists (Dan, 1963: 223-224, 232, 235). Thus, in the early state period there were few unidentified or totally independent groups and organizations in Israeli politics. Cooperative activity in Israel had its conflict and competition, but its salient characteristic was that it was highly structured.

The existence of a predominating network with channels leading into the political center made the price of group independence almost intolerable. Despite the socioeconomic changes that started to take place in Israel in those years and the appearance of numerous new professional, managerial, bureaucratic, and economic interests, most associations opted for affiliation rather than being cut off from the network. Political power was more important at that time in Israel than economic power. Private organizations depended on political power for the distribution of tangible economic resources and private persons, for the distribution of social rewards. Consequently, only few independent groups and organizations could operate for long through alternative channels outside the network. Significant independent pressure groups or enduring new parties did not appear.

"Mobilized participation," according to Huntington and Nelson, is the case of leaders mobilizing others through coercion, persuasion, or material inducements. They also note that the distinction between mobilized and autonomous participation is blurred and there are many mixed cases (1976: 7-8). Israel is one of these mixed cases. Coercion was excluded, but pressures and manipulation were not. Furthermore, it can be seen in retrospect that many groups and organizations which started in the 1950s because of semimobilized participation later resorted to autonomous cooperative activities. The best example of this phenomenon is the loyal party branches and workers' councils organized by Mapai and the Histadrut in new development towns. In the mid-1960s they resorted to independent activities (Weiss, 1973: 182-190). The main reason for this development was the genuine group-based nature of mobilized participation in Israel. What began as central pressure to conform developed into group power not to conform when the external conditions changed in the political system as a whole. By that time most groups already knew how to use the organizational channels for political participation.

The second question with regard to cooperative activity concerns the level of participation within the group or organizations, not in the political system as a whole. The yishuv institutions were informal and small enough to enable a great deal of rank and file participation. The Histadrut, the parties, and even the Zionist Congress were ideologically committed to members' participation, even though direct participation was fully exercised only in the kibbutz movements. With the increased size and bureaucratization of institutions during the state period, indirect representation became dominant. Internal nomination of party leaders by a series of indirect votes was culminating in an elaborate process of selection through sectoral representation and "nominating committees." For instance, between a Mapai member and his national leaders in the 1950s, the following bodies existed: the Conference (Veida) elected every few years comprising close to 2,000 delegates; the Council (Moetza) elected by the Conference and made up of 405 members; the Central Committee (Merkaz), the supreme body of the party, operating between Council meetings and elected by them with a membership of 130 (1950-56) and 196 (1958); and the Secretariat (Mazkirut), elected by the Central Committee comprising 8 members (1951), 19 members (1954), and 31 members (1960). The growing size of the Secretariat resulted in the establishment of the Bureau (Lishka) in 1962 with 7 members. Similar patterns can be found in other parties and other organizations, including the Histadrut, which did not develop formal procedures for electing rank and file workers to its overall governing bodies.

Hence, the high membership figures in political organizations did not reflect internal democratic participation. Even the more active and relatively more autonomous local and regional groups and organizations were often subject to the same pattern of conflict regulation, accommodation, and cooptation. Group representation in the party or the national organization was frequently a case of selection from above (symbolic representatives), in which the group itself did not participate (Seligman, 1964: 56-86; Czudnowski, 1970: 230). This method of recruitment caused these "representatives" to be more loyal to the party than to their group. In order to rise to leadership roles, one needed a "critical linkage position in a communication network" and "control over the flow and distribution of information" (Czudnowski in Greenstein and Polsby, 1975: Vol. II, 232). However, a position within the group was not enough in Israel. The relevant communication network was the whole political system and especially the party channels. Despite the competitive conditions, group-based cooperative activity was structured and effectively constrained by the existence of powerful parent organizations.

As in the other modes of participation, group cooperative activity also started to change in the 1960s. Here perhaps the seeds sown by mobilized participation, especially of the local level, proved to be instrumental in the long run. The first clear signs of independent group activity were manifested in the economic recession of 1966-1967. Strikes were a common phenomenon in Israeli political culture, used by the Histadrut and occasionally by groups of workers even without their trade union consent.

Figure 10.4 shows the increase in the number of strikes in 1965 and 1966. Many of these strikes were unauthorized and directed against both the government and the Histadrut. This was perhaps the first time autonomous cooperative activity was exercised in Israel on such a wide scale.

The internal political processes within the parties were also beginning to open up at that period, albeit slowly. Although no Israeli party had primaries, the omnipotence of the tiny nominating committee started to fade, and some form of elections of the candidates for the Knesset — usually in the party's council — took place.[8] If to all these are added the appearance of independent political groups and unaffiliated pressure groups, the transformation in the cooperative mode of participation in Israel becomes evident. All these occurred later, in the period not discussed in this book, but the origins can be traced to the earlier group activity, however structured and constrained.

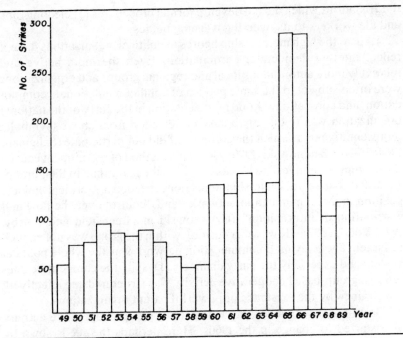

Figure 10.4 Number of Yearly Strikes in Israel (1949-1969)
SOURCES: Statistical Abstract of Israel, No. 12 (1961: 391) and No. 31 (1980: 348).

INDIVIDUAL CAMPAIGN ACTIVITIES

This mode of participation requires a personal decision by the individual to commit him or herself to political work. It can take different forms, some of them related to the other modes of participation presented above, such as joining a political party, working for the party between campaigns, or being a candidate for public office (Milbrath and Goel, 1977: 13). Here the focus will be on voluntary involvement of individuals in election campaigns as an illustration of this mode of participation.

In contrast to the single act of casting a vote, which is simple and secret, personal involvement in the election campaigns represents an intensive form of committed participation. People usually do not invest their time, money, and reputation unless they are convinced that their contribution could make a difference. If individuals try to persuade others to vote in a certain way, or if they work for the party, they are actually trying to expand their influence beyond their own single vote.

Campaign activity communicates the preference of the active citizen to other citizens as well as to party candidates with whom he or she may be in contact. It requires a great deal of initiative as well as cooperation with others. Above all, it is an attempt to use communication in order to have a more direct impact on steering.

Given the low sense of efficacy, it is no wonder that individual voluntary participation in campaigns was not developed in Israel. The difference between participation in national versus local campaigns was not great; therefore, only national campaigns will be examined here. The means at the disposal of individuals in Israel to participate in political campaigns were weak compared to their counterparts in countries with direct election systems. The political channels in general and during elections in particular were dominated by the parties and the affiliated organizations. Consequently, those Israelis who took part personally in the campaign — and many did — were usually party officials or paid workers. On election day, they represented their parties in the voting stations or, together with some volunteers, helped get the voters to cast their ballots, but this is not the kind of committed involvement suggested by campaign activity. Some organized groups were directly involved, notably in Histadrut elections. This was certainly the case with regard to kibbutz and moshav members, but these were affiliated with their respective parties and "allotted" by their movement to take part in the election campaigns.

Israelis took part in the campaign passively by consuming election material and attending political meetings and rallies. Their active campaigning, however, was minimal. Few contributed money to their parties' campaigns. One reason is that the electoral system does not enable one to contribute money to a preferred candidate, only to the party as a whole. The parties conducted special fund appeals during elections, soliciting contributions from well-to-do members. Similarly, members were encouraged to pay their dues or to donate a certain proportion of their salary. But most of the campaign funds were derived from the financial, industrial, commercial, and other economic institutions connected in one way or another with the parties (Gutmann, 1963: 710). For instance, the economic enterprises of the Histadrut were "known to contribute quite lavishly to campaign funds in ways which, though not illegal, are kept secret to avoid a public furor" (p. 711). In 1969 a new law was enacted, and since then direct financing of the parties election campaigns has been from the public purse.

Despite their intensive interest in politics and the high voter turnout, few Israelis engaged in door-to-door canvassing or identified themselves

publicly by displaying and distributing campaign materials in the first
five elections reviewed here. In Chapter 7 the changes in the methods of
conducting national election campaigns were presented. The trend was
from direct personal and group approach to mediated mass campaign
supported by meetings of socioeconomic groups (see Table 7.4). Thus
the Israeli voter was not personally active in the campaign, and he or she
often missed a "major learning experience of democratic politics" (Katz
in McQuail, 1972: 353). Moreover, the way Israeli parties conducted the
election campaign in those years shows clearly that they regarded it as
"payday," when their efforts of penetration and maintenance would
materialize. The party's established channels handled the transmission
of election propaganda; thus there was little need to alter the communication network even in election periods. The bigger the party and the
more time it was in power, the easier it was to utilize its channels during
the campaigns. The structured nature of the election campaign and the
low level of citizen voluntary participation reflected accurately the conditions of the political system at that time (compare Nimmo, 1978:
384-388). In short, campaigning was not a common means for Israelis to
participate in the political system. It illustrates very well the low level of
personal commitment, as far as the individual's direct political activity is
concerned.

POLITICAL PARTICIPATION IN ISRAEL

Israel's election campaigns were always fierce and costly, implying
that participation of the citizens was critical. But was it really? The
foregoing discussion compares the four modes of participation in order
to learn something about Israel's path of democratic political development. The degree of participation in each mode can be summarized as
follows:

Responsive
  Voting turnout ....Very High
  Contacting officials on personal issues ....Very High
  Cooperative activity (structured) ....High
Committed
  Cooperative activities (unstructured) ....Low
  Individual participation in campaign
  activities ....Very Low

These modes of participation are not mutually exclusive: there are
combinations, variations, and different forms and channels in which
they can be expressed. However, the evidence for Israel shows some

interesting discrepancies: relatively good opportunities for individual access to the political network but a low sense of efficacy; very high responsive participation but low committed participation.

In Chapter 1 responsive participants were described as listeners who are sometimes personally active and can modify steering, because they force the network to adjust itself to their votes, their complaints, and their membership in parties. They also contribute to the existence of "public opinion," which cannot be ignored in a democracy. But responsive participants are usually activated from above, which may explain their low sense of efficacy. Israeli democracy in the period under review was characterized by such responsive participation.

Participation, even if largely responsive, indicates a relatively high level of democratic political development, simply because citizens are involved with their political system and take part in collective-oriented activities. The fact that these activities are usually organized and the participation highly structured does not make Israel "less democratic," but rather a democratic system with less "committed participation." As presented in Figure 10.1, committed participation is not a more developed form than responsive participation, nor is it a prerequisite for gaining impact on steering. Indeed, the level of participation in the early state period was high enough to disqualify Israel from belonging to the group of countries in which "guided democracy" or "mobilized participation" is practiced (compare Friedgut, 1979: 249-267). Regardless of how "public opinion" is defined, there is a difference between central steering, which takes into consideration public demands and is directly influenced by individuals and groups that have access and autonomous means of participation, and steering which controls participation. Chapter 8 showed that the Israeli system has developed a steering capacity without being insensitive to information coming from below. In this chapter, it was observed that the channels most frequently used by citizens were the established ones, and that individual and group participation was more responsive than committed. The combination of these two observations indicates the existence of a certain type of democratic political development in which steering is activated mainly through citizens' involvement in institutionalized means of participation. It also points out the importance of the *potential* power of the periphery in determining the level of democratic political development.

Does all this make any difference in terms of *influence* on the behavior of the political system? One way of looking into this question is to find out whether the peripheral target groups were not only penetrated and maintained, but could also gain access to and participate in the political system.

The Peripheral Groups:
Access and Participation

In previous chapters the groups that posed penetration challenges to the political center were described. Their political significance to the center was examined, as well as the channels used to penetrate and incorporate them into the political system. There were ideological reasons, apart from political expediency, which caused the center not to neglect these groups, even though it could have done so (at least with regard to some). How did members of these groups view this process? The center was successful in obtaining support and symbolic identification, but what was the content of the upward flow of information coming from these groups? Was there a high degree of political mobility among them also? Did mobility provide access to information resources as a step toward political participation and influence? The fate of peripheral groups, especially those which try to break into the political system, is important for evaluating the impact of participation on steering (Nettl, 1967).

In Israel, some of the target groups on the center's list did not aspire to be incorporated into the political system. There were also significant differences in the type of access sought by different groups and their readiness to become intensively involved. Of special interest are the target groups of Israeli Arabs, the ultra-orthodox, and new immigrants, which — each for its own different reasons — did seek access to and participation in the system. The other target groups are less relevant here; therefore only these three will be examined, each according to the following criteria: individual access, group access, responsive participation, and committed participation.

ISRAELI ARABS

The Arab citizens in Israel do not share the common contents with the Jewish majority and do not identify with the Jewish state. They are, however, interested in gaining access to political resources such as public budgets and to educational and occupational opportunities. They were incorporated into the Israeli political system due to the center's penetration effort, particularly through the military government, Jewish political parties, the state bureaucracy, and special newspapers and radio programs in Arabic. Yet for all practical purposes, they could be regarded as a nonintegrated political community. As individuals, Israeli Arab citizens in the early 1950s lacked opportunities for rapid political mobility. As a group constituting about 16 percent of the population in

1965, they were not organized politically.[9] A group that is expected to show "loyalty to the State but not identification" (Prime Minister's Advisor on Arab Affairs, *Maariv,* Jan. 31, 1967) is in a difficult predicament.

The Arabs in Israel were cut off from their pre-1948 urban centers and political leaders and under a military government until 1965. They were also subject to a rapid modernization process and many other strong influences emanating from the Jewish society. By 1965, two-thirds of the Israeli Arabs were born in the State of Israel; most knew Hebrew, wore Western clothes, and were economically linked to the Israeli system. Their previous social structure had changed a great deal, and a new class of wage earners and urban residents appeared. Expanded opportunities in education created an important group of young intellectuals, while the rise in the standard of living transformed the traditional modes of communication into modern ones (J. Landau, 1971: 88-90). Nevertheless, their access opportunities as individuals or as a group were limited. They did not, for example, have access to institutions which were Jewish and not Israeli (The Jewish Agency, The Jewish National Fund), but which still affected their lives in areas such as settlements and land acquisition. The main outlet for Israeli Arabs to contest decisions of the authorities was an appeal to the Supreme Court. This important channel of access was used, even though the outcome was not always satisfactory from the point of view of the claimants (see Lustick, 1980: 180).

By the mid-1960s a sizable portion of the Arab community in Israel had become more mobile and was ready to translate its interest in access into participation. Even though this interest was pragmatic, it contained an element of recognition of and compliance with the state and its political system. Yet the level of Arab political organization did not increase, because any such development touched immediately on the sensitive issue of the general Arab-Israeli conflict and other delicate questions, such as the military government or confiscation of land by the Jewish State. It was difficult for any Israeli Arab organization to oppose publicly the official Arab line of those days, which called for the destruction of Israel. Conversely, any independent stance of Israeli Arabs on this issue would not have been tolerated by the Israeli government. Arabs in Israel lacked room for political maneuvering. The government opposed unaffiliated Arab organizations because they implied opposition and disloyalty to the state. The result was that no independent Arab parties were established and the mode of operation through pressure groups did not develop.

Politically, Israeli Arabs were affiliated and dominated by the Jewish parties during elections and Jewish institutions between elections. They remained organized in semitraditional circles of extended families, local villages (tribes in the case of the Bedouins), and regions, while major changes were taking place socially and economically. They were linked to the main channels and institutions of the political system through special extensions of the parties, the Histadrut, the bureaucracy, and the mass media. Their participation in the political system was expressed only in national, local, and, to some extent, Histadrut elections.

Arab participation in the national elections was in fact tacit support of the regime. The ruling party and the Arab lists affiliated with it received a majority of the vote. This support was achieved partly because of the existence of the military government (Kollek and Kollek, 1978: 134) and partly because Mapai could effectively control the various Arab groups and their leaders. The fact that Arabs voted also for Jewish parties that had little to do with Arab affairs suggests either ignorance (misinformation) or willingness to "sell" votes. In 1965, for example, the (Jewish) National Religious Party received 4 percent of the Arab vote in the cities and 6 percent in the rural areas, and the right-wing Gahal 0.5 percent and 3 percent, respectively.

As can be seen in Table 10.2, the participation rate of Arabs in the national elections was consistently high and even higher than the Jewish rate. The main reason for the high turnout among Arabs was the intensive election campaign conducted by the parties, which exerted pressure through the heads of villages, families, and tribes. For instance, the high participation of Arab women — who traditionally are not politically oriented — suggests that not all of it was voluntary.

Local elections were characterized by an even higher rate of participation (about 90 percent). The competing lists in these elections were either local, based on family or religious ties, or affiliated with the national parties (mainly in the cities). The nonaffiliated local lists did not succeed in interfering with the dominance of the established parties. Thus, for example, the Communist Party, which was a nonestablishment organization, had less success in local than in national elections (J. Landau, 1971: 221-222). It provided an outlet for voters — mainly young, urban, and better educated — who opposed the government. Support for Mapam increased because of the inclusion of Arabs in its list of candidates for the Knesset and its opposition to the military government. Until 1965, the support of Mapai and its affiliated Arab lists declined gradually, which indicated an increasing level of free choice among Arab voters. Nevertheless, the control of the political center and the dominating party remained firm.

Another responsive mode of participation — contacting officials — was less prevalent among Arab citizens because of legal restrictions and their dependence on their leaders and official authorities. As for

TABLE 10.2   Israeli Arab Votes in National Elections

Election Year	Percentage of Participation	Mapai's Affiliated Arab lists	Mapai	Communist Party	Mapam	All other Parties
		Vote Distribution Among Parties				
1949	79.3	51.7	9.6	22.2	0.2	16.3
1951	85.5	54.8	11.7	16.3	5.6	11.6
1955	92.1	57.8	11.7	15.6	7.3	7.6
1959	88.9	58.5	4.6	11.2	14.4	11.3
1961	85.6	45.6	8.1	22.5	12.0	11.8
1965	87.8	43.8	8.4	23.1	10.2	14.5
Average — Arab vote	86.5					
Average — general vote (1949-1965)	81.8					

SOURCES: J. Landau (1971: 208); Central Bureau of Statistics, *Election Results*, Special Publications No. 51 (1955), No. 166 (1961) and No. 309 (1969); Harari (1978: 22).

cooperative participation, there were several attempts to establish independent Arab parties in Israel (J. Landau, 1971: 90-100). The most serious one was made by El Ard ("the soil"), a group of young Arab intellectuals who called for nonparticipation in the national elections of 1959. A year later they established a company for the publishing, translation, and import of books. Despite opposition from military authorities, they received a Supreme Court decree enabling them to continue their operation. The group mainly attracted nationalistic young Arabs and was active in the years 1962-1964. In 1965 El Ard's request to set up a political party was denied by the Supreme Court on the grounds that the group did not recognize the State of Israel and was trying to utilize the democratic political process to undermine the political system. The organization was subsequently dismantled.

Between 1959 and 1965 about 40,000 Arabs joined the Histadrut (5 percent of the total membership, and with their families over 30 percent of the total Arab population at that time). Most participated in the Histadrut elections and distributed their votes in a way similar to the national elections. For instance, in 1965, 60 percent of the Arab members of the Histadrut voted for Mapai (the Alignment), 20 percent for the Communists, and 13 percent for Mapam (J. Landau, 1973: 7, 15).

Israeli Arabs were autonomous in governing the two Arab cities, 38 local councils, and 17 villages (1966). On a national level, there were 3 Arab or Druze elected Knesset Members in 1949 and either 7 or 8 elected to each subsequent Knesset (4-5 from the lists affiliated with Mapai, 1-2 from the Communist Party, and 1 from Mapam). In terms of their constituency, the Arab Knesset Members who were affiliated with Mapai tended to be less concerned with the Arab-Israeli conflict and more with the local needs of their supporters. As the heads of extended families or villages, they determined the political affiliation of their people and got the votes. In return they could help their supporters with the authorities and the bureaucracy. Those who voted for the Communist Party as the spokesman for their cause as Arabs were perhaps better represented ideologically but less well connected to the existing channels.[10] In sum, access opportunities for Arabs were limited, and despite their high voting turnout in elections, the general level of Arab participation was also low and nonexistent in terms of committed participation. The main transformation in the political activity of Israeli Arabs started with the abolishment of the military government and reopened contacts with Arabs in the occupied territories in 1967.

ULTRA-ORTHODOX GROUPS

The Jewish ultra-orthodox groups adopted a pragmatic and instrumental attitude toward the political system. They did not recognize the Zionist content of the State of Israel but did identify with the Jewish community and were much concerned with the religious character of the society. The Neturei Karta group is an exception because they opted to be complete outsiders: They did not identify with and sought no share in the Israeli state, society, or polity.

The purpose of the political system was to induce these groups to recognize the state and to take part in its secular institutions. National leaders were willing, however, to make concessions in religious affairs and come forward with economic incentives in order to keep them within the political system. The ultra-orthodox groups affiliated with the two Aguda parties did not participate in the political institutions during the yishuv period. In May 1948, however, they recognized the state, signed the Declaration of Independence, and have voted ever since in national and local elections, occasionally even taking part in the cabinet coalition. Nevertheless, they managed to stay aloof by not allowing direct intervention of any of the secular party, bureaucratic, and mass media channels operating in the political system. They established their own parties, organizations, and newspapers and retained independence in their state-supported schools. Their socialization process was entirely different because of their traditional community and family structure, separate schools, and special institutions of higher religious learning (Yeshivot). By agreement, most of the men and all of their women do not serve in the army. What, therefore, are their modes of access and participation in a political system whose overall secular authority they do not accept?

In terms of individual mobility, there is no doubt that members of the ultra-orthodox communities are capable of gaining access to political resources. By choice, however, their way of life is strictly orthodox and their social mobility is very low. Accordingly, individual motivation to take part in politics does not exist. As a group, however, their high degree of organization and internal cohesion enables them to act forcefully in the political system when they decide to do so. They have decided to cooperate since 1948 because they realized they could advance their interests better within the political system than as outsiders.

The two Aguda parties can form ad hoc coalitions with the more extreme Neturei Karta and the more moderate National Religious Party. For instance, in 1959 all the orthodox groups joined forces in violent demonstrations against the opening of a "mixed" (for men and women) public swimming pool in Jerusalem. On many other occasions, the Aguda parties and NRP fought together to pass religious legislation in the Knesset. Moreover, in the 1949 elections, Agudat Israel and Poalei Agudat Israel were part of the "United Religious Front" aimed at advancing religious affairs in the new-born state. The Front did not last long because of the gulf between the NRP and the Aguda parties on both Zionist and orthodox issues, but all participated in the cabinet coalition until 1952 and their activities on religious issues were frequently coordinated.

In addition to their participation in the elections, the Aguda parties were active in selected local councils — dominating, for instance, the council in the city of Bnei Brak and wielding great influence in Jerusalem. Between 1961 and 1969, Poalei Agudat Israel supported the coalition in the Knesset without taking responsibility for a ministerial portfolio, and also cooperated with the Histadrut and with the kibbutz movements. Both Aguda parties had their trusted people in relevant government departments, such as the Education Ministry (in charge of financing their independent schools). On the other hand, they had no part in the Ministry of Religious Affairs, traditionally dominated by the NRP, and refrained from direct involvement in the continuous struggle around the office of the Chief Rabbinate (Birnbaum, 1970: 113-116).

Participation of these ultra-orthodox groups in the Israeli political system was also manifest in selective and carefully planned group pressure carried out by their political parties. Between 1951 and 1959, the two Aguda parties ran jointly in the elections and regularly obtained five to six seats in the Knesset. In 1961 and 1965 they ran separately, with Agudat Israel obtaining four and Poalei Agudat Israel, two seats. There are no data on voting turnout, but their ability to retain their proportional strength indicates that it was high and steady.

As a group, their political successes were impressive. They obtained from the government direct concessions in religious affairs and had a high share of political resources. These include exemptions for women who objected to military service on religious grounds (1951); the recognition of their separate and independent elementary school system to be supported by the state (1953); and the establishment of their own bank with money obtained from the state treasury (1965).

The ultra-orthodox parties also managed to exert a great deal of pressure on the NRP, forcing it from time to time to take uncompromising stands on religious affairs. Some of the major achievements of the NRP in preserving the religious status quo were inspired by the prodding of the more extreme religious groups. The political power of the ultra-orthodox parties was also enhanced by the support of Jewish groups outside of Israel. Rabbi Levin of Agudat Israel alluded to this power in the 1952 Knesset debate over education, warning the House: "The outcry resulting from the destruction of traditional Torah education would be so great that it would be heard everywhere in the world where Jews could be found" (quoted in Birnbaum, 1970: 170).

The political activity of the ultra-orthodox groups carried not only the possibility of violent resistance but also the threat that the clashes between religious and secular Jews would deteriorate into a destructive *Kulturkampf*. Unlike the NRP, which was reluctant to use this argument as a political weapon, the leaders of the ultra-orthodox spoke openly about a possible split among the Jewish people. They could do so because of their lower commitment to the State of Israel and primarily because they could not conceive of a separation between religion and state in Judaism.

The ultra-orthodox groups pose an interesting case regarding access, participation, and democratic political development. They do not identify with the system, yet they score high marks on political access and participation through voting and cooperative action. They are not committed to the political system in its present form, but they are deeply committed to group activity aimed at influencing that system on specific issues. It is easy to dismiss them as a unique case based on the peculiar characteristics of the Israeli election and coalition systems, but there are two additional lessons. First, the Jewish common contents are shared with the rest of society — in spite of the widely divergent interpretation — and this stimulates access and participation. Second, even when the

state is regarded as merely an instrument, if the group is well organized
and the rules of the political game are generally observed, the chances
for access and participation are high.

NEW IMMIGRANTS

The most significant group for examining democratic political development in Israel is that of the newcomers — particularly the Oriental
communities. They were the prime target of penetration, and they were
eager to gain access and become full participants. In previous chapters
the penetrative ability of the political channels and the mobilizing impact
of schools and the IDF were underscored. Now the opportunities for
independent access and participation will be examined.

In the mid-1960s, only 6 percent of the Israeli population was really
veteran — that is, natives whose fathers were also born in Israel. The
rest were either born abroad or children of immigrant fathers: 46 percent
from Asian and African countries, and 48 percent from European and
American countries (see Table 2.4). On arrival, almost all new immigrants were totally dependent on the political system. Their ability to
develop quickly into independent citizens was restricted because of the
objective conditions, but also because "the immigrant was conceived as
an object of socio-political mobilization rather than a subject with an
autonomous will, aspirations and expectations" (Horowitz and Lissak,
1978: 201).

Western immigrants displayed a higher individual ability to gain
access to political resources. They were more mobile socially and politically because the system they found in Israel was not totally alien,
especially if they belonged to one of the party-affiliated movements
before arrival. There is also some evidence that Western immigrants
displayed

> higher percentages of participation than new immigrants from coun-
> tries in which the population could not participate in politics at all, or as
> Jews, were precluded from such activities. . . . Higher political par-
> ticipation may at least be attributed to the educational factor rather
> than the country of origin [Gutmann, 1960: 59].

This advantage of Western immigrants was not displayed in higher
voting rates or in a higher degree of group orientation and cooperative
political activity. No significant party of Western immigrants was formed
after 1948,[11] and their many immigrant associations were politically
weak or strongly dependent on the parties.

Despite the formal openness of the election system, new immigrants distributed their votes among the existing political powers. The result was that Mapai in particular, but also the other established political bodies, consolidated their power. Immigrants were often organized before they even reached Israel, and their ability to break these ties and organize independently in an entirely new system was limited indeed. Without the party and bureaucratic channels, it was simply impossible to gain access to jobs, housing, education, and health services. This imposition was stronger and more effective on Oriental immigrants whose traditional communities facilitated group manipulation and hindered individual mobility.

The main difference, therefore, between an Oriental and a Western immigrant was that the former initially had a lower ability to participate in the system as an autonomous individual, while the latter had better connections to the political network of the veterans. In certain respects the process of political mobilization of Oriental Jews in Israel resembled that of the urban poor in developing nations (Nelson, 1979). The main method was "vertically mobilized participation," and the channels used were traditional leaders, patron-client networks, and party machines.[12] This type of mobilization links individuals to the political network but perpetuates their dependence and impedes their ability to utilize the vertical channels for upward transmission of information. The story of political mobility of the Oriental community in Israel has not yet been fully told. Peres points out the gap in the political representation of the Oriental community and the progress made until 1967, especially in local governments (1976: 123-134). Smooha identifies the important point: Socioeconomic mobility was not automatically translated into political mobility (1978: 40).

All attempts of new Oriental immigrants to establish their own parties during the early state period failed.[13] In retrospect, these were not serious attempts; they did not develop organized pressure groups or powerful immigrant associations capable of exerting pressure on the parties. There were, on the contrary, outbursts of demonstrations and violent riots in the transitory camps, the new development towns, and notably in poor urban areas such as Wadi Salib.

The Wadi Salib riot in May 1959 was a spontaneous and unprecedented act of violence which began among immigrants from Morocco living in a slum in Haifa. In the course of these riots, the local Mapai club and the Haifa Labor Council building were attacked, shops in the commercial district looted, and a number of policemen and demonstrators wounded. The event rapidly transcended the boundaries of

Haifa and those of the Moroccan community of immigrants. Demonstrations broke out in Migdal HaEmek, Tivón, and Beersheva in which
other North African communities of immigrants took part. The leaders
were arrested and sentenced to short prison terms. The reactions of the
city authorities, the party, and the government were typically a combination of personal appeals, public investigation, and new program pro-
posals. There were attempts to induce the leaders to join Mapai, and
even before the Investigation Committee had completed its reports, a
government program was implemented to improve the living conditions
in Wadi Salib (*HaAretz*, July 10, 1959). The leaders formed a party — the
United Organization of North African Immigrants — and ran in the 1959
elections. As with previous ethnic lists, this too was a complete failure
— the list received less than 8,000 votes and hence no place in the
Knesset.

The Wadi Salib riots represented an outburst of deep feeling of
frustration and bitterness among the new immigrants from Morocco and
other North African countries (Bar-Yoseph, 1959). Many years later a
member of a neighborhood committee in Beersheva still remembered
Wadi Salib:

> We ought to demonstrate. Who do they think they are? They want to
> keep us backward in order to prove to everybody that Moroccans are
> dirty and primitive. We studied in Morocco in Alliance [school] and
> here they discriminate against us. You know why they gather us in one
> neighborhood? So that they can surround us with soldiers, the way
> they did in Wadi Salib [quoted in Stahl, 1979: 44].

At the time, Wadi Salib was an isolated event and indicated that new
immigrants from Oriental countries could exert only a low level of
political pressure. It took the second generation, most of whom were
born in Israel, to sustain independent group (and eventually party)
activity in the 1970s.

The low level of political mobility of Oriental Jews was evident in
their disproportionately low representation among the various elites of
the country, especially the political elite (Gurevitch and Winograd, 1976:
368, 376-377). Smooha maintains that "the more powerful the political
position, the less the representation of Oriental Jews," and that Oriental
Jews have been coopted by the veteran Western community in a process
of "controlled gradualism" (1978: 169, 181).

It is easier to analyze this process from the vantage point of the 1970s.
Within one generation, an overwhelming majority of all new immigrants
in Israel were incorporated into the political system. Most of them
became equal citizens — they had access to political resources almost as
much as the veterans, and their participation was equally responsive.

The Oriental communities of new immigrants, however, demonstrate a different path of political development. Although by the mid-1960s the majority were fairly integrated in socioeconomic terms, their individual and group access was lower compared to the rest of society. Moreover, there appeared a hard core of underprivileged who were left behind — many of them a second generation of native Israelis who later displayed alienation (Galnoor, 1974: 46-47).

In sum, Oriental immigrants possessed neither the personal ability nor the group organization to link themselves to the communication network and to become important factors in Israeli politics. The fact that they were divided into many different communities according to countries of origin, languages, customs, and dates of immigration to Israel also limited their ability to act jointly. Nevertheless, their participation as expressed in voting was high, and the long-run trend has been toward the crystallization of political consciousness, group awareness of political inequality, and a readiness to use the rules of the democratic game to change their situation.

THE PERIPHERY IN ISRAELI DEMOCRACY

In the first part of this chapter, the general sense of efficacy and the modes of participation in Israel were presented. Next, some peripheral groups were used as an illustration of the concrete difficulties of and the opportunities for access and participation. What are the general conclusions from these examples?

Taken together, these divergent groups confirm the conclusions of the previous chapter regarding access in general. First, access opportunities for individuals were medium to wide, whereas groups, particularly the nonestablished ones, had a narrow choice and restricted opportunities for independent transmission of information. They had to operate through the established channels, which were centrally coordinated.

Second, the modes of participation of these groups were by and large similar to that of the general population. The voting turnout rate of Israeli Arabs, the ultra-orthodox, and new immigrants was high, whereas independent group organization and cooperative activity was very low (except, as pointed out, in the special case of the ultra-orthodox). The point here is not that these groups were fully integrated, or that their access and participation were identical to those of the rest of society, but that — despite their more peripheral status — their modes of political behavior resembled those of the other groups.

Third, the more general conclusion is that these groups were not left outside the Israeli political system despite their peripheral status. Efforts by the political center to penetrate and maintain the support of these groups have been described. But even if the purpose was merely to guarantee acquiescence (of Israeli Arabs), recognition of the political system (by the ultra-orthodox), and integration (of Oriental Jews), the result was that eventually these groups acquired access opportunities and did participate. These examples indicate, therefore, that the Israeli system was not just politically developed but that it already contained a relatively strong democratic component.

The democratic component becomes even more visible in light of the fact that the Israeli political center could have tried to use other means in order to penetrate and maintain the loyalty of these groups. The Israeli Arab population could have been subject to special emergency rules, at least initially, which would deny them the right to vote. There were, of course, good reasons why the ruling parties assumed they would obtain most of these votes; and there were considerations of world public opinion. But the fact is that the Israeli political system did not ignore such considerations and Israeli Arabs were given the right to vote in the January 1949 elections before the war was over.

The anti-Zionist, ultra-orthodox Jews represent a more convincing example. They could have been asked to pledge allegiance to the state and its laws before having the right to vote and send representatives to the Knesset, but they were not; and the reasons derived from the "common contents" explain, in my opinion, why no Jewish group could be excluded. Similarly, new immigrants could have been asked to reside a certain period in the country, or at least to learn Hebrew, before becoming full citizens, but they were granted citizenship on arrival. The fact that these entirely different groups participated in divergent ways and different degrees in Israeli politics indicates something about the level of democratic political development.

These examples reinforce the earlier conclusion that Zionism as a political ideology contained democratic elements. In the early state period, Israel was already in the process of democratic political development, manifested in opportunities for individual access and responsive participation of the entire population. No group was peripheral to the extent that its members did not take part, in one way or another, in this process.

Impact on Steering

"Put the steering wheel in our faithful hands" [Mapai slogan in the 1961 elections]

In Hebrew the words "leadership" and "steering" are derived from the same root. The foregoing campaign slogan implies leadership, responsibility, and direction. Does it also imply that the role of the voters ends once they decide in whose hands to put the wheel? What difference do access and participation make in terms of system's steering? Impact on steering requires not only general opportunities, or even actual transmission of information, but power to participate in the decision-making process (Lasswell and Kaplan, 1950: 75). Did Israeli citizens have such power? In the discussion in Chapter 8, the focus was on the emergence of central steering capacity as an indicator of political development. In this concluding section, Israelis' power to influence central steering will not be measured or illustrated through specific case studies. Rather, I will discuss citizens' capacity to influence steering as an indicator of democratic political development. This capacity is based, first, on access and participation of individuals and groups. In addition, I will examine now three systemic conditions which characterize the environment in which the process of democratic political development takes place: political equality, feedback, and openness.

POLITICAL EQUALITY

In Israel, as in many other countries, the test of democracy is viewed in terms of citizen participation, particularly in free elections. Israelis tend to identify democracy with the existence of an elected Knesset and with competition among parties. Additional democratic requirements such as freedom of expression, freedom to form and join organizations, eligibility for public office, and equality in other areas of political participation besides voting are secondary. For instance, the discrepancy between low efficacy, high voting turnout, and low commitment to other forms of participation was not regarded as an issue for great concern in the early state period. The 1961 election, resulting from the Lavon Affair, was the first time the general question of "Israeli democracy" was seriously debated during the campaign.

Political equality is used here to mean that information transmitted by citizens has an equal chance to exert pressure and to influence steering. The many other aspects of political equality will be ignored in order to concentrate on the process of converting information into pressure.

There is first the question of equality before the law and of civil rights legally guaranteed. Constitutional democracy is a prerequisite for turning the modern person into an informed participant citizen (Inkeles and

Smith, 1974: 17). Formally, the Israeli legal framework measures up on this criterion, despite the general restrictions on autonomous participation, the more coercive penetration methods used for Israeli Arabs, and the paternalistic approach toward Oriental immigrants. Even taken together, these reservations do not justify a negative conclusion regarding the existence of constitutional democracy in Israel.

But two or even three decades of sovereign experience with democracy are not enough to develop firm norms of political equality and to guarantee individual rights. The boundaries between state privileges and civil freedoms are still ill-defined, and the prospects for developing an accepted code of civil rights have been hindered by controversies in many areas, particularly regarding the role of religion in the state. Also noted was the precarious position of nonestablished groups in the state and the influence of security pressures on individual rights. One consequence is that the communication network in Israel is functionally open (on a selective basis), but the people's right to know has not been formally recognized. The gap in Israel between the citizen's individual access and the low level of committed participation confirms the observation made with regard to other countries:

> If one of the criteria for successful democratic functioning is relative equality of political activity, access, and influence, our volume indicates how difficult it is to achieve such equality. The "natural" tendency for certain citizens to take greater advantage of participatory opportunities must be overcome [Verba et al., 1978: 308].

Overall, it can be said that in the period under review the political system in Israel was generally responsive, there was little use of coercion, and there was no widespread alienation. Nevertheless, there was still political inequality, as defined above, to be overcome. Citizens' participation was largely organized, usually from above, and there were groups which could take greater advantages of participatory opportunities.

In terms of the probability of transmitting information that could exert pressure and influence central steering, the conclusion is qualified. Until the mid-1960s, impact on steering was mediated by the existence of a powerful communication network and prescribed channels. The contribution of political equality to the process of democratic political development was therefore manifested chiefly in citizens' responsive participation: enhancing the stability of the political system on the one hand, and constraining the sense of efficacy and committed participation, particularly of peripheral groups, on the other.

FEEDBACK

Feedback was defined as information that is corrective or aimed at changing the course of steering. Whereas citizens' responsive participation usually produces feedback capable of marginal corrections, committed participation is often change-oriented. In Israel, the mediating channels — the parties, the bureaucracy, and the mass media — were predominant in carrying feedback information. Consequently, most of this information was what Easton terms "systemic feedback" — that is, responsive information about the general nature and consequences of government decisions (1965b: 363). One can assume that by the time this information reached the political center, it carried little pressure that could drastically modify behavior. The impact of the mediating channel was toward moderation of new demands and correction of serious deviations. Not only were the diagonal organizational channels the most crowded ones (see Figure 1.2), but they also dictated a certain conformity in the feedback information.

Feedback as such does not guarantee citizens' impact on steering. Although absolutely necessary for central steering, the content of the information can be carefully screened or fabricated. In Israel the stabilizing nature of the feedback mechanisms was quite apparent. High voting turnout was not only achieved, it was acclaimed as the most prominent indication of democratic participation. In addition, the widespread practice of citizen complaints to officials on personal matters served as a useful corrective mechanism for both government and citizens. The "rest" of the political process, however, was dominated by the parties and their established affiliations. These were powerful organizations, and they could do much directly without "involving" the government: provide jobs, promise favors, and deliver on the basis of "votes for benefits" exchanges. Thus the function of screening and minimizing demands, which usually causes great stress in political systems, was effectively performed by the intermediary bodies in Israel.

What is the conclusion from this regarding impact on steering? The Israeli political system was not aloof.[14] Responsibility for responding to demands and needs was delegated to the parties and increasingly later to the bureaucracy and the mass media. Therefore, the established channels did provide an outlet for feedback information to reach, if not the center directly, the important party and bureaucratic relay junctions in the network. Some of the demands could be answered directly by these mediating organizations, others were selectively transferred upward, and some were side-stepped. In any case, this mechanism did provide an opportunity for impact on steering, albeit one that is carefully controlled and tuned to the preferences of the political center. For instance, the dominating Mapai party responded through direct cooptation and accommodation. In 1951, the nonsocialist General Zionist Party gained 20 seats in the Knesset compared to 7 previously and was invited to join the coalition cabinet.

Despite institutional constraints and the fact that the political system was dominated by one party for a long period, Israel had a responsive democratic mechanism that functioned through established channels and without frequent alterations of parties in office (Etzioni, 1959: 213). As for the expression of mass or popular opinion (Lane and Sears, 1964; Nimmo, 1978: 242-244), more formal means were not developed in Israel in the period under review. Israel has had no constitutional provisions for a referendum or a plebiscite, and these have not yet been attempted. Also, the "machinery of observability" (Merton, 1968: 409), such as public opinion polls and other forms of political questionnaires, was scarcely used in the early state period, and for a good reason. The forum for influencing government policy was not the general public but the more confined circles of the established parties and the affiliated groups (Eisenstadt, 1965b). The most prominent device was the general elections, which, "like a steering mechanism that is partially loose, gets a slow response to its directives, and is susceptible to tampering, to boot" (Converse in Greenstein and Polsby, 1975: Vol. 4, 77).

Nevertheless, accountability was not totally absent in the Israeli political system, because of the importance of elections and because of the role of the intermediary bodies. On the eve of the 1967 war the two principal rivals of Mapai — Herut and Rafi — joined the government coalition in response to public opinion. Compared to the past, this was an exception, but it was also an indicator of things to come. Since 1967, feedback has become more change-oriented; public opinion, a more vocal and independent factor; and the government, much more responsive. This reached a climax after the 1973 war, when the general mood in society, protest movements, and public demonstrations helped to bring down the cabinet of Prime Minister Meir.

In terms of feedback, even before the mid-1960s the Israeli polity could be classified as a "high information system," in which the legitimacy of political norms requires responsiveness to information generated from below (Apter, 1971: 14). However, a distinction should be made between citizens' ability to have an impact on large collective outcomes as opposed to narrower governmental actions, relevant mainly to a smaller number of people (Verba et al., 1978: 311). In Israel, feedback had an important impact on the former only through elections and on the latter through group affiliations and direct contacts between officials and citizens. In general, the impact was more clearly felt in particularized outcomes.

OPENNESS

The state exacts the utmost degree of obedience and sacrifice from its citizens, but at the same time treats them as children by maintaining an

excess of secrecy and a censorship of news and expressions of opinion
that renders the spirits of those thus intellectually oppressed defense-
less against every unfavorable turn of events and every sinister rumor
[Freud, 1958: 211-212].

Openness here means conditions in the society and in the polity that
enhance political equality and feedback and enable citizens' access and
participation. In Chapter 1 complete openness was described in negative
terms: absence of any deliberate interference in the free flow of information. The question here is, where should Israel be placed on the continuum of closed-open political systems?

Laws in Israel establish the principle that secrecy is the rule and
disclosure the exception. In a comparative study of ten relatively
"open" democratic systems, Israel was classified as "less open" because the people's right to know was less valued than the government's
privilege to conceal information (Galnoor, 1977: 282-284). The differences among democracies regarding openness are negligible compared
to the differences between them and the closed nondemocratic systems.
Israel, for instance, is "less open," but it is nevertheless functionally
open and pluralist — it enables access and participation as well as
competition between political interests. Participation in Israel was voluntary, but the alternative sources of information that could nourish such
activities were few and the choice restricted. Similarly, the people's right
to know was recognized in Israel more as a slogan and less as a norm.

The fact that feedback was mediated in the Israeli political system
also had a constraining effect on openness. The organizational channels
provided relatively effective means for transmitting information, but
they also played a regulatory role. Most of the communication arrangements were based on the principle of exchange, not of openness. This is
not peculiar to the Israeli system, but the high level of structuring did
create many opportunities for "closing" the network to unwanted elements or to those who were regarded as outsiders. It should be noted,
however, that even a controlled network cannot be free of leaks, deliberate or undeliberate.

Assuming that there is less than complete openness in Israel, what
does this mean in terms of citizens' impact on steering? The simple
answer is that the impact on steering did not correspond to the level of
participation. The low sense of efficacy in Israel suggests that citizens
did not feel they had a say in government affairs. However, by and large,
they did not feel alienated and they tended to be responsive participants,
assuming correctly that they could not change major things, but perhaps
they could make the system more responsive.

Because the flow of information in the Israeli political system was
relatively open, there was no need to invest enormous political resources

or use coercive measures to keep the lid on. One can even say that in that period a certain balance existed between developing steering capacity and democratic development expressed in citizens' impact on steering. The first contributed to stability and avoidance of breakdowns and to the achievement of goals such as winning wars or raising the standard of living. The second contributed to nonprogrammed steering capable of frequent adjustments to new demands. The Israeli periphery at that time was politically docile because it enjoyed (a) high steering capacity required for coping with the external threats and other collective efforts and (b) a certain degree of responsiveness from the political system, at least to the pressing needs of most individuals and groups. This may be viewed as an example of "coexistence" between a relatively high profile of steering capacity (see Table 8.2) and relative openness.

In that period the Israeli polity did resemble the *fixed* sound system described in Chapter 1. The responsive participant citizens did not "compose the music" and had little control over the channels and their content. They could, however, activate the system, choose among a limited number of programs, and make it respond to certain preferences. They could modify, but not change altogether; they had impact, but it was restricted.

The trend, moreover, in Israel's democratic development, was in the direction of a citizen becoming less the passive listener and more the active participant. This was connected to the general socioeconomic development of the country and the appearance of "mass" symptoms in the society and in politics. In a mass society more people are in direct contact with the center (Shils, 1975: 506). Such contact can result in *less* impact on steering because individuals and groups can be more easily manipulated through mass political communication. In Israel, however, the initial mass symptoms were manifested during the 1960s in the breakdown of the previously rigid party dominance of the political communication network.

The trend was toward greater openness. Already mentioned was the impact of the split within Mapai on the general behavior of other participants in the system. We may also note an increase in the number of leaks and in the political sensitivity of the information that circulated freely during Eshkol's premiership starting in 1963. Eventually, new modes of activity outside the electoral process started to emerge — action groups and citizen movements — and a general opening-up of the political system. This also started to strain the balance between steering capacity and openness, with its increased opportunity to have an impact on steering. But such a process is the price participants in a democratic system must pay: They sacrifice a "splendid ship" for a continuous struggle to keep the raft of democracy afloat . . . and their feet are always in the water.

NOTES

1. In his study of political participation in the USSR, Friedgut argued that the exclusion of nonvoluntary participation may be a correct approach for homogeneous and advanced societies, but in Communist systems the definition should encompass any nonobligatory involvement of citizens in public affairs (1979: 17-20). In other words, even mobilized participation such as parading or voting in ceremonial elections should be included because it is one of the energizing mechanisms of the Soviet political system. No one can argue against the need to study mobilized activities of citizens, but why call it "participation"? Most of the activities listed by Friedgut, including ceremonies and expressions of general support, were included in the Israeli study, but the term "participation" is preserved for voluntary and autonomous activities. Besides, the distinctions suggested here among penetration, maintenance, access, and participation solve most of the difficulties inherent in comparing different political systems.

2. McPherson et al., measured the stability and reliability over time of people's attitudes regarding four items: that politics is too complex for them to understand; that voting is the only way to influence government; that public officials don't care about them; and that they don't have a say about what government does. They found that only the latter two items are "reliable, reasonably stable and almost uncontaminated by systematic measurement error" (1977: 520).

3. For instance, Pinchas Sapir hands a coin to a beggar in New York. "Where are you from?" asks the beggar, "I haven't seen you around." "I am the Israeli Finance Minister, " replies Sapir. "Thank you very much," says the beggar and returns the coin, "I don't take money from colleagues." Many of these jokes were collected and published in a small booklet entitled *All Eshkol Jokes* referring to Prime Minister Eshkol, who at that time was the main target. The booklet was not identified by publisher and carried no date of publication.

4. In subsequent years, special radio programs and letters of complaints to newspapers became one of the most effective means of Israeli citizens to have their complaints heard by the bureaucracy and often redressed as well (Galnoor, 1977: 194).

5. In the 1960s, about 60 percent of Israelis owned flats in cooperative apartment buildings and were legal partners of the building with the other tenants (Central Bureau of Statistics, 1976: 105).

6. In 1969 there were 231 kibbutzim of which 90 percent were affiliated with the three major labor movements: 78 with Mapam, 76 with Mapai, and 56 with Ahdut HaAvoda. Among the others, 11 were affiliated with the National Religious Party, 5 with the Progressive Party, 3 with Poalei Agudat Israel, and 2 with other parties. The total population in kibbutzim was then over 84,000 — about 3.4 percent of the Jewish population in Israel (Statistical Abstract of Israel, 1970: 33, 35).

7. Kibbutz members could be found in the political institutions of the country as well as in the bureaucracy and the mass media. Their rate of voting, group political activity, and participation in the election campaigns was remarkably high. The kibbutz and moshav movements were overrepresented in many central decision points in the political system. For instance, in 1965 there were 19 kibbutz members (16 percent) in the sixth Knesset, 7 ministers in the cabinet, and 2 deputy ministers. They were also overrepresented within Mapai and the other labor parties (Czudnowski, 1970: 237).

8. In the Labor Alignment since 1974, there have been recurring open competitions in the conference over the leadership of the party. In 1977 the new Democratic Movement for Change introduced direct elections by party members of the party's list of candidates for the Knesset.

9. The issue of the possible contradiction between "Arabism" and "Israelism" of Arabs in Israel is outside the scope of this book. See Peres and Davis (1969), J. Landau (1971), Beeri (1972), Nakhleh (1975), Smooha (1978), and Lustick (1980).

10. In 1965 the Communist Party split into a predominantly Arab faction (Rakah) and a Jewish faction (Maki). The former gained most of the Communist Arab votes in the 1965 elections. On the history of the Israeli Communist Party, see Nahas (1976).

11. In 1942 the Association of Immigrants from Central Europe established the New Immigration (Aliya Hadasha) Party. Significantly, most members were immigrants from Germany who generally had lower chances of political mobility in a system dominated by Eastern European Jews. In 1948 this party united with other factions and established the Progressive Party.

12. Vertically mobilized participation occurs "when people are induced to behave in ways designed to influence the composition or the actions of the government, but those taking part are uninterested in, and sometimes unaware of, the impact of their action on the government. They are acting on instructions, motivated largely or wholly by loyalty, affection, deference or fear of a leader" (Nelson, 1979: 168).

13. Organizations of the Oriental community during the yishuv period were significant and relatively powerful — for example the National Representative of the Sephardic Jews, or the Association of the Yemenites. The Sephardic and Yemenite Parties were represented in the yishuv organs and in the First and Second Knessets; shortly afterwards they joined the nonethnic parties. These organizations, however, represented a *veteran* Oriental community which lived in Palestine for generations, not new immigrants.

14. Prime Minister Golda Meir's statement on this issue reflects her strong, albeit naive, belief that the Israeli political system is still an intimate one:

> I can state absolutely that I do not know a cabinet minister who does not have constant contact with the public in different areas. . . . Of course the contact is not perfect, but I do not accept the notion that there is any distancing. We are so much involved that it is impossible to be disconnected [in a 1972 interview; Caspi, 1976: 268].

11

CONCLUSION

"Seek ye first the political heaven
and then all else will follow."
(KWAME NKRUMAH)

This book opened with a question, "Why offer yet another approach to the study of politics?" The answer was tentatively put forth that the communication approach enables one to study the raw materials of political interaction and, in particular, to analyze the infrastructure of political systems and their steering capacity. In this concluding chapter, the three main threads that ran through the other chapters will be woven together: the development of the Israeli polity, political development versus democratic political development, and the application of the political communication approach to other systems.

Israel:
A Developed Political System

The Israeli case study is proposed as a test of the proposition that democratic political development is a special case of political development. Political development was defined as movement in the direction of creating steering capacity. In the period reviewed in this book (1920s-1960s), the Israeli political system rapidly developed its steering capacity to the point of being included among the politically developed countries in the world. This development was evident on many levels.

(1) The minimum prerequisite of common contents was met from the very beginning and permitted the political system to emerge and start developing. Zionism as a locus of identification provided the common ground for both political and nonpolitical contents and enabled leaders to translate them into political action. All this was manifested in a considerable degree of consensus concerning Zionist goals and in the legitimization of the Jewish state as the means for attaining those goals. Consensus enhanced a climate of political tolerance, and in this case it contributed to political mechanisms based on negotiations, compromises, and coalitions. Israel, which was low on social integration but high on common contents, could therefore use its political system as a rather independent vehicle in the pursuit of collective goals.

(2) As a communication network, the Israeli political system proved successful in establishing links between those who steer (the political center), those who help steer (the secondary centers), and the passengers (the periphery). An important feature of the Israeli network was its reliance on the power of organizations and its dedication to institution-building. Indeed, some parts of the network, particularly the parties, were operating long before the political center was of significance. Israeli politics has been anchored in well-developed organizations, which provided, among other things, hierarchy and a division of labor. This network enabled the center to control without eliminating the independent yet supportive role of the secondary centers. Despite the existence of multiple secondary centers and the high degree of redundancy and overlap, the network showed endurance, as evidenced by the high survival rate of many institutions established during the yishuv period. The network was also reliable as far as the intake of information from the environment was concerned, and adaptable to new circumstances.

(3) Within the network, the Israeli political center operated through channels whose main task was to cross the boundaries between polity and society. The primary efforts were directed toward the penetration of problematic target groups, such as new immigrants or Israeli Arabs, and toward the maintenance of the loyalty and support of the periphery through means such as political socialization, regulation, and control of information. Despite a great deal of stress, no rival center emerged within the Israeli political system.

(4) The main channels — parties, bureaucracy, and the mass media — combined to create effective penetration and maintenance capabilities. The established parties were the dominant institutions in the political system, due to their ability to hold together the organizational maze and to coordinate the vertical, diagonal, and horizontal flows of information. The most important contribution of the parties to steer-

ing was not policy-making or direct coercion, but their ability to function as a clearinghouse in the network and to provide some order to the highly complex political system. Mapai's activities in particular — especially those geared toward the penetration and maintenance of groups in the periphery — were effective not only for mobilizing support for the party but also for the political development of the entire national system. Its dominating position in the system enhanced both coordination and stability. Mapai and the other established parties were not independent of the political center; indeed, they functioned to mutually reinforce the links between the center, the secondary centers, and the periphery. Most parties were mini-networks engaged not only in political communication but also in social, cultural, and economic activities. This contributed to the overall political development, because — despite the fierce competition among them — the rules of the political game were generally observed.

(5) Compared to the parties, the Israeli state bureaucracy was a late starter, but it marked the beginning of the structural differentiation required for further political development. The bureaucracy provided more "professional" channels and also a higher degree of overall legitimacy and officialdom. It could also use coercive means more directly. To some extent, the new state bureaucracy began to replace the parties, not only in the vertical communication between the polity and society but also in the horizontal communication within the political center. The bureaucratic channels contributed to the centralization of an otherwise fragmented network by monopolizing official power, by further politicizing the society through increased dependence of people on the political center, and by performing nonbureaucratic roles. It also cooperated with the parties in penetrating target groups. The bureaucracy was very active in "civic mobilization" — fostering the use of educational and health services, the payment of taxes, or obedience to court orders, for example. In addition, Israeli bureaucrats were committed to the common goals and to the extension and maintenance of the political system. In the short run, the bureaucracy served the existing regime and the dominating party; in the long run, it served the development of the political system as a whole. Gradually, the bureaucracy took over the maintenance function, especially through its control over tangible and intangible political resources. Thus in certain respects Israeli bureaucracy resembled the party-state bureaucracy in Communist countries, while in other respects it was representative — responsible to the elected political leaders and responsive to the needs of the people. As time passed, the bureaucracy grew more professional, more universalistic in outlook, and more independent of the political parties.

(6) Israeli mass communications were closely associated with the structure and modes of performance of the political system. There were direct links between the mass media and party channels, and there was indirect but strong influence of the political center on the distribution of information. The mass channels strengthened the steering capacity of the system in a number of ways: reinforcing the penetration and maintenance efforts through diffusion of national solidarity and ideological messages, providing a centralized and partly monopolized communication channel, legitimizing the political system, and sending special messages to target groups. Gradually, their contribution was felt more in maintenance and in forging identification with and support for the political system through the manipulation of political symbols. As time passed, the mass media channels in Israel became increasingly independent of both the party and the bureaucratic channels, and of the political center.

(7) These three main channels enabled the political system to perform the integrative (penetration) and stabilizing (maintenance) functions. By the end of the period under review (mid-1960s) there was still a great deal of interlocking in their operations. The parties' strongest contribution to steering was coordination; the bureaucracy (centralization); and the mass media (reinforcement). The first two are channels based primarily on organizations; hence their advantage in both personal contacts and centralized control. The latter are channels based on mass technology; hence their advantage in the diffusion of information, flexibility, and adaptability to other channels. The three channels, if they are adequately differentiated, and yet operating with some synchronization, can be described as a "winning combination" for political development.

On the basis of these features, it was concluded that Israel's steering capacity was rather developed in almost all components. The political system secured compliance with little investment in coercion, kept a stable course while managing conflicts, and made binding decisions. Indeed, the steering capacity of the yishuv political system was already developed: politics was "autonomous" within the broader social system; the center held a pivotal position in the network, enabling it to exchange information with the relevant environments; and most diffusion and legibility barriers were overcome. During the early state period, steering capacity was further developed because the political system confirmed its exclusiveness to the driver's seat, established its monopoly on official symbols, and proved its ability to avoid incapacitating breakdowns. The only significant change in the other direction during the state period was the increasing problem of information diffusion and legibility resulting from drastic changes in the composition of the population. Whether analyzed on the basis of the internal process of transformation or in comparison with other new political systems, Israel scored high on steering capacity.

Steering capacity can be achieved with or without popular support for the government and with or without government responsiveness to the needs of the people. Thus, political development is merely a higher capacity to achieve goals, regardless of the desirability of these goals.

We come now to the question of whether Israel was also a *democratic* political system.

Israel:
A Democratically Developed Political System?

Democracy is manifested in the ability of the members of a system to have an impact on steering through access to and participation in the political communication network. Democratic political development is a movement in this direction (or, in more normative terms, toward this goal). The components of political development were discussed primarily from the point of view of the center, whereas democratic political development was presented from the vantage point of the periphery.

In Chapter 10 it was concluded that Israel scored a better-than-average mark on citizens' impact on steering, based on the aggregate indicators political equality, feedback, and openness. Political equality was greater by the mid-1960s, although there were still areas of political inequality. The political system was also responsive to feedback, but a great part of this information circulation was regulated from above and controlled by the party, bureaucratic, and mass media channels. As for openness, the system was functionally pluralist, but the people's right to know was not highly observed, as there was deliberate interference with the free flow of information. Nevertheless, the general trend was clearly toward political equality, less regulated feedback, and greater openness.

(1) Israeli citizens were factors in their political system because, as individuals, they were politically mobile and had the opportunity to link up with the network. Group-based access, however, was highly constrained because new or independent groups had to face imposing barriers (and little tolerance) when they tried to transmit information outside the established channels. Group access was practically blocked by the existence of powerful institutions, and the only choice was to join them. Even the yishuv groups were not ordinary voluntary or pressure groups, because their autonomy was constrained by their parent institution and they had limited options to play an adversary role in the political

system. In the state period, too, access was achieved through belonging, and belonging required some form of affiliation to the established network.

(2) The prevalent mode of gaining access was through the political parties and their extensions. Citizens joined, became members, voted, or reported voting to certain parties — particularly those in power — because this was the most expedient way to gain access to tangible benefits. They could choose among a host of parties and gain access through them, but they could hardly engage in independent group activity in order to transmit uncontrolled information to the political center. Moreover, access to party channels did not entail automatic influence on the party's nominations or internal decision-making. The picture with regard to access to the bureaucratic channels was also mixed. Citizens had some choice between bureaucratic and nonbureaucratic channels: They could complain to officials directly and could practice all kinds of circumventions. The bureaucracy itself was frequently a useful channel for transmitting its clients' needs and demands. At the same time, however, voluntary linkup with this channel was restricted because it was synchronized with the other channels in the political network, especially the parties. The mass media channels were easily accessible as far as information supply was concerned. Yet they were relatively insignificant as society's suggestion box. Israeli mass media were sensitive to needs and demands of citizens, but they did not provide uncontrolled feedback of information from the public to the political center. In sum, in that period Israeli citizens had moderate access to the political network and were not coercively mobilized or "ignored" as outsiders by the political system.

(3) Despite their access to political resources, most Israelis seemed to be rather skeptical about their ability to influence government. This low sense of efficacy was based on a realistic evaluation of politically knowledgeable citizens that an individual's chances to have a direct impact on steering were low. Most were also familiar enough with their system to realize that participation is difficult in a system dominated by powerful institutions. This incongruency in Israel between relatively good opportunities for access and low efficacy is an interesting case of citizens' *realpolitik*. It was apparently influenced by the external pressures that forced a besieged community to value central steering capacity more than citizens' impact on steering. This, however, did not exclude participation altogether, but it caused citizens to prefer certain modes over others.

(4) The prevalent mode of participation in Israeli democracy was responsive, as evidenced by a high turnout on election day and frequent

personal contacts with public officials. Responsive participants are active citizens who can modify steering but not the course. They tend to operate politically within the narrow confines permitted for such activities. Responsive participation required little initiative, and its advantage from the point of view of the political center is that it is performed discreetly through the prescribed channels. Committed participation, on the other hand, is more closely associated with a high sense of efficacy. Israelis were reluctant to commit themselves to political activity requiring direct personal involvement. To be sure, some were politically ignorant, but the average level of political acumen was high enough to permit speculation that most simply concluded that committed participation would not make a difference. Hence, modes of participation such as independent cooperative activity or personal involvement in election campaigns were minimal. These forms of participation would have required efforts to influence the content and direction of political information or to create new channels in order to affect steering more directly.

(5) It is not necessary to judge whether committed participation is "better" than responsive participation or vice versa. The former does, however, represent a different type of democratic political development because of the more intensive involvement of citizens with their political system. Such a process of development was manifested in Israel. In the early state period, the peripheral groups were not left outside the political system: they gained access and were encouraged to participate within the general boundaries of responsive participation. Indeed, some groups (such as lower income groups and new immigrants from Oriental countries) even expressed at that time a higher sense of efficacy than did others (Arian, 1971: 7). In due course, many began to demand more concrete political results, thus demonstrating a higher level of committed participation. It should be reiterated that such a passage from one form of participation to another could engender instability or impair the system's steering capacity. It could signify a movement toward democratic political development, when a dominating elite is thus challenged by the oppressed periphery. It also could be "quasi-democratic" if, for example, committed participation is populistically orchestrated by a demagogic leader.

The profile of Israel's democratic political development in the period from the 1920s to the 1960s is characterized by two concomitant sequences. First, the development of steering capacity was based on common contents and a communication network in which the political center is firmly anchored in powerful institutions and mutually reinforcing channels. Second, the development of citizens' ability to have an impact on steering was based on individual mobility, mediated access to the communication network and the channels, and responsive participation. The coexistence of these two sequences enabled Israel to enjoy both the stability and the goal-oriented purposefulness associated with steering capacity, as well as a certain degree of responsiveness associated with openness and citizens' impact on steering. Since the late 1960s, this balance has changed: There has been, for instance, increased committed participation and more direct impact on steering, accompanied by less stability and greater difficulties in governing (Galnoor, 1980; Galnoor and Diskin, 1981). This would provide another interesting case study of democratic political development: the effect of changing modes of participation on steering capacity.

Comparative Political Communication

I found the communication approach to be a useful tool for the study of Israeli political development. Not all aspects of a political system can be sighted through such a monocle, but the most salient components and significant processes can be elucidated. The Israeli path of political development is not a model for other countries. However, following Deutsch's suggestion of analyzing government as a problem of steering seems to offer promising comparative possibilities. Accordingly, political communication was presented as the infrastructure underlying political behavior. What is more, political development was conceptualized in terms of steering capacity, while democratic political development was conceptualized in terms of impact on steering. One might briefly consider the implications of these concepts for the study of other political systems and for comparative analysis.

What is the comparative value of the communication framework presented in Chapter 1 and used to analyze the Israeli political system? Some of the theoretical implications derived from this analysis of the Israeli case are presented below.

(1) A minimal amount of common contents is a prerequisite for political development. The definition of this minimum as well as its substance vary from system to system. Those which do not meet this requirement are politically undeveloped, even if they are already full-fledged states. Politically developed systems, however, are not immune from tremors due to cracks in the underlying common contents.

(2) Political development starts with the appearance of a political communication network. This divides the political universe into a center (or centers) and a periphery; and it gives some order to the flow of

political information, primarily by distinguishing between horizontal and vertical communication. No two political systems have an identical configuration of their political network, although they can be compared in terms of functions, content of information, direction of flow, and main channels.

(3) In order to ascertain the beginning of political development, one must look for the emergence of political institutions. These are indispensable for politics because they are relatively efficient in communication. Political institutions hide under different names in different systems, but the communication function is based on some hierarchical division of labor and patterned flows of information. This does not preclude overlap and redundancy as functional (or dysfunctional) devices for increasing the adaptability of the communication network.

(4) Political channels of all kinds contribute some permanence to the process of network establishment. Although there are important differences among the channels (for example, parties, the bureaucracy, the mass media), each has a role in strengthening the reticulation of the network. It is useful to analyze the differentiation of the channels and to evaluate their contribution to political development in terms of penetration and maintenance capabilities.

(5) A diachronic analysis of these components must be made in order to determine whether a political system is developing — that is, increasing its steering capacity. In addition, certain features of the steering mechanism itself must be considered, such as its autonomy, monopoly, exclusiveness, and so on. These features permit the comparison of general profiles of steering capacity over different systems as well as changes in one system over time.

(6) The special case of democratic political development begins when, beyond all this, citizens gain access to political resources. This means the opportunity to join the political system via a voluntary linkup with the political communication network. Note that there cannot be a democratic undeveloped political system. This may be possible in small communities, but here we are interested in relatively large and complex systems.

(7) Access is a prerequisite for political participation. One cannot utilize the communication network and its channels unless one is aware of their existence. Once there is access, participation can range from responsive-passive to committed-active, and it is impossible to ascertain whether one combination is generally "more democratic" than another. These are different types or profiles of democratic political development. A citizen's sense of efficacy, however, clearly influences his or her mode of participation. The higher the sense of efficacy, the more the

willingness to undertake committed participation. Voting in elections is not a sufficient indicator for analyzing participation, but it is one of several.

(8) The change over time in opportunities for access and participation must be examined in order to determine whether a political system is democratically developing — increasing the citizen's impact on steering. In addition, certain systemic conditions surrounding the opportunity to have direct influence on the steering mechanism must be examined, such as political equality, feedback, and systemic openness. The variations in citizens' impact on steering among the different systems indicate the unique democratic package within each. Internal transformations reflect what is similar and what is distinct in the separate paths democratic-aspiring systems have had to travel.

(9) The tension between "governability" and "democracy," and between system stability and popular participation, can be explained in terms of the differences between steering capacity and impact on steering. It is possible to show, for example, that the compliance required for central steering is not always compatible with political equality, or that nonresponsive steering and openness do not go well together.

What about the sequence, or "stages," of political development? Democratic political development of complex systems cannot occur without political development, but the processes can and usually do take place simultaneously. A party channel, for instance, can be instrumental for both penetration of the center and for participation of citizens. There can also be proximity in consolidation of the common contents, appearance of the political center, and establishment of the network and the channels — together with access and participatory expectations. In the present study, only certain prerequisites were pointed out, and not in any inevitable internal sequence that adds up to stages. It is not clear whether network construction comes before channels penetration or vice versa. It should be clear, however, that in political communication the interactions count, not necessarily their sequence.

One should be wary of shortcuts in analyzing democratic political development. Different types of access must be considered — and illuminated by the prevalent sense of efficacy — as well as various modes of participation before labeling the system a democracy. Furthermore, in order to understand social change fully and the way a society has internalized democratic values, more is required than the components suggested in this book. It is essential to study the totality of culture and society — that is, its civilization (Nisbet, 1969; 252). No narrow definition of change or growth can capture the richness of human development. Political development is embedded within the total society, historically as well as substantially. It cannot be viewed as merely a response to modern technology or as collective efforts to solve problems of security, welfare, and the constitutional order (Compare Rostow, 1971: 2-3).

The communication approach to the study of politics and of political development cannot ignore the broader context simply because it must start with human interaction as the preliminary basis for its inquiry (Figure 1.1). The *political* communication network is part of the *general* social network. What bridges the imaginary realms of society and its polity is the emergence of common political contents, without which social interactions cannot be translated into political collective efforts.

One should not be misled by viewing politics as collective efforts and, by the Israeli case, to conclude that the communication perspective embraces a *cooperative* model of politics. "More" information flow in the channels does not necessarily add up to political development. A political system whose steering capacity is in the process of degeneration might produce more political interactions than ever before. Similarly, information overflow does not equal openness. Coercive measures often require extending the information load of the communication network to its limits. Communication is a neutral term, because it can result in agreement or disagreement, enhanced or reduced development.

The focus on political communication enables one to strike a useful balance between the "dependent" and "independent" schools in the study of politics. I agree with the motif embodied in Nkrumah's slogan, "Seek ye first the political heaven." Politics is a major vehicle for generating social change. Indeed, Israel is a good case in point for analyzing the independent role of politics and of central steering in political development. Yet I cannot agree with the second part, ". . . and then all else will follow." The "political heaven" is predicated on the presence of other elements in order for the process of political development to ensue. The political communication approach can provide a special monocle which permits one to view both the rudimentary, interactional depth of politics as well as its mundane information exchanges. If "revolutions are always verbose," as Trotsky said, then ordinary politics is just very verbal.

REFERENCES AND BIBLIOGRAPHY

ADLER, C. (1969) "The role of education in the integration of ethnic groups in Israel." pp. 17-31 in The Integration from Different Countries of Origin in Israel. Jerusalem: Magnes Press (Hebrew).

AHIMEIR, Y. (1972) "The government subsidizes the Arab press." Journalists Yearbook, 32: 61-81 (Hebrew).

AKE, C. (1967) A Theory of Political Integration. Homewood, IL: Dorsey Press.

AKZIN, B. (1955) "The role of parties in Israeli democracy." Journal of Politics, 17: 509-533.

————— (1961) "The Knesset." International Social Science Journal, 8 (4): 567-582.

AKZIN, B. and Y. DROR (1966) Israel: High-Pressure Planning. Syracuse, NY: Syracuse University Press.

ALLARD, E. and S. ROKKAN [eds.] (1970) Mass Politics. New York: Free Press.

ALMOGI, Y. (1980) Total Commitment. Tel Aviv: Edanim (Hebrew).

ALMOND, G. A. (1970) Political Development. Boston: Little, Brown.

————— and J.S. COLEMAN [eds.] (1960). The Politics of Developing Areas. Princeton, NJ: Princeton University Press.

ALMOND, G. A. and G. B. POWELL, Jr. (1966). Comparative Politics: A Developmental Approach. Boston: Little, Brown.

————— (1978) Comparative Politics: Systems Processes and Policy (2nd ed.). Boston: Little, Brown.

ALMOND, G. A., S. C. FLANAGAN, and R. J. MUNDT [eds.] (1973) Crisis, Choice and Change: Historical Studies of Political Development. Boston: Little, Brown.

ALMOND, G. A. and S. VERBA (1963) The Civic Culture. Princeton, NJ: Princeton University Press.

ALTERMAN, N. (1972) The Seventh Column. (2 Vols.) Tel Aviv: Hakibbutz Hameuchad (Hebrew).

ANTONOVSKY, A. (1963a) "Sociopolitical attitudes in Israel." Amot, 6 (June-July): 11-22 (Hebrew).

————— (1963b) "Class and ideology in Israel." Amot, 2 (August-September): 21-28 (Hebrew).

————— (1966) "Classification of forms, political ideologies and the man in the street." Public Opinion Quarterly, 30: 109-119.

————— and A. ARIAN (1971) Hopes and Fears of Israelis: Consensus in a New Society. Jerusalem: Academic Press.

APTER, D. E. (1971) Choice and the Politics of Allocation: A Developmental Theory. New Haven, CT: Yale University Press.

————— (1973) Political Change: Collected Essays. London: Frank Cass.

ARGOV, M. (1961) "Did the press fulfill its social and public task in the state?" Journalists Yearbook (Hebrew).

ARGYRIS, C. (1974) Behind the Front Page. San Francisco: Jossey-Bass.
ARIAN, A. (1968) Ideological Change in Israel. Cleveland, OH: Case Western Reserve University Press.
——— (1971) Consensus in Israel. New York: General Learning Press.
——— (1972) The Elections in Israel, 1969. Jerusalem: Academic Press.
——— (1973) The Choosing People. Cleveland, OH: Case Western Reserve University Press.
——— [ed.] (1975) The Elections in Israel, 1973. Jerusalem: Academic Press.
——— [ed.] (1980) The Elections in Israel, 1977. Jerusalem: Academic Press.
——— and S. WEISS (1968) "Split-ticket voting is Israel." Megamot, 16, (August) (Hebrew).
ARIAN, D. (1955) "The first five years of the Israeli civil service." Scripta Hierosolymitana, 3: 340-377.
ARONOFF, M.J. (1977) Power and Ritual in the Israeli Labor Party. Amsterdam: Van Goreum.
ARORA, S.K. and H.D. LASSWELL (1969) Political Communication: The Public Language of Political Elites in India and the United States. New York: Holt, Rinehart & Winston.
AVINERI, S. (1980) Varieties of Zionist Thought. Tel Aviv: Am Oved (Hebrew).
AVIZOHAR, M. (1978) Money for All: The Development of Social Security in Israel. Tel Aviv: Hadar (Hebrew).
BACHI, R. (1958) The Challenge of Development. Jerusalem: Hebrew University.
BADER, Y. (1979) The Knesset and I. Jerusalem: Idanim (Hebrew).
BAKER, F. [ed.] (1973) Organizational Systems. Homewood, IL: Richard D. Irwin.
BALDWIN, D.A. (1978) "Power and social exchange." American Political Science Review, 72 (December): 1229-1242.
BANKS, A.S. and R.B. TEXTOR (1963) A Cross-Polity Survey. Cambridge: MIT Press.
BARELAS, A. (1951) "Communication patterns in task-oriented groups," in D. Lerner and H.D. Lasswell (eds.), The Policy Sciences. Stanford: Stanford University Press.
BARKAI, H. (1964) The Public Sector. Jerusalem: Falk Institute (Hebrew).
BARNARD, C.I. (1938) The Functions of the Executive. Cambridge: Harvard University Press.
BARRON, J.A. (1967) "Access to the press — A new first amendment right." Harvard Law Review, 80: 1641-1781.
——— (1973) Freedom of the Press for Whom? The Right of Access to Mass Media. Bloomington: Indiana University Press.
BARRY. B. (1975) "Political accommodation and consociational democracy." British Journal of Political Science, 5 (October): 477-505.
BAR-YOSEF, R. (1959a) "The Moroccans: background of the problem." Molad, 17 (July): 247-251 (Hebrew).
——— (1959b) "The pattern of early socialization in the collective settlements in Israel." Human Relations, 12: 345-360.
——— (1966) Task Area Differentiation in Urban Families in Israel. Jerusalem: Hebrew University (Hebrew).
——— and O.E. SCHILD (1966) "Pressures and defenses in bureaucratic roles." American Journal of Sociology, 71 (May): 665-673.
BARZEL, E. (1976) "The right to speak to whom?" M.A. thesis, Communications Institute, Hebrew University, January (Hebrew).
BAR-ZOHAR, M. (1975-1977) Ben-Gurion (3 vols.). Tel Aviv: Am Oved (Hebrew).

BAY, C. (1958) The Structure of Freedom. Stanford: Stanford University Press.
BEERI, S. (1972) "Bi-nationalism for the future." New Outlook, 15 (7).
BELKOVSKY, Z. [ed.] (1946) The Protocols of the First Zionist Congress. Jerusalem: Reuven Mass (Hebrew).
BELL, D. V. J. (1975) Power, Influence and Authority: An Essay in Political Linguistics. New York: Oxford University Press.
BEN-AHARON, Y. (1977) In the Eye of the Storm. Tel Aviv: Hakibbutz Hameuchad (Hebrew).
BEN-GURION, D. (1974) From Class to Nation. Tel Aviv: Am Oved (Hebrew).
BENJAMIN, R. W. (1972) Patterns of Political Development. New York: David McKay.
BEN-MEIR, Y. and P. KEDEM (1979) "A religious index of the Jewish population in Israel." Megamot, 24 (February): 353-362 (Hebrew).
BENNIS, W. G. (1966) Changing Organizations. New York: McGraw-Hill.
BEN-SIRA, Z. (1978) "The image of political parties and the structure of a political map." European Journal of Political Research, 6: 259-283.
BENTLEY, A. F. (1908) The Process of Government. Chicago: Chicago University Press.
BERLO, D. K. (1960) The Process of Communication. San Francisco: Rinehart Press.
BERNSTEIN, D. (1980) "Immigrants and society. A critical review of the dominant school of Israeli sociology." British Journal of Sociology, 31 (June): 246-264.
BERNSTEIN, M. H. (1957) The Politics of Israel. Princeton, NJ: Princeton University Press.
——— (1959) "Israel's capacity to govern." World Politics, 11 (April): 399-417.
BILSKI, R., I. GALNOOR, D. INBAR, Y. MANOR, and G. SHEFFER [eds.] (1980) Can Planning Replace Politics? The Israeli Experience. The Hague: Nijhoff Publishers.
BINDER, L. (1962) Iran: Political Development in a Changing Society. Berkeley: University of California Press.
——— et al. [eds.] (1971) Crises and Sequences in Political Development. Princeton, NJ: Princeton University Press.
BIRNBAUM, E. (1970) The Politics of Compromise: State and Religion in Israel. Rutherford, NJ: Fairleigh Dickinson University Press.
BLANC, H. (1957) "Hebrew in Israel: trends and problems." Middle East Journal, 11 (Autumn): 397-409.
BLAU, P. M. (1955) Dynamics of Bureaucracy. Chicago: University of Chicago Press.
——— and R. W. SCOTT (1962) Formal Organizations. San Francisco: Chandler.
BLONDEL, J. (1969) An Introduction to Comparative Government. London: Weidenfeld & Nicolson.
——— (1978) Political Parties: A Genuine Case for Discontent? London: Wildwood House.
BLUMLER, J. G. (1972) "Information and democracy: the perspective of the governed." Politico, 27 (4): 625-247.
——— and E. KATZ [eds.] (1974) The Uses of Mass Communications. Beverly Hills, CA: Sage.
BOULDING, K. E. (1978) Ecodynamics: A New Theory of Societal Evolution. Beverly Hills, CA: Sage.
BRANTS, K. and W. KOK, (1976) "Political communication and agenda building." Presented at the IPSA Xth World Congress, Edinburgh, August.
BRECHER, M. (1972) The Foreign Policy System of Israel: Setting, Images, Process. London: Oxford University Press.
——— (1974) Decisions in Israel's Foreign Policy. London: Oxford University Press.

BRICHTA, A. (1976) "Change and continuity in recruitment patterns and the composition of the Israeli political leadership following the Yom Kippur War," pp. 313-337 in In the Wake of the Yom Kippur War. Haifa: Haifa University (Hebrew).
———— (1977) Elections and Democracy. Tel Aviv: Am Oved (Hebrew).
———— and G. BEN-DOR (1974) "Representation and misrepresentation of political elites." Jewish Social Studies, 36: 3-4.
BROGAN, D. W. (1945) The Free State: Some Considerations on Its Practical Value. London: Hamilton.
BRUNNER, R. D. and G. D. BREWER (1971) Organized Complexity: Empirical Theories of Political Development. New York: Free Press.
BRYSON, L. [ed.] (1948) The Communication of Ideas. New York: Harper & Row.
BRZEZINSKY, Z. and S. P. HUNTINGTON (1966) Political Power U.S.A./ U.S.S.R. New York: Viking Press.
CAHANA, R. (1968) Patterns of Israeli National Identity. Jerusalem: Academon (Hebrew).
CAHANA, R. and S. CNAAN (1973) The Behavior of the Press in Times of Security Tension and Its Influence on Public Support for Government. Jerusalem: Eshkol Institute (Hebrew).
CAMPBELL, A., P. CONVERSE, W. E. MILLER, and D. E. STOKES (1960) The American Voter. New York: John Wiley.
CASPI, D. (1976) "Between legislators and electors: the Knesset, members' perception of public attitudes." Ph.D. dissertation, Hebrew University of Jerusalem, April (Hebrew).
———— (1980a). "How representative is the Knesset?" Jerusalem Quarterly, 14 (Winter): 68-81.
———— (1980b). The Growth of the Local Press in Israel. Ramat Gan: Local Government Institute, Bar Ilan University (Hebrew).
Central Bureau of Statistics (1976) Society in Israel: Selected Statistics. Jerusalem.
———— (1978) Daily Newspapers and Periodicals Published in Israel. Series of Education and Culture Statistics. Jerusalem.
CHAFFEE, S. H. [ed.] (1975) Political Communications: Issues and Strategies for Research. Beverly Hills, CA: Sage.
———— and M. J. PETRICK (1975) Using the Mass Media: Communications Problems in American Society. New York: McGraw-Hill.
CHERRY, C. (1970) On Human Communication (2nd ed.). Cambridge: MIT Press.
CLOR, H. M. [ed.] (1974) The Mass Media and Modern Democracy. Chicago: Rand McNally.
CNAAN, H. (1969) The Struggle of the Press. Jerusalem: The Zionist Library (Hebrew).
———— (1971) Israel: The Press. Jerusalem: Government Information Center (Hebrew).
COHEN, H. (1968) The Factors Behind the *Aliya* from Asian and African Countries in the Twentieth Century. Jerusalem: Institute for Contemporary Jewry, Hebrew University (Hebrew).
COHEN, S. (1973) Ha-olam Hazeh (This World). Tel Aviv: Tefahot (Hebrew).
CONVERSE, P. E. (1962) "Information flow and the stability of partisan attitudes." Public Opinion Quarterly, 26 (Winter).
COUTLER, P. (1971-1972) "Democratic political development: systematic model based on regulative policy." Development and Change, 3: 25-61.
CRICK, B. (1962) In Defense of Politics. London: Weidenfeld & Nicolson.

CRITTENDON, J. (1967) "Dimensions of modernization in the American states." American Political Science Review, 61 (December): 989-1001.

CROSSMAN, R. (1975) The Diaries of a Cabinet Minister. Vol. 1 — Minister of Housing. London: Hamish Hamilton and Jonathan Cape.

———— (1976) The Diaries of a Cabinet Minister. Vol. 2 — Lord President of the Council and Leader of the House of Commons (1966-1968). London: Hamish Hamilton and Jonathan Cape.

———— (1978) The Diaries of a Cabinet Minister. Vol. 3 — 1968-1970. New York: Holt, Rinehart & Winston.

CROTTY, W.J. [ed.] (1968) Approaches to the Study of Party Organization. Boston: Allyn & Bacon.

CROZIER, M. (1964) The Bureaucratic Phenomenon. Chicago: University of Chicago Press.

———— S. P. HUNTINGTON, and J. WATANUKI (1975) The Crisis of Democracy. New York: New York University Press.

CURRAN, J., M. GUREVITCH, and J. WOOLLACOTT [eds.] (1977) Mass Communication and Society. London: Edward Arnold and the Open University Press.

CURTIS, M. and M. CHERTOFF [eds.] (1973) Israel: Social Structure and Change. New Brunswick, NJ: Transaction.

CUTRIGHT, P. (1963) "National political development," pp. 569-582 in N. Posby et al. (eds.), Politics and Social Life. Boston: Houghton Mifflin.

CZUDNOWSKI, M. (1970) "Legislative recruitment under proportional representation in Israel: a model and a case-study." Midwest Journal of Political Science, 14 (May).

———— (1976) Comparing Political Behavior. Beverly Hills, CA: Sage.

DAALDER, H. (1966) "Parties, elites and political development in Western Europe," pp. 43-77 in J. LaPalombara and M. Weiner (eds.), Political Parties and Political Development. Princeton: Princeton University Press.

———— (1974) "On building consociational nations: the cases of the Netherlands and Switzerland," pp. 107-124 in K. D. McRae (ed.), Consociational Democracy. Toronto: McLlelland and Stewart.

DAHL, R. (1956) A Preface to Democratic Theory. Chicago: University of Chicago Press.

———— (1971) Polyarchy: Participation and Opposition. New Haven, CT: Yale University Press.

DAN, H. (1963) On an Unpaved Path: The Saga of Solel Boneh. Jerusalem: Schoken (Hebrew).

DANIEL, A. (1972) The Cooperative: The Dream and Its Realization. Tel Aviv: Am Oved (Hebrew).

———— (1976) Labor Enterprises in Israel (2 vols.). Jerusalem: Academic Press.

DANIEL, S. (1966) "The parties and the press." Journalists Yearbook, pp. 46-51 (Hebrew).

DAVIS, M. [ed.] (1975) The Identification of the Nation with the State. Jerusalem: Zionist Library (Hebrew).

DAVISON, W. P. and T. C. YU [eds.] (1974) Mass Communication Research: Major Issues and Future Directions. New York: Praeger.

DAYAN, M. (1969) A New Map — Different Relations. Tel Aviv: Ma'ariv Library (Hebrew).

DeFLEUR, M. (1970) Theories of Mass Communication. New York: David McKay.

DERBER, M. (1970) "Israel wage differential: a persisting problem," pp. 185-201 in S.N. Eisenstadt et al. (eds.), Integration and Development in Israel. Jerusalem: Israel Universities Press.

DESHEN, S. (1978) "Israeli Judiasm: introduction to the major patterns." International Journal of Middle East Studies, 9: 141-169.

DEUTSCH, K.W. (1953) Nationalism and Social Communication. Cambridge: MIT Press.

───── (1961) "Social mobilization and political development." American Political Science Review, 55: 493-514.

───── (1963) The Nerves of Government: Models of Political Communication and Control. New York: Free Press.

───── (1974) Politics and Government: How People Decide Their Fate (2nd ed.). Boston: Houghton Mifflin.

DEVINE, D.J. (1970) The Attentive Public. Chicago: Rand McNally.

───── (1972) The Political Culture of the U.S.A. Boston: Little, Brown.

DIAMANT, F. (1962) "The bureaucratic model: Max Weber rejected, rediscovered, reformed," pp. 59-96 in F. Heady and S. Stokes (eds.) Papers in Comparative Public Administration. Ann Arbor: University of Michigan Press.

DON-YEHIYA, E. (1975) "Religion and coalition: the National Religious Party and coalition formation in Israel," pp. 255-284 in A. Arian (ed.), The Elections in Israel 1973. Jerusalem: Academic Press.

───── (1978) Conflict and Cooperation Between Political Camps: The Religious Camp and the Labor Movement and the Crisis in Israeli Education. Jerusalem: Hebrew University (Hebrew).

───── (1980) "Secularization, negation and integration: perceptions of traditional Judiasm and its conceptualization in socialist Zionism." Kivunim, No. 8 (Summer): 29-46 (Hebrew).

───── and C. LIEBMAN (1972) "The separation of state and religion: slogans and content." Molad (August-September): 71-89 (Hebrew).

DORSEY, J.T., Jr. (1957) "A communication model for administration." Administrative Science Quarterly, 2 (December): 307-324.

───── (1963) "The bureaucracy and political development in Viet Nam," pp. 318-359 in J. LaPalombara (ed.), Bureaucracy and Political Development. Princeton: Princeton University Press.

DOWNS, A. (1967) Inside Bureaucracy. Boston: Little, Brown.

DROR, Y. (1968) Public Policy Making Re-examined. San Francisco: Chandler.

───── (1971) Policy for the Senior Administrative Staff in Israeli Civil Service. Jerusalem: Hebrew University (Hebrew).

DUNN, J. (1979) Western Political Theory in the Face of the Future. Cambridge: Cambridge University Press.

EASTON, D. (1965a) A Framework for Political Analysis. Englewood Cliffs, NJ: Prentice-Hall.

───── (1965b) A Systems Analysis of Political Life. New York: John Wiley.

EDELMAN, M. (1964) The Symbolic Uses of Politics. Urbana: University of Illinois Press.

───── (1971) Politics as Symbolic Action: Mass Arousal and Quiescence. Chicago: Markham.

───── (1974) "The language of participation and the language of resistance." Human Communication Research, 3: 159-170.

EFRAT, E. (1978) Israel Towards Year 2000. Tel Aviv: Achiasaf Publishing House (Hebrew).

EISENSTADT, S. N. (1954) The Absorption of Immigrants. London: Routledge & Kegal Paul.

—— (1955) "Communication systems and social structure: an exploratory comparative study." Public Opinion Quarterly, 19 (3).

—— (1956) "The social conditions of the development of voluntary associations: a case study of Israel." Scripta Hierosolomytana, 3: 104-125.

—— (1965a) Essays on Comparative Institutions. New York: John Wiley.

—— (1965b) "Molding public opinion." Journalists' Yearbook. pp. 169-174 (Hebrew).

—— (1967) Israeli Society. London: Weidenfeld & Nicolson.

—— [ed.] (1968) Comparative Perspective on Social Change. Boston: Little, Brown.

—— [ed.] (1970) Readings in Social Evolution and Change. Oxford: Pergamon.

—— (1973) Tradition, Change and Modernity. New York: John Wiley.

—— (1976-1977) "Change and continuity in Israeli society." Jerusalem Quarterly, 1 (Fall): 28-35; Vol. 2 (Winter): 1-11.

—— R. BAR-YOSEF, and C. ADLER [eds.] (1970) Integration and Development in Israel. Jerusalem: Israel Universities Press (Hebrew).

EISENSTADT, S. N., R. BAR-YOSEF, R. CAHANA, and I. SHELACH (1968) Strata in Israel: A Reader. Jerusalem: Academon Press (Hebrew).

ELAZAR, D. (1976a) Community and polity: The Organization Dynamics of American Jewry. Philadelphia: Jewish Publication Society.

—— (1976b) "Community and state in Israel." Prepared for the sixth seminar of the Institute for Judiasm and Contemporary Thought, Kibbutz Lavi, July.

ELDERSVELD, S. J. (1964) Political Parties: A Behavioral Analysis. Chicago: Rand McNally.

ELIAV, B. (1976) The Yishuv During the Period of the National Home. Jerusalem: Keter Press (Hebrew).

ELLEMERS, J. E. (1961) Some Sociological Comments on Mass Communication in Israel. Gazette 7: 89-105.

ELLUL, J. (1973) Propaganda. New York: Vintage Books.

ELON, A. (1971) The Israelis: Founders and Sons. New York: Holt, Rinehart & Winston.

—— (1975) Herzl. New York: Holt, Rinehart & Winston.

Encyclopaedia of the Social Sciences (1930-1935) 15 vols. Edward Seligman (ed.), New York: Macmillan.

ENGWALL, L. (1973) Newspapers as Organizations. Farmborough: Saxon House.

ENLAE, C. H. (1973) Ethnic Conflict and Political Development. Boston: Little, Brown.

EPSTEIN, L. D. (1968) Political Parties in Western Democracies. New York: Praeger.

—— (1975) "Political parties," pp. 229-277 in F. I. Greenstein and N. W. Polsby (eds.), Handbook of Political Science, Vol. 4. Reading MA: Addison-Wesley.

ETTINGER, S. (1979) Zionism and the Arab Question. Jerusalem: Zalman Shazar Center (Hebrew).

ETZIONI, A. (1959) "Alternative ways to democracy: the example of Israel." Political Science Quarterly, 74: 196-214.

—— (1962) "The decline of Neo-feudalism: the case of Israel," pp. 229-243 in F. Heady and S. Stokes (eds.), Papers in Comparative Public Administration. Ann Arbor: University of Michigan.

—— (1968) The Active Society. London: Collier.

ETZIONI-HALEVY, E. and R. SHAPIRA (1977) Political Culture in Israel. New York: Praeger.

Facts About Israel (1973) Jerusalem: Ministry of Foreign Affairs/Division of Information.

FAGEN, R. (1964) "Relation of communication growth to national political systems in the less developed countries." Journalism Quarterly, 41 (1).
——— (1966) Politics and Communication. Boston: Little, Brown.
FEIN, L. J. (1962) The Political World of Jerusalem's People. Ann Arbor: University of Michigan Press.
——— (1967) Politics in Israel. Boston: Little, Brown.
FINER, S. (1969-1970) "Almond's concept of political systems." Government and Opposition (Winter): 5-21.
FINKLE, J. L. and R. W. GABLE [eds.] (1971) Political Development and Social Change (2nd ed.). New York: John Wiley.
FISCH, H. (1968) The Zionist Revolution: A New Perspective. London: Weidenfeld & Nicolson.
FLANIGAN, W. H. and E. FOGELMAN (1971) "Patterns of democratic development: an historical comparative analysis," in J. V. Gillespie and B. A. Nesvold (eds.), Macro Quantitative Analysis: Conflict Development and Democratization, Vol. 1. Beverly Hills, CA: Sage.
FREUD, S. (1958) "Thoughts on war and death," in On Creativity and the Unconscious. New York: Harper & Row.
FRIEDGUT, T. H. (1979) Political Participation in the USSR. Princeton: Princeton University Press.
FRIEDMAN, M. (1979) Society and Religion — The Non-Zionist Orthodoxy in Eretz Yisrael. Jerusalem: Ben Zvi Institute (Hebrew).
FRIEDRICH, C. J. (1972) The Pathology of Politics. New York: Harper & Row.
FROHOCK, F. M. (1978) "The structure of 'politics.'" American Political Science Review, 72 (September): 859-870.
GABIS, S. T. (1978) "Political secrecy and cultural conflict: a plea for formalism." Administration and Society, 10: 139-175.
GALLIE, W. B. (1966) Pierce and Pragmatism. New York: Dover.
GALNOOR, I. [ed.] (1971) "Social information for developing countries." Annals of the American Academy of Political and Social Science, 393 (January).
——— (1974) "Social indicators for social planning: the case of Israel." Social Indicators Research, 1: 27-57.
——— (1975) "Politics and leaks." Molad, 35-36 (Winter): 67-76 (Hebrew).
——— [ed.] (1977) Government Secrecy in Democracies. New York: Harper & Row.
——— (1978) "Water policy making in Israel." Policy Analysis, 4: 334-367.
——— (1980) "Transformations in the Israeli political system since the Yom Kippur War," pp. 119-148 in A. Arian (ed.), The Elections in Israel, 1977. Jerusalem: Academic Press.
——— and A. DISKIN (1981) "Political distances and parliamentary government: the Israeli Knesset debates over the peace agreements with Egypt." Medina U'Memshal, 18 (Summer) (Hebrew).
GEERTZ, C. [ed.] (1964) Old Societies and New States. London: Free Press.
GEFFNER (KUBERSKY), E. J. (1973) "Attitudes of Arab editorialists in Israel, 1948-1967." Ph. D. dissertation, University of Michigan.
——— (1974) "An Israeli Arab view of Israel." Jewish Social Studies, 36: 134-141.
GERBNER, G. [ed.] (1977) Mass Media Policies in Changing Culture. New York: Wiley Interscience.
GIL, B. (1950) The Demographic Composition of the Histadrut. The Thirtieth Year. Tel Aviv: The Histadrut (Hebrew).
GILADI, D. (1973) The *Yishuv* During the Period of the Forth *Aliya*. Tel Aviv: Am Oved (Hebrew).

GINOR, F. (1979) Socioeconomic Disparities in Israel. Tel Aviv: Horowitz Institute and Transaction Books.

Glasgow University Media Group (1976) Bad-news, Vol. 1. London: Routledge & Kegan Paul.

GLOBERSON, A. (1970) The Administrative Elite of the Israeli Civil Service. Tel Aviv: College of Administration (Hebrew).

────── (1973) "A profile of the bureaucratic elite in Israel." Public Personnel Management, 2 (1); 9-13.

GOLDMAN, E. (1964) Religious Issues in Israeli Political Life. Jerusalem: World Zionist Organization.

GOLDSTEIN, Y. (1975) Mapai (The Israeli Labor Party). Tel Aviv: Am Oved (Hebrew).

────── (1980) On the Way to Hegemony: Mapai: The Realization of its Policy 1930-1936. Tel Aviv: Am Oved (Hebrew).

GORE, W. and J. DYSON [eds.] (1964) The Making of Decisions. New York: Free Press.

GOREN, D. (1976) Secrecy, Security and the Freedom of the Press. Jerusalem: Magnes Press (Hebrew).

GORNI, Y. (1973) Ahdut HaAvoda 1919-1930: Ideological Foundations and Political Method. Tel Aviv: Tel Aviv University and Hakibbutz Hameuchad (Hebrew).

Government Press Office (1972-1973) Newspapers and Periodicals Appearing in Israel. Jerusalem.

GOTHALF, J. (1969) Public Opinion and the Press. Tel Aviv: Am Hasefer (Hebrew).

GOULDING, P. (1974) "Media role in national development: critique of a theoretical orthodoxy." Journal of Communication, 24: 39-53.

GREENSTEIN, F. I. and N. W. POLSBY [eds.] (1975) Handbook of Political Science (8 vols.) Reading, MA: Addison-Wesley.

GREGG, P. M. and A. S. BANKS (1965) "Dimensions of political systems: factor analysis of a cross-polity survey." American Political Science Review, 59 (3): 602-614.

GRIEBER, A. D. (1976) Verbal Behavior and Politics. Urbana: University of Illinois Press.

GRIMSHAW, A. D. (1973) "Sociolinguistics," pp. 49-92 in I. Pool and W. Schramm et al. (eds.), Handbook of Communications. Chicago: Rand McNally.

GROSS, B. M. (1964) The Managing of Organizations (2 vols.). New York: Free Press.

────── (1965) "The managers of national economic change," pp. 101-128 in R. C. Martin (ed.), Public Administration and Democracy. Syracuse, NY: Syracuse University.

GURI, H. (1962) Facing the Glass Booth: The Jerusalem Trial. Tel Aviv: Hakibbutz Hameuchad (Hebrew).

GUETZKOW, H. (1965) "Communication in organizations," pp. 534-573 in G. G. March (ed.), Handbook of Organizations. Chicago: Rand McNally.

GUREVITCH, M. and G. SCHWARTZ (1971) "Television and the Sabbath culture in Israel." Jewish Journal of Sociology, 13 (June): 65-71.

GUREVITCH, M. and A. WINOGRAD (1977) "Who are the Israeli elites?" Jewish Journal of Sociology, 19 (1): 67-79.

GURR, T. R. (1970) Why Men Rebel. Princeton, NJ: Princeton University Press.

GUTMAN, Y. (1981) The Attorney General Versus the Government. Jerusalem: Edanim (Hebrew).

GUTMANN, E. (1960) "Israel." International Social Science Journal, 12 (1): 53-62.

────── (1963) "Comparative political finance: Israel." Journal of Politics, 25 (3): 703-717.

—— and J. M. LANDAU (1975) "The political elite and national leadership in Israel," pp. 163-199 in G. Lenczowsky (ed.), Political Elites in the Middle East. Washington, DC: American Enterprise Institute for Public Policy Research.

HABERMAS, J. (1975) Legitimation Crisis. Boston: Beacon.

—— (1979) Communication and the Evolution of Society. Boston: Beacon.

HACOHEN, D. (1974) Time to Recount. Tel Aviv: Am Oved (Hebrew).

HALEVY, N. and R. KLINOV-MALUL (1968) The Economic Development of Israel. New York: Praeger.

HALKIN, H. (1977) Letters to an American Jewish Friend: A Zionist's Polemic. Philadelphia: Jewish Publication Society of America.

HALL, A. D. and R. E. FAGEN (1968) " Definition of system," pp. 81-92 in W. Buckley (ed.), Modern Systems Research for the Behavioral Scientist. Chicago: Aldine.

HALL, R. H. (1972) Organizations: Structure and Process. Englewood Cliffs, NJ: Prentice-Hall.

HALLORAN, J. D., P. ELLIOT, and G. MURDOCK (1970) Demonstrations and Communication: A Case Study. London: Penguin.

HALPERN, B. (1969) The Idea of the Jewish State (2nd ed.). Cambridge: Harvard University Press.

HANDY, C. B. (1976) Understanding Organizations. Middlesex, England: Penguin.

HARARI, Y. [ed.] (1978) The Elections in the Arab sector, 1977. Givat Haviva, Israel: Center for Arab Studies (Hebrew).

HEADY, F. (1979) Public Administration: A Comparative Perspective (2nd ed.). New York: Marcel Dekker.

HELLER, H (1933) "Political power," pp. 300-305 in Encyclopaedia of the Social Sciences, Vols. 11-12. New York: Macmillan.

HERMAN, S. H. (1973) "The youth: Jews, Israelis or both." Judaism, 22 (Spring): 167-172.

—— (1977) Jewish Identity: A Social Psychological Perspective. Beverly Hills, CA: Sage.

The Histadrut (1977) Statistical Yearbook, 1968-1977. Tel Aviv: Institute for Economic and Social Research, November.

HORNIK, R. (1980) "Communication as complement in development." Journal of Communication, 30 (2): 10-24.

HOROWITZ, D. (1967) The Economics of Israel. New York: Pergamon.

—— (1980) "The Israeli defence forces: A civilianized military in a partially militarized society." Hebrew University (unpublished).

—— and M. LISSAK (1977) Origins of the Israeli Polity. Tel Aviv: Am Oved (Hebrew).

—— (1978) Origins of the Israeli Polity. Chicago: University of Chicago Press.

HUNTINGTON, S. P. (1965) "Political development and political decay." World Politics 27 (April): 38-39.

—— (1968) Political Order in Changing Societies. New Haven, CT: Yale University Press.

—— (1971) "The change to change: modernization, development and politics." Comparative Politics, 3 (3): 283-322.

—— (1974) "Postindustrial politics: how benign will it be?" Comparative Politics, 6 (2): 172-177.

—— and J. M. NELSON (1976) No Easy Choice: Political Participation in Developing Countries. Cambridge: Harvard University Press.

INBAR, M. and C. ADLER (1977) Ethnic Integration in Israel. New Brunswick, NJ: Transaction.

INKELES, A. (1969a) "Participant citizenship in six developing countries." American Political Science Review, 63: 1120-1141.

—— (1969b) "Making men modern: on the causes and consequences of individual change in six developing countries." American Journal of Sociology, 75: 208-225.

—— and R. A. BAUER (1959) The Soviet Citizen. Cambridge: Harvard University Press.

INKELES, A. and D. S. SMITH (1974) Becoming Modern. Cambridge: Harvard University Press.

Institute for Social and Economic Research (1969) The Histadrut Since the Foundation of the State. Tel Aviv: Institute for Social and Economic Research, July (Hebrew).

ISAAC, R. J. (1976) Israel Divided: Ideological Politics in the Jewish State. Baltimore: Johns Hopkins University Press.

JANIS, I. L. (1972) Victims of Group Think. Boston: Houghton Mifflin.

JANOWITZ, M. and B. BERELSON [eds.] (1950) Reader in Public Opinion and Communication. New York: Free Press.

KARIEL, H. S. (1969) Open Systems: Arenas for Political Action. Itasca, IL: Peacock.

KARSEL, G. (1964) The History of the Israeli Hebrew Press. Jerusalem: Zionist Library.

KATZ, E. and B. DANET [eds.] (1973a) Bureaucracy and the Public. New York: Basic Books.

—— (1973b) "Communication between bureaucracy and the public: a review of the literature," pp. 666-705 in I. Pool et al. (eds.), Handbook of Communication. Chicago: Rand McNally.

KATZ, E. and S. N. EISENSTADT (1960) "Some sociological observations on the response of Israeli organizations to new immigrants." Administrative Science Quarterly, 5: 113-183.

KATZ, E. and J. J. FELDMAN (1962) "The debates in the light of research: a survey of surveys," in S. Kraus (ed.), The Great Debates. Bloomington: Indiana University Press.

KATZ, E. and M. GUREVITCH (1973) The Culture of Leisure in Israel. Tel Aviv: Am Oved (Hebrew).

KATZ, E. et al. (1976) The Secularizaiton of Leisure: Culture and Communication in Israel. London: Faber and Faber.

KATZ, E. and G. WEDELL (1977) Broadcasting in the Third World. Cambridge: Harvard University Press.

KATZNELSON, I. and M. KESSELMAN (1975) The Politics of Power: A Critical Introduction to American Government. New York: Harcourt Brace Jovanovich.

KAUTSKY, J. (1972) The Political Consequences of Modernization. New York: John Wiley.

KEESING, F. M. and M. M. KEESING (1956) Elite Communication in Samoa. Stanford: Stanford University Press.

KEY, V. O. (1961) Public Opinion and American Democracy. New York: Alfred A. Knopf.

KIM. Y. C. (1964) "The concept of political culture in comparative politics." Journal of Politics, 26 (May): 313-336.

KIMMERLING, B. (1973) The Struggle over Land. Jerusalem: Department of Sociology, Hebrew University (Hebrew).

KING. A. (1969) "Political parties in western democracies: some sceptical reflections." Polity, 2 (2): 111-141.

KLAPPER, J. (1960) The Effects of Mass Communication. New York: Free Press.

KLEIN, R. (1973) "The powers of the press." Political Quarterly, 44 (1): 33-46.

KOLLEK, T. and A. KOLLEK (1978) For Jerusalem: A Life. New York: Random House.
KORNHAUSER, W. (1959) The Politics of Mass Society. New York: Free Press.
KRAINES, O. (1976) The Impossible Dilemma: Who Is a Jew in the State of Israel? New York: Bloch Publishing.
KRAUS, S. and D. DAVIS (1976) The Effects of Mass Communication on Political Behavior. University Park: Pennsylvania State University Press.
KRISTAL, H. (1974) "Political positions of the daily press in the Lavon affair." State and Government, 6: 81-99 (Hebrew).
KUHN, A. (1974) The Logic of Social Systems. San Francisco: Jossey-Bass.
KURZWEIL, B. (1953) "The new 'Canaanites' in Israel." Judaism, 2 (January): 3-15.
LAHAV, P. (1978) "Governmental regulation of the press: a study of Israel's press ordinance." Israel Law Review, 13 (2): 230-250.
────── and A. MANOR [eds.] (1967) Source Reader on Citizens' Rights. Jerusalem: Academon (Hebrew).
LAM, Z. (1970) "Zionism: ideology and reality." Molad, 17 (December) (Hebrew).
LIPSET, S. M. and S. ROKKAN [eds.] (1967) Party Systems and Voter Alignments. New York: Free Press.
LANDAU, J. M. (1971) The Arabs in Israel. A Political Study. Tel Aviv: Maarachot (Hebrew).
────── (1973) "The Arabs and the Histadrut," in I. Avrech and D. Giladi (eds.), Labor and Society in Israel. Tel Aviv: Department of Labor Studies, Tel Aviv University.
LANDAU, M. (1969) "Redundancy, rationality and the problem of duplication and overlap." Public Administration Review, 29 (4): 346-358.
LANE, R. E. and D. O. SEARS (1964) Public Opinion. Englewood Cliffs, NJ: Prentice-Hall.
LAPALOMBARA, J. [ed.] (1963) Bureaucracy and Political Development. Princeton, NJ: Princeton University Press.
────── (1971) "Penetration: a crisis of governmental capacity," pp. 205-232 in L. Binder et al. (eds.), Crises and Sequences in Political Development. Princeton, NJ: Princeton University Press.
────── and M. WEINER [eds.] (1966) Political Parties and Political Development. Princeton, NJ: Princeton University Press.
LAQUEUR, W. (1972) A History of Zionism. London: Weidenfeld & Nicolson.
LASSWELL, H. D. (1927) Propaganda Technique in World War I. Cambridge: MIT Press.
────── (1949) Language and Politics. New York: Stewart.
────── (1958) Politics: Who Gets What, When, How (3rd ed.). New York: Meridian Books.
────── (1972) "Communication research and public policy." Public Opinion Quarterly, 36 (3): 301-310.
────── and A. KAPLAN, (1950) Power and Society: A Framework for Political Inquiry. New Haven, CT: Yale University Press.
LASSWELL, M. et al. (1965) The Language of Politics: Studies in Quantitative Semantics. Cambridge: MIT Press.
LEACH, E. R. (1976) Culture and Communication: The Logic by Which Symbols Are Connected. Cambridge: Cambridge University Press.
LEAVITT, H. J. (1964) Managerial Psychology (2nd ed.). Chicago: University of Chicago Press.
LERNER, D. (1958) The Passing of Traditional Society. New York: Free Press.
────── (1963) "Toward a communication theory of modernization," in W. L. Pye (ed.),

Communications and Political Development. Princeton, NJ: Princeton University Press.

——— (1973-1974) "Notes on communication and the nation-state." Public Opinion Quarterly, 37 (4): 541-550.

LEVY, M. J., Jr. (1966) Modernization and the Structure of Societies. Princeton, NJ: Princeton University Press.

LEVY, S. and L. GUTTMAN, (1976) "Zionism and Jewishness of Israelis." Forum, Jerusalem, No. 1 (24): 39-50.

LIEBMAN, C. S. (1975) "Religion and political integration in Israel." Jewish Journal of Sociology, 17 (1): 17-27.

——— (1977) Pressures Without Sanctions: The Influences of World Jewry on Israeli Policy. Ranberry, NJ: Associated University Press.

LIEBMAN, C. S. and E. DON-YEHIYA (1979) "Traditional religion and civil religion." (unpublished)

LIJPHART, A. (1968) The Politics of Accommodation: Pluralism and Democracy in the Netherlands. Berkeley: University of California Press.

——— (1969) "Consociational democracy." World Politics, 21 (2): 207-225.

——— (1977) Democracy in Plural Societies: A Comparative Exploration. New Haven, CT: Yale University Press.

LIKHOVSKI, E. S. (1971) Israel's Parliament. Oxford: Clarendon Press.

LIN, N. (1971) "Information flow, influence flow and decision-making process." Journalism Quarterly, 48 (1): 33-40.

LINDBLOM, C. (1965) The Intelligence of Democracy. New York: Free Press.

LINDSAY, A. D. (1943) The Modern Democratic State. New York: Oxford University Press.

LINENBERG, R. (1972) "Attitudes in the Israeli press towards the Kfar Kassem affair." State and Government, 2 (1): 48-64 (Hebrew).

LIPPMANN, W. (1961) Public Opinion. New York: Macmillan.

LIPSET, S. M. (1959) Political Man. London: Heinemann.

——— and S. ROKKAN [eds.] (1967) Party Systems and Voter Alignment: Cross National Perspectives. New York: Free Press.

LISSAK, M. (1964) "Images of society and status in the yishuv and Israeli society: patterns of change in the ideology and the class structure." Molad, 22 (November): 495-503 (Hebrew).

——— (1969) Social Mobility in Israel. Jerusalem: Israel Universities Press.

——— (1971) "The Israel Defence Forces as an agent of socialization and education: a research in a democratic society," pp. 327-339 in M. R. Van Gills (ed.), The Perceived Role of Military. Rotterdam: Rotterdam University.

——— (1972) "Continuity and change in the voting patterns of Oriental Jews," pp. 264-277 in A. Arian (ed.), Elections in Israel, 1969. Jerusalem: Academic Press.

——— and E. GUTMANN [eds.] (1977) The Israeli Political System. Tel Aviv: Am Oved (Hebrew).

LITTLEJOHN, S. W. (1978) Theories of Human Communication. Columbus, OH: Charles E. Merrill.

LIU, A. P. L. (1975) Communications and National Integration in Communist China. Berkeley: University of California Press.

LIVNEH, E. (1972) Israel and the Crisis in Western Civilization. Jerusalem: Schocken (Hebrew).

LORWIN, V. R. (1971) "Segmented pluralism: ideological cleavages and political cohesion in the smaller European democracies." Comparative Politics, 3 (2).

LUCE, R. D. and H. RAIFFA [eds.] (1957) Games and Decisions. New York: John Wiley.

LUSTICK, I. (1975) "Stability in deeply divided societies: consociationalism versus control." World Politics, 21 (3): 325-344.

―――― (1980) Arabs in the Jewish State. Austin: University of Texas Press.

LUTTWAK, E. (1968) Coup d'Etat. London: Penguin.

―――― and D. HOROWITZ (1975) The Israeli Army. London: Allen Lane.

MANIS, J. G. and B. N. MELTZER [eds.] (1972) Symbolic Interaction. Boston: Allyn & Bacon.

MANSEN, R. J. and B. M. RUSSET (1973) "The political entrepreneur: the utility of small polyarchies." Presented at the IXth World Congress of the International Political Science Association, Montreal, Canada, August.

MARCH, D. (1971) "Political socialization: the implicit assumptions questioned." British Journal of Political Science, 1, Part 4 (October): 453-465.

MARCH, G. J. and H. A. SIMON (1958) Organizations. New York: John Wiley.

MARINI, F. [ed.] (1971) Towards a New Public Administration. Scranton, PA: Chandler.

MARNELL, W. H. (1973) The Right to Know: Media and the Common Good. New York: Seabury Press.

MARVICK, D. (1970) "Party cadres and receptive partisan voters in the 1967 Indian national elections." Asian Survey, 10: 949-966.

―――― (1973) "Communication in political parties," pp. 722-754 in I. Pool et al. (eds.), Handbook of Communication. Chicago: Rand McNally.

MATRAS, J. (1965) Social Change in Israel. Chicago: Aldine.

McCORMICK, J. and M. MacINNES [eds.] (1962) Versions of Censorship. Chicago: Aldine.

McCRONE, D. J. and C. F. CNUDDE (1967) "Toward a communication theory of democratic political development." American Political Science Review 61 (March): 72-79.

McLUHAN, M. (1964) Understanding Media. New York: McGraw-Hill.

―――― (1967) The Medium is the Message. New York: Bentham.

MacPHERSON, C. B. (1973) Democratic Theory: Essays in Retrieval. Oxford: Clarendon.

McPHERSON, J. M., S. WELCH and C. CLARK (1977) "The stability and reliability of political efficacy: using path analysis to test alternative models." American Political Science Review, 71 (June): 509-521.

McQUAIL, D. [ed.] (1972) Sociology of Mass Communications. Middlesex, England: Penguin.

McRAE, K. [ed.] (1974) Consociational Democracy: Political Accommodation in Segmented Societies. Ottawa: McClelland and Stewart.

MEDDING, P. Y. (1972) Mapai in Israel: Political Organization and Government in a New Society. Cambridge: Cambridge University Press.

―――― (1978) "The politics of Jewry as a mobilized diaspora." Presented at the Canada-Israel Workshop, December.

MEIR, G. (1975) My Life. London: Weidenfeld & Nicolson.

MERRIAM, C. E. (1934) Political Power: Its Composition and Incidence. New York: McGraw-Hill.

―――― (1945) Systematic Politics. Chicago: University of Chicago Press.

MERTON, R. K. (1968) Social Theory and Social Structure. New York: Free Press.

MILBRATH, L. (1965) Political Participation. Chicago: Rand McNally.

―――― and M. L. GOEL (1977) Political Participation (2nd ed.). Chicago: Rand McNally.

MILLER, G. (1963) Language and Communication. New York: McGraw-Hill.
—— (1967) The Psychology of Communication: Seven Essays. New York: Basic Books.
MISHAL, N. (1978) "The Broadcasting Authority: political dynamics." M.A. thesis, Bar Ilan University, Israel (Hebrew).
MOHAMMADI, A.S. (1980) "Communication and revolution in Iran." Presented at the World Communications: Decisions for the Eighties Conference. Annenberg School of Communications, University of Pennsylvania, Philadelphia, May.
MONTGOMERY, J. D. (1969) "The quest for political development." Comparative Politics, 1: 285-295.
MOORE, D. C. (1976) The Politics of Deference. Sussex, England. Harvester Press.
MUELLER, C. (1973) The Politics of Communication. London: Oxford University Press.
MURPHY, R. D. (1977) Mass Communication and Human Interaction. Boston: Houghton Mifflin.
NACHMIAS, D. (1974) "Coalition politics in Israel." Comparative Political Studies, 7 (3): 316-331.
—— (1976) "The right wing opposition in Israel." Political Studies, 24 (3): 268-280.
NAHAS, D. H. (1976) The Israeli Communist Party. London: Croom Helm.
NAKHLEH, K. (1975) "Cultural determinants of Palestinian collective identity: the case of the Arabs in Israel." New Outlook, 8 (7): 31-40.
NELSON, J. M. (1979) Access to Power: Politics and the Urban Poor in Developing Nations. Princeton, NJ: Princeton University Press.
NETTL, J. P. (1967) Political Mobilization: A Sociological Analysis of Methods and Concepts. London: Faber & Faber.
—— (1968) "State as a conceptual variable." World Politics, 20 (4): 559-592.
NETZER, S. (1980) Notes from My Journal. Tel Aviv: Am Oved (Hebrew).
NEUBAUER, D. E. (1967) "Some conditions of democracy." American Political Science Review, 61: 1002-1009.
NIE, N. H., B. POWELL, and K. PREWITT (1969) "Social structure and political participation: developmental relationships." American Political Science Review, 63: 361-378.
NIE, N. H. and S. VERBA (1975) "Political participation," Vol. 4. pp. 1-74 in F. Greenstein and N.W. Polsby (eds.), Handbook of Political Science, Reading, MA: Addison-Wesley.
NIMMO, D. (1978) Political Communication and Public Opinion in America. Santa Monica, CA: Goodyear.
—— [ed.] (1980) Communication Yearbook 4. New Brunswick, NJ: Transaction.
NISBET, R. A. (1969) Social Change and History. London: Oxford University Press.
NORDLINGER, E. A. (1968) "Political development: time sequences and rates of change." World Politics, 20: 494-520.
OFER, G. (1967) The Service Industries in a Developing Economy: Israel as a Case Study. New York: Praeger.
OWENS, E. and R. SHAW (1974) Development Reconsidered: Bridging the Gap Between Government and the People. Lexington, MA: D.C. Heath.
OZ, A. (1979) Under this Blazing Light. Tel Aviv: Sifriat Poalim (Hebrew).
PACKENHAM, R. A. (1970) "Political development research," in M. Haas and H. Kariel (eds.), Approaches to the Study of Political Development. San Francisco: Chandler Books.
PALTIEL, K. Z. (1975) "The Israeli coalition system." Government and Opposition, 10 (4).

PARRY, G. (1970) Political Elites. New York: Praeger.
PARSONS, T. (1966) Societies: Evolutionary and Comparative Perspective. Englewood Cliffs, NJ: Prentice-Hall.
——— (1969) Politics and Social Structure. New York: Free Press.
——— (1971) The System of Modern Societies. Englewood Cliffs, NJ: Prentice-Hall.
PATEMAN, C. (1970) Participation and Democratic Theory. Cambridge: Cambridge University Press.
PATINKIN, D. (1959) The Israeli Economy: The First Decade. Jerusalem: Falk Foundation.
PELEG, R. and A. BENJAMIN (1977) Higher Education and the Arabs in Israel. Tel Aviv: Am Oved (Hebrew).
PERLMUTTER, A. (1969) Military and Politics in Israel. London: Frank Cass.
——— (1978) Politics and the Military in Israel 1967-1977. London: Frank Cass.
PERES, Y. (1976) Ethnic Relations in Israel. Tel Aviv: University of Tel Aviv (Hebrew).
——— and N. Y. DAVIS (1969) "Some observations on the national identity of the Israeli Arab." Human Relations, 22 (3).
PERETZ, D. (1979) Government and Politics in Israel. Boulder, CO: Westview Press.
PERI, Y. and M. LISSAK (1976) "Retired officers in Israel and the emergence of a new elite," pp. 175-192 in G. Harries-Jenkins and J. Van Doorn (eds.), The Military and the Problems of Legitimacy. Beverly Hills, CA: Sage.
Plato (1945) The Republic of Plato. Oxford: Oxford University Press.
POLLAK, A. N. (1945) The Hebrew Yishuv at the End of the War. Merhavia, Israel: Sifriyat Hapoalim (Hebrew).
POOL, I. de S. (1963) "The mass media and politics in the modernization process," in W.L. Pye (ed.), Communication and Political Development. Princeton, NJ: Princeton University Press.
——— (1973) "Communication Systems," pp. 3-26 in I. Pool et al. (eds), Handbook of Organizations. Chicago: Rand McNally.
——— (1976). "Government and the media." American Political Science Review, 70 (4): 1234-1241.
——— et al. (1970). The Prestige Press: A Comparative Study of Political Symbols. Cambridge: MIT Press.
——— [eds.] (1973) Handbook of Communication. Chicago: Rand McNally.
PRATT, R.B. (1973) "The underdeveloped political science of development." Studies in Comparative International Development, 8: 88-112.
PYE, W.L. (1962) Politics, Personality and Nation Building. New Haven, CT: Yale University Press.
——— [ed.] (1963) Communications and Political Development. Princeton, NJ: Princeton University Press.
——— (1966) Aspects of Political Development. Boston: Little, Brown.
——— (1972) "Culture and political science: problems in the evaluation of the concept of political culture." Social Science Quarterly, 53: 285-296.
——— and S. VERBA [eds.] (1965) Political Culture and Political Development. Princeton: Princeton University Press.
QUANDT, W. B. (1970) The Comparative Study of Political Elites. Beverly Hills, CA: Sage.
RAE, D. W. and M. TAYLOR (1970) The Analysis of Political Cleavages. New Haven, CT: Yale University Press.
RAPOPORT, A. and W.J. HORVATH (1959) "Thoughts on organization theory and a review of two conferences." General Systems Yearbook, 4: 87-93.

RENSHON, S. A. [ed.] (1977) Handbook of Political Socialization. New York: Free Press.
REUVENY, J. (1974) The Israeli Civil Service, 1948-1973. Ramat Gan, Israel: Massada (Hebrew).
RIKER, W. (1962) The Theory of Political Coalitions. New Haven, CT: Yale University Press.
RIGGS. F. W. (1964) Administration in Developing Countries: The Theory of Prismatic Society. Boston: Houghton Mifflin.
———— (1967) "The 'Sala' model: an ecological approach to the study of comparative administration," in N. Raphaeli (ed.), Readings in Comparative Public Administration. Boston: Allyn & Bacon.
RITTERBAND, P. (1978) Education, Employment and Migration: Israel in Comparative Perspective. Cambridge: Cambridge University Press.
ROBUSHKA, A. and K. A. SHEPSLE (1972) Politics in Plural Societies: A Theory of Democratic Instability. Columbus, OH: Charles E. Merrill.
ROGERS, E. (1976) "Communication and development: the passing of the dominant paradigm." Communication Research, 3 (2): 221-222.
———— and L. KINCAID (1981) Communication Networks. New York: Free Press.
ROGERS, E. with F. F. SHOEMAKER (1971) Communication of Innovations (2nd ed.). New York: Free Press.
ROSEN, H. M. (1971) Jewish-Arab Relations in Israel and the Organizations Responsible for Their Cultivation. Jerusalem: The American Jewish Committee (Hebrew).
ROSENAU, J. (1974) Citizenship Between Elections. New York: Free Press.
ROSENFELD, S. [ed.] (1978) Headline: Maariv — 30 years, 1948-1978. Tel Aviv: Maariv Publications (Hebrew).
ROSENSTEIN, Z. (1946) The Histadrut. Tel Aviv: Hava'ad Hapoel (Hebrew).
ROSENTHAL, U. (1978) Political Order: Rewards, Punishments and Political Stability. Alphen: Sijthoff & Noordhoff.
ROSTOW, W. W. (1960) The Stages of Economic Growth. Cambridge: Cambridge University Press.
———— (1971) Politics and the Stages of Growth. Cambridge: Cambridge University Press.
ROTH, A. and E. FRANKEL [eds.] (1978) Front Page: The Jerusalem Post 1932-1978. Jerusalem: Jerusalem Palestine Post.
ROURKE, F. E. (1969) Bureaucracy, Politics and Public Policy. Boston: Little, Brown.
RUBEN, B. D. [ed.] (1977) Communication Yearbook 1. New Brunswick, NJ: Transaction.
———— (1978) Communication Yearbook 2. New Brunswick, NJ: Transaction.
RUBEN, B. D. and J. Y. KIM [eds.] (1975) General Systems Theory and Human Communication. New York: Hyden Book.
RUBIN, B. (1977) Media, Politics and Democracy. New York: Oxford University Press.
RUBINSTEIN, A. (1974) Constitutional Law in Israel (2nd ed.). Tel Aviv: Schocken (Hebrew).
RUSSETT, B. M., H. R. ALKER, Jr., K. W. DEUTSCH, and H. D. LASSWELL (1964) World Handbook of Political and Social Indicators. New Haven, CT: Yale University Press.
RUSTOW, D. A. (1970) "Transition to democracy: toward a dynamic model." Comparative Politics, 2: 337-363.
SAGER, S. (1971-1972) "Pre-state influences on Israel's parliamentary system." Parliamentary Affairs, 25 (1): 29-49.

SALPETER, E. and Y. ELITZUR (1973) The Establishment — Who Rules in Israel. Ramat Gan, Israel: Levin-Epstein (Hebrew).

SAMET, M. (1979) Religion and State in Israel. Jerusalem: Kaplan School, Hebrew University (Hebrew).

SANDERS, J. (1962a) "The seriousness of humor." East Europe, 2 (2): 21-29.

———— (1962b) "The tactful satirists." East Europe, 2 (3): 23-27.

SARTORI, G. (1970) "Concept misformation in comparative politics." American Political Science Review, 64 (December): 1033-1053.

SCHELLING, T. C. (1960) The Strategy of Conflict. Cambridge: Harvard University Press.

SCHIFF, G. S. (1977) Tradition and Politics: The Religious Parties of Israel. Detroit: Wayne State University Press.

SCHILLER, H. I. (1973) The Mind Managers. Boston: Beacon.

SCHNALL, D. J. (1979) Radical Dissent in Contemporary Israeli Politics. New York: Praeger.

SCHOLEM, G. (1974) "Israel and the diaspora." Molad, 6 (April/June): 17-23 (Hebrew).

SCHRAMM, W. (1954) The Process and Effects of Mass Communication. Urbana: University of Illinois Press.

———— (1964) Mass Media and National Development: The Role of Information in the Developing Countries. Stanford: Stanford University Press.

———— and D. LERNER [eds.] (1976) Communication and Change: The Last Ten Years and the Next. Honolulu: University of Hawaii Press.

SCHRAMM, W. and D. ROBERTS [eds.] (1972) The Process of Mass Communication. Urbana: University of Illinois Press.

SCHWEID, E. (1971) "Ideology, facts and Zionism." Molad, 19-20 (May-June): 56-63.

SCOTT, R. W. (1965) "Theory of organizations," pp. 485-529 in R. Faris (ed.), Handbook of Modern Sociology. Chicago: Rand McNally.

SEGRE, D. V. (1971) Israel: A Society in Transition. London: Oxford University Press.

SELF, P. (1972) Administrative Theories and Politics. London: George Allen & Unwin.

SELIGER, M. (1970) "Fundamental and operative ideology: the two principal dimensions of political argumentation." Policy Sciences, 1: 325-338.

———— (1976) Ideology and Politics. London: George Allen & Unwin.

SELIGMAN, L. G. (1964) Leadership in a New Nation: Political Development in Israel. Englewood Cliffs, NJ: Prentice-Hall.

———— (1967) "Political parties and the recruitment of political leadership," in L. J. Edinger (ed.), Political Leadership in Industrialized Societies. New York: John Wiley.

SELZNICK, P. (1952) Organizational Weapon: A Study of Bolshevik Strategy and Tactics. New York: McGraw-Hill.

———— (1956) Leadership in Administration. New York: Harper & Row.

———— (1969) Law, Society and Industrial Justice. New York: Russell Sage Foundation.

SEYMOUR-URE, C. (1968) The Press, Politics and the Public. London: Methuen.

———— (1974) The Political Impact of Mass Media. London: Constable.

SHAPIRA, A. (1980) Berl. Tel Aviv: Am Oved (Hebrew).

SHAPIRA, J. (1975) The Historic Ahdut HaAvoda: The Power of a Political Organization. Tel Aviv: Am Oved University Library (Hebrew).

———— (1977) Democracy in Israel. Ramat Gan, Israel: Massada (Hebrew).

SHAPIRA, R. and E. ETZIONI-HALEVY (1973) Who Is the Israeli Student? Tel Aviv: Am Oved (Hebrew).

SHAPIRA, R., C. ADLER, M. LERNER, and R. PELEG (1979) Blue Shirt and White Collar. Tel Aviv: Am Oved, Institute for the Study of Work and Society (Hebrew).
SHARKANSKY, I. (1975) The United States: A Study of a Developing Country. New York: Longman.
────── (1978) "How to cope with the bureaucracy." Jerusalem Quarterly, 6 (Winter): 80-93.
SHARETT, M. (1955) "Socialism in Israel — How?" Molad, 13 (Hebrew).
────── (1978) Personal Diaries (9 vols.). Tel Aviv: Maariv Library (Hebrew).
SHAVIT, Y. (1976) The Hunting Season: Ha-sayzon. Tel Aviv: Hadar (Hebrew).
SHEFFER, G. (1980) "The UJA and the State of Israel." Kivunim, 7 (May): 9-26 (Hebrew).
SHEFFER, G. and Y. MANOR (1980) "Fund raising: money is not enough," pp. 283-299 in R. Bilski et al. (eds.), Can Planning Replace Politics? The Israeli Experience. The Hague: Nijhoff Publishers.
SHERF, Z. (1959) Three Days. Tel Aviv: Am Oved (Hebrew).
SHILS, E. (1958) "The concentration and dispersion of charisma." World Politics, 10 (October): 1-19.
────── (1966) Political Development in the New States. The Hague: Mouton.
────── (1974) The Torment of Secrecy (rev. ed.). Carbondale: University of Southern Illinois Press.
────── (1975) Center and Periphery. Chicago: University of Chicago Press.
SHONFELD, A. (1965) Modern Capitalism. London: Oxford University Press.
SHUVAL, J. (1963) Immigrants on the Threshhold. New York: Atherton.
SIGAL, L. (1974) Reporters and Officials. Lexington, MA: D.C. Heath.
SIMON, H. A. (1957) Administrative Behavior: A Study of Decision-Making Processes in Administration Organizations (2nd ed.). New York: Free Press.
────── (1965) The Shape of Automation for Men and Management. New York: Harper & Row.
────── (1969) The Sciences of the Artificial. Cambridge: MIT Press.
SIMONS, H. and J. A. CALIFANO [eds.] (1976) The Media and the Law. New York: Praeger.
SINGH, K.J. and B. M. GROSS (1979) "Mass line communication: the leadership of political movements." Prepared for delivery at the International Political Science Association Congress, Moscow.
SMITH, A. G. [ed.] (1966) Communication and Culture. New York: Holt, Rinehart & Winston.
SMITH, A. (1978) The Politics of Information: Problems of Policy in Modern Media. London: Macmillan.
SMITH. D. E. (1970) Religion and Political Development. Boston: Little, Brown.
SMITH, H. (1969) Everything about Elections in Israel. Tel Aviv: Adi (Hebrew).
SMOOHA, S. (1978) Israel: Pluralism and Conflict. London: Routledge & Kegal Paul.
SPRINZAK, E. (1973) Beginnings of Politics of Delegitimation in Israel, 1967-1972. Jerusalem: Hebrew University (Hebrew).
────── (1981) "Gush Emunim: the iceberg model of political extremism." State, Government and International Relations, 17 (Spring): 22-49 (Hebrew).
STAHL, A. (1979) Ethnic Strife in Israel. Tel Aviv: Am Oved (Hebrew).
STARBUCK, W. H. (1965) "Organizational growth and development," pp. 451-583 in J. March (ed.), Handbook of Organization. Chicago: Rand McNally.
State of Israel (1973) Newspapers and Periodicals Appearing in Israel, 1972-1973. Jerusalem: Government Press Office.

Statistical Abstract of Israel (annual) Jerusalem: Central Bureau of Statistics (English and Hebrew).

STOCK E. (1954) "The press of Israel: its growth in freedom." Journalism Quarterly, 31 (Fall.).

—— (1972) "The reconstitution of the Jewish Agency: a political analysis." American Jewish Yearbook. 73: 178-193.

STURMAN, D. (1979) "Bureaucratic utopia." Crossroads, 4 (Autumn): 69-120.

TALMON, Y. (1965) "The family in a revolutionary movement," in M. F. Nimkoff (ed.), Comparative Family Systems. Boston: Houghton Mifflin.

TARROW, S. (1977) Between Center and Periphery: Grassroots Politicians in Italy and France. New Haven, CT: Yale University Press.

TAYLOR, C. L. and M. C. HUDSON (1972) World Handbook of Political and Social Indicators (2nd ed.). New Haven, CT: Yale University Press.

TEHERANIAN, M. et al. [eds.] (1977) Communication Policy for National Development. London: Routledge & Kegal Paul.

TEXTOR, R. B. (1967) A Cross-Cultural Summary. New Haven, CT: HRAF Press.

THOMPSON, D. F. (1970) The Democratic Citizen. Cambridge: Cambridge University Press.

THOMPSON, V. A. (1961) Modern Organizations. New York: Alfred A. Knopf.

—— (1969) Bureaucracy and Innovation. Alabama: University of Alabama Press.

—— (1973) Organizations as Systems. Morristown, NY: General Learning Press.

TRUMAN, D. B. (1951) The Governmental Process. New York: Alfred A. Knopf.

UNGER, R. M. (1975) Knowledge and Politics. New York: Free Press.

URBACH, E. E. (1979) "Center and periphery in Jewish historical consciousness: contemporary implications," pp. 1-22 in Y. Beck (ed.), Jewish Identity Today. Jerusalem: World Zionist Organization.

USSISHKIN, M. (1943) "The voice of the land." Presented to the Conference of Teachers of the Jewish National Fund, Jerusalem, 1929.

VARDI-AGMON, G. (1970) The Hebrew Press in Eretz Israel, 1863-1904. Tel Aviv University and Hakibbutz Hameuchad (Hebrew).

VERBA, S. and N. H. NIE (1972) Participation in America: Social Equality and Political Democracy. New York: Harper & Row.

—— and J. O. KIM (1971) The Modes of Democratic Participation: A Cross-National Comparison. Beverly Hills, CA: Sage.

—— (1978) Participation and Political Equality: A Seven Nation Comparison. London: Cambridge University Press.

VICKERS, G. (1957) "Control, stability and choice." General Systems Yearbook, 2: 1-8.

VITAL, D. (1978) The Origins of Zionism. Tel Aviv: Am Oved (Hebrew).

WEINER, M. (1962) The Politics of Society: Public Pressure and Political Response in India. Chicago: University of Chicago Press.

—— (1967) Party Building in a New Nation. Chicago: University of Chicago Press.

WEINER, M. and J. LAPALOMBARA [eds.] (1968) Political Parties and Political Development. Princeton, NJ: Princeton University Press.

WEINTRAUB, D. (1971) Immigration and Social Change. New York: Humanities Press.

WEISS, S. (1973) Local Government in Israel. Tel Aviv: Am Oved (Hebrew).

—— (1977a) "The Ninth Knesset: an initial analysis of its composition and patterns of recruitment of Knesset members." State, Government and International Relations, 11 (Winter): 26-39 (Hebrew).

—— (1977b) The Knesset — Function and Output. Tel Aviv: Ahiasaf (Hebrew).

WEISS, S. and A. ARIAN (1969) "Split ticket voting in Israel." Western Political Quarterly, 22 (2).

WEITZ, R. and A. ROKACH (1968) Agricultural Development. Dordrecht-Holland: D. Reidel.

WEINER, N. (1954) The Human Use of Human Beings (2nd ed.). New York: Double-day.

——— (1961) Cybernetics (2nd ed.). New York: John Wiley.

WILDAVSKY, A. (1979) The Art and Craft of Policy Analysis. London: Macmillan.

WILENSKY, H.L. (1964) "Mass society and mass culture." American Sociological Review, 29 (April).

——— (1967) Organizational Intelligence. New York: Basic Books.

WILSON, J.Q. (1973) Political Organizations. New York: Basic Books.

WISEMAN, H.V. (1966) Political Systems: Some Sociological Approaches. New York: Praeger.

YAACOBI, G. (1972) The Power of Quality. Haifa: Shikmona (Hebrew).

——— (1980) The Government. Tel Aviv: Am Oved (Hebrew).

YARON, Z. (1976) Religion in Israel. New York: American Jewish Yearbook.

YATZIV, G. (1974) The Class Basis of Party Affiliation. Ph.D. dissertation, Hebrew University of Jerusalem (Hebrew).

YISHAI, Y. (1978) Factionalization in the Labor Movement: Faction B in Mapai. Tel Aviv: Am Oved (Hebrew).

YOUNG, C. (1976) The Politics of Cultural Pluralism. Madison: University of Wisconsin Press.

YUCHTMAN, E. and G. FISHELZON (1970) "Inequality and income distribution." Economics Quarterly, 17: 75-88 (Hebrew).

ZAMIR, Y. (1975) Judgment in Administrative Matters. Jerusalem: Faculty of Law, Hebrew University (Hebrew).

ZIDON, A. (1967) Knesset: The Parliament of Israel. New York: Herzl Press.

ZLOCZOWER, A. (1972) "Occupation, mobility and social class." Social Science Information, 11: 329-357.

ZUCKERMAN, A. (1975) "Political cleavage: a conceptual and theoretical analysis." British Journal of Political Science, 5, Part 1 (January): 231-248.

INDEX

Access: 14, 15, 21-24, 27, 300-327,
   331-332, 372-373, 376-377
   definition of: 21, 301
   of groups: 310-314, 331, 348-359,
      372
   of individuals: 307-310, 331, 338,
      358, 372
Agranat Commission of Inquiry: 68,
   78n
Agriculture: 44-46, 70, 126, 200, 275,
   239. See Ministry of Agriculture.
   ideologies: 58, 99, 103, 141, 142
   settlements: 55, 70, 122, 142
Ahad Ha'am: 98
Aliya, as symbol: 96-98, 247. See
   Immigration.
Almogi, Yosef: 181, 317
Alterman, Nathan: 92, 106, 109n
Aran, Zalman: 175
Arlozorov, Haim: 282
Arab countries: 32, 39
Arabs in Israel: 49-51, 56, 95, 107, 133,
   139, 146, 158n, 173, 185, 198, 203,
   206, 210, 214-215, 224, 240, 260,
   274, 290, 306, 359, 367n. See
   Military Government, Target
   Groups.
   cleavage: 49-51, 127, 146, 183, 273,
      274
   as peripheral group: 333, 335,
      348-352
   political organizations: 51, 72, 74,
      133, 174, 348-349, 351
   voting: 50, 350-351
   workers: 63, 71, 233, 235
Arab-Israeli Conflict: 32, 36, 37, 49,
   50, 51, 63, 89, 119, 120, 133, 183,
   282, 299n, 349
Arabic Language: 50, 54, 94, 133, 224,
   226, 233, 235, 240, 241, 260

Armistice Agreements: 6, 38, 63
Associations: 17, 114, 126, 144, 161,
   164, 175
   professional: 24, 59, 67, 70, 146,
      152, 153, 157n, 312, 319
   voluntary: 23, 166, 259, 311-312
Attachment, as symbol: 104-105. See
   Pioneering.
Autonomy, of citizens: 22, 23, 24-27,
   28, 137, 301, 307, 311, 324-326
   of political camps: 76, 113, 115, 121,
      125, 126, 151
   of political steering: 19, 146,
      270-272, 291, 297

Balfour Declaration: 48, 80
Begin, Menahem: 73, 74, 299n
Ben-Aharon, Itzhak: 111, 181
Ben-Gurion, David: 38, 65, 66, 72,
   73, 77n, 85, 92, 93, 100, 114, 115,
   119, 129, 130, 142, 157n, 158n, 175,
   176, 181, 193, 234, 235, 238, 249,
   258, 263n, 283, 285, 286, 299n,
   302, 303
Ben Yehuda, Eliezer: 94, 95
Ben-Zvi, Itzhak: 100
Bible: 42, 51, 54, 94
   as symbol: 91-93, 102, 210, 247
Black Panthers, in Israel: 47, 57, 108
Borders: 10, 36, 39, 91
Breakdown, of political systems:
   19-20, 31, 34n, 267, 270, 278,
   281-287, 292, 294, 297, 365
Britain: 63, 230
British Government in Palestine: 47,
   53, 61, 68, 69, 91, 117, 118, 179,
   193, 195-196, 223, 243, 273
   army: 105, 156, 172, 196
   broadcasting services: 117, 233
   influence of: 65, 68, 193, 276

British Mandate on Palestine: 35, 69, 77n, 91, 119, 124
Brit Shalom: 183
Bunt: 81, 298n, 304
Bureaucracy: 13, 15, 16, 121, 184, 189-217, 317, 336-338, 366n, 370
  access to: 317-322
  as channels: 3, 13, 15, 16, 23, 33n, 133, 135, 136, 138, 172, 189-217, 373
  nonbureaucratic roles: 189, 206-209, 318
  red tape: 198, 204, 206, 320, 321, 326n
  ruling: 191, 192, 198, 208
  and service delivery: 187, 198, 204-206

Cabinet: 53, 67, 69, 99, 121, 158n, 163, 287. See Coalitions.
  of national unity: 61, 64, 176, 287, 363
Camps: see Civic, Labor, Political, Religious Camps.
Canaanites Movement: 86-87, 91, 107, 109n, 183, 312
Censorship: 37, 165, 229, 243, 246.
Center: see Political Center.
Central Guidance Cluster: 14, 18, 112
Channels: 15-17, 26, 115, 139, 140-141, 146, 160-161, 261-263, 278, 307-324, 337, 345, 369; definition of: 3-4, 8. See Bureaucratic, Mass Media, Party Channels.
  political, definition of: 3, 160
  choice and access opportunities: 33n, 314-325
  interlocking: 191, 194, 195, 199, 203, 214-217, 220, 235, 262-263, 371
  nonpolitical: 17, 160
Civic Camp: 59-64, 70, 73, 77n, 106, 114, 123, 129, 144, 167
Civil Service: 65, 68, 75-76, 142, 196, 197, 200, 211, 216, 217n, 293. See Bureaucracy.
  Commission: 68, 217n
  nominations: 196-197, 208, 213
  Union: 196, 197
Cleavages: 48-58, 76, 305-306
Coalitions: agreements: 67, 195. See Knesset.

in cabinet: 53, 61, 65, 67, 71, 99, 122, 135, 149, 167, 184, 293, 294
  grand: 76-77
  as political mechanism: 59, 65, 107, 122, 125, 127, 149, 262, 287, 362
Coercion: 10, 19, 20, 31, 112, 126, 133, 163, 192, 198, 246, 270, 275, 281, 289-290, 342, 365, 371, 378
Collective Efforts, as politics: 5, 10-12, 118, 129, 131, 162, 191, 284, 378
Communication: 2-3, 5, 112, 160, 223, 267, 288, 375-378
  political, definition of: 6-9. See Channels, Information Flow; Network.
Communism, ideologies: 48, 65, 81, 103, 115, 164, 221, 302, 304. See Party, Communist.
Communist Regimes: 164, 172, 183, 194, 198, 230, 246, 314, 370
Comptroller General: 65, 67, 337
Compliance: 10, 20, 131, 138, 159, 274, 281, 289-291, 371, 377
Consensus, national, Zionist: 58-61, 88-89, 97, 107-109, 117, 129, 178, 194, 228, 231, 242, 245, 262, 287, 369
Conflict: 3, 5, 10, 182, 188n, 271, 289, 343
Constitution: 41, 64, 65-66, 68, 76, 293. See Laws, Basic.
Contents, common, political: 9-12, 20, 31, 79, 128, 133, 182, 233, 266, 292, 294, 354, 369, 375; definition of: 10
  nonpolitical: 2-3, 88-101, 271
Coordination: 8, 13, 14, 114, 115, 121, 122, 125, 130, 162-164, 180-185, 187, 200, 211, 371
Courts: 13, 40, 51, 53, 67-68, 117, 135, 195, 197, 274, 293, 337-338
  High Court of Justice: 68, 78n, 337, 338
  Supreme Court: 67, 68, 99, 338, 349, 351
Culture: 43, 58, 83, 85, 88-101, 104, 109n, 138, 233, 312
  art: 43, 64, 103, 233
  dance: 42, 103
  Hebrew: See Hebrew Language.

Jewish: 41, 82, 100, 134
Literature: 91, 94, 101, 102, 103, 233,
320, 326n
Music and Song: 35, 43, 93, 102,
103, 104, 137, 233, 247, 320
Political: See Political Culture.
Cybernetics: 7-8, 33n, 147, 270

Dayan, Moshe: 175, 176, 244, 263n,
287
Decisions, binding: 5, 6, 18, 266, 289,
371
Decision-Making: 2, 8, 13, 14, 18, 21,
29, 122, 153, 156, 180, 181, 192,
200, 206, 278, 288-289, 299n, 360
Democracy: 14, 28, 64-66, 268, 300,
372, 377
consociational: 76-77, 127-128, 294
in Israel: 75, 142, 144, 156, 163, 256,
301-307, 313-314, 326, 360
Democratic Political Development:
9, 20-31, 191, 221, 326, 328-329,
347, 359-366, 372-377; definition
of: 20. See Steering, impact on.
Development Towns: 144, 152, 167,
175, 276, 335, 342, 356
Diaspora: 39-41, 43, 48-49, 54-56, 66,
70, 82-83, 85, 93, 98, 106, 122, 126
attitudes in Israel: 85-87, 96-97,
299n
Oriental: 84
as target group: 134, 173, 185, 215,
240, 260
Western: 83-84, 304
Differentiation: 11, 13, 19, 152, 153,
160, 190, 243, 272
Diffusion, of information: 13, 19,
279-281, 287, 297, 371
Druzes: 50, 351

Eban, Abba: 175, 176
Economic and Social Development:
9, 37, 41, 43-47, 56-57, 106, 174,
187, 205, 212, 269, 296, 306
Economy of Israel: 42, 57, 63, 108,
135, 138, 160, 184, 198, 206, 258,
267, 283
recessions: 32, 44, 57, 282, 283,
286, 331, 343-344

Education: 43, 44, 47, 56, 103, 104,
120, 130, 137, 145, 197, 215-216,
224, 233, 308, 354
Jewish: 40, 134
political: 136, 145
Efficacy: 8, 22, 27, 329-331, 332, 345,
347, 364, 366n, 373; definition of:
24
Egypt: 38, 299n
Intelligence operation in: 38, 77n,
188n, 230, 283, 285
Eichman Trial: 97, 105
Einstein, Albert: 104
Elections, campaigns: 25-27, 253-256,
278, 344-346
financing: 78n, 333, 345
in Histadrut: 114, 115, 169-170, 197,
320, 333-334
of Knesset: 22, 27, 31, 65, 71-74,
176, 185, 197, 320, 333-335
in local authorities: 65, 69, 73, 123,
157n, 169-170, 333-335
proportional system: 65, 66, 71, 76,
157n, 284, 293, 314-315
results: 72, 169-171, 287. See
Voting.
Elites: See Leadership.
Employment and Occupation: 43,
44-46, 47, 56-57, 138, 197, 201, 308
Emergency Regulations: 37, 188n
Equality, political: 14, 24, 258,
360-361, 372; definition of: 28
Eshkol, Levi: 130, 175, 181, 200, 242,
244, 258, 287, 365, 366n
Etzel: 59, 61, 73, 105, 120, 121, 166,
188n, 233, 273, 282-284, 285
Europe: 36, 58, 96, 168
Holocaust: 43, 48, 55, 97, 103, 106,
207, 267, 282, 284, 285
ideological influences: 42, 103, 302,
304
Jewish communities in: 52, 54, 55,
80, 119
Exclusiveness, of steering: 19, 31,
274-277, 297

Farmers: 28, 42, 80, 90, 275
associations: 59, 114, 144, 157n, 226
Feedback: 28-29, 31, 112, 153, 177-180,
209, 219, 220, 257-259, 275, 278,
280-281, 290, 324, 361-363, 372;

definition of: 29. See Information Flow.
Films and Newsreels: 37, 39, 40, 121, 125, 130, 142, 149, 230, 238, 240, 244
policy orientations: 63, 84, 285
France: 210, 230

Gadna: 145, 216, 263n
Games theory: 33n, 148
Gaza Strip: 38, 50, 120, 240
Germany, West: 39, 244, 263n
reparations from: 40, 44, 64, 188n, 283, 285
Golan Heights: 38
Groups: 17, 27, 29, 75-76, 272, 310-314, 339-343. See Access, Participation.
interest, pressure: 23, 123, 150, 164, 182, 183, 187, 190, 259, 268, 307, 311, 316, 330, 337, 343
nonpolitical: 138-139, 145, 151, 159, 185, 216, 241, 260, 294
peripheral: 28, 126, 133-139, 174, 338, 348-359, 374. See Periphery.

Haganah: 61, 105, 116, 120, 166, 195, 233, 275, 282, 284
Haifa: 223, 276, 317, 321, 356
Halacha (religious law): 51, 62, 66, 83, 100, 274
Haolam Hazeh (weekly): 183, 228, 242, 248, 263n, 312. See Party.
Health: 43, 44, 47, 118, 122, 166, 201. See Histadrut, Sick Fund.
Hebrew Language: 42, 43, 58, 61, 83, 86, 87, 92-96, 109n, 210, 224-226, 233, 247, 248
Hebrews: See Canaanites.
Herzl, Theodor: 48, 69, 86, 91, 94, 101
Hess, Moses: 109n, 234
Histadrut: 59, 62, 70-71, 76, 77, 77n, 149, 163, 181, 340-341. See Labor Camp.
companies: 59, 62, 116, 121, 188n, 200-203, 204, 320, 341, 345
Elected Assembly: See Elections.
in Israel: 121, 136, 144, 151, 188n, 213, 248, 283, 286, 312, 313, 321, 343
representation in: 57, 61, 71

Sick Fund (Kupat Holim): 70-71, 116, 144, 166, 201
in yishuv: 70-71, 114-117, 119, 120, 166, 193-194, 225, 226, 233-235, 303
Housing: 43, 56, 116, 121, 122, 151, 197, 204, 308

Israeli Defence Force: 61, 66, 69, 105, 106, 135, 143, 161, 172, 184, 188n, 195, 200, 237, 263n, 274, 285, 286, 309
radio station: 238, 247
Ideologies: 48, 62-63, 80, 88, 101-109 (passim), 114, 129, 156, 183, 184, 231-235, 253, 302-305
changes in: 138-139, 143
Ideological Camps: See Political Camps
Immigrants, as peripheral groups: 355-358, 359. See Oriental Jews, Western Jews.
as target group: 41, 135-136, 146, 173, 185, 203, 207, 240, 259, 315
Immigration: 54-58, 96-98, 113, 144
mass: 42, 55-56, 80, 97, 135, 229, 246, 267, 283
to Israel: 40, 55-56, 96-98, 109n, 142
to Palestine: 36, 55-56, 115, 118, 120, 124, 141
responsibility for: 47, 70, 122
selective: 96-98, 109n
Impact on Steering: See Steering.
Independence, Day: 98, 100, 105, 245
Declaration of: 42, 64, 65, 91-92, 233, 250, 352
War: See Wars.
India: 16, 168, 191, 217n, 299n
Industry: 17, 43, 45-56, 341
Industrialists' Association: 59, 76, 149, 167, 226, 312
Information Flow: 4, 7-8, 13, 14, 16, 17-18, 111, 127, 140, 146, 153, 159, 181, 204, 236, 266, 271, 292, 295, 305, 376; definition of: 17-18
directions (diagonal, horizontal, vertical): 16, 21, 25-26, 28, 126, 129, 136, 148-149, 179-180, 189, 192, 198, 207, 213, 219, 261, 267, 273, 277-279, 330, 332, 336, 370

leaks: 151, 181, 229, 258, 296, 364,
    365
legibility: 19-20, 280-281, 287, 297,
    371
monopoly and control of: 13, 14, 19,
    27, 30, 179, 183, 199, 212-213,
    237-239, 258, 272-277, 286, 297,
    320
as pressure: 26, 331-347 (passim),
    360-363
transmission and intake: 19, 26,
    220, 263, 270, 277-279, 287, 295,
    297, 308
Information Bureaus and
    Spokesmen: 23, 93, 228, 236, 244
Ingathering of the Exiles: 40, 48, 98,
    106, 206
Institution-Building: 8, 12, 13, 14, 17,
    112-120, 124, 146, 154, 160, 166,
    170, 191, 325, 369, 376
Institutions, National: 113, 116,
    117-120, 124-125, 179, 193, 195,
    196, 232
Integration: 48-64 (passim), 77n, 139,
    146, 161, 191, 263, 290
disintegration: 48, 88, 108, 120, 182,
    261, 268
national: 10, 81
social and cultural: 8, 10-12, 18, 48
Interaction, political: 1, 3, 5-6, 81,
    130, 220, 378
Interest Groups: See Groups.
Iran: 55, 56, 91, 222, 244
Israel, as case study: 31-33
as Jewish center: 40-41, 48-49, 82,
    98, 125-126, 134
as Jewish state: 50, 96, 98, 109n,
    110n, 274, 348
shelter for Jews: 40-41, 82, 97, 106
Israeli Broadcasting Authority: 75,
    238, 242, 258
Israeliness: 43, 48-49, 58, 82-88, 96.
    See Contents, Common.
Italy: 109n

Jabotinsky, Zeev: 61, 100, 109n
Jerusalem: 36, 52, 54, 55, 90, 99, 101,
    102, 133, 223, 233, 240, 353
Jewish Agency, in Israel: 61, 69-70,
    75, 77, 121-122, 134, 136, 151, 163,

166, 174, 195, 200, 201, 215, 240,
    260, 273, 320, 349
in yishuv: 40, 69-70, 113, 119, 120,
    121, 125, 146, 166, 172, 193
Jewish National Fund (Keren
    Kayemet): 49, 91, 102, 103, 122,
    215, 349
Jewish, support for Israel: 40-41,
    48-49, 77n, 122, 133, 173
Jews, definition problems: 51, 78n.
    See Jewishness, Judaism.
of Mosaic confession: 83-84
Jewishness: 40, 42, 49, 50-54, 56,
    81-86, 88, 89, 96. See Contents,
    Common.
Jewish Colonization Association: 113
Jordan, Kingdom of: 38, 91
Jordan River: 63, 77, 91
Judaism: 40, 48-49, 53, 81-82, 83, 87,
    89, 98, 124, 354. See Contents,
    Common.
Judiciary: See Courts.

Kastner, Israel: 283, 285
Katznelson, Berl: 104, 130, 233, 234,
    303
Kfar Kassem: 78n, 228
Kibbutz: 43, 99, 104, 116, 141, 171, 172,
    303, 333, 340, 342, 345, 366n
movements: 59, 73, 157n, 167, 205,
    283, 285, 340. See Labor Camp.
and political affiliations: 53, 54,
    130, 143, 166, 175, 241
Knesset: 60, 65, 66, 67, 68, 71-75, 101,
    121, 169-171, 212, 285, 293, 317,
    324, 360. See Elections, Parties.
as Constituent Assembly: 66, 293
representation in: 57, 61, 127, 164,
    188n, 197, 251-252, 317
Knesset Israel (in yishuv): 117, 118,
    166
Kollek, Teddy: 92, 238
Kook, Abraham: 53
Kupat Holim: See Histadrut, Sick
    Fund.

Land of Israel (Eretz Yisrael): 42, 54,
    82, 83, 86-90 (passim), 92, 99, 101,
    124, 247
Labor Party Alignment: See Parties.

Labor, Political Camp: 58-64, 70-71,
    104, 106, 111, 114-115, 120, 121,
    124-125, 129, 130, 144, 146, 163,
    184, 196, 201, 276, 281, 285, 302,
    304, 318, 341
Languages: in Israel: 55, 93-96, 133.
    See Arabic, Hebrew.
    and Mass Media: 225-226
    political: 11, 12, 109n. See
    Contents, Common.
    and politics: 10, 13, 28, 160, 273
Lavon Affair: 32, 43n, 68, 77n, 78n,
    158n, 216, 230, 231, 239, 244, 249,
    283, 286, 287, 296, 318, 360
Lavon, Pinhas: 77n, 181, 230, 249,
    283, 286
Law of Return (1950): 40, 97, 109n
Laws, Basic: 66, 68, 293
Leadership: 14, 16, 28, 77n, 107, 121,
    127, 158n, 222, 250-253, 302
    in Israel: 39, 107, 114, 127-130, 137,
    145, 154, 164, 170, 188n, 199, 286,
    359
    Jewish: 134
    recruitment of: 173-177, 342, 357
League of Nations: 53, 69, 119
Lebanon: 38
Legitimization: 16, 64, 114, 126, 135,
    161, 191, 245-249 (passim), 273
Lehi: 59, 61, 121, 188n, 282
Likud: See Parties.
Local Authorities: 44, 57, 68-69, 123,
    152, 153, 164, 174, 175, 188n, 195,
    203, 210, 273, 293, 306, 351, 353,
    356
    elections in: 65, 69, 73, 123, 157n,
    168, 169-170, 333, 350
    municipal government center: 157n

Maintenance: 16-17, 133, 140-146, 162,
    335, 346, 369, 371; definition of:
    16, 140. See Steering Capacity.
    by bureaucracy: 209-214
    by mass media: 241-259
    by parties: 162, 177-185
Mapai: See Parties.
Mass: channels: 17, 139, 141, 253-256,
    324
    society: 16, 138, 152, 156, 220, 365
    politics: 101, 138, 161, 170, 180, 187,
    190, 220, 221, 242, 365

Mass Media: 12, 16-17, 22, 23, 27, 133,
    135, 217-264, 308, 371. See
    Newspapers, Radio and
    Television.
    access to: 322-324
    as channels: 15, 16, 220-222, 337,
    373
    editors' profile: 250-252
    and education: 224
    mission: 232-236, 243-245
    organizations: 219-220
    and politics: 221-222, 226-231, 239,
    249, 250-253, 264n
    and society: 223-226
    technology: 24, 218, 221, 242, 279
Meir, Golda: 130, 175, 181, 286, 299n,
    363, 367n
Membership: in parties: 113, 136, 166,
    167-171, 172, 339
    in political system: 22, 24, 133, 135,
    180, 343
Military: 54, 238, 268. See IDF.
    and politics: 69, 175, 195, 200, 212
    service: 15, 37, 51, 53, 135, 138, 143,
    269, 274, 354
Military Government: 50, 133, 203,
    210, 214, 274, 285, 349, 350. See
    Arabs in Israel
Ministries: Agriculture: 76, 200,
    201-202, 338
    Commerce and Industry: 76, 213,
    228, 313
    Defense: 69, 77n, 175, 184, 195, 216,
    258, 286
    Education and Culture: 70, 145,
    158n, 184, 211, 215-216, 319, 353
    Finance: 211
    Foreign Affairs: 184, 195, 240, 260
    Health: 201
    Housing: 204
    Interior: 68, 69, 109n, 123, 165, 184,
    188n
    Justice: 184
    Labor: 70, 99, 184, 202, 204
    Police: 69, 184, 200
    Religious Affairs: 184, 274, 338, 353
    Welfare: 151, 184, 200
Minorities in Israel: See Arabs.
Mobility: 22, 33n, 218, 356.
    political: 22, 24, 307-310, 338, 357.
    See Access.

Mobilization: 18, 22, 104, 131-133, 164,
   171-173, 208, 263, 268, 287, 355
Modernization: 22, 23, 47, 107, 128,
   138, 141-146 (passim), 152, 161,
   189, 216, 272, 295, 308
Monopoly: See Information Flow.
Moshav: 143-144, 153, 157n, 166,
   167-168, 175, 205, 333, 345
Moslem Countries: 39, 50, 55, 56, 84,
   90, 96

Namir, Mordechai: 201
Nation-Building: 8, 136, 42-43, 112,
   114, 191
National Committee (Vaad Leumi):
   118, 120, 158n, 172, 193, 195, 200,
   275
National Insurance: 44, 47
National Labor Federation: 167
Nationalism: 82, 103-104. See
   Ideologies.
Navon, Itzhak: 238
Neturei-Karta: 51-52, 83, 294, 352,
   353
Netzer, Shraga: 176, 181, 199n
Network: 178, 188n, 346; definition
   of: 3
   political: 3, 8, 12-15, 21, 111-158, 172,
      177, 226-229, 275, 308, 369;
      definition of: 12-13
Newspapers: 16, 17, 23, 94, 133, 135,
   149, 224-228, 231-236, 241-242,
   248, 322, 323, 366n. See
   Mass-Media, Press.
   Editors' Committee: 243-244, 246
Noise: in communication: 20, 141,
   155, 156, 213, 219, 263

Officials: contacts with: 25-26
Openness: 29-31, 179, 183, 241, 288,
   296, 363-366, 372, 377, 378;
   definition of: 29, 364
Oren, Mordechai: 230
Organizations: 1-2, 3, 8, 12, 13, 14, 17,
   23, 111, 112, 155, 162, 192, 265, 369
Organizational: extensions: 165-167,
   190, 203
   maze: 113, 121, 123, 126, 153, 165,
      206, 369
   theory: 13, 140, 153, 209, 298n

Oriental Jews: 54-58, 84, 97, 138, 190,
   207, 306, 330, 354-358, 367n. See
   Immigrants.
   mobility of: 308, 327
   and religion: 56, 83, 84, 93, 144
   as target group: 136-137, 139, 165,
      174, 185, 203, 206, 240-241, 255,
      260
Overlap: See Redundancy.

Palestine: 40, 77n, 91, 133. See
   Arab-Israeli Conflict.
   and immigration: 36, 52
   and partition plan: 49, 64, 91
   settlements in: 36, 39, 113
Palestine Jewish Colonization
   Association: 113
Palmach: 105, 166, 200, 273, 282, 285,
   311
Participation: 8, 24-27, 138, 152, 159,
   161, 301, 328-359, 366n, 373-374,
   376-377; definition of: 24, 328.
   See Efficacy.
   active: 24, 329, 332, 346, 365
   committed: 25-27, 29, 339-347, 362,
      374-275
   modes of: 25-27, 331-347, 365, 373,
      375, 377
   in nondemocratic systems: 15, 31,
      342, 347, 364, 366n
   responsive: 25-27, 29, 332-339, 347,
      359, 361, 364, 374-375
Parties: 57, 71-74, 113-115, 118,
   119-120, 134, 138, 148, 150, 152,
   159-188, 316, 332, 343, 369-370
   access to: 314-318
   as channels: 13-15, 138, 161-163,
      254-256, 373
   party machine: 172, 175, 188n, 356
   Agudat Israel: 52-53, 59, 62, 64,
      72-74, 83, 135, 171, 248, 352-354
   Ahdut-HaAvoda: 72-73, 114, 115,
      119, 171, 176, 184, 244, 250, 263n,
      287
   Alignment/Labor Party: 72-73, 114,
      119, 166, 168, 176, 186, 287, 303,
      315, 341, 367n; internal structure:
      176, 181, 188n, 286
   Arab Lists: 72, 74, 197, 318, 349-352
   Citizens' Rights Movement: 72

Communist Parties: 59, 72, 74, 133, 171, 184, 185, 186, 196, 235, 240, 250, 262, 294, 315, 350-352, 367n
Democratic Movement for Change (DMC): 72, 73, 74, 115, 178, 367n
Free Center: 72
Gahal: 72, 170, 350
General Zionists: 59, 63, 72-73, 119, 158n, 167, 170, 171, 174, 184, 186, 196, 197, 226, 255, 303, 304, 311, 362
Haolam Hazeh: 72, 183, 242
Herut: 59, 61, 62-63, 64, 72-73, 100, 115, 122, 166, 167, 171, 173, 174, 184, 186, 196, 200, 244, 250, 262, 276, 285, 286, 294, 320, 324
Liberals: 72, 73. See General Zionists.
Likud: 59, 72-74, 171
Mapai: in Israel: 60, 62-63, 72-74, 121, 122, 125, 133, 140, 151, 156, 164, 166-171, 173-184 (passim), 187, 197, 201, 211, 213, 225-232 (passim), 239, 246, 249, 251, 255, 262, 283, 285-287, 315, 317, 342, 350, 351, 356, 357, 359, 362, 365, 370; in yishuv: 59-60, 65, 73, 114-117, 119, 125, 166, 187, 194, 225, 234, 282, 303
Mapam: 62, 63, 65, 72-73, 115, 133, 170, 171, 184, 197, 200, 230, 235, 240, 246, 248, 250, 302, 350, 351
National Religious Party (NRP): 53-54, 59, 62, 72-74, 85, 166, 171, 173, 179, 184, 197, 216, 226, 232, 262, 303, 318, 350, 353, 354
Poalei Agudat Israel: 52-54, 59, 62, 72, 74, 83, 135, 171, 197, 248, 352-354
Progressives (Independent Liberals): 71, 72, 74, 167, 184, 196, 197, 226, 250, 255, 318, 367n
Rafi: 72-73, 115, 176, 178, 283, 287, 341
State List: 72
Party Key: 75, 77, 122, 125, 141, 148, 182, 196, 197, 284, 294
Peace Treaty (Israel-Egypt): 38
Penetration: 8, 131-140, 160, 307, 326, 335, 346, 369, 371; definition of: 16, 132. See Steering Capacity.

by bureaucracy: 199-209
and cooptation: 205, 212-213, 295, 313, 317, 341
by mass media: 231-242
by parties: 165-177
Peres, Shimon: 175, 176
Periphery: 13-16, 23, 126, 130-146, 148-152, 161, 179, 186, 203, 271, 275-276, 318, 347, 358-359, 365, 369, 375; definition of: 15, 130-131. See Groups, Peripheral.
Pioneering: 40, 42, 43, 55, 99, 102-106 (passim), 117, 129, 137, 138, 206, 233, 305. See Ideologies.
State-encouraged: 142-143, 276. See Statism.
Police: 65, 69, 117, 195, 198, 200, 315
Policy-Making: See Decision-Making.
Political Actors: See Leadership.
Political Camps: 57-64, 76, 106, 124-125, 141, 149, 156, 157n, 178, 233, 256, 258, 285
Political Center: 17-18, 23, 25, 31, 107, 112-130, 139, 146-153, 155-157, 160, 161, 175, 190, 199, 243, 266-267, 276, 288, 292, 325, 359, 369, 375; definition of: 14, 112
secondary centers: 13-14, 114, 116, 121, 125-127, 148-151, 163, 200, 246, 275-276, 311, 369; definition of: 14, 126
affiliated organizations: 157n, 164, 167
Political Channels: See Channels.
Political Culture: 30, 33n, 57, 107, 128, 136, 137, 141, 145, 213, 272, 305, 314, 320, 336, 339, 343
Political Development: 8-20, 77n, 107, 162-163, 183, 188n, 193, 194, 199, 221, 263, 269, 287-297, 368-372, 375, 377; definition of: 19, 265. See Democratic Political Development.
Political Institutions: See Institution-Building, Organizations.
Political Jokes: 198, 331, 366n
Political Network: See Network.
Political Order: 5, 131, 172, 245, 292-293

Political Stability: 47, 128, 140, 156,
    177, 180, 186, 187, 192, 209,
    211-213, 261-263, 270, 280, 285,
    291-296, 365, 374, 375. See
    Breakdown.
Political System (Polity): 1-2, 81, 131,
    378; definition of: 4-6
    of Israel, formal: 64-74, 77n
    of Jews: 40, 80-81
Power: 4-5, 10, 13, 14, 25, 153, 161, 195.
    See Symbols.
    political: 1-2, 17, 23, 81, 113, 114,
    127, 132, 163, 307, 341
Presidents (of Israel): 66, 67, 100, 104,
    106, 238, 293
Press, Freedom of: 65, 75, 189, 230
Professional Associations: See
    Associations.
Propaganda: 13, 15, 164, 213, 220, 222,
    240, 246, 263n, 301, 323
Provisional Council: 65, 120, 250, 293
Provisional Government: 61, 65, 120,
    188n, 195, 273
Public Opinion: 164, 249, 259, 278,
    330, 347, 363
Public Relations: 220, 228, 236, 256,
    301

Rabbinical Courts: 51, 53, 274
Rabin, Itzhak: 99, 212, 299n
Radio: 16, 23, 117, 133, 221, 224, 227,
    237-239, 244, 245, 247, 253,
    255-256, 324, 366n
Recruitment: bureaucratic: 212-213,
    321. See Bureaucracy.
    political: 8, 164. See Leadership.
Redundancy and Overlap (in
    Network): 122, 127, 147, 153-155,
    166, 170, 179, 200, 203, 296, 376
Regulation: 193, 204-205, 214, 268
    of mass media: 257-259
Religion: 14, 48, 50-54, 56, 62, 81-110
    (passim), 117, 272
    and State: 51, 54, 66, 68, 78n, 99,
    135, 165, 273, 274, 353-354, 361
    status quo: 53-54, 62, 274, 354
Religious: camp: 59-64, 70-76,
    106-107, 114, 129, 146, 158n, 304
    cleavage: 50-54, 57, 58, 215, 274,
    354

Representatives Assembly (of
    yishuv): 60, 80, 117-118, 168, 169,
    303
Resources: distribution: 61, 140, 148,
    150, 182, 211, 268, 307, 341
    political: 18, 21, 22, 25, 27, 36,
    124-126, 131, 147-150, 164, 171,
    307, 364
Revisionist Movement: 58, 59, 61, 65,
    73, 100, 120, 121, 167, 226, 234,
    250, 273, 275, 281-282, 284, 285,
    302, 303, 304
Right to Know: 28, 75, 231, 249, 301,
    361, 364, 372
Rumors: 17, 280, 299n

Sadat, Anwar: 299n
Sapir, Pinhas: 130, 366n
Secondary Centers: See Political
    Center.
Secrecy: 68, 149, 213, 229-231, 243,
    249, 257-258, 363
Security: 37, 68, 76, 78n, 106, 117, 121,
    125, 130, 142, 149, 165, 172,
    228-231, 244, 268, 288
    secret service: 197, 246
Settlements: in Israel: 70, 78n, 273,
    295, 319, 349
    in Palestine: 36, 39, 43, 55, 58, 69,
    80, 92, 104, 113, 118
Sharett, Moshe: 65, 130, 165, 181, 237,
    239, 246, 283
Shazar, Zalman: 100, 130
Sinai: 38, 285
Socialism: 44, 47, 58, 62, 90, 100, 103,
    104-106, 148, 184, 194, 234, 303.
    See Ideologies, Zionism.
Socialization, Political: 2, 7, 103,
    109n, 135, 136, 137, 138, 140-146,
    161, 172; definition of: 140
    by bureaucracy: 207-208
    in families: 138, 141, 144-146, 309
    by mass media: 233, 238, 264n, 309
    in military: 143, 145, 146, 161, 208,
    216, 309
    by parties: 143, 146, 161
    in places of work: 17, 161, 309
    in schools: 12, 17, 22, 54, 92, 103,
    104, 138, 141, 144-146, 215, 272,
    309

Soviet Union: 49, 103, 115, 183, 184, 186, 221, 302
Sports: 54, 58, 106, 144, 166, 228, 245, 319
Stability: See Political stability.
Standard of Living: 47, 150, 152, 205
State-Building: 8, 10, 37, 77n, 108, 114
State Sovereignty: 39, 42, 105-107, 210
Statism (Mamlachtiut): 106, 131, 141-144, 275
Steering: 13, 18-20, 21, 25-26, 147, 155, 206, 237, 261-263, 265-299, 347, 359; definition of: 1, 8. See Political Development.
   capacity: 14, 18-19, 21, 27, 133, 150, 159, 191, 204, 231, 263, 269-297, 298n, 347, 365, 368-372, 374-376, 378; definition of: 19
   impact on: 21, 24, 27-31, 301, 326, 328, 330, 339, 359-365, 372-375. See Democratic Political Development.
   and outcome: 266, 268-269, 288-296. See Decision-Making.
   pathologies: 267, 296
   profiles: 297-298, 365, 376
   programmed: 1, 30, 365
Suez Canal: 38
Symbols: 2, 8, 10, 11, 14, 19, 31, 89, 109n, 111, 118, 124, 140, 273-274, 329, 331
   agricultural: 58, 99, 103, 104, 106, 210
   anthem: 102, 274
   archaeology: 93, 101, 103, 105, 109n, 172, 247
   ceremonies: 101
   coins and stamps: 93, 101, 103, 110n
   emblem: 93, 101-102
   flag: 102, 106, 210, 247
   holidays and the Sabbath: 52, 98-100, 102, 103, 105
   military: 39, 102, 105, 142, 210, 247, 274
   pageants: 104
   political: 19, 101-107, 184, 210, 222, 245, 247, 262
   religious: 90, 98, 102, 304
   of state: 66, 93, 98, 101, 104, 105-107, 178, 210, 217n, 236, 246-247, 272-274, 297

Syria: 38
Systems Theory: 13, 298n. See Political Systems

Target Groups: 14, 17, 132-139, 177, 201, 279, 280, 369
   and bureaucracy: 214-217
   and mass media: 235, 239-242, 259-260
   and parties: 172, 185-187
Taxation: 15, 22, 37, 52, 65, 118, 134, 138, 147, 158n, 198, 213, 315
Tel-Aviv: 43, 123, 223, 233, 276
Television: 12, 16, 23, 78n, 99, 221, 223, 239, 253, 322, 323
Trade Unions: See Histadrut.
Transportation: 70, 77n, 99, 160, 223, 253, 341
Turkey: 91, 95

Uganda: Jewish State in: 86
Ultra-Orthodox: 50-54, 81, 83, 95, 96, 99, 108, 146, 153, 205, 271, 274, 304, 359. See Neturei-Karta.
   as peripheral group: 352-355
   as target group: 133-134, 139, 185, 215, 260
United Nations: 49, 64, 91, 106, 175, 188n
United States: 80, 119, 168, 172, 175, 245, 314, 335
Universities: 44, 70, 95, 122, 150, 224
Urbanization: 22, 44-45, 137, 141, 160, 275. See Mobility.

Violence: 10, 24, 120, 155, 166, 273, 281, 291, 293, 353, 356-357
Voluntary: citizens' behavior: 17, 23, 24, 142. See Access, Participation.
   political system in yishuv: 80, 144, 156, 164, 186, 267, 271
Volunteers' Group (Shurat Hamitnadvim): 183, 188n, 312
Voting: 13, 17, 23, 25, 59, 164, 187, 315. See Elections.
   as participation: 25-27, 332-335, 377
   stable patterns: 178, 185, 356
   turnout: 333-335

Wadi Salib, riots: 283, 356-357
Wars: 18, 37-39, 67, 105, 133, 245, 268,
    278, 281, 293
  of 1947-1949: 37, 38, 42, 49-50, 267,
    268, 284, 285
  of 1956: 38, 145, 228, 258, 268, 285
  of 1967: 32, 38, 64, 87, 133, 138, 145,
    176, 240, 258, 268, 283, 286, 295,
    299n
  of 1969-1970: 38
  of 1973: 38, 74, 78n, 138, 139, 268,
    363
Weizmann, Haim: 100, 129
Welfare Services: 41, 44-47, 70, 109n,
    118, 121, 122, 135, 142, 152
West Bank: 38, 50, 78n, 120, 240
Western, countries: 39, 63, 198, 272,
    300
  Jews: 48, 53, 54-58, 97, 258, 335,
    354-355; as target group: 240-241.
    See Immigration.
Women's Organization: 315
World War II: 36, 43, 48, 55, 97, 103,
    105, 106, 245, 285
Workers, committees: 57, 73, 116, 117,
    153, 166
  councils: 116, 156, 164, 166, 174, 181,
    317, 342, 356. See Histadrut.

Yaari, Meir: 246
Yishuv, languages: 94-95
  mass media in: 223, 226-227,
    231-236
  old: 55, 94, 271, 305, 367n
  parties and politics: 58-65, 72-76
    (passim), 138, 141, 161-162, 297

political institutions: 60, 69-71,
    112-120, 124-126, 146, 157, 179,
    193-195, 202, 273, 275, 284, 303
  voluntary community: 61, 75, 104,
    141, 148, 194, 199
Young People: 143, 145-146, 158n,
    175, 309-310
  as target group: 137-138, 139, 141,
    166, 173, 185, 208, 216, 241, 260
Youth Movements: 23, 54, 104, 137,
    138, 141, 142, 146, 157n, 161, 166,
    167, 172, 208, 216, 311

Zionism: as common denominator:
    54, 58, 59-60, 61, 88-89, 108. See
    Consensus.
  as ideology: 42, 55, 58, 81, 88-109,
    145, 165, 244, 302-305, 359
  and non-Zionists in Diaspora: 81,
    83-84, 266, 298n
  and non-Zionists in Israel: 53, 59,
    115, 247, 352. See Arabs,
    Neturei-Karta, Ultra-Orthodox.
  varieties of: 85-86, 129, 302, 326n
Zionist: Congress: 48, 61, 69, 80-81,
    86, 94, 113, 119, 124, 194, 342
  Executive: 69-70, 119
  Movement: 10, 36-37, 39-40, 42,
    48-49, 53-58 (passim), 80, 85-86,
    88, 118, 120, 124-126, 132, 266,
    281, 302, 303-304
  New Federation: 59, 120, 282
  Organizations: 61, 69, 77, 113, 114,
    116, 118-119, 120, 121, 122, 124,
    134, 166, 181, 272, 273, 282

ABOUT THE AUTHOR

Itzhak Galnoor is Head of the Political Science Department, Hebrew University of Jerusalem (1979-1981). He has taught and conducted research in the United States, Canada, and Great Britain, and has written on Israeli politics, comparative government and administration, and political communications. His most recent publications include "Transformation in the Israeli Political System Since the Yom Kippur War," in A. Arian (ed.), *The Elections in Israel — 1977* (Jerusalem: Academic Press, 1980); *Can Planning Replace Politics? The Israeli Experience* (The Hague: M. Nijhoff, 1980; coauthor); and *Government Secrecy in Democracies* (New York: Harper & Row, 1977; editor)

I AM GONNA TELL

One Mother's Fight for Justice After
Discovering Her Child's Sexual Abuse

Jane T. Doe

iUniverse LLC
Bloomington

I Am Gonna Tell
One Mother's Fight for Justice After Discovering Her Child's Sexual Abuse

iUniverse books may be ordered through booksellers or by contacting:

iUniverse LLC
1663 Liberty Drive
Bloomington, IN 47403
www.iuniverse.com
1-800-Authors (1-800-288-4677)

ISBN: 978-1-4917-1096-8 (sc)
ISBN: 978-1-4917-1098-2 (hc)
ISBN: 978-1-4917-1097-5 (e)

Library of Congress Control Number: 2013918814

Printed in the United States of America.

iUniverse rev. date: 11/11/2013

PREFACE

I say the word "I" a lot in this book. I say this not because I think this
has happened to me or that *I* am the victim; I am fully aware that
my daughter, Michelle, is the victim. I say "My walk through Hell,"
because everything is depending on me now. It's my job to do what
is right, it's my job to believe and protect my daughter, it's my job to
help her, it's my job to know this has happened to my daughter, but
it's also my job to pretend like everything is fine and will be well. My
job is to help all my kids through this; it was my deserving burden
to know that as their mother, I have failed so miserably that I don't
deserve to live, to smile, to ever be happy, but only to endure the
rest of my life knowing that this happened to her. I will suffer and
loathe myself to the end of my days, but all the time I will pretend
that I am fine for the sake of those around me.

In the past, I often said to people with arrogance how I would
make sure that none of my kids ever became one of those statistics.
Since my kids could talk, I prided myself on the fact that I educated
them, watched over them with men, all men, any man or any

woman, regardless of family or friend relation. I watched, I talked, I informed, and I educated. It would never, ever happen to one of mine. NEVER. I was a super freak when it came to this. And I was so sure this would never touch our family. I was an idiot. Nobody can watch twenty four hours a day or seven days a week. There are way too many of the "evil ones" out there. And make no mistake, as I say that, my blame does not ease.

There were times when my family members or friends would say, "Michelle is exactly like you! She looks like you, walks like you, talks like you, everything!" I would retort back, "My daughter will never be like me, she will never bear the burdens that I do. She will be so much better than me, she will never ever have my life." They would stare back at me as if I had just slapped them across the face, and really I had. They had no idea of what secrets I kept. I felt so strongly convicted with what I was saying that I always said it a bit too aggressively. And there I was, watching Michelle become exactly like me. She had her secrets too. And I was so ashamed.

THE PREPARATION

On Saturday night I had a dream; it was a bizarre, disturbing, and beautiful dream all at the same time. Jesus came down from Heaven and brought me up from the Earth to meet somewhere in between worlds. He stood right next to me so close that his body was part of mine. I couldn't see his face, but I knew him and who he was. He spoke to me saying, "Jane, you have to go to Hell for a while." I remember I became slightly confused. I didn't know what I had done, but I trusted him and listened to what He had to tell me. He was pointing at a thick orange line and in it was a set of numbers. There was nothing else around us; it was just Jesus, me and the orange line. He continued saying, "You will go to Hell. It won't be forever, just for a time. Then, Jane, you will come back." I had some relief then, but I was definitely afraid. He paused for a moment so that the reality of what he was saying could sink into my soul. He finished then stating very clearly, "Although you have to go for a while I want you to know, *I will be there* with you every step of the way. I won't leave you, I will stay with you, I'll be right there."

Comfort rushed through my body.

And then . . . I woke up.

This story is based on true events; however, names, places and descriptions have been changed.

1

We were your typical family next door. I had a routine type of life and I liked it that way. My days consisted of waking up in the early morning, getting my youngest out of bed, fighting with the kids to brush their teeth, grabbing my morning coffee drink, kissing my handsome husband goodbye as he left for work, taking my three kids to school and going to work myself. Sometimes we had my husband's three kids with us too and that made the days crazier than usual. Friends and family referred to us as *The Brady Bunch* when we were all together. On the weekends, we would do some kind of family activity: clean the house, catch up on the laundry, watch a movie or two, attend church and be the basic, happy family from next door. It was challenging at times and very routine, but to me, it was heaven. My life was perfect.

It was a Monday just like any other Monday. I was at work when my cell phone rang. I answered it. My twelve year old daughter's middle school was calling to verify my home address. Why were they calling? They knew my parents' address. It was the address I used so my kids could go to school in that district. I irritably confirmed the address of my parents' home and hung up the phone. I hated being interrupted at work for no good reason. If it had been an emergency, that would have been one thing, but to confirm an address was not what I would consider an urgent matter. I continued thinking, "That was a very odd phone call." I wondered if they knew I actually lived a few blocks away in another school district and were busting me for it. I certainly wasn't alone in what I did. Parents did that every day in order for their kids to attend the better schools. My concern over the call came and went, and I finished my day in ignorant bliss.

I did not think anymore about the earlier phone call from school. When I got off work and ended the daily routine of pushing papers around my desk, I proceeded to my parents' home. This was where my children would be waiting for me to pick them up at 4:05 pm, as usual. As I pulled up the driveway I received another phone call on my cell phone; this time from a social worker named Karen. She informed me that she was on her way to my parents' home and would need to meet and interview my two boys. She went on to tell me she had already met with my daughter, Michelle, and after she completed the interviews with my sons, Will and Aidan, she would meet with me to explain what exactly was going on. She tried to reassure me that at this time, it wasn't anything I needed to worry about. I took that reassurance. "Don't borrow trouble, Jane," I thought. "If she says it's no big deal then it's no big deal." Although I must admit even with her reassurance, my heart started pounding quite rapidly.

Karen arrived at my parents' home shortly after I did. She was about my age, late 30s, but she had long, brown hair. She stood about 5'6" and her build was on the thin side. She seemed very pleasant and easy to talk to. Under different circumstances, she seemed like someone I would want to be friends with and meet periodically for coffee and "girl talk." She was completely disarming. I had no problems letting my kids talk with her. I told them they could tell her anything they wanted to, or anything she wanted to know, because we had absolutely nothing to hide.

Karen said they needed to go someplace private to talk. We decided the back patio was the best place as it offered the most privacy. My daughter, Michelle, had already been "interviewed" at school and so my oldest son, Will, spoke with Karen first. It felt like hours before he came in and my youngest son, Aidan was asked to go out. Actually, it was only ten minutes or so, but as I sat and tried to act cool, calm and collected,—I was in a state of panic. My mind raced as I tried to think of what this could possibly be about. Aidan was only interviewed for about 5 minutes and I was so relieved when it was my turn. Finally, I would find out what this was all about. It was worse than my worst nightmare.

Karen began. A friend of a friend of a friend reported that my daughter, Michelle, told her that her step-father, Jake, had been touching her "private parts." Before I had time to react, she added that it was more than likely a mistake. BAM!!! Wha . . . . huh? Whoa! Instantly everything closed in around me. I had an overwhelming fear coupled with a slap of shock, a slice of denial and topped off with a speck of relief, all in an instant that this was all, "no big deal and probably just a mistake."

Karen explained that the school had called in to report it to the social services agency and that is how she came to be sitting at my parents' home, outside on the back patio. Again, she tried to reassure me that this was more than likely a mistake. My boys had denied that anything inappropriate was happening at home. My daughter, Michelle, had reacted normally for someone her age when interviewed at school. She, too, had denied everything. She denied saying anything to anyone, denied those things were taking place, and denied having any problems with her stepfather. I let relief wash over me like a soothing, flowing waterfall and allowed that to calm me down. I so much wanted this to be something my daughter said to someone to see what they would say or what they would do, or . . . I couldn't think of any logical reason why anyone would say this if it wasn't true, but this was just a mistake, right? It was some kind of misunderstanding, misinterpretation, misguided torpedo of hate or gossip or jealousy, just a mistake. My mind continued trying to think of reasons why she would say that or why someone would say she said that if she hadn't, but I couldn't. My mind just went blank. I needed this to be a mistake so, I simply grabbed on to the words the social worker had said to me that this was all just a false accusation, just-a-mistake.

As I talked with Karen, alarms exploded in my mind. I knew things about my husband's family, but decided to keep those secrets quiet for now. Things like the fact that my husband comes from two generations of child molesters. I know, I know, you're thinking, "What an idiot." My husband's sister admitted she was molested by her father and grandfather. But my daughter was denying everything and denying she had talked to anyone and said anything to anyone. So I was A-okay. This was all a lie, an untruth, a misunderstanding. Again I held on to that as if it was the last life boat leaving the Titanic. I remained focused on the bottom line: that this was just a simple mistake. So I kept my mouth shut and turned a deaf ear to those alarms I heard blaring in my head. "We're good, we are all fine, nothing is wrong here, we're good," I kept screaming internally.

Karen suggested that after she left, I should have a long private talk with Michelle. She told me I should keep a watchful eye out for certain changes. Things like if Michelle stopped wanting to be around Jake and grades in school falling inexplicably, just to name a few. I realized that these were things that had already happened, but I still remained silent. I just wanted Karen to leave so I could sort this all out. She said I needed to make sure all of the lines of communication were open. She said I needed to make sure I still had the kind of relationship that I thought I had with Michelle. "Reassure her that she can tell you anything," Karen kept saying. "Make sure she knows she can trust you. Make sure she understands that you will believe her." I heard her words. It seemed like she still had some doubts that all this was a "mistake" and that did not sit well with me.

I defensively informed this social worker that I diligently did all those things already and more. I have always watched everyone around my kids; I was like a hawk. I had even been chastised by my family for being overly protective. I was sure nothing like this would ever happen to one of my kids. "None of my kids will ever become a statistic," I said as confidently as I could, but I knew I was on the verge of panic. I was trying to convince myself just as much as I was trying to convince her that I was a good mother.

I related the story of how many years ago I had dated a guy I had known for fifteen years. During one of his visits I got a creepy feeling that he liked my daughter more than he liked me. He bought her presents like he he had with me and I felt he was actually more comfortable around her. So off we went to the airport where I barely slowed the car down for him to get out. I popped the trunk, let him remove his bags and as he closed the trunk, I sped off and never spoke to him again. To this day I don't think he knows what happened or why I did what I did. But this was my daughter. What kind of mother would I be if I didn't act on those uneasy feelings? What if something happened to her from this guy? Then I would be as much to blame as the pervert. Case closed, class dismissed. That was how I had dated. That is, before I met and married Jake.

My feathers got ruffled and I puffed up with that false sense of pride and an indignant, condescending attitude as I told Karen that as well as being very careful, I've often asked my daughter questions. I've educated my children about this type of thing and have been very cautious. I was a mother who was going to make sure none of my kids ever had anything like this happen to them. She seemed convinced then or at least she pretended to be and left my parents' house with a promise from me to do what she asked; talk with Michelle. "I am good, we are good, it's all good," I kept privately reassuring myself. However, because of what I knew and wasn't telling Karen, I took her advice and kept my promise to talk to Michelle. This would be where it all started I guess. This was the moment our lives changed forever. This was the start of my walk through Hell, my daughter's nightmare uncovered, my worst fear realized. This was the beginning of the end of my life.

2

Before I went to talk to Michelle, I devised a plan. I would do and say all the correct things and she would respond with all the right answers. I got a glass of water, went to the bathroom and flashed my daughter one of those "mom looks" to let her know she was about to be questioned more thoroughly. With that sharp look I watched her recoil. Something inside my head scolded me and I reprimanded myself for setting up this talk for the outcome I wanted. That was not right. That was not the way to get to the truth of what was happening. When I finished in the bathroom I emerged with a softer expression and sat down next to my daughter, who was already sitting on the floor. That's when I had my first "feeling," about all of this. Something told me that I needed to be gentle, not stern or negative. "Look at her," something said in my mind, "Look at how scared she is." Then the mad mother inside me jumped in and quickly responded, "She better be scared, she's in for it now! I'm going to bust her butt for bringing this drama on us." And again the softer side kicked in saying in a louder voice, "She is just a child and she is scared; back off and listen to her. She may have something to tell you if you are ready to hear it." "If you are ready to hear it," the voice echoed again. These two opposite voices within me had this conversation back and forth in debate of how I was to approach it all. In the end, it was the kinder, gentler, more loving Mother that won and I was grateful for that. Kindness, patience, and understanding were what she desperately needed.

She would be fine, I thought, and I would be fine. I would find out she was fine, and we would then go home and laugh about this stupid and crazy event in our lives. She's fine.

I thought of how I would tell my husband, Jake, and how I needed to choose my words carefully so I didn't hurt his feelings. I thought about Michelle and Jake's relationship, how it seemed so tense lately and I hoped this wouldn't damage it further. A little warning bell rang again in my mind. Her moody, pre-pubescent attitude had already put a strain on them and I wanted to be aware of how this might play out later at home. I did not want their relationship to be any more negative than it had already become. I briefly thought how odd it was that I cared more for Jake's feelings than my own or my daughter's. I wondered when that had happened, how I could have taken on the role of his "keeper and protector," and why did I accept that position. Another alarm rang out.

I asked Michelle what I thought were all the right questions. "Has Jake ever touched you? Has he ever made you feel uncomfortable? Has he ever looked at you in a weird way? Has he ever said anything to you that may have been sexual?" Her responses were the same every time. "No," she said. I asked if she had told someone that Jake had touched her. Again, she said, "No." I repeatedly asked if he had ever done anything like that to her, she said, "No." Every question I asked I thought for sure I would get her pre-teenage attitude of, "Mom, puh-leeeese, this is ridiculous! Leave me alone, it's a waste of time. Come on, of course this stuff isn't true . . . DUH!" I wanted to see her roll her eyes at me, shrug her shoulders, and shake her head in disgust. Instead, all I was getting was a simple and quiet, "No," as she sat perfectly still on the floor, her legs folded up with her knees against her chest and her arms hugging those legs tightly, watching me. And with each question, I watched my daughter withdraw more and more like she was trying to sink in to the floor and disappear. She became more introverted and more afraid. This girl was not my daughter.

Michelle was an incredible, outspoken, creative, adventurous, loud and crazy daughter. She was the one who could sing and dance in front of anyone: family, friends, or strangers. She could not find a rollercoaster big enough, high enough, fast enough, or scary enough, to frighten her. She loved school, had lots of friends, and was a social butterfly. This girl in front of me was not that girl. As I sat and compared these two opposites, the one I remembered and the one I saw before me, I realized that my daughter hadn't been that girl I remembered for a very long time. I wondered when that change took place and how I had missed it. Internally, the warning lights flashed and the alarms rang again telling me, begging me, to wake up to reality. Reluctantly I started to comply.

When I looked at Michelle, she looked like a scared animal, ready to run and hide. Warning! Danger! Those bells and alarms became louder and louder. I desperately tried to get her to tell me it all never happened, to say that this was all some crazy mistake started by a girl that was jealous of her or something like that, because that was really what I wanted to hear. That was the only thing I had prepared myself to hear. The conversation did not go as planned; I was not getting what I wanted or needed. Instead, ice cold water was being thrown in my face with every one of her answers.

I started flashing back to different things that had been going on in our house and I instantly started to piece things together. With that, I again had the feeling my daughter had something to say, but I knew it wasn't going to be what I wanted to hear. I could feel with my heart and with that I decided to let go of my ears. I couldn't listen to what she was saying. Instead, I had to "feel" what she was expressing because those two things were very different. I could see in how she was behaving, reacting, talking, not talking and carrying herself. This girl was my daughter, whether or not she was the fearless girl I remembered, and this girl had something to say. She desperately wanted to tell me, but I needed to be a good mother and get her to a "safe" place where she could talk to me. With no experience with this part, I simply acted on impulse. I took her into the next room for total privacy. I felt the presence of God and Jesus with me and with her. After all, I had been prepared by Him just two days before.

The direct approach definitely didn't work. As hard as I tried, I couldn't get her to say anything. I continued to run on instinct and changed tactics whenever I hit a brick wall. I felt like a wide receiver, dodging and weaving in an attempt to find ways to reach her. I asked what I could do to get her to talk. She said, "I don't know." The alarm rang again, the voice in my mind screaming "OH MY GOD," so loudly in my mind it felt as if my ears were ringing. I knew because of that response she had secrets. My reasoning kicked in and I knew without a doubt at that moment that if there truly wasn't anything to talk about, she would have said, "Get me to talk? God, Mom, I am talking; there's just nothing to say." Only I knew she did have something to say, and I needed to get her feeling safe enough to open up.

I tried not to get frustrated. She was so guarded, so withdrawn and so uncharacteristically introverted. I kept talking, bobbing and weaving at the walls she was putting up. "Would a candy bar do the trick?" I asked with a funny smile on my face, hoping this would lighten the mood and get her to come out of herself a bit. It did, and Michelle smiled, but still said, "No." Again, I was confident there was something more. I then asked her what would keep her from telling me everything.

With those words, she sunk back into herself; I literally watched her recoil into a shell like a turtle and then she said in a very, very timid voice, "I don't know." My heart broke. She said "I don't know." She didn't say, "No, nothing, I'm good. All is well." She said she didn't know what it was that kept her from talking to me. So again, I changed my approach. I told her we could whisper things to each other so that nobody else could hear and they wouldn't know. I started telling her again as I had in the past: that I would always believe her; that I would always choose her; and I would always take her side. Still, she remained withdrawn and timid, which was so unlike my girl. I kept whispering reassurances to no avail. The blockade was up, so again I changed. I simply pleaded with her to tell me what was happening so that I could fix it and make it all go away. I begged her to let me help with whatever was wrong; to give me the chance to fix what was broken. "Give me a chance, believe in me and give me a chance," I cried.

Suddenly, she exploded into a fit of tears. I thought for one brief second that she was laughing. "Oh God, please let it be laughter," I hoped, still clinging to that last shred of denial and ignorant bliss I had been living under. Clearly, she had not just burst into an embarrassed girlish laugh where this was all just a huge mistake. She was literally breaking down. And with that breakdown, she said she was "afraid."

Then I knew without any doubts, this was very real. Denial was over, and my daughter had something extremely important to confide in me. I needed to find a way to get it out, but I thought I was going to vomit. I had to struggle to breathe and to keep my pain from Michelle. I knew that I could not let her see any emotions or reactions. Over and over, I asked what she was afraid of. At first she kept repeating she didn't know. I knew she did know and I had to get it out, as much for my sake as it was for hers. I just held on to her. I decided not to speak. Instead, I just sat there and waited while I squeezed all the love and strength I could into her little body.

Finally, after what felt like an eternity, she whispered to me, "Going to court . . . the police." My heart started to pound harder and I was afraid she could feel it, as she was sticking herself to my chest like a newly sprouted appendage. I tried to slow it down so that Michelle wouldn't know what was happening inside me. My breathing became quite labored, but I wanted desperately to be strong for her. I didn't want her to know how sick I was, how disgusted I was with myself for not seeing this sooner—for not doing something sooner—and how scared I was for her, for what this was going to mean and what the next few days were going to bring to our family. I knew that I shouldn't react to anything she was saying, but my body wasn't cooperating.

I tried the logical, "talk it through" approach first, asking, "What about court scares you?" She clammed up again and I was afraid I had just lost my chance. I thought of those crime dramas on TV. I knew she watched those shows. I knew that was what was running through her mind at the speed of light. I had to put to rest the fears that I suspected she had one at a time since she wasn't telling me outright. I explained to her that real life court is not anything like how it is on TV. I told her the police are not like how they are on TV and neither are detectives. "Things are very different in real life," I said. She looked at me then and I could tell she was listening, hanging onto my words, trying to be reassured, hoping I would say what she needed to hear so she could release all of it. I quickly told her, in a nonchalant manner, that I knew police men and women that I thought were such awesome people. I told her she had had them over for dinner so many times and she just didn't know they were police officers. She said, "Really?" and her tone was different, more alert and much stronger. "Okay, she's back," I thought. "She's back; don't blow it." The pressure was intense to do and say the right things, as I knew I wasn't going to get a second chance. However, I ran out of ideas, tactics, and strategies and my heart was ready to explode. I was about to throw up all over my daughter as we clung to each other and I knew this conversation needed to come to an end. So, I played my last card . . . my final try . . . my one last ditch effort that was all I could think of to do. I lied. I flat out lied.

I slowly and quietly told her that if she told me and whispered it to me, I wouldn't tell anyone else and we could just keep it to ourselves as a Mother and Michelle secret. And with that, surprisingly, she exploded. That was what brought it all out. The dam broke, the geyser gushed, and the volcano erupted. She believed me. It spilled out of her with such shame and fear and violence. She told me it was true, all true and that she had told her best friend, but her best friend swore she didn't tell anyone and . . . She told me it was true. That's all I heard blasting through my head. She said it was all true. It was true. True. TRUE.

I started to die just then. I could feel myself shriveling up like a dying flower, but a desire to know more kept me going. Maybe it was just a misunderstanding? Maybe this was one of "those things." I tried to rationalize what was one of "those things," and although I couldn't come up with one, I just wanted this to be one of "those things." My mind went into a preservation mode and just kept repeating "one of those things." No other explanation, no other reasoning, no definition, just that phrase that could wrap this all up in a package so that our lives could continue on as it was; so that my life could go on as it had.

I steadied my voice and asked her, "What did he do?" Timidly, she said how he would come in to her room at night when she was mostly half asleep and start to "rub" her. Okay, he rubbed her. My mind raced against what I was hearing and tried to think of how that was really innocent and perhaps she had taken it wrong. Then I thought with panic that maybe it was a dream. Or better yet, maybe it was someone else entirely and not my husband at all. Then with such shame and out of complete desperation, I hoped that it was perhaps my oldest son. Yes, I had even wished that it was my son more than my husband. I would sacrifice my son in order to keep the man I thought I knew so well and loved so much. I would choose him over my first born, my own son. My pathetic mind was exploring every possibility it could in order to keep the one I referred to as "my soul mate, the one God made just for me."

I asked her where he would rub her and she said, "He'd start with my back and then go down, all the way down and through to my front . . ." She sobbed and broke apart in my arms. I died inside. I think I actually felt my heart break for both me and my daughter and for totally different reasons. Her sobbing was almost screaming out of her, bordering on hysteria. She clung to me and I squeezed her right back. "God please help me," I prayed. In my mind I yelled for Him to hear me, "GOD HELP ME." The next second I suddenly felt composed. I asked her how many times this had happened, honestly, I was hoping for the "once or twice," answer, which could then be brought back to this being a mistake. Just a mistake. Just a time of where my husband was sleepwalking or . . . something. I was secretly grasping at straws. Instead I got a, "I don't know, about ten, I guess." TEN, I heard ten, she just said ten, the number ten, way after one or two, not three or four, passed five or six all the way to ten. Ten. TEN.

I died again in that moment. How many times could I die in this life? How many times could I feel the life leave my body? My heart shattered to pieces. I had failed. I was a failure. I had one mission, one goal that I clung to my entire adult life to be a good parent, to never let sexual abuse happen to my children and I failed. My insides ripped open and busted apart, I felt my heart explode while beating a thousand times per minute. It was hell. Pure agony unlike anything I had ever experienced, heard, dreamt, or thought about. I died. Trying to breathe was impossible. The air barely came in to my lungs as I knew they were torn open too. My stomach burned and twisted and whatever that was left in there from lunch was trying to come up. This was surely what dying slowly must have felt like. All the while, I knew I deserved this pain. I deserved all of it and more.

Then Michelle looked at me with so much fear again that I was jolted out of my self-loathing. She was about to say something else. In that split second I thought, "What else is she going to say? Oh God, please, I'm not sure how much more I can take." Then she asked me something she was so afraid to ask. She needed to put me to the test. She needed to know if all those times I said all those reassuring things was a lie. She wanted protection from the thing she was most afraid of, something scarier to her than my husband.

"You do believe me don't you?" And there is was. This was her fear; the biggest, baddest, ugliest, monster there was. This was my test. "GOD," I screamed in my head, "Help me. I don't want to believe any of this, I don't want to hear or listen or believe any of it." My mind was reeling and splitting and cracking open, but I replied very slowly and softly, "Of course I do. I will always believe you, I will always choose you; I will always take your side."

She then started to cry in such a different way. I felt her relax in my arms. I felt her relief as her little body went limp. I just sat there and held her, trying to just have a temporary triumph that we had succeeded in getting the truth out. It was out. She was free from bearing the burden alone. She told her secret. That evil, dark, dirty secret that had changed my daughter from the most outgoing, loving, adventurous child to this moody, introverted, secretive, angry and complex female person. My mind wouldn't let me stop there though. It screamed and raced chaotically. I feared my heart pounding must have been hurting her head that it was beating against. She just sobbed ever so softly, oblivious to what was happening in my physical body and my mind. Thank God for that. I was grateful for that.

I told her I was so very proud of her. Inside I screamed, "WHY DIDN'T YOU TELL ME SOONER? WHY DIDN'T YOU CALL OUT FOR ME? WHY DIDN'T YOU TELL HIM, 'NO' OR 'STOP?' WHY? WHY? WHY?" But even as I thought them, I knew none of those questions mattered. I had done the right thing, said the right things, and would continue to do the right things. I just told her I loved her so much, and I'm so glad she told someone and that I was so thankful that person told someone. We sat together on the loveseat in the living room and cried. I held on to her for life and breath and she did the same to me. As we cried she asked if we could stay at Grandma's house and live there. I reassured her that we would never go back to our house and she would never have to see Jake again. Michelle was so fragile and I didn't know if what I was saying was entirely true or not, but in her delicate, most vulnerable state, I knew she needed to feel safe and comforted.

About a half hour later, Michelle asked to go to her friend's house; she needed another kind of comfort. This was her best friend, Nicole, from next door. The friend she told . . . the one I loved, and perhaps now hated, but was grateful towards for telling. "Yes, go." I whispered. And off she went, still upset, but at the same time relieved and probably a million other emotions I'll never know about. I wanted her to be a kid. "Go be a child," I whispered to myself. "Be an innocent child," although I knew those days had been taken from her a long time ago.

3

I struggled with feeling like a zombie: cold, numb, and dead. Then, my heart would begin racing at the speed of light, threatening to burst out of my chest. An internal meltdown was hidden under a fake smile for the sake of my daughter's well being. As I went through the motions, I remembered a movie I had seen where a man and his wife had the most wonderful, loving marriage and lots of beautiful children. However, one of the daughters had shown mixed signals for her father much like the relationship between Michelle and Jake. The girl in the movie had tried to talk to her mother one night while being tucked into bed. That mother was in denial. She didn't listen to what her daughter was trying to tell her. I remember knowing what that girl wanted to say—it seemed to be so obvious. It was horrible to watch then and even worse to see how my life was currently mirroring this movie. It was called, *Liar Liar Between Father and Daughter.*

I remembered my own experience and doing that denial thing too when Michelle had tried to tell me in her own way. I didn't listen either. My memory started to place images and replay events in my conscious mind; I couldn't believe what I was seeing. I couldn't believe I had been so stupid. I couldn't understand how someone so smart could deny everything that was so obvious. How could this happen? How could I have not seen or recognized what was happening right in front of me? I started getting hit with one memory after another of Michelle trying to tell me. Those small and subtle signals were there, but I just kept wrapping it up in a nice package of, "Oh she's going through puberty and is hormonal and becoming modest and doesn't want him around her anymore." Or when she came up behind me and grabbed or patted my bum. I would tell her, "That is called unwanted touching and is not allowed." She would sort of awkwardly giggle and reply, "Well, that's what Jake does." I would always tell her in quick retort, "Yes, but he's my husband." I instantly thought she meant that is what she saw him doing to me, not what he was doing to her. I never even thought of any other reason for what she was saying and doing. I had rationalized everything. I put it in a place so that I could continue living the nice life I had created. I stayed in denial, and apparently I loved it there.

I felt each slap in the face and every punch in my gut with all the memories of how she tried to tell me. I must have been the world's stupidest person. The signs I missed previously slammed, kicked, and stung me. My head flung from side to side as my eyes squinted shut. Weird sounds escaped my mouth. I looked like someone being smacked around by a ghost. I couldn't stop the thoughts or these waking nightmares of everything I had missed or, more accurately, dismissed. One by one they came: relentless and unstoppable, taking no mercy as they physically pummeled my body, mind, and spirit.

Internally, I began to list the signs I had missed:

1. My daughter had become increasingly and violently modest of her body, even in front of me. She would lash out and yell if someone caught her changing clothes. I attributed that to puberty. After all, that seemed normal for her age.

2. She started locking her bedroom door no matter how much I scolded her for it. I punished her because I worried that if I needed to come in at night or if the house caught on fire, I better be able to get in. Jake would tell me when she locked her door innocently saying, "I heard Michelle go into her room tonight and lock her door, is that okay?" No matter how much trouble she got into, she would not obey me. She wanted privacy and I justified that as understandable because she was growing up.

3. She would not shower anymore. She smelled. She fought with me over it and when she would cave in, she did it only when I was right there in the next room watching TV; those showers were so fast, it was no wonder her body still smelled afterwards. I thought it was a puberty thing since Jake's own daughters went through the same "phase" when we met and moved in together. Only recently did they seem to "grow out of that." And so Michelle would grow out of it too, someday.

4. When dressing for bed on those few times Jake wasn't home yet and her door was unlocked, I caught Michelle putting a lot of clothes and undergarments on before putting on her pajamas. When I asked why she was layering her clothes, she just said she didn't know and that it just made her more comfortable. "Okay," I thought, "I have a weird daughter; she likes a lot of clothes on." Once again, *puberty* was my answer, that wonderfully neat package I could tie up in a pretty bow so that I could continue on with my ignorant life.

5. Whenever I left, she wanted to go with me, even if I was going somewhere she hated to go to in the past. If I wouldn't let her come with me she pleaded to go to a friend's house. I thought she just missed me or needed constant attention.

6. Once, she very timidly told me one day that Jake came into her room and rubbed her back and that it made her feel uncomfortable. I told her I would take care of that and the

fear and relief that washed over her face was way too much for something so innocent. When I repeated to him what she said, and admonished him that he better not do that anymore, he nonchalantly replied, "Oh, okay." So with that, it was never given any more thought. He didn't cower or blow up or act like he had done anything wrong. I never thought, "Why in the hell was he going in there to rub her back?" My selfish mind wouldn't face reality and simply thought, "He's such a kind and loving man to these girls, what a good father."

7.   Michelle made a comment in front of a friend of mine, "I don't want Mom and Jake together because he is way too hairy." I passed that off as his arms and legs were too hairy. I even asked her about it with the answer in the question: "You meant his arms and legs were too hairy, right, Honey?"

8.   A few months earlier, Jake and I split for several months because the kids weren't getting along and Michelle was begging me to leave. Later, when we reconciled, Michelle was upset and didn't want him coming over to our apartment, and didn't want us to get back together. However, she saw me crying for him every day during that time. The way Michelle saw it, my pain and suffering would end if we reunited, so she never said why she wanted us apart. She was going to unselfishly and quietly put herself in danger for her mother's happiness, but she was the only one of the kids who wasn't for reconciliation and I never asked why.

9.   Michelle now had to sleep with the light on. I thought she must be sneaking to watch scary movies.

10. Michelle had angry outbursts of emotions that were completely irrational and totally violent. Well, only irrational to someone who didn't know what she had been going through. Again: I assumed puberty.

11. Her grades fell suddenly when she used to be such a great student. I thought it must be a difficult adjustment going from grade school to middle school.

12. Michelle started to suffer from nightmares. Again, my excuse was puberty and watching bad TV.

13. She hated Jake. Michelle no longer wanted him around her, and she certainly did not want to be around him. My explanation: "Teenagers: you just can't figure them out."

14. Michelle went from being meticulously clean and organized to having this obstacle course type of mess surrounding her bed. Her room was a nightmare and again, I simply attributed it to her pre-teen changes.

I felt like I was obviously the most selfish, stupid, pathetic, sorry excuse for a mother . . . . and with the internal beating, there was the negative chatter that would come to occupy my thoughts. "I don't deserve to live. This is my fault." Self-loathing came flooding in; that is the only way to describe it. A disgusting, shameful, vile feeling that said this was just as much my fault as it was the sick, twisted man who did it. I wanted to die. I wanted God to send down a bolt of lightning and kill me, to rip open my body and shred it to pieces. I would have taken matters in to my own hands if I wasn't already so consumed and overwhelmed with the violent "wake up" bashing I was going through.

I wished my thoughts would have stopped there, but they didn't. I moved on to all the signs in my husband that I dismissed or put in to a nice category that I could live with. I remembered almost every night making love to Jake and falling asleep in his arms. And then I remembered many times waking up to find him missing from our bed. I would call out to him to find out where he was, perhaps in our bathroom, but he never answered. I would then get up and go out in to the hallway and there he would be coming up the dark stairwell as if he was just returning from downstairs. I knew now though he hadn't been downstairs, he had been right next door; in that bedroom right next door, Michelle's bedroom. But I let it go when this was all happening. I ignored that feeling that something wasn't right and continued to sleep soundly as my daughter was being violated only a few feet away from me time and time again.

I remembered lying in bed sleeping and being woken up by the feeling that someone was watching me. I would catch Jake staring at me inches from my face. He was so close I could smell his breath, feel it blowing hot air on my skin. My eyes would pop open and as I startled him I would ask, "What are you doing?" He would reply, "I was just checking to see if you were asleep." Another punch slammed in to my stomach. How stupid was I? I never questioned this? I never stopped to wonder. What the hell did he care if I was asleep yet or not? Never did I question him. Again, the guilt consumed me.

The movie I had remembered played on in my mind: the mom and dad were intimate all the time—he was a loving and attentive husband. Things were so great on the outside. Then the bomb dropped: the daughter told someone at school that her father was molesting her. The family imploded—everyone took a side with either the father or the daughter. The mother was confused and in between both of them. She was doing the right things for her kids' sake, but she didn't believe it. They had a wonderful marriage and an incredible sex life. How was any of this possible? But it was possible, it was true. It was all true. There was an older daughter, who was grown up and married with her own baby daughter, and she let the father live with her because she was sure he was innocent. She hated her little sister for doing this to their father. That eldest daughter helped him with his legal defense and supported him in every way. My mind replayed this entire movie in my head so vividly I almost needed popcorn and a soda to go along with it. I was dying as I watched my life in that movie I had seen once upon a time. That mother who loved her husband and didn't fully believe her daughter but who couldn't turn her back on all the signs she was now realizing.

When someone would disrespect the father from the movie in such a way, he would grab that child and say in a stern voice, "I'll show you." Then he would take them and rape them in private, when all the while, the mother thought they were just getting a spanking. I remembered when I disrespected my husband or caught him making a stupid mistake, Jake would teasingly grab me and bend me over the couch, the bed, or the drain board and pretend to hump me, all the while saying, "I'll show you." Even before this bomb exploded in my life, I always thought of that movie whenever he did that to me.

There were just as many signs from Jake as there were from Michelle. I just wrapped them up in the cozy blanket called denial. The movie ended where the man was found guilty: he had molested all the children, including the eldest daughter that was helping and supported him. In the end she, too, broke her silence and testified against him. That oldest daughter had hoped it was only her he had molested, since he had promised her that he would never do it again. She had to help him with his legal problems and make her own sister out to be a liar so that she could convince herself that he was a changed man. So she could live with herself for not telling and, in doing so, enabling him to do this to her younger brother and sisters. She had to make this all go away so she could continue to live her life, but she finally broke her silence when she saw signs that the father was turning towards her own child, his grandchild. She saw him for what he really was: a sick, twisted, child-molesting monster. And then the man went to jail.

"Just breathe," I said to myself. "Just breathe. Think of what's next." I had to think of all the things that were yet to come. Would this happen to us? Would there be others out there. Will Jake's sister and father defend him because of their own secrets? I was scared and too tired to fight, but I wanted Jake to pay for what he had done. "Just breathe," I kept telling myself over and over again. My chest was so tight it felt like something heavy was sitting on top of me, pressing against me so that drawing in air was like trying to swim through quicksand. It just wasn't happening.

4

I still had to undo the lie I had told, that beautiful, ugly lie that got Michelle to talk. The one that said we didn't have to tell anyone else. With my newfound information, I needed to make a phone call. I had to call Karen, the social worker, and tell her to come back. I had to call her and tell her that we were, "one of those families—another statistic." But first I had to ask Michelle to give me permission to tell Karen. I didn't want to cause Michelle any more harm or make her feel any more powerless; I needed to make her feel like she was the one making the decisions and in control. How in the world was that going to happen? "Wait, breathe, relax and wait," I kept saying over and over and over again. "Smile, you can do this." I became my own cheerleader. I didn't know how I could take another breath, another step, and put another perky inflection in my voice. After all, I had already died and I was becoming more of a ghost every second.

The words, "I can't," crept in to my mind a lot. "I can't do this . . ." kept whispering in my mind. Other things whispered too; terrible, negative thoughts of how I could just end my pain and be done, that I really didn't have to endure this. Having three kids kept the cheerleader voice coming back though. "I know you can make it. I know you can do it. You can do it." And then, quietly: "I'll stay with you. I won't leave you." I had remembered the dream. He is with me. He prepared me and He thinks I can do this. So I made dinner and I acted as if everything was normal and going to be just fine. I was the best liar I knew. Well, except for my husband, of course.

I still secretly wanted this to be a false accusation. Something a pre-teen does to her step-father because he scolded her and made her go to bed early. I secretly hoped for another breakdown from Michelle, where she would admit to being a liar. In the meantime though, I had to do what was right, just in case. Just in case I had actually raised the bravest child in the world who was a fighter: a strong and brave fighter; a better and more beautiful and stronger person than I could ever hope to be. Just in case this was all true and my daughter truly was the most awesome person I had ever met, I would continue to do what was right. Just in case.

My heart and my head were in the worst conflict I'd ever witnessed. One screamed profanity at me for being so incredibly stupid when all the signs were there. The other one, broken and bleeding, said, "You will lose the only man you ever loved and the one God made for you, your soul mate who you know could never do this to anyone." They pounded on me and whether my heart was going the speed of light or my head swirling with that same relentless pace, I only knew that they were killing me. In the meantime, my daughter needed the benefit of the doubt or else she would die. I have to do the right thing. "I will be with you every step of the way," I remembered Him saying. Then I would breathe. Comfort would wash over me and for brief moments at a time, I could relax and let go.

My phone beeped that I had a text message. It was from my loving, sick, twisted husband. "I'm thinking of someone special . . . can you guess who?" it said. Instantly I was on fire. I felt like some kind of comic book superpower that would say, "Flame on," and their body would be engulfed in flames. My hands curled into claws and my adrenaline kicked into overdrive. My reasoning told me to keep quiet and ignore the phone, but insanity won the battle. I replied in that moment of hot fury: "Probably my daughter, you sick son of a bitch." It was all I could say—all I could think to say—and then my head started to spin. The room began to go dark and unsteady around me. I wanted to kill him and I wanted him to deny it at the same time. But he never did. He never denied it. I kept thinking if that was me, I would be going crazy to talk to that person and let them know I could never do such a thing. If that was me, I would be calling that person to say, "Hey I don't know what that was about, but I can assure you I have never done . . ." He never did that either.

About an hour later my phone started to ring every five minutes for about a half an hour. He left a few strange voicemails, strange in the way that he pretended as if nothing was happening, nothing was going on and that he was simply surprised to go home to an unoccupied house. One voicemail said in a very nice normal tone, "Hi Honey. Uh, what is going on? Can you call me back please? Okay . . . bye." The next one wasn't quite as perky, but still relatively normal saying, "Hello, it's me; can you call me back? I think you have your phone off." The next one was slightly more concerned, "Your brother is here picking up clothes for you and the kids. What is going on? Is everything okay? Can you call me back, please?" And finally in a somewhat shaky voice: "I don't know what this is about: I'm upset, I'm confused, and I deserve a phone call. I deserve that much." It was funny how this was all about him, as was everything else. His concern was first for himself. He successfully played the role of "helpless victim" throughout his entire life. He surrounded himself with people who would take on the role of "mother hen" or "protector." I, too, was one of those people. Somewhere along the way I became his keeper, his mother, anything that would let him play the "victim" and keep me busy being his "guardian."

I felt like I couldn't have any contact with Jake. If I did, I would die. I knew I would kill myself if I saw him or spoke to him and I didn't even want to hear any more voicemails, so I was thankful when the phone quit ringing. I expected him to show up, since he knew where we were: just at Mom and Dad's, just a few short blocks away from our home. He never came, never denied what he had done, never left another voicemail or text message. Just silence. Simple bittersweet silence that I was very thankful for.

I had called my brother, George, earlier during the course of making dinner. I whispered to him what happened so that nobody would hear. So that I didn't even have to hear what I was saying. So that I didn't have to choose my heart or my head. "Just whisper it and that way it's not so real." Who knows where that thinking comes from, but it worked for Michelle and then it worked for me too. He came immediately to help.

He went to our house, saw Jake, and brought some things back to my Mom and Dad's house where this was all taking place. I asked him what Jake was doing and how it went. Even then, I still cared for him in some insane, dysfunctional way. He told me Jake asked him what was happening since he only knew of some sort of sick message about Michelle . . . and my brother responded to him by saying, "I don't know, and I don't want to know; I'm just here because my sister asked me to come and get some things for her and the kids." George said when he left; Jake was in our bedroom crying.

Again, I became confused, filled with emotions that made no sense. I didn't understand why I would care what Jake was doing or how he was handling all this. Something inside me remained his protector or perhaps I was so used to unknowingly being in that role, I just couldn't quit. One insane second I wanted to call him and beg him to talk to me. The next second I wanted to vomit and then the next I wanted to hurt him. After all deranged thoughts had come and gone, I knew that I couldn't see or speak to him ever again.

My brother, George, went home then. Not wanting to do any more or perhaps even know any more. George went home back to his family to cherish what he had there. He had done all he could that night for me and my kids. It was more than anyone could ask for. For that I was grateful.

Over dinner, Michelle asked me what would happen to Jake now. I couldn't believe she brought it up all on her own; this was my chance to lead her in the right direction, to lead her to our next decision. Everything was moving so fast. I responded by saying, "That is entirely up to you. You will have to ask God to help you do what is right, and then you will have to tell me what to do next." She sat quietly playing with her food, so I went on to say, "Unfortunately, child molesters don't molest only one child in their entire life and be done with it. I wish that were true. The sad reality is that they do this to many children and they usually keep on going from victim to victim if they aren't stopped and put in jail . . . but that is up to you to decide, up to you to tell me what to do." As I sat there staring blankly at my plate, trying my best to seem nonchalant about the whole thing, I screamed a prayer at God. I pleaded with Him to give her the strength to tell, the will to fight and the courage to put Jake in jail.

I was desperate for Michelle to do the right thing. The part of me that still harbored thoughts of Jake's innocence wanted Michelle to tell so that I would know this was the truth. If she was willing to step out and tell someone else besides me, who had promised to keep this a secret, then I could be sure that this was real. Although denial would be over, I was already in a state of pathetic resistance. I knew what I knew, but it was too intense to accept easily; I remained in that confusion of demented resistance.

Michelle sat silently nibbling on her dinner. I could feel her pull away; I could see her mind racing and trying to piece things together. She didn't want to be the one responsible for sending someone to jail, but at the same time, she wanted him to go there for her safety's sake. Her little mind was spinning and working. My poor daughter once again had to make an adult decision at only twelve years old. I knew I needed to help her, so I stepped in and said, "We could just call Karen, the social worker, and talk to her and see what she says we should do. I believe she will help us do what we have to—I trust her." Michelle nodded her head slowly in agreement. She wanted me to call the social worker. There was my daughter, so strong, so brave, and only twelve years old.

I was relieved she wanted to tell, but scared for her because I didn't really know what this meant. I didn't know what my daughter was going to have to further suffer through. I've seen all the television shows about what lawyers do to rape victims in court, and witnesses and mothers who drop cases because their children become incapacitated from the stress. Because of my lack of experience, I believed TV and now, I had to convince myself that real life was not like what we see on *Law and Order*. This was easier said than done. What would the next step do to my baby? I had no idea who would come to our house after Karen. Honestly, I didn't really know what the next step actually was. My daughter was scared to death and so was I, but I told her over and over again, "Courageous people and heroes do what they have to do. Even when they are so scared of what they are doing, they do it anyway. Those are the people who are brave. It's because they are so scared, but they do what is right anyway, and that includes you."

"Okay," she said again, "call Karen." With relief, I softly smiled, trying not to make too much out of this huge feat. There she goes again: that amazing daughter of mine, surprising me at every turn. Unfortunately, those thoughts and feelings were short lived. Fear washed over me, and then panic slammed into me like a bus. What outside influences was I opening us up to? What would our lives turn into? Will our future be nothing but court dates, therapy sessions, and interviews? The darkness instantly swept in, tempting me to keep this a secret. Instead, I kept listening to my own private cheerleader. I asked her to cheer louder, harder, and more fervently each time I felt her shrinking and fading. I wanted to block out the thoughts that kept coming. "What would this phone call bring? What would this next step cause?"

I dialed the number from the business card Karen gave me, knowing that it was too late to actually reach her, so I left a detailed message of who I was and what had happened after she left and that she needed to call me ASAP. I explained everything. I really had to acknowledge that this wasn't some sort of nightmare, it was real. I had just taken a huge step into reality. "No going back now," I said to no one but myself. Our journey had officially begun: this was now well on its way, the path mapped out, the road ahead would soon become very clear and I was shaking so badly I had to sit down before I fell down.

That first night at my parents' house was very long. Time seemed to stop and hurry by all at once; I didn't know what was up or down or sideways. A confused part of me missed my husband. I wanted him to comfort me and hold me and tell me it would all be okay, but with the next thought I realized he was the one who caused this. He was the one who hurt my daughter. I felt so sick, alone, ashamed . . . lost. I couldn't believe this was happening. I just wanted it all to go away. I kept thinking of Jake. Inside, I kept wondering what he was doing and what he was thinking. That first night, the first night of many that would find us apart. If only I had kissed him goodbye a little longer. If only I had taken his scent in deeper when I hugged him that morning and squeezed him a little tighter. If only I had known that would be the last time I would be able to touch him in a loving way. And then I would snap back as I remembered what he did, all that my daughter had revealed. Those memories of loving Jake turned black with evil; every memory bringing with it a vile, repulsive feeling. I felt dirty and sick to my stomach for even thinking of him, for even wanting to remember an affectionate feeling about him. I couldn't help it, though. I wanted to remember something good, but every time I did, the thought expanded to who he actually was: a child molester; a predator; a sex offender; a pervert and a monster.

A struggle ensued all night long. I felt so incredibly stupid that I had fallen in love with the thing I hated the most. What was wrong with me? Why couldn't I find a good guy? Why did I keep making mistakes? Why did he prey on me? Why was I such an easy target? What did I do? What did I say? Why can't I ever be happy? One question after another consumed me every minute. My mind reeled with inadequate answers that explained nothing and simply left me worn out. I just wanted it all to end, but this was just the beginning. I had just opened the door and stepped in; I hadn't even started walking down this path and already, I felt like I couldn't go on.

When we went upstairs to bed, my mother told us which rooms were to be ours, but we ended up all cuddling together on the floor in the den. Well, all except for my oldest son, Will. He wasn't having anything to do with this lynching of Jake. He hated his sister for causing this. He was angry and hurt, and most of all, he wanted to be alone. At times, I tried to ask him, "What if it is true, Will? What would you want us to do?" He kept silent, not wanting to acknowledge that that was even a possibility. I remembered that damn movie again. How reality was mirroring that damn movie. How the children were dividing, how the family seemed to split in two as it fell apart.

Later that night, since I couldn't sleep myself, I found Will outside the house sitting on the bricks, crying. He was so angry—fourteen years old, confused, and full of resentment towards his sister and me. I tried to explain that I was doing what I felt was best for us as a family, that that is my job. I told him that I knew he didn't understand and that he was angry, but he would simply have to hang on until the day came when he did understand. The fact that the step-father he loved so much had committed such horrible crimes would destroy him. This was the step-father that had introduced him to mechanics, which had changed his life and showed him how great fathers could really be, but he was also the perverted man who had stolen his sister's childhood. All I could do was wait and watch for the fallout so I could help pick up the pieces. This nightmare continued to affect everyone. It was an ugly, chocking vine that had been planted in my daughter and allowed to grow while I watched and watered and fed it. This weed spread its evil disease through my family and the only thing I could do was painfully watch it, and wait as the horrifying movie of my life played on.

5

The next morning I was up and ready to start strong for the kids. I got them all ready for school in our normal way. I got ready for work, pretending I could go to my job because everything was fine. I told Michelle that Karen may come back to her school and that she needed to tell her the truth this time. She said she was okay and that she was doing okay. I held on to the "okays." They were my band-aids that kept me from bleeding to death.

When I arrived at work, I wondered how I got there. I wondered why everything looked so different: it felt different, smelled different, as if it was all completely foreign. I wondered what I was even doing there. I couldn't think. I couldn't remember why I had come, and then I heard a manager talking to my close friend, Agnes, who was also my boss, "Uh, you better go over there and see what's up with her." Agnes came over to me and I looked into her sweet concerned face and I grabbed a hold of her. I squeezed and couldn't stop myself from squeezing her; I wanted to say it, but I didn't know how. I wanted to scream and yell and kill and hate and love and die. Mostly,

I wanted to die. "Please don't let go or I will die," I cried. My friend was shocked as this was not the ignorantly blissful woman she knew.

I tried to tell her what happened, but I was so sick. My body then felt like it turned black with the evil taint of what had been done to my daughter and to me. I held on to Agnes, hoping to soak in her goodness, but it didn't work. As I held on for life I could feel I was contaminating her (not to mention scaring her). Agnes's eyes were large with shock and she kept asking "what, what, what's happened, what's wrong, what?" Each time I started to speak, to tell her about the disgusting happenings in our home, each time my mouth started to form a word, I thought I would vomit. Eventually and agonizingly I whispered what Jake had been doing to Michelle and then I watched Agnes recoil, her goodness shriveled away to be replaced with a horrified expression. My shame overwhelmed me and I no longer wanted to be touched so I let go. I felt like I was rotting. My skin needed to be peeled from my body so I could feel pain and torture the way my daughter had been tortured for so long. I needed to somehow cut out my heart, but I couldn't touch myself to pull off my skin. It disgusted me to touch my chest where my heart was. It needed to come off and my heart needed to come out. I was self-loathing at its finest. I was breaking and eventually I broke completely.

A common mistake people make in this type of situation is to try and comfort the person in pain. We tend to want to fix it right away or to mask it, or simply apply a bandage. You cannot comfort someone who feels this way. You cannot tell someone they don't deserve to die when they know they do just as you cannot tell someone the sky is purple when clearly it is blue. My friend and boss, Agnes, tried helping me. She wanted to bandage me up, to make it all go away, and to fix it. She started to call all the church members who were in place for times of crisis. She called everyone she knew. Nobody was available. I called the social worker again, but she still wasn't available. I was alone and truly feeling the effects of what had just happened the evening before. It consumed every part of me. From my hair to my toes, from my bowels to my brain and its evil stench was shutting down all my senses and reason and self-preservation. All that remained was agony and self-loathing. And so I loved it; it consumed me and I loved it like my long-lost best friend. This was what I deserved.

The minutes ticked by where nobody called back and I knew it was because I deserved to be alone. I didn't deserve to have anyone comfort or help me. I deserved to die. Agnes pleaded with me to stop the bad things coming out of my mouth, but I couldn't. It was like I was possessed by something demonic. She needed to stop being so nice to me and to start treating me like the thing I was, an enabler who served her daughter up to a child molester. I, too, was just as responsible as the man who did this to my baby. If this knowledge didn't kill me then I would take matters in to my own hands and dispense the justice on my body. My wrists were calling for me to touch them, to scrape them, to cut them open. I could feel this pulsating type of pressure just under the surface that needed to be released. And with that I knew it was time to leave.

As I got up to make my quick exit people suddenly started to call and I started to get answers and make appointments. I talked to my counselor, who had helped me in the past, and then I talked to the leader of our church. Both their sadness and compassion was a momentary life stabilizer. I grabbed on to it. Not because I deserved it, but because I had three kids who needed me. Three kids who would die without me. Three, not one, but three, not just me, but three others who needed their mom. The three people I would paint the smile on my face for. The three kids who would keep me alive for another day. I, at least, had to make sure they would be okay, so that became the plan. I knew I needed to just hang in there until they were cared for and then I could check out. I could end this suffering that was unlike any other I would ever experience.

My church leader gave me the name and number of someone in our congregation that I knew by face, but not by name. She was in my shoes twelve years earlier. She walked where I had walked and felt what I was feeling. She was me a long time ago and yet still alive and well and made it through. I left work and called her. I went to her home. I was still falling apart, but now I was with someone who would let me fall apart without wanting to fix the broken body, mind and spirit sitting before her. She knew what I was feeling and understood the dark place I was in. She lived there at one time too. She knew where I was. I selfishly didn't care that I was bringing up all her demons and pulling her back into that ugly place. I threw her a rope so to speak so she could join me in my hell and she surprisingly came running to where I was, not to try and pull me free of it, but to actually come and join me where I was.

With that support, I cracked, but I had someone physically there with me, someone who had been there before and left it to live again. I grabbed a hold of her and confided in her everything: even my secret desire that this would end up being a lie and I could once again love that man I had built my world around. She understood all of it. I didn't shock her. I didn't disgust her. She just accepted all of it. She just wanted to hold my hand and walk through it with me if I wanted her to. And at that moment I did. I clung to her life as if it were my own. I wanted to give some of this to her to carry for me and in a way she did. Knowing that there was someone who actually survived this was oxygen for my lungs.

The day went by in a flash and then I left my new friend to meet with Karen again at my parent's home, which was now officially our family's home again. She showed up on time and we waited together for Michelle to get home from school. In the meantime, Karen did her best to console me and let me know that this was a normal way to have things come out. It was all going to be okay and there were things in place to help us get through all of it. I believed her. I had to believe her. I had no other choice.

Michelle came home and they went to go "interview" alone upstairs in her room. I waited downstairs with my boys for what seemed like an eternity. I hoped Michelle was being honest and truthful and that she was okay and not breaking down again. I wanted to be there if she was breaking down again. I needed to be there for her if that's what was happening. Finally they emerged from the room. Michelle seemed okay and went to the couch to watch TV while Karen and I spoke. She said that Michelle was consistent with what I told her that Michelle had divulged to me. I found out later that she had actually divulged even more . . .

more of the sick, twisted things he had done. I guessed that even more facts would eventually come out; and that was to be expected. This filth had gotten away with doing these things at least ten times or even more. He undoubtedly progressed further knowing that the incompetent mother who was right next door sleeping away, trusting that wonderful handsome man, and he was free to do as he pleased. I knew that I had a severely cruel reality check coming. That was okay, I deserved it.

Karen informed me that the next step was to call the police and have them come take their official report. Michelle withdrew. She didn't want a policeman coming over. Fear sprung up in her again. I had always tried to get my kids to wave at the firemen in the truck when we sat at a red light next to each other. I tried to get them to wave at policemen who drove by. I tried instilling that respect for them that I was raised with, but clearly I had failed and the goddamn television had won. I wished there were no such thing as cable, or satellite dish, I wished there were still only five channels, with *Lawrence Welk* on Sundays along with bowling or golf. I wanted nothing more than *Popeye* cartoons followed by the family film festival movie and shows like *Happy Days, Eight is Enough, Laverne and Shirley, The Love Boat,* and *Little House on the Prairie.* Stupid me for allowing a satellite television in every room. Going home after school to Grandpa and Grandma's house just to sit and listen while Grandpa watched his Crime Scene CSI dramas, *Law and Order, Cops* and Special Victims Unit stuff. If that's Michelle's frame of reference, God only knows what she's thinking.

"Breathe, think, and calm her down," those whispers said. I did, enough at least so that when the officer came, she went into the other room along with Karen. This time the boys and I went upstairs; while they did their thing downstairs in the dining room. Time went by and by and by and by and then came reality: cold, harsh, and cruel. Karen, Officer Olden, the policeman, and I sat at the dining room table as he told me how consistent my daughter had been. He told me she was very brave and that he had given her his card. He wanted my information and asked for my driver's license. He said that he needed things off of it that he didn't want to ask me. For some reason, I thought that he must need my weight. I didn't know why and I couldn't think clearly, but I didn't care either. I think that he just wanted to let Karen do the talking then, which she did. She told me of a few more things that Michelle had divulged. Gross things and all the while, I could see Jake's face in my face checking to see if I was asleep. As Karen talked, those haunting memories kept flashing through my mind.

How close Jake's face was to mine, only inches away so that I could smell and feel his breath. Checking, searching, waiting for my breathing to be so even and deep that there was no doubt he was now free to go a few feet down the hall, right next door and steal my daughter's innocence. He was the devil, the epitome of a "wolf in sheep's clothing." I wanted to hurt him. I wanted to dig my nails into his flesh and rip it off from head to toe. I wanted to reach in and pull his eyes out so he could never look at me or my daughter again. The hatred consumed me instantly. I wanted my hands to bury into his body and tear every organ out so he could see them. I wanted to rip his intestines out and show him his disgusting filth. I just wanted him to die an agonizingly slow painful death. I wanted to die myself. I wanted the same things done to me because I knew I was certainly just as much to blame.

I confessed to Karen and Officer Olden about Jake's family history. They both stopped and looked over at me and then quickly went back to what they were doing, but I got the message. "Duh, what did you expect?" was the unspoken phrase. I told him that Jake's grandfather was a child molester and he had molested all his daughters. One of the daughters had even had her father's child; that child was a grown man who was slightly retarded from being inbred. I went on to tell him of Jake's father and how he had molested Jake's sisters, all three of them. They asked me with some shock because I hadn't disclosed this earlier, if this was all "confirmed," and I said yes, because at one time, all the kids were removed from the home by Social Services with the exception of my husband Jake.

As they wrote, I went on, disclosing more family secrets. I told them of the anonymous letter I had received a few short months after our wedding. The letter told me to watch out for Jake's father,

Jake Sr. who was a child molester. It went on to say that if Jake really cared for me then he would have told me all of this. He would have protected my children from his father. The letter of course was right. Looking back, I should have left and divorced him right then and there. That letter was absolutely one hundred percent correct and if Jake had loved me, he would have put me and my kids' well-being above his own shame and pain, and told me of his father. How could I have been so stupid? This was just as much my fault as it was Jake's. Officer Olden spoke then, bringing me back to the present time and place. He wanted a copy of that letter and I told him that I would find it and bring it to him.

I wondered what happened to the woman who once upon a time wouldn't consider dating anyone she got the "creeps" from. I silently wondered how I could let all this stuff go. At one time in my life, I was so dedicated to my kids that I put their happiness above my own . . . obviously those days had been over since I met Jake. I let major warning signs go for the sake of my selfish love. I remembered telling my oldest son, Will, during my courtship with Jake, "Don't ruin this for me, do you understand? I want him, for the first time in my life; I want the man and not the other way around." Well, I certainly got what I wanted didn't I? I got that man and everything that came with him. I deserved this. My daughter did not, but I certainly did deserve this.

Again, I felt like the biggest moron this side of creation. I should have moved out right then and there when I received that letter. I should have taken my kids and ran, but Jake denied it all. He told me to call his sister and talk to her about it. He didn't want to discuss it any further. He kept urging me to call her. I wanted to work it out with him directly, but he wasn't having it. I finally let it all go. I let Jake off the hook, but his sister, Julie, had other plans.

Instead of Julie telling me it was all a lie, she told me it was all true and to keep my daughter away from her father, Jake Sr. She told me about the sexual abuse she had endured at the hands of her father and grandfather. She said that Social Services came in and took all the girls out of the home and placed them in foster care-all except for Julie. She was taken and given to the grandparents, her father's parents, where her grandfather did what her father had done and so much more. I was completely and utterly horrified at what I was hearing. I had no idea why she was telling me all of this and why she hadn't told me before since she knew her father was coming to our house regularly. I was so pissed off and I felt betrayed, but instead I responded by saying that I wouldn't repeat what she had said, especially not to her father. For some sick reason, she didn't want him knowing that she was telling people about what he had done. She cared about what her father thought of her and their relationship.

At that time, I went against my instincts and against my past, against my values and beliefs for the sake of this man that I loved. I agreed to keep all this "hush hush." In doing so, I agreed to help protect the molester from knowing that we all knew who and what he was. Above all else, I too kept society from knowing they needed to protect their kids from this evil man.

Julie and her father seemed to have a strange relationship, but I never suspected he had done these things to her. She hugged him when he came around, she loved him, yet she was also very jealous of his love and adoration of me. Although again, hindsight being 20/20, I often thought it was alarming how insistent he was at having my children go with him alone one by one so that he could, "get to know" each of them. I always told him, "No, we are way too busy." At least my maternal instincts and internal warnings were working those days. Still, I was upset with Julie for not telling me all this sooner, but who was I to judge: I had secrets too. The difference was that she knew exactly what he was. And that was pretty much the end of our relationship. She betrayed me. She put my children in harm's way. She was no longer welcome in my heart.

God, I loved my husband. Even after this newfound information of his family secrets was thrust upon me, I still wanted him more than anyone else in the world. I still thought of him as being this innocent victim who had terrible burdens to bear because of his childhood. How sad it was that still today as an adult he couldn't face them. He had insisted I go to Julie for that information because he knew she would tell me the truth when he could not. I loved him even more, but was angry that he hadn't protected us from his dad.

Jake never could face any of it. Or at least that's what I thought at the time. That mistake in judgment cost us everything.

Julie never suspected Jake was the one I should be watching out for, or at least that's what I would like to think. She, like me, loved to live in the wonderful world of denial. She didn't want to think that her one sibling left alive, the one she loved most, her baby brother she adored, would have turned out to be just like the other men in the family. He, too, would be one of those, "evil ones," that would do the same to innocent children. Unfortunately by refusing to face the truth she enabled him to victimize others. Then, in order to live with herself, her brother, and father, she rallied towards Jake's defense and went into complete resistance of reality. She recanted all her previous statements of abuse from the men in the family, denied sexual abuse had ever occurred to anyone in the family at all. She had to. It was self-preservation. It was sad to watch her claws come out for her brother. Julie protected her lies, her secrets, and his secrets so that she didn't have to confront what had been done to her. Just like in that movie. It was so twisted.

6

My panic emerged in an instant and my concern shifted from my daughter to that of my step-children. Jake's biological children—his teenage girls, aged sixteen and fourteen. "Oh God, the fourteen year old. Oh God." That barrel ride down the mountain started anew. The pain in my stomach made me think an alien was trying to cut his way out. All the signs they had been exhibiting were the same as my daughter. I informed the officer and Karen. I told them now that my time in Denial-Ville was over. I was thinking and remembering all the things about my step-daughters. Although we never really got along, I truly loved them. I especially loved the fourteen year old. The one that was so feisty and moody and so much like me . . . that tortuous journey down the mountain continued. The officer and social worker heard my panic and immediately Karen told me she would take care of them tomorrow. "Relax, I've got it scheduled already. They won't be allowed to go anywhere near their dad." I was not relieved because I knew their mom, and I knew she would deny all of this—just like I did at first. Karen had to then disclose to me that they are one hundred percent sure this happened to Michelle and because of that they are putting things in to place that would prevent the ex-wife from letting the kids see their father. There would not be any visitation.

If Jake's ex-wife, Christy, went against that, the children would be put into protective custody. A little relief finally washed over me and I could temporarily breathe. If just for that minute only, I could breathe.

Officer Olden said he wanted to go talk to Jake. He said he was going to his home—our home—to question Jake and depending on how Jake responded, it would determine whether or not he arrested him. He said he would call me either way. He would call. I needed that information. I needed to know what was happening at every moment. I needed the power or control of knowing who, what, where, when, and how. It was lasting air. Without the information, I would suffocate.

Before he left, Officer Olden shook my hand three different times and said, "I'm sorry this is happening to you and your family." I thought he was genuinely sorry. He repeated Jake's arrest would depend on how the "interview" went. He said it would depend on how Jake reacted. Karen and the officer left. They were obviously burdened with another one of these "things" happening again to an innocent child. I saw how heavy they walked. They were sharing my load, but for a different reason. It seemed to me like the officer did not want to leave. He saw my pain and as a typical man and police officer, he wanted to fix it right then and there. He knew though that he had a mission to accomplish and wanted to complete it more than he wanted to keep me from my agony. He was human, but he had a job. I felt that and was so grateful that God had him doing this. He wasn't a cynical robot in uniform detached without compassion. He was human too and I caught it, I felt it. And I was so thankful.

Time stood still that night. I kept my cell phone in my pocket. Something was wrong: it wasn't ringing. The silence was buzzing too loudly in my head; I just wanted the phone to ring. I kept checking to make sure it was on and that the ringer was loud enough so I would hear it. I took a tranquilizer. It helped me stop shaking as I walked around the house pretending that everything was normal. I continued to pace up the stairs, down the stairs, around the house, back and forth, waiting, checking, watching, and wondering what was happening to my husband. It seemed that somehow I still cared for him, but I didn't know how or why.

Hours later the phone rang. Officer Olden told me he had Jake down at the station. He had gotten Jake to "crack" somewhat but he needed more information from us to get him to come all the way out with a confession. Instantly I felt burdened with the responsibility of getting Jake to talk. I said, "Okay, what do you want to know? How can I help?" He asked me if there was any way that Michelle was making this up. I said no, that she wasn't the type who would make up something like this. Next, he asked if I was one hundred percent sure this happened and I said, "I'd be lying if I said yes." I was still clinging to the hope that he would tell me this was all a big mistake. Although I was ninety-nine percent sure it was true. I was only ninety-nine percent sure because my blinders were now off and everything was clicking into place. I was remembering things and realizing things, and recognizing everything as if there was a giant neon sign that was showing me everything and I just wasn't looking or watching, but now I could no longer deny it. "Yes, this is all true, I know it is, but the tiny one percent of me who loved and trusted this man I thought God gave to me, doesn't want to believe it and that's the only reason I am not one hundred percent certain." He took a deep sigh then and said he understood.

He asked to speak with Michelle next so he could get some additional information from her and so I gave her the phone. He talked with her for ten minutes or so, I'm guessing. She seemed okay when she gave the phone back to me. I listened to Officer Olden say he was going back to arrest Jake, that Michelle was very consistent and that was what he needed to hear. He also needed that anonymous letter. He said after he reads Jake his rights and arrests him, he didn't know what would happen, only that Jake would then be transferred to the county jail, but that he will call me when it was over. Again, being informed was keeping me alive. I looked forward to the next phone call, the next bit of information, the next morsel of news that would sustain me through another hour of this dark journey I was on.

7

The next day was Wednesday. My kids were all at school and I was free to fall apart again. I went to talk with a close friend that I hadn't visited in several years. I missed her so much. I wanted to be with her and be comforted by her. I needed her to sit with me and say nothing, the way she usually did. Just be with me. I needed her strength and her assurance and inspiration to continue living. I needed her to tell me how important it was to live through this for the kids' sake. I was becoming desperate and dark. So I drove to the cemetery where her body was laid to rest. It had been so long that I had forgotten exactly where she was. I paced up and down the area called "sheltering trees" and still thought that was funny since there were only about six trees on the entire area so named. I searched for Elora, my Elora, my friend. I became increasingly agitated that I couldn't find her and at the same time, it felt appropriate because I didn't deserve such comfort. I prayed to God that He just let me find her so I could read the words on her grave marker. I implored Him because I couldn't walk anymore. The lack of food and sleep was taking its toll and I was about to collapse. And so He did. There she was, there it was and there it said. It was a quote from her suicide letter, "The love we give to each other is all that matters and is what is remembered, the suffering disappears, love remains."

"Thank you," I whispered both to her and to God. I desperately wanted to be reassured that things would be better. I needed to know that one day Michelle's burden would ease and someday she would be able to love and trust again. Someday she may even find someone special and "normal," who would love her and she would be able to love him back. I wanted her to know what love is. Hypocritical of me I know because I knew now there really was no such thing. It was too twisted and too dark. You never really know anyone. Never.

My Elora knew that. She was in my shoes a long, long time ago and she decided to leave this world and the agony of it, leaving her daughter to be raised by grandparents. The pain of knowing her husband molested their daughter was too much and she gave up. She left. I envied her, hated her, and respected her for it somehow. I was now in her shoes and understood all of it. I now knew Elora. I was closer to her now than I had ever been in life. I knew who she really was. I understood why she decided to leave. I wanted to be her, or with her and didn't at the same time. My poor Elora was like so many of us, molested as children by a family friend—the scars left by those experiences made her choices in life seem questionable at best. She grew up to marry a molester and when that grotesquely unfolded, her mind snapped. After several months of enduring the pain and agony in so many ways, on so many levels, she "checked out." That deathly realization came flooding in with such clarity, I no longer mourned her. For the first time in ten years since her death, I was done grieving over the loss of her. She was better off. I would be better off, but I also knew that my children would not and that kept me alive that day.

When I returned to my car to drive away, I was suddenly sucked into the self-loathing state that was quickly becoming my comfort zone. I drove to Elora's parents' home. I needed her father. The one who struggled daily and showed me more than anyone else the effect a suicide has on family members. I needed to be reminded of the pain it causes to everyone else; the survivors. Her father, Mark, wanted to go take a walk, but I couldn't. My feet were too heavy to lift. So we sat and talked and I fell apart again. He tried telling me how I needed to find the things that would make me feel better and how I needed to simply do all those things, but he wasn't listening. I didn't want to feel better. I didn't deserve to feel better. I only deserved to suffer. I couldn't figure out why nobody understood that.

Next, I drove to the house of the devil—my house. I searched for the "anonymous" letter I promised to give to Officer Olden and found it. I left in a hurry before I vomited up bile as there was nothing else in my system. It disgusted me to be in that place. It physically hurt me to pass by that room where my daughter had been hurt. I couldn't get out fast enough. I ran. I took it to the police station and gave it to the front desk officer. She was matter of fact and I don't think I liked her, but she gave me a copy to keep and took the original letter. Maybe she knew who and what I was and was treating me accordingly. "Good for her" I thought. "Good for her for seeing that I'm no better than he is." For the first time in my life I didn't feel "slighted" by anyone. I felt that the mistreatment was so fitting that I was thankful.

The cell phone glued to my hip rang and it was Officer Olden. He said that around midnight Jake had cracked and admitted to almost everything. He said that yes it did happen and it happened over and over, but it was an accident. When asked how that accident happens over and over again, Jake replied that he didn't know. The officer told me Jake was arrested and went to the county jail where he should stay until being released on a high set bail and that I would definitely be notified of his release beforehand. I felt good about that. Everything was happening so fast and I was very grateful. Officer Olden also said that in case he does make bail, I should get a restraining order just for peace of mind. I took his words and wanted to follow every bit of it. I let him do the thinking for me as to what to do next.

When I hung up the phone, I drove to the county courthouse. Unfortunately, it was the lunch hour and there was nobody around to answer my questions. Being resourceful, I made my way up to the seventh floor where the "Order for Protection," issues were handled. I sat, then got up, and wandered around a bit feeling incredibly alone, overwhelmed, and so nervous that I started shaking. There were a few clerks there to accept the completed applications, but nobody at the information booth. The stack of papers I was given was almost an inch thick and the three inch long dull pencil I was given hardly worked. I was so embarrassed and ashamed. I felt like everyone knew why I was there and they were all staring at me. The papers I was filling out did not make any sense. Nothing seemed to be pertaining to me or my situation; it was a stack that mostly contained information on how to fill out the paperwork and what the definition of "domestic violence," was. I was confused and, while I tried hard not to, I started to cry. Then people really were staring at me, so I ran for it. I fled down the many flights of stairs as if a maniac was chasing me, out the area of guarded entrances and exits and back to my car and away from all those people. I hoped I'd never see any of them again.

On my way home, my cell phone rang over and over again. Someone obviously wanted to speak with me urgently. So I eventually pulled over to listen to the messages that were being left on my phone, causing it to beep constantly. To my surprise, it was Christy, Jake's ex-wife. She had called me because one of her daughters had been "interviewed" at school by Social Services and afterwards, she called her mom to tell her that something serious was going on. Her mother, in turn, called me to find out why her kids were not allowed over to our house or to be with their father, Jake. She just kept calling and calling and leaving messages, so I finally called her back. The only thing I could think of in answer to her many questions was to tell her, "I can only tell you it's not because they are in danger from me." She was almost yelling at me, saying, that Jake could never hurt any child, ever. She knew that because she was married to him for fifteen years.

I could feel her hatred and anger towards me coming through the phone like lightning bolts. Her words were full of pain and they pierced and cut me. I told her to go ahead and hate me if she wanted to, but she had better take those blinders off and get her girls some help. That stopped her dead in her tracks. She kept saying, "My daughters," in total disbelief, that her daughters could somehow be involved or affected. Still it was like talking to a brick wall. I couldn't blame her though because I was just like her just two days before.

Jake's ex-wife, Christy, denied that molestation was even a possibility and she vehemently defended Jake. I had become so frustrated and angry at her insistence of Jake's innocence. She wouldn't let me get a word in, but when she paused long enough to take a breath, I finally told her that he was arrested the night before and that during his "interview," he broke down and basically confessed, except he said, "It was an accident." Blah, blah, blah, was all Christy heard. I was the nightmare new wife who was creating problems. I was the one who was going to throw a wrench into her Hawaiian vacation plans since she and her husband were due to leave the following week and Jake and I were suppose to keep the kids. I just kept telling her to watch her daughters, to talk specifically to her fourteen year old, Cindy. That statement infuriated Christy and she finally hung up on me. The silence rang in my ears and I felt like I had just been electrocuted. I wanted to scream at her, to call her back and to accuse her, to threaten her, and hate her, but I couldn't. I was her, just two days earlier.

I sat in my car shaking and crying, bordering on full blown hysteria. I kept wishing I had never answered my phone and never called her back. Christy was relentless when she wanted something. Relentless, is the key word in describing her, but I hoped I had planted a seed in her as well. I hoped her girls would tell. I especially worried for the fourteen year old, Cindy. All the signs were there flashing in my mind, each slapping and beating me down one after the other. Michelle was following in Cindy's footsteps, as I had said on so many occasions. "It must be a phase and a hormonal thing, because Michelle is doing exactly what Cindy did." I had remembered a time when Cindy wouldn't shower at our house. Her hair would get greasy and her body smell was quite offensive by the time the weekend visit was over. I wondered how she could stand herself. I always brushed it off as a phase and wrapped it in to a nice, neat package that I could understand and easily live with.

I remembered Cindy's insistence on having someone else spend the night with her when she came over, especially if her older sister was sleeping at her mom's or another friend's house. Cindy would have an emotional meltdown unless someone was allowed to come over. When all else failed she would beg my daughter to sleep with her, even though she hated Michelle and treated her so badly. What was equally as shocking was the fact that Michelle, without hesitation, would agree. She would eagerly go into Cindy's room. I never asked, "Why?" "Why would you want my daughter to sleep with you when you hate her so much?" And to Michelle, "Why would you want to spend the night in her room when she treats you like crap?" I was so ashamed that I had never stopped to ask that all too important question. "Why?" What was I thinking? This all seemed so obvious to me now.

Christy called me again later that evening. She was different now: worried, concerned, and had some compassion in her voice. This was new. She told me that the social worker, Karen, and Officer Olden had come to her home and met with Christy's father and her and explained everything. Karen later told me that because I had disclosed to Christy that it was my daughter who was the victim it gave her a little more freedom to disclose a bit more to Christy. We were all glad for that because Karen was able to let Christy and her family, know that this was one hundred percent true and that Jake had (mostly) admitted it during his interview with the police. Christy had her denial blinders off and was now watching her daughters more closely. Although she was resistant to all of it, she couldn't deny what was being told to her by law enforcement and Social Services. She had taken a baby step towards reality. For that, I was grateful.

8

The next day Christy called again. She was quickly becoming a nuisance. Her girls wanted to get some of their stuff from the house and wanted me to meet them over there to do it. I didn't think I could go inside that place again. It was like walking into Hell. I knew I could just wait outside and let them get whatever they needed. So I did. I was shaking as I drove over. I stood on the porch and waited for them for what seemed like hours, but I couldn't bring myself to go inside. The outside of the house was just as bad, though; it had a darkness surrounding it. Just driving up, it looked as if it was haunted. Now it seemed like something you saw on a Halloween card. You could sense that evil was everywhere. They showed up and the girls embraced me. Erica and Cindy gave me genuine hugs that I had never received from before. Cindy held on to me for quite a long time. Cindy, the one who had always hated me for unknown reasons; she held on to me and cried. I just squeezed her tightly and let her cry and all her hatred and mood swings seem to now make perfect sense to me.

As the girls went in the house and up to their room, Christy and I talked. She told me how concerned she was since the girls had not defended their dad. Neither had said that they were sure Michelle was lying or that they knew this wasn't true. They both just wanted to know if Michelle was okay and to tell her that they loved her. They loved her? Since when? They always hated Michelle. I wanted to scream at Christy. I wanted to grab her and shake her and yell at her that her daughters were telling her something. I wanted Christy to listen to them. I wanted her to see what I was seeing, but I couldn't do that and Christy wasn't there yet. She was still in denial on some level, but at least she was concerned: that was all I cared about. Christy was watching and seeing some things although it was still from her front row seat at the movie called Disbelief. I understood. Sometimes I sat in that movie, too.

The girls emerged from the inside with just a few pieces of clothing in their hands. I was surprised that they didn't have more. I curiously thought, "What was the importance of that t-shirt? What was so important that we had to come here again?" Both girls just had simple, non-descript things; nothing looked significant. I didn't understand. Did they just want to see me? Before they left, I gave them all a hug goodbye. Erica, the oldest daughter, started to cry. I whispered in her ear so that no one else could hear: "Remember the good things about him, that's what I'm going to do." Saying that aloud made her cry even harder which brought a flood of emotions from me that I could not control. I broke the embrace and hurried to my car. I had to cover my mouth as the sobbing was exploding out with sound. I almost collapsed from the emotional pain, but I didn't want the girls to see me in such a way, and it made me hurry even faster to my car. *Get away* was all I could think of to do, and I did.

Thursday came and I wanted to go to work. I needed a break from my life. I needed to dive head first into paperwork, copies, faxes, scanners and phone calls so I could be free from my pain for a time. I truly needed to become someone else, which quickly made me wonder if this was how multiple personalities developed. That was a scary thought. I couldn't handle this life, let alone another person's, but I needed to disassociate.

Work went well, as both my managers knew what was happening. They piled the work on my desk so I wouldn't have time to think. Don't think, don't feel, and don't exist; I never even went to the bathroom that day. I just worked, and I was so grateful.

Later that night, reality came crashing back when Christy called . . . again. "Please, God, let her daughters tell." Each time my cell phone rang and I saw her name appear on the screen, I prayed that one of the girls had told. Then I would pray that they hadn't. I struggled and fought with what telling and not telling would cause them; it was a violent war going on inside me. My stomach had a knife sticking into it that was cutting deeply and exposing vital organs. It hurt so badly at times I would double over. I took more tranquilizers to help calm the torment going on in my head, but nothing helped what was happening in my heart. My legs ached and my feet were so heavy I felt like I was wearing cement shoes. Then the medicine would kick in and I could cope. Well, it wasn't really coping since it made me more of a zombie, but at least I could function . . . sort of.

When I spoke with Christy, she shocked me by saying, "Jake's getting released from jail right now." How did she know before me? Had my phone rang, but I didn't hear it? Was it on? Did they forget that Michelle was the victim and that we were supposed to be notified of this? The world suddenly exploded and a bright light flashed in my eyes. I wasn't sure what had just happened or if I had just heard some kind of thunder, but as I tried to gather my senses, Christy kept talking at a fast and furious pace. "His sister, Julie, was at the jail with their father and an attorney getting him released." I wondered how that was possible since I didn't get the phone call the officer said I would get: I was supposed to be informed of that. "How is this possible?" I asked. "How can Julie be down there with the father that molested her when she was a child, bailing out her brother for doing the same thing?" Christy kept saying that Julie had called and left messages for her daughters saying that "Your prayers have been answered: your dad is coming home and they're not pressing any charges against him." I was jolted into such confusion in that moment that my body hurt from the blow. I secretly hoped it was true. I secretly wanted this to be a mistake. I secretly and ashamedly wanted more than anything just to have a messed up daughter who needed intensive therapy so I could go back to my life. Unfortunately though, that just wasn't the truth.

My happy, beautiful, perfect life; the one where my only concern was if we could cover all the bills this month, buy the family a few new things, and still get the dog neutered. My head and my heart went into that battle. It disgusted me to hope this; I went in to self-loathing spirals with bouts of hope that my husband was the man I thought he was. I wanted to believe that my husband, Jake, was a kind, loving, decent man who really was just a victim. I would rather have that, than be the world's most idiotic and selfish mother who ever lived. It made me sick. I took more tranquilizers: I had already started to run low on those.

Anger ran in and out of me. I didn't know where to go, who to call or what to do. My reasoning kept saying that I needed to find out, but in the meantime, I couldn't let Michelle know anything was any different than it was earlier that morning. He was in jail, she was safe and she knew it. I wanted her to be normal. I wanted her to skip rope and still play with dolls. I wanted to erase the last few years and make her go back to being an innocent child. I paced outside and watched all the neighborhood kids playing.

I called my local police station and asked for the Watch Commander. He was stern and said he didn't know anything; I had to call the D.A. in the morning because he had no information to give me. I desperately wanted to hear him say he knew this happened to my daughter. "Keep doing what is right by her," but he never said it. I needed the encouragement. When I asked him how a man can pretty much confess and then be released without being arraigned, he said that Jake never confessed. At that moment, I felt that I had been punched in the gut so hard I couldn't breathe; the air wouldn't come. Had Officer Olden told me he got Jake to confess so that I would be proud of him? Did Officer Olden just need an ego-stroking? Was he like every other policeman I've ever met who just had that knight in shining armor syndrome and he just needed to be viewed as a hero?

"Oh, God, please help me," was all I could think. My agony and confusion was intense. I didn't know what to believe and the world just started to spin. Nobody was available. Karen was at home as she should be, not in her office, Officer Olden was off until Monday and I was left with this asshole Watch Commander who didn't want to give me any information and just wanted to get off the phone. I asked again, hoping I misheard him, "You said my husband did not confess—is there a chance this is not true?" Then he backpedalled, saying, "Ma'am, I don't have the report; I wasn't there, I don't know." Then I was more confused than before and I was getting nowhere. I had no access to any information and since it was after 5:00 pm, I would just have to wait until the next day. Again, I was helpless and out of control and worse: I was left alone to deal with all of it. Not only did I have my children and my own dysfunctional self to deal with, but I now had the legal system to handle and that was showing itself to be quite inefficient. The emotional storm was like a tornado. I didn't know how to think, feel, say or act. My mind was in pieces that kept getting caught up in that storm. I tried grabbing this piece or that one, but when I did, it seemed to make me lose the other piece I had in my hand; I couldn't get a hold of anything long enough to make sense of it. There was nobody available who could help me. I felt dizzy and confused. I couldn't fix myself or right myself. I was a mess. Finally, I decided that for now my kids needed me. So I shut off the phone, went into my zombie state of being that didn't feel or know anything about anything and went inside to get my kids ready for bed and ready for another day in Hell.

9

There was Michelle, cuddled in bed, still looking afraid, but somewhat relaxed at the same time. It was a contradiction, I know, but that was what I saw. A child who was going through so many different things, all her own that I would never know. She was so brave. I was so proud of her. She was doing more than I would do. More than I had done. I loved her so much in that moment, but even more than that, I respected her for the first time in her life. I would never respect anyone else like I now respected her.

We all went to bed, my daughter and I in one bed, my youngest son on the floor next to me and my oldest in another part of the house, completely detached from us. That was something I couldn't deal with; he would unfortunately have to wait. I had no idea what was happening with him, but I knew it was a violent, emotional storm. Much like mine but for entirely different reasons, I was sure. Still: he would have to wait. My sanity and life were on the line every moment of every day which directly affected the lives of all the kids and the rest of my family. I did only the absolute bottom line, the bear necessity and not one thing more. I couldn't. Breathing was the maximum I was allowed and fighting the powerful, sometimes overwhelming urge to hurt myself was the other.

Friday came and went with more, "Sorry, I don't have any information for you." Or I would hear, "You'll have to speak with Officer Olden, but he won't be in until next Monday." It was frustrating to say the least. I couldn't imagine going through the entire weekend feeling like I did. I was confused and scared and I doubted everything that had taken place. The questions raced through my mind: Was this all just a mistake? Was Jake really innocent and they let him go because they knew that to be the truth? Did something else happen? Is this just a strategy the D.A. used to let him go free so he could metaphorically hang himself? I didn't know what was happening or why. That added salt to all the wounds and made me a nervous wreck; I paced the floor, walked the halls and the neighborhood, and took tranquilizers like they were candy.

Since Jake and Christy had been married for so long, Julie, Jake's sister, had developed a close friendship with Christy's sisters. And apparently, they still kept in touch. Christy called me first thing Saturday morning to say that Julie had told one of Christy's sisters that Jake was released because the D.A. had made a mistake. They had double-booked an arraignment for another inmate and skipped Jake altogether. When an attorney showed up to get Jake released, he discovered the mistake and the D.A. literally let him walk out of jail right then and there. That was the real story. Again, confusion washed over me. Insanity lurked just inside my ears, pulsing right there about to whisper something to me that would make me die, that would let me die. I didn't know what to believe. I just listened as Christy rattle on and on saying that Julie was now harassing her daughters, my step-daughters, Erica and Cindy, and Julie was angry with them for not returning their dad's phone call. The phone call where he left a message happily saying, "Hi honey, I'm out, I love you. Call me." No denial of what he'd been accused of, no concern, no remorse and above all (because of Julie) no need to face the reality of the situation he found himself in the middle of. It was an event that would undoubtedly leave any sane man scared to death. Not

Jake, though; his voice sounded as if nothing was happening and perhaps in his mind, nothing had happened.

Christy also expressed her concern as to why her kids did not want to rally to their father's defense, did not want to speak with him, and definitely did not want to see him. They told their mom they only wanted to make sure that Michelle was okay and that she knew they loved her. Concern flashed over me and my face felt like it was on fire. I wanted Christy to see what I was seeing, but she was too busy dealing with Julie. Julie was pissed off, trying desperately to create a surrounding for her brother that was completely free from this terrible reality, but nobody was being very cooperative with her which made her lash out. Christy said Julie had called and screamed at her for not making the kids talk to their dad.

Christy informed Julie she had to follow Child Protective Services and do what was right by her kids while still staying neutral. This was apparently not what Julie wanted to hear: she yelled at all of them and hung up when it became clear she wasn't going to get her way. I felt sorry for my step-daughters for having an aunt, so desperate for her own self-preservation that she was not rational or, at the very least, erring on the side of caution. My step-daughters were upset. They needed love and compassion, not an aunt who was losing her mind. Their world as they knew it had completely fallen apart as well and the only thing they had was their mom. For the first time, I had love in my heart for Christy. Genuine love because she was doing right by her kids, my step-kids. It was all I needed in order to let them go. I had to let go, at least for now.

My loud and intrusive cell phone rang. "What the hell else could possibly go wrong now?" I asked myself, knowing that's what that damn phone seemed to always bring. It was my eight year old, Aiden's, teacher; she spoke with a frustrated and aggressive tone. I just listened as she told me my child was out of control that week. She wanted me in for a meeting right away. I just said, "Okay," to everything and let her vent about my son being disruptive, unable to stay on task, blah, blah, blah. We set the appointment for a meeting; I hung up the phone, and just collapsed. I had reached the end. I was maxed out. I was so thankful that everyone was still at school and unable to see me lying on my legs in a chair, doubled over, unable to pick my body up or lift my head. "God, you have a sense of humor," was all I could say to Him right then. Exactly how much more did He think I could handle? Whatever was next in coming, He was so wrong because I was way past being done and was totally overloaded. Life didn't stop. No matter what was happening, everything else kept happening and moving on too. I was being attacked from all sides. This was affecting all of us and nobody understood any of it, including my son's teacher, including me.

I was already at the end of my rope. I already had the most terrible thing to deal with, but now I had people calling me for other problems as well? No, this was not the way life worked. You get one terrible tragedy at a time and that's it. You get one thing here, one thing there; you deal with it and move forward. You don't get hit from all sides. Why wasn't life co-operating? Why didn't life understand that I had already received my tragedy? I just wanted to sleep. I needed rest and food—neither of which was available to me. The bed too far away from where I sat doubled over and food just took too much effort to prepare. Several hours later, when I noticed the sun had gone down, I went downstairs and ate a piece of bread and drank water. It was all I deserved anyway.

It was in that moment that I decided to write everything down. Since life didn't have a magical pause button for me to press while I dealt with all this stuff with Jake and the justice system, my family, and Christy's family, I would need some way of unloading it. I would keep a record of everything that was happening to me; write it and expunge it from my being so I didn't have to carry it anymore. I decided in that moment that I could give it all away to a computer. And that is exactly what I did. I wrote it all down, gave it all to the computer; my confessor: my new best friend called, Dell. Maybe one day it may even help someone else. Maybe this way, I would be able to survive this entire ordeal. It was either this or slit my wrists.

I thought of cutting my wrists often and how much it would probably hurt. I thought that pain would be welcomed and very much deserved. It was my escape. I daydreamed of it like someone would envision a Caribbean cruise or a trip to Jamaica. I explored thoughts of my final release. "What would I use? Oh yes, I would go and buy a straight razor. Where would I do it? Oh, I better make sure the kids aren't the ones to find me." The razors, blood, and pain: it was a relief to imagine. I was falling again into darkness. That was my cue to find Michelle and make sure she was alright.

She was ready to snuggle up in our bed and so was I. I asked Michelle how she was doing and she immediately asked me what I meant. I specified, saying, "With all that's been happening." She answered in a much worn out voice, "Scared . . . nervous . . . and sort of happy." I let out a deep and obvious sigh which really caught her attention. I told her that meant she was normal and I was so happy to hear that my daughter was so normal. She became slightly amused and confused and asked me what I meant. I told her that if she had replied to me that she was fine, I would be worried about her. "It is very normal to have a bunch of different emotions about all this." I told her I was glad she was reacting as she should be. She smiled at me and looked relaxed. So while in the comfort of our room, I took that opening and asked her questions that had been weighing on my mind.

"Why . . ." I asked her, "All those times we had talked, the times I tried to ask you if anything was going on that I should know about . . . why didn't you tell me?" Since receiving that anonymous letter in the mail I had been more alert. I brought up all the occasions when I specifically asked about Jake and his father and any inappropriate touching or uncomfortable feelings. As if I was stupid, she looked at me with a stern, solid face and a bitter tone of reprimand as she replied, "You asked me on the way to school. You asked me in my room where it was happening. You asked me when I knew Jake would be home soon. You asked me in the car going to the grocery store. What did you think I would say? How did you think I would answer you?" And there it was. Her words were honest; true and accurate spears that pierced my heart. I could feel my throat swell up and my heart pound in my ears as I held back my tears. Looking back on it she was right. I had set the stage for the answers I wanted to hear: I had it all laid out for the responses

I needed. There was no way she could tell me anything other than, "No, there's nothing going on."

If I had been a good mother, a good communicator, a person who actually wanted to know if anything truly was happening to my daughter—I would have taken her somewhere safe, private, and away from our home where time didn't matter. If I was anyone other than who I was, I would have used common sense; I would have seen the signs and paid closer attention to all of it. I would have "heard" my daughter.

The guilt consumed me as the truth of her words set in. I couldn't help myself and I started to cry. Michelle's face became so sad and slightly shocked at my reaction. I owed her the biggest and most sincere apology anyone had ever given in this world. I told her how sorry I was for not protecting her, for not loving her more than I loved my husband, for not seeing and hearing what she needed me to know. Tears welled up in her big green eyes and she said, "You didn't know." But that wasn't entirely true. I told her how I looked back and thought of times when she was trying to tell me. She nodded her head, started to cry and said, "Yes, I did." My chest seemed to cave in on itself. The only thing I could do was repeat that I was sorry; I was so sorry. The bravest, most wonderful person I'd ever known said she forgave me, but this was something I knew I would never ever forgive myself. For now, however, my daughter wanted me next to her and I was too tired to do anything else. I lay down beside her and passed out. I slept an entire five hours that night. Although it was still induced by heavy amounts of tranquilizers, it was good.

10

Of course, just like the daily mail and the delivery of the newspaper, Christy called again. She was even more concerned for Erica than she had been for Cindy. Erica had an emotional meltdown at a movie theater the night before over a make-up bag she had just purchased and put under the movie seat that was stolen during the movie: an absolute meltdown where security was called to help contain and control an inconsolable child. I started to cry with Christy. A sad pain was in my heart for my stepdaughter, for someone else's daughter—for a possible victim who may be one step closer to telling a hidden secret. I didn't know. I just felt so awful and I wanted the pain to stop. I wanted Christy to stop calling me, but at the same time I wanted to be reassured that she was still doing everything to protect her children. I wanted and needed to know that she was keeping those blinders off to the real possibility these girls were also molested. It seemed like she was doing that.

I needed to let go of them and hang on to what was happening in my house. I needed to get through the weekend. That way I could reach Monday which held promises of information. Why wasn't life cooperating? I expressed my sincerest love and sadness for Christy and her family's situation and just hung up the phone. I couldn't handle much more of anything else and I didn't understand why it was me that Christy kept calling.

I drove to the store at 3:00 pm and wondered where my Saturday went, although I was grateful it was nearly over. I looked around the grocery store I had been to a million times over in my life and recognized nothing. I was different and so was the store. Everything had changed: the color, the smells, the people, lights; but again, just like at work, I knew the change was inside me. I knew I was going crazy.

My therapist wanted to see me earlier than normal that day. I drove to his office and was thankful I could release some of what I was feeling in a safe, nonjudgmental environment. He understood everything, or so he said. He listened as I wept on and on for what seemed like two days, but in actuality, it was only a little over an hour. When that was over, I felt a little better, completely wiped out but somewhat better. I had unloaded what really was two days worth of emotions. I was seeing him every two to three days. I was then able to go home and paint that smile on and do what needed to be done.

Sunday came and I needed to attend church. I was scared though, thinking that Jake would have the audacity to show up. Deep inside I knew he wouldn't because of his non-confrontational personality. However, my fear persisted so I went early to talk to the bishop, the leader of the congregation. I told him a little of what was going through my mind, life, heart, and family. He kept picking at his finger nails, unable to look at me, unable to withstand the pain he saw in my face for any length of time. I could see him suffer, but I didn't know exactly why, nor did I care.

I was being consumed again with disgust for myself. I thought of my escape plan that included my forearms and a razor blade. That release I savored and planned on when I became completely and utterly defeated. It gave me some sort of control to have finally decided how I would accomplish the task. Not that day, though.

Instead I went to a church meeting and sat with a friend in the back. After the first hour, I managed to make it to the second meeting and sit by the door—I needed the ability to make a quick getaway in case Jake showed up. He could show up and be totally oblivious to there being an issue with his freedom.

The topic of the day was "Partaking of the Sacrament." A good one, I thought, so I was eager to snap out of my zombie-like state and try to listen. Towards the end of the class, I heard the teacher say something about being "worthy" to take the sacrament which is the bread and water, the symbolic body and blood of Christ. He asked if anyone had a question and I most certainly did. My whole reason for being there was to partake of the sacrament and recharge with His Spirit inside me; however I definitely wasn't worthy. I was an unworthy, sinful, loathsome, sorry excuse for a mother. I asked, "Is it possible just to partake because we needed it and not because we are worthy to partake of it?" The teacher, not knowing what was happening in my life, didn't agree and told me so. I broke down. My reason for getting up this morning, my reason for attending church, just popped like a balloon. I needed a quick escape but couldn't get up out of my chair and out the door fast enough as I burst in to tears while screaming out that I was definitely not worthy. "I am not worthy." And no, that was not funny.

My friend held on to me and helped me out the door and to the nearest couch before I collapsed like a rag doll in her arms. I didn't care that I had snot running down my face, mascara mixed with tears making Alice Cooper type black lines down my cheeks or that I was making a spectacle of myself. Nothing mattered; I wasn't worthy and I couldn't escape from myself, my pain, or the agony of being me. I hysterically cried right there in the middle of the foyer. I couldn't contain or control myself. After a time, I heard whispers from people around us that perhaps my husband, Jake, had died. In a way, he did. It definitely felt as if I was in mourning. I had lost not just one person, but three. I lost my daughter, my husband, and myself. I lost an entire life. Sacrament meeting came and went as I stayed in a daze, but I partook of the Sacrament and asked for God's forgiveness. I prayed for strength and knew this was where Jesʋ

wanted me to be. He said, "I'll stay with you," and I was counting on it. I stayed on tranquilizers for the remainder of the day to help numb the pain but nothing worked. Nothing helped. I felt angry with Michelle. I caught myself several times snapping at her for no reason. It made me feel worse about myself. My poor, beautiful, no-longer-innocent daughter had such an ugly tainted experience in her life at the tender age of twelve. Her innocence was gone. I was a failure and here I was scolding and blaming her for my pain. I was sick.

I ate my candy which was actually Xanax, a tranquilizer, for the rest of the day and night until sleep finally took me. Sleep, it was supposed to provide relief. It was supposed to be a time where I could forget who and what I was. It was supposed to be a temporary release, but God had other plans for me. Or perhaps it was the devil. I didn't know which, but it certainly gave me no kind of relief. At 2:00 am, my eyes popped open. A vivid memory I was obviously trying to suppress came out in a painful flash: I almost caught him. "You bastard, I almost caught you," I whispered aloud. I remembered a night when I awoke to find Jake missing in bed. I looked everywhere for him. I called out to him. I looked in every bedroom and he wasn't anywhere. Then I went downstairs to find the lights out and the house empty. When I went back upstairs there he was in bed. When I asked where he was, he said he had been in the bathroom and I accepted that. I accepted that when I knew goddamn well he wasn't in that bathroom. I had checked that bathroom. I guess I was just too tired to get into a discussion in the middle of the night. Perhaps I just wasn't ready to deal with reality, I don't know. Now shame took over. Shame, guilt, agony, and a burning urge to filet my wrists. I needed those emotions to find a way out of me. I needed to cause myself true physical pain and perhaps then the emotional pain would subside.

I needed air. I couldn't breathe and I was gasping for some oxygen. I ran for the front door, to get outside and inhale the cool night. It was dead silent outside. The sky was dark and I could barely see. It gave me life. I momentarily felt free. I wanted to run and keep on running, but those kids were right there, upstairs, counting

on me. The pressure of that was suffocating. I struggled to be free. I wanted to color my hair, change my name, and move to some small town in the middle of nowhere. Nowhere-ville and become Nowhere Woman with no past, no future, no kids, no life and most importantly: no memories. I needed that life but it was never going to happen and I painfully knew it. What's done is done. How long could I possibly go on this way? I sat and cried on the bricks in front of my parent's home. I cried there that early morning, and I kept on crying until the sun came up.

The newspapers were being delivered. A van drove slowly down the street and the loud, intrusive "smack" sounds were getting closer and closer. People started coming out of their homes in their nightclothes to get the morning paper. They had cups of coffee in their hands and waved at each other. It was their morning routine. I had one of those once, I thought. I used to have one that was just about perfect. Although I didn't retrieve or read a delivered newspaper, I did cherish my crazy mornings with all the kids. Other people started showing up walking their dogs. They all seemed as if they hadn't a care in the world. There were no child molesters in their lives; no pain, no suffering, just happy little dogs and blissful lives. I hated them. I hated all of them. I started to seethe. When I had finally had enough of what I was seeing, I went inside.

Monday came and went while still in a deep haze. I was so tired. I didn't know how I had gotten to this terrible place. I had such a wonderful life and I had been thankful for it. I knew I had a beautiful life and that I had been so blessed. What happened? Why? I was too tired. The pressure of keeping it together for my kids was now becoming unbearable. I needed release. The urge to cut myself, although quite foreign, became comforting to me at the same time. I kept thinking that I was in control of something. If I were to cut my wrists, I would do it because I wanted to. If I didn't cut myself, that too was because I did not want to. It was a small element of control.

Food became the next thing. I didn't eat. At first it was because I couldn't without vomiting. Then, it became all about torturing me by only eating bread and water. Finally, it was something I could control. Eat, don't eat, it was my decision what I did to my once-beautiful and happy body was completely my decision and had nothing to do with anyone else. "Jesus, I'm screwed up. Please, just stay with me," was all I could whisper. Whenever I found myself alone, which was never often enough, I prayed in hushed whispers. "Jesus, just stay with me," and He did.

Karen, the social worker, called me to tell me why Jake got out of jail. She confirmed that the D.A. made a mistake and double-booked an arraignment for another inmate and forgot all about Jake. Unfortunately, this was to be the first of many mistakes in this case. When Jake's sister showed up with an attorney, he caught the mistake and Jake walked out free. No arraignment, no charges, no slap on the wrist, no reprimand, no nothing. She told me to hang in there and to keep the ex-wife at bay. My focus needed to be on Michelle and nobody else. She was right, of course, so that was easy to comply with. I welcomed having someone tell me what to do; I needed someone else to tell me what to do. I didn't want to think or be responsible for anything anymore. I needed to be free.

11

Officer Olden called later that day. I hadn't heard from him in so many days that it seemed like months had gone by. He asked me if Michelle would be up to calling and trying to get Jake to confess again on tape. I said, "Yes, she can do it." I was excited to hear that someone was finally doing something about this. A voice, barely audible, whispered, "no." I could hardly make it out as I kept listening to the officer tell me what needed to happen. Then it spoke up a bit louder "NO." And finally I was snapped out of my stupidity and saved myself from almost making another Mother of the Year, mistake. I realized that it wouldn't work and would be way too traumatizing for Michelle. She is just a small child. I told him that I would do it. "I will do it, I know I can." I actually needed to confront Jake—I needed to get straight and do right by my child. I needed to save her from any more suffering. I needed to keep her completely out of this investigation and out of this phone call. I owed it to her.

Although I agreed to make the call, I dreaded doing it too. My heart raced as the idea of just talking to Jake flashed in my mind.

What if he pleaded with me to come home? What if he denied it all to the point where I believed him over my daughter? What if hearing his voice caused me . . . A million other questions came flooding in. I had to plan out what I would say. I needed to make sure I was ready for every possible scenario. That way, I could follow my script. I had a whole day to complete it. It was also an entire day to dread what would more than likely be a terrible traumatic experience.

I sat up half the night going over and over what I would say and what I would do so that I would be prepared. Officer Olden and I would call Jake and get him to spill his guts and we would succeed and Michelle would never know about this. She would never know that the D.A. needed more information, more evidence than just her word. I was ready to get him to confess, I was ready to do right by my daughter. I needed to do right by her.

The next day, when the kids went to school, a friend of mine drove me to the police station. She stayed outside as I went in. I sat in the empty lobby and waited. The room was earth toned and very basic and non-descript. I began dissecting every inch of the place, looking for something of comfort. I started reading every pamphlet, every notice on the walls, listening to the TV in the corner talk about terrorism and how to cope. I read a poster by the secretive locked door on the side of the room and found a misspelled word. That struck me as being funny, in an odd sort of way so I told the lady on the other side of the glass. She didn't seem to care. I did care. I cared that my police department had posters with misspelled words and things in the lobby on "How to Handle Terrorism," but nothing on "How to Handle Your Life When Sexual Abuse Hits Home." I became angry then, which led to feeling more anxious, as if the success of everything was solely on me. The weight of the case against my husband, the evidence, and the responsibility in obtaining evidence, all of it was mine and mine alone.

I felt so much pressure and I wanted to run. Before I could act on my "flight" instinct Officer Olden came out from behind the locked door. It was too late to back out, too late to run and hide. There I was: walking down a hallway and with so much at stake. Breathing was at times difficult, but I was committed to succeeding. I would pass this test. It was good versus evil and the old saying, "Good guys finished last," was not happening that day. I would triumph over this devil and then feel worthy of life and have justice for my daughter.

As I was being led to the first room I was surprised at the difference between what TV depicts and what a real police department looks like. There were no people, no officers, no criminals, and, most shockingly, there was no sound. Or perhaps my brain had shut down my listening devices in order to do what must be done, I didn't know. It was just so odd to be in a police station and not hear sirens or the radio of the crimes being committed or phones ringing with calls coming in. In that first room we went into, Officer Olden explained what we were going to do and why. After he prepared me, we went back out to the hall and into another large room. It was the detective's room. It was the size of two normal living rooms put together with desks all around the outer walls. Nothing significant except again, it was empty with just me, Officer Olden and one other guy who was pretending not to notice us. Everything there was cold, still and lifeless with no sounds coming from anywhere.

One wall caught my attention and I couldn't help but look. The wall had "death" on it. It had different angled pictures of a bloody person and I just couldn't help but stare in horror. That was where the similarity between a TV police station and a real one began and ended. There was still no ugly tiled floor, smoking detectives, hand cuffed criminals or prostitutes shouting obscenities. Nothing, it was all empty, but for some reason, it still terrified me.

Officer Olden had everything ready. I called Jake twice on his cell phone, but he didn't answer. I couldn't believe that all the worrying and planning was going to end because he wasn't answering his phone. I had not planned on that being a scenario at all. We decided to call his work phone. He answered and sounded completely different. He seemed resolved, strong and focused. He had never been that way before, but it seemed like he was just as prepared for this call as I was. I did my best. I tried to get him to talk, but I failed. He was more prepared than I had given him credit for. His sister had built a stronger more defensive wall around him than I could penetrate. Their wickedness was greater than anything moral I could conjure. I had no idea what I was dealing with. I was so unprepared. I pleaded with Jake to seek help. He stayed silent. I begged him to talk, he stayed silent. I told him we could get him help and then go back to how things were, but still, he stayed silent. And after all that, I failed. Jake said absolutely nothing.

Officer Olden disconnected the call and said I had done very well, but I didn't believe him. The other guy who pretended not to notice us tried to join in and say that he was impressed with me. They were liars and not very good ones either. I struggled between hope and failure, wanting to try again and being defeated. Both officers told me it was over, that was the "one shot." "The D.A.'s office would have to handle it from here on out." I wanted to scream and fight and jump up and down in frustration. I wanted to explode, but in the end I simply allowed Officer Olden to walk me outside and to my friend's car.

I couldn't understand why I wasn't able to do anything right. I couldn't detect a pedophile. More than that, I was in love with one. I couldn't protect my daughter, and I couldn't even get the sick, twisted s.o.b. to acknowledge any part of what he had done. A pedophile was smarter than I was. A child molester was better at everything; more clever than I was. Self-loathing flooded every pore, every crevice, and every ounce of me, in and out of my soul. I was finished. I was dead. I decided right then, to make that so.

I became very aware that that day was to be my last day on earth. I decided in an instant that I would slit my wrists with the razors I kept in the corner of the garage. It was weird how I suddenly remembered where they were. I had them the whole time. My mind raced and planned out all the details. I was shocked to be so smart and clear all of a sudden, but couldn't get someone to talk about the truth of his actions. Nevertheless, I planned. A numbness washed over me as my mind explored its final end. I felt relieved and glad that this was going to be over, at least for me.

I envisioned that my kids would be at school or at my parents' home safe and sound. They wouldn't know where I was or what I was doing. I would drive to the beach. It was beautiful there. I would drive down into the beach parking lot. My car would face the ocean.

There I could sit and watch the sun set, just off to the right, for the very last time. The waves would rhythmically wash in and pull out. I would slice the length of my arms from wrist as far up to the elbow as I could stand. I wouldn't cut too deeply on my left arm so that I would still have strength when I cut my right arm. That cut would be the deepest. The smell of the ocean air would soothe me. The sound of the waves and the birds would be peaceful. I would wait, watching and listening as the blood pulsed out of my veins and dripped onto my lap where my hands would be resting. Finally, someone I had never met would discover me and call 911. It would be beautiful and serene and more than I deserved. Still though, it would be perfect.

My friend drove me across the street, back to work in total silence. She had heard the police officer try and reassure me that I had done a good job even though he had not confessed. She knew that I had failed. It didn't matter anymore to me though. I was simply annoyed that I had to go back to work and pretend like there was going to be a future for me. I couldn't live with myself and this life I had given my kids. I felt let down by God, let down by my parents and family, let down by my husband of course and most importantly, let down by myself. I slipped further in to a zombie-like state of being. I went on automatic pilot. I worked and worked without thinking and without worrying about anything anymore. Today was to be my last day and for that I was grateful.

After a time, I don't know how long, I was brought to the present by an irritating beeping. It was my cell phone. It stated I had a message from someone. I figured it was probably from Christy, as she called all the time, so I didn't bother checking it. Whatever she had to say didn't matter anymore. I was done. However, the constant flickering red light that kept reminding me there was an unread message was so annoying that I decided to look at it. When I opened my flip phone, I was shocked to see it was from Jake. My mind seemed to explode instantly and my chest swelled up with pressure. I couldn't seem to read it fast enough and when I read it, my mind couldn't comprehend what I was seeing. I nearly collapsed out of my chair and onto the floor when I finally understood what it said. Jake was stating he wanted help for his problem. Jake said he wanted help, he wanted to talk, and he was reaching out to me. Was this enough? Did he more or less just confess? I sprung up from my desk and begged one of my managers to read the text message. I thought perhaps I was in a state of delusion. I wondered if my mind had gone in to some kind of "survival mode" and was playing tricks on me. I thought that maybe something inside was trying to keep me from ending my life when the work day was over so it was making me hallucinate. My boss saw what I saw. He said, "Yes, Jake is asking you for help."

I didn't know what to do; my entire life and its ending had just changed in an instant. I immediately called Officer Olden. I went from being lifeless to having some hope in a matter of a few seconds and it was exhausting. Over the office landline phone, the officer told me what to say over the text messages. With his help on my office phone, Jake and I had a brief but important conversation. Jake asked for help and said he was ready for it. I followed Officer Olden's direction and gave Jake a phone number to call. "Oh God we are almost there," I said to myself over and over again. I hoped this would be enough. I hoped this would seal the deal and Michelle would be spared a traumatic court trial and all that would entail. I felt triumphant and let that temporarily consume me. We were one step closer! After the back and forth text messages was finished, I went back to my work day with a renewed sense of self-worth. I had life in me again. Maybe Jake really wasn't smarter than I was.

Some of the joy and relief vanished as quickly as it had come. After all was said and done, I was still me, and what was done to Michelle had still been done. I tried to hang on to the jubilant feeling of justice being served. I listened to some music. "Don't give up." Josh Groban's song kept playing in my mind, keeping me alive. So I played his *Awake* CD. I played that song, "Don't Give Up," over and over again. He was singing to me. Thanks to him and a conversation where my sick husband was basically confessing, that day was not going to be my last.

The life that included the happenings of my other kids was now coming into play. Later that afternoon, I had to see my youngest son's teacher. It was good and bad that life didn't stop for our problems;

I had to keep going because I had other responsibilities. His teacher wanted to share her disappointment over my son's behavior. My youngest son, Aidan, had been acting out. He was disruptive, disrespectful, mean, and didn't do any of his assigned work. She was angry and frustrated; she was venting to me. What did I expect? Did I really think this situation didn't affect him? Although her timing sucked, it was perfect as well. Some sort of fighting instinct kicked in and I spoke up to her. I told her I allow only one phone call to be nasty and frustrated and rude per year and that was all I would permit. She had just used hers, so from now on she needed to call me before she felt that way. I believe she read or saw something that told her not to mess with me because she calmly and very quickly explained what she wanted to do and ended the meeting. I left to go back to my Hell, but I was in control and very thankful to her for letting me, score one, in the meeting. I could make it through one more day. I was going to make it.

Unfortunately, the day's drama hit me like a massive wave of cement. No matter how many times I fought to keep my head above water, life was still happening so that I felt as if I was drowning. My body, head and even my teeth hurt from the trauma. I needed my therapist. I didn't know how much longer I could keep swimming. I drove to my therapist's office and went into a full on state of panic. I paced, shook, and rambled on about nothing and everything that had happened. After an hour of that I slumped onto his couch and shut down. I was too tired emotionally and now, I was physically exhausted. My therapist and I were having long sessions to keep me alive and I was grateful. We made another appointment for another three days later: three days was the maximum I could handle without venting and he knew it. I was not right and just barely functioning and on the verge of a complete break of my psyche. He was committed to not letting me die and for that, I was grateful.

12

Wednesday came and went, but without so much haze. I felt depressed but no longer desperate. Officer Olden called to let me know that Jake had called the phone number I had given him for help. He took that step, but still needed to do a little more. Again, I felt like we were headed in the right direction for the full confession we needed. The one that would spare Michelle from court, the one that would give me some sort of closure and the one that would land that sick son of a bitch in jail. I needed it. Unfortunately the day wore on without Jake making any other moves. I risked sending him another text message that read, "Did you call? When do you start therapy?" He did not reply and as time went by, my mood sank. My depression and self-loathing slowly and quite discreetly crept back in. He was obviously just "playing" me. Just doing what he did best. I was his puppet. How long had I been under his control and not even realize it? He was such an, "aw shucks," kind of guy. One that never made you feel threatened or worried around him; he was so disarming, gentle and kind. It was all just a ploy. He pulled the strings and I behaved in whatever way he wanted and I never realized it until now. God, I had been so stupid. I was so weak and so controlled and I really thought I was the one who ran the show. How funny the pictures were in my mind. They came to me vividly: I was dressed like Pinocchio getting all the laughs and attention, but at the end, everyone would applaud Jake as he walked onto the stage and everyone saw that it was he who told that puppet what to do. I was a simple marionette. I was a total joke.

That night when Michelle and I snuggled into bed, I could feel her sadness. It rolled over me in waves. It consumed me as I watched her remember terrible things. It slowly but surely took hold of her body, mind and spirit, and all I could do was watch. I sank down deeper along with her and just tried to let her know that I loved her. I knew she needed help. I wasn't qualified to deal with the fallout from what Jake had done to her. Eventually, I asked if she would go to counseling. "No, I'm done and I don't want to talk about it anymore, I don't want to remember it anymore," she adamantly answered. Then I asked, "You want to try and just forget all of it, don't you? Just pretend that it never happened?" "Yes," she said in such a weak, childlike voice. I was instantly reminded that she was only twelve. Just twelve years old. In a soft voice, I quietly told her that we can never really forget these kinds of things. That they make us act out later in life if we don't deal with them as we should. I then divulged my secret. It was something I vowed I would never ever do. However, at this moment, it seemed like it was a promise that I had to break. I told my daughter that I am the way I am because, "I never told." Instantly, she snapped out of her hell. "This happened to you?" "Yes, it did, but I never told anyone." We whispered back and forth about why I never told and who it was and I reassured her that my monster had died long ago. She was bonded to me then. She knew I understood everything that she felt. It killed me to know my daughter now knew me, too. She knew who I was and why I was: something I often swore she would never know. Never.

We slept soundly that night with our common bond discovered. It sickened me. I wanted to share ice skating lessons with her, a favorite TV show to watch, or a fondness for a certain kind of music or food, but not this. Not a sick, twisted experience that would stick us together in a forging of evil. We were bonded with our same experience of pain and suffering. Again, I knew I was a failure and I truly did want to die.

The next day I received several calls from the ex-wife, Christy. I couldn't answer the phone. I knew she was calling to update me on her court appearance with Jake. She had said that her attorney was putting in for an emergency, one hundred percent custody order where Jake had only limited and supervised visitation. She was going on vacation again and didn't want him coming to see the kids. The girls had asked their mom if they were allowed to dial 911 if their dad showed up while she was gone. That gave her the mindset to put it in writing just to help give her some peace of mind while she was away. But I didn't want to know about anything going on in her house. I couldn't handle anymore. I was fully loaded and deep fried, so I hit my "ignore" button. With one quick touch to my phone, I could pick and choose who I talked to, and who I heard from. I wished life was like that. Especially then.

I went through my work days wondering how I could even be there. I fought the incredibly powerful urge to run out. I often glanced at the door. I wanted to leave and get in to my car to drive away, and keep right on driving and driving until I was somewhere brand new. I replaced meals with Xanax and didn't care who saw me. "Time for a little lunch," I said to no one in particular as I popped the top of the medicine bottle. It was a bit amusing in a sick way, but then again, I was in a really bad place.

My daily chores were done in a fog of nothingness. I washed dishes and literally crushed a wine glass in my hand as I held it. I saw glass everywhere in the sink and wondered why I did not see blood. When I looked down at my hands there was nothing but broken glass. I was shocked at the amount of force I was using to wash dishes without realizing it. I was also disappointed that the glass did not shred my skin as it should have.

At dinner time, Michelle remained very withdrawn. "God help her," was all I could think of. She was getting worse by the day. The boys went out to play and Michelle stayed with me. She asked to make cookies and, of course, I said she could. While in the kitchen, she asked me if I still loved Jake. She said my youngest son, Aiden, said that I did. I told her that Aiden had caught me while on the phone talking with someone and that I didn't know what he was asking or what I was saying, although that wasn't entirely true. I hated Jake, but I also still loved him as well. He was also a man that never existed. I loved someone who was not real, but how could I explain that to a twelve year old when I didn't really understand my own feelings myself? I kept it simple and told her that I did not love him anymore, that I was over and done with him. I tried to show her strength just then and not let on to how devastatingly broken I was. She believed me and I was grateful.

Later that night I escaped to my computer. I wanted to be alone. I wanted to write my thoughts and feelings and be truthful and real to someone or something. I kept coming back to my best friend, Dell: the computer who took it all in without asking me any questions or passing any judgments. The machine that didn't lie and tell me what a good mother I was, or how strong I was, or how I would make it through this. Dell just absorbed it all without doing or saying anything in return. And again, for that, I was grateful.

The next day brought more of the same. I was settling in to this new life. It had been almost two weeks since I had opened Pandora's Box. Two weeks since the bomb was dropped. Two long weeks of walking through Hell. I went to therapy and confessed I couldn't take it any longer as I usually said, but there I was, still alive. I felt so old and tired. I told my therapist that I wouldn't make it and expressed all my thoughts of suicide. God had definitely made a mistake thinking I could live through this.

Elora was the one who knew me. Only she knew what I was feeling and only I knew what she had felt before she took her life. I was going to be with her sooner than I thought, but I had a few things to take care of first. The most important one being that Jake go to jail. I didn't want to give up on that. I wanted the world to know that he was a sexual predator, a wolf in sheep's clothing. I wanted justice for my daughter. That became my quest. That mission kept me alive for the time being. That and those frequent every-other-day trips to my therapist.

In the meantime I had to watch as Michelle suffered. Her life was painful. She went in and out of depressive states. I could see it when she remembered things, or when her thoughts turned black. It cut me deeper than any razor ever could. In a way I resented having to watch her go through that and sometimes I found myself being overly critical of her. I resented wanting justice for her and not being able to end my own suffering.

I wanted to cut. I never understood why someone would self harm until this happened. The realization was shocking but comforting too. I thought the pain needed to be brought to a physical sense and then there would be something I could control, especially since I wasn't doing the job of controlling anything else. The emotional agony of watching my daughter struggle was too difficult to bear. I needed some kind of release. I needed to inflict pain on my body to help get rid of the pain I was experiencing emotionally. However, each time I felt that horrible urge, I neither had the means nor was I in the proper, private place. I grew to resent that as well.

Monday came again. Time was passing too quickly without circumstances changing. The longer time went on, the more real this became and the harder it was to undo. The more difficult it was to try and believe that this was all just a terrible nightmare. To simply believe this was one of those real ones that when you wake up you think, "Oh, thank God, that was just a dream." I grew increasingly angry. Every moment of my life contained a harsh reality of something I didn't deserve or maybe something I did deserve, but didn't want. The resentment, bitterness, anger and hatred grew. It was directed everywhere, to everyone and everything.

When the world came crashing down on our family, Social Services said, "I know it's hard, but we'll help you get through this every step of the way. It won't be easy, but we'll try and help you as much as possible." Well, I had to call bullshit on that one. I had been left alone. Alone to deal with all of it, alone to carry the load, and all alone to suffer what I felt when I saw my children suffering through things. We were all completely and utterly alone. I had questions and I demanded answers from . . . nobody, because nobody was ever available. Where was all this help? Where was all the "support for what you're going through?" Where the hell were they as I watched my daughter slip in and out of her own hell? Two whole weeks had gone by with no referrals for counseling. More than two whole weeks of torment and torture and devastation in our family. We were a mess and getting worse by the day.

The anger was a violent storm fighting inside me every second. I had a kind of mortal combat, a brutal war raging that I couldn't get away from. It felt as if it was just under the surface of my skin, waiting for the chance to lash out. I was a walking time bomb. There was a compassionate love I still harbored for Jake; the thoughts were full of pity and sorrow. I believed he was a victim himself when he was a child and I knew he was, at the very least, the third generation of child molesters in his family lineage. My ignorant belief was that he couldn't help himself—he was a good person, but couldn't help following in his father's and grandfather's footsteps. He loved, I felt that love, and I knew that love. He was caring and kind and compassionate. He loved and was worthy of my love. The other side didn't support those thoughts at all. I was filled with memory after memory and fact upon fact of experiences where Jake was cunning and manipulative. Each time my love surfaced, it was met with the knowledge of just how calculating and scheming he was.

Somebody was going to pay for this and it didn't look like it would be Jake. I called Officer Olden and, as usual, I had to leave a message as he wasn't working. Of course he isn't working! Of course nobody answers their frigging phone. Where was the D.A.? What was happening with Jake? Why wasn't he rotting in a jail cell being pawed and touched and groped by some gangbanger named Smokey? Why wasn't he being made to suffer for what he had done to my baby? God help me, I was angry. I didn't know if that was better than the self-loathing or not because that raging nightmare inside was becoming too close to being let loose.

At work, I kept myself buried under a mountain of paperwork. I thought if I had too much to do then I wouldn't be able to go anywhere or hurt anyone, but I often found myself still looking at the door. I wanted to get up and bolt out of there. Through the hall, outside, down the stairs, into the car and drive, drive, drive to somewhere else. I longed to be free. What I really wanted was just to forget, but that wasn't going to happen. The kids and I were all simply going to settle into our new lives, with our new personalities and our new tainted experience that would make us do, say and act certain ways for the rest of our lives. There wasn't one single thing I could do to change any of it. I was powerless. I was weak and I was most certainly a failure. All I could do was watch this new movie as it played out in front of me, helpless as to its conclusion, unable to change the plot as it thickened or unfolded. Completely out of control. I gave up then and gave in.

Those first two weeks was hell. It was a nightmare. Nobody could ever know what life was like unless they've lived it. I could never explain it, never share it, and never describe it in a way for anyone else to come close to knowing what that was like. Hell. I can't imagine anything worse happening to me. Maybe I was being punished? Perhaps this was happening because it was always my worst fear in life and God is teaching me this lesson. The Bible teaches us that our greatest weaknesses will one day become our greatest strength. Is God giving me my worst nightmare to teach me and make me stronger? Was He trying to show me that I could survive anything as long as I had faith in Him? Was He testing me? Was this a sick test? Were He and the Devil debating over which way I would go, as they did with Job?

I was twisting inside and again I felt like I had eaten broken glass. The pain was excruciating, but I loved it. "Just desserts," I thought to myself. For once in my life, the pain did not trigger my anxiety attacks. It just felt appropriate. My body and mind were in agony and I deserved it. All that anger and rage kept me alive. It was such a violent storm that was getting more powerful and intense. I often found myself barely able to contain it, but just as quick as the anger came, it would leave.

I started to finally settle in to a workable routine again. Officer Olden didn't return any of my calls and perhaps that was a blessing. The veracity of life set in more and more each day. I could no longer fight it, hide from it, or deny it. This was now my life. This was now Michelle's life. My kids and I had been damaged in such a way that nothing would ever be the same again. Done. It was time I took back some control. It was time for me to sink or swim. I found Michelle a therapist without any help from Social Services. Funny how they disappeared once the can of worms was opened. We went to school and work and did our chores in order to live in my parents' home. Everything continued on as usual in life as if nothing had changed . . . on the outside. That was both depressing and comforting. I knew that in a year, things would look so much differently. Things would be different for us some day. We just had to get there. Unfortunately, this was just not that day.

13

My oldest son, Will, came home from school with news that his step-sister, Cindy, was talking to him again in person. She had been trying to talk to my kids via the internet, but I kept all communications, phones, internet things, etc., to a minimum. She asked Will why we hadn't moved out of our house yet. How in the world would she know that? I was immediately slapped in the face with that one. This meant that while her mom was on vacation and had a protective custody order put in place, these girls had still gone over there to our home—to their dad's home. Cindy had disclosed that Erica's boyfriend was now living in the house, too. Jake had moved him in. I was hurt, angry and frustrated. I didn't know what to do or what to say or how to react. These kids were so messed up: one day they never wanted to see their dad again and the next they were going over there? I didn't get it. I had to keep reminding myself that they were just children, and I knew this was an extremely manipulative tactic on Jake's part. Letting Erica's boyfriend move in as a way of getting his girls back, being the "good guy," a hero of sorts. "What a

puppet master he is," I kept mumbling to myself. I waited for Christy
to call me. I wanted reassurance that she was still doing what was
right by her kids. I still believed Cindy had something to say. I didn't
want her to keep it for the rest of her life. She reminded me of myself.
And that most definitely was not a good thing.

Officer Olden called me back, finally. It had been over a week
since I had spoken with him last. He said that he knew I had
been through hell and didn't want to contribute to my emotional
rollercoaster but at the same time wanted to keep me informed. I
replied that I appreciated that and to please tell me anything new.
He said that although he hadn't heard it from the D.A.'s mouth, he
did hear it from someone down the chain of that office that in their
opinion the D.A. had more than enough to prosecute. He said there
was a meeting that took place with Jake and this investigator and it
was enough. Again, though, this was not confirmed so, "don't get
your hopes up," but he said they were moving forward and should
have enough to proceed. He was still waiting for a call from the D.A.
directly and until that call came, we still had to sit and endure the
hurry up and wait.

I was overwhelmed with hope. I knew I shouldn't have been but
I couldn't help it. The D.A. was moving forward. Someone there
cared enough about my daughter to dedicate manpower to meeting
Jake and getting him to talk. They actually set up a meeting with
him, they actually followed through. In my mind, I tried to keep it
"unconfirmed," but this was such a huge step in the right direction. I
asked the officer if I could call him in a week, but he asked me not to.
He said he wanted me to just wait for his call or a call from the D.A.
The bubble popped somewhat, but I still felt that a small victory was
now on our side. It may take time, more time than should be allowed
in my opinion, but we had a victory. I swam in it. I let it feed me,
giving me hope and purpose. I let it sustain my life a little longer.

Then Christy called. She was finally back from vacation. She
told me of the goings on at mine and Jake's house. I told her I knew
because "Cindy talks to Will at school." She told me how angry
she was at what Jake had done and how she called everyone and let
them know her opinion. Christy, true to form as usual, she always

let everyone know what she was thinking and how she felt about everything. She wasn't one to hold back and now I was grateful for that. I was again reassured she was doing her best for her kids and keeping the visitations supervised. She informed me that when Jake came over, the kids didn't really want to talk to him. And he weirdly acted as if nothing was going on. Christy said he was in complete denial over any wrongdoing.

On their last visit with Jake, a few days prior to the call that gave me hope; Jake asked to speak with Christy outside away from kids' earshot. He told her that the good news was the D.A. was not pressing any charges and he and Julie were attending "Self Help" classes. I just laughed at that. Christy asked if I knew about that and I asked her right back, "Why would Jake attend "self help," classes if he didn't do anything wrong?" She said she didn't know. Then I informed her that the D.A was pressing charges and this was far from over. I so badly wanted to tell her everything but I knew of her shreds of denial and her inability to keep things to herself so I kept my explanation about everything I knew, to a minimum.

I told Christy that I had proof on my cell phone of Jake confessing and that I would one day get together with her and show her all of it. I explained very briefly of the conversation I just had with the officer on this case, but I didn't go into detail about our, "sting phone call operation." I simply told her that I had proof and that it was downloaded to the police and the D.A. and there was a lot more to the story than I could talk about right then. She said she understood and asked me again what I thought of her daughter, Cindy, being molested. I heard her pain. I knew she wanted me to reassure her that if Cindy hadn't talked yet, then she probably wasn't molested by Jake. I knew she wanted me to tell her she was free and clear, but I couldn't. My mind knew that she was a victim just as much as my daughter was. I felt sorry for Christy which was something new to our relationship. At least my wondering was done. At least I was passed the denial, hope, suspicion phase, and had now just moved on to wanting to help, cope and deal with it all.

I reminded Christy again of what the officer had told me weeks ago during Jake's arrest. He felt very strongly that Cindy was also a victim, so much so that he called Karen to make sure she interviewed that family and put an order into play to not let Jake near his kids. Christy's voice broke off. She didn't want to hear any of that and wasn't prepared for what I had to say regarding her daughters. I completely understood her pain. I felt sorry for her.

My next move forward was to get an attorney. I wanted a good one who would handle my divorce so I wouldn't have to think about it. I called Christy's attorney against Jake; she seemed like the obvious choice. I'd seen her in action and she was a fantastic ball of fire. I called and made an appointment. I also set Michelle's appointment with her therapist. I was taking control without realizing it. I quit one of my jobs, because I couldn't handle very many things anymore. I hadn't gone in to that job since this all started, anyway. I made all the appointments for everything. I was moving deeper and deeper down this new life's path. I had officially accepted everything that was going to happen. This was all real, I couldn't change it or undo it, and I accepted all of it and was finally starting to deal with it. It was a definite step in a healthy direction for me.

Then the inevitable of living in such a small city happened. I was driving to the local drug store. As I was trying to find a parking spot Jake walked right across my path, just in front of my car. I instantly thought my mind was playing tricks on me. But it wasn't. It felt like I had been slapped in the face. That was him, right there just a few feet away. He wouldn't make eye contact, but he obviously saw me before I saw him. I couldn't believe this was happening. I froze and then nearly vomited. I parked my car watching the entire time where he was going. I watched and violently shook as he walked to his truck and I continued to watch as he drove away. He was undoubtedly watching where I went to as well because he kept driving away at less than a snail's pace. Again, I was frozen in shock. I felt so sick and, for some unknown reason, violated. He was in my space. It was easier to deal with all of this when I didn't see him. There was no way I could handle knowing he lived and breathed the same way I did. I hated knowing he was still free. "I can't do this," started in on me again. Those hateful dark whispers lurked in my head urging me to give up. They continued with fury. To say that at that moment I was enraged was a complete understatement.

I bought the birthday card I was at the store for and went home in an ugly wrath. Self-doubt rammed in to me and I was once again fighting to breathe. "I can't do this, I won't make it," kept repeating over and over in my mind. I went for the Xanax to help numb my feelings. The feeling of nothing is better than all this. Did I cause this? Did I let Jake down in some way? Did I bring this into our family? Why was he walking around free? Why was he living a seemingly normal life while we're living at my parents' home? Why was he eating at the local sub shop as if nothing had happened? Why was he living normally like nothing had happened? He looked normal! He looked like he wasn't suffering at all! This wasn't a man who just lost the love of his life! This wasn't a man who was living in fear of losing his freedom! This wasn't someone clearly in pain over what he had caused to his family! This man looked like he hadn't a care in the world! He was your everyday Joe Blow!

I was on fire. Why didn't I floor it and just run him over? Justice was taking too long. This wasn't fair! My life is in ruin and he has everything! "Oh God, where are you? Please help me," was all I could pray. I ran to my computer and hoped that the drugs would kick in fast and take pity on my pain. I started to write more and try and give it to the computer. I played my favorite CD and my inspiring song, but I fell in to self-doubt and despair nonetheless. No, I wasn't going to make it. I wasn't going to and remain sane. I wanted to pace and cry and beat my fists against my head. I felt like those crazy people you see on the streets, the poor homeless. Could this be why they are like that? Could this be the cause of their insanity? Would I end up like them one day? All my questions fell on nobody, they reached no one, I was alone, in agony, in pain. I kept swirling down deeper and deeper into darkness and despair. The devil started to whisper things about hurting myself in order to cope. I needed a release. Then, came the effects of the Xanax and the negative chatter eased up. I went numb and drifted into the zombie-like state that was both good and bad. I liked it better there. At least then, I stopped crying.

I fell back in to needing to be "in control" of something, so I quit eating again. It seemed like the only thing that had nothing to do with anyone else. Nobody could tell me what to and what not to eat. Nobody had anything to do with what went into my body. I wasn't waiting on anyone else to make a decision about that or anything surrounding my food. Those decisions were based on me and me alone. I had total control of it, or at least that's what I thought. I took control of myself, but I was just starving myself and accomplishing nothing. It was just a band-aid. Something insignificant and oh so temporary that left me weak and unable to think clearly. It definitely did more harm than good. It didn't matter however, because it was power. I was the only one who had control over that. No police officer, D.A., attorney, judge, mother, daughter, friend, phone call, nobody had anything to say about it. It was all me. It was the only thing I had so I held on to it so tightly. I had control over something that no one could take away.

The weight fell off of me faster and faster. Days went by where I could hardly think straight from the lack of food. On those days I ate protein to keep from passing out. I indulged in a sugary tea and that kept me going. My clothes began to hang on me and the dark circles around my eyes looked deeper. My skin became pale and plastic looking. I looked the same as how I felt inside and I liked that too. I was in control.

It had been another week and a half since I spoke to Officer Olden last. I decided to call the D.A. and find out the new status of all this. A young woman answered the phone and I explained who I was and why I was calling. It was something I did the same way every time I called. She told me the case was still rejected and sent back with my local police department. I felt like I had just spontaneously combusted. "How is that possible, I was told over a week ago that you guys had more than enough evidence to prosecute and that evidence was sent to your office last week?" I irritatingly blurted out. She put me on hold several times to check in several different places to see if there had been any new developments. Each search resulted in the same response from her, "No, there's nothing new, no evidence, nothing."

With that information and in a state of total confusion I called and of course had to leave a message for Officer Olden. This time however, I left a ten-minute voicemail explaining how I must have been daft because I did NOT understand how there could be evidence and in someone's opinion "enough evidence to move forward," and then the D.A.'s office saying the case hadn't had any updates or any evidence logged in, ever. I ended the lengthy message with a demand for a return phone call, from someone who had a clue, to explain things to me.

One day I'm up, the next I'm down. The emotional rollercoaster ride I was on was making me sick to say the least. I was so exhausted from my physical and emotional state being dependent on what someone else said to me. This was going to kill me for sure if my starvation didn't do it first. I took two steps forward and I'm able to function just to take two steps back and feel totally defeated. My moods, my health, my everything, depended on the phone and what was being told to me from the person on the other end. I hated and resented it. I couldn't find much comfort in what I was doing for my daughter. I was getting her help, but the pretense that all was well everywhere else in my life was beating me down.

The next day Officer Olden called. His words were like daggers through my heart. They cut me deeper than anything I could've done to myself. He told me the evidence against my husband had been lost. There was no change in the status of the case because the D.A. didn't show this evidence ever being logged in and his records show that the evidence was sent to them a long time ago. So there we were, back at square one. We had a rejected case because we needed more evidence and the evidence we had was gone or, "misplaced." Jake had his sister and she had built the Great Wall of China around him. There was no way we would be lucky enough to get him to talk again. That luck was gone. His ignorance was gone. He had an attorney and his sister who were controlling his every thought. This case was going nowhere.

Officer Olden kept trying to tell me "it's not over," but I knew it was. The D.A.'s office had screwed up twice now on this case and my husband was walking around a free man. He wouldn't ever have to

answer to anyone for what he did to my daughter and that was just
the sad reality of it. My life was over. Michelle's innocence was lost
and he would never have to suffer for any of the damage he caused.
I was defeated.

My mood sank so low I didn't want to go anywhere or do
anything at that point. I was finished. I felt so badly beaten down
I didn't care what happened to anyone anymore. The world sucked
and that was the bottom line. I wanted to take some control and
end things on my terms. I wanted to take my own life the way I
wanted to and when I wanted to. I needed my suffering to stop. I
needed the thoughts I had of Jake to stop. He won. People like him
won. This was no place for me and I couldn't stay around and carry
my burdens and watch my daughter's pain anymore. I couldn't
pretend any longer that we were all getting better when I knew from
experience she would have a lifetime of pain, ugliness, darkness, and
bad decisions because of it, waiting in her future. She would never
get better. She would only get better at hiding it. She would only
get better at pretending. She would be just like me and I couldn't
deal with that.

I thought of Jake twenty-four hours a day, seven days a week.
My disruptive sleep was always about him. Everything in my life
was about him. I couldn't believe he had done this. I couldn't believe
it when my therapist told me, "If I was a betting man, I'd bet he
was molested as a child. That is what the statistics say and it's a sad
reality." My heart broke for Jake having to suffer through that as a
child. The mercy I had in my heart felt sorry and understood what
he had done and what motivated him. Then the mother in me ripped
through all of it and I fumed at what he had done to my daughter.
My thoughts were everywhere at once and it was near impossible
for me to get control of them. They were fickle: darting furiously
between feeling sorry for Jake, to hating him and wanting him to
suffer.

Sometimes I wondered if I had somehow caused him to do
this to Michelle. Did I give him too much love? Too much trust?
Did I enable him to reach into his darker side and express it? Did
I somehow let him down? Did I make him this way by wanting to

always talk about his father's past? Has he cheated on me? Could I have a disease? Should I see a doctor? The questions were never ending and all over the place. The pain and confusion was never ending.

Christy called to tell me about her day in court. She had to appear because Jake was trying to get his partial custody of his children back. She read me Jake's sworn declaration where he says that the false accusations against him came from his sick and twisted wife, me, whom he was trying to divorce. She read on that my daughter is known throughout the entire family to be a liar and a drama queen who has always been in need of attention. She (Michelle) was known to make up stories in order to get this attention. Christy continued on, but all I heard was a buzzing in my ears at that point. The loudest buzzing or humming type of sound took over. I heard words from the phone but they were intermittent and inaudible.

The salt in my wounds sizzled and burned. I couldn't believe what I was hearing. The secret wishes I had been harboring about Jake were dissolving fast. I guess I wanted him to show up in court, if we ever made it that far, and confess and ask for help. Until Christy's call, I had hoped that there was still some tiny piece of him that I really did know. That he did possess qualities that were lovable. I wanted to think he really was the man that I loved or that at the least there was a small part of him that was that man. But he kept showing over and over again that he was not. He had not been that man and would never be that man. That was a harsh and bitter reality for me to come to terms with. I was waking up to the fact that I never knew Jake. I never knew the real Jake. All the tender moments were false. He was not a good person. He was not a loving father and husband. He was not someone who was good, but just couldn't shake a terrible trauma he had experienced as a child. He was a liar. He was a really good liar. He did things that were evil and was able to hide them with ease.

"Let's pray," he would say. "Heavenly Father we are so very thankful for all your many blessings. Please bless our marriage and keep us thankful for what we have; please help Jane become more Christ-like, and please help us make good choices as we go throughout our day, in Christ's name we pray, Amen." Liar. He was nothing but a manipulative liar. Make me more Christ-like! He would pray for me and throw it in there that I needed help, that I needed to be more Christ-like, when all the while he was sneaking in to my daughter's bedroom and touching her. Everything was now contaminated. Every memory was disgusting to me. Every tender moment was now viewed as a malicious, loathsome event that haunted me. He was one of the devil's minions and I was once in love with him. I was stupid enough to be with him. I had made that demonic being my entire life, my whole world.

I would never survive this education I was waking up to. My heart could not withstand this new information. Whenever I thought my heart couldn't break any further, I was shocked to feel how wrong I was. The pain in my chest was unbearable during these informative sessions. I was grateful when the agony would travel to my stomach and give my heart a rest. My poor stomach however was not as grateful. It turned and flipped and ripped like nothing I had ever felt before. Death would be such a welcomed state and it just couldn't come quickly enough.

Christy's call ended with her telling me how pissed off she was at how Jake made her out to be such a bad mother. At how he tried to paint the image of having a slut for a daughter, a twisted wife, an incompetent ex-wife, a dramatic, deceitful step-daughter and how he was such a victim in all of this by every single one of us. He had tried in vain to play the part of the poor, innocent man who was the victim of terrible circumstances. Although he had put on a good show and talked a great game, thankfully, he lost. The judge awarded him two more supervised hours of visitation, but added that the supervisor needed to be court appointed and he had to pay for it. It was a small victory for us, but enough for me to grab hold of it as my temporary life preserver. I glued myself to it to sustain me for another day. Just at least for the rest of that day.

I called my pastor at church and asked for a special blessing. I reached out to the people who had gotten me this far through this nightmare. I was surprised though at the attitude I was getting. They wanted to move on. They wanted me to move on. The bishop was no different; he wanted me to not dwell on this because it would destroy my life. Like I had a life? What a joke. There was no life to destroy. That had ended on September sixteenth at 5:27pm. My daughter's ended a year and a half before that. There was no life to move on to.

I received my half-assed blessing from the pastor and left. I needed some comfort and some kind of companionship from someone who sympathized with me. I called my other friend, the one who walked through this hell somewhat like mine a long time ago. Her words shocked me. She said that since Michelle was no longer in any danger and since Jake was not stalking me or threatening me in anyway, I should really, "Move on." I couldn't believe what I had been hearing. Had the world gone completely mad along with me? This was now what people felt? I guess they thought that since it had been over a month. Just over a month, an eternity in hell and at the same time a New York minute. In their eyes, we should be all better and get on with our lives. They didn't understand. They didn't know what this was like or how this was affecting my children, my family, me.

There was nothing to move on to. I had nothing to look forward to, no life, no goals, no wishes and no dreams. I was simply going through the motions until God called me home. People just did not understand what had happened, what was happening and what was still going to happen. I was in agony and the only one who understood any of it was dead. I was completely alone and getting really pissed off.

14

I watched day after day as my children fell apart. Life for us was an up and down wild ride that none of us wanted to be on. We tried to be normal and pose as a normal family for the neighbors, but we were anything but. Day after day I analyzed every move Michelle made, every word she spoke, every outfit she wore, every smile, every frown, everything. Absolutely everything she said and did, I filed away in my mind to process at a later time or think or rationalize the who, what, where, when and why's. It was exhausting, but I couldn't help myself. I wanted so badly to see her getting better. I wanted to see her be her and not me. Every day I was saddened to observe her doing exactly what I had done as a child with secrets. It tore me apart. My daughter wasn't getting any better; she was acting out and expressing her torment. She was angry and confused and I could see it and feel it in almost everything she did. It made me sick. I felt so guilty for ruining her life because that is exactly what I had done. She was ruined and I held that responsibility. Although I took her to therapy every week, I knew that therapy would be a lifelong commitment and necessity for her. Someone I loved did things to Michelle that caused us a financial burden as well as all the emotional scarring and baggage that would follow all of us forever. Someone else did this and he didn't have any problem living his life. That infuriated me.

My oldest son, Will, became more and more distant. He was angry with Michelle, which was becoming obvious to everyone in the house including her. I tried so hard to explain things to him, but his fourteen year old mind just couldn't deal with it. He withdrew. Luckily he skateboarded and that kept him busy and out of trouble. He had nice friends that I encouraged him to be around as much as possible. I had no idea if that was the right thing to do in the long run or not. I guessed I'd find that out someday. My youngest son, Aiden, was my energy sponge. He drained me of anything and everything I may have had left. Nothing made him happy, nothing was good enough, sweet enough, or rich enough. He was the child I had to do cartwheels for and still he wouldn't smile. Both boys had to be put on hold for a while until this immediate crisis with Michelle was handled or, at the very least, made to be more stable. Still, I had to just watch and let everything happen as it was, having no power or control over any of it.

And then there was me, the new me. I was angry and bitter and came to realize that I didn't want people to know who I was. I didn't want anyone to even know my name. I wanted to hide or blend in with the crowd, but I was also angry and I wanted justice for my daughter and for me. I hated knowing that Jake was living in our beautiful home with all of our beautiful things. I kept coming back to the bottom line. Jake molested my daughter. He wasn't being punished, and now he was living a free life in our house with lovely things. We were removed from our home, living in two bedrooms in someone else's house, with only a week's worth of clothes on our backs and absolutely nothing else. Nothing. How was this possible? How was this fair? This was tragedy on top of something so unjust and I guess that's what kept me alive for a time. I fought our circumstance. I wanted to change that we had nothing, and that he had taken everything. I needed to know that Jake would someday be left with nothing but the clothes on his back and big scarlet letters across his forehead that read, "Child Molester."

I kept calling the D.A.'s office. I wanted Jake to go to jail. I couldn't stand seeing his truck everywhere I drove never knowing if that was actually him or not. At the very least I wanted him to have a conviction on his record. I wanted him to have to move thirty miles away from us and register somewhere as a sex offender. I wanted to know that he was convicted of what he had done to my daughter. I needed all of that and more. I was told that all evidence had finally been recovered, but the investigator was on vacation and would be out for two more weeks. Again, I had to wait. The frustration at the legal system was enough to drive a sane woman to the brink of self-destruction and I was by no means starting this journey as a sane woman.

I had nothing else to do but wait. The days rolled into weeks and as I kept calling the D.A.'s office I received one excuse after another. The D.A.'s investigator at first said, "I'm reviewing it, call me back next week." Then it became, "I gave it to the D.A. to decide if she is going to prosecute or not." That was an ugly phone call. I backed the investigator into a corner and asked "Why on earth wouldn't the D.A. prosecute?" So he let me have the ugly reality of it. This was not just about my daughter. There was a bigger picture involved. If the D.A. tried my husband and he was found *Not Guilty*, then when another victim came forward, they would not be able to use this evidence against him. If they tried my husband and got a conviction, he would receive a slap on the wrist and still the D.A. would never again be allowed to bring up this case in anything against him in the future. They were more than likely going to wait and combine this case with another victim should another victim ever come forward or be found. That was the sad reality I had to face.

As I sat in my car in front of my office listening to the special investigator tell me all this, I, once again felt defeated, knocked down, and totally obliterated. The fact of the matter was that my daughter was nothing more than a statistic. We didn't mean anything to anyone. Her innocence, her life, my life, meant nothing more to the D.A.'s office than a fly buzzing by. It couldn't I supposed or else these people would never be able to do the jobs they did. We were probably just viewed as a case number. I asked the investigator, "What am I supposed to do now? I have nothing, he has everything, I have to start over, and now you tell me your office probably won't even prosecute? How am I supposed to live with that?" He very curtly replied, "You have to move on and do what you would normally do." Period. That was the end. Those were his consoling words, his educated response to a woman living in Hell. "Move on."

I could see why people snapped and took matters into their own hands, but I couldn't do that either. There was a part of me that still hoped Jake would come forward, confess, bare his soul to God and the D.A. and beg for forgiveness from me and mercy from the court. That was an unrealistic hope and definitely a waste of time, but I harbored that secret desire nonetheless. Again I had nothing else to do but to wait and pray that justice would somehow be served.

The next several phone calls were met with more excuses of evidence being misplaced and given to the D.A. in pieces and then that the D.A. herself was on vacation. I couldn't believe this was how our legal system worked, especially when it came to these types of crimes. I knew the snail's pace combined with some incompetence, along with a desensitized attitude towards the victim would eventually result in the D.A. doing absolutely nothing. We were a series of case numbers only. No more, no less. Still, I hoped that somewhere, somehow, someone would stand up and make this a crime punishable by death and that Jake would be convicted.

I was tired. This life had worn me out. I wanted to escape from the waiting of the justice system, the falling apart of my family, the emotional train wreck that was my daughter and of course the nightmarish existence of just being me. It had now been two months since this all happened. Time was uncooperative when I demanded it speed by so I could see where I'd be in a year and unrelenting when it stood perfectly still during my bouts of agonizing emotional pain. There was nothing left for me to do, so I killed time and fell into a routine. I took the kids to school, Michelle to therapy, myself to work and also got involved in church activities. I did anything and everything to mask the storm and chaos that was constantly raging inside me. My physical symptoms of stress eased up some during that time. I started sleeping more and even eating. On the surface we looked like we were going to be okay. On the outside, I pretended we were going to be okay. I continued to wait for the official decision from the unresponsive D.A.

15

I had time enough to reflect on everything we had been through in the last two months, then two years, and finally the last three years plus, since I'd been with Jake. It seemed like a lifetime ago when I'd met him in a class at a church for people who were recovering from divorce, but I remembered every detail like it was yesterday.

It was autumn, the trees were turning colors and life seemed to be starting a new chapter. A new school year was starting for the kids and fresh choices were waiting to be made just around the corner. As I drove home from work I saw a big banner sign hanging from posts at the end of the parking area for a relatively new church that had moved into town. It said, "Divorce Recovery," and listed all the information on how to sign up for classes and get emotional support. Something whispered in my mind to join and see what I could learn, so I did.

The following month, classes began on Monday evenings. When I first walked in to the huge warehouse type of building I thought that there must be several hundred people going to attend. There wasn't, it ended up being about a hundred of us. We were a diverse group of people from every age, nationality, and social standing. Some had been divorced for years and some were still in marriages that were failing, and everything in between. That's when I saw Jake.

He stuck out like a sore thumb. He was so young and handsome, wearing his black leather jacket and blue jeans. He was tall with black hair and the biggest most beautiful green eyes I had ever seen. My heart skipped a beat when I saw him. The first night we were all together in one huge introductory meeting. The following classes they broke us up into smaller groups. I was so surprised when Jake and I were seated at the same table. I thought it was a nice coincidence. Our first few meetings in the smaller circles consisted of everyone sharing their own personal failed love story. It was sad and sometimes even pathetic the way these people clung to their hatred and bitterness. Almost everyone in the group had such terrible stories to tell. At first I simply sat and listened to all the tales of the cheating spouses and the custody battles that followed. After a few weeks the group wanted Jake and I to talk, as we were the only ones who hadn't shared anything yet. When I deferred to him, he said he wanted to hear all about me. That made me smile, having someone want to hear about me. It had been several years since anyone cared at all about anything I had to say. That ignited in me a need to talk to Jake all the more, so I chatted up a storm.

I told the group that I had been previously married, three kids, divorced for several years and that I only joined the group to see if I could learn anything new and to get out of the house, blah blah blah. Jake seemed so interested in me. He watched me intently as he hung onto my every word. I wasn't bitter and complaining or whining over spilled milk. I was simply there to have some adult time. After I completed telling my life in a "nutshell," I looked over at him. Those eyes, so beautiful and deep, stared back at me as if he had just memorized everything I had said, every angle of my face and every streak in my hair. It made me feel wanted, accepted, interesting and most importantly, desired.

Next he told his story. He was a year older than I, also had three kids, but was currently going through his divorce even though his wife was already engaged to someone else. He seemed like he was there just to have some adult time and see what he could learn as well. It seemed like we were destined to meet. He asked if our group wanted to exchange phone numbers so we could call on each other throughout the week just in case we needed some emotional support. I thought he was such a kind and caring man to have such concern for everyone. Of course we did the number exchange thing and later he confessed it had all been a ploy to get my phone number. That excited me to know someone wanted me. Someone was willing to be creative and put forth effort in order to get to know me. And of course that was the beginning of me falling head over heels in love.

We connected and everyone in our group knew it. It wasn't long before Jake and I started going out afterwards for coffee and then soon after skipping group entirely just to be together. At that point I thought I had found my soul mate. I knew that this was all destined to happen. I got caught up in falling in love and I let myself fall long and hard for that man. Something inside me whispered that he would, like the others, break my heart. I simply whispered back that he was worth it.

Halloween came during those early days of our courtship. Jake came to my parent's home and walked with my children and me through the neighborhood as we went trick or treating. He was so patient with my kids. He seemed like such a family man, just wanting a good woman to love and children to care for. I didn't want to go too fast in a relationship with him because of his marital status. I wanted to do everything right because I knew he was my soul mate. As we crossed the street he took my hand and I felt dizzy at his touch. He was so strong and so masculine. As we walked up the curb on the other side, I let go. After all, I didn't want him thinking I was "easy." He later told me that my playing "hard to get" only fueled his fire for me. Of course I had no idea at the time that the fire was from Hell.

He did everything right. He was the most romantic, charming, kind, gentle, loving, man I had ever met. That was all wrapped up in quite a handsome package, too. He was perfect. For the first time in my life I wanted someone, I wanted him. I thought for sure God made him for me from the top of his head down to his toes, from his insides out, he was exactly what I always wanted. There could never be anyone else in the world for me except Jake. "I finally found the one," I kept thinking over and over again. I was incredibly happy, floating on air, soaring above the clouds and smiling permanently from ear to ear every night and every day. It was an amazing time in my life. He was Mr. Right and then some.

On a date that I'll never forget, Jake and I went roller skating. It was a magical night in the skating rink. The lights were dim, music like Barry White was playing and soft glowing balls of light overhead made all of us gals look younger and more attractive. Jake and I skated and sometimes held hands, sometimes skated apart so we could watch each other and sometimes we fell and made fools of ourselves. It was fun and romantic. At one point we took a break and sat on the benches. As we watched all the couples and wannabe couples skating around, Jake looked over at me. His dreamy eyes made me melt and I often said silent prayers thanking God for giving me this man. Jake moved in closer and whispered in my ear, "What would you do if I kissed you right now?" My heart started beating a hundred times per second as I replied, "I'd kiss you right back." And then he leaned in and he kissed me so softly, gently, sweetly and lovingly, I thought I had died and gone to heaven. It was by far the greatest kiss I had ever experienced and I had kissed a lot of frogs to get to this prince. I was after all, thirty-six years old with three kids and two ex-husbands. I knew without a doubt, without any reservations, without holding anything back that this was the man I was meant for. I would do whatever it took to marry him. I was hooked, cooked, and done for. There would never be anyone else for me except him.

This fact was reiterated many times by others who saw us together. One night while we were eating at one those all night pancake houses, a bus boy came up to us and said, "I have to tell you, it is obvious you guys were meant for each other. You look so good together and so in-love and happy I just had to tell you." Again I said a silent prayer thanking God for giving me Jake. Soon after that we wanted to move in together and see each other every morning, every night and every in between. It was a wonderful period in my life. My life; it had been full of contention, disappointment, failures and too much sadness for one person to have. However, things had changed. My life would never resemble any of the things it had before. If I had my way, life would be full of happiness, joy and too much love for one person to have.

The night I met his children I instantly clicked with his youngest son. He became my little love, my sweetest angel. He was the same age as my youngest, but slightly younger in his skills, intellect and personality due to having autism. I adored him like he was my baby. The feeling was mutual too as I often caught him gazing over at me, his head slightly tilted with a smile on his face. Sometimes he would plunk himself down right on my lap and I would ask him, "Do you want me to hold you like a baby?" He would say, "Yes," and so I would. I couldn't imagine ever being without this innocent child in my life. I often thought that he should have been born to me. I loved him that much from the start. In my heart, it was just another sign that Jake and I were destined to be with one another.

Jake's two older girls weren't as easy to understand or get to know. Although when I met Cindy I thought I knew her. She behaved in such a way that I thought she was exactly like I was at that age. It never dawned on me that it was because we shared the same secrets. At first they liked me okay, but soon after we had all moved in together, it became apparent they didn't like me and didn't want me with their dad. I tried so hard to ease their minds as to my "status" with him, always letting them know that they came first before me and that I was okay with that. They would write notes on their dad's cell phone that read, "My kids are number one" or "I love my kids!" and they made sure I saw it. I would smile and tell them, "That's right and that's how it should be." However it seemed the harder I tried to love them and have them accept me and the kids, the more they didn't like me and the more they pulled away. I attributed this to their mom, thinking that she must be sabotaging our happiness. It seemed for every little thing that went wrong, I was to blame and they took all their frustrations out on me. At first this only fed my desire to connect with them. I loved their dad so much that I wanted to love them and have them love me back too. I tried everything I could think of, but in the end they hated me and we all knew it.

Unfortunately, that intense dislike spilled over on to my kids. At first we had girls in one room and boys in the other. We were often referred to as, *The Brady Bunch*, but we were anything but. It wasn't long before Cindy and Erica started doing mean things to Michelle, not that my kids were angels mind you, but these girls were older and were capable of more. They made Michelle the butt of every joke, painted her face like a clown and told her it was a "make-over," often scared her with horror stories, and sometimes even hit her. So we put my kids in one room and his in the other. It helped for a time, but it was obvious that the girls were trying to ruin our relationship. As hard as we tried to maintain the status quo, since we were so perfect for one another, the strain of the kids' relationship was causing arguments.

We wanted to get married and do what was right in God's eyes. We wanted to show the kids that we were committed to each other and set a better example then what they had been shown previously. We wanted the Lord's blessings for our relationship and knew He would help us with this problem. However, Jake's divorce was still in process since there were custody issues to work out. Our hands were tied and we couldn't move forward but we loved each other too much to move backwards, so we hung in there. Our love for each other remained the focus of our world. It was passionate, sexual, blissful, romantic, and honest. At least on my part it was honest.

So many nights we would lie in bed and I would ask him, "Tell me a secret. Tell me something nobody else in the world knows about you." He would always say the same thing, "I have no secrets from you. You know everything." I, on the other hand, always answered him, divulging my innermost demons, secrets, thoughts, and feelings. I mistakenly held nothing back. I shared it all with no idea that was all being taken in and would one day be used against me. I had no clue that he was processing everything, filing it away so he could use it to manipulate situations and know exactly when and how to take advantage of me and my daughter. It disgusted me to think of how open I was, how much I shared with him, and how I basically invited him in to do these terrible things.

Time went on; life moved forward and yes, there were signs that I ignored. Jake wasn't perfect by any means, I just thought he was perfect for me. I saw things in his daughters that troubled me. For example, the not taking a shower when they were with us for four days in a row, the back talk, disrespect towards all of us without having any consequences from Jake, the way they yelled, "Now!" and how Jake would take off running to do whatever they wanted; the way Jake made excuses for anything and everything bad that went on in our house, the way he let his ex-wife, Christy, run our household when it came to those kids. There were a multitude of things that went on, but I attributed it all to Jake becoming your typical "Disneyland Dad" and part-time parent who wouldn't spend any of the precious time he had with his kids being a disciplinarian. Again, I wrapped it all up in a nice livable package. I made excuses for everything he was and everything he wasn't. If only I had stopped just once to look and really see how far beyond that, the situation went. If only . . .

Although I was blindly in love, I still kept a close watch on the goings on where my children and Jake were concerned. I looked for any and all signs that Jake could be something other than what I thought, what I hoped. I watched out for him wanting to be alone with any of them. That never happened. I watched for him to walk in on them changing clothes or showering. That never happened. I even sometimes tried to bait him during intimate conversations to see if he was secretly attracted to younger girls. Nope, that never happened either. I thought I was so sly in weeding out anything that may be suspicious. I was arrogant at my confidence in knowing more than he did about what I was doing and searching for.

In that first year, all my children adored him. They often begged me to let them call him "Dad." I would never concede to that, but it was a sure good sign that he was a great guy. My children loved him, what else was there? Later, after we were married, when things changed, when their opinions of him changed, I still held on to them thinking he was the greatest guy in the world. As time went on things became dramatically different. They had suddenly and inexplicably no longer wanted to call him "Dad." My daughter no longer wanted us together, she didn't hang on him and try and hug him all the time. She didn't want to sit by him at the movies. She no longer wanted that fatherly attention she was previously desperate for. Still though, I told people that my children loved Jake. He was the father they never had.

I often wonder why, as women, we do that? We have a courtship and experience wonderful things in the first year. And we let that form our permanent everlasting opinion of our spouses. We can later have years and years of neglect, so-so love making, arguments, never getting flowers or poems, even abuse, but still we hold on to the opinion of him from that first 6 months or so. Why? Why did I continue to tell people that my children loved Jake? Why did I keep telling people that Jake was such a good man? He surely didn't do the things a good man would do in all these situations. In fact there were times when he acted sneaky, evil, conniving, and manipulative. But I continued to think that he was such a great guy and I was so lucky to have him. I always said those silent prayers thanking God for giving me this man.

In retrospect, yes, there were signs, but not enough for me to doubt the man I knew God made just for me. While I thought I was the smart one and he was the simpleminded "Aw shucks, Honey, I'm just a good man looking for a good woman-" he was the puppet master. Here I thought everyone watched and saw that I was the root of this family and that I kept it all together by working so hard physically and emotionally. The reality was that Jake pulled all the strings. He simply sat back and reaped the rewards. I was killing myself to protect Jake, to work at keeping everyone and everything together. To show the world we were the *The Brady Bunch*, Jake would say something that was bothering him like, "Michelle isn't being very nice to me lately. Do you know what is going on? I'm feeling mistreated, what should I do?" Then I would jump to his defense. Spring into action to fix whatever was broken. Run to scold and reprimand my daughter for hurting Jake's precious feelings. Sometimes I laugh at how easy I made it all for him. The puppet master had the perfect puppet he called "Wife." The stage was set exactly right for him and I was mindless doing his evil bidding.

16

I had no idea that child molesters had control over what they did and when they did it. Although I had no compassion for them, I honestly thought that they were all molested as children and, as a result, had a vile compulsion they couldn't control. I believed it was just an ugly taint that festered in their souls needing constant gratification. It's what drove them and kept them alive and functioning day after day. They had one purpose and one purpose only and that was to have their hands on a child as often as possible. I mistakenly thought: PEDOPHILES DID NOT LEAD NORMAL LIVES. I was convinced they were jobless, single men that walked around preying on stupid women who used drugs and drank massive amounts of alcohol so they could easily get a hold of their kids. They were obvious in their desires for children always asking to baby sit or take kids somewhere alone. They were greasy and slimy and were always looking to hug the kids or ask if your kids would give them a hug. They wanted kids to sit on their lap and they always had toys to give out in an effort to buy their affections. You had to be quite a neglectful mother to have this happen to one of your kids. You had to be an idiot not to notice and recognize that the man in your living room, or at your front door, or living in the corner house, was a predator waiting for you to turn your back. After all, pedophiles did not lead normal lives.

How and why I had painted such a picture, I'll never know. I thought I had done all the right things, waiting, watching, and testing. My daughter loved Jake, she trusted him. Other than the few flaws I mentioned before, he didn't do or say or act in any way to warn me, for more than a year. I thought I was safe. I thought she was safe. How could a sick, twisted, predator go for over a year without trying something? How could he have such self control for all those months and not be compelled to walk into the bathroom where she showered and start doing things to her? How could he maintain that façade for so long and not ask me to take the boys for a weekend getaway while he and Michelle had daddy-daughter time? This did not compute with what I thought pedophiles were. Surely they could only act normal for a few months before that uncontrollable desire reared its ugly head.

My ignorance opened the door for Jake, and he walked right in, sat down, and simply waited in complete control of everyone and everything until the one hundred percent trust was there for him to do whatever he wanted, whenever he wanted. Why me? How could I have been so stupid? How did I let this happen? Why didn't I know better and why wasn't anyone out there teaching us unsuspecting women about this?

I instantly developed an obsession for knowledge on this disgusting subject. It was accompanied by a need to save every woman and child in the free world from all pedophiles. Over time, that naturally felt more like a psychosis rather than a mission. Some days it was a terrible, needful burden and other days it was simply my duty and still other days it was just something I did. Most of the time it nearly killed me to open that door, to look inside and continuously revisit the horror that had destroyed my family, but I did it anyway. Like I said, it became an obsession.

As I did the research on the internet, I found myself developing new habits. I often caught myself reading with my finger tips covering my lips. Sometimes I sat and twisted a lock of my hair until strands started falling out. Often times the muscles in one arm would twitch uncontrollably or I'd find that I had been flexing a muscle in some part of my body for so long that the pain would eventually grab my attention. I was shocked to discover the "new me." I had become so different, so foreign. The new mannerisms carried over into my daily life at work, driving in the car, and even during conversations with people. Although these mannerisms were of little consequence, I sometimes wondered when and if they would end: would the old me ever come back?

During my course of gross study, I discovered that most websites or articles very neatly and conveniently wrapped up pedophiles into categories that made them seem so distant; so far and few between. It was definitely over-simplified, like something to keep society from living in fear. Unfortunately, it kept us all ignorant as well and left our lives open to people like Jake.

To break down these demons and put them into neat and tidy categories for the sake of societal labeling was and is outrageous. They are not opportunistic. Jake planned and manipulated everyone around him so he could eventually get to my child. He was cunning and devious and most of all, he was patient. That was something I never thought they had-patience. It was a characteristic that made everything even more calculating and wicked.

I often found myself applying the data I learned to my husband and his family. Although almost all the information of his relatives had all been disclosed by third parties, Jake's grandfather had allegedly molested all his children both male and female. He strived to get his hands on children constantly. His own daughter had his baby: an inbred baby boy who grew up being semi-mentally challenged. The stories I heard suggested that Jake's grandfather seemed, at some point in his life, to prefer sexual relations with his children and not his wife. He molested his granddaughter when she was living with him as well, a fact that she herself confirmed. It sickened me to think that this entire family knew what the patriarch was and still allowed a grand-daughter to live with them. And most repulsive was his wife, so groomed, that she never said a word; all the silence perpetuated more victims. The entire family's silence enabled more victims; victims like my daughter.

There was also Jake's father. He allegedly molested all his children too. He was constantly striving to have his hands on children. Family functions made him feel like a kid in a candy store. He tried to have his biological grandchildren on his lap at all times, he tried to get my children to go away with him "one on one, to get to know each other." His whole purpose was to be alone with children. What category do they fit in to? Are they dangerous to other children or just the ones they're related to? I was not married into or part of his family when he tried incessantly to get my children alone with him, so would my children have been safe? I don't think so.

I, for one, can tell when someone is creepy and gives off the bad vibe. Therefore, I can warn my children to stay away from that individual. I can keep a close watch on that guy. And I can even harass him until he moves away. I however, could not figure out who the most prevalent pedophile was, as they do LEAD COMPLETELY NORMAL LIVES. Are you afraid of the one who grabs a child off the street and rapes them once or the one that can come into your house, build your trust and rape your child repeatedly for years and years? Ultimately, BOTH are evil, both can be deadly, both will destroy your family and both will take away the trust, security, stability and normalcy from your child and your life. All predators will devastate everything.

17

The phone call finally came that said the D.A. decided to file charges against my husband, for real this time. I was relieved and felt validated when I heard the news. There was always a catch however. "We need one more thing," the D.A.'s investigator said. Michelle was going to have to have a recorded interview and go through all the gruesome details again. This didn't totally surprise me because I figured that at some point she was going to have to tell someone other than just me, a social worker and a police officer; someone from the district attorney's office needed to hear all this so that he or she could file the proper charges. Although I had no background in the criminal justice system, I was getting a crash course in it anyway, regardless of whether or not I was up for it.

At that time, it had been four months since this all came out. Four long, emotional months of therapy, roller coaster rides, pain and suffering for all of us. I wondered how much Michelle had forgotten about, or had made herself forget. I wanted so much to forget Jake—forget what had happened to my daughter. I knew

Michelle was doing the same and because she was a child, she would be more successful at forgetting than I was. Would it be good for her to be forced into remembering? Would this re-traumatize her? I had more questions that needed answering. I had concerns and wanted to help her get through this, but as usual, there was never anyone I could call. For these things, I was not grateful.

Michelle's recorded appointment/ interview took more time in coming than I had hoped. It seemed everything the criminal justice system needed to do, took so long. The wait was agonizing. Didn't they know there was a pedophile that was free to do whatever he wanted to more victims? Didn't they realize that the longer he was free, the longer they took to prosecute him, the more victims he would have, the more lives he would ruin? The winter holidays were mixed in there and they all came and went without a word as to when this re-traumatizing of sorts would take place. So much more time passed without any word. Again, nobody seemed to know anything. One day, it was Officer Olden doing the scheduling; then, I would get a call saying it's been given to another detective; and then it was someone else with the district attorney's office. Why didn't any of these people talk to each other? Why wasn't there just one person to lead us through all this: to schedule appointments, answer questions, and be a liaison between the investigation, criminal justice system and our own family implosion?

Those wasted holidays were another nightmare. It was a time when the world was celebrating and enjoying time off from work, exchanging gifts, family dinners and Christmas music. These were all things I hated, all the Christmas greetings, smiles, and happy holiday wishes. These people didn't live in the real world like I did. They had no idea what was lurking somewhere in their family or extended family. How was I supposed to celebrate anything anymore, or ever again? There was no way I would be able to suffer through more pretend cheer. I would have rather slit my wrists and I didn't care who knew it. However, whether I was a willing victim of the holidays or not, they still came and went without any phone calls, without any progress, without much hope. For that, I was not grateful.

The only thing I could do was to once again start at the beginning. I began calling the local police department. I tried getting a hold of the so-called new guy, Detective DeSilva. I wanted to introduce myself as the latest thorn in his side. In fact, that is exactly what I said on his voicemail. "Hello, my name is . . . and I'm going to be the new thorn in your side . . ." I half expected a call back from a man with some anger in his voice exerting his authority over me and letting me know I was not to call him, but that he would call me. It wouldn't work however; I had been desensitized to the police's power. I no longer looked at them as having any knowledge or competency when it came to the law. Yes, they did deserve respect, but not for what they knew, just for helping out when a life threatening emergency was at your door step. Other than that, we were totally equal. The uniform didn't make them any better or worse than the rest of us. This was their job, their chosen profession and just like anyone else at work, they too made mistakes.

Detective DeSilva returned my calls and what he said reinforced what I felt about the police department. He notified me that he was unaware this was even his case or had anything to do with it. He wanted to know who gave me his direct line and who informed me he was on this case. I had to laugh inside. It just did not surprise me in the least. Why would I think any of this would go smoothly? Nothing had yet and now the detective supposedly assigned to our case didn't even know who we were. Could this get any worse? Could it move any slower? Was there anyone who knew anything of use to us? And of course at the end of the day, the answer to that question was just silence.

The new detective said he would look into all this. After he did some research on our case, he took care of business immediately and scheduled our appointment. This was a nice change. When dealing with my daughter and me, Detective DeSilva was someone who seemed to understand the emotions involved. When we spoke, his voice sounded caring with its quiet tones. I pictured him being a man of small stature who was older with children of his own; I imagined he probably had grandchildren who were Michelle's age. Perhaps the horror of this case falling on his desk wasn't something he was going to dismiss as a chore, but embrace as a way of being there to help us get through it. During his two days of calls and inquiries, he called me several times to give me status as to what was happening. I found that in this nightmare, knowledge of who, what, where, when and how was so comforting and Detective DeSilva understood that, too. I was grateful for him.

We were given less than a day's notice for Michelle's appointment. Whether that was a good or bad thing, I didn't know. I called Linda, my daughter's therapist, and she had an emergency over-the-phone session with Michelle. She did her best to prepare her emotionally for the retelling of her terrible ordeal. I didn't believe that did much good because that evening, I found my daughter curled up in a little ball, hiding in the corner of an unused bedroom. My poor, young child having so much resting on her shoulders, clearly it was taking its toll. My heart broke seeing her in that state, but I had to be strong for her. I had to lend her all the influence I could conjure in hopes that it would be enough for her to do what was needed. I approached her, gathered her up in my arms as best I could without carrying her, and simply told her it was time for bed. Tonight, we were going to watch, *The Princess Diaries*. The sweet movie with happy thoughts and happy endings comforted her and she slept soundly, for a change. I was thankful for that.

The next day we went to her interview. The building was a regular, non-descriptive, four story office building with only the address in huge numbers on the outside. Inside, there was one reception area with a sheriff sitting behind a desk; there was nothing else around. No other people, no directory on the wall with lists of people's names and suite numbers. There was nothing except an empty foyer with a tall desk and a sheriff behind it. I don't even remember there being a picture on any of the walls. It was a blank place to be. It was a building you would only be at if given specific instructions to be there. It wasn't a place you went to by mistake looking for this office, that doctor, this business or something else. This was situated and constructed and decorated (or lack thereof), for one reason and one reason only: you were there for one of those TV types of interviews. One of those scary ones you see on *Law and Order*, where you knew people were watching and waiting and grilling you for answers. This was going to be a terrifying experience. Michelle was not going to be okay when this was over. She wasn't going to be, and neither would I.

I knew from the detective's instructions that we were to go upstairs. The staircase was secure and visible just past the sheriff standing in the corner. Nobody would be able to go up without the officer allowing it. We walked past the sheriff to the staircase. I was surprised he didn't stop us to ask any questions. It seemed he was a protector of sorts and yet he didn't even glance our way. As soon as we started up the stairs, there were big arrows colorfully painted on the walls. The atmosphere changed in an instant. First we were at some non-descriptive foyer, and the next we were in an enchanted, happy place. As we walked up the stairs the cute murals materialized with large, happy, cartoon characters everywhere. The more steps you climbed, the bigger and brighter the pictures became.

We followed the bright neon arrows and pictures that directed us where to go. The office door we went into looked like a regular doctor's office at first. There were chairs around the edge of the room with magazines on a coffee table. More happy, colorful cartoon characters were painted on the walls making everything seem super friendly. There was a lady sitting behind a glass window who immediately asked for our names. I checked us in and within two minutes, a young woman came out from another door within the waiting room. She took Michelle for what was referred to as "playtime." There was a large window from the waiting room where I could watch where Michelle went to. She couldn't see me, but I could watch her and a few other kids playing. I noticed each child was paired with an adult who seemed like some sort of buddy.

Inside that very large room was every toy, playhouse, craft table, and book you could imagine. To my surprise, Karen, the social worker, was in there with Michelle. She came out, asked me a few questions, which I comfortably answered her; she was so easy to talk to. She said she was very pleased with Michelle's progress. It seemed as though she had "blossomed," was how she put it and we were a testament as to what a safe home environment and therapy could do for a child. I was glad she had noticed that since I had not, but really it was of little comfort. I knew the things Michelle was exhibiting at home, like still not showering regularly and if she did, it was with her clothes on. I knew Michelle was broken, even if she could still function in public. Karen then disappeared back into the other room, letting me know it was time for them to begin. I wasn't sure what that meant exactly, but I knew it would be difficult for Michelle.

After the playing part was over-which was simply to ease the child's anxieties and get them ready to talk-Michelle was taken in to a side room off of that giant playroom. Everything happened in that secret place where nobody could see. When I could no longer see Michelle, as the door closed behind her, I sat down in the regular looking waiting room and waited. Two painstakingly-long hours which seemed more like an entire day, went by. I chewed off all my finger nails, read every magazine and brochure in the waiting room and still kept on waiting and worrying about my daughter. I sent many text messages to anyone who would respond just trying to stay distracted from why I was really there. At one point, a lady came into the waiting area and asked me if I wanted some juice and cookies. I politely declined, knowing those would be wasted on my ever increasingly sensitive stomach.

Detective DeSilva and Karen finally emerged. I was surprised to meet the detective and even more surprised to see how my mental picture of him was so wrong. He was very tall and slightly younger than I. He seemed like a big, brown teddy bear. This was probably a good thing for Michelle. They told me Michelle did great and was doing fine back in the large playroom. The room now was being used to decompress Michelle with more play therapy to help her transition from what she had just talked about. She had told everything again and her story remained very consistent. Consistency was something I was terrified of. The thing that worried me the most, the monster hidden in my closet, was that Michelle would one day tell them that Jake had done much more than she was telling. I was dreading the day that she became so comfortable with talking about it that she would be able to vocalize every detail. My thoughts were that pedophiles often progressed. The more they did and the more they could do, the more they did do as there was nothing and no one to stop them. Michelle had been suffering in silence for so long. I often times imagined he had done so much more to her and she just wasn't ready to tell.

Detective DeSilva and Karen informed me that Michelle was now making some jewelry and picking out a stuffed animal to take home and that it shouldn't be too much longer. This interviewing process was really set up in a fantastic way. They did try hard to make it as comfortable for the child as possible. There was the playtime before hand, to make the child more comfortable. After that, there was the actual interview, in another room, just off the playroom. This was followed up by decompression playtime to transition the child back into a more typical state of being. It was a smooth and intelligent way to talk to a kid. Whoever came up with this was brilliant and for that, I was grateful.

Now that Michelle's interview was all on video tape things would progress more quickly from the legal standpoint. Apparently this interview was something that should have been done a long time ago: it was supposed to have been done at the very beginning. Was I surprised at the error? Not at all. Once the D.A.'s office had this, they could and would move forward, or so I was told. It was just another piece of information that made me shake my head back and forth as to why these professionals who did this day in and day out, couldn't seem to get this case together. A mother without a college education and no legal experience had a better handle on how to track everything more than they did.

I informed them that I wanted to be notified of everything, from the arraignment to the trial, so I could be there. I needed to be involved in every aspect of the case. I felt as if I missed something, then they would miss something and Jake would then go free. Detective DeSilva said that usually these cases plea bargain out to a lesser offense to avoid the burden of a trial. It didn't matter to me though; this was now on its way to being over. I wanted it to be over and I wanted to be there to see it.

18

The next few weeks were, once again, very quiet—too quiet. I called the D.A.'s office to check on the status of things, but as usual there was no answer and no return phone call. The children and I just kept going day after day with our somewhat normal routines. And I kept right on calling for a status of a trial that seemed like it would never come.

More odd quirks surfaced, with regards to my daughter. She had more problems, my boys had issues, and I developed more weird tics myself. Life continued on. I kept calling and was relentless in my pursuit for justice. With one call, that was finally answered, I learned that the D.A.'s office had questions for me. They were waiting for the detective from the police department to call me so that I could answer the questions, then they would relay that back to the D.A.'s office that I was currently on the phone with. It was a ridiculous way of doing things, but that was the way it was. I needed to be contacted by Detective DeSilva to ask me questions that the district attorney's investigator needed answered, then relayed to the prosecuting attorney. Why the prosecuting attorney's investigator couldn't call me and ask me the questions, I will never know. Why he couldn't ask me right then as I was on the phone with him, again, I will never know. It was such a waste of precious time; time when a pedophile was running free to create more victims.

I received promise after promise that this would be the last thing they needed before they started proceedings. I continued to call the detective at the police department to answer these unknown but all-important questions. Finally, after a week of me trying to connect with someone, we talked and I answered the stupidest questions I'd ever heard. It seemed to me they were just buying time. It started to feel like they wanted another victim to appear and make their case stronger. Or perhaps they were just testing the waters to see if I would eventually give up and disappear.

Another week without any word from anyone slipped by. I called the prosecuting attorney's office and spoke with the investigator again. I nearly fell off my chair when he asked me the exact same questions that Detective DeSilva had asked. I frustratingly gave him the exact same answers. Why didn't he just ask me in the first place? Why did I have to go back to the detective just to end up being asked again by the D.A.'s investigator whom I was on the phone with weeks ago in the first place! He was the one who told me there were more questions and here I was . . . talking to him . . . answering him . . . with the same answers . . . to the same questions. Why did we just wait all these weeks if he was going to have to hear it for himself anyway? This seemed like the most ineffective and inefficient way to handle a criminal case! These people acted like it was the very first time they had ever investigated or tried to prosecute a crime. The questions were so inane that I can't even recall what they were. Ridiculous was and is the only thing I can remember.

A few weeks later, my status-inquiring phone calls to the D.A. were finally answered with another piece of evidence being lost, or "misplaced" as they liked to call it. It was Michelle's videotaped interview this time. I told the D.A.'s investigator I was about to "stroke out" on him out of frustration. Although he said that he understood, I didn't think he did. Wasn't he embarrassed that the evidence kept getting lost? I could feel the room swirling as my blood pressure rose. I thought for sure I was about to pass out. How could this many mistakes happen? Didn't we already talk about this piece of evidence? Didn't we already locate all the missing evidence from before? The D.A's investigator had no answers for me. I was helpless. These were the people in charge and these were the ones I had to rely on to get justice for my daughter. This was of little comfort. This, I was not grateful for.

As I worked trying to locate the missing tapes and making sure they were given to the right person, I wasn't at all shocked to learn that we wouldn't be able to even locate them until the following week. The evidence clerk was supposedly on vacation until then. This, of course, was just another ploy at wasting time; I think they just wanted a break from my continuous phone calls. However, the only thing this accomplished was making me feel like they were incompetent and stupid and putting me on edge, to say the least. It made me think that without my direct and forceful participation, this case would be lost along with all the evidence that kept growing legs and walking off.

Too much time again had passed since all the evidence had been logged in . . . successfully. Everything was now in the hands of the female prosecuting attorney. She was assigned to the case, and it was now her decision when to file formal charges. The only thing left to do at this point was to wait. Patience was not one of my strong suits, but I had definitely gotten better at it. However, too much time was passing by. I wondered if the prosecutor was looking at the videotape of my daughter and seeing her as an older girl. At this point, a long time had gone by and my daughter had grown significantly since she was actively being molested. Was the prosecutor looking at a tall preteen, whom she didn't believe would keep quiet for so long? Was she not seeing the innocent, little girl who had been violated starting when she was only ten years old? What would it take for her to make her decision to prosecute and make it official?

I somehow needed to show her that my daughter was small and pure. She needed to see her for the innocent child she was. I desperately went on a hunt for pictures. It was the only thing I could think of to do and it would be a difficult task, since we weren't living in our home with our own things. However, over the years, I had given my parents enough photos and memorabilia that this was not impossible. It was just going to be difficult. I needed pictures of any kind, school pictures, holiday pictures, even Jake's and my wedding photos. These were a more accurate depiction of what Michelle looked like back when he first started molesting her.

In a box in one of the unused rooms, I found several photos. One brought me to raging tears. It was of Michelle and Jake dancing at our wedding. She was so little, lanky and thin. She had a short bob haircut up to her earlobes. She looked adorable, happy and excited. They were dancing together and Michelle was gazing up at him as if she finally had the dad she had always wanted. She had an expression of excitement and happiness as if the whole world was going to be a magical place. Jake looked back adoringly at her and I, of course, saw it for what it was. He was a wolf, licking his lips and salivating at a future meal. It was sickening to look at the picture of them. She, being so innocent, and he, getting ready to pounce.

It was hard not to remember that day while looking at my daughter's beautiful face, her beautiful eyes looking so eager about the future. I was so happy to be marrying my soul mate, the man God made just for me. However, I was nervous, too, and not in the normal way either. Something was nagging at me. Things were not right with all our kids and here we were, making this all a permanent family. We had our closest friends and family present, and our pastor married us in our church. I wore a light blue tea length dress. My youngest son walked me down the aisle while the rest of our children were the groomsmen and bridesmaids. The ceremony was quick with the reception being held in the large gymnasium right after. Everyone danced and took lots of pictures. It ended up being a wonderful day. My kids were so happy, but Jake's daughters seemed reluctant to participate. No matter how hard I tried, they were never happy. Why didn't I stop to ask why? Instead, I assumed it was the same old story, with them perceiving me as the wicked stepmother. I mistakenly thought I just needed more time to show them who I was.

As I looked at these photos and remembered those days, I was unaware that tears had flooded my face, snot was running freely from my nose, and that I was barely breathing. The sudden bursting forth of emotion was too much again and I had to try hard to catch my breath. I wanted so badly to go back in time, to that day and stop all of it. Why didn't anyone tell me this before I married him? Why didn't his daughters or nieces or someone tell me he was a child molester before I married him on that day? My daughter wasn't his first victim, the way it was going; she wouldn't even be his last-so why hadn't anyone else told me what he was? In a flash, the pain and questions consumed me. I saw my Michelle in these few photos. She was sweet, so full of life, trusting, beautiful and wholesome. She was, in a word, fearless. Then, I came across her school photo that was taken a year later. The comparison was horrifying. In the school picture she was hidden behind long, messy, dirty hair. She didn't really smile in the picture. Her expression was pained and she looked very tired. She wore too many clothes for our hot weather. She was almost unrecognizable. There was even a darkness that seemed to surround her where before all the pictures were bright. How did I not notice this change? How could I not see?

I was enraged at myself and in such emotional pain as I haphazardly scribbled out a note for the prosecutor. I wrote something to the effect that these pictures were of my daughter before and during the time she was being molested. These were how she looked back then. She wasn't the older preteen in the video, (not that that would have made it less offensive), but she was younger and trusting and so innocent. Jake was the one who changed all that; he was the one who took that all away. He was the one who needed to be punished. And she, the prosecuting attorney, was the one to make it so.

I drove the photos and letter to the police department and asked the receptionist behind the glass to give it to Detective DeSilva. It was all that was left inside me. There wasn't anything else for me to do. If all of this wasn't enough, then nothing would ever be enough. In my eyes and in my heart, this was and should have been more than sufficient. Michelle was worth it. She deserved to have her word be believed. There shouldn't have to be another victim before he went to prison. Another child should not have to suffer and then come forward in order to hold him accountable. Why wouldn't anyone else come forward? If you were a victim, why would you not tell? I had to take a good long look in the mirror in order to have that question answered. I was the expert on that answer.

Another Friday came and went as I resolved to become more self-reliant in the matter of case monitoring and information. There had to be some sort of access to all this online. You could "Google," just about anything so there must be a way to see when the district attorney's office would file charges. After a few hours, I found the county website and discovered that I was able to access all kinds of things. It was amazing. I could look up and see if someone even had a traffic ticket. Then you could "Google" the charge and see what the codes meant and why they had been ticketed. It felt empowering to finally not have to call someone else, but to have all the access I wanted and needed at a time of my choosing. For this I was grateful.

While at the computer, I checked the county website again. I couldn't believe my eyes when I saw new charges under Jake's name. He had three new counts. I clicked on them and saw he had formally been charged with three counts of "lewd and/or lascivious acts against a child under 14." Finally, this was on its way to being over! Six long, agonizing and mind breaking months had gone by. In fact, it was six months to the day since we had reported the sexual abuse. It took exactly six months to have a prosecutor file charges against a pedophile. That, in and of itself, didn't seem right. But at least there it was.

I wondered why Jake was not in jail and why there were only three charges against him. This was something I wasn't able to find out over the internet, so back to the beginning I went. I called the D.A's office over and over again, but I received no answer and no return call. I had all these questions of course, but one of them was crying out to be heard: how much longer before I could live again? Of course, there was no answer. More days would pass before I heard anything further. These days were torture. They ate away at me like a flesh-eating disease. How and why the officials in these positions didn't know this was how it all felt was mindboggling. They either didn't know, didn't care, or maybe even both.

Days and days later, I received a call from Detective DeSilva. He finally had a warrant and was going to arrest my husband. At last, some vindication, some justice, some triumph for our side. He asked where they could find Jake because they had done a stake out at his house—our house—and he wasn't home. He said they had showed up at 9:00am in the morning and stayed there until 5:00pm. I let out a sort of frustrated burst of air as I asked why they thought he would be at home during a work day? Who did they think he was? This was not the creepy guy living in his mother's basement. Why did everyone, including the police officers, think that this was what a pedophile was?

I informed him that he'd find him at work, holding down his job, working for a living. Then I had to tell him where Jake worked and who he worked for. Really? Wasn't there some kind of database they had access to in order to locate the criminals they were searching for? Did the police really have to rely on someone who had absolutely no contact with a person for over six months to give them the information they needed? Detective DeSilva said he was going to make a scene about it and arrest him at his work and make sure everyone knew what he was being arrested for. I suppose he was trying to make up for seeming inept and making me feel so discouraged about his competency. After it was all over, he would call me back and relay how it all went down. I had a slight smile on my face all day that day. It seemed that Jake's good fortune was at an end. His luck and the protection of his sister was finally coming to a close.

19

All day, I waited. I watched my phone and waited for that irritating beeping or ringing. I was still just searching for something to let me know that the deed was done and that this was over. I was hoping I would feel relieved—more content, in a way—or safer after he was arrested. As the day wore on, my fake smile was replaced with lines of worry. I wrung my hands, paced in my office, and took constant bathroom breaks. The minutes seemed like hours, the hours seemed like days; it was definitely one of the longest eight hours of my life. The call I was waiting for finally came a little after 5:00 pm. I was already home from work. My heart raced as I answered my phone. I didn't want any distractions or interruptions as I listened to the detective, so I went back outside, listening intently to the voice on the other end. He relayed the day's events quickly and without emotion. Why I was shocked at that point was laughable, but astounded I was, along with a million other emotions as well. I took in every syllable of his pathetic tale of the day's events.

Jake worked as a mechanic at a car dealership in town and the detective found his work place with ease, only to find that the entire business had closed down and moved. The detectives had to go knocking on all the nearby businesses just to find one that knew where the car dealership had moved to; the information came from a nearby plumbing business. So off the police officers went to find the newly relocated place. Again, the new location was found with little effort, but the day was wearing on and they needed to get there by 5:00 pm. When they arrived, they staked it out watching for any sign of Jake. They didn't see him anywhere, so they thought it best just to storm in. Unable to find Jake, they went into an office and spoke with a shocked manager and an owner. The detectives asked where Jake was and informed them that they were there to arrest him. During this brief conversation, one of the officers noticed a nice looking, middle aged, blonde woman leave the area and go into an adjacent office, which made the officer very suspicious; his first thought was that perhaps they were hiding Jake. Then the owner of the car dealership informed the detectives that Jake no longer worked there: he was let go some time back for reasons the owner did not disclose. However, the owner or someone who worked for the dealership still had contact with Jake and told the detective where he now worked. So it was back to square one in locating that place and fast, because the work day was quickly coming to a close. If they didn't find him immediately, chances were, they weren't going to, at least not that day.

All the police officers went off to the next location where Jake supposedly worked in hopes of having this wild goose chase come to an end. This was now location number three, or four if you counted our house where they had mistakenly staked out initially. Once again, they found the next site rather quickly, but by the time they arrived there, unsurprisingly, Jake had fled. He was nowhere to be found. In fact, the garage radio was still playing music and tools were scattered on the ground next to a car-it was obvious that a person had just fled this location and left in a major hurry.

At this point, I could hear the frustration in Detective DeSilva's voice; it was apparent that this was one long day for him as well. He had one arrest warrant to enforce and he didn't expect it was going to take this long or be this difficult to apprehend a simple pedophile. Yet again, Jake and his entourage had been underestimated. This added not only to my own irritation, but it instilled a fear factor as well. Who was Jake and how did he keep getting away from being held accountable for his actions? Who were these people that kept helping him and why?

The law enforcement officers searched the premises when they came across the manager of the place. While still in shock, the boss relayed to the officers what had just taken place literally seconds before they arrived:

"Jake received a phone call on his cell phone and then literally dropped his tools and ran. He came in here, clearly out of breath, said he had some personal family problems to take care of, needed to get a lawyer and would most likely be gone for a few days."

The manager told him that was okay and then Jake ran out of there fast, got his keys, got into his car and sped away. The manager then wanted to know what was going on, but by now, the officers just wanted to go home. Detective DeSilva knew it was the blonde woman from Jake's previous employer that had tipped Jake off. He knew by the way she had reacted to everything that she was up to no good. An officer's instincts, intuition, whatever it was, he called it right. And then, Jake was on the run.

So there it was. After all that, they left to go make their reports back at the police station and make that bitter and disappointing phone call to me. As I listened to the detective, I felt so defeated. Again Jake's luck had prevailed. The detective tried to reassure me that this was just temporary and that Jake couldn't hide forever, but I knew otherwise. Jake would somehow come out of this unscathed, like he had with everything else so far. That wave of depression and sense of loss washed over me in an instant, so familiar. I was brought back to that place of hopelessness. As I walked back into the house, my visiting sister-in-law and my mother could see on my face that the day's events had not gone on as planned. I closed my eyes, dropped and shook my head, the tears pouring down like a waterfall from my eyes, let them know that once again, Jake was free, and we had lost.

The next day, I found myself alone at work. It was one of those rare occasions where everyone was out of the office for one reason or another. I realized that I was nervous for my own safety. Something could happen to me and nobody would even know. I was there, totally alone, completely unprotected and I didn't even have the strength or the will to fight, should anything happen. My thoughts turned to a desperate concern for Michelle. I was becoming acutely aware that I didn't know Jake at all. I didn't know who he knew, who had loyalties towards him or why. What was he capable of? What were his friends and family capable of doing?

I called Michelle's school to let them know what was happening. I'm sure the person I spoke with heard the desperation and panic in my voice. They were sensitive and proactive to the situation and had everything under control instantly. My daughter was safe and would stay that way, under their protection, until I came to get her. There was no need to worry about her. They reassured me they would have her covertly under supervision at every second of the day. For that, I was grateful.

All day, while at work I watched my computer screen. It was on an official, county internet page that showed the status of my husband's arrest. "Husband:" I loathed that word. Right now that status said, *Fugitive*. His hearing information was there as well and that said, *Failed to appear*. I kept hitting the update button to show me the most current, up to the second information. That dark cloudy mist swirled around me as I worked that morning. The scary whispers stayed in my mind as well. They spoke of horrible things that Jake could do to me or Michelle in his desperate state. I watched the door to my office for any sign that someone could be there just on the other side, listening to see if I was alone, waiting for the perfect moment to enter and do those awful things that my imagination kept thinking about. My eyes went from the door to the computer monitor, back and forth, like watching a tennis match. I was a wreck that was slowly sinking deeper and deeper into despair with a touch of irrational panic on the side. My stomach churned and made noises and I felt so sick. The pain in my jaw from clenching my teeth was also painful and it was wearing me down; the physical suffering was almost as bad as the emotional. I didn't even want to engage the thoughts of how we would cope if Jake decided to stay on the run. I couldn't handle one day of the *Fugitive* status, let alone many days or, heaven forbid, years.

One of my internet updates showed that Jake had been released on bail. That was utterly confusing because his status still showed *Fugitive*. One update click more and that, too, stated *Heard*. "Heard what?" I asked aloud to no one in particular. What was happening? I frantically updated and read every page and suddenly, it only said he was out on bail until his court date of April 25th. How did this all happen? I couldn't believe what my eyes were telling me. Yesterday he was a fugitive and today he's out on bail? I immediately called the D.A.'s investigator and asked him what in the world was going on. He confirmed the tale of someone with such incredible luck on his side; he said he was somewhat amazed as well.

Jake showed up in court while arraignments were going on for multiple offenders. He appeared with a criminal lawyer, a bail bondsman and of course, his sister, Julie. All key players on hand and ready for them to sign on the dotted line and walk Jake out of the court room without so much as a slap on the wrist. He was free, not even one night in jail. The investigator kept warning me that this was not a quick event. He informed me that this entire criminal court process would most likely take a year and a half, possibly more. There would be pre trial after pre trial of exchanging evidence and then a preliminary hearing and finally a jury trial. All of this would be done over the course of a year or two while we all went on with our lives. While Jake went on with his life. He was hardly missing a beat. How simple it all was for Jake. How easily someone was making his court process: it was just another nuisance. It was nothing more than a fly buzzing around a picnic. A wave of your hand and the fly flies away and all is well with the sun still shining on his face. This was his life and the person who was taking care of all of this for him was his sister. No doubt it was his sick, victimized sister who had a need to make all this disappear for her baby brother. They were peculiar and dysfunctional, behaving more like lovers at times than brother and sister.

I kept speculating why Jake's sister, Julie, didn't use her money for therapy. At some point, she had to know or, at the very least, suspect these charges now officially brought against him may be true. Why not, at that point, talk about therapy? Take all that money she was spending: retaining the criminal attorney; the $10,000 dollars cash for the $100,000 bail; not to mention retaining of the family lawyer who had been representing him in the custody disputes of his children . . . All that money spent for a man who belonged in prison. Why not spend the small fortune more productively? The questions came one after the other, unanswered. The wonderings of my brain wouldn't cease and after a long exhausting work day of doing nothing but rambling on to no one, I went home.

The familiar darkness swirled around me and I became increasingly depressed. This was it. My life had become nothing more than what I had been afraid of; counseling appointments for my daughter, calls for updates on a case that was about as productive as watching grass grow, and a dangerous hermit-like lifestyle that I had adopted and was perfecting. It was everything I didn't want. I had three kids who needed me. Other than that, I had nothing to live for. I simply couldn't get past what had been done to Michelle, to our family, to me. I couldn't overcome the self-loathing, guilt, depression, and mixed emotions I had for myself and Jake.

The whispers came, relentless in their pursuit, still demanding my death. They knew me so well; they knew exactly what to say. My mind clouded over with the most profound sense of sadness I had ever known. My heart ached in my chest with such bleeding pain and massive pressure, it was almost impossible to breathe. I kept seeing his face, his eyes, his smile and wondered still how he could've done this. The lack of remorse shown by his actions spoke volumes of my existence in relation to him. I was just a puppet, a toy, and play thing to occupy his time until it broke, was lost, or he became bored with it, trading it in for something new. My suffering was never given any consideration by him. I was of absolutely no consequence.

I found out through his ex-wife's grapevine that he had moved on and had even acquired a new girlfriend to go with his new life.

She was now his new toy, his new puppet; I was so quickly and easily replaced. I agonized over whether or not he had gained a new child to torture as well. And unfortunately, I found out the new puppet did have a daughter. Of course she did. He wouldn't be with her if she didn't. My desperation and loss of control continued to suffocate me. I still wondered if the devil would win and eventually would convince me to give him my life. It was a daily struggle, a moment to moment struggle, to say the least.

I sometimes found hope and a sense of purpose when I emailed everyone I could think of who could affect change. I contacted celebrities who fought for and supported causes, my local politicians, radio personalities, etc. I wanted laws to become better. I wanted to let other women know who and what was lurking out there waiting to enter their lives. I wanted to let victims know they weren't alone. I needed to stop this from happening to someone else's son or daughter. In the end, however, nobody wrote back, nobody called; nobody cared until it hit their home. I didn't blame them. I wouldn't want to give this horror a glance either, much less dedicate part of my life to it if I didn't have to. But I did have to now. This was who and what I was. I was a victim of sorts, and someone who couldn't undo something terrible that had been done. This was now my life, the life that would continue on throughout the criminal court proceedings. The year or two that the D.A.'s office told me it would take. This was it. Despair, depression, hate, anger, bitterness, pain, agony, none of these words came close to describing what I felt. In the end, however, this was what life would be like for the next one or two years, or so I thought.

20

The hopelessness I fell into became harder and harder to conceal. My children all knew that their mother had changed. Although I had played off their concern as nothing more than just being tired from work: they knew it was not that simple. There just didn't seem to be a way back to being myself. I had become uncharacteristically thin and my hair kept falling out in large chunks; there were days when I was afraid to even touch my head out of fear of how much hair I would find in my hand, on the brush or dropped onto my lap. I now kept my head lowered at all times when I walked. I rarely looked anyone in the eye and certainly never talked to strangers. I felt like I wanted to just stay in a corner of a room and not interact with anyone anymore.

Everything felt broken; my body, my mind and definitely my spirit. My reflection in the mirror was no longer recognizable so I stayed away from them—one look in the morning was all I could handle seeing. Just a quick glance as I threw what was left of my long, beautiful, thick hair up with a clip, a few swipes of a lipstick, a little mascara and that was it. So far away from the woman who had once been in front of a camera for local business ads. I wasn't much of a model back in my early twenties, but it was something I did for fun and because of that, I used to care about how I looked; now I couldn't care less. I was actually disgusted as to who and what I saw looking back at me.

Although I was busy hating myself and my life, I still took care of my children. I was still able to go through the motions of being a mom. I took my daughter to therapy every week. It was a place almost an hour away from where we lived, but it gave us time to bond and talk about anything we wanted to talk about. I hoped that one day she would realize just how much I loved her and how she was one of the most important kids in the whole wide world to me. Her therapist seemed to really care about her as well. So much so, that her therapist, Lisa, always brought out CDs into the waiting room for me to listen to while she was inside with Michelle. They were CDs on how to be a good parent. This was obviously a subject I needed serious help in or so she thought anyway. If I was a good parent, then this wouldn't have happened to Michelle in the first place, right? So I politely took the CDs every week, popped in the one where I had left off the week before, and listened intently on what I could do better as a mother. Mostly though, if I was alone in the waiting area, I just sat and quietly cried as the man talked into my ears, from the educational CD, telling me how to think, act and treat my children better. It seemed that even he knew I wasn't good enough.

I felt awful that people naturally assumed I was a bad mother in every way and needed help with day to day life. It was a terrible feeling to think that everyone I came in contact with thought I was no better than some crack addicted prostitute who couldn't care less whether her children even had food. After all, those were the only people who were victims of sexual abuse right? Was I deserving of this kind of treatment? I didn't know. How did I even get to this place? That was a constant thought in my head. It was only six months ago that I owned my own home with my husband, had beautiful things, and took all my kids on shopping sprees whenever I had a larger than normal paycheck. My days and nights consisted of being at home, with them, always doing family things. Where did I go wrong to make people think that I was this monster?

It seemed like the more people knew, the more they had heard, or the more Michelle or I revealed, the worse I was treated. They acted like they knew everything that had happened and so they were entitled to pass judgment. Everyone seemed to look at me differently. Most of my brothers and sisters quit communicating with me. Distant relatives always had harsh words for me about this decision or that one, if they spoke to me at all. I became like someone with leprosy or another highly contagious disease. In their eyes I was suddenly not good at anything and not good enough for anything. They all frequently reminded me that this entire issue was my fault. It was a harsh slap in the face when people who knew about us and what had happened started and continued to treat me so poorly or just avoided me completely.

My daughter had somehow become a saint and I, the ultimate sinner. She was not only a victim of Jake, but of me as well. If she said, "jump," and I didn't do it, I was looked at as a criminal. It encompassed all aspects of our lives: what I chose to cook for dinner was not good enough, the time I let Michelle go out and play was not the right time, being unable or unavailable to help with homework was despicable to everyone, I was sleeping too much or sleeping too little, I didn't make enough money; my kids weren't seeing the right doctors, the kids weren't wearing the right clothes, the list was never ending. I was surprised they weren't complaining about how I breathed: certainly there was a right and wrong way to do that, too.

There was one thing however, that I experienced that was worse than any of those things I just mentioned. It crushed me and not only was it insensitive, but also totally unjustified. I was no longer trusted with anyone's child. I was no longer the one people called to watch over their little ones. Somehow, what my husband had done became my crime. I was, in some way, as guilty and responsible as well as he was. The lack of confidence from my family was unfounded and hurtful to the point of physical pain. When my nieces would visit which was so seldom anyway, they were pulled away from me as if the plague showed infectiously on my skin. I couldn't figure out what made everyone so afraid to leave me alone in the same room with one of their kids. I was the same woman they called less than a year ago to babysit. I was exactly the same if not more cautious and protective than before. Did they really think that I was suddenly a child molester too? Was that really a disease you could catch? The isolation and the obvious distaste for me and my choices was one thing, but not being able to be a part of my nieces and nephews lives for something I did not do, felt like an over-reaction: inappropriate, it was so wrong and I felt so insulted.

Not only were the children made to stay away, but the adults kept their distance also. As soon as I walked into a room full of family or friends, it would empty out in a matter of seconds. They would ask me cordially how I was doing and whether or not I told them the truth about the court case, or if I lied and said, "I'm fine," I would still find myself constantly alone. It felt like some kind of sick game where I was the only one playing along, but eventually, I started to count the seconds it took for everyone to leave once I entered a room. I'd be lying if I said that didn't destroy me as well. Yes, to be left in solitude to deal with everything and to be treated with such disdain was painful. Although I thought I deserved it, I didn't feel that they were the ones who should be criticizing me. I was the only one who should have passed judgment on me, me and God and nobody else.

My family wasn't the type to talk about negative or uncomfortable things. Someone could be dying of cancer, but it would never be discussed. We didn't talk about such things. If one of us was out of a job, lost a relationship or was even in a minor car accident, it was all hushed up. I knew they all wanted everything swept under the rug and I had forgotten my broom and dustpan and was not complying. We all knew that was how it had been dealt with when we were children. It seemed like back in the "good ol' days" that was how things were handled. We were told to smile, hum a nice little tune as everything went under a rug. Then you sat quietly in a chair, looking neat and pretty and never said a word. But it was wrong then and was wrong now and I didn't care how much they were repulsed by me for wanting justice for Michelle. She was not

Jake's first victim, but I was going to make sure she was his last even if they all hated me for it; even if they all ended up completely removing me from their lives.

Outside of the home, life was just as crazy. One evening, while on the way to my therapy, I spotted Jake's sister, Julie, sitting in a car at the end of the block. Apparently, she had forgotten that I was with Jake, Julie and her husband when they bought that car from the dealership where Jake worked. It had been several years earlier, and it was for Julie's husband, Ryan, but it was a distinctive luxury car. I knew it was her from half way down the street. It was a nice enough car that people would notice it and there was Julie, sitting in it, unmoving, probably wondering frantically how to act as someone drove by since she was not getting out of the car. As I ever so slowly approached in a family member's vehicle, she looked like she was trying to disguise herself and her real purpose in being there. It was almost comical to see her looking down into her lap as I approached in a t-bone direction, turned, and then ultimately drove by. I guess I wasn't supposed to remember the car or what she looked like, even in her oversized glasses and big floppy hat. Who wore an outfit like that in the winter time in the early evening hours? Did she think people would believe she was about to get out of her car and start doing yard work at the house she was in front of? Did she think that nobody knew who the people were who lived there or what they looked like?

Living in the same neighborhood for over thirty years made it so everyone knew everyone. This was a very small community which was nice and when people came to visit someone, we all knew they didn't live here; they were just friends of that family or extended family. Julie stuck out like a sore thumb and didn't even realize it. I immediately called my mother to have her bring Michelle inside the house. I didn't know what Julie was doing there, what she planned to do, or what she had hoped to see, but I wasn't taking any chances either. I only knew that Jake's family that I was dealing with was extremely bizarre and totally unpredictable. I also had to come to the realization that this was all going to get very ugly before it was over. None of these people were anything like I thought they were; none of them were what they seemed or pretended to be. It would be so much easier if bad people wore signs or had a unique look to them, but they don't. I only knew that one of them was sitting in a car at the end of my street watching my daughter play with her best friend outside, in the front yard.

My daily life still consisted of going to work. There were times when getting out of bed was almost impossible, but for the most part, I faked it through my regular routine. One particular morning, as I was driving to work, my steering wheel locked up. The car was still moving, but it was now nearly out of my control. Of course this scared me to the point where I thought my heart was about to explode as I struggled to regain power over my car. Thankfully, I wasn't too far away from the house, still driving barely twenty five miles per hour through our neighborhood and was able to use all my strength to go around the block and back in our driveway. By the time I got home I was sweating and out of breath from the strain of navigating the broken steering of the car. I felt so grateful that I was alone, without the kids, not on the freeway doing sixty five miles per hour or taking a sharp turn somewhere. I didn't want to even give those thoughts any mental processing time. The what if's on that were terrifying. I had never had such a thing happen and I had never heard of this type of problem occurring in any car. I just kept wondering what in the world happened. One day everything was fine, my car ran perfectly and the next morning it had all changed in a second. There was no sound of something breaking, no leaking of fluid or grinding noise that would have possibly alerted me to a problem, there was just suddenly and inexplicably, almost no ability to steer this car.

This was just another one of those things that happened at a really bad time in one's life. People say, "When it rains it pours" and apparently, my monsoon season had only just begun. Losing my husband, my daughter in a way, my house and now my car seemed like a lot to go through at one time. I think the first two were definitely the hardest. Losing everything else that was materialistic was just the icing on the cake, or more accurately, the straw that broke the camel's back, or my back anyway.

Things became very foggy. I once again started to function on autopilot. I had to be able to get Michelle to therapy every week so getting the car back up and running became a priority. Luckily, my dad had a mechanic friend named Jim. He was a handy man type of fellow who didn't hold down any regular jobs. He knew quite a bit about a whole lot of different things, but seemed to love his day to day freedom and a little of the bubbly more than getting a regular paycheck. Normally, a person with that type of background wouldn't have been my preference, but since money was so tight and his schedule so flexible, he seemed the right choice. He came over within a day or two and immediately started working on the car. For this, I was very grateful.

One day, as I rode my bicycle up the driveway, coming home from work, I was met by Jim, the mechanic/ handyman, along with my father. They had troubled looks on their faces and I was not only shocked, but horrified to find out why. At first I thought this must be a way more expensive problem then we had originally discussed and I was going to be riding my bike a lot longer than anticipated. What they told me turned my world upside down and made it clear that money was no longer the issue, but something much worse. It wasn't more expensive, it was just more sinister. Jim informed me that the entire engine had had all its nuts, bolts and screws removed from it. Every day when he came over to work on the car, he had been bringing a pocket full of screws, nuts and bolts. The more he put back into the engine, the more he found were missing. This was also the reason why the steering mechanism didn't just go out, but literally, snapped off. There was nothing holding it into place. As I was driving the car, things were shaking and becoming loose. It was only a matter of time before serious parts would start to break, the first one being the steering.

Jim stared at me intently, making sure I understood the severity of what he was saying. I did, I got it, and this wasn't an accident. I let him know I appreciated everything he was doing, and then I turned and escaped into the house. I wanted nothing more to do with this situation, I just wanted it fixed and gone. My mind went back into that realm where it seemed to explode into a million pieces and I just went back to being numb. I once loved that man. I once thought he loved me. Was I one of those women who had a husband who was trying to kill her? Was I someone people watched on the six o'clock news about how their estranged husband committed murder? This was not and could not be my life. I was not a made for TV movie. I was not so stupid that I didn't know the difference between a good man and a murderer right? Everything, time and time again, kept telling me that everything I thought, everything I believed about him, was false. How did we get to this place? Where do I go now? What can I do about this? They were all just unanswered questions that kept circling my mind.

There was no way I could prove my husband had done this so there was no use in calling the police. I was also not one hundred percent sure Jake had done this, since I was still in an emotional battle between my feelings and my new-found knowledge and facts. I wanted so much to believe that the man I fell in love with, the man I married and believed God made for me, would never do this. It had to be a coincidence. It just had to be. If it wasn't, then I didn't know anything about anyone. Yes, my husband was a mechanic, as well; he used to drive my car because it got better gas mileage than one of our other, larger vehicles. Yes, he was the only one who ever worked on the car so he knew it inside and out like the back of his hand. His finger prints would be everywhere. Nevertheless, that didn't matter because this had to be a mistake. However, at that moment, I just wasn't sure, I had a ticking time bomb for a car that I had been driving all this time with my kids and I didn't even know it. Sometimes, ignorance really was bliss, but unfortunately, those days were also over and reality would be exposed more and more every day.

21

The first of what would end up being many pre-trials was quickly approaching. It seemed like it took forever to get here, but now was just right around the corner and I didn't feel ready. I had put in for the day off from work and was going to do my best to attend not only this one, but every single one after it, if there were any more.

As the date of April 25th drew nearer, I developed a nervous tic just below my left eye. It never stopped and was quite embarrassing as well as extremely annoying. I could tell when people noticed it so I started to put my fingers on my face when engaged in conversation. I found that when I pulled or put pressure on that area, it would stop for a minute or two, just long enough to finish the conversation so that I could move on. After having this happen incessantly for more than a week I went to the doctor. If everything that had gone on wasn't making me crazy enough, this nervous tic was definitely doing the job. I had hoped there was some kind of medication I could take to alleviate the symptoms of stress. My scary hair loss, the feeling of broken glass in my stomach, and now this never-ending tic were just too much to handle anymore. Unfortunately, other than sedatives—which I already had and ingested like candy—there wasn't much else my doctor could do. We both talked about the importance of therapy and hanging in there and that was about it. She reassured me the tic and other symptoms were temporary and would all go away once the trial was over. I prayed she was right, but knew the end wouldn't come quickly enough.

It seemed I wasn't the only one suffering lately. Surprisingly, it wasn't Michelle, but my young eight year old son, Aidan. He started suffering from severe headaches and was acting out a lot more than usual. One evening while my aunt was visiting and helping him with his homework, Aidan went temporarily blind. Thankfully, my aunt could be quite calm in situations like these and was able to keep her composure as she finished talking my son through the situation, until his sight returned, and she could send him upstairs to play. She then relayed to me what was happening with him. This, I thought, had to be a joke or she was exaggerating as she usually liked to do about things. There was no way (and I mean no way) life could or would give someone all of these things to handle at once. Something was just being blown out of proportion or this was just "one of those things" that some kids get one time and never comes back . . . something. I didn't know what this could be, but I knew for sure that this wasn't going to be anything serious. Life could not be that cruel, even to someone like me, even to a failure like me; it just couldn't be this horrible.

We started with Aidan's regular doctor. He wanted Aidan to see an eye doctor. We did everything in small steps and I was so grateful to have my aunt there to take Aidan to these appointments and help me as I was still trying desperately to hold down my job. The eye doctor said Aidan's eyes were fine, so back to his regular doctor they went. Then they were off to an eye surgeon, again, his eyes and everything attached to them were fine. During this time and all these appointments, Aidan continued to have headaches and problems at school and often complained about seeing spots and other things that weren't there. After another appointment with his regular doctor, we ended up seeing a pediatric neurologist.

She scheduled an MRI right away, but said that Aidan was fine and didn't think there was anything wrong with him. Of course, this was a huge relief and I was grateful we were simply just going through all the steps you were supposed to in order to get his certificate of perfect health. We were covering all our bases. Everything was good, everything was fine, we were going to be fine and all would come out fine. Fine, fine, fine, was all I kept thinking and saying . . . again. Nothing and no other word existed, just, "fine." And so we moved on.

Pre-Trial #1 April 25th

With all of Aidan's medical appointments, my physical stress symptoms and the car issues, my ducks were not quite in a row as I prepared to go to the pre-trial. I was scared not knowing what to expect or where the court house was and of course seeing Jake again held the most fear. I still had such a mixed up set of emotions in regard to him and didn't know if that day would be the day I decided to kill him or if I would simply scream out my hatred and frustration and totally lose control. I asked a friend to go with me and she said she could only meet me there. I became a nervous wreck, totally unsure if I was going to be able to handle it.

I used the internet to get directions and came up with a plan. I would go there, check it out, look at him, and then leave. Nobody dictated what I had to do or how long I had to stay. My eye was twitching uncontrollably and my stomach was making me nearly double over in pain. However, I knew, this had to be done and that I had to do it. I followed the driving instructions and easily found the place. As I was walking up to the courthouse steps I found my friend, Meagan. She was walking around looking lost so she stuck out like a sore thumb among the people who walked purposefully in different directions with their obvious destinations. Together, Meagan and I went inside, went through the metal detectors, and found our courtroom. I kept telling myself that I didn't have to stay. I wasn't here because I was in trouble, I was there because I wanted to be and that meant I could leave anytime. This was going to be over and be over quickly.

We entered the courtroom very quietly and found seats in the back right-hand corner. I saw Jake instantly amongst all the people. He wore one of the suits I had bought him for church and sat next to his sister, Julie. They were giggling and chatting as if they were sitting in a movie theatre waiting for the show to begin. They seemed like a couple on a date, not two siblings waiting for sexual molestation charges to be brought against him. Did he not get why he was here? Did she not think this was any big deal either? Could they actually discard this and what he had done to my daughter—to me—as if we were nothing more than a fly on a wall? Did they not understand that he ruined our family, my daughter's life, my life? They were laughing. How could they be laughing? He should have been crying and shaking and begging for my forgiveness. Seeing this behavior from them was totally unexpected. I was instantly on fire and felt all my fears about killing him and not being able to control myself, come to the surface.

I realized I was holding a pen in my hand. I was gripping it like a knife and thought I could easily stab him. My muscles ached and it made me realize I had been transfixed on Jake and Julie while clutching this weapon. My thoughts went to how quickly I could jump over the aisles of chairs and people and thrust the pen into his neck before anyone could stop me. I wondered how many seconds it would take me to reach him. I wondered if I could do it faster than it would take for the bailiff to stop me. As I took a deep breath I gripped the arm rests of the chair I was in. "Don't let me get up," I whispered to my friend Meagan. "Don't let me hurt him." Then I lowered my head and stared at the harmless pen that I had mentally turned into a slayer of the wicked. A pen, a tool used to write with, homework, love letters, etc. and now, a destroyer of evil. It was an amazing thing I held. It could do so many different things . . . I just hung on to the arm rests, ensuring they would keep me in my seat, telling myself that this would be over soon.

I decided it would be best to look at the other people sitting in the gallery. How many were there because they too, were in trouble?

Which ones were there to observe, which were victims, perpetrators, or just innocent friends? The courtroom really was situated like a movie theater. There was seating on the left side of the large room, rows of seats in the middle and then a grouping on the right side. They were separated by aisles where one would be able to stand and scoot over to the closest aisle and go up to the wooden gate that divides the gallery of people from the attorney's desks and the judge's bench. That side of the divider was like the movie screen. The judge's bench was taller and perfectly in the middle than the rest of the wooden desks in the room. On the far right-hand side were two rows of seats where a jury would be seated. Instead of jurors, there were attorneys sitting, waiting for their cases to be called. They were all just chatting away, sipping on their morning coffee from one coffee house or another. They acted as if they did this every day, all day long and it was all no big deal. I guess to them, it wasn't. Nothing they talked about or dealt with had anything at all to do with their children, family or their freedom. On the left-hand side of the judge was a court clerk. Next to her was a bailiff and in front of the judge, down low and off to one side, was the court reporter. She looked as bored as a kid in summer school. She had absolutely nothing to do except wait until the judge came in so she could start typing up what everyone was saying. It was a huge display of stories ready to be acted out like a live play instead of on a big white screen.

Without warning, the bailiff demanded the attention of everyone in the room. With his loud and commanding voice he informed us that if we chewed gum, ate or drank anything, had a cell phone ring, spoke, or made eye contact or motions of any kind to anyone while the judge was seated, then we would be asked to leave and our case would be pushed back to the end of the day. Meagan and I both got rid of our gum and she hurried to turn off her cell phone. I had left mine in the car. As we sat in the back next to the nearest exit for easy escape, the clerk called out each case name. One by one, each case was being continued for one reason or another and I hoped above all other hopes that ours would not go like that.

Once their case was called, the accused would stand up from wherever he or she was sitting and go up to the gate; the offender's attorney would stand from the other side of the gate where they were sitting in that jury area, walk over, and stand next to the accused with the gate in between them. Then they would be addressed by the judge, respond, set a new pre-trial date and move on to the next case. It was done very quickly with no drama like on TV and without any conclusions. It seemed like everyone just kept putting things off for one reason or another and would just have to come back in another month or two.

As I sat shaking and feeling like my breakfast had consisted of broken glass, I was entranced at the inner workings of criminal court. I found it to be as addictive as my tranquilizers and couldn't get up and walk out once it had all started. It was fascinating to see all the different players who were involved in each case that was being called. I wondered silently what each charge and code meant, what the accused had done, who the victims were, if any, in the gallery, etc. I couldn't help but be completely consumed with everything going on around me. I was enthralled and couldn't move. Luckily, this made me want to stay and so did Meagan. This, I would come to realize later, was probably the best decision I made that day.

As I watched and waited for our case to be called, for Jake's name to be called, I held on to my plan. The plan, the only plan, the only possibility I had prepared for was to have all the evidence presented to Jake and his attorney. It would all be stated in court, everyone would hear, including me, Jake would then leave and meet with his attorney, and they would decide it would be time to change their plea from *Not Guilty*, to *Guilty*. Then we would be done. I had that all ready and processed in my mind. I had prayed for that enough times that it was sure to happen because God loved me. I felt like this was all common sense anyway, and this was the only possible outcome. We were simply here to go through the motions. Somewhere deep inside Jake, he was a good man; he was partly the man I knew and loved. He would see he was caught, know it was the right thing to do, and end this nightmare. I knew that underneath everything, he must have loved me a little and would do right by me.

Nothing was further from the truth. The clerk sitting next to the judge called out my husband's name. Jake stood up in his fine suit with his fresh haircut and looking as handsome as ever. He seemed so sure of himself and acted as if he knew what was going to happen. Jake, his attorney and our prosecutor, spoke to the judge, but Meagan and I were sitting so far in the back of the court room we could hardly make out anything they were saying. Then the attorneys and the judge disappeared into the judge's chambers. Nobody else's cases had done this before now. I had no idea what was happening, what they were doing, or how long they would be gone. Jake and Julie seemed to know. They weren't nervous and didn't look confused like Meagan and I certainly did. Even the other members of the gallery seemed to take notice that something out of the ordinary had happened.

I took a deep breath and remembered the words previously said to me, "Criminal Justice is justice for the criminal, not the victim." I looked over at Jake, he had sat back down, and I saw him whispering to his sister Julie and he was laughing. I couldn't believe he was smiling and laughing. I hadn't done either of those things in more than six months. However, there he was, seeming as if nothing would ever happen to him, no accountability, no court, definitely no jail, and ultimately, there was no remorse, no sadness for what he had done.

The judge and attorneys returned in less than five minutes and then spoke on the record for all of five seconds. Just that quick, it was all over. I couldn't even hear what had been said. Jake and Julie got up and left with their attorney and the prosecutor went on to another case. "What just happened?" I kept frantically asking my friend. "What did they say?" She just kept saying she didn't know. I was so confused and instantly angry. I was regretting my decision to allow my pen to remain a simple pen. I had missed my only opportunity to make this right, to give justice to my daughter. It was over, and they were now gone.

Although Jake, Julie and his attorney had left, I decided I wasn't going anywhere. I wanted to find out what in the world had just happened, what was said behind closed doors and what was going to happen next. There was no way that after the hell I had walked through for the last six months, that I would let this be over in five seconds without so much as a word to me or from me. I wanted to know everything. I planted my ass firmly in that chair and wasn't going to let anything, anyone or even an act of God move me from there until I had some answers.

I couldn't help the rage that was starting to flow freely inside me like molten lava. I hadn't erupted yet, but I was seething, letting all of those sitting around me know that they shouldn't even glance my way. I had to say something and say it to someone who would truly listen and do something about all of this. He was not going to walk away, he was not going to go free, and he was not going to molest any other children. So Meagan and I sat and waited for the right moment to get the D.A.'s attention. I needed to speak with her and find out what had just happened. I needed to know what Jake's position was with the case and help the prosecutor fight it and convict him. I realized I could hear a deep guttural growl coming out of me as we waited, but even hearing it; I didn't care and wasn't going to make myself stop.

When the judge announced a break and got up and left the room, I asked Meagan to go ask if I could speak with the prosecutor for our case. I didn't know what the legalities were regarding that, so she seemed like the obvious choice to inquire whether or not this was permitted. Thankfully, Meagan was quick to do what I asked and grabbed the attorney before she had time to disappear along with all the other attorneys leaving the room. I saw the prosecutor nod yes, that she would speak with me, as she scanned around the room to see if she could find the person they were talking about. When our eyes met, she made a beeline for me. She seemed to know exactly who I was. I was a bit stunned at how matter of fact she was, with no small talk or pleasantries being exchanged. She was not about to waste any of her valuable time on me as she directed us to go outside the courtroom, into the hallway, and take a seat on a bench.

As she came over I noticed how professionally she was dressed. I liked her sense of style and she was very much in control and assertive in a surprisingly competent way given the last six months of hiccups in the case. We sat together, the three of us and she explained what the defense's position was. I was horrified to hear the most outlandish reasoning, scenarios, and above all mudslinging that Jake and Julie were saying. Jake had stooped to an all-time low and I couldn't help but have my mouth drop to the floor as I repeated the words, "What?" over and over again. I found it rather odd that I could be shocked at what Jake had to say. Why would I expect anything else from a child molester? Why did I keep thinking that he was going to own up to what he had done and take his lashings like a man? Why did his lies bring me to my knees time and time again when he is nothing more than a monster?

She described how Jake had turned in a videotape of my daughter skateboarding outside his home—our home. They said that she was not a victim, but a cunning liar and she was taunting him. Jake said that Michelle was so jealous of his relationship with his own daughters that she decided to make all this up in order to hurt him. The proof of that defense was the video. It was a video where a little girl was playing outside with one of her best friends; the defense had twisted it into a thing where a deceitful little girl was manipulating and mocking this poor man who was now the victim of an appalling accusation. They also had her CAST interview (the recorded interview they had Michelle do inside the non-descript building with the playroom). Another video where my daughter testified to what Jake did to her and then in that video when asked if Jake was "fair," she said, "no." This, in the defense's mind, was proof that my daughter was angry at Jake for no reason. She was nothing more than a jealous, spoiled little brat and liar.

Two videos were all it took to make the prosecuting attorney regret her decision to file charges. Two easily explainable recordings were distorted to get a child molester off. Seriously? Why? Because he was so handsome? Because he had perfected his "Aw Shucks" persona? This was all it took for people to dismiss a case? Enraged and barely containable, I explained to Lydia, the prosecutor, that we lived less than a mile away from Jake. When we lived in our house with Jake, Michelle made three very good friends on that street. Two times and only two times, I had allowed Michelle over to one of their homes to play under the direct supervision of the friend's mother who knew about Jake and what he was. And for God's sake, why wasn't I in that video tape? I was sitting in my car, just down the block, watching my daughter the entire time. She was only allowed over there twice for about 30 to 40 minutes because that was all I could handle. Michelle was trying to be as normal as possible and I was trying to help her. She was trying to play with her friends that she had been missing since we had left our home to go live with my parents. After weeks of begging to go over there to play, and me finally allowing it, those were now the reasons why Jake wasn't going to be charged? And Michelle was right about the unfairness of Jake when it came to his children. He did anything they asked, but what did that prove?

Next she informed me that another defense of theirs was that Jake and I were going to be divorced and that I was such a vindictive woman I had made my daughter tell these lies in order to hurt him. Again, they showed the CAST interview where my daughter seemed to be easily led to say what anyone wanted to hear. Obviously, this was something I conjured up and was making her lie about Jake so that I could retaliate against him for leaving me. Again, Jake was painted as the victim in all this. He just wanted a divorce and I was so deranged, I was going to make my daughter walk through hell in order to punish him for leaving me. It was a ridiculous defense that was easily disputed. When this was brought out and we had a Social Worker at our house from Child Protective Services, telling me about the rumor of sorts my daughter had told someone, I was the person who defended Jake. I was the one who said there was no way this could possibly have happened. I was the one who dismissed this person and her accusations against my husband. And it was she, Karen, the social worker, who told me to have another talk with my daughter to make sure all was well. Now, I was being accused of being a monster? How ugly was this going to get?

As if this ridiculousness wasn't enough, Jake had one more defense to add to his case. It was his *big finale*, the kicker, the topper, the, "if all else fails:" his defense was that Jake's own autistic son slept in the same bed as Michelle and if she truly was molested, then it was by his son and not him. I was sure I had misunderstood the prosecutor. I knew that I had somewhere during that brief presentation of information I had somehow lost all train of thought, including my listening skills and had gone off to some other world for peace. I had to ask several times for her to repeat what she was saying because I didn't seem to understand her correctly. That incessant buzzing in my ears kept coming and going so that I was unable to make out the fullness of what Lydia, the prosecutor, was telling me. After several attempts of explaining their defense strategies, it actually took Lydia and my friend, Meagan, to make me understand what they were saying. Jake was accusing his own son. A son who never slept with my daughter in her bed, who was four years younger and smaller than Michelle was, and who was the sweetest, most innocent boy of all boys I had ever met. I had the most difficult time wrapping my head around this defense.

The man I had once loved like no other in the world was throwing his most loving, innocent son under the bus to save his own neck; I couldn't comprehend this no matter how many times Lydia explained it to me. There was absolutely no way we understood correctly what Jake and Julie were throwing out there. When Lydia finally convinced me that this really was the truth of his words, my heart and soul wilted away like a dying flower in fast forward motion. I could feel my entire body start to shrink in on itself. My hands wrapped around my chest in a hugging position and rested on my shoulder and upper arm area. My legs crossed and my head lowered as I stared down to my feet. This was not going as planned. This was not how a loving husband and father handled his problems. Who in the hell was Jake? Who had I been living with? Who had I been sleeping with? I instantly felt terrified, vulnerable and shocked. What was I thinking bringing this form of malevolence into our family, into my bed?

I took one issue at a time with Lydia. I explained away everything that had made her doubt her decision to file charges against Jake. The video of my daughter playing outside the house was our attempt at normalcy. The CAST video where my daughter was obviously angry at Jake was pretty typical of a child being molested by someone she once loved, even though she couldn't seem to remember the time in the beginning when she worshiped Jake. I was not a vindictive woman who wanted to get back at my husband for wanting a divorce. Those women who made headlines for doing just that had made it so that when molestation accusations really were what was happening, this was the perfect defense. Did people not care about what kind of damage there were creating by making false allegations against others?

And finally, the one that devastated me the most was the one about his own son being the monster in our house. I made sure Lydia understood that my stepson was so much younger and such an innocent angel, there was no way that he could do anything like this and there was no way that Michelle wouldn't be able to distinguish between a grown man and a little boy. Michelle would have also been able to put this little one in his place had he ever done anything that was inappropriate. Michelle was not reserved in her emotions about bad behavior with her stepsiblings. She was quite vocal about everyone and everything regarding our blended family. Everything, except being molested by a man she knew I loved so much.

Lydia seemed relieved. She said she was glad I had stayed and waited to talk with her. She again informed me that she had been regretting her decision to file charges against Jake, but that now, she was back on track and ready to move forward. I didn't know whether or not she thought this would make me feel better, but the only thing it did was make me feel like I had to be present and to fight this all the way to the end. This whole day made me think that without my direct input and presence at every pre-trial, Jake was going to walk away a free man. I could even picture him with his sister as they left the courthouse. They would obtain a *Not Guilty* verdict and leave walking arm in arm, laughing and talking as if nothing at all had ever happened. He would be free to move on to his next victim, his next prey, destroying everything that was possible in her life, too. He would ruin his next victim's life and her mother's too, just as he had with me and Michelle. And although I was now only a fragment of a person, one way or another, there was just no way I was going to let that happen.

Jake,

I'm not sure where to begin. Why? This is one of a million questions that play over and over again in my mind. It took me quite a while to realize that you never actually loved me. Looking back, I doubt you even liked me. I was just a woman with the right kind of child at the right age of your liking. There were so many times when I thought I was the one in control. Turns out, it was you all along. Does that make you proud of yourself? I often wonder how many victims you have created. Do you think about them or their families? Are they notches on your bed post? Is there any part of you that is real or was it always just the means toward the ending you wanted? All these questions and so many more that I will never have answered. I think I'm okay with that now. It took a very long time, but I eventually got to a place of acceptance. I realize that you are an evil person with disgusting motives in everything that you do and say. Of course you hide that well under an "Aw Shucks, I'm just a good man looking for a good woman," façade. I think the one that I love the best is, "You make me want to be a better man." I can't help but laugh at that now. For all the games you played, sweet nothings you whispered and lives you've destroyed, you are the one I feel the most sorry for. You will never know what living or loving is really like. You will never know how to smell the flowers, soak up the sunshine on your face, or feel the cool ocean breeze on your skin and be able to enjoy it. To truly be grateful for those things and more will always escape you and those like you. Evil cannot enjoy anything good, righteous or beautiful. You will never know any of these things because you will always have wicked intentions hiding under the surface. You are the epitome of a wolf in sheep's clothing. So, goodbye to you. I know that is something we always said we would never say to each other. However, it is in those words that I have closure in my heart for a husband who never existed, to a man who was not real.

Goodbye to you forever.

Jane

Here's a Sneak Peek at:

I am Gonna Tell, Too
By
Jane T. Doe

Jake's attorney walked into the courtroom and looked at me. To him, I apparently stuck out like a distracted deer among the hunter. He was quite unmistakable as well. I nicknamed his attorney; "Big Boy," due to his large stature and his even larger than life attitude. It was obvious with the way he carried himself that he thought he was the ultimate and most untouchable defense attorney in the business. He never had any problem acknowledging or trying to intimidate me in his own way. He made that brief glance which held a quick conversation. A sort of, "There she is again, but who do you think will win today? It won't be you." He sat with Jake and whispered to him, no doubt saying that I was once again there sitting behind him. After a few more words were exchanged they both laughed. Apparently making light of why they were there or perhaps even discussing and making fun of me. I didn't know and I didn't much care. This was part of the long haul, and I was in it for that.

The D.A. noticed me sitting in the back and instantly came to my side. As he started to talk, the judge called out our case name. He quickly said, "They're going to continue and I will tell you why after." I nodded my understanding of what he said and then waited and listened. Jake stood up with his attorney and I could only see the back of his head. I imagined Jake probably had a smile on his face. He was probably feeling very confident about the case against him. After all, this was one child's word against his. The D.A. stood up front on one side of the courtroom. Jake's attorney on the other side. Big Boy said that he had a conflict in his schedule and he wouldn't be able to attend the jury trial that was due to start the following week. The judge asked "The People?" meaning the D.A. and if Aaron, the new prosecutor, had a problem with that. He said, "No objection your honor." My head tilted back and I looked up into the ceiling. For a moment I tried to take in strength from the nothingness of the ceiling. Nothing existed up there. I tried to pretend the white ceiling tiles were clouds. I took a deep breath and stared towards the front once again. The defense attorney picked a date over two months away. It was a date that was nearing our two year anniversary of this horror. The previous D.A.'s investigator's words echoed in my mind. "This whole process will take on the average of two years."

There I was watching it all unfold in the exact time frame I had been told about so long ago. The judge granted the continued trial date. As Jake and his attorney left the courtroom, Aaron, the D.A., motioned for me to wait, as if I was going to go anywhere without an explanation. He walked back over to me and led me out into the hallway. He asked me about Michelle and let me know he could see on my face that this was dragging on way too long. I teared up as I let him know that Michelle was now struggling with an eating disorder and that we were dealing with all the typical things that come with being molested. I could see the hint of sorrow in his eyes, just there for only a split second, but I caught it and I was grateful.

He then informed me of the police department's detective's inability to reach a parent of a witness. He said that was why he did not contest the defense's motion to continue. Aaron said there was testimony he needed in order to have the case irrefutable. We needed evidence that only the police detective could bring to the table. At that moment I couldn't wait to race out of there and start making phone calls. I had a million and one questions, what was the problem, what testimony did they need, what were they looking for and finally, how could I help. But he didn't have the time for any of that. I was one of many cases in his huge stack of files.

I left the courtroom and the tears began to flow freely down my face. I started texting Christy the information that was relayed to me and she quickly called me back. I started to lose my composure and yelled at her my frustration. Nobody was coming forward as they should have and yes, I was implying her and her daughters. There was my uncle too, who witnessed firsthand Jake's inappropriate touching of Michelle at a skating rink, parents of other victims who didn't want to get involved, babysitters, nieces, friends of friends, the list went on. My rage grew throughout the conversation and continued on throughout the day. Everyone involved in this case, everyone who knew Jake, was leaving everything to my daughter. A child, the youngest of all of them, had to be the adult, all alone and stand up to a monster that everyone else was afraid to fight. Christy vowed to help and make phone calls so I left her to it.

I spun out of control . . .